Assassinations and Executions

# Assassinations and Executions

*An Encyclopedia of Political Violence, 1900 through 2000*

REVISED EDITION

HARRIS M. LENTZ III

McFarland & Company, Inc., Publishers
*Jefferson, North Carolina, and London*

**Library of Congress Cataloguing-in-Publication Data**

Lentz, Harris M.
 Assassinations and executions : an encyclopedia of political violence,
1900 through 2000 / Harris M. Lentz III.— Rev. ed.
  p.  cm.
 Includes bibliographical references and index.
 ISBN 0-7864-1388-3 (illustrated case binding : 50# alkaline paper)
 1. Assassination — History — Chronology.  2. Executions and
executioners — History — Chronology.  I. Title.
 HV6278.L45  2002
 909.81— dc21                                        2002003871

British Library cataloguing data are available

Manufactured in the United States of America

*Cover images (top to bottom):* Funeral cortege of Archduke Ferdinand, Mahatma
Gandhi, John F. Kennedy, Tsar Nicholas II and family, the body of General Lucio
Blanco, and funeral painting of Michael Collins by Sir John Lavery
*(All images ©2002 Art Today, except* John F. Kennedy *©2002 Library of Congress)*

*McFarland & Company, Inc., Publishers*
 *Box 611, Jefferson, North Carolina 28640*
  *www.mcfarlandpub.com*

To my friend Doy L. Daniels, Jr.

....let us sit upon the ground
And tell sad stories of the death of kings;
How some have been deposed, some slain in war,
Some haunted by the ghosts they have deposed,
Some poison'd by their wives, some sleeping kill'd;
All murder'd; for within the hollow crown
That rounds the mortal temples of a king
Keeps Death his court, and there the antick sits,
Scoffing his state and grinning at his pomp;
Allowing him a breath, a little scene,
To monarchize, be fear'd, and kill with looks,
Infusing him with self and vain conceit,
As if this flesh which walls about our life
Were brass impregnable; and humour'd thus
Comes at the last, and with a little pin
Bores through his castle wall, and farewell king!

—William Shakespeare, *Richard II* (III.ii)

# ACKNOWLEDGMENTS

I would like to take this opportunity to thank the many people whose assistance and support have made this book possible. I would like to give special thanks to my mother, Helene Z. Lentz, my sister, Nikki Walker, and my friend Carla Clark. Also thanks to Kent Nelson, Anne Taylor, David Hyde, S. Newton Anderson, Andy Branham, Joy Martin, Tony Pruitt, Bobby Matthews, Jimmy Walker, George and Leona Alsup, Betty Alsup, Toni Cerritto, Fred Davis, Louis and Carol Baird, Doy L. Daniels, Jr., Paul Geary, Dale Warren, Dr. Mark Heffington, Rosa Burnett and the staff at State Technical Institute library, Denise Tansil, John Janovich, Jenny Byczek, Jake Miller, Hal Stansbury, Blaine Lester, the fine folks at J. Alexanders, James Gattas, the University of Memphis Library and the Memphis and Shelby County public libraries.

# CONTENTS

# PREFACE

The purpose of this book is to present a concise look at the many world leaders who met their end in a violent manner during the 20th century. This book primarily deals with those leaders who have perished as victims of political assassination, though some whose deaths have traditionally been recorded as "executions" are also included. Often an execution is merely an assassination given legal justification. (A leader is deemed "assassinated" if he perishes during a coup, but "executed" if his killing is subsequent to his fall from power.) The inclusion of such executions broadens the scope to include the many victims of the purges of Stalin and Hitler, as well as those Nazi leaders whose crimes against humanity resulted in their justified execution.

The entries in this book are from the 20th century, covering 1900 through 2000. I have offered in the Prologue a brief summary of the deaths of major leaders whose assassinations fell before this period. I have also included in the body of the book unsuccessful assassination attempts against major world figures. (Names of victims of unsuccessful attempts are given in Roman type, while names of persons actually killed are given in boldface.)

Selecting the individuals to be included has sometimes been difficult. Naturally I have attempted to include all heads of state and government who perished in political violence. I have also endeavored to include the other major world figures who so died. I have made an attempt to record the deaths of ambassadors, leading national figures, and military officers. Serious difficulties arise, however, with various nations in Africa, South America and Asia, where political violence has often seemed to be a way of life. It would be virtually impossible to name every victim of political violence in El Salvador, Guatemala or Colombia, record the victims of Pol Pot's massacre in Cambodia, or list those who perished under Macias Nguema in Equatorial Guinea, Idi Amin in Uganda, or the Duvaliers in Haiti. In these cases I have attempted to give an overview of these violent situations and record the deaths of notable figures.

The entries in this book are generally listed in chronological order. It has not always been possible to determine the exact date of some of the assassinations and killings recorded, so using available information I have endeavored to list them as closely as possible to their proper order. I have also varied from the strict chronological format in several special cases. When the assassinations or executions of several individuals occurring in a particular year were directly related to one another, such as victims of the purges of Stalin, Hitler, and Amin, or the violent political upheavals in Ethiopia or Iran, I have grouped these incidents together in one entry, even though the actual deaths may have been several months apart. I felt that this would better clarify the impact and ramifications of the initial and succeeding deaths.

In writing this book I have attempted to give the facts regarding the assassination, including the manner, the motive, and the assailant, when known. I have included bio-graphical information on some of the major victims. I have also attempted to record the immediate effects of the assassination on the political climate of the day. In some cases I have also recorded the final fate of the assassins, who, on occasion, have themselves become victims of the same violence they unleash, thus deserving their own passages in this book.

# PROLOGUE

The term assassin, originally *hashshashin*, or taker of hashish, was derived from the eleventh century Isma'ili sect of the Shi'ite Moslims. It was used to describe the followers of Hasan ibn al-Sabah, the "Old Man of the Mountain," who, for several centuries, gained great power in the Middle East by violence and threats of violence against the area's rulers. European crusaders brought the word and legend back from Syria, and it soon became a common term used to describe someone who commits premeditated murder by sudden assault.

Though episodes of political murders date back through biblical times, and likely before recorded history, the murder of Julius Caesar, the legendary Roman general and dictator, is perhaps the best-known historical assassination. He was stabbed to death in 44 B.C. in the Roman Senate by a band of political opponents.

Caesar was but the first in a long line of leaders of the Roman Empire to so perish. Gaius Caesar, known as Caligula, was murdered along with his family by members of the Praetorian Guard in A.D. 41, and his uncle and successor, the Emperor Claudius I, was poisoned by his wife, Agrippina the Younger, in A.D. 54. She was, in turn, executed by the order of her son, the Emperor Nero, in A.D. 59. Nero was also responsible for the executions of his wife, Octavia, and the daughter of the late Claudius,

Claudia Antonia, before he took his own life during an army rebellion in A.D. 68.

Other slain emperors include Servius Sulpicius Galba and Aulus Vitellius in 69, Domitian in 96, Lucius Aelius Aurelius Commodus in 192, Decimus Clodius Septimus Albinus in 197, Publius Septimus Geta in 212, Caracalla in 217, Elagabalus in 222, Marcus Aurelius Alexander Severus in 235, Marcus Julius Philippus in 249, Aurelian in 275, Marcus Claudius Tacitus in 276, Carinus in 285, Flavius Julius Constans in 350, Valentinian II in 392, Maximus Tyrannus in 422, Valentinian III in 455, and Anthemius in 472.

Many emperors of the Eastern Roman Empire in Constantinople were also recorded as victims of political violence. Valens was killed by the Goths in 378. Flavius Tiberius Mauricius was murdered in 602 by Phocas, who succeeded him. Phocas was, in turn, overthrown and executed eight years later. Others include Constantine III in 641, Constans II in 668, Justinian II in 711, Anastasius II in 721, Constantine VI, who was murdered by order of his mother in 797, Romanus IV Diogenes in 1972, Alexius II Comnenus in 1183, and Alexius IV Angelius, who was murdered by Alexius VI in 1204. Alexius V, who served shortly as emperor himself, was thrown from a column in Constantinople by crusaders later in the year.

Other early assassinations include those

1

of Visigoth kings Theodoric II in 466 and Alaric II in 407. Gundimar II, the king of Burgundy, was murdered in 532, and the Ostrogoth king Theodat was slain in 536. Totila, another king of the Ostrogoths, was killed in battle in 552. Alboin, the king of the Lombards, was poisoned by his wife in 572. Two kings of the Franks, Sigebert I in 575, and Chilperic I in 584, were also assassinated. Brunhilde, the Queen of Austrasia, was executed by being dragged behind a wild horse in 613. King Oswald of the Northumbrians died in battle in 642, and Newt, son of Ander, a Northumbrian prince, was defeated in battle and beheaded in 676.

In Persia, several rules also perished. King Ormizd IV was deposed and murdered in 590, and Khosrau II was killed in battle in 628. His nine-year-old successor, Ardashir III, was murdered by his general in 630.

In 644 Omar I, the second caliph, or deputy to the Prophet Mohammed, was assassinated by a Persian slave. The third and fourth Moslem caliphs were also murdered, Othman in 656, and Ali in 661.

Abd-er-Rahman, the Arabian emir of Spain, died in battle in 732, and Marwan II, the caliph of Ommiad, was overthrown and murdered in 750. Ethelbert, the king of the East Angles, was beheaded in 794, and Al-Amin, the caliph of Baghdad, was murdered by his brother in 813. Leo V, the Byzantine emperor, was assassinated on Christmas Day in 820.

Several Roman Catholic popes also perished as victims of political violence. John VIII was murdered in 882, and Stephen VI was strangled in prison in 897. Benedict VI was also strangled in 974, and Christophorus, an antipope, was murdered in prison in 904.

William I, the duke of Normandy, was assassinated by the count of Flanders in 943 and, on May 26, 946, Edmund I, the king of England, was stabbed to death. Edward the Martyr, who ruled as England's king for three years, was murdered by an agent of his stepmother on March 18, 978.

In Norway, King Haakon the Great was murdered by his soldiers in a pigsty in 995. In Scotland, King Duncan I was defeated in battle and murdered in 1040. His successor, Macbeth, was killed in battle by Malcolm III in March of 1057, in a tale dramatized by William Shakespeare. Sancho II, the king of Spain, died in battle in 1072, and Sancho IV, the king of Navarre, was murdered by his brother in 1076. Denmark's King Canute IV was murdered by a mob on July 10, 1086.

King William II of England was assassinated while on a hunting trip on August 2, 1100. Charles the Good, Count of Flanders, was murdered at Bruges in 1127, and Randulf de Gernons, Earl of Chester, an Anglo-Norman leader, was poisoned in 1153. In 1157 King Canute V of Denmark was assassinated by Sweyn III. Sweyn was killed in battle later in the year. Two kings of Norway were assassinated, Eystein II in 1157, and Haakon II in 1162. Charles VII, king of the Swedes and Goths, was assassinated in 1167.

On December 25, 1180, Thomas à Becket, the archbishop of Canterbury, was murdered in his cathedral by knights from the court of King Henry II of England.

Conrad, Marquis of Montferrat, the Italian leader of the Third Crusade who became king of Jerusalem, was murdered by an assassin in 1192. Baldwin I, the leader of the Fourth Crusade and emperor of Constantinople, was murdered following his defeat in battle in 1205. Engelbert I, the French Roman Catholic archbishop of Cologne, was slain in 1225.

In 1240, Raziya, the queen of Delhi, was murdered, and on August 9, 1250, Eric IV, the king of Denmark, was murdered by his brother. Conradin, the king of Jerusalem and Sicily, was defeated in battle and beheaded on October 29, 1268, and Przemsyl II, the king of Poland, was assassinated in 1296. In 1306, Vaclav II, another Polish king, was assassinated. Adolf of Nassau, the king of Germany, was killed in battle in 1298, and King Albert I of Germany was murdered in 1308. Scottish rebel leader William Wallace was executed by the British in 1306.

King Edward II of England was deposed and executed in September of 1327. Pedro the

Cruel, the king of Castile and Leon, was murdered by his brother in 1369. In 1381, Wat Tyler, an English peasant leader, was executed for treason. Charles of Durazzo, the king of Naples and Hungary, was assassinated in Hungary on February 27, 1386, and King Richard II of England was presumed murdered in prison in February of 1400.

On May 30, 1431, Joan of Arc, a heroine of France, was burned at the stake. King Henry VI of England was murdered in the Tower of London on February 18, 1478. Edward V, the fourteen-year-old king of England, was smothered with his brother, Richard Plantagenet, the Duke of York, by the order of King Richard III on June 26, 1483. Richard III himself died in battle on August 22, 1845. James III, the king of Scotland, was murdered during a revolt on June 11, 1488.

Mohammed X, the Moslem king of Granada, was deposed and assassinated in 1500, and Cesare Borgia, an Italian nobleman and Roman Catholic cardinal, was killed during the siege of Vienna on March 12, 1507. On September 9, 1513, James IV, the king of Scotland, was defeated and killed by the army of England's King Henry VIII.

Vasco Nunez De Balboa, the Spanish explorer who discovered the Pacific Ocean, was condemned for treason and beheaded in Panama in 1519. Ferdinand Magellan, the Portuguese explorer who led the first expedition to circumnavigate the globe, was killed by natives on the Pacific island of Mactan on April 27, 1521.

Guatemotzin, the last Aztec emperor of Mexico, was executed by Cortes in 1525, and Atahualpa, the last king of the Incan Empire of Peru, was strangled by order of Francisco Pizarro on August 29, 1533. His son, Prince Huascar, was also murdered. Pizarro was himself assassinated by followers of Diego de Almargo on June 26, 1541. De Almargo, the Spanish governor of Peru, was, in turn, deposed and executed in 1542.

In 1535 Sir Thomas More, a leading British statesman, and Saint John Fischer, the English Roman Catholic bishop of Rochester, were beheaded by the order of King Henry VIII. Anne Boleyn, King Henry's second queen, was beheaded on May 19, 1536, and Catherine Howard, Henry's fifth queen, was beheaded for adultery in 1542. Thomas Cromwell, Earl of Essex, an advisor to King Henry and a leader of the Reformation, was executed for treason on July 28, 1540.

Ibraham Pasha, the grand vizier of Turkey, was strangled by order of the Sultan in 1536, and David Beaton, a Scottish Roman Catholic cardinal in France, was murdered by Reformationists in 1546.

Lady Jane Grey, who served as England's queen for less than a month in 1553, was beheaded on February 12, 1554. Her father, Henry Grey, Duke of Suffolk, was executed for treason later in the year.

In 1555 Hugh Latimer and Nicholas Ridley, English Reformationist leaders, were burned at the stake for heresy. Thomas Cranmer, the first archbishop of Canterbury of the Church of England, was also burned at the stake on March 21, 1556.

Henry Stewart, Lord Darnley, the second husband of Mary, Queen of Scots, was killed in Edinburgh when his house was blown up on February 9, 1567. Queen Mary as herself beheaded by the order of Queen Elizabeth I of England on February 8, 1587.

William the Silent, the king of Holland, was assassinated on July 10, 1584. Louis II De Lorraine, the French Roman Catholic archbishop of Reimes, was assassinated in 1588, and Henry III, the king of France, was murdered by a monk on August 2, 1589. In 1591 Dimitri Ivanovich, the Czarevitch of Russia and the son of Ivan the Terrible, was murdered. Czar Feodor II of Russia was killed by the Boyars on June 1, 1605, and Czar Dimitri I was murdered on May 17, 1606.

On January 31, 1608, Guy Fawkes, Henry Garnett, Thomas Winter, Robert Winter, Robert Keyes, and Ambrose Rokewood were hanged for conspiring to blow up the English Parliament in the Gunpowder Plot.

King Henry IV of France was murdered by a religious fanatic on May 14, 1610, and British nobleman George Villiers, the first

Duke of Buckingham, was assassinated in August of 1628. Ibrahim, the sultan of the Ottoman Empire, was overthrown and murdered in 1648, and King Charles I of Great Britain was deposed and executed on January 30, 1649.

In 1681, Oliver Plunket, an Irish Roman Catholic prelate, was hanged for treason, and Donald Cargill, the Scottish leader of the Covenanters, was beheaded as a traitor.

Govind Singh, the guru of the Sikhs of India, was murdered in 1709, and Nadir, the shah of Persia, was assassinated in 1747. On July 17, 1762, Czar Peter III of Russia was deposed by his wife, Catherine the Great, and assassinated. Emelyan I. Pugachev, a Russian Cossack rebel leader, was executed by order of Catherine on January 11, 1775.

American patriot Nathan Hale was hanged by the British for treason on September 22, 1776, and Major John Andre, a British army officer, was hanged as a spy on October 2, 1780. Button Gwinnett, a signer of America's Declaration of Independence, was slain in a duel in 1777.

Jose Gabriel Condorcanqui, known as Tupac Amaru, a Peruvian rebel leader, was captured and executed in 1781. Nicolae Horea, a rebel leader in Romania, was put to death in 1785, and Jacques Vincent Oje, a Haitian rebel, was executed in 1791.

On March 16, 1792, Gustavus III, the king of Sweden, was shot to death during an aristocratic plot.

Following the French Revolution, King Louis XVI of France was executed on January 21, 1793. His wife, Marie Antoinette, was put to death on October 16, 1793. Many other prominent French royalists and revolutionaries were also guillotined during this period, including Armand de Coetnempren, Count of Kersaint, Jacques Pierre Brissot, Armand Gensonne, Louis Philippe Joseph, Duc d'Orleans, Jean Bailly, the mayor of Paris, Countess Marie DuBarry, Anacharsis Cloots, Georges Jacques Danton, Camille Desmoulins, Jean Baptiste Gobel, the Roman Catholic archbishop of Paris, Marguerite Elie Gaudet, Louis Saint-Just, and Maximilien Robespierre. Jean Paul Marat, a leading figure in the Revolution, was stabbed to death in his bath on July 13, 1793.

Luft Ali Akhan, the shah of Persia, was assassinated in 1795. His successor Agha Mohammed Khan, was murdered in 1797. On March 23, 1801, Czar Paul I of Russia was assassinated by soldiers. Alexander Hamilton, a leading figure in the American Revolution and the United States' first secretary of the treasury, was mortally wounded in a duel with Aaron Burr on July 11, 1804.

Jean Jacques Dessalines, the emperor of Haiti, was assassinated on October 17, 1806, and Mustafa IV, the sultan of Turkey, was deposed and murdered in 1808. In 1812 Spencer Perceval the prime minister of England, was assassinated. Jose Miguel de Carrera, a former head of state of Chile, was captured and executed in 1821, and Ali, the Turkish pasha of Janina, was deposed and shot in 1822. On July 19, 1824, Agustin de Iturbide, the deposed emperor of Mexico, was executed, and Manuel Dorrego, the provisional president of Argentina, was executed by rebels in 1828.

Chaka, the chief of the Zulu tribe in Africa, was assassinated in 1828, and Antonio Jose de Sucre, a former president of Bolivia, was assassinated on June 4, 1830. Vicente Guerrero, an ex-president of Mexico, was shot by rebels on February 14, 1831, and Felipe Santiago Salaverry, the president of Peru, was executed in 1836.

The king of Afghanistan, Shah Shuja, was murdered in 1842, and Francisco Morazan, the former president of the Central American Federation, was captured and shot on September 15, 1842. Braulio Carrillo, the exiled president of Costa Rica, was executed in 1845.

Denis Affre, the Roman Catholic archbishop of Paris, was killed during a revolt on June 27, 1848, and Archbishop Marie-Dominique-Auguste Sibour, his successor, was stabbed to death by a mad priest in 1857.

Abbas I, the pasha of Egypt, was murdered by slaves in 1854, and Tantia Topi, an Indian Hindu rebel leader, was hanged for insurrection in 1859. John Brown, the American abolitionist who led the raid on Harper's Ferry, was hanged for treason on December 2,

1859, and William Walker, an American adventurer who served as president of Nicaragua from 1856 to 1857, was court-martialed and shot in Honduras on September 12, 1860.

Danilo I, the prince of Montenegro, was assassinated in 1860, and Santo Guardila, the president of Honduras, was murdered in 1861. In 1863 Radama II, the king of Madagascar, was assassinated. Ignacio Comonfort, a former president of Mexico, was ambushed and slain in 1863, and Omar El-Hadj, a Sudanese leader, was killed by opponents in 1864.

Abraham Lincoln, the sixteenth president of the United States, was shot to death by actor John Wilkes Booth while attending a play in Washington, D.C. on April 14, 1865.

Maximilian, the emperor of Mexico, was deposed by rebels led by Benito Juarez and executed on June 19, 1867, along with Gen. Miguel Miramon and Gen. Tomas Mejia.

Venancio Florez, the president of Uruguay, was killed during a rebellion on February 19, 1868. Irish-Canadian journalist and politician Thomas D. McGee was shot to death in Ottawa on April 7, 1868, and Michael, the prince of Serbia, was assassinated on June 10, 1868.

Musajiro, the Japanese minister of defense, was murdered by radical nationalists in 1869. Justo Jose de Urquiza, a former president of Argentina, was assassinated by political rivals with his two sons on April 11, 1870. Francisco Solano Lopez, the dictator of Paraguay, was killed in battle by Brazilian soldiers on March 1, 1870. Juan Prim y Prats, a leading Spanish statesman and soldier, was assassinated in Madrid on December 18, 1870.

Cirilo Antonio Rivarola, the first president of the Republic of Paraguay, was killed in December of 1871, shortly after leaving office. Georges Darboy, the archbishop of Paris, was held hostage and killed by French revolutionaries during the Paris Commune revolt on May 24, 1871. French Socialist politician and revolutionary leader Charles-Theophile Ferre was court-martialed and shot for his role in the Paris Commune revolt on November 28, 1871.

Richard Southwell Bourke, Lord Mayo, the British viceroy of India, was stabbed to death by a Moslem assassin in 1872. Jose Balta, the president of Peru, was killed during an army uprising on July 22, 1872, and Augustin Morales, the President of Bolivia, was assassinated on November 24, 1872.

Cuban revolutionary leader Carlos Manuel de Cespedes was killed by Spanish soldiers in 1874. President Gabriel Garcia Moreno of Ecuador was slain by an assassin on August 6, 1875.

Charles Caldwell, a black state senator from Mississippi, was killed by a gang of Ku Klux Klan members on December 25, 1875.

Abdul-Aziz, the sultan of Turkey, was deposed and likely murdered on June 2, 1876. Hussein Avni Pasha, the Turkish grand vizier and minister of war and leader of the coup that ousted Sultan Abdul-Aziz, was also shot and killed in 1876. On June 24, 1876, Gen. George Armstrong Custer, was killed in battle by Indians at the Little Bighorn River in Montana. Crazy Horse, a Sioux Indian chief who had participated in the Battle of Little Bighorn, was killed by United States soldiers while he was attempting to escape from Ft. Robinson on September 5, 1877.

Juan Bautista Gil, the president of Paraguay, was assassinated on April 12, 1877. Saigo Takamori, a Japanese general and statesman, was killed while leading the unsuccessful Satsuma rebellion on September 14, 1877.

Toshimichi Okubo, a leading Japanese statesman, was assassinated on May 14, 1878. Manuel Pardo, the former president of Peru, was assassinated in Lima in 1878. Gen. N.V. Mesentsov, the Russian prefect of police for Moscow, was stabbed to death in the streets of Moscow on August 16, 1878.

Mehemet Ali Pasha, a Turkish army leader, was killed by a mob of rebels in Albania on September 7, 1878. Gen. Kropotkin, a Russian military advisor to the Czar, was slain by revolutionaries in Kharkov in 1879, and Francis Cadell, a Scottish explorer who had mapped the Murray River in Australia, was murdered by his crew in 1879.

Alexander II, the czar of Russia, fatally

injured by two small bombs thrown at his carriage by revolutionaries on March 1, 1881.

James A. Garfield became the second president of the United States to be assassinated, when he was shot twice in his back at a Washington train station by Charles J. Guiteau on July 2, 1881. The president died of his wounds eleven weeks later on September 19, 1881.

Lord Frederick Charles Cavendish, the chief secretary for Ireland, was stabbed to death in Phoenix Park by members of an Irish secret society known as "The Invincibles, on May 5, 1882. Edward Henry Palmer, an English Orientalist and explorer, was murdered by Arab brigands on August 11, 1882. Midhat Pasha, the former Turkish grand vizier, was murdered in prison on May 8, 1883.

Col. William Hicks, a British soldier who was the leader of the army of the khedive of Egypt, was killed by the forces on the Mahdi on November 4, 1883. Charles George Gordon, who had been sent to Khartoum to evacuate the city before the Madhi's forces conquered it, was butchered by triumphant invaders when they overran Khartoum on January 26, 1885.

Justo Rufino Barrios, the president of Guatemala, was killed in battle in El Salvador on April 2, 1885. Japanese education minister Viscount Mori Arinori was also assassinated in 1885 by nationalist fanatics.

Louis Riel, the leader of a rebellion of the French half-breeds, known as the Metis, in Canada, was convicted of treason and executed on November 16, 1885.

John IV, the king of Ethiopia, was killed in battle at Metamma in March of 1889. Francisco Menendez, the president of El Salvador, was ousted from office on June 22, 1885, and died the same day.

Sitting Bull, the American Indian chief of the Teton Dakota Prairie Sioux tribe, was killed while under arrest by American soldiers on September 15, 1890.

Khristo Belchev, the Bulgarian finance minister, was assassinated by Macedonians in 1891. James Wallace Quinton, the British Commissioners in Assam, was stabbed to death in Manipur Province in 1891.

German explorer Mehmed Emin Pasha was brutally murdered in Africa by agents of a slave trader on October 23, 1892. Jules Ferry, a former premier of France, was shot and killed by a religious fanatic on March 17, 1893.

Hilarion Daza, the exiled former president of Bolivia, was killed by an angry mob when he tried to return to his country on March 1, 1894. The president of France, Marie Francois Sadi Carnot, was stabbed to death by an Italian anarchist on June 24, 1894.

Queen Min of Korea was brutally murdered by agents of the Japanese on April 8, 1895. Jose Julian Marti, a Cuban revolutionary, was killed in battle against the Spanish on April 11, 1895. Stefan Stambulov, the former prime minister of Bulgaria, was murdered in the streets of Sofia on July 15, 1895.

Nasir Ad-Din, the shah of Persia, was assassinated on May 1, 1896. Jose Rizal y Mercado, a Philippine nationalist leader, was tried on charges of insurrection and shot on December 30, 1896.

Antonio Canovas del Castillo, the premier of Spain, was assassinated by an anarchist on August 8, 1897. Juan Idiarte Borda, the president of Uruguay, was killed following a populist revolt on August 5, 1897.

Jose Maria Reina Barrio, the president of Guatemala, was assassinated by a rebel on February 8, 1898. Empress Elizabeth of Austria, the consort of Emperor Francis Joseph I, was slain in an attack by an Italian anarchist on a boat dock in Geneva, Switzerland, on September 10, 1898.

Ulises Heureaux, the president of the Dominican Republic, was assassinated by political enemies on July 26, 1899. 'Abdullahi ibn Mohammed, a disciple of the Mahdi who became known as "the Khalifa," was killed in battle against Egyptian forces led by Sir. F.R. Wingate on November 24, 1899.

# ASSASSINATIONS AND EXECUTIONS

## 1900

- **William Goebel** (1856–1900), Democratic gubernatorial nominee in the Kentucky election of 1899, was shot and seriously wounded on January 30, 1900. He died of his injuries four days later. Goebel was born in Sullivan County, Pennsylvania, on January 4, 1856. He was narrowly defeated by the Republican nominee, Taylor, but he contested the election, charging fraud. The matter was sent to be settled by the Kentucky legislature, but Goebel was shot by an unknown assailant wielding a rifle on January 30, 1900, while walking up a sidewalk leading to the Capitol building in Frankfort. The legislature decided in Goebel's favor, and he was sworn in as governor as he lay dying from his wounds. He died four days later, on February 3, and was succeeded by Lt. Gov. J.C.W. Beckham. Many Republican leaders and office holders were implicated in the assassination and several were convicted, though most convictions were overturned on appeal. Caleb Powers (1869–1932), the Republican secretary of state for Kentucky, was sentenced to life in prison for complicity in the crime. He appealed and was reconvicted several times before being granted a full pardon by Governor Augustus Willson in June of 1908. Powers was subsequently elected to Congress for the first of four terms in 1911. A notary public named Henry Yountsey was convicted of the actual shooting and did not appeal, receiving a life sentence.

- **Baron Klemens von Ketteler** (1853–1900), who had served as the German minister to Peking from 1899, was murdered on June 19, 1900, by Chinese Nationalists. Von Ketteler had previously served as Germany's minister to Mexico from 1896 to 1899. The murder of von Ketteler coincided with attacks on foreign legations throughout Peking by young members of a nationalist secret society known as "The Society of Harmonious Fists." The outbreak of anti–Western violence, which had the tacit support of Empress Tzu Hsi, became known as the Boxer Rebellion. The rising was suppressed by a six-nation expeditionary force, and a later German expedition took punitive action against the supporters of the Boxers in retaliation for von Ketteler's murder.

- **Umberto I**, the king of Italy, was shot and killed by an anarchist at Monza while traveling to his summer retreat on July 29, 1900. Umberto Ranieri Carlo Emmanuele Giovanni Mario Ferdinando Eugenior was born in Turin in Piedmont on March 15, 1844, the son of King Victor Emmanuel II and Adelaide, Archduchess of Austria. He was given a military education and entered the army in March of 1858. He saw action in Solferino in 1859 and against the Austrians at Custozza in 1866. He held the title Prince of Piedmont, and married Princess Margherita Teresa Giovanna of Savoy in April of 1868. A son, the future king Victor Emmanuel III, was born in November of 1869. Umberto succeeded his father to the throne of Italy on January 9, 1878. Umberto's reign was initially tranquil, despite conflict with republicans on the left and Catholic clericals on the right. In foreign affairs Umberto supported the government's alliances with Germany and Austria-Hungary. He also promoted increased spending for the Italian armed forces. During the later years of his reign Umberto often tried to interfere in parliament's selection of prime ministers, further alienating republican sentiments. He remained Italy's king until his murder in July of 1900.

His assassin, anarchist Gaetano Bresci, was a former silk weaver from Paterson, New Jersey. Bresci confessed that the killing had been planned with other anarchists in the United States. He was convicted of the murder and, on August 2, was sentenced to life imprisonment at Santo Sefano Prison at Ventotene Island. Bresci was found dead in the prison on May 22, 1901, reportedly a suicide, but more likely murdered by a guard.

# 1901

- In early 1900, **F.C. Sitwell**, the traveling commissioner for the British colonial authorities in the Gambia, was shot and killed at Sankandi village in Kiang West district, while attempting to enforce a decision over a rice dispute in the area. Sitwell's replacement, **F.E. Silva**, the chief of Battelling, **Mansa Koto**, and six constables were also killed in the assault. This action led the British and French governments to join forces in a military effort to pacify the region. **Fodi Kabba Dumbuya**, a Marabout warlord who instigated the rebellion, was defeated and killed at the town of Medina in March of 1901. The Marabout chief of Sankandi, **Dari Bana Dabo**, sought to escape, but was captured by the French. He was turned over to the British authorities and executed for his participation in the revolt.

- **Nikolai Pavlovich Bogolepov**, the Russian minister of education, was killed on February 14, 1901, by an expelled student. Bogolepov was born in Moscow on November 27, 1846. He was educated in law at Moscow University, where he served as a professor after completing his doctorate in 1881. He served as rector of the University from 1883 to 1895. He became supervisor of the Moscow educational district in 1895 and was appointed minister of education in 1898. He attempted to implement reforms in Russia's educational system. He was shot in the neck by a former student, Peter V. Karpovich, on February 14, 1901, and died of his wounds the following month on March 2, 1901.

- **William McKinley** became the third United States president to die by an assassin's bullet. McKinley was born on January 29, 1843, in Niles, Ohio. He served during the Civil War and later practiced law in Canton, Ohio. He was elected as a Republican member of the United States House of Representatives in 1876 and served until 1883. He again served in congress from 1885 until 1891. In 1890, as chairman of the House Ways and Means Committee, he was instrumental in passing the McKinley Tariff. From 1892 until 1896 he served as governor of Ohio and, in 1896, he was elected president of the United States.

On February 15, 1898, during McKinley's first term of office, the United States battleship *Maine*, while on an official visit to

Cuba, was sunk by a mine while in the Havana harbor. The United States subsequently became involved in Cuba's fight for independence from Spain, resulting in the Spanish-American War. Following the United States victory, a peace treaty was signed in December of 1898, which resulted in Spain's granting independence to Cuba and relinquishing Puerto Rico, Guam and the Philippines to United States control. Filipino independence fighters, under the leadership of Emilio Aquinaldo, then transferred their hostilities from their Spanish rulers to the new United States occupation forces. The guerrilla forces continued their battle for independence until Aquinaldo's capture the following year.

McKinley was reelected president in 1900 and was at the start of his second term of office when he was shot by Leon Czolgosz, an anarchist, at the Temple of Music at the Pan-American exposition in Buffalo, New York, on September 6, 1901. Czolgosz, who had been inspired to commit the assassination after having read accounts of the murder of Italy's King Umberto (q.v.) the previous year, approached the president following the completion of his speech. The assassin had a gun in his hand with a handkerchief wrapped around it. As he drew near McKinley, as if to shake his hand, Czolgosz fired two shots into the president before being wrestled to the ground.

McKinley's wounds were not immediately considered serious, but his condition worsened, and he died on September 14. Czolgosz was tried and convicted of murder and executed in the electric chair on October 29, 1901.

# 1902

• **Dimitri Sergeevich Sipiagin**, the Russian minister of the interior, was murdered by a revolutionary in St. Petersburg, on April 2, 1902. Sipiagin was born to a noble family in 1853. He served as deputy governor of Kharkov Province from 1886 until 1887 and was governor of Kurland from 1888 until 1891. He subsequently served as governor of Moscow Province until 1893, when he became assistant minister of state domains. The following year he was named assistant minister of the interior. He was named to head the czar's private chancellery in 1895. Sipiagin was appointed minister of the interior in October of 1899. He was a leading reactionary in the government and a close associate of the finance minister, Sergei Witte. Sipiagin was shot to death by Stefan Balmashev, a Social Revolutionary, who fired a pistol at the minister at close range at Marinskii Palace, where the state council was meeting. Balmashev was seized and court-martialed. He was convicted of the murder and hanged.

• **M. Kanzchev**, a Bulgarian cabinet minister, was assassinated in Sofia in 1902.

# 1903

• **James Buchanan Marcum** (Jan. 9, 1858–1903), the chairman of the state Republican party in Kentucky, was shot to death on the steps of the Breathitt County Courthouse in Jackson, Kentucky, on May 4, 1903. Marcum's assailants were Curtis Jett and Tom White, who were acting as agents of James H. Hargis, the Breathitt County judge.

• **Ahmadu Attahiru**, the ruler of the Sokoto Caliphate in Northern Nigeria, was killed by British forces in July of 1903. Attahiru had become Caliph in 1902 and opposed the British incursion in his territory. He was repelled by the British and fled into exile. He was deposed in March of 1903. British forces pursued Attahiru and he was killed in July of 1903.

• **Alexander Obrenovich** was murdered with his wife in the royal palace by rebel soldiers on July 11, 1903. Alexander was born on

August 14, 1876, the only son of King Milan of Serbia. He was proclaimed King of Serbia under a regency council on March 6, 1889, upon the abdication of his father. On April 13, 1893, Alexander assumed full authority as king and dismissed the regency council. The following year he abolished the constitution of 1888 and restored the earlier conservative constitution of 1869. In 1900 Alexander married **Madame Draga Mashin** (1867–1903), a former lady-in-waiting to his mother. This act proved to be very unpopular with his government and the Serbian people. He attempted to restore confidence in his reign by instituting a new constitution in 1901, but he suspended it arbitrarily when he felt the need. On July 11, 1903, a group of officers conspired to remove the king. Alexander's palace was surrounded by mutinous officers, and the royal couple was ultimately found hiding in a secret room behind the private bath. Alexander and Draga were then repeatedly shot and butchered with sabers before their bodies were thrown from a window into the courtyard beneath.

- **N.M. Bogdanovich**, the Russian governor of Ufa, was assassinated by Social Revolutionaries in Kiev in 1903.

- **Andrew H. Green**, a leading political figure in New York City, was shot to death in front of his home on Park Avenue in New York on November 13, 1903. Reportedly, his murderer had mistaken him for someone else. Green was born near Worcester, Massachusetts, on October 6, 1820. He was instrumental in creating New York's Central Park, and was involved in the establishment of the New York Public Library and the Bronx Zoo.

# 1904

- **Bogoslovski**, he Russian governor of the Caucasas, was killed by local separatists in 1904, following Russia's persecution of the Armenian church in that region.

- **Nikolai Bobrikov** (1839–1904), the Russian governor general of Finland, was shot and killed on June 16, 1904. Bobrikov attended the General Staff Academy and was chief of the guard unit in St. Petersburg from 1884 until 1898. He was subsequently appointed governor general of Finland in August of 1898. Bobrikov supported the abolition of the Finnish constitution guaranteeing Finnish autonomy and the Russification of Finland. Evgenii Shauman, a nationalist student and the son of a Finnish senator, assassinated Bobrikov and committed suicide following the attack.

- **Vyacheslav K. Plehve**, the Russian minister of the interior, was assassinated on July 28, 1904. Plehve was born in the Kaluga province of Russia on April 20, 1846. A member of the department of justice from 1867, Plehve was named to the ministry of the interior as police director in 1881, following the assassination of Czar Alexander II. His success in abating terrorist activities resulted in his appointment as deputy minister of the interior in 1885 and head of the Imperial Chancellery in 1894. In April of 1902 Plehve became minister of the interior following the assassination of Dimitri Sipiagin (q.v.). His ruthless suppression of dissent earned him the enmity of various organizations and resulted in his assassination by Social Revolutionary Egor S. Sazonov in the streets of St. Petersburg on July 28, 1904. The assassination occurred while Plehve was driving to a railway station in St. Petersburg and a bomb was tossed under his carriage. Sazonov was apprehended and sentenced to life imprisonment.

- **Jose Francisco Chaves**, a leading political figure in New Mexico, was assassinated by an unknown assailant in Pinos Wells, New Mexico, on November 26, 1904. Chaves was born in Los Padillas, Mexico (now Bernalillo County, New Mexico) on June 27, 1833. He served in the Union Army as a colonel during the Civil War. He was a delegate to the U.S. Congress from New Mexico Territory from 1865 to 1867 and from 1869 to 1871. Chaves also served as a delegate to New Mexico state constitutional convention in 1889. He was appointed New Mexico's superintendent of public instruction in 1903, a post he held at the time of his murder.

# 1905

• **Count Pavel Andreevich Shuvalov**, the Russian prefect of police in Moscow, was killed by a Social Revolutionary agent in 1905.

• **M. Johnson**, the procurator of the Finnish senate and a leading supporter of Russification for Finland, was assassinated in February of 1905.

• **Grand Duke Sergius**, a son of Czar Alexander II and commander in chief of the military district of Moscow, was killed in Moscow on February 17, 1905, by a bomb tossed at his carriage by Social Revolutionary I.P. Koliaev. Sergei Aleksandrovich Romanov was born on April 29, 1857. He was appointed governor general of Moscow and commander of the military district by his father in 1891. He was a leader of the conservative faction in the court of his nephew, Czar Nicholas II (q.v.).

• **John McPherson Pinckney**, a congressman from Texas, was assaulted and killed during a meeting of the Waller County Prohibition League in Hempstad, Texas, on April 24, 1905. Pinckney was born on May 4, 1845. He served in the Confederate Army during the Civil War and was a state court judge in Texas from 1900 to 1903. He served as a U.S. Representative from Texas from 1903. Pinckney's brother and three others were also killed in the riot at the Waller County Courthouse.

• **Harry St. George Galt**, the British acting sub-commissioner of Uganda's Western Province, was killed by a spear-throwing tribesman near the Ibanda camp in Uganda on May 19, 1905. The killer was identified as a native peasant known as Rutaraka, who was subsequently murdered by two other tribesmen, Gabrieli and Isaka. It was believed that Gabrieli and Isaka were involved in the plot to murder Galt, and that several native chieftains were also part of the conspiracy. Galt's murder damaged relations between Britain and its colony, leading to a lengthy suspension of several treaties and agreements.

• **Frank Steunenberg**, who had served as governor of Idaho from 1897 until 1901, was killed by a bomb planted at the front gate of his home on December 30, 1905. Steunenberg was born Keokuk, Iowa, on August 8, 1861. A Democrat, he had served two terms of office as Idaho's governor. It was during his administration that the Western Federation of Miners rioted and Steunenberg called in federal assistance in maintaining order. Harry Orchard (1866–1954) admitted planting the bomb which killed Steunenberg at the order of officials of the Western Federation of Miners, but no convictions of union leaders resulted from the subsequent trial of labor leaders William D. "Big Bill" Haywood (1869–1928), Charles H. Moyers and George D. Pettibone. Orchard was sentenced to life imprisonment for his role in the murder of Steunenberg and other union foes.

# 1906

• Russian Orthodox priest and labor leader **Georgii Apollonovich Gapon** was lynched on March 28, 1906, by Social Revolutionaries in Ozerki, near St. Petersburg, who believed him to be a spy for the czarist police. Gapon was born in 1870 and graduated from the Poltava seminary in 1893. He founded the Assembly of Russian Factory and Mill Workers in St. Petersburg in 1903. Gapon went into hiding when the workers' march on the capital on January 9, 1905, turned violent. He briefly fled Russia. He was recruited to spy on the Social Revolutionary Party by the Russian secret police after his return. His role with the police was exposed and he was condemned to death by the revolutionary council and hanged.

• **Prof. Mikhail Yakovlevich Gertsenstein**, a member of the Russian Duma, was shot to death in Terioki in 1906 by a fanatical anti–Semite after Gerstenstein had accused members of the Russian nobility of corruption. Another Jewish member of the Duma, **Dr. Iolloss**, was also murdered in 1906. Aleksandr I. Dubrovin (q.v.), a journalist and the chairman of the Union of Russian People, was accused of instigating their murder.

On May 31, 1906, King Alfonso XIII of Spain (1886–1941) and his wife, Queen Victoria (1887–1969), survived an assassination attempt following their marriage in Madrid. An assassin threw a bomb as the couple's carriage departed the cathedral. The king and queen were uninjured in the assault, but over thirty spectators were killed. An anarchist, Matteo Morales, was responsible for the assassination attempt.

• **General Mann**, who was responsible for putting down the riots in Moscow, was shot to death at the Peterhof railway station in 1906.

• **Alfa Seydou** (1865–1906), the leader of a rebellion against the French in southern Niger in 1905, was captured and executed in 1906. Seydou, who was from a noble family from Kobakitanda, stirred up anti–European sentiment that spread from Niger into Nigeria. He was known as the "Blind Marabout" due to his blindness. The revolt erupted into violence in December of 1905 and Seydou was forced to flee to Nigeria. He was executed there after attempting to continue his revolt.

• **Vladimir Fedorovich von der Launits** (1855–1906), the governor of St. Petersburg, was assassinated by Social Revolutionaries in 1906. Von der Launits joined the Russian army in 1873 and served as Marshal of Nobility of Kharkov Uezd from 1895. He became vice-governor of Arkhangelsk in 1901 and was acting governor of Tambov from 1902. Von der Launits served as governor of St. Petersburg from 1905 until his death.

• **Dmitrii F. Trepov** (1855–1906), the military governor-general of St. Petersburg, was assassinated by Vera Zasulich, a revolutionary. She was subsequently acquitted of the crime. Trepov had served as Moscow's chief of police from 1896 until 1906.

• **Count Aleksei Pavlovich Ignatieff** (1842–1906) was assassinated by Social Revolutionary S.N. Il'inskii in Kiev on December 9, 1906. Ignatieff served in the Russian cavalry and was governor general of Irkutsk from 1885 until 1889. He subsequently served as governor general of Kiev Province until 1896, when he was named to the state council. He was considered a leading reactionary in the government and was the founder of the League of True Russians. He was a supporter of harsh measures against revolutionary activity.

• **General Liarpiarski**, the military governor of Warsaw, Poland, was killed in 1906.

• **Arthur Brown**, a former United States Senator, was shot to death in a Washington, D.C., hotel room by a woman who claimed to be the mother of his children on December 12, 1906. Brown was born on March 8, 1843. A Republican attorney, he rose through the ranks of the local party in Utah before being selected as that state's first U.S. Senator in 1896. Allegations of an affair with a much younger woman forced his resignation the following year in March of 1897. Brown's refusal to marry the woman led to his death.

# 1907

• **Dimitur Petkov**, the prime minister of Bulgaria, was shot to death on a Sofia street on February 26, 1907. Two members of his cabinet, Nicolai Genadiev (q.v.) and Gen. Michail Savov, were also injured in the assault. Petkov was born in 1858. He was a leader of the pro–Austrian Stambulovist party and served in the Bulgarian cabinet. He was called upon by King Ferdinand to head the government on November 14, 1906. His ministry was marked by widespread corruption and profiteering. He continued to head Bulgaria until his murder in March of 1907. His assassin, Alexander Petrov, was captured immediately and tried for the murder. Newspaper editor Ivan Ikonomov and journalist Matei Gerov are tried for instigating the murder. Petrov is convicted and hanged on July 3, 1907. Ikonomov served three years in prison for complicity and Gerov was acquitted.

- **Manuel Lisandro Barillas**, the former president of Guatemala, was assassinated in Mexico on April 7, 1907. Lisandro Barillas was born on January 17, 1864. He was owner of one of the largest coffee plantations in Guatemala. Lisandro Barillas was named provisional president of Guatemala after the resignation of Alejandro Sinibaldi on April 8, 1885. He was subsequently elected president and retained office until March 15, 1892.

- **Amin As-Soltan, Ali Asghar Khan** was born in 1858, the son of Aqa Ibrahim, a leading advisor to the Shah. He was Persia's most powerful political figure from the 1880s. He served as prime minister under Nasir ad-Din Shah and instituted Iran's pro–Russian policies in 1892. He was dismissed as prime minister following the assassination of Nasir ad-Din Shah in 1896, but returned as premier in 1898. Amin as-Soltan, having been given the title of Atabak, was unpopular with the progressives, who believed he was leading Iran to Russian control. He was again dismissed in September of 1903, and embarked on a world tour. In January of 1907 he was reappointed as premier by Mohammad Ali Shah, who had succeeded to the throne. Shortly after his appointment, Amin as-Soltan was stabbed to death by members of a radical group on August 31, 1907. The Shah attempted to use Soltan's killing as an excuse to crush the radicals, but the action instead encouraged them and increased their strength.

# 1908

- **King Carlos I** and **Crown Prince Luis Philippe** of Portugal were assassinated on February 1, 1908. Carlos was born in Lisbon on September 23, 1863. He was the son of King Luis of Portugal and Princess Pia of Savoy. Carlos married Marie Amelie of Orleans, the daughter of the Comte de Paris, in 1886. He succeeded to the throne upon his father's death on October 19, 1889. His reign was soon beset with both international and domestic crises. Portugal's economic condition deteriorated under mounting debts and oppressive taxes. Corruption in the government and the inability of the government to secure additional loans brought about calls for the establishment of a republic. Carlos dissolved the parliament in May of 1907 and granted dictatorial powers to Premier Joao Franco. Rioting took place throughout the country amid renewed calls for the abolishment of the monarchy. Another revolt broke out in late January of 1908 and the royal family returned to Lisbon from Vila Vicosa. Upon their arrival in Lisbon on February 1, 1908, two radical Republican gunmen ambushed and shot Carlos and the Crown Prince Louis Philippe to death in the royal carriage.

- **Count Andrzej Potocki** (1861–1908), the Hapsburg governor of Polish Galicia from 1903, was murdered by a Ukrainian nationalist.

- In June of 1908, following a coup d'état against the constitutional assembly of Persia by Mohammad Ali Shah, several prominent progressive leaders were arrested and executed. **Jamal Ad-Din Esfahani** and **Malek Al-Motakallemin**, both radical preachers from Isfahar, and **Mirza Jahangir Khan**, the editor of the newspaper *Sur-e Esrafil*, were executed on the orders of the shah.

- **Edward Ward Carmack**, a prominent Tennessee newspaper editor and political figure, was shot to death by political rivals on the streets of Nashville on November 9, 1908.

Carmack was born in Sumner County, Tennessee, on November 5, 1858. He was elected to the Tennessee state legislature in 1884 and, soon after, served as editor of the *Columbia Herald*. In 1888 he became editor of the *Nashville American*, and, forum years later, the *Memphis Commercial Appeal*. He used these forums to advance his position as a proponent of prohibition. In 1897 Carmack was elected to the United States Congress, and, in 1901, he was elected to the Senate. Rather than run for reelection in 1906, he chose to challenge Malcolm Patterson for governor of Tennessee, and was defeated. He continued his fight to eliminate liquor sales in the state as, again, editor of the *Nashville American*. He was slain by Duncan B. Cooper and his son, Robin, while campaigning to enact his prohibition policies before the Tennessee state legislature. The Coopers were political allies of Governor Patterson and were subsequently pardoned by the governor for the murder of Carmack.

• **Tsai-t'ien**, the emperor of China, died on November 14, 1908. He had been a virtual prisoner of the Dowager Empress for many years and it was considered likely that he had been poisoned shortly before or after her death. The Dowager Empress died the following day, but possibly predeceased him with his death only being announced first. Tsai-t'ien (Te-tsung) was born on August 14, 1871. He was the second son of Prince I-huan and the grandson of Emperor Hsuan-tsung. His cousin, Emperor Mu-tsung died on January 12, 1875, and his maternal aunt, the Dowager Empress Tz'u Hsi (Hsiao-ch'in), chose him as successor to the throne. He ascended the throne on February 25, 1875, with the Dowager Empresses Tz'u Hsi and Hsiao-chen as co-regents. The title Kwang Hsu was chosen to designate the years of his reign. Tsai-t'ien was proclaimed of age on February 7, 1887. He married a cousin on February 26, 1889, who became known as Empress Hsiao-ting. Dowager Empress Tz'u Hsi still retained considerable power at the court. Her use of funds designated for naval construction to build an imperial pleasure garden was instrumental in

China's defeat by Japan in the war of 1895. Tsai-t'ien initiated a reform movement with the intention of removing Tz'u Hsi from power. She anticipated the coup attempt and returned to Peking from her summer palace in September of 1898. The Emperor was confined on the palace grounds and she acted in his name to crush the reform movement. The influence of court officials and foreign diplomats prevented Tsai-t'ien from being murdered or dethroned. The Dowager Empress resented foreign influence in China and sponsored an anti-foreign movement known as the Boxer uprising in 1900. Foreign troops entered Peking to put down the uprising on August 14, 1900, and Tz'u-Hsi fled the palace for a period, bringing the Emperor with her. She continued to rule in his name and returned to Peking soon afterward. Tsai-t'ien remained a virtual prisoner until his death on November 14, 1908.

# 1909

• **Howard Baskerville** (1885–1909), an American missionary in Iran, was killed with Iranian revolutionaries on April 19, 1909, while leading the defense of the city of Tabriz from siege. Baskerville, a graduate of Princeton Theological Seminary, came to Iran in 1907. He became involved with the nationalist Iranian Constitution Movement.

• **Sir William Curzon Wyllie**, the British political aide-de-camp of the India office, was assassinated by an Indian Hindu nationalist at the Imperial Institute in London on July 2, 1909. A Parsi doctor, **Cowasjee Lalkaka**, who had rushed to Wyllie's aid, was also shot, dying several days later. The assassin, Madan Lal Dhingra (1883–1909), was tried and convicted of the murders and was hanged in London on August 17, 1909.

• **Jilali ibn Dris al-Yusfi al-Zarhuni**, known as **Bu Hmara** (master of the donkey), was executed on September 15, 1909, after a lengthy rebellion against Moroccan government. Al-Zarhuni had begun his rebellion in 1902 after the Sultan had refused to honor the sanctity of a shrine. Bu Hmara's forces withstood several assaults by loyalist troops. His forces were wiped in 1908 by a Berber army and Bu Hmara was captured on August 11, 1909. He was brought to Fez, and publicly executed on September 15, 1909.

• **Prince Hirobumi Ito**, a Japanese statesman and former premier, was killed while in Manchuria on October 26, 1909. Ito was born in Choshu on September 2, 1842, to a Samurai family. Following the overthrow of the shogunate and the restoration of imperial powers under Emperor Mutsuhito, Ito served in the foreign ministry. He soon became governor of Hyogo Prefecture. He became minister of public works in 1873. He was named home minister in 1878, becoming one of Japan's leading political figures. He became the first prime minister of Japan under the new cabinet system on December 22, 1885. He resigned as prime minister to head the privy council on April 30, 1888. Ito was instrumental in the promulgation of a constitution in 1889. He also became head of the upper house, the House of Peers, in 1890. He again headed the government from August 8, 1892. He remained prime minister until September 18, 1896. He again headed the government from January 12, 1898, until June 30, 1898, when he resigned over the issues of imposing additional land taxes. He formed a new government as prime minister on October 19, 1900. He resigned from office on June 2, 1901. Ito subsequently traveled to Russia to establish better trade relations. He returned to Japan to again head the privy council in 1903. After the Russo-Japanese War, Ito signed the Korean-Japanese Convention in 1905 which granted Japan full authority over Korea's foreign affairs. He became the first Japanese resident general of Korea in 1906. He forced the abdication of the Korean emperor and established the country as a Japanese protectorate. He resigned in 1909 to again head the privy council. Ito was touring Manchuria when he was assassinated at a railway station in Harbin by An Chung Gun, a Korean nationalist, on October 26, 1909.

• **Francisco Ferrer Guardia** (1859–1909), a Spanish educator and Socialist politician, was court-martialed and executed in October of 1909 for having taken part in anarchist riots in Barcelona.

• **Arthur Jackson**, the British district magistrate of Naski, India, was shot to death at his farewell party in India in December 1909.

# 1910

• **Butrus Ghali Pasha**, the premier of Egypt since 1908, was shot to death on February 19, 1910, on the steps of the ministry of justice, two days after he had introduced a bill for an extension of the Suez Canal company's concession. Butrus was born in a village near Beni-Suef, Egypt, in 1846. He was an influential leader in the Coptic Church and was instrumental in attempts to modernized the church in the late 1800s. He began his career in government service during the reign of Khedive Tawfiq, serving as minister of justice, finance and foreign affairs in various governments. Butrus served as foreign minister in the government of Mustafa Fahmi, and was involved in negotiations with the British over the Sudan. He succeeded Fahmi as prime minister in 1908 with the support of the British. He earned the enmity of the nationalists because of his conciliatory attitude toward the British, typified by his willingness to begin negotiations to extend the lease for the Suez Canal. Butrus was assassinated by Ibrahim Warddani, a young Moslem nationalist and pharmacist. Warddani claimed that he had shot the premier because Ghali had presided over the Denshaway Tribunal, which had, in 1906, sentenced four peasants to death for the killing of a British officer. Warddini's other motives included the revival of the Press Law and Ghali's Suez canal policy. Warddani was tried and executed on June 30, 1910.

- **Sayyed Abdollah Behbehani**, a prominent Persian politician and leader of the Moderate party, was assassinated by left-wing extremists in 1910.
- **William J. Gaynor** (Feb. 2, 1848–1913), the mayor of New York City from 1909 to 1913, was shot in the throat and seriously wounded on August 3, 1910, by James Gallagher, a discharged city employee, while on the deck of a ship, the *Kaiser Wilhelm der Grosse*, preparing for a vacation in Europe. Mayor Gaynor, a justice on the New York Supreme Court from 1893 until his election as mayor in 1910, remained in office until his death three years later on September 10, 1913, still suffering from lingering effects of his injury.
- **Miguel Bombarda**, a Portuguese psychiatrist and Republican leader, was murdered on October 3, 1910, by a mad patient. Bombarda's assassination led to an uprising that deposed Portugal's King Manuel II.

# 1911

- **Robert Ashe**, the British district magistrate of Tinevelly, was killed in Madras, India, in June of 1911.
- **Pyotr Arkadyevich Stolypin**, the Russian prime minister, was shot by an assassin on September 14, 1911. Stolypin was born in Dresden, Saxony, on April 14, 1862, the son of a Russian general. He was educated in St. Petersburg, and entered government in the ministry of domains. He was placed in charge of the Royal estates at Kovno in 1888. He was appointed governor of Grodno in 1902 and was named governor of Saratof the following year. He gained the notice of Emperor Nicholas II, who named Stolypin minister of the interior in May of 1906. He was appointed premier two months later on July 23, 1906. Stolypin was instrumental in the dismissal of the First Duma, Russia's legislative body, and subsequently ruled by executive decree. He instituted a series of reforms to enhance the welfare of the peasantry. He also began a policy of ruthless suppression against accused terrorists and rebels, thousands of whom were executed by "Stolypin's necktie," which became synonymous with the hangman's noose. He survived an attempt on his life August 25, 1906, when a bomb exploded during a party at his summer residence, seriously injuring many guests and two of his children. Stolypin again ruled by executive decree from June of 1907, and altered the constitution by Imperial decree to limit the franchise for future elections. He gained the enmity of most of - Russia's political factions because of his disregard for constitutional niceties. Stolypin was shot twice and critically wounded by Socialist Revolutionary terrorist Dmitry Bogrov while attending a performance at the Kiev opera on September 14, 1911. He died three days later in a Kiev hospital on September 17, 1911. Bogrov was subsequently hanged for the crime.

- **Ramon Caceres**, the president of the Dominican Republic, was slain on November 19, 1911. Caceres was born to a prosperous family in Moca on December 15, 1866. He was a leading opponent of the regime of President Ulises Heureaux (q.v.) in the 1890s. Caceres assassinated Heureaux at a rally in Moca on July 26, 1899. The nation's political situation remained unstable over the next several years and Caceres briefly went into exile in 1903. He returned to the Dominican Republic to serve as Carlos Morales' vice-president in 1904. Caceres succeeded to the presidency following Morales' resignation on January 13, 1906. He presided over a period of peace and prosperity in the Dominican Republic. He initiated numerous public works programs and reformed the constitution. He withstood several plots against his administration until November 19, 1911, when he was assassinated by political opponents. His death led to direct United States military intervention in the Dominican Republic from 1916 until 1924.

# 1912

• **General Pedro Montero**, the Ecuadorian revolutionary leader who had been proclaimed president by his troops in Guayaquil, Ecuador, following the death of President Emilio Estrada, was killed by a mob on January 24, 1912. Montero had been court-martialed for his participation in the revolt and was sentenced to sixteen years imprisonment. A mob, angered by what they considered too light a sentence, dragged Montero from the courtroom, riddled his body with bullets, cut off his head, and burned his remains in a bonfire. Montero, an ally of Eloy Alfaro (q.v.), had been the chief of the military in the Guayaquil district. He had formed a provisional ministry and awaited the return of Alfaro from exile. On January 23, 1912, government troops, led by General Leonidas Plaza, defeated the rebels and captured the leaders.

• Former Ecuadorian president **Eloy Alfaro** was killed on January 28, 1912. Alfaro and other revolutionary leaders, including his brothers **General Flavio Alfaro**, ex-minister of war and commander in chief of the revolutionary forces, and **General Medardo Alfaro**, and **General Ulpiano Paez** and **General Manuel Serrano**, were dragged from their jail cells and lynched by an angry mob.

Jose Eloy Alfaro Delgado was born in Monteristi, Manabi, Ecuador, on June 25, 1842. He was a supporter of General Jose Maria Urvina and was instrumental in the revolts against the regime of President Gabriel Garcia Moreno in 1865 and 1871. The failure of the revolts led to Alfaro's exile in Panama, where he continued to promote liberal causes in Ecuador and throughout Latin America. He returned to Ecuador in 1893 to lead a revolt against President Luis Cordero. Cordero was ousted in April of 1895 and Alfaro became Ecuador's leader on June 18, 1895. He called a constituent assembly which authored a new constitution and Alfaro was elected president of Ecuador in 1897. He completed

his term of office on September 1, 1901, and was succeeded by Leonidas Plaza Gutierrez. Alfaro led the revolt against the subsequent presidency of Lizardo Garcia and became president after his defeat of the government troops on January 16, 1906. He again convened a constitutional convention which chose him as president on January 2, 1907. His second term of office was marked by an attempt to reduce the power of the Roman Catholic church in Ecuador. He instituted laws to separate the church and state and church property not used for religious purposes was seized in 1908. He instituted reforms in education and public health and oversaw the opening of the Quito and Guayaquil Railroad. Alfaro stepped down from office on August 11, 1911, and Emilio Estrada was elected as his successor. Alfaro went into exile in Europe, but when Estrada died several months later a civil war ensued. Alfaro returned to Ecuador in an attempt to return to power in January of 1912. He was arrested and imprisoned in Guayaquil with other rebel leaders shortly after his return.

• Slavko Cuvaj (1851–1931), the ban, or governor, of Croatia, was seriously injured in an assassination attempt when a bomb was thrown at him by a young Croat student on June 8, 1912. Cuvaj subsequently resigned from office and left the country.

• **Michel Cincinnatus Leconte**, the president of Haiti, was killed in an explosion which destroyed the Palais National on August 8, 1912. The explosion occurred when a large stockpile of arms and ammunition stored in the basement of the presidential palace was ignited. It remains a mystery whether the explosion was an accident, though there is evidence to suggest that Leconte was murdered before the detonation, as his charred body was found dismembered after the explosion.

Leconte was educated in Haiti and in Europe. He was active in the revolt that ousted President Etienne Salomon in August of 1888. He held various government positions and served in the government of Pierre Nord Alexis as minister of the interior in 1906.

He was a leading figure in Northern Haiti, and was active in the military revolt that deposed President Antoine Simon. Leconte became president of Haiti on August 14, 1911. His regime was beset by opposition from the time he took power. He began making limited reforms in the country, advancing education and building barracks for the military. He also undertook an ambitious public works program and made significant strides against government corruption.

• On October 14, 1912, Theodore Roosevelt (1858–1919), the president of the United States from 1901 until 1909, was shot and wounded by John N. Schrank (1876–1943) before addressing a crowd in Milwaukee, Wisconsin. Roosevelt was in the midst of a campaign for the presidency on the Progressive (or Bull Moose) party ticket. Following his shooting in front of the Gilpatrick Hotel, Roosevelt proceeded to the Milwaukee Auditorium and gave his speech to the crowd before seeking medical attention. Roosevelt recovered from his wounds and went on to place second, ahead of Republican incumbent William Howard Taft, in the election. Schrank was judged insane and sentenced to the Central State Hospital in Wisconsin, where he remained until his death over thirty years later.

• **Jose Canalejas y Mendes**, the premier of Spain, was slain by an anarchist on November 12, 1912. Canalejas was born to a wealthy family in El Ferrol on July 31, 1854. He entered politics in 1881 and was elected to the Cortes from Soria. Two years later he was named to the prime minister's department as an undersecretary. He joined the cabinet as minister of public works and justice in 1888 and served as minister of finance in 1894. He stepped down from Praxades Mateo Sagasta's cabinet in 1902, feeling the government was not going far enough in settling the question of religious orders. He served as president of the Chamber of Deputies in 1906. Canalejas, a leftist member of the Liberal Party, succeeded Segismundo Moret as prime minister on February 8, 1910. His government was faced with a railway strike in mid–1912. He responded by compelling the workers to return to their jobs by conscripting them into the military. He also attempted to decentralize the Spanish government to give more power to the provinces. Canalejas was shot to death by Manuel Pardinas, a young anarchist, while entering the ministry of the interior for a conference on November 12, 1912. The assassin fired two shots at the premier and then killed himself.

# 1913

• **Nazim Pasha**, the Turkish minister of war, and two other Turkish officials were assassinated during a cabinet meeting on January 23, 1913, by a group of young revolutionaries led by Enver Bey.

• **Manuel Enrique Araujo**, the president of El Salvador, died on February 8, 1913, of wounds received in an assassination attempt. Araujo was trained as a physician. He entered politics and served in the national assembly. He also served as mayor of San Salvador. He became president of El Salvador on February 28, 1911. During his term of office he established the national guard and reorganized the army. He also encouraged industrial development in the country. Araujo was stabbed by an assassin on February 4, 1913. He died four days later on February 8, 1913.

• **Francisco I. Madero**, the president of Mexico, and **Jose Pino Suarez**, his vice-president, were slain on February 23, 1913, after having been overthrown and arrested by General Victoriano Huerta.

Madero was born to a wealthy family in Parras, Coahuila, on October 30, 1873. Madero soon became active in politics and formed the Benito Juarez Democratic Club in 1905. He was defeated for the governorship of Coahuila that year. He formed the National Antireelectionist Party to challenge dictator Porfirio Diaz. Madero was arrested in June of 1910 on the eve of the election. He fled to San

Antonio, Texas, after his release and issued a call for an armed rebellion against Diaz. The revolution began on November 10, 1910. The government was unable to suppress the rebellion and Diaz resigned on May 25, 1911. Madero was the candidate of the Constitutional Progressive Party and won the election by a wide margin. He assumed office on November 6, 1911. His government tried to introduce social legislation and political reforms that led to a rightist rebellion led by Pascual Orozco. The government forces under General Victoriano Huerta suppressed the rebellion. Followers of Emiliano Zapata also revolted against the government, claiming Madero was going too slowly in implementing land reform and other promises made during the revolution. A military revolt led by Felix Diaz erupted within the federal army in early 1913. General Huerta, with the approval of United States Ambassador Henry Lane Wilson, betrayed Madero and joined with the rebels. Madero was forced to resign on February 18, 1913, and was arrested. He and his vice-president, Jose Maria Pino Suarez, were murdered while being transferred to prison on February 22, 1913, allegedly while trying to escape.

• **Sung Chiao-jen**, a leading member of the Chinese Kuomintang and an associate of Sun Yat-sen, was assassinated, presumably by agents of Yuan Shih-ka'i, the provisional president of China, in March of 1913.

• **George I**, the king of Greece, was assassinated on March 18, 1913. The monarch was shot to death by a Greek named Alexandros Schinas, while he was walking in the streets of Salonika. George I was born Prince William of Schleswig-Holstein in Copenhagen, Denmark, on December 24, 1845. When King Otho of Greece was forced to abdicated in October of 1862 Prince William was nominated by Great Britain, France and Russia to ascend to the throne. The Greek national assembly accepted the nomination on March 30, 1863, and he claimed the throne as king of the Hellenes on October 31, 1863. A new constitution was promulgated the following year and George reigned as a constitutional monarch. George was a popular monarch during most of his fifty year reign, which ended with his assassination. He was succeeded by his son, Constantine I.

• **Tancrede Auguste**, the president of Haiti, died on May 2, 1913. His death was largely thought to be the result of poisoning. Auguste was a prosperous planter and businessman from Cape Haitian. He served in President Tiresias Simon Sam's government as minister of the interior and police from 1896 until 1902. He was elected president on August 8, 1912, following the death of Michel Cincinnatus Leconte. Auguste suffered from poor health in the latter part of his term, remaining president until his death.

• **Mahmud Sevket**, the Turkish grand vizier, was assassinated on June 11, 1913, in Istanbul. Sevket was born in 1858, in Baghdad, and was educated in Constantinople. He subsequently served in the Turkish army. He was stationed in Germany for nine years, rising to the rank of general in 1901. He supported the Young Turk Revolution in 1908 and, as inspector general and commander of the Third Army, he suppressed a counter-revolution the following year. Following the abdication of Sultan Abdul-Hamid II, Sevket became minister of war. Following an insurrection by members of the Committee of Union and Progress (CUP) and the subsequent resignation of Kamil Pasa as Grand Vizier, Sevket assumed that office on January 23, 1913. He was assassinated by opponents of the CUP on June 11, 1913.

• **Abe**, the director of the Japanese foreign office's political affairs bureau, was murdered in Tokyo by militant Japanese nationalists on September 5, 1913.

# 1914

• **Gaston Calmette** (1858–1914), a French journalist, was shot and killed on March 15, 1914. Calmette was the editor of *Le Figaro* from 1913, and had tried to expose the financial corruption of the French government, particularly the policies of Joseph Caillaux, the minister of finance. Calmette was murdered by Mme. Caillaux in his office while he was preparing further incriminating evidence against her husband. Mme. Caillaux was acquitted in the subsequent trial, but the scandal resulted in the resignation of her husband.

• **Archduke Francis Ferdinand** of Austria and his wife, **Countess Sophie Chotek**, Duchess of Hohenberg, were assassinated on June 28, 1914, by Gavrilo Princip, a Serbian nationalist student, while on a visit to Sarajevo, Bosnia. Francis Ferdinand was born in Graz on December 18, 1863, the son of Archduke Charles Louis. He became the heir apparent to the crown of Emperor Francis Joseph of Austria, his uncle, following the suicide of the emperor's only son, Archduke Rudolf, on January 30, 1889. On July 1, 1900, Francis Ferdinand married Countess Sophie Chotek, following a bitter confrontation with his uncle, and only after renouncing the future rights of succession for their children. Francis Ferdinand used his prestige and office to attempt a reconciliation with the Russians and to effect a solution to Hungary's internal problems. His assassination was considered to be the immediate cause of the First World War. Twenty-five people were tried and convicted in connection with the assassinations, including Danilo Ilic, who was sentenced to be hanged for his part in organizing the conspiracy. Gavrilo Princip, who had fired the fatal shots, was sentenced to twenty years in prison. He died of tuberculosis in April of 1918.

• Abbas II (1874–1944), the khedive of Egypt, was shot and wounded in an assassination attempt by an Egyptian student in July 1914 while he was visiting Constantinople. Abbas, who had served as khedive of Egypt since January of 1892, was deposed by the British and sent into exile the following December.

• French Socialist leader **Jean Leon Jaures** was assassinated on July 31, 1914, while dining in a Paris cafe. His assailant was Raoul Villain, a right-wing fanatic. Jaures was born on September 3, 1859, in Tarn. He was a teacher and writer when he was elected a deputy from Tarn in 1885. Four years later he was defeated for reelection and returned to teaching. During this period he also authored several important essays on philosophy. He returned to the chamber of deputies in 1893 and served until 1899. He was again elected in 1902, serving until his death. He was the leader of the French Socialist party in the chamber during much of his tenure. In 1904 he was a founder and editor of *L'Humanite*, the Socialist newspaper. Jaures was active in seeking a Franco-German reconciliation, and opposed militarist legislation prior to the First World War. His assassination removed the most prominent and respected Socialist leader from the French scene. Villain, his assassin, was himself murdered in Spain in 1936, by leftists revenging the murder of Jaures.

• **Chief Douala Rudolf Manga Bell** (1873–1914), a tribal leader in Cameroon, was executed by firing squad by the German colonial authorities on August 8, 1914. Manga Bell had become King in 1910. He opposed the colonial leaders until his arrest and deposition in August of 1913. He and fellow anti-colonialist **Martin-Paul Samba** (1875–14), the traditional chief of the Ebolowa, were executed the following year, shortly after the outbreak of World War I.

• **John Schuyler Crosby**, a former Governor of Montana Territory, was attacked and beaten by a deranged servant in 1914 and died in Newport, Rhode Island, several months later on August 8, 1914. Crosby was born in Albany, New York, on September 19, 1839. He served as a colonel in the Union Army during the Civil War. Crosby was Governor of Montana Territory from 1883 until 1884.

• **Jacobus Hercules De la Rey** was shot and killed by a police patrol in Johannesburg, South Africa, on September 15, 1914. De la Rey was born in 1847 in the Orange Free State and was raised in Transvaal. He entered the South African parliament in 1893, and on the advent of the South African War in 1899, he became a general. He conducted many successful guerrilla campaigns against the British, and was considered a worthy and honorable foe. Following the conclusion of the war, De la Rey became a leading supporter of Louis Botha, and was active in his political party, Het Volt ("The People"). He was a representative in the legislative assembly from 1907 until 1910, and from 1910 to 1914, he was a member of the Union of South Africa's first senate. He sided with the rebels seeking to restore republican independence at the start of the First World War, but was shot to death before he could lead the rebellion. His killing was instrumental in staring the revolt which began the month following his death.

# 1915

Joao Chagas (1863–1925), the premier designate of Portugal, was shot and seriously wounded in 1915 by **Joao De Freitas**, a member of the Portuguese senate, who was slain by Chagas' bodyguards. Chagas briefly served as Portugal's prime minister in 1911. He was a supporter of the Allies against Germany, but the seriousness of his wounds, which included the loss of his right eye, prevented him from forming a government. He recovered to serve as a member of the Portuguese delegation to the Versailles Peace Conference. Chagas died in Lisbon on May 28, 1925.

• **Mijiddorjiyn Handdorj** (1871– 1915), the foreign minister of Mongolia, was assassinated in February of 1915. Handdorj headed the foreign ministry in the government of the Bogd Khan from November of 1911. He negotiated the Mongolian-Russian treaty the following year.

• **Oreste Zamor**, the former president of Haiti, was executed with numerous other political prisoners on July 27, 1915, while imprisoned in Port-au-Prince. Zamor was a leading military figure in the northern region of Haiti. He and his brother, Charles, led a military revolt against the regime of President Michel Oreste, that ousted the government

on January 27, 1914. He was chosen by the chamber of deputies to replace Oreste as president on February 8, 1914. Haiti's economy continued to deteriorate under Zamor's rule and his administration came into conflict with European interests in the country. He was faced with widespread revolt, and was forced to resign on October 29, 1914. Zamor was arrested in early 1915 by the government of Jean Guillaume Sam and was jailed in Port-au-Prince. As Sam's government began to collapse, the jail commandant ordered the execution of all political prisoners being held and Zamor was brutally executed on July 27, 1915.

• **Jean Vilbrun Guillaume Sam**, the president of Haiti, was murdered by a mob on July 28, 1915. Sam was the son of Tiresias Simon Sam, who served as Haiti's president from 1896 until 1902. The younger Sam was the leader of the Haitian revolution in January of 1915. He became president of Haiti on March 4, 1915. He was faced with a rebellion in the north led by Rosalvo Bobo and took repressive measures against his political opponents. Sam ordered the execution of several hundred of his political opponents on July 27, 1915, including former president Oreste Zamor (q.v.). Following a revolution against his oppressive rule, he took refuge in the French Legation in Port-au-Prince on July 28, 1915. An angry mob stormed the legation, dragging Sam into the streets. He was then impaled on the iron fence surrounding the legation and torn to pieces, with the remnants of his corpse being drug through the streets. His regime and the subsequent civil disorders led to American military intervention in August of 1915.

# 1916

On Easter Monday, April 24, 1916, the Easter Rising in Dublin took place, with the leaders of the rebellion proclaiming Ireland as an independent republic. The rebellion was quickly put down by the British, and many

Republican leader who took part were executed or imprisoned. The more prominent leaders killed included **Patrick Henry Pearse**, **James Connolly**, **Sir Roger David Casement**, and **Thomas MacDonagh** (1878–1916), a poet. Other insurgent leaders who were executed by firing squad within twelve days of the rising included **Tom Clarke**, **Joseph Plunkett**, **Edward Daly**, **Michael O'Hanrahan**, **Willie Pearse**, **John MacBride**, **Eamon Ceannt**, **Michael Mallin**, **Sean Heuston**, **Cornelius Colbert** and **Sean MacDermott**.

Patrick Pearse was born on November 10, 1879, in Dublin. He was a writer and poet of some renown when he became active in the movement for Irish independence. He was a proponent of a teaching system incorporating Irish traditions and culture, and, in 1906, founded St. Enda's College in Dublin based on these attributes. He also authored several essays on education. He was active in the Irish Republican Brotherhood, becoming a member of its ruling council in 1914. Later in the year, when the Republican movement splintered, Pearse became director of organization of the more extreme Nationalist faction. During the First World War he opposed assistance to Great Britain. At the time of the Easter Rising, Pearse was commander-in-chief of the Nationalist forces, which announced independence. On the steps of the general post office in Dublin, Pearse proclaimed himself president of the Irish provisional government. On April 29, 1916, he surrendered to the British forces and, following a court-martial, was executed by firing squad on May 3, 1916, at Kilmainham Prison.

James Connolly was born June 5, 1870, in County Monaghan, Ireland. An early Irish Socialist leader, Connolly became active in the formation of trade unions, working with James Larkin. At the start of World War I, Connolly took charge of the Irish labor movement in Larkin's absence. He called for non-participation in the Allied war effort and the overthrow of all capitalistic states. He accompanied Pearse during the Easter Rising in Dublin. He was captured by the British and, on May 12, 1916, was executed at Kilmainham Prison.

Sir Roger David Casement was born in County Dublin on September 1, 1864. He became associated with the British consular service, serving as consul to various African colonies from 1892 to 1903. He also served in diplomatic posts in South America, notably Brazil, from 1906 until 1911. Casement gained an international reputation for his exposé of the slave trade in areas in which he had served, particularly the Congo and Peru. His investigation in these matters led to changes in the colonial administration and earned Casement a knighthood in 1911. The following year he retired and returned to Ireland. He became active in Nationalist activities and opposed Irish assistance to Britain in World War I. During the war he undertook a mission to Germany to seek aid in achieving Irish independence. Casement, hearing of the proposed Easter Rising, returned to Ireland aboard a German submarine, bringing arms to the Irish rebels. The ship was captured; Casement was arrested on April 24, 1916. He was tried and convicted of treason and, on August 3, 1916, was hanged in London at Pentonville Prison.

- **Shafiq Mu'ayyad al-Azm**, a Syrian nationalist leader, was charged with treason and hanged by a Turkish military tribunal in Damascus on May 6, 1916. Azm represented Damascus as a member of the Ottoman Empire's Lower Chamber of Deputies from 1908. He was a leader of Arab interests in the chamber and a critic of the ruling Committee of Union and Progress.

- **Karl Sturgkh**, the Austrian prime minister, was assassinated in Vienna on October 21, 1916. Sturgkh was born in Graz on October 30, 1859, to an impoverished noble family in Styria. He entered politics and was elected a deputy to the Reichsrath, or parliament. He served as a director in the ministry of public works in 1894. He served as Ernst von Koerber's parliamentary lieutenant from 1900 until 1904. He gained a reputation as an expert in educational matters and received the patronage of Rudolf Sieghart, a leading financier and newspaper publisher. Sturgkh headed the public works ministry from 1909 and was called upon to head the government on November 3, 1911. Sturgkh remained minister president of Austria following Archduke Francis Ferdinand's assassination on June 28, 1914, and the subsequent events leading to World War I. Sturgkh headed the government in the early years of the war and, despite entreaties, refused to convene parliament. He remained minister president until October 21, 1916, when he was shot to death by radical Socialist Friedrich Adler (1879–1960), while having lunch at a Vienna hotel. Adler claimed he killed the prime minister as a protest against the First World War. He was convicted of the crime and sentenced to death. This sentence was subsequently commuted and, two years later, Adler was released from prison.

• **Sultan 'Ali Dinar** of Darfur renounced his allegiance to the government of the Sudan in 1916, resulting in a battle with troops commanded by Lt. Col. P.J. Kelly near El Fasher in May of 1916. Dinar's army was routed, and the Sultan fled to Jabal Marrah, where he was killed on November 6, 1916.

• **Charles Foucauld**, a French soldier and adventurer, was assassinated in North Africa December 1, 1916. Foucauld was born September 15, 1858, in Strasbourg. He served in the French army in Algeria before embarking on a personal exploration of North Africa and the Middle East. During this period he became interested in religion, and in 1890 he became a Trappist monk. In 1897 he left the order and in 1901 he was ordained into the priesthood. He then returned to North Africa, settling with the Tauregs in the Hoggar mountains. He was largely responsible for retaining the area's loyalty to France, and it was for this reason that his assassination was accomplished by the rebellious Senusi in Tripoli.

• **Grigori E. Rasputin**, the Russian mystic and advisor to the court of Czar Nicholas II (q.v.), was murdered on December 31, 1916, by a group of Russian noblemen who perceived him to be a baneful influence on the emperor. Rasputin was born in 172 at Pokrovskoe, near Tyumen. At an early age he

devoted himself to a life of religion, though of an unorthodox sort. Having a magnetic personality, and likely possessed of hypnotic powers, Rasputin gained a large following among the peasantry. In 1903 he began a pilgrimage to St. Petersburg, where he became a part of aristocratic circles. In 1905 he gained the attention of the court of the Romanovs. His efforts to comfort and cure the heir apparent, Alexis (q.v.), a hemophiliac, won him the lasting gratitude of Czarina Alexandra (q.v.). She considered him a holy man who had been sent by God to ensure the czar's continued rule. Rasputin exercised his newly won powers by advocating strong, autocratic measures against the czar's opponents.

Following the outbreak of World War I and Nicholas' absence from the capital as field commander, Rasputin gained near absolute control of Russia through the empress. His debauchery and reputation for moral corruption brought him the hatred and contempt of many leading Russian politicians, and his position of power brought him the jealousy of many others. The major opposition to his influence was espoused by the rightists in the court, who eventually effected his execution. A group of conspirators, headed by Prince Felix F. Yousupov (1887–1967), took it upon themselves to dispose of Rasputin, feeling they were ridding the empire of a malevolent individual who threatened the entire dynasty. On the evening of December 30, 1916, Rasputin was lured to what he presumed to be a party at the home of Prince Yousupov. After an attempt to poison him had seemingly no effect, the conspirators shot and stabbed him. He was then bound and thrown, still alive, into an icy river, where he finally perished.

# 1917

• **Vice-Admiral Adrian Nepenin** (1871–1917), the commander of the Russian Baltic Fleet, was murdered during on March 17, 1917, at Sveaborg Naval Port in

Helsinki. Dozens of other admirals and officers were also killed by rioting soldiers including **Admiral Robert Viren**, the Chief Officer of the Port of Kronstadt.

• **Jose Manuel Pando**, the former president of Bolivia, was assassinated by political opponents on June 15, 1917. Pando had served as Brazil's president from October of 1899 until August of 1904. Pando was born in Arica on December 25, 1848. He studied medicine in La Paz before joining the army in 1871 to oppose the dictatorship of Mariano Melgarejo. He served with distinction in the War of the Pacific from 1879 until 1884, and rose to the rank of lieutenant colonel. He was the commander of the victorious Liberal forces during the civil war of 1899. Pando became head of the ruling junta on October 6, 1899, following the resignation of President Severo Fernandez Alonso. Pando's government initiated many public works programs, developing roads and railroads. He attempted to put down a Brazilian-sponsored separatist movement in the rubber-rich Acre region in the Amazon basin. Bolivia was forced to cede much of the region to Brazil with the Treaty of Petropolis in 1903. He completed his term of office on August 14, 1904. Pando remained active in politics and formed the Republican Party in 1914 after breaking with the Liberals.

• **Dragutin Dimitrijevic**, a Serbian army officer and nationalist leader, was executed on June 27, 1917, along with two of his associates, **Ljobomir Vulovic** and **Rade Malobatic**. Dimitrijevic, who was also known as Colonel Apis, was born in August of 1876 in Belgrade. As a member of the army, he was active in the conspiracy that resulted in the assassination of King Alexander (q.v.) in 1903. He became a leading member of the cadre of officers that ruled the army under the new king. In 1911 he was the founder of the secret society known as "Union or Death," which sought the unification of all the Serbs. The society, commonly known as the Black Hand, was instrumental in the assassination of Archduke Francis Ferdinand (q.v.) in 1914. In December of 1916 Dimitrijevic was arrested

on charges of attempting the assassination of the regent Alexander (q.v.). Though his guilt was not full proved, it granted his political opponents the opportunity to remove a leading obstacle in the way of their control of the army, and Dimitrijevic's subsequent court-martial resulted in a sentence of death.

• **Mata Hari**, the Dutch dancer who became a spy during World War I, died by firing squad on October 15, 1917. She was born Gertrude Zelle August 7, 1876, in the Netherlands. She learned oriental dances while in Java with her husband, Captain Campbell MacLeod. Following their divorce she returned to Europe and, taking the name of Mata Hari, began a career as a dancer. After settling in Paris in 1908, she soon became an agent of the German government, using her connections in French society and government circles to learn French military information. The French eventually learned of her intrigues and, in July of 1917, she was tried by a French court-martial and sentenced to death by firing squad.

• **Nikolai N. Dukhonin** (1876–1917), the commander-in-chief of Russian armed forces during the 1917 revolution, was shot to death by soldiers in revolt on December 3, 1917, after refusing to begin peace negotiations with the Germans.

• **Ivan L. Goremykin**, the former Russian prime minister, his wife, and brother-in-law were killed by robbers at their country house in Sotchy, on the Black Sea, on December 11, 1917. Goremykin was born to a prominent family in Novgorod province on October 27, 1839. He began a decade long period of service in Poland, where he was named commissioner of peasant affairs. He was named vice-governor of Plotsk in 1866 and Keletsk in 1869. He returned to St. Petersburg in 1873, where he entered the ministry of interior as a member of the provisional committee for peasant affairs. He replaced Ivan Durnovo as minister of interior in October of 1895. He subsequently served on the state council, where he exercised little influence over the next six years. In April of 1906 Goremykin was named head of the council of ministers.

Goremykin was dismissed by the Emperor in favor of Pyotr Stolypin (q.v.) on July 8, 1905. He held no major position in subsequent governments until February 11, 1914, when he was again called upon by Nicholas II (q.v.) to replace Vladimir Kokovtsev as chairman of the council of ministers. He continued to support the Emperor in the face of growing unrest throughout the country. His increasing inability to effectively serve as a buffer between the government and the Duma led to his dismissal on February 2, 1916. He subsequently retired from politics. Goremykin was forced to flee to the Caucasus following the Bolshevik revolution in 1917. He was killed there on December 11, 1917.

• **Andrei Ivanovich Shingarev** (1869–1917), a deputy of the fourth Duma and the minister of agriculture, and later finance, in the first cabinet of the Russian provisional government in 1917, and **Fyodor Fedorovich Kokoshkin** (1871–1917), a professor of constitutional law at Moscow University and deputy of the fourth Duma who served as state comptroller of the provisional government, were murdered by two Kronstadt sailors assigned to guard them after being transferred from prison to a hospital ward in December of 1917.

# 1918

• **Metropolitan Vladimir** was tortured and shot to death on January 25, 1918, at the Lavra Monastery in Russia, by men dressed in military uniforms. Vladimir was born in the province of Tombovsk on January 1, 1848. He was named archbishop in 1898 and Metropolitan of Moscow and Kolomna in 1898. He served as Metropolitan of Petrograph from 1915 until a disagreement with Czar Nicholas (q.v.) over his advisor, Rasputin (q.v.), resulted in his transfer to Metropolitan of Kiev.

• **General Lavr Georgievich Kornilov** (1870–1918), a leader of the anti–Bolshevik forces in Russia, was killed at his headquarters by a shell on April 13, 1918. Kornilov was a graduate of he Nicholas Academy of the General Staff. He served in the Russo-Japanese War and was military attaché in China from 1907 to 1911. He served in the Russian army during World War I. He was taken prisoner by the Austrians, but effected an escape in 19116. He served as commander in chief of the Russian Armies from July until September of 1917. Kornilov was subsequently arrested for several months before his release the following December. He co-founded the anti–Bolshevik Volunteer army movement and led the First Kuban campaign before his death.

• **General Count Wilhelm Von Mirbach-Harff**, the German ambassador to Moscow, was assassinated on July 16, 1918, by two members of the Social Revolutionary party. Mirbach-Harff had become his nation's ambassador to Russia following the signing of the Brest Litovsk Treaty earlier in the year. His killing was intended to force resumption of hostilities with Germany and was followed by an attempted coup. The rising was suppressed, and peace was maintained by the two countries.

• In mid–July much of the Russian royal family was executed by the Bolsheviks, who had held them in captivity since the Revolution of 1917.

**Grand Duke Michael Alexandrovich Romanoff** (Nov. 22, 1878–1918), the czar's younger brother, who had declined succession to the throne after Nicholas' abdication on March 15, 1917, was exiled to Perm in the Ural region in February of 1918. On July 10, 1918, the grand duke and his English secretary were murdered by Cheka agents under the leadership of Miasnikov. Their bodies were presumably burned, as they were never located.

On July 18, 1918, the Russian royal family was executed. **Czar Nicholas II**, his wife, the **Czarina Alexandra**, and their five children, the **Czarevitch Alexis** (Aug. 12, 1904–18) and the **Grand Duchesses Olga**

(Nov. 15, 1895–1918), **Tatiana** (June 10, 1897–1918), **Marie** (June 26, 1899–1918) and **Anastasia** (June 18, 1901–18), were all slain. Several members of their household, including the czar's personal physician Dr. Evgeni Sergeevich Botkin, servants Alexis Trupp and Anna Stefanova Demidova and cook Ivan Kharitonov, were also executed with them in Ekaterinburg by a Bolshevik firing squad, led by Jakov Yurosky (1878–1938), under orders from the chairman of the Ural soviet, Aleksandr G. Beloborodov (1891–1938). The royal family had been held under arrest at various locations in Russia following the abdication of Nicholas on March 15, 1917.

Nicholas II was born on May 18, 1868, in Tsarskoe Selo. He was the eldest son of the future Emperor Alexander III and his consort Maria Fedorovna, Princess Dagmar of Denmark. Nicholas' father ascended to the throne as Emperor of Russia following the assassination of Alexander II in March of 1881. He succeeded his father as emperor following Alexander II's death on November 1, 1894, and he was crowned as Nicholas II on May 26, 1895. He married Alexandra, the daughter of German Grand Duke Louis IV of Hesse-Darmstadt on November 26, 1894. His wife was a strong-willed woman who wielded vast influence with the Emperor, despite her unpopularity with the Royal Court and the populace. Nicholas ruled Russia as an autocrat whose absolute power over the country was granted by God. He distrusted his ministers and was unyielding in his view that the government would exercise no powers not derived from the throne. He continued his father's policy of Russification, which resulted in increasing dissatisfaction by the non–Russian ethnic people of the Empire. Nicholas tried to expand Russia's sphere of influence in Asia in the early 1900s. His policy toward Korea sparked the Russo-Japanese War of 1904, which ultimately resulted in the defeat of Russia's Baltic Fleet in May of 1905. The subsequent peace settlement forced Russia to abandon all claims to Korea, though it was allowed to maintain influence in northern Manchuria. The cost of the war in lives and

money sparked a workers' rebellion in St. Petersburg on January 22, 1905, when police fired into a crowd of peaceful demonstrators, killing nearly 1,000. Riots and strikes took place throughout Russia, culminating in a general strike in October of 1905. Nicholas was forced to issue a proclamation allowing the establishment of an elected legislature, the Duma. The Duma attempted to institute numerous political reforms, which the Emperor refused to consider. Nicholas and his prime minister, Pyotr Stolypin (q.v.), dismissed the Duma in July of 1906, setting the stage for the election of the Second Duma. This legislature was even more reform-minded than the first, which made agreement between it and the Emperor's government impossible. The Second Duma was dissolved in June of 1907 and Nicholas subsequently reneged on many of the political reforms of 1905. Though two more Dumas were subsequently selected, Nicholas continued to rule Russia as an absolute monarch with the able assistance of Stolypin until the latter's murder in 1911. International tensions were on the rise throughout Europe, and Russia entered World War I against Germany and the Austro-Hungarian Empire as an ally of Great Britain and France. The Russian army was ill-prepared for the battle ahead and suffered numerous casualties during the invasion of East Prussia in August of 1914. Nicholas took personal command of the Russian armies in September of 1915, leaving the country largely in the hands of the Empress. She had allied herself with Grigori Rasputin (q.v.), a self-styled holy man. Rasputin was considered a malign influence on the Royal Court and government, whose authority was derived largely from his ability to control the hemophiliac bleeding of the young Czarevitch Alexis. The Empress' German background also led to distrust and allegations of treason against her and her advisor. Members of the Royal Court took matters in their own hand and orchestrated the brutal murder of Rasputin at the end of December of 1916. With Nicholas still absent from the capital, rioting broke out in Petrograd in March of 1917. The Emperor sent troops to restore order, but the government resigned and calls for Nicholas' abdication increased. Amidst widespread civil unrest the Emperor agreed to renounce the throne on March 15, 1917, in favor of his brother, the Grand Duke Michael (q.v.), who declined the crown. Nicholas was initially held at Tsarskoe Selo, before being taken with his family to Tobolsk, in Western Siberia. They were held prisoner for over a year by the Bolsheviks. The Royal Family was removed to Ekaterinburg in the Urals in April of 1918. The approach of the White Russian army on Ekaterinburg led to an order by the Bolshevik leadership to prevent the rescue of Nicholas. The local captors executed the Emperor, his wife and five children, and other members of the Royal Court during the night of July 29, 1918. The bodies were burned and the remains were unceremoniously dumped into an abandoned mineshaft.

Alexandra, the wife of Nicholas II, was born June 6, 1872, in Darmstadt, Germany. She was the daughter of Grand Duke Louis IV of Hesse-Darmstadt. She changed her name from Alix Victoria Helene Luise Beatrix to Alexandra Feodorovna on her marriage to the czar on November 26, 1894. In 1904, after having given birth to four daughters, she gave Nicholas a male heir to the throne, the Czarevitch Alexis. The czarevitch was a sickly child, suffering from hemophilia. His condition kept Alexandra in a constant state of nervous anxiety, and led her to place her faith in Grigori Rasputin (q.v.), a disreputable holy man who seemed to bring comfort to her son. Through Alexandra, Rasputin gained great influence in the court, which added to the discontent of the populace and the displeasure of Russian society. Following the start of World War I and the czar's absence from the capital while serving as commander-in-chief of the army, Alexandra and Rasputin were left in virtual control of the government. Her German heritage nurtured the distrust of many prominent Russians, some even suspecting her as being an agent of the Germans. Rasputin's assassination in 1916 served only to make her more extreme in her belief of Nicholas' God-given right to rule. Her influence and

unpopular nature were thus largely responsible for the revolution of March 1917, following which she accompanied her husband and family to their exile and eventual death.

On July 18, 1918, the Russian **Grand Dukes Sergius Mikhailovich Romanoff** (Sept. 25, 1869–1918), **Ivan Constantinovich Romanoff** (July 5, 1886–1918), **Constantine Constantinovich Romanoff** (Dec. 24, 1890–1918) and **Igor Constantinovich Romanoff** (May 29, 1895–1918), the **Grand Duchess Elisabeth Feodorovna Romanoff** (1864–1918), widow of Grand Duke Sergius Alexandrovich (q.v.) and **Prince Vladimir Paley** (1896–1918), the son of Grand Duke Paul, who were being held at Alapayevsk following the ouster of the monarchy, were brutally murdered by the Bolsheviks. Grand Duke Sergius was shot, while the others are thrown into a mine near Ekaterinburg and grenades hurled after them.

• **Herman Von Eichhorn** (1848–1918), the German field marshal who led the Tenth Army against the Russians during the First World War, was assassinated in the Ukraine on July 31, 1918. Eichhorn had also commanded the Eichhorn military group in Kurland from 1916 until 1918.

• **Moses Solomonovich Uritsky**, the local head of the Russian Bolshevik security police, or Cheka, was shot and killed by a Social Revolutionary student on August 13, 1918.

• Lenin (1870–1924), who led the Bolshevik Revolution in Russia and served as premier of the Soviet Union from 1917, was seriously injured in an assassination attempt on August 30, 1918. Lenin was shot twice by Fanya Kaplan (1893–1918), a revolutionary. Kaplan was seized by guards and summarily executed. He recovered from his injuries and returned to his duties. Doctors removed the bullet from his neck four years later. His health further deteriorated, with him suffering from periods of semi-paralysis. Lenin suffered a major stroke on March 10, 1923, losing the power of speech. He remained seriously ill until his death in Gorky on January 21, 1924.

- **Aleksandr D. Protopopov** (1866–1918), the Russian czar's last minister of the interior, was executed in September of 1918. Protopopov had served as a member of the Octoberist party in the third and fourth Duma, he served as vice-chairman of the Duma from 1914 to 1916. An ally of Grigori Rasputin (q.v.), Protopopov was named as Russia's minister of the interior on October 1, 1916. His reactionary policies further inflamed the population against the government and the royal family. Following the Revolution of March 1917, Protopopov was arrested and imprisoned in the Peter and Paul Fortress. He was held there until his execution by the order of the Communist Cheka.

- **Aleksandr Ivanovich Dubrovin** (1855–1918) was a founder and leader of the Union of Russian People. A physician, he also edited *Russkoe Znamia* and was considered responsible for the murders of Russian Duma members Mikhail Gertsensenstein and Dr. Iolloss (q.v.) in 1906. He was an opponent of Prime Minister Petr Stolypin (q.v.) and was forced to resign his position with the Union of Russian People in 1910. He remained an outspoken critic of the government and was shot by the Bolsheviks in 1918.

- Many other leading Russian politicians were executed during the year by the Bolshevik regime. Those killed included **Aleksei Nikolaevich Khvostov** (1872–1918), the former governor of Vologda (1906–10) and **Nizhnii Novgorod** (1910–12) and the Russian minister of the interior from 1915 to 1916 in August; **Ivan Gregorevich Shcheglovitov** (1861–1918), minister of justice from 1906 to 1915 and president of the state council in 1917; **Nicholas Alekseevich Maklakov** (1871–1918), a member of the state council and minister of the interior from 1912 to 1915; **Stepan Petrovich Beletsky** (1873–1918), the vice governor of Samara (1907–09), director of the police department (1912–15) and deputy minister of the interior from 1916 to 1917; **N.A. Dobrovolsky** (1854–1918), minister of justice from October 1916 to February 1917; **Vladimir Fedorovich Trepov** (1860–1918), governor of Taurida in 1902, a senator in 1905 and member of the State Council from 1901 to 1911, he was also chairman of the Supervisory Council of the International Commercial Bank of St. Petersburg until 1917; **Roman Vatslavovich Malinovsky** (1878–1918), a Social Democratic deputy in the fourth Duma who worked as an agent for the interior ministry; and **I.F. Manasevich-Maanuilov** (1869–1918), an agent of the Russian police; **General Nikolai V. Russky** (1854–1918), the commander-in-chief of the Northern Front, was captured and shot by Bolshevik sailors in Kislovodsk. Russky's predecessor as Northern Front commander, **Pavel Karl Rennenkampf** (1854–1918), was also executed by the Bolsheviks after refusing to accept a commission in the newly-formed Red Army.

- **Count Istvan Tisza**, the former prime minister of Hungary, was murdered by a group of discharged soldiers on October 3, 1918, who charged him with responsibility for involving Hungary in the First World War.

  Tisza was born in Budapest on April 22, 1861. He was the son of Kalman Tisza, who served as Hungary's prime minister from 1875 until 1890. The younger Tisza worked in the interior ministry and was elected to parliament in 1886. He was named prime minister on November 3, 1903. His government fell on June 18, 1905, over his efforts to override parliamentary obstruction to his policies. He formed the Party of National Work in 1910 and became speaker of the lower house of parliament in May of 1912. He again headed the government as prime minister from June 10, 1913. He was initially opposed to Austria-Hungary's war with Serbia in 1914, but soon became a supporter of the war effort. He led Hungary during most of the First World War before stepping down on June 5, 1917. Tisza was held responsible for Hungary's misfortunes during the war and was shot to death at his home in Pest by soldiers on October 31, 1918, soon after the revolution broke out.

- **Sidonio Cardoso de Silva Paes**, the president of Portugal, was shot and killed on

December 14, 1918. Paes was born in Cam-
inha, Minho district, in 1872. He became active in politics, joining the moderate republican Unionist Party. Paes served in the cabinet
as minister of public works and finance in
1911. He served as Portugal's minister to Berlin
from 1912 until March of 1916. Paes was a
major in the army reserve and led the military
coup in December of 1917, that ousted the
government of Afonso Da Costa. Paes assumed power as head of state and government
on December 8, 1917, calling his regime "the
New Republic." He was elected president in
the spring of 1918, and was officially installed
in office on May 10, 1918. He continued Portugal's pro–Allied policy during World War I.
Opposition to his government mounted in the
summer of 1918. A counter-revolutionary movement led by the Democrats was suppressed in
October of 1918. There was an unsuccessful
attempt to shoot Paes on December 6, 1918.
Paes was shot to death by Jose Julio da Costa,
a Democratic fanatic, at Rossio railway station
in Lisbon on December 14, 1918. His assassin
was immediately slain by a mob.

• **Bio Guera**, the chief of Gbekou, led an
uprising against the colonial government of
French Dahomey in September of 1916. The
revolt spread throughout the Bembereke-
Kandi region until the French authorities suppressed it the following year. Bio Guera was
killed by French forces on December 19, 1918.

---

# 1919

---

• **Ag Mohammed Wau Teguidda
Kaocen** (1888–1919), a leader of the Taureg
revolt against the French in Air, Niger, in
1916, was captured and hanged in Mourzouk
on January 5, 1919. Kaocen was a leading opponent of French control in the area. He had
warred against the French in Chad and the
Sudan before leading an attack on Agadez in
December of 1916. He held the French troops
there under siege until March of 1917. Rein-
forcements arrives and crushed his rebel-

lion. He was captured and executed two years
later.

• German Socialist leaders **Rosa Luxemborg** and **Karl Liebknecht** were arrested
and murdered by right-wing Freikorps troops
on January 15, 1919, while being transferred to
a West Berlin prison.

Rosa Luxemborg was born on March 5,
1870, in Russian Poland. She became involved
in the Polish Socialist movement and was
forced to flee to Switzerland to escape imprisonment for her political activities. In 1893 she
became the leader of the Social Democratic
Party of Poland with the non-nationalistic
aim of spreading Socialism throughout Poland
and the Soviet Union. In 1898 she settled in
Germany, joining the German Social Democratic Party. She and Karl Liebknecht became
leaders of the extreme left wing of the German Socialist movement. At the start of the
First World War in 1914, she and Liebknecht
founded the Spartacus League to promote
their view of establishing Communism through
proletarian democracy. She was imprisoned
during the war, but her writings still greatly
influenced the Socialist movement. Following
her release from prison in November of 1918,
Luxemborg was instrumental in transforming
the Spartacus League into the German Communist party. Early the next year she was
arrested and murdered.

Karl Liebknecht was born in Leipzig on
August 13, 1871. He became involved with the
extreme left wing of the Social Democratic
party and became internationally known for
his promotion of Socialism. He was elected to
the German Reichstag in 1912. He opposed
the German war effort in 1914, breaking with
the leadership of the Social Democratic party
in doing so. He was subsequently expelled
from the party in early 1916 and arrested later
in the year for his anti-war activities. On
November 9, 1918, following his release from
prison, Liebknecht declared Berlin a German
Socialist Republic and, with Rosa Luxemborg,
transformed their Spartacus League into the
German Communist party. Shortly thereafter
the Communist rising against the central gov-

ernment of Friedrich Ebert was crushed and Liebknecht, with Luxemborg, was arrested and murdered.

• **Grand Duke Nikolai Mikhailovich Romanoff** (Apr. 14, 1859–1919) of Russia, the grandson of Czar Nicholas I and a leading Russian historian, and **Grand Duke Paul Aleksandrovich Romanoff** (Sept. 29, 1860–1919), the son of Czar Alexander II (q.v.), were executed in Petrograd on January 28, 1919. **Grand Duke George Michaelovich Romanoff** (Oct. 11, 1863–1919) and **Prince Dmitri Constantinovich Romanoff** (June 1, 1860–1919) were also slain by the Bolsheviks at this time.

• **Georgii Stepanovich Khrustalev-Nosar** (1877–1919), the former first chairman of the St. Petersburg Soviet of Workers' Deputies during the Russian Revolution of 1905, was shot and killed by the Bolsheviks in 1919. Khrustalev-Nosar joined the Mensheviks in 1907. He subsequently abandoned politics to work as a journalist for the rightist press. During the Civil War he formed the Khrustalev Republic in the Ukraine. He was captured and killed by the Bolsheviks in 1919.

• **Habibullah Khan**, the amir of Afghanistan, was shot to death on February 20, 1919, in the Laghman Valley by one of his subjects. Habibullah was born in Tashkent on July 3, 1872. He was the son of Emir Abdurrahman Khan. He succeeded his father to the throne on October 3, 1901. He continued the modernization of Afghanistan begun by his father, establishing the Habibia school in 1904. He also introduced electricity and automobiles into the country and modernized medical facilities. He maintained peaceful relations with the British and the Russians and secured domestic stability within the country. Habibullah also maintained Afghanistan's neutrality during the First World War. He was assassinated at his camp in Kalagosh in the Laghman Valley.

• **Kurt Eisner**, a leading German Socialist politician, was assassinated in Munich by a German student on February 21, 1919. Eis-

ner was born on May 14, 1867, in Berlin. He was a journalist on several German newspapers, including the *Frankefurter Zeitung* and the Berlin *Vorwarts*. In 1907 he became editor of the Nuremburg Socialist newspaper, *Socialist Frankische Tagespost*, serving until 1910, when he became a citizen of Bavaria. He joined the Independent Social Democratic Party (USPD) in 1917, in opposition to the German war effort. He was instrumental in the Munich revolution of 1918 that resulted in the overthrow of the monarchy and, on November 7, 1918, he proclaimed the establishment of the Bavarian republic, becoming its first prime minister and minister of foreign affairs. Three months later he was assassinated in Munich by Count A. von Arco-Valley, a right-wing student.

• **Emiliano Zapata**, the Mexican revolutionary leader, was ambushed and killed on April 10, 1919. Zapata was born in Anenecuilco, Morelos, Mexico in 1877. He was active in Francisco Madero's (q.v.) revolution against President Profirio Diaz in 1910. Zapata continued the revolution after the fall of Diaz and into the administrations of Maderos, Victoriano Huerta and Venustiano Carranza (q.v.). Zapata was a proponent of agrarian reform and continued to pressure the government to accede to his demands for a fair distribution of land to the poor. He allied himself with Pancho Villa (q.v.) from 1914 and 1915 and maintained control of the province of Morelos during much of his rebel activities. He was ambushed and killed by Jesus Guajardo, acting under the orders of a Carranza ally, General Pablo Gonzalez.

• **Otto Neuring**, the German Socialist war minister of Saxony, was assassinated in Dresden by soldiers protesting a pay cut on April 12, 1919.

• **Radko Dmitriev** (1859–1919), a Bulgarian-born Russian army general, was captured and murdered by the Bolsheviks in 1919.

• **Jose Joaquin Tinoco**, the minister of war of Costa Rica and brother of President Federico Tinoco, was assassinated in August of 1919 by opponents of the government. President Tinoco subsequently resigned from office and went into exile.

• **Hugo Haase** (1863–1919), a German Socialist leader and president of the German Social Democratic party, was assassinated in Berlin by right-wing gunmen on October 8, 1919. Haase had served as a member of the German Reichstag in 1897 and organized the independent Socialist party in 1917, in disagreement with the government's war policy. He served as a member of the coalition cabinet from November to December of 1918.

---

# 1920

---

• **Aleksandr V. Kolchak**, the Russian naval officer who led the "White" Russian forces from 1918 to 1920, was executed by the Bolsheviks on February 7, 1920. Kolchak's interior minister in the anti–Communist government, **Viktor N. Pepeliaev** (1884–1920), who had served as a member of the fourth Duma, was also executed at this time. Aleksandr Kolchak was born in 1873 and had served in the First World War as a rear admiral, commanding the Black Sea fleet. Following the Revolution of June of 1917, he went to the United States for a period, then returned to Omsk, in Russia, where he became absolute ruler of the White Russian forces there. Though his armies were initially successful in battling the Bolshevik forces, later military reversals and the loss of support from the Allies resulted in the fall of Omsk on November 14, 1919. Moving his command post to Irkutsk, Kolchak was forced to resign his position on January 4, 1920, following an insurrection there. He was captured by the Bolsheviks soon after and executed. His body was thrown into the Angara River.

• **Abderahman Tegama Agh Bakhari**, the sultan of Agadez, in Niger, was murdered in his prison cell by the French authorities on April 29, 1920. Tegama was born in Dogarawa in 1880. He was a participant in the re-

bellion against the French in 1916. He fled Niger, but was captured in May of 1919. Tegama was imprisoned by the French and was killed without a trial while in custody, though his death was originally announced as a suicide.

• **Mokhtar Kodogo** (1880–1920), a leader of an uprising against the French colonial forces in the Air, Niger, in 1916, was captured and killed near Zouar on May 11, 1920. Kodogo was the brother of Kaocen (q.v.), the leader of the rebellion. After the revolt failed Kodogo continued his battle against the French until his death.

• **Venustiano Carranza**, a Mexican revolutionist and president, was murdered on May 21, 1920. Carranza was born to a wealthy family in Cuatrocienegas, Coahuila, on December 29, 1859. Carranza became active in politics in 1887 as a supporter of Bernardo Reyes. He served as a state deputy and federal senator. Carranza was defeated for the governorship of Coahuila in 1909. He supported Francisco Madero's (q.v.) candidacy for president against Porfirio Diaz in 1910 and took part in the subsequent revolt that ousted Diaz in May of 1911. Carranza served as governor of Coahuila during Madero's presidency. After Madero's overthrow and murder in February of 1913 Carranza led a revolt against General Victoriano Huerta. His revolutionary army defeated Huerta's forces and drove the dictator into exile in July of 1914. Carranza became provisional president on July 15, 1914. His government was opposed by Pancho Villa and Emiliano Zapata. Alvaro Obregon, a Carranza loyalist, defeated Villa's rebels in mid–1915. Carranza was inaugurated as constitutional president in May of 1917. Mexico's economy suffered during Carranza's administration and the currency collapsed. He mandated a constitutional convention in 1917 that produced a new radical constitution that supported agrarian and labor reform and anticlericalism. Carranza maintained Mexico's neutrality during the First World War. Carranza attempted to secure Ignacio Bonnillas as his successor in the presidential election of 1920. The military supported Alvaro Obregon and led a coup that ousted Carranza. He fled Mexico City for Veracruz on horseback. He was ambushed and killed by troops under Rodolfo Herrera at Tlaxcalaltongo, Puebla State, on May 21, 1920.

• Albanian politician **Essad Pasha** was assassinated on June 13, 1920. Essad Toptani was born in Tirana in 1863. He became head of the powerful Toptani family after the murder of his brother, Ghani Bey. He was a leader of the Young Turk movement in the Ottoman Empire in 1908, entering the Turkish parliament as a deputy for Albania. He was placed in charge of the Ottoman army, commanding the forces at Shkoder. He surrendered the area to Montenegrin troops in 1913. Toptani, who was known as Essad Pasha, was named minister of internal affairs and of war under William of Wied for several months in 1914, until he was arrested on charges of treason in May of 1914. He was sent to Italy, but returned to Albania following William's departure. He raised an army that occupied Tirana and forced the Senate to name him head of state on October 5, 1914. He continued to rule central Albania until February 24, 1916, when he accompanied the Serbs against Austria-Hungary in Salonika. He attended the peace conference after the conclusion of World War I in an attempt to represent Albania. He subsequently retired to Paris, where he was instrumental in an unsuccessful coup attempt against the Albanian government in 1920. Essad Pasha was shot to death in Paris on June 13, 1920, while leaving the Hotel Continental by Avni Rustemi, an Albanian student.

# 1921

• **Nikolai Stepanovich Gumilev** (1886–1921), a leading Russian poet and a founder of the Acmeiest school of poetry in 1912, was executed by the Bolsheviks in 1921 for allegedly conspiring against the government. Gumilev's poems include those found in the collection *The Pillar of Fire* (1912).

• Premier **Eduardo Dato y Iradier** of Spain was assassinated by anarchists in Madrid on March 8, 1921. Dato was born in Corunna on August 12, 1856. He studied law before entering politics. Dato served as secretary of state for the interior from 1892 and was named to the cabinet as minister of the interior in 1899. He returned to the cabinet as minister of justice in 1903. Dato was elected mayor of Madrid in 1907 and also served as speaker of the House of Representatives. He was a member of the moderate wing of the Conservative Party, becoming party leader in 1913. He was named to head the government as prime minister on October 27, 1913. Despite his sympathies for the Allied cause, Dato maintained Spain's neutrality in the early days of World War I. He stepped down from office on December 6, 1915. He again briefly headed the government from June 9, 1917, until October 27, 1917, when Spain was beset by labor strikes and civil unrest. He used harsh measures to suppress the workers' movement. Dato served as secretary of state for foreign affairs in 1918. He returned to head the government on May 5, 1920, and attempted to breach the rift in the Conservative Party. Dato continued to serve as prime minister until he was shot to death by two anarchists while driving near his home in Madrid on March 8, 1921.

• Turkish political leader **Mehmed Talat Pasha** was shot and killed on March 15, 1921, while in exile in Berlin. Mehmed Talat Pasha was born in 1874 in Edirne, Turkey, and became a leader of the Young Turk movement during the revolution. In 1909 he became minister of the interior and later president of the Society of Union and Progress, the Young Turks' political party. He again served as minister of the interior at the star of the First World War. He served as minister of the interior and grand vizier from February 4, 1917 until October 8, 1918. Talat was considered responsible for the Turkish policy of genocide against Armenians, in which more than 500,000 were reported massacred. He went into exile following Turkey's defeat by the Allies in 1918. Talat was shot and killed in Berlin by an Armenian, Saro Melikian (1897–1960), on March 15, 1921. Melikian claimed to have acted in revenge for his people. He confessed to the crime, but was acquitted of the murder by a German court.

- **Karl Gareis**, a Socialist deputy in the Bavarian Landtag, was shot to death in front of his Munich home by a member of the right-wing paramilitary Einwohnerwehr on June 10, 1921.

- **Milorad Draskovic** (1873–1921), minister of the interior for the provisional Yugoslavian government from 1920, was shot and killed by a Bosnian Communist on July 21, 1921. Draskovic had retired earlier in the year following a previous attempt on his life.

- German statesman **Matthias Erzberger** was shot and killed by nationalists on August 26, 1921. Erzberger was born in Wurttemberg on September 20, 1875. He became a member of the German Reichstag in 1903, establishing himself as the leader of the left wing of the Centre party. He opposed the German war policy and was a proponent of a negotiated peace. In 1918 he became secretary of state without portfolio and chaired the armistice commission later in the year. He resigned his office in 1920, following charges of questionable financial practices while in office. He was assassinated while vacationing in the Black Forest. His assassins were not brought to trial until the late 1940s, after the conclusion of World War II.

- **Baron Roman Nikolaus Von Ungern-Sternberg** (1885–1921), a Russian Czarist army general who fought against the Bolsheviks in eastern Siberia, was captured and shot on September 15, 1921. Ungern-Sternberg had captured and occupied much of Mongolia in the Spring of 1921. The Mongolian revolutionary army and units of the Soviet Red Army defeated Ungern-Sternberg. He was captured at Tarialan in August of 1921 and executed the following month in Irkutsk.

- **Dr. Antonio Granjo** (1881–1921), the premier of Portugal, was shot to death on October 19, 1921. Granjo was called upon to head the government on July 17, 1920. He initiated

reforms in the colonial administration. He introduced a measure calling for the amnesty of Monarchist rebels still imprisoned from a rebellion the previous year. He stepped down on November 16, 1920, when the Republicans opposed his amnesty measure. He served in the cabinet as minister of commerce before again being called upon to head the government on August 28, 1921. A military coup forced Granjo's resignation on October 19, 1921. He and several members of his cabinet, including **Antonio Machado Dos Santos**, a founder of the Portuguese Republic and member of the ruling triumvirate in 1917, **Jose Carlos De Maia**, Granjo's minister of marine and of the colonies, and **Carlos Silva**, were murdered by a group of rebels the night of October 19, 1921. Granjo was drug from the home of his finance minister, Francisco Cunha Leal, taken to the arsenal and shot to death by a band of men in sailors' uniforms.

- Prime Minister **Takashi Hara** of Japan was assassinated in Tokyo on November 4, 1921. Hara was born at Morioka on February 9, 1856. He served as the consul in Tientsin before being appointed charge d'affaires in Paris in 1886. He served as ambassador to Korea in 1896, but returned to Tokyo in 1897 to resume journalism. He became the editor of a leading Osaka newspaper. He joined Hirobumi Ito's political party Rikken Seiyukai in 1900 and was elected to the Diet. He was named to Ito's cabinet as minister of communications in 1900. He became home minister in Kimmochi Saionji's cabinet in 1906 and again in 1911. He again held that position in several other cabinets in 1912 and from 1913 until 1914. He subsequently retired from the government to serve as president of the Seiyukai party. He was called upon to form a government on September 29, 1918, after Masatake Terauichi's cabinet was forced to resign during the rice riots. He formed Japan's first party government. He initiated moderate electoral reforms, but opposed the universal suffrage movement. He continued to head the government until November 4, 1921, when he was stabbed to death by a young right-wing fanatic at the Tokyo railway station.

- **Sait Halim Pasa**, a former Turkish grand vizier, was slain by an Armenian in Rome on December 6, 1921. Halim was born in Cairo in 1863. He was an Egyptian prince and became active in Ottoman politics in the early 1900s. He was elected to the parliament, where he became affiliated with the Committee of Union and Progress. He was chosen as Grand Vizier on June 12, 1913, following the assassination of Mahmud Sevket (q.v.). He was largely a figurehead during his term of office, with the real power residing with the CUP leadership. He was involved in the negotiations with Germany that resulted in an alliance with the Ottoman Empire during World War I. He resigned in protest over the conduct of war policy on February 3, 1917. Sait Halim was arrested by the Allies following the occupation of Constantinople in 1918. He went into exile in Rome, where he remained until his assassination.

- Paul Konduriotis (1855–1935), the regent of Greece following the death of King Alexander in October of 1920, was shot by three former soldiers at his office on December 21, 1921. Konduriotis recovered from his injuries and later served as president of Greece from April of 1924 to March of 1926.

# 1922

- German statesman and industrialist **Walther Rathenau** was killed in Germany by right-wing nationalists while going to his office on January 24, 1922. Rathenau was born in Berlin on September 29, 1867. He became a director of the family-owned Allgemeine Elektrizitats-Gesellschaft, a leading German power industry, in 1899. He became the company's president in 1915. During the First World War Rathenau was instrumental in managing the disposition of raw materials needed for the war effort. He was active in

preparing the German delegation to the Versailles Peace Conference in 1919 and the London Conference of 1921. He served as minister of reconstruction in 1921 and was the German representative to the Cannes Conference of 1922. As Germany's foreign minister, he signed the Rapallo treaty with Russia. His career earned him the admiration of many, but the hatred of the fanatical nationalist elements. Soon after Rathenau's murder his two assailants were killed during a shoot-out with the police while trying to flee the country.

- **Heikki Ritavuori** (1880–1922), Finnish minister of the interior, was assassinated by right-wing extremists in front of his home in Helsinki on February 14, 1922. Ritavuori had served as interior minister from 1919 to 1920 and again from 1921 until his death.

- **Ahmed Jemal Pasha**, a Turkish army officer and political leader, was killed in 1922 by two Armenian nationalist gunmen while traveling to Tbilisi. Jemal was born in Istanbul in 1872. He served in the army and became a member of the military administration in Istanbul following the revolution of 1908. During the First World War Jemal was recognized as one of the three most powerful figures in the Turkish government. He was unsuccessful in his attempt to invade Egypt in 1914 and was later made governor of Syria. Following the armistice of 1918, Jemal went into exile in Germany, and later accepted a position to train the Afghan army. He was subsequently court-martialed and sentenced to death in absentia by the Ottoman government. His assassination was the result of his barbarous treatment of Armenians during his term of office in Syria.

- **Vladimir Dmitrievich Nabokov** (1870–1922), a Russian law professor who served as head of the chancellery of the provisional government in 1917, was shot to death by two right-wing extremists in Berlin, Germany, on March 28, 1922. A leading liberal democrat, he fled Russia with his family after the revolution. He settled in Berlin, where he edited the newspaper *The Rudder*. He was killed saving the life of the assassins' target, politician Pavel Milukov. Nabokov was the father of the famed novelist Vladimir Nabokov, author of *Lolita*.

• British army officer **Sir Henry Hughes Wilson** was slain by two Irish Nationalists in front of his London home on June 22, 1922. Wilson was born in County Longford, Ireland, on May 5, 1854. Joining the army, he served in Burma from 1885 to 1887 and fought in the South African war from 1899 to 1902. He became commandant of the Camberley Staff College in 1908 and, in 1910, served as director of military operations. In this position he was a proponent of military cooperation with France in the event of war in Europe. In 1914 and 1915 he served as the British liaison officer with the French army headquarters and became a member of the Allied Supreme War Council in 1917. He became chief of the British general staff in February of 1918 and was promoted to field marshal in 1919. In 1922 he left his position in the army and was elected to parliament from Northern Ireland, where his position on Ireland earned him the enmity of the Sinn Fein and cost him his life. Two members of the Irish Republican Army, Reginald Dunne (aka John O'Brien) and Joseph O'Sullivan (aka James Connelly), were tried and convicted of Wilson's assassination. They were hanged in Wandsworth Prison on August 10, 1922.

• **Enver Pasha**, the leader of the Young Turk Revolution in Turkey in July of 1908, was killed leading an attack against Bolshevik troops near Dushanbe on August 4, 1922. Enver was born in Constantinople on November 23, 1881. He attended the War Academy, graduating in 1902. He worked with the Committee of Union and Progress (CUP) to overthrow the government of the Ottoman Empire in 1908. Enver subsequently served as military attaché to Berlin, returning to the capital the following year to crush a counter-revolutionary rebellion. Enver continued to serve in the Ottoman army, becoming minister of war in January of 1914. After the Ottoman's defeat during World War I, Enver went into exile to continue the fight against

the Allied occupation of Ottoman territories. He joined the Turkistan resistance movement in 1921 to fight the Bolsheviks and was killed in battle the following year.

• **Metropolitan Veniamin** of Petrograd (1874–1922), who had refused to relinquish church property to the Bolsheviks, was arrested on May 29, 1922, and convicted of anti-state activities. He was shot to death on August 12, 1922, along with **Archimandrite Sergius** and two laymen, **Yuri Novitsky** and **Ioann Kovsharov**. Veniamin had previously served as archbishop of Petrograd from 1917. Veniamin was born Vasily Pavlovich Kazansky in Olonetz Gubernia in 1874.

• Irish Republic leader **Michael Collins** was ambushed and killed on August 22, 1922, near Brandon in County Cork, Ireland. Collins was born in Clonakilty, County Cork, on October 16, 1890. He served in the British civil service in London from 1906, working as a postal clerk. He became involved with Irish nationalism and joined the Irish Republican brotherhood in 1909. Collins returned to Dublin in 1916 and took part in the Easter Rising. He was captured and interned in Frongoch, Wales, until December of 1916. He was elected to the Irish assembly, the dail eire-ann, in December of 1918 as a member of the Sinn Fein. He declared his support for the Irish Republic and served as the Sinn Fein minister of home affairs. He was instrumental in arranging nationalist leader Eamon De Valera's escape from prison in February of 1919. Collins also served as director of organization and intelligence of the Irish Republican Army. After the truce with Great Britain in July of 1921, Collins and Arthur Griffith represented the Irish nationalists at the negotiations in London at the end of the year. He signed the treaty with Great Britain on December 6, 1921, and persuaded the dail to approve it by a narrow margin. Collins became chairman of the provisional government. Civil war soon broke out between the government and followers of Eamon De Valera, who opposed the treaty. Collins became head of state following the death of Arthur Griffith on August 12, 1922. He continued to lead the army in putting down the rebellion. His party was ambushed at Beal-na-Blath on August 22, 1922, while traveling from Skibereen to Cork. Collins was shot and killed.

• **Dogsomyn Bodo**, the head of the Mongolia government, and **Dambyn Chagdarjav**, the former Mongolian prime minister, were purged and executed with fifteen other Mongolia political leaders on August 31, 1922.

Bodo was born in 1885 in Tov Province, Mongolia. He was a lama and served in the autonomous government. He also worked as an instructor of translators at the Russian consulate in Urga and became a leading Mongolian journalist. Bodo was selected as prime minister of the people's government in July of 1921, also serving as minister of foreign affairs. Bodo was forced to resign from the government in January of 1922. He was subsequently arrested and charged with conspiring against the government.

Dambyn Chagdarjav was born in Ih Shav' in 1880. He was a wealthy Mongolian lama who joined the revolutionary movement. He was a member of the Mongolian delegation to Russia seeking help in 1920. He was an ally of Bodo and headed the provisional government from March 31, 1921, until July of 1921. He subsequently went to organize activities in Northwest Mongolia. He was purged and executed with Bodo in September of 1922.

• **Robert Erskine Childers**, the Irish writer and Republic leader was tried and executed on November 24, 1922, during the Irish Civil War. Childers, who was born in London on June 25, 1870, had been active in the struggle for Ireland's independence. He was well known as a novelist and authored *The Riddle of the Sands* in 1903. He fought with British forces during the First World War, and served in the 1917 convention to determine home rule for Ireland. As a Sinn Fein deputy, he was active in the negotiations concerning the Anglo-Irish treaty, but did not support the final agreement. He joined the republican dissenters in the subsequent Civil War, and was tried and executed after being arrested for possessing an unauthorized pistol.

• Former Greek prime ministers **Dimitrios Gounaris**, **Petros Protopapadakis** and **Nikolaos Stratos** were executed by order of General Nikolaos Plastiras after an anti–Royalist revolution on November 28, 1922. Also executed were **Theotokis**, the former Greek war minister, **Baltassiz**, a former cabinet minister, and **General Hadjanestis**, the former commander of the Greek armed forces. The Greek leaders were tried and convicted in connection with the Greek military disaster in Asia Minor.

Dimitrios Gounaris was born in 1866. He became active in politics and served in Dimitrios Rallis' cabinet as minister of finance from 1908 until 1909. He became a leader of the Royalist Party and briefly headed the government as prime minister. He served from March 10, 1915, until August 23, 1915, following Eleutherios Venizelos' resignation because of a conflict with King Constantine over Greece's participation in World War I. Gounaris was deported after the abdication of King Constantine in June of 1917. He returned to Athens after Constantine reclaimed the throne in December of 1920. He returned to the government as minister of war before becoming prime minister on April 2, 1921. The Allies were unable to achieve a peace settlement between Greece and Turkey, with conflicts continuing in Asia Minor. Gounaris resigned the premiership in March of 1922, but quickly resumed his position. He again resigned on May 16, 1922. He was arrested in September of 1922 when a military revolt forced the abdication of King Constantine.

Petros Protopapadakis was born in 1860. He served in Dimitrios Gounaris' cabinet as minister of finance in 1915. He returned with the cabinet in Gounaris' second government in 1921, serving as minister of finance of supplies. Protopapadakis became prime minister on May 22, 1922. He was forced to resign on September 10, 1922, and was arrested.

Nikolaos Stratos was born in 1872. He entered politics in 1909. He was named to Eleutherios Venizelos' cabinet as minister of marine the following year. He subsequently left the Venezelist Party to become an Independent Royalist. Stratos headed a brief interim government from May 16, 1922, until May 22, 1922, following the resignation of Dimitrios Gounaris.

• **Gabriel Narutowicz** was killed by a madman on December 16, 1922, shortly after assuming office as the first president of the Polish Republic. Narutowicz was born in Teleze, Lithuania, on March 3, 1865. He was educated in St. Petersburg and Zurich, where he trained as an engineer. He was subsequently a professor at Zurich University. Narutowicz was named to the government as minister of public works in June of 1920. He subsequently served as foreign minister in Julian Nowak's government in 1922. He was supported by the parties of the left in the presidential election in 1922. He was elected to the presidency after a bitter campaign against the nationalists. He succeeded Jozef Pilsudski on December 11, 1922. Several days later Narutowicz was shot three times in the back by Niewadomski, a deranged artist, while attending an exhibition of paintings at the Palace of Fine Arts on December 16, 1922. His assassin was tried, sentenced to death and executed.

# 1923

• **Damdiny Suhe Baator** (1893–1923), a leader of the Mongolian People's Party's armed forces, died, likely from poisoning, on February 22, 1923. Suhe Baator was made commander in chief of the army in February 1921 and served in the provisional people's government. He was instrumental in driving the Chinese from Kyakhta and was named minister of the army in July of 1921. He retained his positions until his death two years later.

• **Vaclav Vaclavovic Vorovsky** (1871–1923), a Bolshevik politician and diplomat, was assassinated on May 10, 1923, in Lausanne, Switzerland, during a conference between the Soviet Union and the Western powers concerning the Turkish question. A Russian-born Swiss, Maurice Conradi, was identified as the assassin. Vorovsky served as the Bolshevik government's representative to Scandinavia from 1917 until 1921, when he became the Soviet minister to Rome. He was involved with the International Economic Conference in Genoa in 1922.

• **Juan Cardinal Soldevilla y Romero**, the Roman Catholic archbishop of Saragossa, Spain, since 1901, was shot and killed by two young assassins on June 4, 1923. Cardinal Soldevilla was born in Fuente de la Pena, Spain, on October 29, 1843. He attended the Seminaries of Valladolid, Tuy and Compostella before his ordination as a priest. Soldevilla worked in the archdiocese of Valladolid and served as secretary to the Bishop of Orense from 1875 until 1883. He was cathedral canon of Valladolid from 1883. Soldevilla was selected as Bishop of Tarazona in February of 1889. He was elevated to Archbishop of Saragossa in December of 1901. He was created a cardinal priest by Pope Benedict XV on December 15, 1919. As the Vatican's spokesman in Spain and a leading reactionary, the cardinal had gained many enemies among Republicans and Socialists. Soldevilla was seated in his car at a monastery near Saragossa at the time of his murder. His assassins were two anarchists, Francisco Ascaso (q.v.) and Buenaventura Durruti (q.v.), both of whom were killed early in the Spanish Civil War.

• Bulgaria statesman and former prime minister **Aleksandr Stambolski** was slain by his opponents on June 14, 1923. Stambolski was born in Slavovitsa on March 1, 1879. He was educated at the agricultural college in Halle, Germany. He returned to Bulgaria in 1897 and became a journalist, serving as editor of the Agrarian newspaper from 1902. He was elected to the Sobranye in 1908 and served as leader of the Agrarians. Stambolski opposed King Ferdinand's policies during the Balkan War and threatened the king against entering into an alliance with Germany and the Central Powers during the First World

War. Ferdinand ordered Stambolski's arrest in 1915 and he was court-martialed and sentenced to life imprisonment. Stambolski was released in September of 1918 and raised an army of insurrectionists that forced Ferdinand's abdication. Stambolski supported the new king, Boris III, and joined the government as minister of public works in January of 1919. He was named prime minister on October 19, 1919, and signed the Treaty of Neuilly in France the following year. He remained in power after his party was victorious in parliamentary elections in March of 1920. His government complied with the terms of the peace treaty with the Allies and sought to improve relations with Yugoslavia. Stambolski was ousted by a military coup on June 9, 1923. He was at his native village of Slavovitsa when news of the coup reached him. He tried to flee the country but was found and shot to death by rebels when he resisted arrest on June 14, 1923.

- **Nicolai Genadiev**, a member of the Bulgarian cabinet and former foreign minister, was assassinated in the streets of Sofia in 1923. Genadiev had survived a previous assassination attempt in February of 1907, when Bulgarian prime minister Dimitur Petkov (q.v.) was killed. Genadiev had succeeded Petkov as head of the People's Liberal Party.

- **General Juan Cristonomo Gomez**, who had been named vice president of Venezuela the previous year by President Juan Vicente Gomez, was assassinated in his sleep in Caracas on June 29, 1923.

- **Francisco "Pancho" Villa**, the Mexican bandit and revolutionary leader, was shot and killed in Parral, Chihuahua, on July 20, 1923. Pancho Villa was born Doroteo Arango on June 5, 1878, in Durango, Mexico. He spent his early life as the leader of a group of bandits. In 1910 he joined Francesco Madero's (q.v.) revolution against the regime of General Profirio Diaz. In 1912 Villa was sentenced to death while serving in the army under General Victoriano Huerta. His sentence was commuted, and Villa escaped from prison and went to the United States. He returned to

Mexico following the death of Madero and joined forces with Venustiano Carranza (q.v.) in battle against Huerta. Following Huerta's defeat in 1914, Villa and Carranza began battling among themselves. Carranza defeated Villa's forces in 1915. Villa continued to harass both the Mexican and United States governments with a series of raids across the United States border. Brig. Gen. John J. Pershing was sent to Mexico to capture Villa for his activities north of the border, but failed in his mission. Following the overthrow of Carranza in 1920, Villa retired from his revolutionary activities and received a ranch in Durango from the government. It was during his period of retirement that he was ambushed and killed by a group of gunmen led by Mexican congressman Jesus Salas Barrazas (d. 1957). Barrazas was convicted of the murder, but served virtually no time in prison for the crime.

# 1924

- **Heinz Orbis**, the German pro–French separatist leader in the Rhenish Palatinate, was shot to death on January 8, 1924, in Speyer by four right-wing nationalists while dining in a hotel restaurant. Four of his colleagues were also killed during the attack.

- **Petko D. Petkov**, who had succeeded the slain Aleksandr Stamboliski (q.v.) as head of the Bulgarian party, was shot and killed by political opponents in the streets of Sofia in 1924. Another leading Bulgarian statesman, **Todor Strashimirov**, was also killed in 1924.

- Italian Socialist leader **Giacomo Matteotti** was kidnapped by Fascists in Rome on June 10, 1924. He was taken outside of the city and brutally murdered. His body was not discovered until August 16, 1924. Matteotti was born on May 22, 1885, in Rovigo, Italy. He was first elected to the chamber of deputies as a member of the Italian Socialist party in May of 1919. Shortly before his death he also became the secretary general of the Socialist party. Matteotti was a leading critic of the

Fascists and of Benito Mussolini (q.v.). His murder provoked numerous anti–Fascist demonstrations, but with little result. The six Fascists who perpetrated the crime were identified as Amerigo Dumini, Augusto Malacria, Filippo Panzeri, Amleto Poveromo, Giuseppe Viola and Albino Volpi. They were alleged to have been hired by Fascist leaders Cesare Rossi, Francisco Giunta, Giovanni Marinelli and Filippo Filippelli. Following a trial in 1926, light sentences were handed down to those assassins tried and not acquitted. Another trial in 1947, after World War II, resulted in a sentence of 30 years imprisonment for Dumini, Poveromo and Viola.

• **Yaakov de Haan** (1881–1924), a Dutch-born Jewish journalist and an opponent of Zionism, was shot to death in Jerusalem by two Haganah gunmen on June 30, 1924. He was a leader of the Ashkenazi Council and made pro–Arab reports to the League of Nations. His actions gained him the enmity of the Zionist leadership and led to his murder.

• **Robert Whitney Imbrie** (1883–1924), an American diplomat, was killed in Tehran, Iran, on July 18, 1924, after he was assaulted by Muslim worshippers who objected to his taking of pictures at a religious celebration. Imbrie was an attorney who had served in diplomatic positions in Russia and Finland. He was named vice-consul in Tehran in 1923. His murder damaged relations between the United States and Iran and halted negotiations by American oil companies interested in developing oil in northern Iran.

• **Danzan Khorloo**, a leader of the Mongolian People's party and commander-in-chief of the Mongolia army, was executed as a "Japanese spy" in August of 1914 following an "anti–Russian" speech made at the Mongolian People's party's third congress in Urya. Danzan was born in Sayn-Hoyon-Han Province in 1873. He was a leading revolutionary figure in Mongolia, serving as commander in chief of the army and secretary of the central committee. He served as minister of finance in Bodo's government from 1921.

He was named to head the government as prime minister in 1923. He was a capitalist and nationalist who favored trade with China and supported limiting the scope of the revolution. Danzan was purged in August of 1924.

• **Todor Aleksandrov**, a Macedonian nationalist and leader of the Internal Macedonian Revolutionary Organization (IMRO), was assassinated on August 31, 1924. Aleksandrov had been instrumental in aligning the IMRO with other nationalist organizations and had signed an agreement with Bulgarian Communists to attempt to form a Balkan federation, with Macedonia as an integral part. He was murdered en route to an IMRO meeting, where he hoped to explain his position. His assassination caused an increase of violence within Macedonia.

• **Sir Lee Stack** (1868–1924), the British governor general of the Sudan and the sirdar (commander-in-chief) of the English-trained Egyptian army, was shot and seriously wounded on November 19, 1924, while driving through the streets Cairo by Egyptian terrorists. He died the following day. Stack had held his positions since 1919. Field Marshal Allenby, the British high commissioner for Egypt and the Sudan, held the Egyptian Wafd government of Premier Sa'd Zaghlul responsible for the murder, and forced the government's resignation.

# 1925

• **General Kosta Georgiev**, a high-ranking Bulgarian army officer, was shot and killed on April 15, 1925, while outside the war ministry. Georgiev's assassination followed an unsuccessful attempt on the life of King Boris III (q.v.). At Georgiev's funeral at the cathedral of Sveta Nedelya, in Sofia, a bomb exploded, killing nearly 125 people. The government proclaimed martial law and executed five persons for the crime.

• **Boris V. Savinkov** (1879–1925), a leading Russian revolutionary, died in prison in May of 1925. His death was officially announced as a suicide. Savinkov had joined the Socialist-Revolutionary party in 1903. He had been active in the assassination of Interior Minister Plehve (q.v.) in 1904. Savinkov served in the army during the First World War and, in 1917, as deputy minister of war, became one of the most powerful figures in the provisional government. Following the Bolshevik revolution, Savinkov went into exile in Paris, seeking Allied help in toppling the Bolshevik regime. He returned to Russia on August 18, 1924, and was promptly arrested, tried, and sentenced to death. His sentence was commuted to life imprisonment at death Prison. A year later he was dead.

# 1926

• **Giovanni Amendola**, an Italian journalist died in Cannes, France, on April 6, 1926, as a result of injuries inflicted on him by Fascists who had attacked him at Montecatini, an Italian spa. Amendola, who was born in Rome on April 15, 1882, was a leading opponent of Fascism. He was elected to parliament in 1919, and in 1922, served as the Italian minister for colonies. Following the assumption of power by Benito Mussolini (q.v.), Amendola frequently attacked the dictator in a series of columns in his newspaper, *Il Mondo*. He withdrew from parliament following the murder of Giacomo Matteotti (q.v.) in 1924, and continued to oppose Mussolini and Fascism until his death.

• **Simon Petlyura**, the Ukranian nationalist leader, was shot to death in Paris on May 25, 1926. Petlyura was born in Poltava on May 17, 1879. He was a founder of the Ukrainian Social Democratic Workers' Party in 1905. He was editor of the Socialist newspaper *Slovo* in Kiev until 1909 and published the Moscow weekly *Ukrainskaya Zhizn* from 1912 until 1914. He served in the Russian army during the First World War. After the Russian revolution in March of 1917, Petlyura became a member of the Ukrainian Central Council. He served as minister of war after the formation of an autonomous Ukrainian government in June of 1917. He was forced from the government when the Germans occupied the Ukraine in April of 1918. He returned to power as commander-in-chief of the Ukrainian army in November of 1918. He was recognized as head of state the following February. The Soviet and White Russian armies contested Petlyura's forces in the Ukraine over the next several years. Petlyura turned to Poland for assistance. A treaty with Polish leader Jozef Pilsudski in April of 1920 led to the Russo-Polish War. The Soviets forced Petlyura and the Polish from the Ukraine and Petlyura formed a government-in-exile in Warsaw. He soon moved to Paris where he continued to head the exile government. Petlyura was shot to death in the streets of Paris by Shalom Schwarzbard, a Jewish student who held Petlyura responsible for the persecution of Ukrainian Jews, on May 25, 1926. Schwarzbard confessed to the killing, but was found not guilty by a French jury.

• **Javid Bey** (1875–1926), a leading Turkish politician, was executed in Turkey on August 26, 1926, for plotting against the regime of Mustafa Kemal. Javid was a member of the Committee of Union and Progress and had served as minister of finance and public works in several Turkish government. **Dr. Nazim Kemal**, another early Committee of Union and Progress member, was also put to death at this time.

# 1927

• **Kevin Christopher O'Higgins** was shot to death near Dublin on July 10, 1927. O'Higgins was born in Queen's County, Ireland, on June 7, 1882. He joined the Sinn Fein movement in 1916. Following the Easter Rising, he was arrested. While imprisoned he was elected to the parliament. As a member of the revolutionary Dail, O'Higgins supported the creation of the Irish Free State in 1921. He was minister of economic affairs in the fist provisional government in 1922, and became vice president of the executive council in 1923. He was the founder and leader of the Civil Guard, established to restore order during the insurrection by the Republicans. A proponent of Ireland's continued membership in the British Commonwealth, O'Higgins also served on the committee which created the Irish Constitution. He was murdered amidst the continuing controversy surrounding Ireland's relationship to Great Britain.

• **Nicola Sacco** (1891–1927) and **Bartolomeo Vanzetti** (1888–1927), were executed in the electric chair on August 23, 1927, after having been convicted of robbery and murder in a 1921 trial. The two Italian immigrants had been accused of robbing a Massachusetts shoe company paymaster and killing him and his guard on April 15, 1920. The defendants were anarchists, and it was believed that their radical political beliefs were instrumental in their conviction. The trial was widely denounced by Socialists and others who believed Sacco and Vanzetti did not receive a fair trial. The Massachusetts Supreme Court denied a new trial on appeal in 1927. A three-man special panel appointed by Massachusetts governor Alvan T. Fuller ruled that proper judicial procedures had been followed in the original trial and the two men should be executed as sentenced.

• In October of 1927, Mexican army officers and politicians who opposed the anti-Catholic policies of President Plutarco Elias Calles and the presumed election of his hand-picked candidate, General Alvaro Obregon (q.v.), in the presidential campaign, broke out in open revolt against the government. The revolution was quickly put down and many of the leaders were captured and executed. **General Francisco Serrano** and **General Arnulfo R. Gomez**, the zone commander

of the Mexican State of Vera Cruz, both of whom were considered leading opposition candidates against General Obregon for the election scheduled in 1928, were among those executed. **General Alfred Rueda Quijano**, **General Adalberto Palacios**, **Colonel Salvado Costanos**, **Major Francisco Meza Perez** and several dozen other generals and legislators were also executed during October and November of 1927.

• **Prince Pavel Dmitrievich Dolgorukov** (1866–1927) was arrested and shot after returning to Russia with a forged passport in 1927. Dolgorukov was a member of the Union of Liberation and a founder of the Cadet party. He served in the Second State Duma and was a supporter of the anti–Bolshevik forces. Dolgorukov left Russian in 1920. He returned four years later and was arrested. He escaped to Poland, but again returned in 1927. He was captured and imprisoned before his execution.

• Jesuit priest **Miguel Pro** was executed on November 23, 1927, after being accused of conspiracy against Mexican president Alvaro Obregon (q.v.). Pro was born in Concepcion del Oro, Zacatecas, Mexico, on January 13, 1891. In 1911 he joined the Jesuit order, but was forced to flee Mexico under the anti-clerical measures of President Carranza (q.v.) in 1914. He did not return to his homeland until 1926 and was then still required to stay in hiding and conduct worship services in secret. After three years of clandestine operations, he was located by the Mexican authorities and condemned with little evidence of his guilt.

# 1928

• **Chang Shao-tseng**, a leading Chinese military figure, was murdered in Tientsin on March 21, 1928. Chang commanded a division of the Chinese Army in 1911 and supported the revolutionary movement that ousted the Manchu dynasty. He was named military governor of Shansi Province in 1912. Chang became military inspector general in 1916. He served as acting minister of war before becoming premier from January of 1923. He stepped down in June 6, 1923, and fled to Tientsin when President Li Yuan-hung was forced from office.

• **General Luis Mena**, who had served as acting president of Nicaragua in 1910, was assassinated in Ponelova on May 20, 1928. Mena, who led the revolt against President Jose Sanos Zelaya in 1909, became acting president of Nicaragua in early 1910 after Zelaya fled the country. He relinquished the presidency shortly afterward to Juan M. Estrada, and served in the new administration as minister of war. Following United States intervention, Estrada was forced to leave office, and Adolfo Diaz became president. In November of 1911 General Mena was selected as president by the Nicaraguan congress, but the election was nullified, and Diaz resumed the office. Mena began an insurrection against Diaz, but was forced to flee to Panama, where he remained until 1913. At the time of his death he was actively supporting the candidacy of General Maria Jose Moncada, the Liberal party nominee, for the presidency.

• **Stefan Radic** (1871–1928), the founder and leader of the Croatian Peasant party, was assassinated in parliament with his nephew, **Paul Radic**, and **Dr. George Basaritchik** on June 20, 1928. Radic had served as a member of the legislature of Yugoslavia and was minister of education from 1925 to 1926.

• **Alvaro Obregon Salido**, the former president of Mexico, was shot to death on July 17, 1928, shortly before taking office to serve another term. Obregon was born on a farm in Alamos, Sonora, on February 19, 1890. He entered politics and was elected mayor of Huatabampo in 1911. He supported the presidency of Francisco Madero against Pascual Orozco's rebellion in 1912. Obregon joined Venustiano Carranza's revolt against President Victoriano Huerta, after the ouster and murder of Madero in February of 1913. Obregon's forces achieved victory over the government forces and Huerta was driven from office in July of 1914. Obregon remained loyal to Carranza against Pancho Villa and Emiliano Zapata, who continued to war against the government. He inflicted serious defeats on the rebels. Obregon was instrumental in the more radical elements of the new Mexican constitution enacted in 1917. Obregon was a candidate for the presidency in 1920. Carranza attempted to arrange the election of Ignacio Bonnillas as his successor and Obregon joined in a rebellion against the government. Carranza was ousted and murdered in May of 1920 and Obregon was subsequently elected president. He took office on December 1, 1920. His government implemented numerous social and economic reforms. He crushed a rebellion led by Adolfo de la Huerta in late 1923. He supported the election of Plutarco Elias Calles as his successor and left office on December 1, 1924. Obregon again ran for the presidency in 1928. He was reelected in a violent and bitter campaign. Obregon returned to Mexico City to attend a victory celebration. He was shot to death while dining on July 17, 1928, by Jose de Leon Toral, a Roman Catholic seminary student who opposed Obregon's anticlerical policies.

• **Chang Tso-lin**, the Chinese warlord of Manchuria, was killed by a bomb planted by Japanese extremists on October 10, 1928. Chang was born to a peasant family in Haich'eng, Fengtien, in 1873. He entered the military while in his teens and saw action in the Sino-Japanese War in 1894 and 1895. He returned to Fengtien after the war to organize a local militia. Chang's forces allied with the Japanese in the Russo-Japanese War in 1904 and 1905. He continued to rise in influence under the presidency of Yuan Shih-k'ai. To advance his position, he threatened to lead a Manchurian independence drive in 1915, and was named military governor of Fengtien to insure his support of the Peking government. Chang supported Premier Tuan Ch'i-jui in his power struggle against President Feng Kuo-chang in 1918 and was rewarded with the post of inspector general of the Three Eastern Provinces in September of 1918. He remained allied with Tuan until 1920, when he joined with the Chihli faction led by Ts'ao K'un to force Tuan from power. He subsequently broke with Ts'ao and his forces were defeated in a battle with the Chihli faction in May of 1922. He still maintained much of his power in Manchuria. He again challenged the Peking government in October of 1924 and achieved victory with the assistance of defecting Chihli general Feng Yu-hsiang. He subsequently broke with Feng, who allied himself with other military leaders to challenge Chang's power. Chang received assistance from the Japanese to retain power. Military conflicts continued over the next several years with various factions fighting against Cang and each other. Chang claimed the title of president of the central government in Peking on June 18, 1927. The Nationalist army, now under Chiang Kai-shek, continued its advance on Peking. The Japanese pressured Chang to withdraw from Peking so as not to jeopardize Japanese interests in Manchuria. Chang abandoned Peking to go to Mukden in early June of 1928. A bomb exploded under the private railway car he was traveling in while passing over a bridge on the morning of October 4, 1928. He died of his injuries several days later on October 10, 1928. His position was assumed by his son, Chang Hsueh-liang.

# 1929

• **Habibullah Ghazi**, a brigand chief formerly known as Bacha Sakao, deposed King Amanullah Khan of Afghanistan in January of 1929. Bachai Saqqao was a member of the Pejatk tribe from north of Kabul. He served in the Afghan army before taking to the hills as a brigand leader. Known as "the Water Boy of the North," he was the leader of a rebellion against Amanollah Khan in 1929, forcing the ouster of Amanollah and his

brother, Inayatullah. Bachai Saqqao claimed the throne on January 17, 1929, and took the name Habibollah Ghazi. During his brief reign Habibullah executed many prominent Afghanistani politicians, including two of the deposed emperor's brothers and **Mohammed Osman**, the former governor of Kandahar and a leading advisor to the former emperor. Amanollah's cousin, Mohammed Nadir Shah, returned to Afghanistan to lead government troops against the usurper. They drove him from the capital on October 13, 1929. Bachai Saqqao was captured and executed with many of his followers on November 3, 1929.

• **Julio Antonio Mella**, the founder of the Cuban Communist Party, was murdered in Mexico on January 11, 1929. Mella, a law student, was an opponent of the dictatorship of Gerardo Machado. He founded the Cuban Communist Party in 1925. He was arrested on several occasions and went into exile after his release. Mella traveled to the Soviet Union before settling in Mexico. Mella was assassinated there, likely by agents of Machado, in 1929.

# 1930

• During 1930 the first Stalin purge trials in the Ukraine took place. Thirteen Ukrainian leaders, including **Serhiy Efremov**, were tried and executed.

• **Nguyen Thai Hoc**, the leader of the pro-independence Viet Nam Quoc Dan Dang, or Nationalist party, was guillotined with twelve of his followers by the French colonial authorities in February of 1930. Nguyen Thai Hoc was executed shortly after a rebellion by Vietnamese soldiers at the French garrison at Yen Bay.

• **Ras Gugsa Wele** (1877–1930), the husband of Ethiopian Empress Zauditu, was killed in battle while leading a rebellion against the government on March 31, 1930. Gugsa Wele was known as a poet and author. A nephew of Empress Taytu, he led troops during the battle of Adwa in 1895. He married Zauditu, the daughter of Emperor Menelek II, in 1900 and became governor of Begemder the following year. When Empress Taytu lost power, Gugsa Wele was dismissed from his governorship in 1910. He separated from Zauditu in 1916 as a precondition for her assume the throne as empress. She did reward him with the return of the governorship of Begemder. In 1929 Gugsa Wele was accused of disloyalty to the government by the regent, Haile Selassie. He was killed in battle with government troops two days before the death of the empress.

• **Dr. Albert von Baligand**, the German minister to Portugal, was assassinated in Lisbon on June 7, 1930.

• **Yuko Hamaguchi**, the prime minister of Japan, was shot and seriously wounded by a right-wing assassin on November 14, 1930. Hamaguchi died six months later of his wounds on March 10, 1931. Hamaguchi was born Yuko Mizoguchi in Kochi Prefecture in April of 1870. He married into the wealthy Hamaguchi family in 1889 and adopted his wife's surname. He worked in the ministry of finance after graduation from the University of Tokyo and was elected to the house of representatives in 1915. He served as minister of finance in Takaaki Kato's cabinets in 1924 and 1925. He served as home minister in Reijiro Wakatsuki's government in 1926. He became leader of the Minseito party in 1927. He was asked to form a government on July 2, 1929, following the resignation of Giichi Tanaka. Hamaguchi oversaw a policy of financial austerity to improve Japan's economy. He came into conflict with the army and rival parties over his government's acceptance of the disarmament measures agreed to at the London Naval Conference in 1930. Hamaguchi was shot and seriously injured by Tomeo Sagoya, a young right-wing extremist, at the Tokyo train station on November 14, 1930. Baron Shidehara, the foreign minister, acted as head

of the government while Hamaguchi recuperated. He attempted to resume his duties on March 10, 1931, but was unable to. He underwent two more surgeries and stepped down on April 13, 1931. Hamaguchi died in Tokyo of his injuries several months later on August 25, 1931.

# 1931

• The Stalin purge trials continued in the Ukraine during 1931. During the trial of the "National Centre" many politicians, including **Vsevolod Holubovych**, were sentenced to death.

• **Sardar Bhagat Singh** (1907–31), an Indian revolutionary, was executed on March 23, 1931. Singh was the founder and first secretary of the Naujawan Bharat Sabha, or Indian Youth Association, in 1925. In 1928 Singh was active in the formation of Hindustan Socialist Republic Association, and took part in the murder of J.P. Saunders, a Lahore police officer, on December 17, 1928. In April of 1929 Singh and another revolutionary bombed the Indian Legislative Assembly. Singh was arrested following this incident and sentenced to life imprisonment. He was later tried for the murder of the police official and received a death sentence. He was executed with two other revolutionaries.

• **Sidi 'Umar Al-Mukhtar**, a Bedouin Sanusiya sheikh, was captured by Italian troops under the command of Marshal Rodolfo Graziani (q.v.) and hanged on September 16, 1931. Mukhtar was born to the Minifa tribe in 1862 at was educated at Janzur and Giarabub at Sanusi schools. He was instrumental in leading the Cyrenaican resistance movement against the Italians from 1911. He became a guerrilla leader against the Italians occupation in 1923, and his capture largely ended organized resistance to the Italian in Libya.

# 1932

- **Junnosuke Inouye** (1869–1932), the Japanese minister of finance, was slain on February 9, 1932, by a young member of the ultra-nationalist League of Blood as he was entering a meeting hall in Tokyo to give a speech. Inouye had also served as governor of the Bank of Japan in 1924 and from 1927 until 1928.

- **Dan Takuma**, a leading Japanese businessman, was assassinated on March 5, 1932, at his office by nationalists who resented the powerful role of high finance in the Japanese government. Takuma was born in 1858 and studied mining engineering in the United States. From 1888 Takuma worked with the Hose of Mitsui and joined the Mitsui Trading company following its founding in 1909. His success brought increased wealth and power to the Mitsui family, and, during the 1920s, Takuma was considered one of the most powerful figures in Japan.

- **Paul Doumer**, the president of the French Republic, was assassinated on May 6, 1932. Doumer was born in Aurillac, Cantal, on March 22, 1857. He became involved in politics and was elected to the chamber of deputies as a Radical in 1888. He served as minister of finance in Leon Bourgeois' government in 1895 and 1896. He was appointed governor of Indochina in January of 1897, where he remained for the five years. He returned to France in 1902 where he formed a Radical Party dissident group in opposition to the government of Emile Combes. He was elected president of the chamber of deputies in January of 1905. He was defeated for the presidency of France by Armand Fallieres in 1906. He served on the senate committee for military affairs during World War I, during which four of his sons were killed. Doumer served in several cabinets as minister of finance in 1921 through 1922 and 1925 through 1926. He was elected president of the senate in 1927. Doumer succeeded Gaston Doumergue as president of France on June 13, 1931. His administration was cut short by his assassination by fanatic Russian émigré Pavel Gorgulov on May 6, 1932. Doumer was shot in the head and arm by Gorgulov while attending a charity book auction in Paris. He died of his wounds fourteen hours later.

- **Tsuyoshi Inukai**, the prime minister of Japan, was assassinated on May 16, 1932. Inukai was born in Niwase, Okayama Prefecture, in 1855. He became active in politics, joining the Kaishinto party in 1882. He was elected to the house of representatives in 1890. He briefly served as minister of education in Shigenobu Okuma's cabinet in 1898. He formed the Kokuminto party in 1910 and was an opponent of the government of Taro Katsura. He was an advocate of universal suffrage and opposed increased military expenditures. Inukai was named minister of communications in Gombei Yamamoto's cabinet in 1923. He again headed that ministry in Takaaki Kato's coalition government in 1924. He merged his party with the Seiyukai in 1925 and announced his retirement from the cabinet and politics. His supporters refused to accept his retirement and reelected him to the Diet. He became leader of the Seiyukai party following the death of Giinchi Tanaka in 1929. He was called upon to form a government on December 13, 1931, following the collapse of Reijiro Wakatsuki's government. His party won a majority in elections in 1932 and embarked on an effort to improve Japan's economy. His proposal to recognize Chinese sovereignty over Manchuria brought him into conflict with the military. Inukai was shot to death at his official residence in Tokyo during an uprising by rightist military officers on May 16, 1932, when nine young officers broke into his home and shot him in the neck and stomach. His killing was intended to give more power to the armed forces. His assailants, including Lt. Yamagishi, their leader, were all tried and convicted of his murder, but served no time in prison.

- **Gombyn Sodnom** (1903–32), the Mongolian minister of trade and industry from 1930, was killed in Arhangay Province in May of 1932.

---

# 1933

---

• During 1933 the Stalin purge trials continued in the Ukraine. **Yury Kotsiubinsky**, the deputy premier of the Ukrainian Communist government, and other prominent Ukrainian leaders, were tried and executed on orders of the Soviet secret police.

• **Professor Theodor Lessin**, a German writer and teacher, was murdered in 1933 in the Czechoslovakian spa of Marianske Lazne by agents of Adolf Hitler. Lessin, a champion of pacifism and humanitarianism, had become a prominent target of German nationalists.

• On February 15, 1933, an assassination attempt was made against United States president-elect Franklin D. Roosevelt (1882–1945), following a speech made from a motorcade at Miami Bayfront Park in Florida. Guiseppe Zangara (1901–33), an Italian immigrant and anti-capitalist, missed his target, instead shooting **Anton J. Cermak** (May 9, 1873–1933), the mayor of Chicago, who was one of the dignitaries greeting Roosevelt. Cermak, who had served as Chicago's mayor from 1931 and was an unsuccessful candidate for the U.S. Senate from Illinois in 1928, died of his wounds on March 6, 1933. Zangara was tried and, on March 20, 1933, electrocuted.

• **Luis Manuel Sanchez Cerro**, the president of Peru, was shot and killed on April 30, 1933. Sanchez Cerro was born in Piura in 1889. He graduated from the Chorrillos Military Academy in 1910. He participated in the military uprising that ousted President Guillermo Billinghurst in 1914. He participated in an unsuccessful attempt to overthrow President Augusto Leguia in 1922. He was imprisoned for his part in the revolt but was subsequently released and promoted

by Leguia to lieutenant colonel. He led another military coup against Leguia and ousted the president on August 25, 1930. He headed the ruling military junta from August 27, 1930, until opposition in the armed forces forced his resignation on March 1, 1931. He subsequently founded the revolutionary Union Party and successfully contested the presidential election in October of 1931, defeating Victor Raul Haya de la Torre's Aprista Party. Sanchez Cerro assumed office on December 8, 1931, and embarked on a ruthless campaign to crush the opposition Aprista Party. Many of its members were arrested or deported. Sanchez Cerro put down several rebellions and survived an assassination attempt in 1932. He was shot to death by Abelardo Hurtado De Mendoza, an Aprista member, in Lima on April 30, 1933. The assassin was subsequently slain by presidential guards.

• **Tsengeltiyn Jigjidjav** (1894–1933), the former prime minister of Mongolia, was shot to death at his home in a suburb of Ulan Bator on May 22, 1933. Jigjidjav served as Mongolia's prime minister from April of 1930 until July of 1932. He subsequently served as minister of trade, transport and communications until his death.

• **Assis Khan** (1877–1933), the elder brother of King Nadir (q.v.) of Afghanistan, was shot and killed by an Afghanistani student in Berlin on June 6, 1933.

• **Hayim Arlosoroff** (1899–1933) was murdered by two unknown assassins in Palestine while walking with his wife on a beach in Tel Aviv in June of 1933. Arlosoroff was born in the Ukraine and raised in Germany from 1905. He became active in Zionist affairs as a young man and was cofounder of the Ha-Po'el ha-Tzai'r party in 1918. The party subsequently merged with the Tze'irei Zion to become the Histadrut or Union, party. Arlosoroff remained a leader of the Histadrut and went to Palestine in 1921. He was a representative of Zionist interests at the League of Nations in Geneva in 1926. In the early 1930s Arlosoroff attempted to negotiated with the Nazis in Germany for increased Jewish emigration to Palestine. After a visit to Germany he was murdered. Two extremist Zionists were charged with the murder, but their convictions were overturned because of lack of evidence.

- **Sardar Mohammed Nadir Shah**, the king of Afghanistan, was the victim of an assassination on November 8, 1933. Nadir Shah was born in Deradun, in Northern India, on April 10, 1880. He rose from being a stable boy to serve in the Afghan army, attaining the rank of general. He served his cousin, Amanullah Khan, as Afghanistan's minister to France from 1924 until 1928. When Amanullah was ousted by the brigand leader Bacha Sakao (q.v.) in January of 1919 Nadir Shah returned to Afghanistan and took command of the loyalist army. He defeated Bacha Sakao after a long campaign and was awarded the throne on October 16, 1929. He put down several other revolts soon after. Nadir Shah instituted political reforms and introduced a new constitution providing for an elected legislature in 1930. He was assassinated in Kabul at the palace courtyard while awarding school prizes on November 8, 1933.

- **Ion Gheorghe Duca**, the premier of Romania, was shot and killed in Sinaia on December 30, 1933. Duca was born in Bucharest on December 20, 1879. He began his political career with his election to the chamber of deputies as a member of the National Liberal Party in 1907. He entered the government in 1914 as minister of education, serving throughout World War I until 1918. He was named foreign minister in 1922, and was a strong supporter of the Polish alliance and the Little Entente. He remained foreign minister until 1926. He succeeded Vintila Bratianu as leader of the National Liberal Party in December of 1930. Duca was named to head the government as prime minister by King Carol on November 14, 1933. His government moved to outlaw the Fascist Iron Guard movement in anticipation of elections in December of 1933, which the Liberal Party won handily. Duca was shot to death soon afterwards by Radu Constantinescu, an Iron Guard sympathizer. The prime minister was shot four times in the head while waiting on a platform at the Sinaia train station after a meeting with King Carol on December 30, 1933.

# 1934

- **Marinus van der Lubbe**, an unemployed Dutch bricklayer, was executed at Leipzig Prison on January 10, 1934, on charges of burning the German Reichstag on February 27, 1933. Van der Lubbe had been discovered inside the burning building by police and confessed to the charges. The Nazis used the fire as an excuse to arrest political opponents and dissolve civil liberties. It had been speculated that the fire was planned by Hermann Goering and carried out by Nazi agents, with van der Lubbe serving as a convenient scapegoat. He was tried by the Leipzig Supreme Court near the end of 1933 and condemned to death.

- **Cesar Augusto Sandino**, a Nicaraguan rebel leader, was assassinated in the Nicaraguan capital of Managua on February 21, 1934, by members of the National Guard. Sandino was born in 1893, the son of a farmer. In 1926 he fought with Nicaraguan vice-president Juan Bautista Sacasa in support of Sacasa's claim to the presidency. Following the intervention of the United States Marines, Sandino refused to abandon his fight. The United States forces, along with the Nicaraguan National Guard, under the command of General Anastasio Somoza Garcia (q.v.), attempted to destroy Sandino and his followers. He was forced to retreat to the mountains of northern Nicaragua and adopt guerrilla tactics. The failure of the superior forces of the United States and Nicaraguan governments to suppress the revolt led to President Franklin Roosevelt's decision to withdraw the marines in 1933. Following the removal of the American troops, Sandino expressed his willingness to negotiate with the administration of Juan Bautista Sacasa, who had become president following the 1932 elections. Sandino petitioned the government for the right to establish a semi-autonomous agricultural colony at his stronghold in Nueva Segovia. While the administration was willing to accept his terms, General Somoza and the National Guard opposed any negotiations, still hoping to gain an outright victory in battle. On February 21, 1934, following a dinner with the president, Sandino and several of his aides were seized by members of the National Guard and murdered. General Sandino soon seized the Nicaraguan presidency himself. Sandino's assassination led to his establishment as a martyr and a symbol of nationalism throughout Latin America. Years later, those who were inspired by his activities and operated under the name of Sandinistas seized power in Nicaragua by deposing the son of the man who ordered Sandino murdered.

• **Jambyn Lhumbe** (1902–34), a leading Mongolian Communist who served as secretary of the party's Central Committee, was arrested on charges of counterrevolutionary activity and executed on June 30, 1934.

• On June 30, 1934, Adolf Hitler conducted a purge of members of the German Nazi party, liquidating numerous members of his own paramilitary force of brown-shirts, or Sturmabteilungen (SA), including their leader, **Ernst Roehm**. Other German leaders who were viewed as possible threats to Hitler's rule also perished during the so-called "Night of the Long Knives." Among those killed were former German chancellor **Kurt von Schleicher**, early Nazi party member **Gregor Strasser**, and former Bavarian State Commissioner **Gustav von Kahr**. **Edmund Heines** (1897–1934), a close associate of Rohm and the group leader of the SA in the Breslau district, also perished. Other killed during the purge included **General Kurt von Bredow**, an associate of General Schleicher; **Obergruppenfuehrer Schneidhuber**, the chief of police of Munich; **Father Bernhard Stempfle** of the

Hieronmymite Order, who had assisted Hitler in the editing of *Mein Kampf;* and **Erich Klausener**, a leader of Catholic Action, who was slain in his office at the Ministry of Communications. Chancellor Franz von Papen managed to escape with his life, but his principal secretary, **Herbert von Bose**, and **Edgar Jung**, a Munich lawyer and writer who served as von Papen's advisor, were both killed.

Ernst Roehm was born on November 28, 1887, in Munich. He joined the army in 1906 and served during the First World war. He was a founder of the Nazi party and formed his own brown-shirt paramilitary group, known as the Sturmabteilungen, or SA. He was an early supporter of Adolf Hitler, and participated in the Munich "Beer Hall Putsch" on November 8, 1923, for which he was briefly imprisoned. In 1931 Roehm reorganized the SA and, in 1933, led a national revolution in Bavaria, becoming the Reich secretary of state there. He was in disagreement with Hitler over what he perceived as Hitler's unwillingness to continued the revolution after the Nazi's leader's selection as chancellor. Hitler was still not ready to challenge the power of the Germany army, and realized the Wehrmacht was strongly opposed to Roehm and the SA. in order to appease the army while consolidating his power, Hitler ordered a purge of the SA on charges of conspiracy, with Roehm being one of the first victims.

Kurt von Schleicher was born in Brandenburg on April 7, 1882. He entered the army in 1900 and was named to the general staff in 1913. Von Schleicher rose through the ranks, making many powerful military and political contacts along the way. He served as aide-de-camp to General Hans von Seeckt from 1923. He was promoted to colonel in 1926 and became a leading force in the Reichswehr ministry. His power increased following the appointment of Wilhelm Groener, his former commanding officer, as defense minister in 1928. Von Schleicher was named to the newly created position of chief of the ministerial staff at the Reichswehr, with the rank of major general, in 1929. Von Schleicher was instrumental in bringing about the collapse of Heinrich Bruning's government in June of 1932. He served as minister of defense in Franz von Papen's subsequent government. His resignation from the cabinet brought about von Papen's resignation, and von Schleicher was called upon to head the government on December 2, 1932. He was a powerful opponent of Adolf Hitler and the Nazis, and worked to insure that the Reichswehr was in a position to curtail excesses by the Nazis. Von Schleicher was forced to resign on January 28, 1933, following an agreement between Hitler and von Papen that resulted in President Paul von Hindenburg offering the reins of government to the Nazi leader. Von Schleicher retired to private life, but was still viewed as a powerful opponent of the Nazis. When Hitler dispatched the Schutzstaffel (SS) to eliminate his rivals and opponents on June 30, 1934, in an event known as the "Night of the Long Knives," von Schleicher was high on the list. Accused of conspiring against the government, von Schleicher and his wife were shot to death by the SS at their Berlin flat, allegedly while resisting arrest.

Gregor Strasser was born in Lower Bavaria on May 31, 1892. He served in the German army during the First World War, and later joined the rightist Freikorps in Bavaria. In 1923 he participated in Hitler's "Beer Hall Putsch," and was briefly imprisoned following its failure. In 1924 Strasser was elected as a member of the Bavarian legislature and was subsequently released from prison. While Hitler was still serving a prison term, Strasser became the co-chairman of the Nationalist Socialist party, and used his organizational skills to greatly expand the party. He, with his brother Otto Strasser, founded the *Berliner Arbeiterzeitung*, a weekly Nazi newspaper. Strasser remained one of Hitler's greatest rivals for power in the Nazi organization. Strasser was an advocate of more Socialistic ideals than Hitler was willing to commit to, and Strasser opposed the many compromises Hitler made with the military and the wealthy industrialists. Strasser was

propaganda minister for the party from 1926 until 1932, when he resigned his party posts after Hitler opposed his acceptance of a cabinet position in the government of General Kurt von Schleicher. Strasser remained inactive in politics, but was still viewed by Hitler as a potential rival. Due to the possible threat he presented to Hitler's power in the Nazi party, Strasser was murdered during Hitler's purge.

Gustav von Kahr (1862–1934) was general commissioner of state in Bavaria at the time of Hitler's "Beer Hall Putsch." He participated in the revolt under duress, and abandoned Hitler as soon as opportunity allowed. The putsch failed, and von Kahr was apparently never forgiven for his betrayal. He later served as the president of the administrative court of justice from 1924 to 1930. During the Nazi purge of 1934, von Kahr, a nearly forgotten figure from Germany's past, was murdered while in retirement.

• German anarchist **Erich Muhsam** died in prison on July 10, 1934. Muhsam, who was born in Berlin on April 6, 1878, was a leading German Jewish playwright and was active in the Bavarian Socialist Revolution of 1918. After serving a term in prison for his activities, he became an outspoken critic of the Nazis. He was arrested by the Nazis shortly after the Reichstag fire in February of 1933, and was imprisoned in several concentration camps, where he was subjected to brutal treatment. His badly beaten body was found hanged in the latrine at Oramenberg shortly after Hitler's "Night of the Long Knives."

• **Engelberg Dollfuss**, the chancellor of Austria, was murdered in the chancellery in Vienna by Austrian Nazi rebels on July 25, 1934. Dollfuss was born in Kirnberg an der Mank in Lower Austria on October 4, 1892. He was educated at the Universities of Vienna and Berlin, where he studied economics and law. He became active in politics, serving as secretary of the Lower Austrian Peasant Union. He directed the chamber of agriculture in Lower Austria from 1927, gaining a reputation as an expert in agricultural matters.

He served as president of the Austrian federal railways from 1930, and was named to the cabinet as minister of agriculture in March of 1931. He was called on by the Clerical Christian Socialist Party to form a government as chancellor on May 20, 1932. He was attacked in the chamber by nationalist elements in July of 1932 when he accepted a League of Nations loan agreement that required Austria to forgo a customs union with Germany. Dollfuss began to govern in an increasingly authoritarian manner. He formed the Patriotic Front in May of 1933. He sought an alliance with Benito Mussolini's government in Italy and began to base Austria's government on the Fascist model. Dollfuss promoted a new constitution in May of 1934 which established him as a virtual dictator. He ruthlessly suppressed and dissolved the Social Democratic Party before moving against the Nazi Party in May of 1934. Civil violence erupted throughout the country. Dollfuss was assassinated in the chancellery in Vienna during an abortive Nazi coup attempt on July 25, 1934.

• On October 9, 1934, **King Alexander I** of Yugoslavia and **Jean Louis Barthou**, the foreign minister of France, were assassinated by Vlada Cherzozensky, a Croatian terrorist, in Marseille, when the gunman fired a pistol at the two leaders when he jumped onto the running board of their car. Alexander was hit by two shots and died instantly. Barthou was shot once, and died several hours later. Cherzozensky was seized by an angry crowd and shot by a policemen. He died of his wounds soon afterwards. Other conspirators were subsequently captured and sentenced to prison. The leader of the conspiracy to kill King Alexander, Ante Pavelic (1889–1959), escaped capture.

Alexander was born in Cetinje on December 16, 1888. He was the second son of Peter Karageorgevich and Zorka. He spent much of his youth in exile in Geneva with his father. He was sent to St. Petersburg in 1899. His father gained the throne of Serbia in 1903. Alexander returned to Serbia in 1909 and became heir to the throne when his brother,

George, renounced his right of succession in March of 1909. Alexander commanded the Serbian army during the first Balkan War of 1912 and distinguished himself at the battle of Kumanovo. Alexander was named regent of Serbia on June 24, 1914, due to the poor health of his father. He also served as commander in chief of the armed forces. He remained at army headquarters during World War I and returned to Belgrade in October of 1918. Alexander remained regent of the newly formed kingdom of the Serbs, Croats and Slovenes on December 1, 1918. The constituent assembly passed a new constitution in June of 1921 and Alexander narrowly escaped an assassination attempt after swearing allegiance to the constitution. He succeeded as king upon the death of his father on August 16, 1921. He married Marie, daughter of Ferdinand I of Rumania, on June 8, 1922. They had three children: Peter in 1923, Tomislav in 1928 and Andrei in 1929. Political conflict between the Serbs and Croats escalated in the kingdom following the murder of two Croatian politicians on the floor of the Skupstina, or parliament, in June of 1928. Alexander felt compelled to abolish the constitution in January of 1929 and assume full powers to keep the country from splitting apart. He changed the name of the kingdom to Yugoslavia on October 3, 1929 and promoted a new constitution in September of 1931. Yugoslavia's relationship with its neighbors Italy and Hungary was strained during the early 1930s. Alexander survived another assassination attempt in 1933. He was murdered in Marseilles, France, by Vlada Cherzozensky, a Croatian terrorist, on October 9, 1934, and succeeded by his son, Peter.

Jean-Louis Barthou was born in Oloron-Sainte-Marie on August 25, 1862. He was educated as a lawyer and elected to the chamber of deputies in 1889. He entered Charles Dupuy's cabinet as minister of public works in 1894. He served as minister of the interior under Jules Meline in 1896. He returned to head the public works ministry in 1906 under Ferdinand Sarrien, retaining that position under Georges Clemenceau through 1909. He was named to head the government as premier on March 21, 1913. He enacted legislation that mandated three-year military service. Barthou's government resigned on December 10, 1913. He served as minister of state in 1917 and became minister of war under Aristide Briand in 1921. He served as minister of justice in 1922 and represented France at the Genoa Conference later in the year. He was subsequently elected to the senate. He returned to the ministry of justice in 1926. Barthou was named foreign minister in Gaston Doumergue's coalition government in 1934. He attempted to negotiate a pact between France and Yugoslavia. Barthou arranged a state visit to France by Yugoslavia's King Alexander I. During the visit Barthou was killed while unsuccessfully attempting to thwart the assassination of the King by a Croatian terrorist in Marseille on October 9, 1934.

- **Sergei M. Kirov**, a leading Soviet politician, was assassinated in Leningrad on December 1, 1934. Kirov was born in Russia on March 27, 1886. He joined the Bolsheviks in 1905 and was active in the revolution of that year. He served several terms in prison during the reign of the czar, and was active in the revolution of 1917. Following the success of the revolution, he took part in the wars against the counter-revolutionaries in northern Caucasia. In 1921 Kirov was named the first secretary of the Azerbaijan Communist party and, in 1926, he became secretary of the party's organization in Leningrad. In 1930 he became a member of the ruling Politburo and was a close aide to Joseph Stalin. In 1934 Kirov was involved with Stalin's opponents on the central committee. He was shot to death in Leningrad by Leonid Nikolayev, presumably on the orders of Stalin. Nikolayev and others were executed shortly after, and Kirov's murder was used as a pretext by Stalin to initiate the purge trials to eliminate his rivals and opponents.

# 1935

- **Ch'u Ch'iu-Pai** (1899–1935), an early Chinese Communist leader, was arrested and executed as a leftist extremist in 1935. Ch'u became the chairman of the Communist party in China in 1927. His administration was marked by a policy of insurrection, which caused his removal in 1928 and his eventual execution

- **Antonio Guiteras** (1904–35) former Cuban Secretary of the Interior, War and Navy, was killed on May 8, 1935, in a fight between the army and navy forces and a group of rebels, which he led, at Fort Morillo, near the City of Matanzas, Cuba.

- **Maj. Gen. Tetsuzan Nagata**, the chief of the Military Affairs Bureau in the Tokyo War Office, was assassinated on August 12, 1935. Nagata, who was considered a moderate, was killed by three stokes of a sword wielded by Lt. Col. Sabura Aizawa, following Nagata's dismissal of some of the more militant war office personnel. Aizawa was tried for the murder and executed on July 3, 1936.

- Louisiana politician and United States Senator **Huey P. Long** was shot and fatally injured near his office in Baton Rouge by Dr. Carl Austin Weiss (1906–35) on September 8, 1935. Weiss was in turn slain by Long's bodyguards, who fired over 60 bullets into the senator's assailant.

Huey Long was born in Winnfield, Louisiana, in 1893 and began his political career practicing law. His oratory skills and political demagoguery resulted in Long's election as Louisiana's governor in 1928. He served in that position as a virtual dictator and became known as "the Kingfish." He retained a firm control on the Louisiana legislature after his election to the United States Senate in 1930 and initiated a series of welfare measures as part of his "Share the Wealth" campaign. Long attained a national prominence as a leading opponent of President Franklin Roosevelt and was considered a likely challenger for the

Democratic presidential nomination of 1936. Long's assailant was the son-in-law of a prominent Louisiana jurist who was a political opponent of Long. It is believed that Weiss shot Long because of the senator's attacks on the reputation of his wife's family. There is still doubt if the bullet that killed Huey Long was actually fired by his alleged assassin or was a ricochet fired by one of his own bodyguards. Long lived for two days after the shooting, finally succumbing to his injuries on September 10, 1935.

- Mobster **Dutch Schultz** (Arthur Flegenheimer) (1902–35), was shot to death by mob hitmen in a Newark, New Jersey, restaurant on October 23, 1935. Several of Schultz's associates, **Abbadabba Berman** (1880–35), Lulu Rosenkrantz, and Abe Landau, were also killed with two hitmen burst into the restaurant to kill Schultz. It was believed that Schultz's hit had been ordered by mob leader Lucky Luciano (1897–62) when he learned that Schultz was planning the assassination of New York District Attorney Thomas E. Dewey (1902–71). The mob feared that Dewey's murder would bring increased pressure on their activities.

- **Chuan-fang Sun** (1885–1935), Chinese marshal and formerly one of the country's most powerful war lords, was assassinated by a young Chinese woman in Tientsin, China, on November 13, 1935.

- **Sheikh Izz Al-Din Al-Qassam**, the leader of the Palestinians' first revolt against British rule, was killed during fighting against British forces on November 19, 1935. Qassam, a preacher, educator and member of the Muslim Brotherhood, had called for a jihad against the British and Zionists in Palestine. His death marked the start of a four year Arab revolt in the area.

# 1936

- **Wilhelm Gusloff**, a German Nazi agent operating in Switzerland, was assassinated at Davos by David Frankfurter, a Jewish student, on February 4, 1936.

- **Maxim Gorky**, the famed Russian writer and dramatist, died suddenly on June 18, 1936, while undergoing medical treatment. It was alleged that he was assassinated by poisoning at the hands of agents of Josef Stalin or by Stalin's enemies. Born Alexei Maximovich Peshko on March 28, 1968, in Nizhniy-Novgorod, Russia, Gorky began writing in 1892. An early supporter of the revolutionary movement, he took part in the 1905 revolution. Gorky was in exile in Capri from 1906 to 1913. He supported the ouster of the Czar and became head of the State Publishing House. Plagued by poor health, Gorky spent year abroad in the early 1920s. He returned to Russia in 1928, to work on his unfinished *The Life of Klim Sangin*. His better known works also include the play *The Lower Depths* (1902) and the memoir *My Childhood* (1914).

- On February 26, 1936, Japanese right-wing militarists conducted a purge of moderate Japanese statesmen and politicians. Former Prime Minister **Viscount Makota Saito** (1858–1936), a Japanese admiral and close advisor to the emperor, was shot and killed while returning from a dinner at the American embassy. Another former prime minister **Viscount Korekiyo Takahashi** was shot and hacked to death with a sword. **General Jotaro Watanabe** (1878–1936), the inspector general of military training, was murdered in his home.

Makota Saito was born in Iwate Prefecture in 1858. He attended the Naval Academy and rose through the ranks of the navy. He served as vice minister of the navy during the Russo-Japanese War from 1904 until 1905. He became minister of the navy the following year and was promoted to admiral in 1912. He stepped down from the cabinet in April of

1914 when Gombei Yamamoto's government collapsed following a bribery scandal involving naval officers. He was appointed governor general of Korea in 1919, and adopted a moderate policy there. He retained that position until 1927. Following the assassination of Tsuyoshi Inukai by rebel military officers Saito was called upon to form a government of national unity on May 26, 1932. His government recognized the puppet state of Manchukuo in Japanese-controlled Manchuria and withdrew from the League of Nations. His government resigned on July 4, 1934, following a bribery scandal involving officials at the ministry of finance.

Korekiyo Takahashi was born in Sendal in July of 1854. He began his education in Nagasaki before emigrating to the United States in 1870. He returned to Japan several years later to work as a clerk in the department of education. He became the first director of the newly formed Japanese Bureau of Patents and soon entered the banking industry. He became governor of the Central Bank of Japan in 1911. Takahashi served in various cabinets as minister of finance from 1913 until 1914 and in 1918. He was named to head the government as prime minister on November 13, 1921, following the assassination of Takashi Hara (q.v.). His government collapsed on June 12, 1922, following criticism of his handling of negotiations for the naval vessels treaty between Japan, the United States and Great Britain. He again served in the cabinet as finance minister in 1927 and from 1931. Takahashi also led a short-lived government following the assassination of Tsoyoshi Inukai (q.v.) on May 16, 1932, until Makoto Saito formed a government on May 26, 1932. He remained in the government as finance minister until May of 1934, when he stepped down for reasons of advanced age. He was asked to resume his position in November of 1934 following an economic downturn. He retained office until his murder.

Several of the rebels' targets survived the attempts on their lives. Prime Minister Keisuke Okada (1868–1952) hid in the toilet of his house upon hearing the arrival of the muti-

neers. His brother-in-law was killed by the armed band by mistake. The emperor's grand chamberlain, Admiral Suzuki (1867–1948) was injured by assailants, but recovered from his wounds. Other prominent Japanese had also been marked for assassination, including Prince Saionji (1849–1940) and Count Nobuaki Makino (1861–1949), but were not found by the assassins. The rebellion was quickly put down by government troops and most of those involved were arrested and court-martialed in secret. Thirteen of the rebels, as well as **Kita Ikki**, a leading right-wing writer and agitator, were executed on July 3, 1936.

• **Jose Calvo Sotelo**, a Spanish Monarchist political leader and minister of finance in Miguel Primo De Rivera's government, was shot and killed by left-wing Asaltus gunmen on July 12, 1936. He was murdered immediately after the killing of **Lt. Jose Castillo** by Falangists. Castillo's comrades blamed Calvo Sotelo's speeches in the Cortes for Castillo's slaying. Captain Condes of the Civil Guard and his aides took Calvo Sotelo from his home and shot him to death. His body was dumped beside a cemetery outside of Madrid. Condes went into hiding following the murder, and died during the early days of the Civil War.

• **Michael Stelescu**, the founder and leader of the Romanian Fascist organization "The Brothers of the Cross," was murdered on July 16, 1936, while in a hospital. Stelescu's group had merged with a similar organization led by Corneliu Codreanu (q.v.) to become the Iron Guard. Stelescu was presumably killed by Iron Guardists following his disagreement with Codreanu over the issue of closer ties with Nazi Germany.

• On July 17, 1936, Spanish Republican **General Quintero Romerales**, having discovered plans of the Nationalist uprising in the Moroccan town of Melilla, was arrested by Colonel Seguia. He was subsequently shot with the Mayor of Melilla. Later in the month **General Julio Mena Fuenco** and **General Domingo Batet Mestres** (1872–

1936), both Loyalists, were shot and killed following the military rising in Burgos. Loyalist **General Miguel Nunez De Prado** was killed by General Miguel Cabanellas after he was sent to confirm Cabanellas' loyalty. Cabanellas joined the military rising and shot Nunez. Other Republican generals executed by the Nationalists in the early days of the Civil War included **General Molero Lobero** (1870–1936) of Valldolid, **General Enrique Salcedo Molinvero** (1871–1936) of Corunna, **General Caridad Pita**, the military governor of Corunna, **General Campins** of Granada, **General Lopez De Ochoa y Portuondo** (1877–1936), and **Admiral Manuel Azarola Grusillon**, the commander of the arsenal at El Ferrol.

• **Federico Garcia Lorca**, the Spanish poet and playwright, was arrested in his home town of Granada for harboring left-wing sympathies. He was condemned to death by the commander of the Falangist militia and executed on August 19, 1936. Garcia Lorca was born in Fuente Vaqueros, Granada, on June 5, 1898. His better known works include *Thus Five Years Pass*, *The Public* and *Dona Rosita*. Much of his work was banned during the Franco dictatorship. His play, *The House of Barnardo Alba*, was not produced in Spain until 1950.

• On August 23, 1936, Spanish Republican forces executed a number of leading rightist leaders who had been imprisoned in Model Prison in Madrid. They included **Melquiades Alvarez y Gonzalez** (1864–1936) and **Jose Martinez De Velasco** (1875–1936), two prominent rightists; **Fernando Primo De Rivera**, the brother of Jose Antonio Primo De Rivera (q.v.); **Julio Ruiz De Alda y Miqueleiz** (1897–1936), a leading Falangist; **Dr. Jose Maria Albinana y Sanz** (1833–1936), a leader of the Nationalist party; and **General Rafael Villegas Montesinos**.

• Spanish military leader **Manuel Goded Llopis** (1882–1936) was tried and executed for treason in August of 1936, following his participation in the Nationalist rising in Barcelona. Goded Llopis served in the Spanish army, and assisted Miguel Primo De Rivera in seizing power in Spain in 1923. He later broke with the dictator due to Primo's treatment of the army and, in 1929, was involved in the unsuccessful Andalusian rising. When the Spanish Republic was formed, Goded Llopis was named inspector general of the army. Following his support of the unsuccessful Sanjurjo coup in August of 1932, Goded Llopis was dismissed from his posts and arrested. He was later released and made joint chief of staff with General Francisco Franco in October of 1934. He was subsequently named the director of the air force. In early 1936 Goded Llopis became a major figure in the Nationalist rising. He was captured by Loyalist forces on July 19, while leading an assault on Barcelona. He was court-martialed and executed in the castle of Montjuich on August 11, 1936.

• **Joaquin Fanjul Goni** (1880–1936), a right-wing Spanish soldier and politician, was executed for treason in 1936. Fanjul Goni was a leading conservative figure in the Spanish army. He served with distinction in Morocco and, following the establishment of the republic, became actively involved in conservative politics. He served in the Cortes and, in May of 1935, was named undersecretary of war by Gil Robles. He became involved in the Nationalist rising early in 1936 and, on July 18, was captured by the Loyalists during his unsuccessful attempt to capture Madrid. He was subsequently court-martialed and shot for treason.

• Republican forces murdered numerous members of the Roman Catholic clergy in Spain, including a number of bishops. Killed during the early days of the Civil War were **Manuel Basulto Jimenez**, bishop of Jaen; **Salvio Huix Miralpeix** (1877–1936), bishop of Lerida; **Miguel Serra Sucarrats** (1867–1936), bishop of Segorbe; **Cruz Laplana Laguna** (1876–1936), bishop of Cuenca; **Manuel Irurita Almandoz** (1876–1936), bishop of Barcelona; **Diego Ventaja Milan** (1882–1936), bishop of

Almeria; **Juan Medina Olmos** (1869–1936), bishop of Guadix; **Narciso De Estenaga y Echevarria** (1882–1936), bishop of Ciudad Real; **Manuel Borras Ferrer**, suffragan bishop of Tarragona; **Juan De Ponce**, apostolic administrator of Orihuela; and **Florencio Asensio Barroso** (1876–1936), apostolic administrator of Barbastro and titular bishop of Epirus.

• The first of the major Soviet purge trials of the Stalin regime concluded on August 24, 1936. This trial, known as the "Trial of the Trotsky-Zinoviev Terrorist Center," ended with the shooting of Lenin's close associate **Grigori E. Zinoviev**; **Lev B. Kamenev**, a Politburo member since 1919; and **G.E. Evdokimov**, a former member of the Secretariat. Thirteen other defendants were also convicted, including the Trotskyites **Ivan M. Smirnov**, an ex–Central Committee member; **Sergei V. Mrachkovsky**, a fighter, **V.A. Ter-Vaganian**, an intellectual Armenian; and **E.A. Dreitzer**, head of Trotsky's bodyguards. Other defendants included **Ivan P. Bakayev**, **Valentin Olbert**, **K.B. Berman-Yurin**, **Fritz David**, **Moissei Lurye**, **Nathan Lurye**, **Isak Reingold**, **E.S. Holtzman** and **Richard Pickel**. All were convicted of treason and most were executed. Another Politburo member, Mikhail P. Tomsky, committed suicide on August 22, 1936, after having been implicated.

Grigori Evseevich Zinoviev was born in September of 1883 in the Ukraine. He joined with the Bolsheviks in 1901 and was active in the 1905 revolution. He was a close aide to Lenin during his period of exile from 1909 until 1917, and returned with him to Russia following the March Revolution. Zinoviev, along with Kamenev, were leaders of the right-wing bloc of the Bolsheviks who opposed Lenin's seizure of power, during a Socialist coalition government. As leader of the Communist party in Petrograd, Zinoviev was named a candidate member of the ruling Politburo and full member two years later. He was chairman of the Communist International Executive Committee from 1919 to 1926, and

was a leading candidate to succeeded Lenin at the time of Lenin's death in 1924. Zinoviev initially aided Stalin in his struggle against Trotsky, but later broke with him. This move led to his expulsion from the Communist party and his subsequent trial and execution.

Lev Borisovich Kamenev was born in Tylis on July 22, 1883. He joined the Social Democratic Party in 1901 and was soon engaged in revolutionary activities. He left Russia in 1908 and became a close associate of Lenin. He returned to St. Petersburg in 1914 to direct Bolshevik activities in Russia. He was arrested the following year and banished to Siberia. He returned to St. Petersburg at the outbreak of the revolution in March of 1917 and was the principal Bolshevik leader in the country until the return of Lenin. Kamenev soon broke with Lenin over the issue of joining with other Socialist parties to form a coalition government. He was elected to the politburo in October of 1917 and briefly served as chairman of the Presidium of the Supreme Soviet in November of 1917. He joined with Josef Stalin and Grigori E. Zinoviev in opposition to Leon Trotsky in 1923. He subsequently broke with Stalin and was removed from his party positions in 1926. He served as Soviet ambassador to Italy the following year. His opposition to Stalin's regime led to his ouster from the Communist party and his arrest in 1935. He was subsequently tried for treason and sentenced to prison, but was retried the following year and executed.

• **Ramiro De Maeztu y Whitney**, a Spanish political journalist, was shot and killed by Republicans in Madrid on October 29, 1936. Maeztu y Whitney was born on May 4, 1874, in Victoria, Spain. He served as a political correspondent for various Spanish newspapers in London from 1906 to 1916, and later supported the dictatorship of Miguel Primo De Rivera. Following the establishment of the Spanish Republic, he opposed the government through a series of political articles and books. He was murdered shortly after the outbreak of the Spanish Civil War.

• Ethiopian freedom fighters continued to attack the occupying Italian forces in Ethiopia during 1936. A small group of soldiers attacked Addis Ababa in July of 1936. **Abune Petros**, a leading figure in the Ethiopian church, was arrested and executed by a firing squad in a public square by the Italian occupiers on July 29, 1936. Another leader of the Ethiopian church, **Abune Markos**, was also executed by the occupation forces. **Abera Kasa** (1905–36), the son of the emperor's advisor, Kasu Haylu, and a leader of the band that carried out the attack, surrendered and was executed on December 21, 1936.

Abune Petros was born to a farming family in Fiche in 1892. He was given the baptismal name Hayle Maryam and became a priest with the Ethiopian Orthodox Church. He taught at the Debre-Menkrat monastery church in Wolamo until 1924, when he became head teacher at the church in Lake Zewai. He became a bishop, or abune, of the church in 1928, leading the church in the central and eastern part of Ethiopia. Abune Petros accompanied Emperor Haile Selassie's forces into battle against the Italian invaders in 1932. He continued to opposed the occupation forces after the defeat of the Ethiopian army.

• **Jafar el-Askari**, the former prime minister of Iraq, was assassinated on October 30, 1936. Askari was born in Baghdad in 1887. He was the son of a military leader of the Ottoman Empire. He graduated from the Ottoman military academy in 1904 and served in the Ottoman army during World War I. He was captured by the British during the war and made a daring escape from his captors in Egypt. He subsequently joined the Arab Nationalist movement with his brother-in-law, Nuri as-Sa'id (q.v.), and joined T.E. Lawrence's Arab revolt against the Turks. Askari became a close associate of Feisal, who became king of Syria in 1920. Feisal was removed from power by the French, but was supported in his claim of the Iraqi throne in 1921. He served as minister of defense in the first Iraqi government. He headed the government from November 22, 1923, until August 3, 1924, and again from November 21, 1926, until December 31, 1927. He remained active in government affairs, serving in the cabinet as minister of defense and foreign affairs in 1931 and 1932. He continued to be a major figure in Iraqi politics and was again serving as minister of defense when he was murdered by insurgent troops under the orders of General Bakr Sidqi (q.v.) on October 30, 1936.

• **Jose Antonio Primo De Rivera**, the son of the former Spanish dictator General Miguel Primo De Rivera, was executed on November 20, 1936. Jose Antonio was born in Madrid on April 24, 1903. He became active in politics at an early age, and was a leading conservative spokesman at the time of his election as a deputy in the Cortes in 1933. The same year he founded the right-wing Falange party, which he led until his death. Jose Antonio lost his seat in the Cortes in 1936 and was arrested soon afterward. He was again elected to the Cortes while imprisoned, but his election was nullified by the Republican government. Jose Antonio remained imprisoned through the start of the Spanish Civil War, and was eventually tried and convicted of treason on November 18, 1936. He was executed in Alicante prison two days later.

• Spanish anarchist **Buenaventura Durruti** was shot and killed in front of Model Prison in Madrid on November 21, 1936. Durruti was born in 1896, and first became involved in the anarchist movement in 1917, by sabotaging railway lines in Leon. In 1923 he, along with Francisco Ascaso, assassinated Cardinal De Soldeville (q.v.), the archbishop of Saragossa, and the following year the two made an unsuccessful attempt on the life of King Alfonso XIII of Spain. Following a brief period of imprisonment, Durruti became active in the Federation Anarchista Iberica (FAI), and orchestrated many acts of political violence prior to the start of the Spanish Civil War. When the Nationalist rising began, Durruti served on the Anti-Fascist Militia Committee, which ruled Catalonia. He led an anarchist army against the Nationalist forces in Saragosa, and later led his column in defense of Madrid. Speculation exists that Durruti was shot in the back by his own men, but there is also evidence to suggest that his shooting was an accident that occurred when his aide's machine pistol caught on a car door, firing a bullet into Durruti's chest.

# 1937

• In January of 1937 the Soviet purge trials continued with the trial known as the "Trial of the Anti-Soviet Trotskyite Center." The defendants included Politburo member **Grigori Sokolnikov**, journalist **Karl Radek**, **Grigori L. Pyatakov**, **Leonid P. Serebryako**, **A.A. Shestov**, **M.S. Stroilov**, **B.O. Norkin**, **N.I. Muralov**, **Valentin Arnold**, **Yakov Livshits**, **I.A. Knayev**, **A.S. Rataichak**, and five others. Most of the defendants were convicted, and the sentences ranged from execution to imprisonment.

Grigori Yakovlevich Sokolnikov was born in 1888 and became a member of the Bolshevik faction in 1905. He lived in exile until the Revolution of 1917, and served as a member of the Russian delegation which negotiated the Brest Litovsky peace treaty with Germany in 1918. Sokolnikov served as the assistant people's commissar of finance in 1922, and was the Soviet ambassador to Great Britain from 1929 to 1932. At the time of his arrest he was the assistant commissar for the timber industry. He was sentenced to ten years' imprisonment following the trial, but reportedly died in a prison camp in 1939.

Karl Bernadovich Radek was born in Lwow, Gallicia, in 1885. He became a member of the Social Democrat party of Poland and Lithuania in 1901, and served as a journalist on numerous left-wing publications in Poland and Germany. He accompanied Lenin across Germany following the Russian Revolution of 1917. Returning to Germany he was instrumental in the establishment of the German Communist party. Following his arrest he returned to the Soviet Union in 1920. He was charged with being a follower of Leon Trotsky (q.v.), and was dismissed from the Communist party in 1925, but was later readmitted. Following his trial for treasonable activities he was sentenced to ten years' imprisonment, but was reportedly murdered in a prison camp in 1939.

Grigori L. Pyatakov was born in 1890. He served as the assistant commissar for heavy industries from 1931 to 1937. He was tried for treason as a follower of Leon Trotsky (q.v.), and was executed on January 31, 1937.

• Soviet politician **Grigori Konstantinovich Ordzhonikidze** was forced to commit suicide on February 18, 1937, by order of Josef Stalin. Ordzhonikidze was born in Georgia, Russian on October 27, 1886. He joined the Bolsheviks in 1903. Following a period of exile in Germany, he returned to Russia in 1907 and was arrested on several occasions. After the 1917 Revolution Ordzhonikidze became a member of the Bolshevik Communist Party Committee. In January of 1918 he was appointed commissar extraordinary for the Ukraine. In 1926 he became a candidate member of the Politburo and served in several important positions. In 1930 he became the chairman of the Council of National economy and a member of the Politburo. He became people's commissar for heavy industry in 1932. Ordzhonikidze, a supporter of Stalin, became a victim of Stalin's distrust of potential rivals.

• **Nikolai Aleksandrovich Uglanov** (1886–1937), a member of the Politburo from 1926 until his ouster in 1929, was shot during the Stalin purges in 1937.

• In February of 1937 an attempt was made on the life of Marshal Rodolfo Graziani (1882–1955), the Italian viceroy of Ethiopia. Graziani was uninjured in the attack, but the Italian army retaliated cruelly against the Ethiopian people.

• In 1937 Mohammad Reza Khan, the Shah of Iran, imprisoned several former members of his government whom he considered rivals to his leadership. **Prince Firouz Mirza Nosrat-ed-Dowleh**, the oldest son of former Iranian Prime Minister Prince Abdol Hossein Farmanfarma, had served as Minister of Foreign Affairs in 1919 and was the Shah's Minister of Finance. He was imprisoned with **Seyyed Hassan Modaress**, a member of the Majlis, and **Abdul Hossein Teymourtash**, the Shah's Minister of Court. The three were executed later in the year.

• **Ras Desta Demtew** (1892–1937), a leader of Ethiopian guerrilla forces against the Italian occupiers, was captured and executed in 1937. Demtew had been a supporter of Haile Selassie during his regency. He served as governor of Sidamo and Borana from 1924. Demtew had made efforts to modernize the region. He became commander in chief of the military in southern Ethiopia in 1935 and one of the leading resistance fighters.

• Spanish General **Emilio Mola Vidal** was killed when his plane crashed under suspicious circumstances on June 3, 1937. Mola was born in 1887. He was the last director general of security under the Spanish monarchy. He supported the right-wing coup in 1936, which resulted in the Spanish Civil War. He served in the junta which governed Nationalist Spain. Mola's power diminished after General Francisco Franco was selected to lead the combined forces of Falangists and Carlists.

• On June 12, 1937, executions were carried out against a number of leading Soviet military leaders during the Soviet army purge trials. It has been estimated that over 35,000 Russian army officers, representing over half of the officers corps, were executed during the year. Among those tried and executed were **Marshal Mikhail Tukhachevski**; **General Iona E. Yakir** (1896–1937), commander of the Kiev Military District and Central Committee member; **General Ieronim P. Uborevich** (1896–1937), commander of the Byelorussian Military District; **General R.P. Eideman**, head of the civil defense organization "Osoaviakhim"; **General Kork**, head of the Military Academy; **Corps Cmdr. Vi-**

**tovt Putna**, military attaché in London; **Corps Cmdr. Feldman**, head of the Red Army administration; and **Corps Cmdr. Primakov**, deputy commander of the Leningrad Military District. **Yan Gamarnik**, head of the political administration of the Red Army and first deputy commissar of defense, committed suicide on June 1, 1937, after having been implicated in the trials.

Mikhail Nikolaevich Tukhachevski was born in Smolensk province in 1893. He served in the Russian army during the First World War and joined the Communist party and the Red Army in 1918. He led a successful campaign against the White Army during the Civil War. He was commander of the War Academy from 1921 to 1922, before returning to command the Western Army Group. Tukhachevski became chief of the general staff of the Red Army in 1925, serving in that position for three years. In 1934 he was elected as a candidate member of the Communist Party's Central Committee and was made a marshal of the army in 1935. He was executed following Stalin's purge of the army.

• Purge trials and executions against Communist party members continued throughout the year, claiming victims from the Soviet Union and many other countries. **Karl Yanovich Bauman** (1892–1937), a member of the Politburo from 1929 to 1930, was tried and shot in October of 1937.

Ten of the twelve arrested leaders of the Hungarian Revolution were killed, including **Deszo Bokani**, theorist **Lajos Magyar**, and **Jozsef Pogany**, who under the name John Pepper was the Comintern's representative to the American Communist party.

Romanian Communist leaders **Marcel Pauker** and **Alexandru Dobrogeanu** were shot during the year, as was Italian Communist party member **Edmondo Peluso**.

Beginning in 1937, all twelve members of the Polish Communist party's Central Committee present in Russia, and several hundred others, were executed. These included Polish Communist leaders **Adolf S. Warski**, **Wera Kostrzewa**, and **Budzyn-**

**ski**, who were shot on August 20, 1937. **Jerzy Ring** and **Henryk Henrykowski**, Polish Politburo members, and **Henry Walecki**, the Polish Communist party representative to the Executive Committee and Control Commission of the Comintern, were also purged.

**Panas Lyubchenko**, the premier of the Ukraine, was ordered to Moscow and executed.

Much of the Yugoslav Central Committee perished in 1937, including **Milan Gorkic** (1890–1937), the general secretary of the Yugoslav Communist party, and **Vlada Copic**, the Yugoslav party's organization secretary. Gorkic had become active in the Communist party in 1918, and was a founding member of the Yugoslav Communist party. From 1922 until 1937 he lived in Moscow, becoming the leader of the Yugoslav party. Following his execution, Josip Broz Tito succeeded him in that position.

On June 16, 1937, **Andres Nin**, the Spanish political secretary of POUM (Marxist Party of Catalonia), was arrested in Spain. He was tortured and killed by agents of Stalin. **Jose Diaz**, the secretary general of the Spanish Communist party, jumped, or was pushed, from a window in Moscow.

During the summer of 1937, **Nikolai Smernov**, the Soviet NKVD resident in France, was recalled to Moscow and executed.

**Ignace Reiss** (1899–1937), a former Communist party functionary and NKVD resident in Switzerland, was shot to death in Lausanne, Switzerland, on September 4, 1937. Reiss, formerly Poretskii, fought with the Bolsheviks during the 1917 Revolution. Afterwards he became an agent of the Cheka, the Soviet security police, in Poland, Austria and Germany. He had refused an order to return to the Soviet Union during the Stalin purges and was likely killed by Soviet agents.

• **General Bakr Sidqi**, the leader of the Iraqi army, was assassinated on August 11, 1937. Sidqi was born in Kir Tuk, Kurdestan, in 1890. He was the son of the Ottoman provincial governor. He entered the Turkish army in 1908, where he gained a reputation for ruthlessness. He fought with the Ottoman army during the First World War. He joined King Feisal's army in Iraq as a general after the war. Sidqi's massacre of unarmed Assyrians in Mosul Province forced his dismissal in 1933, but he was soon reinstated. Sidqi led a military coup against the government on October 30, 1936, during which time defense minister Jafar el-Askari was slain and the government of Yasin al-Hashimi was forced to resign. Sidqi established himself as chief of the general staff and military dictator of Iraq. He controlled the army and the government under a warrant from King Ghazi until August 11, 1937, when he and **Major Muhammad 'Ali Jawad**, commander of the Iraqi Air Force, were shot to death at the airport in Mosul. The assassin was identified as Muhammad 'Ali Yallafari, and Iraqi soldier and distant relative of slain defense minister el-Askari.

• **General Gelegdorjiyn Demid** (1907–37), the commander-in-chief of the Mongolia army, was poisoned while traveling to Moscow aboard a Trans-Siberian Trailway train on August 22, 1937. A revolutionary leader during the 1920s, he had served as Mongolia's minister of war from 1930.

• **Lewis Andrews** (1896–1937), the British district commissioner of Galilee in Palestine, was assassinated on September 26, 1937, during an Arab revolt. His murder was believed to have been orchestrated by followers of Sheikh Izz al-Din al-Qassam (q.v.), a leader of the revolt who had been killed two years earlier. A report calling for the partition of Palestine into Jewish and Arab areas, with Galilee part of the Jewish state, directly preceded the assassination.

• **Peljidiyn Gendung** (1892–1937) was a leading figure in Mongolia's revolutionary movement. He served as chairman of the Presidium of the Little Hural from November of 1924 until November of 1927. He replaced Anandyn Amor (q.v.) as prime minister and foreign minister in July of 1932. His government implemented the "New Turn" policy. He negotiated the Treaty of Friendship with the Soviet Union in March of 1936. He was expelled from the presidium of the central committee and removed from office in March of 1936. Gendung was charged with conspiring with General Demid (q.v.) in counterrevolutionary and pro–Japanese activities. He was arrested in July of 1937 and executed in Moscow on November 26, 1937. **Sodnombaljiryn Buyannemeh** (1901–37), a leading Mongolian journalist, historian and playwright who worked with the Mongolian Communist party, was arrested by Soviet authorities in September of 1937 for counterrevolutionary activities. He was executed on October 27, 1937. Mongolian party leader **Hasochiryn Luvsandorj** (1910–37), who edited the party's newspaper from 1934, was executed on November 16, 1937.

# 1938

• In March of 1938 the third major Soviet purge trial began. This trial was known as the "Trial of the Anti-Soviet Rightists and Trotskyites." The defendants in this trial included **Nikolai I. Bukharin**, a Politburo member since 1924; **Aleksei Rykov**, a Politburo member since 1922 and Lenin's successor as prime minister; **Nikolai N. Krestinsky** (1883–1938), a Politburo member from 1919 to 1927 and former ambassador to Berlin; and **Genrikh G. Yagoda**, who as head of the NKVD inaugurated the Soviet system of forced labor. Other defendants included **Khristian Rakovsky**, the former Soviet ambassador to France; **Fayzullah Khodhayev**, the prime minister of the Uzbek Soviet Socialist Republic; **Akmal Ikramov**, the Uzbek Communist party leader; and **Arkady Rosenglots, V.I. Ivanov, M.A. Chernov, G.F. Grinko, Izaak Zelensky, V.F. Sharangovich, Sergei Bessonov, P.T. Zubarev, Prof. D. Pletnev, Dr. L. Levin, Dr. I.N. Kazako, Boris Kamkov, Vladimir Karelin, P.P. Kryuchkov, P.P. Bulano** and **V.A. Maximov-Dikov-**

**sky**. As in early show trials, most of the defendants were executed or imprisoned. Of those that received prison sentences, most did not survive their incarceration.

Nikolai Ivanovich Bukharin was born in Moscow on October 9, 1888. He was an early supporter of the Bolsheviks and was imprisoned in 1911. He went into exile throughout Europe, meeting Lenin in Vienna in 1913. He settled briefly in New York City in 1916 and edited *Novy mir*, the Communist newspaper. Bukharin returned to Russia at the start of the revolution in 1917. He was elected to the Central Committee of the Soviet Communist party and became the editor of *Pravda*. Bukharin was selected as a member of the ruling Politburo in 1924. He supported Stalin in his struggle against Leon Trotsky (q.v.), but broke with Stalin in 1928 over economic and political matters. In November of 1929 he was expelled from the Politburo, and his political power was seriously diminished. In March of 1938 he was arrested and tried as an alleged member of a counter-revolutionary organization. He was sentenced to death and shot.

Aleksei Ivanovich Rykov was born in Saratov on February 13, 1881. He joined the Social Democratic Workers' Party in 1899 and became an active revolutionary soon after. He was arrested and deported several times but was able to escape and return to Russia. He supported Lenin in his break with the Bolshevik leadership in 1904, and was active in the revolution the following year. He spent several years abroad before returning to Russia in 1911. He was again arrested and banished to Siberia in 1913. He was released at the start of the revolution in March of 1916. Rykov supported a conciliatory policy with other Socialist factions and the formation of a coalition government. After the revolution in November of 1917 Rykov served in Lenin's first government as people's commissar of the interior. He served as chairman of the supreme council of national economy from 1918 until 1921 and was deputy chairman of the council of people's commissars from 1921. He succeeded Lenin as chairman on February 2, 1924. He initially supported Josef Stalin against party rival Leon Trotsky, but soon broke with Stalin to become a leader of the "Right Opposition." Stalin emerged from the conflict victorious and Rykov was replaced as chairman of the people's commissars on December 19, 1930. He subsequently served as people's commissar for communications until his dismissal from the government in 1936. Rykov was expelled from the party in 1937 and arrested for treason the following year. He was sentenced to be executed and was shot to death in Moscow on March 14, 1938.

Khristian Georgievich Rakovski was born in Bulgaria on August 13, 1873. His homeland was annexed by Romania in 1878, and he subsequently served in the Romanian army. During the early years of the First World War Rakovsky was arrested as a subversive. He was freed by the Russians following the 1917 Revolution, and became a member of the Communist party's Central Committee in 1919. Later in the year he was named president of the Soviet of People's Commissars of the Ukraine. He was also named as the Soviet charge d'affaires in London in 1924, and was the Soviet ambassador to France from 1926 to 1927. His support for Leon Trotsky (q.v.) resulted in his expulsion from the Communist party in 1927. He was tried in March of 1939 and sentenced to twenty years imprisonment. He is presumed to have died in the early 1940s while serving his term in a concentration camp.

Genrikh Grigoryevich Yagoda was born in 1891 and, as commissar of internal affairs, was instrumental in carrying out the early stages of the Stalin purges. He became head of the NKVD in 1934, serving until September of 1936, when he was demoted to the position of commissar of posts and telegraphs. He was arrested soon after and was himself tried during the purges. He was convicted of treason and executed.

• **Hasan Sidqi al-Dajani**, a Palestinian politician and lawyer, was assassinated in Haifa during the Arab revolt in 1938. Dajani was a founder of the Liberal Party in 1930.

He was leader of the Arab Car Owner's and Drivers' Association and instigated a general strike protesting British rule in 1936.

• **Yan E. Rudzutak**, a Politburo member since 1926, was tried and shot on July 19, 1938. Rudzutak was born on August 15, 1887. He was a leading trade unionist and an ally of Stalin before he was purged and executed.

• **Jan K. Berzin** (1889–1938), the Soviet advisor to the Republican government during the Spanish Civil War, was recalled to Moscow in 1937. He was arrested and executed in 1938. Berzin, a Communist Party member since 1905, worked as a secret police officer from 1919 and was head of military intelligence from 1924 until 1935.

• **Vasilii Konstantinovich Bliukher** (1890–1938), the leading Soviet advisor to the Chinese Communists, was also recalled to Russia and executed in 1938. Bliukher was a leading Red Army commander during the civil war.

• Earlier in the year **A.A. Slutsky**, the head of the Soviet NKVD foreign department, died in Moscow. His death was officially announced as a heart attack, but poisoning by cyanide seemed the more likely cause.

• Throughout the year Stalin's agents purged the Communist ranks both inside and outside the Soviet Union. Many members of the German Communist party were killed during the year. **Heinz Neumann**, former member of the German Communist Politburo and a member of the Comintern living in the Hotel Lux, was arrested on April 28, 1937. German politburo members **Herman Remmele**, **Fritz Schulte** and **Herman Schubert**; **Hans Kippenberger**, head of the party's military apparatus; **Leo Flieg**, organization secretary of the German Central Committee; **Heinrich Suskind** and **Werner Hirsch**, editors-in-chief of the German Communist newspaper *Rote Fahne*, along with four assistant editors; and **Hugo Eberlein**, German Comintern delegate, all vanished and were presumed killed during the purges.

- **Jantsangiyn Damdinsuren** (1897–1938), who served a leader of the Mongolian government from November of 1927 to January of 1929, was also accused of counterrevolutionary activity and executed in 1938. Damdinsuren had also served in the government as deputy prime minister and minister of agriculture in 1929. He remained a leader of the collective farm system in Mongolia during the 1930s, also heading the livestock department until his arrest and execution.

- **G.A. Agabekov**, the former Soviet OGPU resident in Turkey, was murdered in Belgium in 1938.

- **Lev Sedov** (1906–38), the son of exile Soviet Communist leader Leon Trotsky (q.v.), died in a Paris hospital on February 17, 1938. He was admitted suffering from a minor ailment, but later was found wandering the halls in a disoriented state. He died shortly thereafter, presumably poisoned by a Soviet agent.

- **Han Fu-Chu** (1890–1938), a leading Chinese general from the Shantung province, was shot for treason in Hankow by troops of Chiang Kai-shek. General Han sided with the Nationalist government against his former ally, Fen Yu-hsiang, in 1929. In 1930 he became governor of Shantung province. He was still serving in that position in 1937 when war broke out with Japan. He was ordered shot in 1938 by Ching for suspected treasonous activities with the Japanese.

- **Walter Gempp** (1878–1938), the chief of the Berlin Fire Department, was strangled and killed on May 2, 1938, while imprisoned by the Nazis. Gempp had gained the animosity of leading Nazis following the Reichstag fire in February of 1933. He claimed that his department had been prevented from performing its duty adequately by high-ranking Nazi officials. His testimony at the trial of those accused of setting the fire was damaging to the case of the prosecution. In September of 1937 Gempp was arrested and convicted of malpractice. His death occurred while he was awaiting an appeal.

- **Colonel Evhen Konovalets** (1891–1938), the leader of the underground Ukrainian Nationalists (OUN) in Poland, was assassinated on May 23, 1938 in Rotterdam, the Netherlands, by Stalinist agent Pavel Sudoplatov with a bomb rigged in a box of chocolates.

- **T'ang Shao-yi**, the former premier of China, was murdered at his home in Shanghai by several axe-wielding men on September 30, 1938. T'ang Shao-yi was born in Hsingshan, Kwangtung, in 1860. He was appointed as a customs official in Tientsin in 1901 and was sent on a diplomatic mission to Tibet in 1904. He was forced to resign from his positions in Peking in 1907. He subsequently served as governor of Fengtien until mid– 1909. He returned to prominence in Peking when Yuan Shih-k'ai became head of the government in December of 1911. Yuan named T'ang premier on February 14, 1912, when he became president. Conflicts soon developed between Yuan and T'ang and T'ang stepped down as premier on June 16, 1912. He retired from public life to enter business in Shanghai. T'ang returned to the government after Yuan's death in June of 1916. He soon became allied with Sun Yat-sen's Kuomintang and opposed China's entry into the First World War. He became minister of finance in Sun's Canton government in mid–1917. He remained part of the Canton government after Sun left in early 1919. He retired the following October to return to Hsiangshan, where he lived quietly. He again briefly headed the government from August 5, 1922, until September 19, 1922. He served on several commissions in the National Government in the 1930s. He fled to the French concession in Shanghai after the start of the Sino-Japanese War in 1937. The identities and motives of his killers were never discerned.

- **Major General Yordan Peyeff**, chief of staff of the Bulgarian Army, was assassinated in Sofia, Bulgaria, on October 9, 1938.

- **Ernst Von Rath** was killed by a young Polish Jew, Herschel Grynszpan, on November 7, 1938. Von Rath, the embassy's councilor and an anti–Nazi, was killed when Gryn-szpan went to the German embassy intend-ing to shoot the ambassador in revenge for the expulsion of Jews from Poland, includ-ing his family. The killing of von Rath was used as an excuse by the German Nazis to fur-ther persecution of German Jews, and led di-rectly to the so-called "Crystal Night," in which angry mobs smashed the store win-dows of Jewish shopkeepers. Grynszpan was held in a French prison until the German occupation. He is presumed to have per-ished in a concentration camp during World War II.

• **Corneliu Zelea Codreanu**, the founder and leader of the Romanian Fascist organization the Iron Guard, was shot and killed, reportedly while trying to escape from prison, on November 30, 1938. Co-dreanu was born on September 13, 1899, in Iasi. He became involved with anti–Semitic groups while in college and, in 1923, founded the National Christian League. He was tried and acquitted in 1925 on charges of mur-dering a police official and subsequently left the country. He returned to Romania in 1927, and the following year he merged his organization, now called the Legion of the Archangel Michael, with Michael Stelescu's (q.v.) Brothers of the Cross. The new organi-zation, led by Codreanu, became known as the Iron Guard. The Guard became the leading voice of Romanian Fascism, becom-ing closely associated with Adolf Hitler's Nazi Germany. Iron Guardists were respon-sible for many anti–Semitic terrorist activi-ties and were implicated in the 1933 assassi-nation of Romanian prime minister Ion Duca (q.v.). In 1938 the Guard was ordered dis-banded, and Codreanu and many of his fol-lowers were ordered arrested by Armand Ca-linescu (q.v.), the minister of the interior. Codreanu and thirteen of his followers were shot and killed while in transit between two prisons.

# 1939

• **Vlas Yakovlevich Chubar** (1891–1939), the premier of the Ukraine in 1923 and a Soviet politburo member from 1935, was shot during the Stalin purges in February of 1939. **Stanislav V. Kossior** (1889–1939), the first secretary of the Ukrainian Commu-nist Party from 1928 to 1938, was also exe-cuted at this time. **Pavel P. Postyshev** (1887–1939), a member of the Soviet Polit-buro from 1934 until he was expelled in Jan-uary of 1938, was executed on February 22, 1939.

• During the year **Nikolai Ivanovich Yezhov**, the Communist politician who, as commissar for internal affairs and leader of the NKVD from September of 1936, had or-chestrated the Stalinist purges during their bloodiest period, himself fell victim to them. Yezhov, who was born in 1895, had joined the Communist party in 1917 and became a member of its Central Committee in 1927. As an ally of Stalin, his powers increased, until he replaced Genrikh Yagoda (q.v.) as director of the purges. He organized the major show tri-als of 1936 through 1938 and the purge of the army. He was also responsible for the elimi-nation of dissident elements in the NKVD. The ear of the purges became known as the "Yezhovshchina" due to his activities. As Stalin's interest in the purges decreased in 1938, Yezhov fell out of power and was sub-sequently arrested and shot.

• **Feodor F. Raskolnikov** (1892–1939), the former commander in chief of the Soviet Red Navy, was founded murdered in exile in France in 1939. Raskolnikov had headed the sailor's mutiny in the spring of 1917 and be-came commander in chief of the Navy after the revolution. He later served as a Soviet diplomat and government official, until he fled the Soviet Union in 1939 to avoid the purges. He subsequently issued a statement critical of Stalin, and was killed, presumably by Soviet agents, soon afterwards.

• On February 5, 1939, several Spanish Nationalist leaders who had been held by the Republican forces in prison at Gerona were murdered when Gerona fell to the Nationalists. They included **Anselmo Polanco y Fontecha** (1883–1939), the bishop of Teruel, and **Colonel Rey D'Harcourt**.

• **Ghazi ibn Faisal**, the king of Iraq, was killed in a car accident on April 4, 1939. Though the exact circumstances of his death remain obscure, his cousin, future regent Abdul-Ilah (q.v.) and his sister Aliya, Ghazi's estranged wife, were suspected of involvement. Ghazi was born in 1912. He was the son of King Faisal of Iraq and succeeded to the throne on September 9, 1933, following the death of his father. He continued Faisal's policy of modernization in the country. His reign was challenged by dissident elements, who staged an unsuccessful rebellion in 1935. Jafar el-Askari (q.v.), the King's defense minister and leading advisor, was killed prior to a military coup led by General Bakr Sidqi (q.v.) in October of 1936. Sidqi was assassinated the following year and Nuri as-Said (q.v.) became prime minister and leading advisor to the King. Ghazi signed a treaty of alliance with Saudi Arabia in 1937, and maintained close relationships with Great Britain, France and the United States. He retained the throne until his death on April 4, 1939.

• **German Busch**, the president of Bolivia, reportedly committed suicide at his home in La Paz on August 23, 1939. Some of his supporters claimed that Busch had been the victim of a political assassination. German Busch Becerra was born in Trinidad, El Beni, on March 23, 1903. He attended the Military College and entered the army as a cadet. He rose through the ranks, becoming a colonel during the Chaco War from 1932 until 1935. He was a leader of the military coup that ousted the government of Jose Luis Tejeda in May of 1936. Busch ousted his fellow junta member Jose David Toro as president on July 13, 1937. Busch adopted a new constitution and was elected constitutional president in May of 1938. He continued the policy of military socialism, and encouraged the unionization of tin miners. He remained president until his death in August of 1939.

• **Ralph Cairns**, a British police official in Palestine, was assassinated in 1939 by the Irgun zwei Leumi, a Jewish underground terrorist organization.

• Romanian prime minister **Armand Calinescu** was assassinated by members of the Fascist Iron Guard on September 21, 1939. Calinescu was born in Pitesti on May 22, 1893. He became active in politics as a member of the Peasant Party, and was elected to the parliament in 1926. He served in several governmental positions in the late 1920s and early 1930s. He became a close advisor to King Carol II and served in Octavian Goga's cabinet as minister of the interior from December of 1937 until February of 1938. He was an opponent of Corneliu Zelea Codreanu's (q.v.) Iron Guard, and was instrumental in arranging the arrest and subsequent execution of Codreanu and many of his followers. He was instrumental in the establishment of King Carol's Royal Dictatorship and was a strong supporter of Romanian neutrality during World War II. He remained minister of the interior in Miron Cristea's government from February of 1938 and also assumed the post of vice-premier, handling many executive duties as Cristea's health failed. Calinescu was named to succeed Cristea as prime minister following his death on March 6, 1939. His tenure was cut short when he was shot to death by Iron Guardists in retaliation for the execution of Codreanu. He was ambushed while driving through the streets of Bucharest from his office to his home on September 21, 1939.

• Hungarian Communist leader **Bela Kun** was executed on November 30, 1939, a victim of the Stalin purges in the Soviet Union. Kun was born in Szilagycseh, Transylvania, on February 20, 1886. He was educated in Cluj and joined the Social Democratic Party in 1902. He served in the army during the First World War and was taken prisoner in Russia in 1916. He joined the Bolshevik party the following year. He became chairman of the International Federation of Communist Prisoners of War and took part in the defense of Petrograd. He returned to Budapest in November of 1918 and founded the Communist Party of Hungary. Kun was arrested in February of 1919 and remained imprisoned until the Hungarian Soviet Republic was proclaimed on March 21, 1919. Kun became people's commissar for foreign affairs and leader of the country. The Soviet Republic was ousted by the Romanians and counterrevolutionary forces under Admiral Miklos Horthy. Kun emigrated to Austria, where he was interned and expelled to the Soviet Union in 1920. He became a member of the executive committee of the Communist International (Comintern) the following year. Kun reappeared in Vienna in 1928, where he was again arrested before being allowed to return to the Soviet Union. He continued to be an active participant in the Communist movement before falling out of favor with Soviet leader Josef Stalin. He was arrested in May of 1937 and imprisoned at Butyrka prison in Moscow, where he was executed two years later.

# 1940

- **Seyyid Rustum Haydar**, the Iraqi finance minister, was assassinated on January 18, 1940. Haydar had served as minister of finance in the first government of Prime Minister Nuri as-Said (q.v.) in 1931. When Nuri returned to power in 1938, Haydar again became finance minister. He was the subject of much criticism by Arab nationalists for his support of Nuri's pro–British policies. Haydar was shot by Husayn Rawzi Tawfig, a former government employee. Haydar died of his wounds four days later. Tawfiq was tried and convicted of the murder and hanged on March 27, 1940.

- **Sir Michael Francis O'Dwyer**, a British colonial officer who had served in India, was shot and killed on March 13, 1940,

at a public meeting in London. O'Dwyer, who was born in 1864, was revenue commissioner in the Punjab from 1901 to 1908. He became lieutenant governor of the region in 1913. He incurred much hostility because of his autocratic rule, and he was held responsible for the massacre of Indians at Amritsar. Following his retirement and the publication of his autobiography, he remained a leading symbol of the excesses of the British colonial empire. This hostility resulted in his assassination by an East Indian, Mahomed Singh Azad. Lord Zetland, the secretary of state for Indian, and Sir Louis Dane and Lord Lamington, two former British administrators in India, were also injured in the attack

- **Losolyn Laagan**, the chairman of the Presidium of the Little Hural and Mongolia's head of state from April of 1930 until July of 1932, was charged was counterrevolutionary activities and executed on May 4, 1940.

- **Abd Al-Rahman Shahbandar** (1880–1940), a leading Syrian nationalist, was assassinated in Syria in June of 1940. A supporter of the Arab Revolt during World War I, Shahbandar had briefly served as foreign minister under Amir Faisal. He went into exile from Syria following the French occupation in 1920. He returned two years later to form the Iron Hand Society to fight for Syrian independence. He was arrested by the French on several occasions. He was also a founder of the Syrian nationalist party, the People's Party, in 1925, and led an unsuccessful revolt in 1927. He spent the next decade in exile, returning to Syria in 1937, where he was an opponent of Syrian Prime Minister Jamil Mardam. Mardam and other National Bloc leaders where accused by the French of complicity in Shahbandar's murder, forcing them to flee the country.

- In June of 1940, following the German occupation of Poland, many prominent Polish political leaders were shot, including **Macief Rataj** (1884–1940), the former speaker of the sejm, and **Mieczyslaw Niedzialkowski** (1893–1940), the Socialist leader. Also executed during this period was **Stefan**

**Starzynski** (1893–1940), who had served as mayor of Warsaw from 1937 until 1938, and had led the defense of Warsaw against the German occupation army.

• **Italo Balbo**, the marshal of the Italian air force, was killed when his plane was shot down at Tobruk, Libya, on June 19, 1940. Balbo was born on June 6, 1896, in Ferrara. He became involved in the Italian Fascist movement and led Benito Mussolini's (q.v.) march on Rome at the head of the black-shirt militia in 1922. Balbo was instrumental in creating the Italian air force, serving as undersecretary of air from 1926 and air minister for 1929. In 1933 he was appointed air marshal. Balbo also became a popular rival of Mussolini, and disagreed with Mussolini's policies of cooperation with Nazi Germany. In 1933 he was appointed governor general of Libya. He was killed in Libya on June 19, 1940, when his plane was shot down by Italian troops when it failed to give the correct recognition signals.

• **Samuel H. Chang**, the director of the Post Mercury company and several Chinese newspapers, was shot to death by an assassin in the International settlement of Shanghai on July 19, 1940.

• **Leon Trotsky** was the victim of an assassination attempt by a Stalinist agent on August 20, 1940, dying the following day. Trotsky was born Lev Bronstein on October 26, 1879, in the Ukraine. He became involved in revolutionary activities in 1897, and was arrested soon after. He was exiled to Siberia, but managed a successful escape, joining Lenin in exile. Trotsky broke with Lenin soon after, fearing that Lenin's policies were designed to install a dictatorship. He became a leader of the Menshevik faction, advocating the theory of "constant revolution." He was active in the 1905 Revolution in St Petersburg, and was again arrested and exiled to Siberia. In 1907 he once more escaped, settling in Vienna. During this period he attempted to serve as a conciliator and unite the various Socialist factions. He served as the first editor of *Pravda*, the Communist party newspaper. He was a strong opponent of World War I and was expelled from Germany. He left for France in 1916 and briefly settled in the United States, before returning to Russia following the Revolution in 1917. He gain joined with Lenin's Bolsheviks and was active in the seizure of power in the capital. He served as commissar for foreign affairs in Lenin's first Communist government, and was the leader of the committee whose actions resulted in the Brest-Litovsky peace treaty with Germany. In 1918 he served as leader of the commissariat of war and successfully established a viable Red Army to repel the counter-revolutionaries during the subsequent period of civil war. Following the death of Lenin in 1924, Trotsky was a leading candidate to replace him as leader of the Soviet Communist party, but he was defeated by Stalin, with the assistance of Zinoviev (q.v.) and Kamenev (q.v.). He remained a member of the ruling Politburo, but was removed from his positions of power. In 1926 he again challenged Stalin's power, with the support of both Zinoviev and Kamenev. He again suffered defeat as Bukharin (q.v.) and Rykov (q.v.), leaders of the Soviet Communist's right wing, rallied with Stalin to undermine Trotsky. He was subsequently removed from his positions and expelled from the party. The following year he was forced into exile, finally settling in Mexico in 1937. He remained a consistent enemy of Stalin and constituted Stalin's only real opponent for the leadership of the Communist movement. Trotsky was denounced and reviled throughout the major purge trials during the late 1930s, and many of his supporters were executed by Stalin's regime. In 1940 Ramon Mercader (1925–78), using the name of Frank Jackson, gained Trotsky's trust and breached his stronghold outside of Mexico City. While reviewing a political paper "Jackson" had authored, Trotsky was attacked by his assailant wielding an alpine axe. Trotsky was mortally wounded and died the following day. Mercader served twenty years in a Mexican prison for his crime, being released in March of 1960. He was later declared a hero of the Soviet Union before his death in Havana, Cuba, on October 18, 1978.

• During 1940 a number of leading Spanish Republican leaders were captured in France by the Vichy government. They included **Luis Companys y Jover** (1883–1940), the Catalan Nationalist leader and president of Catalonia in 1936, and **Jurgen Zugazagoitia**, a former Socialist minister of the interior. They were returned to Spain and executed in October on the orders of Gen. Francisco Franco.

• **Fu Hsiao-en**, the Japanese puppet mayor of Shanghai, China, was assassinated while sleeping in his home in Shanghai on October 11, 1940.

• **Willie Munzenberg** (1889–1940), a leading German Communist and Stalin's propaganda expert in the West, was murdered and hung from a tree in a forest near Grenoble. His decomposed body was found on October 22, 1940. He had refused to return to the Soviet Union during the purges.

• **Andrei S. Bubnov** (1883–1940), a Russian Communist leader during the 1917 revolution, was executed during the Stalin purges in 1940. Bubnov as a member of the Politburo from 1925 and served as commissar of education in Russia from 1929.

• On November 28, 1940, the Fascist Iron Guard of Romania assassinated sixty-four prominent members of the Romanian government, including former prime minister **Nikolae Iorga** and **Virgil Madgearu**, a peasant leader.

Nikolai Iorga was born in Botosani on June 17, 1871. He was educated at the University of Iasi and continued his education in Paris, Berlin and Leipzig. He returned to Romania to join the University of Bucharest as a history professor in 1894. He was an internationally renowned historian of the Romanian people and authored numerous scholarly works. Iorga was also active politically, co-founding the Democratic Nationalist Party in 1910. He served in the chamber of deputies during the 1920s and was called upon to serve as prime minister on April 19, 1931. He relinquished the position to Alexandru Vaida-Voevod on May 31, 1932. He was a supporter of

King Carol II and served as minister without portfolio in the government during the 1930s. He was instrumental in the arrest and trial of Iron Guard leader Corneliu Zelea Codreanu in 1938. Iorga was assassinated by the Iron Guard on November 28, 1940.

• **Raul Fernandez Fiallo**, a professor at the University of Havana, was assassinated near the university campus in Havana by unknown assailants on November 28, 1940.

# 1941

• **Modesto Maidique** (1890–1941), a former Liberal party member of the Cuban senate, was shot and killed in Havana on January 13, 1941.

• **General Walter G. Krivitsky** (1899–41), the former Red Army chief of intelligence for Western Europe until 1937, was found shot to death at the Bellevue Hotel in Washington, D.C. on February 10, 1941. Krivitsky had defected to France in the late 1930s to escape Stalinist purges. Though Krivitsky's death was ruled a suicide, it was suspected that he had been murdered by the Soviet secret police on orders of Stalin.

• **Rudolf Hilferding**, a leading German Social Democratic politician, died in a French prison on February 11, 1941, after having been brutally beaten by the Gestapo. Hilferding was born on August 10, 1877, in Vienna. He became active in the Social Democratic party, serving as a teacher at the party's training center in Berlin. He was the political editor of the Socialist newspaper *Vorwards* from 1907 to 1915, and authored several books on political theory. He was elected as a deputy in the Reichstag in 1924, serving until 1933. In 1923 and from 1928 to 1929 he served as minister of finance in the German cabinet. In 1933 he was forced to flee Germany as the Nazis came to powers, going first to Denmark, then settling in France. He was arrested by Vichy

French police in unoccupied France and turned over to the Gestapo.

• **Juvenal Viegas Silva**, the leader of the Brazilian Communist party, was slain by police while resisting arrest on February 17, 1941.

• **Lodo Van Hamel**, a Dutch naval officer, was accused of spying for England by the German occupation forces. He was executed by the Nazis on June 16, 1941.

• **Dmitrii G. Pavlov** (1897–1941), the commander of the Russian Red Army on the western front, was court-martialed and shot following the German invasion in June of 1941. Pavlov had previously commanded the Russian tanks the fought with the Republican government during the Spanish Civil War.

• **Anandyn Amor** (1886–1941), the former prime minister of Mongolia, was accused of spying for the Japanese and executed in Russia on July 10, 1941. Amor had served in the Mongolian foreign ministry during Mongolia's period of autonomy. He served in several governments as foreign minister and deputy premier during the 1920s. Amor served as prime minister from February of 1928 until April of 1930. He again headed the government from February of 1936 until March of 1939, also holding the position of foreign minister. Amor was accused of counterrevolutionary activities by Khorloghiyin Choibalsan in 1939. He was purged from the government and sent to Moscow to stand trial. He was one of over thirty prominent Mongolian victims of the Stalin purges in the Soviet Union.

• **Dansrangiyn Dogsom** (1884–1941), who served a Mongolia's head of state as chairman of the Presidium of the Little Hural from February of 1936 to July of 1939, was executed on July 30, 1941. **Olziytiyn Badrah** (1895–1941), a leader of the Mongolian Communist Party and former minister of health, was executed on July 7, 1941. Another former health minister, **Soyryn Galindiv** (1907–41), party leaders **Dorjjavyn Luvsansharav** (1900–41) and **Zolbingiyn Shijee** (1901–41), **Renchingiyn Mend** (1901–41), the

minister of trade and industry, **Zunduyn Purevdorj**, minister of livestock, minister of trade **Damdinsurengiyn Shagdarjav** (1902–41), and **Gompilyn Danshiytsoodol** (1905–41), Mongolia's minister of justice, were executed between July 27 and July 30, 1941. Internal affairs ministry officials **Yadamsurengiyn Byambajav** (1910–41), **Sanjiyn Bazarhand** (1912–41), **Nerendoogiyn Chimiddorj** (1914–41), **Chimidiyn Damba** (1900–41), **Delegiyn Galsanpuntsag** (1913–41), **Gendengiyn Jamsran** (1915–41), **Badrahyn Namjil** (1902–41), **Nerenmoriyn Nasantogtoh** (1904–41), **Tsendiyn Sosorjav** (1911–41), **Gurjavyn Tsendsuren** (1903–41), **Bandiyn Vanchinhuu** (1913–41), **Tsevegiyn Dolgorjav** (1913–41), and **Jamtsyn Bayasgalan** (1910–41), were all executed in late July of 1941.

• **Marx Dormoy** (1889–1941), a former French minister of the interior, was killed in an explosion of a time bomb in his hotel room near Montelimar, France, on July 26, 1941. Dormoy was elected to the French Chamber of Deputies in 1936. He became minister of the interior in Leon Blum's Popular Front cabinet in 1936, serving until 1938. He was an opponent of Marshal Petain's fascist government and was interned by German following the occupation of France. He was released in the spring of 1941, but was killed by an assassin several months later.

• **Marcel Gitton**, a former French Communist leader and member of the Chamber of Deputies, was shot in Paris on September 5, 1941. Gitton died the following day of his injuries.

• **Fakhri Bey el-Nashashibi**, the leader of the Arab Defense party, was shot to death while leaving his hotel in Baghdad, Iraq, on November 9, 1941.

# 1942

- **Yves Paringaux**, the chief of staff of the interior ministry of Vichy France, was found murdered on railroad tracks in Melun, France, on January 5, 1942. Paringaux was in charged of overseeing the suppression of anti–Nazi activity.

- **Alfredo Zarate Albarran**, the governor of the State of Mexico, was shot and seriously injured while attending a party at Toluca, the state capital, on March 5, 1942. Fernando Ortiz Rubio, the son of a former Mexican president, was charged in the shooting. Zarate Albarran died of his wounds on March 8, 1942.

- **Juan Peiro Belis** (1887–1942), the anarchist minister of industry in Spain's last Republican government during the Spanish Civil War, was captured in France by the Vichy government and returned to Spain. He was executed on the order of Gen. Francisco Franco in 1942.

- **Hassan Fareed**, the minister of finance, the interior and foreign affairs for the Maldive Islands, was killed in local waters during a Japanese attack on the British ship he was aboard in 1942.

- **General Vladimir Zaimov**, the former Bulgarian minister of the interior, was executed on June 1, 1942, following his court-martial in Sofia. He was convicted of espionage for the Russians.

- **Albert Clement**, the editor of the pro–Nazi newspaper *Le Cri du Peuple*, was shot to death in Paris while leaving his office by members of the French Resistance on June 2, 1942.

- **Reinhard Heydrich**, the German Reich protector of Czechoslovakia, was critically injured by a bomb tossed at his car by two Czech Resistance agents on May 27, 1942. He died in Prague on June 4, 1942. Heydrich was born in Prussian Saxony on March 7, 1904. He served in the right-wing Freikorps after the end of World War I, and later served in the German navy. In the early 1930s he joined the Nazi movement, becoming a protégé of Heinrich Himmler, the head of the S.S. Heydrich served as Himmler's field agent and, in this position, was privy to the many files the S.S. maintained on prominent and powerful Germans. He was instrumental in supplying evidence used as a pretext for Hitler's purge of the S.A. in 1934 during the "Night of the Long Knives." Heydrich soon rose in power to become Himmler's deputy as head of the S.S. and the Gestapo. Following the Anschluss with Austria in 1938, he was placed in charge of police affairs there. The following year he was involved in fabricating a border incident with Poland to justify the German invasion of that country. During the early years of World War II Heydrich was in charge of the mass deportation of Jews and others from German occupied areas in Poland and the Soviet Union, earning the nickname "the Hangman" for his efforts. Soon after, he was placed in direct charge of the establishment and operation of the extermination centers used by the Nazis to liquidate Jews and other "undesirables," with Adolf Eichmann (q.v.) as his second-in-command. Heydrich's main ambition was to supplant Himmler as one of Hitler's most trusted advisors. In September of 1941, he was named Reich protector for Bohemia and Moravia. While serving in this capacity he also retained control of the extermination centers. In May of 1941 Jan Kublis and Joseph Gablitz, two Czechoslovakians who had been trained in England to kill Heydrich, parachuted into Czechoslovakia to perform the assassination. Following their attempt on Heydrich's life, Kublis and Gablitz went into hiding in the Karl Borromaeus Church in Prague. They were betrayed to the Germans by Karel Curda and were killed along with 120 other members of the Czech Resistance in fighting with the S.S. Curda was later killed by members of the Czech underground. Heydrich died of his wounds eight days after the attack. The S.S. conducted a vigorous retaliation for the killing, including the complete destruction of the Czech village of Lidice.

• **General Alois Elias**, the premier of the Protectorate of Bohemia-Moravia from April 1939 until October 1941, was executed by the Nazis on June 19, 1942.

• In 1942 the German Abwehr uncovered many Germans in strategic locations who were supplying the Soviet Union was extensive espionage information. The spy group was known as the "Rote Kapelle," or "Red Orchestra." The leader was **Harold Schulze-Boysen**, who worked in the Luftwaffe espionage bureau. Other associated who were positioned in ministries and military offices included **Arvid Harnack**, an economist in the Ministry of Economics; his wife, **Mildred Fish Harnack**, **Franz Scheliha** in the Foreign Office; **Countess Erika von Brockdorff** in the Ministry of Labor; and **Horst Heilmann** in the Propaganda Ministry. Seventy-five members of this organization were tried for treason and fifty were sentenced to death. The condemned were strangled by a rope, which was attached to a meathook, and slowly hanged.

• **Henry Gachelin**, a leading advisor to French Fascist leader Jacques Doriot, was shot to death in Arpajon, France, on August 7, 1942, while walking from a railway station to his home.

• **Hans Drosch**, the German consul general for Ljubljana, Croatia, died suddenly at a hotel in Ljubljana on August 27, 1942. It was rumored that Drosch had been poisoned by opponents of the Nazi government.

• **Marceli Nowotko** (1893–1942), the leader of the Polish Communist party, was murdered by **Boleslaw Molojec** on November 28, 1942. Nowotko, who was selected by Stalin to lead the Polish Communists, had been accused of collaborating with the Germans during the occupation of Poland. Molojec, who had led the Polish Communist forces in the International Brigades during the Spanish Civil War, was subsequently tried by a Communist party court and executed.

• **Jean Darlan**, who was in charge of the French armed forces under the Vichy regime, was assassinated on December 24, 1942, in Algiers. Jean Louis Xavier Francois Darlan was born in Nerac, Lot-et-Garonne, on August 7, 1881. He attended the French naval school from 1899 and served in the French navy. He served as a commander during the First World War and rose through the ranks to rear admiral in 1929. He was named chief of staff of the navy in December of 1936 and, following his promotion to admiral of the fleet, he became commander in chief of the French navy in August of 1939. Following the fall of France, in 1940, Darlan served Henri-Philippe Petain's Vichy regime as vice premier. He headed the government from February 11, 1941, until April 9, 1942. He subsequently became commander and chief of all Vichy French military forces. He was sent to North Africa to serve as high commissioner in November of 1942. The Allied invasion of Morocco and Algeria began soon after and Darlan ordered the local Vichy French forces to not resist the invasion. He negotiated an armistice with the Allies and brought his forces under the command of the Free French. Darlan was granted authority as chief of state for French Africa, and was to be placed in charge of all French Resistance forces. Darlan was shot and killed in Algiers on December 24, 1942, by Bonnier de la Chappille, a French anti–Fascist, who viewed Darlan as a traitor to France for his earlier collaboration with the Germans. The assassin was quickly tried and executed for his act.

# 1943

• **Carlo Tresca** (1877–1943), an Italian-American labor leader and anti–Fascist spokesman, was murdered in New York City on January 11, 1943. Tresca was born in Sulmona, Italy, on March 8, 1879. He was a Socialist party organizer in Italy in the late 1800s, until he was forced into exile in Switzerland. He settled in the United States in 1904, where he became involved in the labor movement.

He was also an active opponent of Benito Mussolini's (q.v.) government in Italy. Tresca served as editor of *Martello*, a publication he used to vehemently denounce Fascism. He escaped several assassination attempts before he was fatally shot in the head on a New York street. His assailant, who was never apprehended, was believed to have been an agent of Mussolini.

• **Hendrik Alexander Seyffardt** (1871–1943), the chief of staff of the Dutch army from 1929 to 1934, was shot to death in the Hague on February 5, 1943. Seyffardt had come out of retirement during the German occupation of the Netherlands and formed a volunteer military unit called the Vrijkorps, which fought with German troops in Russia. He was killed by Dutch Resistance members as a collaborationist.

• **C. van Ravenzwaal**, a member of Anton Mussert's (q.v.) pro–German government in the Netherlands, was shot to death by members of the Dutch underground resistance on February 12, 1943. Van Ravenzwaal served as minister of social affairs in Mussert's government.

• On February 22, 1943, **Hans Scholl** and his sister, **Sophie Scholl**, were executed by hanging following a trial by the Nazi People's Court. They were active in the "White Rose" resistance group which operated out of Munich University. The Scholls were born in Forchtenberg, Wurttemberg, Hans in 1918, and Sophie in 1921. After meeting Kurt Huber (q.v.), a professor of philosophy, while attending the University of Munich, they joined the resistance to Adolf Hitler's regime. They printed and distributed leaflets denouncing the Nazis, taking the name of their group from the emblem of a white rose which was printed on the leaflets. On February 18 they distributed fliers from the main building at the university, calling on the youth of Germany to rise up against the Nazis. They were subsequently arrested by the Gestapo and executed after a summary trial.

• **Pierre Brossolette**, a leader of the French Resistance, died in prison of injuries received after being tortured by the Gestapo, on March 22, 1943. Brossolette was born on June 15, 1902, at Angouleme. He was a Socialist and served as editor of the party newspaper *Le Populaire* in the late thirties. Following the German occupation of France, Brossolette went to London in 1942, to join General Charles De Gaulle. He subsequently returned to France to serve as a leader of the resistance movement, where he was captured by the Germans.

• **Sotir Yanev**, a leading Bulgarian politician and a minister in the National Assembly, was shot to death by two assassins on April 15, 1943. Yanev was an advisor to King Boris III (q.v.) and president of Bulgaria's foreign affairs commission in the parliament. He was regarded as pro–Nazi and was editor of the newspaper *Slovo*.

• **Isoruku Yamamoto** (1884–1943), the commander-in-chief of the Japanese navy during World War II, was killed on April 18, 1943, when his plane was shot down by United States forces over the Solomon Islands. Yamamoto was instrumental in planning the Japanese attack on Pearl Harbor. His use of Japanese naval air power scored him early victories against the Allies in the Java Sea, but the United States forces were able to defeat Yamamoto's Imperial Navy at the Battle of Midway in June of 1942. Yamamoto was targeted for death when United States intelligence agents were able to decode a Japanese message giving details of a planned inspection tour by Yamamoto.

• **Colonel Atanas Pantev**, the Bulgarian chief of police from 1939 to 1941, was shot and killed in Sofia on May 2, 1943.

• **Wladyslaw Sikorski**, the leader of the Polish government in exile during World War II, died in an airplane crash near Gibraltar on July 4, 1943. Sikorski's difficulties in establishing and maintaining an effective relationship with Joseph Stalin's Soviet government led to speculation that the crash which claimed his life may not have been an accident. Sikorski was born in Tuszowo, in Galicia, on May 20, 1881. He was educated at the

University Technical College at Lwow, where he received a degree in civil engineering. Sikorski became involved in the Polish independence movement and was instrumental in the formation of the Polish army in 1917. He commanded an army corp during the Polish-Ukraine War in 1919 and the Polish-Russian War in 1920. He served as chief of the general staff in 1921. He became prime minister on December 16, 1922, following the assassination of President Gabriel Narutowicz. He stepped down on May 27, 1923. Sikorski served as minister of war from 1924 until 1925. He retired from the army in 1928 in opposition to Jozef Pilsudski's dictatorship. He went to Paris for a decade, returning to Poland in 1938. He went back to Paris following the German occupation of Poland in 1939. He became premier and minister of war in the Polish government-in-exile on September 30, 1939. He also became commander-in-chief of all Polish forces in November of 1939. Sikorski established his headquarters in London after the fall of France, where he remained until his death.

• **Jean Moulin**, another leader of the French Resistance, died on July 8, 1943, in a German prison following brutal beatings. Moulin was born on June 20, 1899, in Beziers. He served in the French civil service as a prefect in the Eure-et-Loir Department. He was removed from his position after his refusal to cooperate with the Germans following the occupation of France. Moulin joined the French Resistance and escaped to London. He returned to France to help organize the maquis, French Resistance guerrilla fighters, as delegate general for General Charles De Gaulle for unoccupied France. He took the code name "Max" and served as the first chairman of the National Council of the Resistance. In June of 1943 he was captured by the Gestapo and imprisoned. He was taken to Germany and subjected to torture and beatings, resulting in his death.

• **Professor Karl Huber**, a professor of philosophy at the University of Munich, was beheaded on July 13, 1943. Huber, who was born on October 24, 1893, in Switzerland, was a leading member of the German resistance to the Nazis in Munich, and had inspired Hans and Sophie Scholl (q.v.) in the formation of the "White Rose" movement. He was arrested in February, along with the Scholls, and sentenced to death.

• **Boris III**, the king of Bulgaria, died mysteriously on August 28, 1943, following a meeting with Adolf Hitler. His death was reported to have been due to a heart attack, but other reports suggest the King may have been shot by an assassin or poisoned. Boris Clement Robert Marie Pius Louis Stanislas Xavier was born in Sofia on January 30, 1894. He was the eldest son of King Ferdinand of Bulgaria and Princess Maria Louisa. Boris was raised in the Orthodox church. He attended the military academy in Sofia and served in the Bulgarian army during the Balkan Wars and World War I. Ferdinand abdicated after Bulgaria's defeat in the First World War and Boris succeeded him to the throne on October 4, 1918. The Agrarian Party under Aleksandr Stambolski (q.v.) governed the country until Stambolski's ouster and murder in June of 1923. The Agrarians and Communists attempted an armed revolt against the subsequent government of Alexander Tsankov and made several unsuccessful attempts on Boris' life in 1925. Boris dismissed Tsankov the following year. He married Princess Giovanni of Savoy, daughter of King Victor Emmanuel II of Italy, in 1930. A military coup in May of 1934 took control of the government, but Boris maintained the throne. He became more active in formulating foreign policy and attempted to maintain Bulgaria's neutrality in the early years of World War II. He was pressured by Germany to sign the Axis pact in March of 1941 and Bulgaria declared war on Great Britain the following December. Boris refused to commit Bulgarian troops to the Russian campaign. Boris had an uncomfortable relationship with Adolf Hitler. His death came shortly after having had a bitter argument with Hitler.

• **Wilhelm Kube**, the German commissioner general for White Russia, was killed in

Minsk on September 22, 1943, by a bomb planted at his headquarters by Russian agents.

• **Bernhard Lichtenberg**, a leading Catholic member of the resistance to the Nazis, died on November 3, 1943, while en route to Dachau concentration camp. Lichtenberg was born in Silesia on December 3, 1875. He became a Catholic priest in 1899 and served in the First World War as a military chaplain. Following the war he joined the Catholic Centre party and served as a city councillor in Berlin. As provost of St. Hedwig's Cathedral in Berlin, Lichtenberg attacked the Nazi program of euthanasia, and publicly prayed for the Jews during church services. He was arrested on October 23, 1941, by the Gestapo, serving two years in Tegel Prison in Berlin. His death occurred while he was being transferred to a concentration camp.

# 1944

• **Kaj Munk** (1898–1944), a Danish playwright and clergyman, was murdered near Silkeborg, Denmark, on January 6, 1944. Munk, an outspoken critic of the Nazis was the author of *An Idealist* (1928), *The Word* (1932), and the anti–Nazi play *He Sits by the Melting Pot* (1938). Local police were forbidden by the Gestapo from investigating the murder.

• Five Italian Fascist leaders were found guilty of treason by a Fascist tribunal at Verona on January 11, 1944. **Count Galeazzo Ciano**, Mussolini's son-in-law and foreign minister from 1936 to 1943, **Emilio De Bono**, former commander-in-chief of Italy's armed forces, **Luciano Gottardi, Giovanni Marinelli** (Oct. 18, 1879–1944)and **Carlo Pareschi** had all voted against Mussolini at the Fascist Grand Council of July 24, 1943. They were all tried and convicted at the insistence of Germany and executed.

Count Galeazzo Ciano was born on March 18, 1903, in Leghorn, Italy. In the 1920s Ciano entered the Italian diplomatic corps, following a brief career in journalism. In April of 1930 he married Edda, the eldest daughter of Benito Mussolini (q.v.) and soon after he was appointed Italy's envoy to China. He served in that position for two years and, in 1934, was named minister of propaganda. In January of 1936 he was appointed by his father-in-law to the position of foreign minister. Ciano was an early advocate of Italy's alliance with Germany and was instrumental in Mussolini's decision to enter Italy into World War II on the side of the Axis powers, following the fall of France in 1940. Ciano's enthusiasm for the German cause soon decreased due to the increasing number of Axis military defeats and the treatment of the Italians by their German allies. In 1942 he began advocating a separate peace with the Allies and, in February of 1943, was removed from his position as foreign minister. He was given the post of ambassador to the Vatican, over the objection of the Germans, who felt he might enter into negotiations with the Allies from that diplomatic position. On July 25, 1943, Ciano voted with the majority of the Fascist Grand Council in forcing Mussolini's resignation. He fled to northern Italy soon after, as the new government began investigating charges that he had used his positions of influence for his personal financial gain. While in hiding, Ciano was lured to Munich by agents of Joachim von Ribbentrop (q.v.), the German foreign minister. He was arrested there by the Gestapo and tried and executed for treason at the insistence of Hitler, who held him personally responsible for Mussolini's ouster.

General Emilio De Bono was born on March 19, 1866, in Cassano d'Adda. He joined the Italian army at an early age, and served on the general staff during Italy's war with Turkey. During the First World War he rose from the rank of regimental commander to that of general. He later became active in Mussolini's Fascist movement and took part in the March on Rome in 1922. He served in the subsequent Fascist government and, following the Italian invasion of Ethiopia in 1935, was named commander-in-chief of the Italian forces. De Bono became decreasingly removed from Mussolini's policies during World War II, and supported his ouster at the Fascist Grand Council in July of 1943. Soon after, he was seized by supporters of the deposed dictator and was among the foes of Mussolini who were tried and executed for treason.

• **Chang Yao-Tso** (1893–1944), the Japanese puppet governor of Kwangtun Province, China, was killed by Nationalists on April 5, 1944.

• **Colonel Demetrio Psarros**, the leader of the Social Liberation Movement (EKKA), an anti–Communist Greek guerrilla army established to resist the German occupation, was murdered in April of 1944. Colonel Psarros was killed by Aris Velouchiotis, a Communist guerrilla fighter. Velouchiotis was himself killed several years later during the Greek civil war.

• Several Polish Communist leaders who had been imprisoned by the Nazis during World War II were executed in 1944. They included Polish Workers Party founders **Pawel Finder** and **Marcjanna Fornalska**.

• On April 10, 1944, President Miguel Avila Camacho (1897–1955) of Mexico narrowly escaped assassination when a gunman fired a revolver into his chest. The president's life was saved by the bullet-proof vest he was wearing. The attempted assassin was identified as Sama Rojas, a pro–Nazi Mexican military officer. Rojas was shot by presidential guards at the scene and died of his injuries several days later.

• **Max Josef Metzger**, a Catholic priest and foe of the Hitler regime, was executed at Brandenburg on April 17, 1944. Father Metzger was born on February 3, 1887. He was ordained a priest in 1911, becoming the curate at Mannheim and Karlsruhe. He was the founder of the Peace League of German Catholics in 1917. In 1942 Father Matzger sent a letter to the Protestant archbishop of Uppsala calling for the removal of the Nazi regime

in Germany. He was arrested by the Gestapo and condemned for treason by the People's Court.

• **Christian Wirth**, the S.S. major who had served as head of the Polish death camp operations, was killed in street fighting with Yugoslav partisans on May 26, 1944. Wirth was born in Wurttenberg in 1885 and served with distinction in the German army during the First World War. In the early 1930s he served with the police in his hometown, and was known for his brutal investigative methods. He rose in rank in the criminal police (KRIPO) and was, in 1939, placed in charge of liquidating the mentally ill by means of lethal injections and poison gas. In 1941 Wirth was sent to Poland to administer the elimination of over two million Jews in death camps at Chelmno, Belzec, Sobidor and Treblinka. He performed his duties with an inhuman vigor and, in 1943, he was sent by Himmler to Yugoslavia. It was there that he perished during a skirmish in the streets of Trieste, possibly the intentional victim of Jewish revenge squads.

• **Professor Marc Bloch**, a French historian at the University of Paris, was arrested, tortured and shot by the Gestapo in France on June 6, 1944. Bloch had been a leading member of the French Resistance, and his execution came two weeks prior to the liberation of France.

• **Philippe Henriot** (1889–1944), the French Vichy minister of propaganda, was shot and killed by members of the French Resistance while in his bedchamber, in Paris, on June 28, 1944. Henriot was a school teacher when he was elected to the French chamber of deputies from Bordeaux. He was associated with the French fascist factions in the chamber during the 1930s. After the German invasion of France Henriot became a leading collaborator with Marshal Petain's Vichy government. He also served as editor of the pro–German weekly newspaper *Gringoire*. He was named minister of information and propaganda in Pierre Laval's (q.v.) government in January of 1944.

• **George Mandel**, a leading French politician was executed on July 7, 1944, by the order of the French Vichy police. Mandel was born on June 5, 1885, near Paris. He became a close advisor to Georges Clemenceau, serving on his personal staff and assisting in the compilation of his journals. In 1919 Mandel was elected to the chamber of deputies, serving until 1924. He was elected once again in 1928, and served until 1940. He served in several cabinet positions during the 1930s. He was named minister of colonies in 1938, serving until 1940, when he was appointed minister of the interior. Mandel was greatly opposed to collaboration with Germany following the fall of France. He was ordered arrested by the collaborationist government of Marshal Petain, but was subsequently released. Mandel traveled to North Africa in the hopes of continuing France's war effort from the colonies, but was arrested in Morocco. He was tried for treason in 1941, and handed over to the Germans in November of 1942. After spending several years in German concentration camps, Mandel was returned to Paris in early July, where he was executed by order of Joseph Darnand (q.v.), the head of the Vichy French police.

• Dr. Jose Antonio Arze, a leading Bolivian leftist, was shot twice in the back and seriously wounded on July 8, 1944. Arze's injuries forced his resignation from the seat in the Bolivian congress which he had won earlier in the year.

• **Georges Barthelemy**, a member of Pierre Laval's (q.v.) pro–German Vichy government in France, was assassinated by members of the French Resistance on July 10, 1944. Barthelemy had served in the French chamber of deputies as a member of the Socialist party before the German occupation of France.

• **Johannes Post** (1907–44), a leader of the Danish Resistance to the German occupation during World War II, was executed by the Nazis on July 16, 1944. Other leading Resistance members were also killed for their opposition to the Germans including **Gerrit Jan van der Veen** (1903–44), banker **Wal-**raven van Hall (1905–44), student leader **Hannie Schaft** (1920–44) and Catholic priest **Titus Brandsma** (1883–44).

• On July 20, 1944, the German anti–Nazi conspiracy made an attempt on the life of Adolf Hitler. A bomb was planted under a conference table in Rastenburg, East Prussia, during a meeting which Hitler was attending. Count Claus von Stauffenberg, who planted the bomb, believed that Hitler had been killed in the attempt, and directed that the plan coup against the Nazi regime proceed. Hitler had instead suffered only minor injuries, and quickly regained control of Germany. Most of the conspirators were rounded up, and many other Resistance leaders not involved in this particular plot were also arrested and tried. Over 150 alleged conspirators were executed as a direct result of the bomb attempt, including thirteen generals and two ambassadors. Fifteen other leading figures in the conspiracy committed suicide.

Though Hitler was not killed during the attack, several others in attendance at the meeting died from their injuries, including **Colonel Heinz Brandt**, the chief of staff to General Heusinger, deputy chief of staff of the army, **General Gunther Korten**, the air force chief of staff; **General Rudolf Schmundt**, an adjutant to Hitler; and **Berger**, the official stenographer.

General Korten, who was born in 1898, was Luftwaffe chief of staff from August 25, 1943, until his death. He was near resigning his position due to difference with Hermann Goering when he was critically injured in the bomb blast, dying two days later.

General Schmundt, who was born on August 13, 1896, was chief of the Wehrmacht Personnel Office and Adolf Hitler's Wehrmacht adjutant at the time of his death. He had previously served as chief of army personnel. He died on October 1, 1944, from wounds suffered in the explosion.

• The first reprisals against the conspirators took place on July 20, 1944, the same day of the plot. After the bomb explosion, **Count Claus Schenk von Stauffenberg** returned to the War Office in Berlin, where he was joined by **Col. Gen. Friedrich Olbricht**, the chief of staff and deputy commander of the Reserve Army; **General Ludwig Beck**, the chief of staff of the German Armed Forces from 1935 to 1938; **Lt. Werner von Haeften**; and **Col. Mertz von Quirnheim**. As it became clear that the attempt on Hitler's life was unsuccessful, they were ordered arrested by the Reserve Army commander, General Friedrich Fromm (q.v.). They were given a summary court-martial, and executed, with the exception of General Beck, who was given the opportunity to take his own life.

Count Claus Schenk von Stauffenberg was born on November 15, 1907, in Upper Franconia. He was strongly influenced by his aristocratic and Roman Catholic upbringing. In 1926 he joined the German army and, in 1930, was commissioned a second lieutenant. In 1936 he entered the General Staff College in Berlin and later served under General Hoepner as a staff officer in Poland and France. Stauffenberg served at the Russian front after Hitler's invasion of the Soviet Union and, through his contact with Russian prisoners of war, became interested in Socialism. He was an early member of the German resistance movement, becoming one of the leading conspirators in the attempt to overthrow the Nazi regime. In 1943 Stauffenberg was gravely injured while serving with the Tenth Panzer Division in North Africa, losing his left eye and his right hand. Following his recovery and return to duty, Stauffenberg was named chief of staff to General Friedrich Olbricht, the deputy commander of the Reserve Army, in Berlin. He was promoted to chief of staff to the commander of the Reserve Army, General Friedrich Fromm, in June of 1944. At this post he was in a position to attend meetings at Hitler's headquarters, and was chosen by the conspirators to carry out the assassination of the Fuhrer. Two earlier plans to kill Hitler, on July 2, 1944, and July 15, 1944, were postponed, as the conspirators were hoping to also eliminate Hermann Goering and Heinrich Himmler. Stauffenberg, as a seriously wounded war hero, was not subjected to the usual vigorous searches conducted by Hitler's security forces, and was able to deliver a bomb in his briefcase on July 20, 1944. He arranged to be called away to the telephone prior to the detonation of the bomb, and returned to Berlin following the blast, convinced that Hitler had been killed. After his arrival in Berlin, Stauffenberg learned that the other conspirators had not taken control of the key installations as planned, but had been awaiting his return. When it was learned later in the night that Hitler had survived the assassination attempt, troops loyal to the Fuhrer arrested Stauffenberg and other key conspirators at the War Ministry on the Bendlerstrasse. Stauffenberg was hastily court-martialed by General Fromm, and executed for treason in the War Ministry courtyard.

Colonel General Friedrich Olbricht was born in Leisnig on October 4, 1888. He served in the German army during the First World War. In 1926 Olbricht served as a general staff officer and, in March of 1940, he was promoted to the post of second in command to the commander of the Replacement Army. He was an early member of the anti–Nazi conspiracy to remove Hitler and, with Claus von Stauffenberg, was instrumental in planning "Operation Valkyrie," which was to have allowed the Resistance to take power in Berlin following the elimination of Hitler. After Stauffenberg's attempt on Hitler's life, Olbricht was to have begun "Valkyrie," but delayed its implementation until Stauffenberg returned to Berlin. The several-hour delay cost the Resistance valuable time and resulted in the failure of the scheme once news reached the capital that Hitler was not dead. Olbricht was swiftly ordered arrested by General Fromm. He was summarily court-martialed and executed with the other conspirators present at the War Ministry.

General Ludwig Beck was born in the Rhineland on June 19 1880. He served on the German general staff from 1911 and saw active duty during the First World War. He rapidly rose in rank and power in the army and, in 1935, was named chief of the army general staff. Beck was a bitter critic of Hitler's adventurous military and foreign policies and frequently clashed with the Fuhrer over these matters. On August 27, 1938, Beck resigned his position in the hopes that his fellow officers would do likewise. He was bitterly disappointed that little attention was paid to his departure, and that Hitler was now free to pursue his policies without a restraining hand at the head of the general staff. Beck became an active conspirator in the plot to remove Hitler, and was to have replaced Hitler as Germany's head of state had the July 20 conspiracy proved successful. Following the failure of the coup, Beck, who had joined with the other conspirators at the War Ministry, was allowed to commit suicide with his pistol. When his first two attempts to end his life failed, an attending sergeant assisted him on a third successful attempt.

Lt. Werner von Haeften was born in Berlin on October 9, 1908. He served in the army during World War II and, in 1942, was sent to the Quartermaster's Office of the German High command. There he became adjutant to Count Claus von Stauffenberg and became an active member of the conspiracy against Hitler. Lt. von Haeften had accompanied Stauffenberg to Hitler's conference in Rastenburg, and was arrested and executed with him following their return to Berlin and the failure of the plot.

On August 8, 1944, more leading anti–Nazi conspirators were executed following their conviction for treason by the People's Court. The Resistance leaders, who had been involved in the July 20 plot against Adolf Hitler, included **Field Marshal Erwin von Witzlebenl**, the highest ranking army officer involved in the conspiracy, **Col. Gen. Erich Hoepner**, a leading tank commander; **Count Peter Yorck von Wartenburg** (1903–44), a founder of the anti–Nazi Kreisau Circle; **Maj. Gen. Helmut Stieff** (1901–44), who prepared the bomb used in the assassination attempt; and **Lt. Gen. Paul von Hase**, **Reserve Lt. Dr. Albecht von Hagen** and **General Staff Lt. Col. Robert Bernardis**.

Erwin von Witzleben was born in Breslau on December 4, 1881. He served in the German army and was appointed a field marshal on July 19, 1940, following the fall of France. Von Wizleben had long been involved in the conspiracy to remove Hitler, and was to have been named as commander-in-chief of the German Wehrmacht had the conspiracy succeeded. He was arrested on the day after the unsuccessful attempt on Hitler's life and was subjected to torture and humiliation prior to his execution.

Erich Hoepner was born on September 14, 1886, in Frankfurt. He was veteran German tank commander who had been humiliated and dismissed by Hitler while serving as commander of the Fourth Armored Corps during the invasion of the Soviet Union. He was to have been the German minister of war in the post–Nazi government.

• Throughout the year more trials took place in the Nazi People's Court and more conspirators were executed. The more prominent included **Wolf Heinrich Graf von Helldorf**, chief of police in Berlin; **Adam von Trott Zu Solz**, a German Abwehr official; **Otto Karl Kiep**, a member of the German Foreign Office; **Karl Heinrich von Stulpnagel**, the German military governor of France from 1942 to 1944; **General Erich Felligiebel** (1888–1944), the German Army's chief signal officer; **Ulrich-Wilhelm Schwerin Schwanenfeld** (1902–44), assistant adjutant to General von Witzleben; **Ulrich von Hassell**, the former German ambassador to Italy; **Joseph Wirmer** (1901–44), a leading Centre party politician; **Wilhelm Leuschner**, a leading trade union member; **Adolf Reichwein**, a leading Social Democratic politician; **Elizabeth von Thaddem**, a leading educator; **Jens Peter Jessen**, an economics professor at the University of Berlin; **Count Friedrich Werner von Schulenberg**, the former German ambassador to the Soviet Union; **Bernhard Letterhaus**, a Catholic labor leader; and **Lt. Col. Caesar von Hofacker**, a member of General von Stulpnagel's staff.

Wolf Heinrich Graf von Heldorf was born on October 14, 1896, in Merseburg. He served during the First World War and was involved in the Kapp Putsch in 1920. He joined the Nazi party in 1926 and, in 1933, was elected to the Reichstag. Von Helldorf was named Berlin's chief of police in July of 1935. During the war von Helldorf became involved in the conspiracy against Hitler, and was arrested following the July 20 coup attempt. He was tried and, on August 15, 1944, executed.

Adam von Trott Zu Solz was born on August 9, 1909, in Potsdam. A leading anti–Nazi, he used his position in the German foreign office and the Abwehr to establish a link between the German Resistance and Allied and American leaders. He was arrested for his role in the July 20 plot, and tried before the People's Court He was hung in Plotzensee Prison on August 26, 1944.

Otto Karl Kiep was born on July 7, 1886, the son of a German diplomat. He joined the German Foreign Office and was named counselor to the German Embassy in Washington in 1927. In 1930 he was appointed consul general in New York. He was recalled to Germany in 1933 following his attendance at a banquet honoring Albert Einstein. During the war Kiep was reinstated in the foreign office and became active in the German resistance movement. He was implicated by the Gestapo for treason after attending a tea party at the home of Elizabeth von Thadden (q.v.), another Resistance leader. He was tried by the People's Court and executed at Plotzensee Prison on August 26, 1944.

Karl Heinrich von Stulpnagel was born on January 22, 1886, in Darmstadt. He was quartermaster general on the German army's general staff from 1938 to 1940. He then served until October of 1941 as commander of the German seventeenth Army following the invasion of Russia. On March 3, 1942, he was named military government of Paris. Stulpnagel had long been an opponent of the Nazi regime and was active in the conspiracy to overthrow Hitler. Following the July 20 attempt on Hitler's life, Stulpnagel successfully ordered the arrest of the senior S.S. and Gestapo officers in France, before it became apparent the coup attempt had failed. He was ordered back to Berlin and unsuccessfully attempted to take his own life en route. Though serious injured, Stulpnagel was tried by the People's Court and, on August 30, 1944, hanged in the Plotzensee Prison courtyard.

Ulrich von Hassell was born in Pomerania in 1881. He joined the German Foreign Office in 1908, and later served in various diplomatic posts throughout Europe. He was the German ambassador to Denmark fro 1926 to 1930, and ambassador to Yugoslavia from 1930 to 1932. In 1932 he was sent to the German embassy in Rome as ambassador to Italy. His dislike for the Nazis resulted in his removal from the diplomatic corps in 1938. He supported a military coup against Hitler, and was involved in several conspiracies against the Nazis' rule. Hassell was long suspected of disloyalty by the Gestapo, and was arrested shortly after the July 20 attempt on Hitler's life. He was tried by the People's Court and, on September 8, 1944, was hanged at Plotzensee Prison.

Elizabeth von Thadden was born on July 29, 1890, in East Prussia. She was the founder and administrator of Schloss Wieblingen, a Protestant boarding school near Heidelberg. During the war she became involved with the German resistance movement. She was implicated by the Gestapo for her activities following a meeting of anti–Nazis at her home, during a tea party organized by Frau Anna Solf. She was tried by the People's Court and, on September 8, 1944, executed.

Wilhelm Leuschner was born on June 15, 1888, in Bayreuth. He was an early member of the Social Democratic party and a leading figure in the German trade union movement. He was arrested by the Nazis in May of 1933 and imprisoned in a concentration camp for nearly a year. Upon his release he became active in the German Resistance, serving as a liaison between the outlawed trade unions and the leaders of the conspiracy. He was arrested shortly after the failure of the July 20 attempt on Hitler's life and was executed on September 29, 1944.

Adolf Reichwein was born on October 3, 1898, in Bad Ems. He joined the Social Democratic party prior to the First World War, and served as a professor at Halle Teachers' College. In 1933, as a leading Socialist, his resignation was forced by the new Nazi regime. He was active in the German Resistance, and was arrested with Julius Leber (q.v.) on July 4, 1944, following a meeting with members of the underground Communist movement. He was tried and executed on October 20, 1944.

Jens Peter Jessen, an economics professor at the University of Berlin, was a member of the Nazi party during the early 1930s, but became disillusioned with them following the rise to power in 1933. He became involved with the Kriesau Circle and other resistance groups, and was arrested following the July 20 plot against Hitler. He was tried and sentenced to death, being executed in November of 1944.

Count Friedrich Werner von Schulenburg (1875–1944) was a leading member of the German diplomatic corps and an architect of the 1939 Non-Aggression Pact between Germany and the Soviet Union. He served as Germany's ambassador to the Soviet Union from 1934 until the German attack in 1941. Schulenburg, a lifelong friend of General Ludwig Beck (q.v.), soon became involved with the conspiracy to remove Hitler. He was arrested following the failure of the July 20 plot, and executed on November 10, 1944.

Bernhard Letterhaus was born on July 10, 1894, in the Rhineland. He became involved in the organization and administration of Catholic labor unions following service in the First World War. In 1928 he was elected union secretary of the Catholic Worker's Association. Letterhaus was an early advocate of resistance to the Nazi regime. During the war he served in the Abwehr and became directly involved in the conspiracy to overthrow Hitler. He was arrested with other conspirators following the July 20 attempt on Hitler's life, and was tried by the People's Court. Letterhaus was executed on November 14, 1944.

Caesar von Hofacker was born on March 2, 1896. He was a cousin of Count von Stauffenberg (q.v.) and shared his convictions that Germany would be better served by the elimination of Adolf Hitler. Serving as a staff officer for Field Marshal von Kluge in France, von Hofacker acted as a liaison between General von Stulpnagel (q.v.), the German military governor of France, and the conspirators in Berlin. He was arrested and tried with General Stulpnagel by the People's Court on August 29. Von Hofacker was sentenced to death for his part in the conspiracy, and executed on December 20, 1944.

Other Resistance leaders who died at the hands of the Gestapo and S.S. during this period included **Gen. Fritz Lindemann, Col. Frh. von Boeselager, Col. Georg Hansen** of the Abewahr, **Dr. Carl Langbehn, Hans Bernd von Haeften**, the brother of Werner von Haeften, **Gen. Hans Count von Sponeck, Major Ludwig von Leonrod, Count Heinrich von Lehndorff, Dr. Carl Sack, Count Berthold von Stauffenberg**, brother of Klaus von Stauffenberg, **Gen. Fritz Thiel**, chief of signals, OKH, and **Gen. Freiharr von Thuengen**, who had been appointed by Gen. Beck to succeed Gen. von Kortzfleisch on the day of the attempt on Hitler's life.

• Another leading member of the conspiracy to replace Hitler, **Field Marshal Erwin Rommel**, was given the option of taking poison or being tried by the People's Court, once his part in the conspiracy became known. Rommel was born on November 15, 1891, in Heidenheim. He served with distinction in the German Third Army during the First World War. His military talents caught the attention of Adolf Hitler and, in February 1941, he was appointed German commander in Libya, leading the Afrika Corps. He became known as the "Desert Fox," and won the respect of the enemy, as well as his superiors, for his strategic abilities. Following the German defeat during the second battle of El Alamein. Rommel was promoted to field marshal and sent to command Army Group B in

France, in anticipation of the Allied invasion. He was injured near St. Lo on July 17, 1944, during an air raid, and sent back to Germany to recover. During the course of the war, Rommel had become increasingly opposed to the Nazi regime and Hitler's war policy. He was approached by the German Resistance and indicated he would support their attempt to overthrow Hitler. Had the July 20 plot succeeded, Rommel, as an extremely popular figure with both the military and general public, was to be named chief of state. His injuries prevented him from taking a direct part in the coup attempt and its aftermath. Following evidence of the field marshal's complicity in the conspiracy, Rommel was arrested by the S.S. On October 14, 1944, Rommel swallowed poison, sparing his family the disgrace of his being executed for treason. The German government announced that he had died from the injures he had suffered in France and he was given a hero's burial.

- **Princess Mafalda**, the daughter King Victor Emmanuel II of Italy, and the wife of Prince Philip of Hesse, died during 1944 at Buchenwald following the desertion of her father from Hitler.

- **Ernst Thaelmann**, the leader of the German Communist party, was shot to death in Buchenwald concentration camp on August 28, 1944, after more than a decade in captivity. Thaelmann was born in Hamburg on April 16, 1886. He joined the German Communist movement in 1903, and was active in the organization of the trade unions in Hamburg. He served as a Communist deputy in the German Reichstag from 1924 until 1933, also serving on the executive committee of the Comintern, the Soviet-dominated governing body of international Communism. Thaelmann, like most leaders of the German far left, failed to recognize the threat of Hitler's brand of fascism, assuming the Nazi party was little worse than the traditional brand of German conservatism. Thaelmann ran for the presidency of the Reich in 1925, gaining few votes. In the 1932 election, won by Paul von Hindenburg, Thaelmann placed

third, behind Adolf Hitler, and received over ten percent of the vote. Thaelmann was arrested soon after the Nazis came to power in 1933, and was sent to Moabit Prison in Berlin. Having spent over a decade in various prisons and concentration camps, Thaelmann was murdered in Buchenwald on August 28, 1944.

- **General Alfredo Noguera Gomez**, an exiled Nicaraguan army officer, was killed in a skirmish with Costa Rican troops on October 9, 1944, while preparing to lead a revolt into Nicaragua from the Costa Rican border. General Gomez, an admirer of Juan Peron of Argentina, wanted to set up a Fascist government in Nicaragua.

- **Belew Zelleqe**, a hero of the Ethiopian Resistance against the Italian occupation, was hanged by the Ethiopian government after being convicted on charges of conspiring to seize power. Other officers, including **Mamo Haylu**, were also hanged at this time.

- **Richard Sorge**, who had served as a spy for the Soviet Union, was executed in Japan on November 7, 1944. Sorge, who had been on close terms with the German Embassy in Tokyo, had been privy to many German and Japanese military secrets while working for the Soviet Union. Sorge was born in Russia in 1895. His father was a German, and Sorge spent much of his youth in Germany. He became a member of the communist party in 1918, and acted as an agent for the comintern throughout Europe and Asia. As a respected journalist for the *Frankfurter Zeitung*, Sorge settled in Tokyo in the early 1930s. He established high-level contacts with the Japanese and the German Embassy there. Sorge served as Russia's leading espionage agent in Asia and was able to relay much valuable and strategic information to Joseph Stalin. Through Sorge's efforts the Soviets were able to learn the exact date of the German invasion of the Soviet Union. Sorge was arrested on October 15, 1941, by the Japanese authorities and, on November 7, 1944, he was executed.

- **Walter Edmund Guinness, First Baron Moyne**, was assassinated by two Israeli terrorists at his home in Cairo, Egypt, on

November 16, 1944. Baron Moyne, who was born in 1880, had served as a member of the British parliament from 1907 to 1931. He served in the cabinet as minister of agriculture from 1925 to 1929 and from 1940 to 1941. He served as colonial secretary and the leader of the House of Lords in 1941 and 1942. In 1942 he was appointed the deputy minister of state in Cairo, a position he held at the time of his death. His assassins were identified as Eliahu Bet-Tsouri (1921–45) and Eliahu Hakim (1924–45), both members of the Stern Gang. They were tried and convicted of the murder on January 10, 1945, and executed on March 22 of that year.

# 1945

• Until virtually the end of World War II many leaders of the anti–Nazi Resistance were executed by the Nazis. These included **Karl Friedrich Goerdeler**, the former lord mayor of Leipzig and the chief civilian leader of the German Resistance; **Deitrich Bonhoeffer**, a German Lutheran pastor; **Admiral Wilhelm Canaris**, the chief of the German Abwehr; **Maj. Gen. Hans Oster**, Canaris' chief of staff at the Abwehr; **Count Helmuth von Moltke** and **Hans von Dohnanyi**, members of the Abwehr staff; **Julius Leber**, a leading Social Democratic politician; **Nikolaus Gross**, a trade union leader; **Alfred Delp**, a Jesuit priest; **Fritz Goerdeler**, the brother of Karl Goerdeler; **Wolf von Harnack**, a leading Social Democratic; **Gen. Arthur Nebe**, the head of the German criminal police; **Albrecht Haushofer**, a professor of political geography; **Klaus Bonhoeffer** (1901–45), a lawyer and the brother of Dietrich Bonhoeffer; and **Count Albrecht von Bernstorff**.

Count Helmuth Graf von Moltke was born in Silesia on March 2, 1907. He was an early opponent of National Socialism and a founder of the Kreisau Circle, whose meetings he hosted at his Silesian estate. During the war, von Moltke served as a legal advisor to the Abwehr. He was arrested by the Gestapo in January of 1944 and, though he head not participated in the July 20 plot against Hitler, he was tried and convicted by the People's Court. He was hanged on January 23, 1945, in the Plotzensee Prison courtyard.

Nikolaus Gross, a German trade union leader, was born on September 30, 1898, in the Ruhr. During the 1930s he served as editor of the *Westdeutschen Arbeiterzeitung*, a German workers' newspaper. He was an early opponent of the Nazis and was arrested by the Gestapo on August 12, 1944, for complicity in the July 20 plot. Following a trial before the People's Court, Gross was executed on January 23, 1945.

Karl Friedrich Goerdeler was born on July 31, 1884, in Schneidemuhl. Following service in the First World War, Goerdler was appointed second burgomeister of Konigsberg in 1922. He served in this post until May 22, 1930, when he became lord mayor of Leipzig. He was an early opponent of Hitler and National Socialism and, on March 31, 1937, was forced by the Nazis to resign his position. He soon became the leading civilian member of the German Resistance, and used his personal prestige to encourage a military coup. Following the defeat of the German army at Stalingrad, Goerdler was able to convince some major figures in the German military to plan for Hitler's overthrow. Goerdler went into hiding following the failure of the July 20 attempt on Hitler's life, which, had the plot succeeded, would have made him the chancellor of Germany. On August 12 he was arrested by the Gestapo in Marienwerder, and tried by the People's Court. He was sentenced to death on September 8, 1944, and hanged in Berlin on February 2, 1945.

Johannes von Popitz was born on December 2, 1884, in Leipzig. He served in the finance ministry during the 1920s, and was minister of finance in Prussia following the 1933 victory of the Nazi party. Von Popitz, a conservative and a monarchist, became involved in the conspiracy against Hitler in 1938. He was instrumental in attempting to persuade Heinrich Himmler to join the conspiracy against Hitler, an act which brought him under the surveillance of the Gestapo. Von Popitz was arrested the day of the unsuccessful attempt on Hitler's life on July 20, 1944. He was tried and condemned to death by the People's Court on October 3, 1944, but was not executed until February 2, 1945.

Alfred Delp was born on September 15, 1907, in Mannheim. He was ordained a Jesuit priest in 1937. For the next four years Delp served as an editor of *Stimmen der Zeit*, a Jesuit journal. He became active in the German Resistance in 1942, and was arrested by the Gestapo shortly after the failure of the July 20 coup attempt. He was tried by the People's Court and sentenced to be executed. He was hanged in the Plotzensee Prison on February 2, 1945.

Wolf Alexander Oskar Ernst von Harnack was born in Marburg on July 15, 1888. A Social Democrat, von Harnack served in various positions in the Prussian civil service prior to the Nazi victory of 1933. A member of the German Resistance, he was arrested immediately after the failure of the July 20, 1944, attempt on Hitler's life. He was tried before the People's Court, and hanged on March 3, 1945.

Arthur Nebe was born on November 13, 1894, and served in the German army during the First World War. Nebe joined the German criminal police (KRIPO) in 1924 and, in 1931, joined the S.S. After Hitler came to power in 1933, Nebe was appointed chief of the state police. In 1941 he was placed in charge of Action Group B, an extermination unit active at the Russian front. During this period Nebe was instrumental in developing new methods of mass execution. Nebe was reportedly repelled by the inhumanity of the system he observed, and joined the German Resistance. He went into hiding following the failure of the plot against Hitler, but was subsequently arrested and tried for treason. It was reported that he was executed on March 21, 1945, but various reports during the 1950s and 1960s allege he survived the war, using his supposed execution to avoid prosecution for war crimes.

Hans von Dohnanyi was born on January 1, 1902, in Vienna. He served on the staff of the Reich Justice Ministry from 1929 until 1938, when he was named to the Leipzig Supreme Court. The following year he was appointed to the Abwehr, serving under Maj. Gen. Hans Oster. He used his position to gather evidence of the illegal activities of the Nazis, to be used to justify the overthrow of Hitler. Von Dohnanyi's involvement with the Resistance was suspected by the Gestapo, and he was first arrested in April of 1943. He was released at that time due to lack of evidence, but was arrested again shortly before the July 20 attempt on Hitler's life. He was sent to the Sachsenhausen concentration camp and, following the discovery of his private papers detailing Nazi atrocities, he was tried for treason. Von Dohnanyi was sentenced to be executed, and was put to death on April 8, 1945.

Dietrich Bonhoeffer was born on February 4, 1906, in Breslau. A theologian and lecturer, he left Germany for London following the Nazis' rise to power in 1933. He returned to Germany in 1935 and founded the anti–Nazi German Confessing Church. He joined the German Resistance against Hitler near the start of World War II, and acted as liaison between the conspirators and the Allies. He was arrested by the Gestapo for subversion on April 5, 1943, and imprisoned. He was sent to Buchenwald following the July 20 attempt on Hitler's life, and was later transferred to Flossenburg concentration camp where, on April 9, 1945, he was executed.

Wilhelm Canaris was born on January 1, 1889, in Westphalia. He served with naval intelligence in Spain and Italy during the First World War, and took part in the Kapp Putsch following the war. On January 1, 1935, he was appointed chief of the Abwehr, the German military intelligence agency. Canaris supported some of the views of the Nazis, particularly their opposition to Communism, but did not favor many of their activities. He, along with his deputy, Hans Oster (q.v.), became involved with the conspiracy against Hitler in the late 1930s. In February of 1944 he was dismissed as Abwehr head and appointed to the Office for Commercial and Economic Warfare. He was an active participant in the July 20 attempt on Hitler's life, and was arrested shortly after the plot's failure. He was imprisoned at Flossenburg concentration camp, and executed for treason on April 9, 1945.

Maj. Gen. Hans Oster was born in Dresden on August 9, 1888. He served as a general staff officer during the First World War I and, in 1933, was named to the Abwehr as head of the Financial and Administrative Department. Oster was an active foe of the Nazis, and used his position in military intelligence to pass on German military plans to the Allies and assist Jews in fleeing from Nazi occupation. He was relieved of duties in April of 1943 and was arrested shortly after the July 20, 1944, plot against Hitler. He was sent to Flossenburg concentration camp, and was executed with his former commanding officer, Wilhelm Canaris (q.v.), on April 9, 1945.

Albrecht Haushofer was born on January 7, 1903, in Munich. He was the son of Professor Karl Haushofer, the founder of Geopoltik. Haushofer was named to the faculty of the University of Berlin as professor of political geography in 1939. He was a close friend of Rudolf Hess, the deputy fuehrer of the German Reich, and was possibly instrumental in planning Hess' flight to England in May of 1941, on a quest for a separate peace with Great Britain. Haushofer was involved in numerous anti–Hitler conspiracies and, in December of 1944, he was arrested by the Gestapo. He was imprisoned in Moabit Prison, in Berlin, and shot by members of the S.S. during the Battle of Berlin, on April 23, 1945.

Julius Leber was born on November 16, 1891, in Alsace. He was an early member of the Social Democratic party and served in the German army during the First World War. During the early 1920s he served as editor of the left-wing newspaper *Volksbote* in Lubeck, and was elected to the Reichstag in 1924. He was a leading opponent of Hitler, and was the target of an unsuccessful assassination attempt

following the Nazis' rise to power in 1933. He was imprisoned by the Nazis following the Reichstag fire later in the year, and spent the next four years in concentration camps. Upon his release he became an active conspirator against Hitler's regime and a close political ally of Count Claus von Stauffenberg (q.v.). He was arrested by the Gestapo prior to the attempt on Hitler's life on July 20, 1944, when he was denounced by a Gestapo spy while attending a meeting with members of the outlawed Communist party. He was sentenced to death on October 20, 1944, by the People's Court and, on July 5, 1945, hanged at Plotzensee Prison in Berlin.

• During 1945 the Communist Vietminh executed a number of prominent Vietnamese politicians whom they considered potential rivals, including moderate leaders **Bui Quang Chieu** and **Pham Quynh**, and **Ta Thu Thau**, the leader of the Trotskyite factor of the Vietnamese Communists.

Bui Quang Chieu (1873–1945), a founder of the Constitutionalist party in French Indo-China, was arrested and killed by the Communists. Bui was a moderate Vietnamese nationalist and the founder of the Constitutionalist party in 1917. His party gained control of the Cochin-Chinese Colonial Council following the elections of 1926, and Bui used his influence to advocate constitutional rights for the Vietnamese. He served in the Council of France Overseas from 1932 to 1941, and was a strong contender to head the first independent Vietnamese government.

Pham Quynh (1892–1945), a Vietnamese writer and politician, was executed by the Communists as a French collaborator. He served as a founder and editor of the *France-Indochine* newspaper and, in 1933, he succeeded Ngo Dinh Diem (q.v.) as chief minister in the government of Bao Dai. His pro–French views resulted in his execution by the Communist Vietminh nationalists in 1945.

• **Colonel Karl Koch**, the S.S. commandant of the Buchenwald concentration camp, was executed by the S.S. on charges of theft and poor discipline. Koch had served as Buchenwald's commandant from its founding in 1937. He and his wife, Ilse (1906–67), known as the "Red Witch of Buchenwald," were notorious for their brutal treatment of the camp prisoners. In 1943 the Kochs were investigated by the S.S. on charges of mismanagement and theft. Following a two year investigation, Karl Koch was convicted of stealing from the Nazi party and was executed by the order of the S.S. district leader, General Josias von Waldeck-Pyrmont (1896–1967). Though Ilse Koch was acquitted by the Nazis, she was arrested and tried by the Allies as a war criminal following the end of the war. After several trials, she was convicted in 1950 and sentenced to life imprisonment. She committed suicide on September 1, 1967.

• **Sigmund Rascher** (1909–45), a Nazi doctor who had carried out secret experiments at the Dachau concentration camp, was arrested and executed for child abduction. Rascher was one of the more notorious Nazi concentration camp doctors who conducted inhuman experimentation on prisoners at Dachau from 1941 to 1942, his experiments, which dealt with the ability of humans to withstand extreme temperature, caught the attention of Heinrich Himmler, who served as Rascher's patron for his barbarous acts. Rascher escaped being tried for war crimes, as he was executed by the Gestapo at Dachau in 1945, after it was learned that the children he claimed were his own had been abducted from other German families.

• **Warren Green Hooper** (May 2, 1904–1945) was a member of Michigan's state house of representatives from 1939 until 1944, and served as a member of the Michigan state senate in 1945. He was called before a grand jury and admitted to taking bribes. Hooper agreed to testify against others, but was shot to death in his car along a highway near Springport, Michigan, on January 11, 1945.

• On February 1, 1945, war crimes trials in Bulgaria, which had begun in December of 1944, culminated in the execution of the three

regents: **Prince Cyril**, brother of the late King Boris III (q.v.); **Bogdan Filov**, who served as premier of Bulgaria from 1940 to 1943; **Lt. Gen. Nikola Mikhov** (1891–1945), the minister of war. Former premiers **Dobri Boshilov** and **Ivan Bagrianov**, were also executed. Other executions included 22 ministers, 68 minister of parliament and eight of King Boris' advisors.

Cyril (Kiril) was born in Sofia on November 17, 1895. He was the son of King Ferdinand of Bulgaria and the younger brother of King Boris III. He became regent following the death of King Boris on August 28, 1943, and the succession to the throne of his minor nephew, King Simeon. Cyril headed the regency council which also included Prime Minister Bogdan Filov and War Minister General Nikola Mikhov. Cyril was ousted as regent by the anti–Fascist Fatherland Front government on September 9, 1944. He was arrested as a war criminal and was tried and executed with the rest of the regency council on February 1, 1945.

Bogdan Filov was born in Stara Zagora on March 28, 1883. He was a leading Bulgarian academician and a member of the Bulgarian Academy of Science from 1929. He served as president of the academy from 1937 until 1940. He was chosen to head the government by King Boris on February 16, 1940. He signed the Vienna Agreement in March of 1941 that brought Bulgaria into World War II on the side of Germany. After King Boris' death in August of 1943 Filov became the leading political figure in the country. He arranged the appointment of a regency council consisting of himself, Prince Cyril and General Nikola Mikhov, the minister of war. He stepped down as prime minister on September 14, 1943, and named Dobri Bozhilov to head the government. He remained a strong supporter of Germany during the war. The regency council was ousted on September 9, 1944, when Kimon Georgiev's Fatherland Front formed a government. Filov was arrested and tried for war crimes. He was executed along with the rest of the regency council and numerous other members of the wartime government on February 1, 1945.

Dobri Bozhilov was born in 1884. He served as minister of finance from 1938. He was named by Bogdan Filov to serve as prime minister on September 14, 1943. Filov largely controlled the government and Bozhilov stepped down on June 1, 1944. He was subsequently named director of the National Bank, where he remained until his removal in August of 1944. Bozhilov was arrested following the establishment of the Fatherland Front government in September of 1944. He was tried for war crimes and was executed on February 1, 1945.

Ivan Bagrianov was born in 1892. He was educated in Germany and commanded a German artillery unit during the First World War. He was a close friend of King Boris and a leading member of the Agrarian Party. He served in various governments until his resignation in 1941. He was chosen to head the government on June 1, 1944. He was considered to be an acceptable candidate to both Germany and the Allies. He attempted to extract Bulgaria from the war by declaring neutrality and Bulgaria withdrew from the conflict in August of 1944. His proposal was unacceptable to the Allies and Russian troops continued to advance. Bagrianov was forced to resign on September 2, 1944. He was arrested after the establishment of the Fatherland Front government later in the month. He was tried as a war criminal and executed on February 1, 1945.

• **Jacques Larsac**, the former police chief of Dijon, France, was hanged by a mob on February 15, 1945. Larsac, who was imprisoned on charges of ruthless treatment of French Resistance members during the occupation, was dragged from his jail cell and killed before he could be tried.

• **Ahmed Maher Pasha**, the premier of Egypt, was shot and killed on February 24, 1945. His assassination took place in the Egyptian parliament in Cairo after announcing Egypt's declaration of war against Axis powers. Maher was born in 1886. He was a leading Egyptian scholar, holding doctorates

in law and economics. He was an early leader of the Nationalist Party and was a supporter of Said Zaghlul. He was involved in the formation of the Wafd Party after World War I. Maher served as minister of education in Zaghlul's first Wafd government in 1924. He was accused of complicity in the assassination of Sir Lee Stack (q.v.), the British Governor-General of the Sudan, and was removed from the government. Though acquitted, the British still viewed Maher with suspicion and vetoed his role in national politics. He resumed an active role in the Wafd leadership in 1927, serving as the secretary of the party's parliamentary group. He became a close ally of Mahmoud Fahmy el-Nokrashy and left the Wafd Party with him in January of 1938 following a conflict with Wafd leader Mustafa el-Nahas. He and Nokrashy formed the Sa'adist Party and joined the government of Maher's brother, Ali Maher, in 1939. Ahmed Maher was a supporter of Egypt joining the Allies in World War II and resigned from the government with other members of his party in September of 1940. Maher formed a government to replace Nahas in October of 1944, and retained office following elections in January of 1945 that were boycotted by the Wafds. Maher announced his government's intentions to enter World War II against Germany in February of 1945. He was assassinated in the Egyptian Parliament in Cairo the following day on February 24, 1945, by Mahmoud Essawy (1917–45), a Fascist sympathizer. His assassin was tried and convicted by a military court and hanged in September of 1945.

• **Col. Gen. Friedrich Fromm** (1888–1945), who as chief of the German Replacement Army had ordered the arrest and execution of the leading participants in the plot against Hitler on July 20, 1944, was tried by the People's Court and executed by firing squad on March 19, 1945.

• **Franz Oppenhof**, who had recently been appointed mayor of Aachen, Germany, by the Allied occupation authorities, was shot to death by three German parachutists on March 25, 1945.

• **Benito Mussolini**, the founder of Fascism and the dictator of Italy from 1922, was executed by Italian partisans near Dongo, on the shores of Lake Como, on April 28, 1945. Executed with Mussolini was his mistress, **Clara Petacci** (Feb. 28, 1912–1945), both of whom were shot by partisan leader Walter Audisio (1909–73) outside the gates of Villa Belmonte. There bodies were hung in the Piazzale Loreto. Also captured and executed at the time were fifteen other Fascist leaders, many of whom were members of Mussolini's government. They included **Achille Starace** (Apr. 18, 1889–1945), the secretary general of the Italian Fascist party from 1932 until 1939, **Alessandro Pavolini** (Sept. 27, 1903–45), the minister of popular culture and party secretary for the Republican Fascists, **Francesco Maria Barraci, Dr. Paolo Zerbini, Ruggero Romano, Fernando Mezzasoma** (Aug. 3, 1907–1945), Fascist minister in the Salo Republic, **Augusto Liverani, Carlo Scorza, Guido Gasti, Goffredo Coppola, Ernesto Daquanno, Mario Luigi, Vitto Casalnuovo, Pietro Salustri, Marcello De Facci** and **Nicolo Bombacci** (Oct. 24, 1879–1945).

Benito Mussolini was born in Predappion on July 29, 1883. He worked as a journalist and schoolteacher as a young man, traveling to Switzerland and Austria. He became active in the Socialist party and was jailed in 1911 for his opposition to Italy's policy during the Libyan conflict. The following year he became editor of the Socialist newspaper *Avanti!*. He initially favored Italy's neutrality during World War I, but soon called for an alliance with Germany and the Triple Entente. He was expelled from the Socialist party for his views. Mussolini served in the Italian army during the war until he was wounded in 1917. In March of 1919 he and several other war veterans formed the Fasci di Combattimento, or Fighting Leagues, in Milan. The Fascist movement was initially unsuccessful, but soon gained support from leading members of the right. The Fascists formed their own paramilitary organization known as the Blackshirts, who were active against the Socialists,

Communists, and other leftist elements. Mussolini became known as "Il Duce", or the leader, and organized the Fascist march on Rome in October of 1922. King Victor Emmanuel III entrusted the government to Mussolini on October 31, 1922, to prevent further violence in the capital. Mussolini faced an early crisis following the assassination of Socialist journalist Giacomo Matteotti in June of 1924. The following year Mussolini began the establishment of the dictatorship which would characterize the remainder of his regime. He negotiated the Lateran Accords with the Vatican in February of 1929. After consolidating his power within Italy he began to concentrate on foreign affairs. He supported Francisco Franco's forces during the Spanish Civil War in the mid–1930s, and defied the League of Nations by conquering Ethiopia. He signed the Rome-Berlin Axis with Hitler's Germany in 1936, and further solidified Italy's military ties with Germany with the "Pact of Steel" in May of 1939. Italy had occupied Albania the previous month, though Mussolini was initially reluctant to enter World War II. Mussolini did not enter Italy into the war until June of 1940, when he felt that Germany was already the victor. A series of military reversals damaged Mussolini's prestige at home and with his allies. He received a vote of nonconfidence from the Fascist Grand Council, which gave King Victor Emmanuel III the opportunity to force Mussolini's ouster on July 25, 1943. He was arrested by the new government and imprisoned at Campo Imperatore in the Abruzzi mountains. He was soon rescued by the Germans and installed as figurehead leader of the occupied Italian Social Republic in northern Italy. As the Allies and anti–Fascist Italian partisans advanced on his position, he fled with his mistress, Clara Petacci, and other supporters. They were captured by Italian Communist partisans led by Walter Audisio (1909–73) near Lake Como. He and his retinue were shot to death at Giulino di Mezzegra on April 28, 1945, and their bodies were hung and displayed in the Milan piazza.

• **Roberto Farinacci**, another former secretary general of the Italian Fascist party, was also executed by Italian partisans on April 28, 1945, in Milan. Farinacci was born in Isernia on October 16, 1892. He was an early follower of Benito Mussolini (q.v.), and was the founder of the fascist daily newspaper *Cremona Nuova*. He was appointed secretary general of the Italian Fascist party on February 12, 1925, but was replaced in March of the following year. He served as a member of the Fascist Grand Council from 1935, and was appointed minister of state in 1938. Farinacci escaped from Rome following the downfall of Mussolini in 1943. He was captured by partisans in April of 1945, and tried and executed for treason.

• **S.S. General Richard Gluecks**, who served as the Nazi inspector of concentration camps during World War II, was murdered, presumably by a Jewish revenge group, on May 10, 1945.

• **Odilo Globocnik**, the S.S. officer who was in charge of the extermination of Jews in Poland during World War II, was also presumed killed by a Jewish revenge group on May 31, 1945. Globocnik was born on April 21, 1904, in Trieste. He joined the Nazi party in 1930 and became a member of the S.S. three years later. He was appointed the Nazi gauleiter of Vienna in 1938, but was dismissed the following year for misconduct. He was reassigned later in 1939 as S.S. leader in Lublin, Poland. In 1943 Globocnik was placed in charge of organizing extermination camps to liquidate Polish Jews. The following year he was placed in charge of the S.S. in the Adriatic region. Following the end of the war Globocnik was captured and murdered by Jewish partisans in Austria.

• **Andre Baillet**, the director general of information in the French Vichy government, was executed at Fort De Chatillon on July 18, 1945. He had been convicted of treason and collaboration with the Germans during a trial that ended on June 20, 1945.

• On August 14–17, 1945, rebel soldiers seized the Imperial Palace in Japan in an attempted coup d'etat to prevent the surrender of Japan. **General Takshi Mori** was slain during the mutiny. Hidemasa Koga, the son-in-law of General Hideki Tojo (q.v.) and a leader of the coup attempt, committed suicide following the coup's failure.

• On August 25, 1945, **John Birch** (1918–45), a Baptist missionary in China, was shot to death by Chinese Communists. Birch had assisted Lt. Col. James Doolittle and his crew when they parachuted into China following the air attack on Tokyo in 1942. He subsequently served as an intelligence officer and interpreter in China under Brig. Gen. Claire Chennault. He was transferred to the Office of Strategic Services in Northern China in May of 1945, and was responsible for leading Japanese occupation troops to the coast following the surrender of Japan. He was seized and killed by a band of Chinese Communists while performing this mission. Birch served as the inspiration and namesake for the extreme anti–Communist John Birch Society, founded by Robert Welch in 1954.

• **Dr. Joseph Pfitzner**, the deputy mayor of Prague, Czechoslovakia, during the German occupation, was hanged in Prague as a traitor on September 6, 1945.

• **General Nicolo Bellomo** of Italy was executed by a firing squad for war crimes on September 11, 1945.

• **Archbishop Anba Theophilus**, the Coptic patriarch of Jerusalem, was shot to death while walking in an Upper Egyptian grain field on October 1, 1945.

• **Joseph Darnand**, a leading French collaborator with the Nazis, and the head of the Milice, the S.S. French police force, was tried for treason. He was sentenced to be executed on October 3, 1945. Darnand had commanded a French S.S. unit on the Russian front in 1943, before returning to France and becoming the secretary general for the maintenance of order. Darnand's Milice was responsible for many brutal acts against members of the French Resistance.

• **Jean-Harold Paquis**, a French propaganda broadcaster during the German occupation, was executed by a firing squad near Paris on October 11, 1945.

• **Pierre Laval**, the French politician who served as premier of Vichy France during much of World War II, was executed as a traitor by a firing squad at the Prison of Fresnes on October 15, 1945. Laval was born in Chateldon, Pyu-de-Dome, on June 28, 1883. He was elected to the chamber of deputies from Aubervilliers in 1914. He began his political career on the extreme left, but moved to the right after becoming a senator in 1926. He served in several governments before becoming premier on January 27, 1931. He stepped down on February 23, 1932. He subsequently served as minister of labor in Andre Tardieu's government from February until June of 1932. Laval was minister of colonies from February until October of 1934 and foreign minister from October of 1934 until May of 1935. He again headed the government as premier from June 7, 1935, until January 25, 1936, also retaining the position of foreign minister. During this term of office he supported an agreement that recognized Italy's claims on Abyssinia. He remained out of the government until after Germany's defeat of France in June of 1940. He entered Henri-Philippe Petain's Vichy government as premier on July 11, 1940. Petain distrusted Laval's ambition and dismissed him in December of 1940. He was subsequently arrested and imprisoned until the Germans arranged his release. He subsequently went to German-occupied Paris. Laval was injured in an assassination attempt in Versailles on August 27, 1941. He returned to power to lead the Vichy government on April 9, 1942. Laval was granted dictatorial powers by Petain shortly after resuming office. The Allies began achieving victory over the German forces and Laval was forced to retreat with the Germans on August 17, 1944. He escaped to Switzerland the following year. He then went to Spain before returning to France to stand trial for treason in July of 1945. He was sentenced to death and, after a failed suicide attempt by poison in the prison of Fresnes, he was shot to death.

• French right-wing journalist **Robert Brasillach** (1909–45) was tried for treason and executed in 1945. Brasillach was a leading collaborationist with the Germans during the occupation of France.

• **Vidkun Quisling**, the Norwegian Fascist leader who betrayed his country to Adolf Hitler and served as Norway's prime minister during the German occupation, was executed for treason on October 24, 1945. Vidkun Abraham Lauritz Jonsson Quisling was born in Fyresdal, Telemark, on July 18, 1887. He attended the Military Academy in 1911 and served in the Norwegian army as a junior member of the general staff. He served as military attaché in Russia and Finland from 1918 until 1921, when he abandoned his military career. He was a relief commissioner in the Soviet Union from 1922 until 1926. He remained in the Soviet Union, where he represented Great Britain's interest, until 1929, when he returned to Norway. He subsequently entered politics and gained a reputation for his extreme rightist positions. He served as minister of defense in the Agrarian cabinets from May of 1931, until the government collapsed in January of 1933. He subsequently broke with the Agrarians to form the National Unification Party (Nasjonal Samling) in May of 1933. His party was unsuccessful at the polls and Quisling moved toward Fascism. Despite a lack of popularity within Norway, he gained the support of Adolf Hitler's Nazi regime in Germany in 1939. Germany invaded Norway on April 9, 1940, and Quisling unilaterally declared himself head of the government when the legitimate Labor government left the capital. His so-called government received no support within the country and he was forced to step down after six days. Because of his support of the occupation forces the name of Quisling became synonymous with traitor. The occupation government was headed by German Reichskommissar Josef Terboven. Quisling's party was the only one allowed to exist during the occupation. He was named to the position of minister president by Terboven on

February 1, 1942. His government attempted to nazify churches and schools and sent many Jews to death in concentration camps. He was reviled by his fellow countrymen and was arrested following Norway's liberation in May of 1945. He was tried for military and civilian treason, illegally changing the constitution, illegal confiscation, theft, and murder. He was convicted and executed by a firing squad on October 24, 1945.

• **Colonel Antonio Brito**, a former Cuban chief of police, was assassinated on November 28, 1945.

• **General Anton Dostler**, the Nazi general and commander of the Seventy-Fifth German Army, was executed by a firing squad in Aversa, Italy, on December 1, 1945. He was tried by the United States Military Tribunal in Rome on October 12, 1945, and convicted of war crimes.

• **Josef Kramer** (1906–45), the S.S. commander of the Kirkenau and Bergen-Belsen concentration camps, was executed for war crimes on December 13, 1945. Kramer had joined the S.S. in 1932 and served as deputy to Rudolf Hoess (q.v.) at Auschwitz from 1940 until 1944. He was named commandant at Belsen in December of 1944. He served in that position, and at Bergen-Belsen, during the final periods of mass slaughter, as the Russian army advanced toward the concentration camp sites. He became known as the "Beast of Belsen" by the world press when the remains of his victims were discovered by the British army. He was tried by a British military court at Luneberg, and was sentenced to death on November 17, 1945. He was executed the following month.

• Nazi **Lt. Gens. Friedrich G. Bernhardt** and **Adolf Hamann** were hanged in Bryansk for war crimes on December 30, 1945.

• **Martin Luther Nsibirwa**, the chief minister, or katikiro, of Buganda, was murdered in front of the Namirembe Cathedral in Buganda in retaliation for his support of a land seizure to expand Makerere College. Nsibirwa served as Buganda's chief minister from 1930 until 1941, when he was forced to resign. The colonial government returned him to office in 1945, shortly before his murder.

# 1946

• **William Joyce**, the British propagandist known as "Lord Haw-Haw" during World War II, was convicted of treason and hanged in Wandworth Prison on January 3, 1946. Joyce was born in the United States in 1906. His mother was English and his father was an American citizen. The family moved to England in 1921, and Joyce became a member of the British Fascist movement. He went to Germany in 1939 and used his wit and talent as a tool for Joseph Goebbel's propaganda machine. During the war he broadcast misleading information about the British war effort and encouraged English soldiers to give up the fight. He was arrested in Germany at the end of the war, and returned to England to stand trial.

• **Sir Amin Osman Pasha** (1900–46), a former Egyptian finance minister, was assassinated in Cairo on January 5, 1946. Osman was educated in England, where he studied law. He returned to Egypt as a lawyer and subsequently became a financial director for Alexandria. He was named minister of finance in 1942, where he began the pension program for government employees. After leaving office he entered private business and served in the senate. He formed the Renaissance League in 1945. Osman's murder was believed to have been by the Muslim Brothers, with assistance from Anwar al-Sadat (q.v.).

• **Dr. Laszlo De Bardossy**, a wartime premier of Hungary, was hanged in Budapest for treason on January 10, 1946. Bardossy was born in Szombathely on December 10, 1880. He headed the press department of the foreign ministry from 1924 until 1931. He served as counselor at the Hungarian legation in London from 1931 until 1934. Bardossy was appointed ambassador to Romania in 1934. He returned to Budapest to serve as foreign minister in February of 1941. He was also named to head the government as prime minister on April 4, 1941, following the suicide of Pal Teleki. Bardossy's government declared war on the Soviet Union in June of 1941. His government stepped down on March 9, 1942. He became chairman of the Fascist United Christian National League the following year. Bardossy collaborated with the Arrow Cross Party during the German occupation in 1944. He was arrested as a war criminal after the war. He was tried by a people's tribunal and sentenced to death in November of 1945. Bardossy was hanged in Budapest on January 10, 1946.

• **Tarrad Moulheim**, a Syrian deputy, was assassinated on January 13, 1946.

• **Lt. Gen. Herman Winkler**, the former Nazi commander of Nikolayev, and six other German officers were hanged on January 17, 1946, for war crimes.

• **General Otto Blaha** and **General Robert Richtermoc**, of the Prague gendarmerie, were hanged for war crimes in Prague on January 21, 1946.

• **Milo Bushati**, who had served as premier of Albania during the German occupation, and regents **Anton Arapi** and **Levi Nossi** were convicted of war crimes and shot in Tirana on February 17, 1946.

• **Jean Luchaire**, the president of the pro–Nazi *Paris Press*, was executed in Paris on February 22, 1946, for treason and collaboration with the Germans.

• On February 23, 1946, **General Tomoyuki Yamashita**, the Japanese commander-in-chief in the Philippines, was executed for war crimes. **Lt. Col. Seichi Ohta**, head of the Japanese Kempei Tai (thought police) of the Philippines, and **Takuma Higashiga**, a civilian interpreter, were also executed.

General Yamashita was born in Tokyo in 1885. He served in the Japanese army during the Russo-Japanese War, World War I, and the Sino-Japanese War. In 1940 he was named inspector general of Japan's aircraft and, in 1941, he was appointed commanding officer of the Twenty-Fifth Army. In that capacity he led the forces that overran Malaya and captured Singapore. In 1942 he was stationed as commanding general of the Japanese army in northern Manchuria. He was appointed commander-in-chief of the Japanese-controlled Philippines in July of 1944, and put up a sturdy defense against the American advance. Yamashita's efforts at resistance proved in vain and, on September 2, 1945, he signed the articles of surrender. He was subsequently arrested on charges of allowing atrocities to take place under his command near the close of the war.

• **Bela Imredy**, a former premier of Hungary, was executed for treason by a firing squad at the Marko jail courtyard in Budapest on February 28, 1946. Imredy had been convicted of war crimes and anti–Jewish activities in November of 1945. Imredy was born in Budapest on December 29, 1891. He was a leading economist and served as director of the National Bank from 1928. He served in Gyula Gombos' government as minister of finance from 1932 until 1935, when he assumed the presidency of the National Bank. He succeeded Kalmas Daranyi as prime minister on May 14, 1938. He continued Hungary's policy of alliance with Nazi Germany. He was forced to step down on February 14, 1939, but remained a leading figure in the right-wing of the government party. He formed the Hungarian Revival Party in September of 1940 and advocated the transformation of Hungary into a Fascist state. He served in Dome Sztojay's government as minister of economic affairs following Germany's occupation of Hungary in March of 1944. Imredy was arrested after the war and tried as a war criminal.

• **Count Fidal Palfy**, the wartime minister of agriculture in Hungary, was hanged for treason in Budapest on March 2, 1946.

• **Ferenc Szalasi**, the pro–Nazi former premier of Hungary, was executed in Budapest for treason on March 12, 1946. Four of his aides, **Joseph Gera**, **Karoly Bereczky**, **Gabor Vaina** and **Ferenc Rajniss**, were also executed at this time.

Ferenc Szalasi was born in Kassa on January 6, 1897. He served in the Hungarian army, rising to the rank of major and serving on the general staff. He became the leader of the right-wing Hungarian Life Association in 1930. He was a proponent of Fascism and formed the Party of the Nation's Will after retiring from the military in 1935. He united his group with other Fascist organizations to form the Hungarian National Socialist Party two years later. The party was banned and Szalasi was arrested for conspiracy against the government in August of 1938. He was released in September of 1940 and became the leader of the Arrow-Cross Party. The regent, Miklos Horthy, was forced by the German occupiers to appoint Szalasi as prime minister on October 16, 1944, after Horthy tried to withdraw Hungary from World War II. Horthy was forced to abdicate and Szalasi also became head of state of a Fascist government. The Arrow-Cross movement conducted terrorist activities against its opponents during the final months of the war. His government fell when Hungary was liberated on April 4, 1945. Szalasi was arrested and sentenced to death by a people's tribunal.

• **Maximilien Blokzijl** (1885–1946), a Dutch Nazi broadcaster during the German occupation, was executed as a traitor in the Hague on March 16, 1946.

• Former Hungarian ministers **Eugen Szoelloesi**, **Baron Gabriel Kemeny** and **Sando Csia** were hanged for treason in Budapest on March 20, 1946.

• **Marcel Bucard**, the French blue-shirt Fascist leader, was executed for treason near Paris on March 20, 1946.

• **Marshal Doeme Sztojay**, another former Hungarian premier, was condemned to death for treason and executed by a firing squad in Budapest on March 22, 1946.

Dome Sztojay was born in Budapest on January 5, 1883. He served in the Hungarian army, rising to the rank of lieutenant general. Sztojay served as military attaché in Berlin from 1927 until 1933 and was named Hungary's ambassador to Germany in 1935. He was a leading supporter of Hungary's alliance with Germany during World War II. He returned to Budapest with German troops to assume control of the government as prime minister on March 22, 1944. His government functioned as a puppet to the German occupation forces and allowed the deportation of Hungarian Jews to death camps in Germany. Sztojay was forced to resign by moderate elements in the government on August 24, 1944, following the withdrawal of Romania from the war. He was arrested as a war criminal after the war and sentenced to death by a people's tribunal.

• **General Masaharu Homma**, who had led the Japanese invasion of the Philippines in 1941, was executed by a firing squad at Los Banos, Luzon, the Philippines, on April 3, 1946. **Lt. Gen. Hikotaro Tajima** was executed with Gen. Homma. Homma was born in Nigata in 1888. A member of the Japanese army, Gen. Homma served as an observer with the British during the First World War. Following a tour of duty as Japanese resident officer in India, Homma was appointed military attach in London in 1930. Shortly after the Japanese attack on Pearl Harbor, Gen. Homma led the Japanese forces that invaded and captured the Philippines. After the defeat of Japan, the general surrendered to the United States military authorities on September 14, 1945. He was brought to trial in Manila on January 3, 1946, on charges that he was responsible for the Bataan "death march" and other atrocities committed during the Japanese occupation. He was convicted on February 11, 1946, and executed two months later.

• **Andor Jaross**, a former Hungarian minister, was executed by firing squad in Budapest on April 11, 1946. He, his undersecretary **Dr. Vitz Laszlo Endre**, and **Laszlo Baky**, a former gendarme chief, had all been sentenced to death for war crimes on January 7, 1946.

• **Maj. Gen. Masataka Kaguragi**, along with four other Japanese officers, was hanged by United States authorities for war crimes in Shanghai on April 22, 1946.

• **Dr. Franz Anton Basch**, the German minority leader in Hungary, was executed for treason in Budapest on April 26, 1946.

• **Anton Mussert** (1894–1946), the Dutch Nazi party leader, was executed for treason on May 7, 1946. Mussert founded the Dutch National Socialist Movement in 1931, patterning his party on Benito Mussolini's Fascism. Following the rise of the Nazi party in Germany, Mussert became an admirer of Adolf Hitler and adopted many of Hitler's ideals, including the persecution of the Dutch Jews. After the German occupation of the Netherlands, Mussert was appointed by Hitler as the "leader of the Netherlands people" in December of 1942. Mussert was arrested following Germany's defeat in 1945, and was convicted of treason and collaboration with the enemy on December 12, 1945. He was executed by a firing squad in a small village near the Hague five months later.

• **Karl-Hermann Frank**, a leader of the Sudenten German party, was hanged for war crimes on May 22, 1946. Frank was born in Karlsbad on January 24, 1898. He became deputy to Konrad Henlein, the leader of the Sudenten German party, and was elected to the Czechoslovak parliament in 1937. After the Nazi occupation, Frank was appointed chief of police in Prague. On August 20, 1943, he was named Reich minister for the Protectorate of Bohemia and Moravia. He was arrested by the Allies at the end of the war, and handed over to the Czechoslovak government. Frank was charged with war crimes, and convicted and hanged near Prague.

• **William Hagelin**, the minister of the interior in Vidkun Quisling's (q.v.) wartime government in Norway, was executed for treason in Oslo on May 22, 1946.

• **Ion Antonescu**, the leader of the pro–German wartime government of Romania, was executed for war crimes on June 1, 1946, near Ft. Jilava. **Mihai Antonescu** (1904–46), who served as Ion Antonescu's deputy prime minister and foreign minister, and **George Alexeanu** and **Gen. Constantin Vasiliu**, two close aides to Antonescu were also executed.

Ion Antonescu was born on June 15, 1882, in Pitesti. He served in the Romanian army during World War I and, in December of 1937, he was named minister of defense. He was dismissed, because of his Fascist leanings, in February of 1938. Following a period of increasing civil disorders, Antonescu was appointed prime minister by King Carol II on September 4, 1940. He later forced the abdication of King Carol and government Romania as a dictator. Romania became closely allied with Nazi Germany and joined in the war against the Soviet Union in June of 1941. Antonescu was ousted by a coup led by King Michael, the son of King Carol, on August 23, 1944. He was imprisoned by the Soviet occupation forces and tried for war crimes.

• **Desider Laszlo**, the chief of staff of the Hungarian army during the war, was convicted of war crimes and shot by a firing squad on June 1, 1946.

• **Chen Kung-Po**, who served as president of Nanking under the Japanese, was executed for treason in Sochow on June 3, 1946.

• **Ananda Mahidol**, the king of Thailand, was shot to death in his chamber at the royal palace on June 9, 1946. Ananda Mahidol was born in Heidelberg, Germany, on September 20, 1925. The king, titled Rama VIII, assumed the throne of Thailand under a regency in 1935, following the abdication of his uncle, King Prajahlipok. The circumstances of his death have remained a mystery, but in 1954 the Thai Supreme Court ruled that the king had been murdered. Three people, including Ananda Mahidol's private secretary, were sentenced to death for complicity in the assassination.

• **Prof. Wen I-To**, a leading Chinese poet and scholar, and **Prof. Li Kung-Po** were murdered by agents of Chiang Kai-shek's Kuominang government on July 11, 1946. The victims were both members of the liberal Democratic League, and had been outspoken critics of the government's intellectual repression in the 1940s.

• **Gen. Draja Mihajlovic**, the Serbian army officer who served as leader of the Free Yugoslavian, or Chetnik, underground army during World War II, was executed for treason in Belgrade on July 17, 1946. The Yugoslavian government convicted Mihajlovic and twenty-three other defendants of treason and collaboration with the Nazis, **Milos Glisich**, a former Chetnik leader; **Radoslave-Rade Radich**, a former Chetnik unit commander; **Oskare Pavlovich**, the former police chief of Zagreb; **Dragomir Yovanovich**, the former police chief of Belgrade; **Tanisiji Dinish**, the former minister of the interior; **Djuro Dokich**, the former minister of commerce; **Velibor Ionich**, the former minister of education; and **Kosta Musicki**, an aide to Yugoslavia's King Peter, were executed with Mihajlovic. The remaining defendants were tried in absentia.

Gen. Mihajlovic was born in Serbia on March 27, 1893. He was serving in the Serbian army at the time of the German attack on Yugoslavia in April of 1941. Mihajlovic organized and led a guerrilla army, called Chetniks, to fight the German occupation forces. The Chetniks originally fought alongside a rival Communist-led resistance army under the leadership of Josip Broz, called Marshal Tito. Mihajlovic was appointed minister of war of the Yugoslav government in exile in January of 1942. Shortly after his appointment, Gen. Mihajlovic was accused of assisting the German army in eliminating his Communist rivals. The Allies began to give increasing support for Marshal Tito's army as Mihajlovic's loyalty was further questioned. After the liberation of Yugoslavia, Gen. Mihajlovic went into hiding, but he was captured by partisans on March 13, 1946. His subsequent trial and condemnation generated much controversy throughout Europe and the United States, but

Mihajlovic was executed despite pleas for mercy from the Western powers.

• On July 20, 1946, **Arthur Greiser**, who served as the Nazi Reich governor of the annexed western regions of Poland during World War II, was hanged for war crimes in Poznan. Greiser was born in Posen on January 22, 1897. He became a member of the Nazi party in 1929, and joined the S.S. in 1930. Greiser was elected deputy president of the Danzig senate in 1933, and became senate president the following year. He held that position until 1939, when he was appointed gauleiter of the Warthegau region in western Poland. He supervised the mass deportation of Poles and Jews from the areas in his jurisdiction. Greiser was captured by the Americans at the end of the war, and handed over to the Polish authorities to stand trial. He was convicted of wartime atrocities and publicly executed.

• **Gualberto Villarroel**, the president of Bolivia, was murdered during a revolt on July 21, 1946. Villarroel was born in 1908 and joined the Bolivian army. He fought against Paraguay in the Chaco War from 1932 until 1935, and became a leading figure in the Bolivian military. Villarroel became president of Bolivia following a military coup in December of 1943. During his administration he implemented reforms that benefited the tin miners and the Bolivian Indians. His labor and land reform programs met with bitter opposition from the tin industry and land owners, and resulted in a rebellion against his regime. The presidential palace in La Paz was attacked by a mob on July 21, 1946, and Villarroel was thrown from a balcony and lynched from a lamppost in the Plaza Murillo below.

• In August of 1946 **Gen. Andrei A. Vlasov**, **Gen. Sergei Bunyachenko**, and five other Soviet generals who had fought alongside the Germans during World War II were hanged for treason in Moscow. **Viktor I. Maltsev** (1894–46), a former Soviet Air Force officer who had helped train Soviet pilots for the German Luftwaffe, was also executed for treason.

Gen. Vlasov was born on September 1,

1900. He became a respected officer in the Soviet Red Army and commanded the Twentieth Army against the Germans in the battle of Moscow. He was captured by the Germans in July of 1941 at the Volkhov front. He was soon convinced by the Germans to lead an anti–Stalinist Russian Army of Liberation, consisting of Russian prisoners of war. The German-sponsored army saw little active members during World War II and surrendered to the Allies in 1945. Vlasov and the other officers were returned to the Soviet Union after the end of the war and condemned as traitors.

• **Vojtech Balu Tuka**, the Slovakian Fascist leader who served as premier and foreign minister in the Nazi-backed regime of Josef Tiso (q.v.) was sentenced to death as a collaborator on August 11, 1946. He was executed in Prague on August 20, 1946.

Tuka was born in 1880 in Slovakia of Hungarian parents. He was a professor at the Hungarian Law Academy in Bratislava. Slovak Populist Party leader Andrej Hlinka named Tuka editor of the party's newspaper *Slovak* in 1922. Tuka organized the para-military group Rodobrana, or Home Defense, the following year. He was elected to the chamber of deputies in 1925. Tuka was arrested and charged with treason in January of 1929. He was found guilty and sentenced to fifteen years in prison. He was amnestied by President Eduard Benes in June of 1937. He was named prime minister of the newly independent Slovakia by President Josef Tiso on November 2, 1939. He also served in the government as foreign minister from July of 1940. Tuka was an admirer of Adolf Hitler and led the country into a close alliance with Nazi Germany during World War II. He came into conflict with President Josef Tiso, but was able to remain head of the government with German support until September 5, 1944. Slovakia was conquered in April of 1945 and Tuka was subsequently arrested.

• **Robert Wagner**, the Reich governor of Alsace-Baden during World War II, was executed for war crimes in Strasbourg on August 14, 1946. Wagner was born in Lindach on October 13, 1895. He was an early follower of National Socialism and served as the Nazi gauleiter in Baden from 1925. In 1940 he was appointed Reich governor of Alsace in occupied France. He was responsible for the mass deportation of Jews in that area, until it was recaptured by the Allies in 1945. Wagner was imprisoned and tried for war crimes by a French military court.

• **Theodor von Renteln**, the Nazi commissioner general of Lithuania during World War II, was hanged by the Russians for war crimes in 1946. Von Renteln was born in Russia on September 14, 1897. He moved to Berlin in his youth and joined the Nazi party in 1928. He was appointed the leader of the Nazi Students' League and the Hitler Youth in 1931, serving until the following year. In August of 1941 von Renteln was appointed commissioner general of Lithuania, and was responsible for Nazi activities in that area. He was captured by the Russians at the conclusion of the war, and tried for atrocities committed during the war.

• Following the conclusion of World War II, many of the leading figures in Nazi Germany were tried before the International Military Tribunal at Nuremberg. Over a period of several years, 199 men were tried by the Tribunal. Thirty-six defendants were sentenced to death, twenty-two received life sentences, 103 received prison terms, 38 were acquitted, and five committed suicide during their trials. On September 30, 1946, the first trial of the major Nazi leaders was concluded. Eleven of the twenty-one defendants were sentenced to death by hanging. The sentence was carried out on October 15, 1946, for ten of the defendants. They included **Joachim von Ribbentrop, Wilhelm Keitel, Ernst Kaltenbrunner, Alfred Rosenberg, Hans Frank, Wilhelm Frick, Julius Streicher, Fritz Sauckel, Alfred Jodl**, and **Arthur Seyss-Inquart**. Hermann Goering (1893–1946), the leader of the German Luftwaffe and Adolf Hitler's second in command, cheated the hangman by taking poison several hours before his scheduled execution.

Joachim von Ribbentrop was born on April 30, 1893, in Wesel. He served in the German army during World War I, and later engaged in business as a wine merchant. He joined the Nazi party, shortly after meeting Adolf Hitler, in August of 1932. He served as the Fuhrer's chief advisor on foreign affairs after Hitler's appointment as chancellor the following year, and, in 1935, was named Germany's ambassador-at-large. He was appointed to Great Britain in August of 1936, serving in that position until he was named minister of foreign affairs in February of 1938. He negotiated the German-Soviet Non-aggression Pact in 1939, and was instrumental in developing the German, Italian, and Japanese alliance the following year. Von Ribbentrop was captured by the British in Hamburg in June of 1945, and indicted for war crimes. He was convicted of being "responsible for war crimes and crimes against humanity because of his activities with respect to occupied countries and Axis satellites," and was hanged at Nuremberg Prison on October 16, 1946.

Gen. Wilhelm Keitel was born on September 22, 1882, in Helmscherode. He served in the German army and was promoted to major general in 1934. In February of 1938 he was named by Adolf Hitler as chief of the armed forces high command. Keitel dictated the terms of armistice to France in June of 1940, and continued to serve as a leading military advisor to Hitler throughout the duration of World War II. Keitel was present at Rastenburg during the bomb attempt on Hitler's life on July 20, 1944, but was uninjured in the explosion. He later served as a member of the court which sentenced many of the military conspirators against the Nazi regime to death. On May 9, 1945, Keitel signed the articles of Germany's unconditional surrender to the Allies, and was subsequently arrested for war crimes. He was tried at Nuremberg by the International Military Tribunal. The verdict convicting him stated that

he "put pressure on Austria… signed the orders for the attack on Belgium and the Netherlands" and had otherwise planned and waged a war of aggression. He was hanged on October 16, 1946.

Ernst Kaltenbrunner was born in Austria on October 4, 1901. He served as a legal advisor to the Austrian Nazi party from 1932, and, after the German occupation in 1938, he was appointed chief of police for Austria. In 1943 Kaltenbrunner, by then a general in the S.S., was appointed chief of the Gestapo and the Nazi Security Police, succeeding Reinhard Heydrich (q.v.). In this position he was directly responsible for numerous atrocities committed by the Nazis. He was captured by an American patrol after Germany's defeat and tried for war crimes. He was found guilty of having "played a leading part in the extermination of the Jews" and hanged on October 16, 1946.

Alfred Rosenberg was born in Estonia on January 12, 1893. He was an early member of the Nazi party, and served as editor of the party newspaper, *Volkischer Beobachter*. He was a leading promoter of anti–Semitism. When Hitler was imprisoned following the unsuccessful Beer Hall Putsch in 1923, Rosenberg was named leader of the Nazi party. He was named to lead the Nazi party's foreign policy office in 1931 and, following Hitler's appointment as German chancellor in 1933, he continued to be a leading spokesman for Nazi philosophy. After the fall of France in 1940, Rosenberg was placed in charge of removing valuable artworks and transporting them to Germany. He was arrested by the Allies after Germany's defeat in World War II, and was tried for war crimes. He was convicted on all four charges and was judged "responsible for plunder throughout invaded countries." He was hanged at Nuremberg Prison on October 16, 1946.

Hans Frank was born in Baden on May 23, 1900. He joined the Nazi party in 1926 and subsequently became Adolf Hitler's legal advisor. In 1933 Frank was appointed state minister of justice. From 1939 until August of 1944 he served as Nazi governor general of Poland and was directly involved in the extermination of Polish Jews. He was arrested after the conclusion of World War II, and was tried at Nuremberg. He was convicted of "willing participation in a program involving the murder of three million Jews," and was hanged on October 16, 1946.

Wilhelm Frick was born in the Palatinate on March 12, 1877. He was an early member of the Nazi party, and participated with Adolf Hitler in the Munich Beer Hal Putsch in 1923. Frick was elected to the German Reichstag in 1924 and was appointed to the position of minister of the interior in Thuringia in 1930. Following the formation of the Nazi government in Germany in 1933, Frick was named minister of the interior for Germany, serving until 1943. On August 24 of that year he was appointed Reich protector of Bohemia and Moravia, serving there until the end of the war. He was captured by the Allies in 1945 and tried for war crimes. He was found guilty at Nuremberg for having been "largely responsible for bringing the German nation under the complete control of the Nazi party ... for the legislation which suppressed trade unions, the church and the Jews." He was hanged on October 16, 1946.

Julius Streicher was born in Upper Bavaria on February 12, 1885. He was the founder of the German Socialist party and, in 1921, he joined his groups with Adolf Hitler's Nazi party. The following year he began publication of *Der Sturmer*, a virulent anti–Semitic journal, which he edited until 1943. In 1925 Streicher was named the Nazi gauleiter of Franconia, a position he held until 1940, when his penchant for obscene conduct resulted in his dismissal. He was arrested following the end of the war, and tried on charges that his writings were used to incite the extermination of Jews. His verdict said, "his persecution of Jews was notorious" and that "as early as 1938 he began to call for the annihilation of the Jewish race." He was hanged at Nuremberg Prison on October 16, 1946.

Fritz Sauckel was born on October 27,

1894, in Hassurt am Main. He joined the Nazi party in 1923 and was appointed gauleiter of Thuringia in 1928. In 1932 he was named minister of the interior in Thuringia and, the following year he was appointed governor. Sauckel was appointed by Hitler as German commissioner general of manpower in occupied territories in 1942. He was arrested by the Allies following the end of World War II and convicted of having had "overall responsibility for the slave labor program." It was further charged that he was "aware of the ruthless methods ... used to obtain laborers and vigorously supported" those methods. He was hanged at Nuremberg Prison on October 16, 1946.

Gen. Alfred Jodl was born on May 10, 1890, in Qurzburg. He served in the German army during World War I and was named to the German general staff in 1919. An early supporter of Adolf Hitler, he was promoted to major general in 1939 and was named chief of the German general staff. He remained in this position for the duration of the war. On May 7, 1945, he signed the articles of surrender for the German army. Gen. Jodl was arrested and charged with war crimes and tried by the International Military Tribunal. He was found guilty of having been "in the strict military sense the actual planner of the war ... active in planning the attack on Czechoslovakia ... in preparing the Norwegian attack ... in planning against Greece and Yugoslavia." He was hanged at Nuremberg Prison on October 16, 1946.

Arthur Seyss-Inquart was born on July 22, 1892, in Moravia. He was a practicing lawyer in Vienna when, in 1931, he joined the Austrian Nazi party. He was a supporter of Anschluss, the Austrian union with Germany, and, under pressure from Germany, Seyss-Inquart was named Austrian minister of the interior on February 16, 1938. Following the resignation of Chancellor Kurt von Schuschnigg in March of 1938, Seyss-Inquart was appointed the Reich governor for Austria, a position he held until April 30, 1939. In October of that year he was named deputy to Hans Frank (q.v.), the Nazi governor of Poland, and the following May he was appointed Reich commissioner for German-occupied Holland. He was arrested by Canadian soldiers following the conclusion of World War II, and was tried for his role in the deportation of Dutch Jews and for the shooting of hostages. He was convicted at Nuremberg of "ruthless application of terrorism," and hanged on October 16, 1946.

Of the remaining defendants, Rudolf Hess (1894–1987), Walter Funk (1890–1960), and Eric Raeder (1876–1960) received life sentences). Baldurr von Schirach (1907–1974) and Albert Speer (1905–1981) were sentenced to twenty years' imprisonment. Constantin von Neurath (1873–1956) was sentenced to fifteen years' imprisonment and Karl Doenitz (1891–1980) was sentenced to ten years' imprisonment. Hjalmar H.G. Schacht (1877–1970), Hans Fritzsche (1900–1953), and Franz von Papen (1879–1969) were acquitted. Robert Ley (1890–1945), the leader of the German Labor Front from 1933 to 1945, was scheduled to have been tried with the other defendants, but committed suicide on October 24, 1945, before the trials commenced. Martin Bormann (1900–45), the Nazi party secretary from 1940 to 1945, was tried and sentenced to death in absentia, but it was later believed that he had been killed on May 1, 1945, while trying to escape from the advancing Russian armies.

A number of other important Nazi figures took their own lives during and after the war, many of whom would have certainly been charged with war crimes. The most prominent suicide was that of Adolf Hitler (1889–1945), the founder and leader of the Nazi party and chancellor of the German Third Reich. He and his mistress, Eva Braun (1912–45), committed suicide in his bunker in Berlin on April 29, 1945. Joseph Goebbels (1897–1945), the leading Nazi propagandist and one of Hitler's closest advisors, killed himself, his wife, and their six children, on May 1, 1945. Heinrich Himmler (1900–45), the head of the Gestapo and the Waffen-S.S. and Hitler's minister of the interior from 1943 to 1945, took poison on May 23, 1945, while

in British custody. Bernhard Rust (1883–1945), the Reich minister of science, education and popular culture from 1934 to 1945; Konrad Henlein (1898–1945), the Reich governor of the Sudentenland; Josef Terboven (1898–1945), the Reich commissar in Norway, Third Reich historian Walter Frank (1905–45); Philip Bouhler (1899–1945), the head of the Nazi euthanasia program; Adm. Hans von Friedeburg (1895–1945), the last supreme commander of the German Navy; and air force general Robert Ritter von Greim (1892–1945) all committed suicide in May of 1945. Josef Burckel (1894–1944), the Nazi governor of Austria, killed himself on September 28, 1944, and Leonard Conti (1900–45), the Reich minister of health, committed suicide on October 6, 1945. Theodor Dannecker (1913–45), the S.S. captain in charge of the deportation of Jews from France, Bulgaria, and Italy, ended his own life on December 10, 1945. Field Marshal Walther Model (1891–1945) chose suicide rather than capture on April 18, 1945. Otto Thierack (1889–1946), the Reich minister of justice and one-time president of the People's Court, killed himself on October 26, 1946. Thierack's successor as president of the People's Court, Roland Freisler (1893–1945), was killed on February 3, 1945, but Allied bombing while he was sitting on the bench. Ludwig Muller (1883–1946), Reich bishop and leader of the German Faith Movement, killed himself in March of 1946. Gen. Otto von Stuelpnagel (1878–1948), the military governor of France from 1940 to 1942, committed suicide on February 6, 1948, and Herbert Backe (1896–1947), the Reich minister of agriculture and food, killed himself on April 6, 1947. Walter Buch (1883–1949), the president of the Nazi party Supreme Court, committed suicide on November 12, 1949, following his conviction for war crimes.

• **Col. Gen. Kurt Daluege** (1897–1946), of the German Nazi Police, was executed for war crimes in Czechoslovakia on October 23, 1946. Daluege had served as deputy protector of Bohemia and Moravia after the assassination of Reinhard Heydrich (q.v.) in 1942, and was responsible for the Nazi retaliation against the Czechs. He was responsible for giving the order to destroy the Czech village of Lidice shortly after Heydrich's death.

• **Gen. Ferenc Szombathely**, the former Hungarian chief of staff, was executed with a number of aides on November 6, 1946, at Novi Sad. He was convicted of war crimes and of having organized the massacre of Serbo-Croatians in 1942.

• **Gen. August Meissner**, head of the Gestapo's regional bureau in Belgrade, Yugoslavia, was hanged in December of 1946, with eight other senior S.S. officers.

• **Marshal Sladko Kvaternik**, the Croatian separatist leader, was hanged in 1946 as a collaborator. Kvaternik was an ally of Croatian leader Ante Pavelic and served as his premier when Pavelic announced Croatia's independence in April of 1941.

• **Otomar Kula**, the Czech anti–Semite leader, was executed in 1946 for war crimes and treason.

# 1947

• **Pyotr N. Krasnov** (1869–1947), a Cossack commander who was a leader of the pro–German Russian Liberation Army, was captured by the British in May of 1945. He was returned to the Soviet Union, where he was tried for treason and hanged in January of 1947. Krasnov led a Cossack division during the First World War. He was commander of the Don Cossacks in 1918, and fought against the Bolsheviks. He left Russia after the civil war and settled in Germany. He joined with Gen. Andrei Vlasov's (q.v.) pro–German forces during World War II. Krasnov and other senior Cossack officers who fought with the Germans were repatriated after the war

and executed including **Gen. Andrei Shkuro**.

• On February 10, 1947, **Brig. Gen. R.W.M. De Winten**, the commander of the British Thirteenth Infantry Brigade, was shot to death in Pola, Italy, by an Italian woman. The assailant was angered over Pola having been given to Yugoslavia following the war.

• **A.E. Conquest**, the deputy superintendent of police in Haifa, Palestine, was assassinated by a Jewish gunman on February 26, 1947.

• **Col. Gen. Alexander Lohr** (1885–1947), a German Luftwaffe officer who commanded troops in the Balkans during World War II, was hanged for war crimes on March 16, 1947, in Yugoslavia. Lohr served in the Austro-Hungarian army during World War I. He served in the army of the Austrian Republic as an air officer following the end of the war, and was named commander of the Austrian air force in 1936. In 1938 Lohr became a general in the German Luftwaffe, taking part in the Polish, Balkans, and Russian campaigns. From 1942 he was stationed in the Balkans, and it was during this period that he was judged to have committed war crimes.

• On March 27, 1947, **Col. Gen. Karol Swierczewski** (1897–1947), the Polish vice minister of national defense, was assassinated near Sanok, Poland, by members of the Ukrainian underground. Gen. Swierczewski had fought with the Russians during World War I and had participated in the Russian Revolution. He later served as a professor in the Moscow Military School. In 1936, during the Spanish Civil War, he served as a military advisor to the republican forces.

• **Qadhi Muhammad**, the leader of a Kurdish separatist movement in Iraq, was hanged with two associated in the main square of Mahabad on March 31, 1947. Qadhi Muhammad was a leading citizen and jurist in Mahabad. He had joined the Kurdish autonomy movement in October of 1944 and founded the Kurdish Democratic Party the following year. He had proclaimed the autonomous Republic of Mahabad in January of 1946. The Iranian army crushed his forces and he surrendered in December of 1946. He was tried and sentenced to death for his rebellion.

• **Rudolf Hoess**, a German S.S. officer who served as director of the Auschwitz concentration camp from 1940 to 1943, was hanged on April 15, 1947, at Auschwitz. Hoess was born on November 25, 1900, in Baden-Baden. He joined the Nazi party in 1922 and the S.S. in 1934. He was stationed at Dachau concentration camp later in the year. Following a tour of duty as Sachsenhausen, from 1938 until 1940, he was appointed commandant at Auschwitz on May 1, 1940. During his three years at Auschwitz he was responsible for the extermination of over two million prisoners. In 1943 he was named deputy inspector general of concentration campus under Richard Gluecks (q.v.). Hoess was captured on March 2, 1946, and given over to the Polish government. He was tried by a Polish military tribunal in March of 1947, and executed the following month.

• **Fernand De Brinon**, a leading French collaborationist with the Germans, was executed by firing squad in Forte De Montrouge on April 15, 1947. De Brinon was born on August 16, 1887, in Libourne, Gironde. He was a leading supporter of Franco-German reconciliation between the wars, and was active in the establishment of the Vichy regime following the German occupation. De Brinon was appointed the Vichy government's ambassador to occupied Paris in November of 1940. Following the collapse of the Vichy regime in September of 1944, he was involved in an attempt to form another pro–German government, but met with little success. He was captured by the Allies near the end of the war and tried for treason.

• **Huynh Phu So**, the founder and prophet of the Hoa Hao, a Vietnamese peasant movement, was executed by Communists on April 16, 1947. Huynh Phu So was born in Hoa Hao village, near the province of Chau Doc in 1919. He began his evangelical calling in 1939, converting over two million people to his movement. He was detained by the French colonial authorities on several occasions. In 1945 he founded the Union of Buddhist Associations and the Movement for Vietnam Independence, and the Vietnamese Democratic Socialist Party in September of 1946. He was ambushed and killed by communists at Doc Vang, in the Plain of Reeds, in 1947.

• **Josef Tiso**, the pro–German president of Slovakia during World War II, was hanged for treason in Bratislava, Czechoslovakia, on April 18, 1947. Tiso was born at Velka Bytca in Hungary on October 13, 1887. He became a Catholic priest in 1909, and became a leading member of the nationalist Slovak People's party following World War I. He was elected chairman of the party when Andrej Hlinka died in August of 1938, and in October of that year became premier of Slovakia. He was selected as president of independent Slovakia on October 26, 1939, and allied his country with the German war effort. He was ousted from office following the Soviet and Czechoslovak capture of the capital of Bratislava in April of 1945. Tiso was arrested by the American army on May 21, 1945, and handed over to the new Czech government. His trial began in Bratislava on December 2, 1946, and Tiso was convicted of "conspiring against the Czechoslovak republic, suppressing democratic freedom and establishing a Fascist dictatorship, warring against Poland and the Soviet Union and committing war crimes."

• On July 12, 1947, United States Senator John W. Bricker (1893–1986) of Ohio was uninjured in a shooting incident in the Senate office building in Washington, D.C. The attempted assassin was identified as William Kaiser, a former police officer. Bricker, a former Ohio governor, had run unsuccessfully for the United States vice presidency on the Republican ticket in 1944.

• **Sir Shafa'at Ahmad Khan**, a member of the Moslem League, was stabbed to death in Simla, India, on July 18, 1947. Khan was murdered shortly after having joined the interim Indian government.

• On July 19, 1947, five armed men attacked the executive council chamber in Rangoon, Burma, assassinating the chairman of the council, **U Aung San**, and seven other members of the council. The council members killed included Aung San's elder brother, Commerce and supplies member **U Ba Win**, education and planning member **Abdul Bazak**, industry and labor member **Mahn Ba Khaing**, Socialist party leader and finance member **Thakin Mya**, transport and communications deputy secretary **Ohn Maung**, frontier areas counselor **Sao Sam Htun**, the sawba of Mong Pawn, and information member **U Ba Choe**. Most of those killed were members of Aung San's political party, the Anti-Fascist People's Freedom League. Several leading opponents of the new government were arrested for complicity in the assassination. On May 8, 1948, six Burmese citizens, including former premier **U Saw**, were executed for their participation in the crime.

U Aung San was born in Burma in 1914. He attended Rangoon University and, as a student there, spent time in prison for subversive activities conducted as a member of a nationalist movement. He fled to Japan near the start of World War II and was trained by the military. Following the Japanese occupation of Burma, Aung San founded the Burmese Anti-Fascist People's Freedom League, joining together the various nationalist movements in Burma to fight with the Allies. After the defeat of the Japanese, Aung San pressured the British into granting autonomy for Burma. He served as defense and external affairs counselor in the first interim government. He succeeded in achieving an agreement with Britain regarding Burmese independence and, in April of 1947 his party won an overwhelming majority in the election of a constituent assembly. Aung San was almost certain to become the leader of independent Burma before his death at the hands of political opponents.

• **Lyuh Woon-Heung**, the chairman of the People's party and a leading Korean anti–Communist, was assassinated on July 19, 1947, in Seoul, South Korea, while riding in a car.

• On September 12, 1947, **Sami Taha** (1916–47), the secretary general of the Arab Labor Federation, was shot and killed on a street in Haifa, Palestine. Taha was a leading political foe of Haj Amin el-Husseini, the exiled grand mufti of Jerusalem.

• **Nikola Dimitrov Petkov**, a leading Bulgarian politician, was hanged in Sofia on September 23, 1947, following a trial which accused him of plotting a coup d'etat. Petkov, who was born in 1889, was an early member of the Bulgarian Agrarian National Union. He was imprisoned on numerous occasions for subversive activities during the 1920s and 1930s. During World War II he became a leader of the Bulgarian Resistance, and achieved victory for his party in September of 1944. His inability to work out a compromise with the Russian-backed Communist party resulted in his resignation the following year. Petkov continued to advocate an Agrarian-Communist coalition government for Bulgaria, and, in June of 1947, he was arrested on charges of planning a military coup. He was subsequently convicted and executed, despite the protests of Great Britain and the United States.

• On October 10, 1947, **Dr. Truong Dinh Tri**, the head of the Hanoi municipal council, was seriously injured in a grenade attack. He died the following day.

• **Alberto Bellardi Ricci**, the retiring Italian minister to Sweden, was stabbed to death by Giuseppe Caopocci, an Italian Fascist and mental patient, on December 25, 1947. Ricci, who had been appointed as Italy's minister to Chile, was attending a farewell party in his honor at the time of his attack.

---

# 1948

---

• **Mohandas K. Gandhi**, the leading Indian Hindu nationalist and spiritual leader, was assassinated by a Hindu extremist on January 30, 1948, while attending a prayer meeting at his residence at Birla House in New Delhi. Gandhi was born in Porbandar, India, on October 2, 1869. He studied law in London in the late 1880s and, after several years of practicing law in India, he went to South Africa in 1893. It was there that he first instituted his non-violent "passive resistance" to what he considered unjust and discriminatory laws. In January of 1915 Gandhi returned to India and soon after began a campaign for the political independence of India from Great Britain. In 1919 he organized the Satyagraha, a movement advocating non-cooperation with the British authorities. His movement escalated during the 1920s, and riots and violence resulted from some of his overenthusiastic followers' confrontations with the British authorities. Gandhi was arrested on charges of sedition in 1922 and sentenced to six years in prison, though he was released two years later for reasons of health. In 1925 he was elected president of the Indian National Congress, and was again imprisoned briefly in 1931 for advocating civil disobedience against the British salt tax. He resigned from leadership of the Congress party in 1934, but remained the leading spokesman for Indian independence. Gandhi was again arrested during World War II and remained in detention until 1944. In 1946 the British announced their intention to withdraw from India, and the following year they decided that Moslem Pakistan would be partitioned from Hindu-dominated India. Gandhi disapproved of this plan, advocating that Indian Hindus and Moslems should live and work together in harmony. Religious riots followed Independence Day on August 15, 1947, and Gandhi soon after announced his intention to fast until the killings ended. The violence rapidly abated due to the tremendous love and respect the Indian people felt for the Mahatma. In January of 1948 he began another fast which resulted in a pact by the Indian government guaranteeing the safety of the Moslem minority. Later in the month Gandhi was shot and killed by Nathuram V. Godse, a

radical Hindu, who felt Gandhi had betrayed the Hindus by criticizing anti–Moslem riots. Godse and other Hindu radicals, including Narayan Dattatraya Apte, Vishnu Ramrishkhma Karkare, Madan Lal, Gopal Vinayak Godse, Dattalraya Sadashiv Parchure, Shankar Kistayya, and Kashmirilal Pahwa, were tried for the murder. Godse and Apte were convicted and hanged at Ambala Jail on November 15, 1949. The other members of the conspiracy were sentenced to prison.

• **Yahya Ben Mohammad Ben Hamid Ed Din**, the imam of Yemen from 1904, was assassinated along with his chief minister, on February 17, 1948. Imam Yahya was born in 1876 and, in 1904 succeeded his father as the head of the Zaidi sect of the Shi'ite Moslems, thus becoming the hereditary monarch of Yemen. Yahya was initially opposed to the Turkish occupation of Yemen, but in 1911 he reached an accommodation with the Sultan which resulted in the independence of Yemen. After the collapse of the Turkish empire following World War I, Yahya became embroiled in several territorial disputes with Great Britain which were not settled until the signing of the Anglo-Yemini treaty in 1934. Later the same year Yahya engaged in a brief and unsuccessful war with Saudi Arabia. Yemen became more involved in regional and international affairs following World War II, joining the Arab League in 1945 and the League of Nations in 1946. There was a premature report of the imam's death by natural causes in January of 1948, and his announced successor was **Sayyid Abdullah Ibn Ahmed Al Wazir**. Yahya was indeed dead by the end of the following month, the victim of an assassination. Sayyid Abdullah proclaimed himself the new imam and a brief civil war broke out, with two of Yahya's sons being killed in street fighting. The murdered imam's eldest son, Ahmad (q.v.), the crown prince, raised an army of royalist supporters and deposed the usurper Sayyid Abdullah, who was tried and executed with many of his followers on April 8, 1948. Ahmad was himself then proclaimed imam of Yemen.

- **Dieter Wisliceny**, a major in the S.S. who was responsible for the deportation and murder of Jews in Eastern Europe, was executed for war crimes in Bratislava, Czechoslovakia, on February 27, 1948. Wisliceny was born in Rugularken on January 13, 1911, and became a member of the Nazi party in 1931. He joined the S.S. in 1934, and in September of 1940 he was appointed an advisor to the Slovak government on handling the extermination of Jews. In 1943 he organized the deportation of Jews from Greece, and the following year he was appointed deputy to Adolf Eichmann (q.v.) in Budapest, Hungary. He was arrested by the Allies at the end of the war and was handed over to the Czechoslovak government to stand trial for wartime atrocities.

- **Jorge Eliecer Gaitan**, a Colombian liberal politician, was shot to death in Bogota on April 9, 1948. Gaitan was born in Bogota on January 26, 1902. He studied law and entered Colombian politics in the late 1920s. He was elected mayor of Bogota in 1935 and served in the cabinet of President Eduardo Santos as minister of labor. Gaitan ran for the presidency of Colombia in 1946 as a Liberal party candidate, but was defeated by Mariano Ospina Perez. In 1947 he became leader of the Liberal party. The following year, while planning another campaign for the presidency, Gaitan was assassinated by Juan Roa Sierra, a chauffeur, in the streets of Bogota. The assassin was subsequently killed by an angry mob.

- On April 20, 1948, Walter P. Reuther (1907–69), the president of the United Auto Workers labor union, was seriously injured by a shotgun blast fired through a window of his home. The labor leader's assailant was not identified, and Reuther recovered from his injuries and resumed his duties. Reuther's brother, Victor Reuther (b. 1912), who was also active in the labor movement, was injured in an assassination attempt the following year. He also recovered from his injuries.

- Mustafa el-Nahas (1876–1965), a former premier of Egypt, was uninjured in an assassination attempt on April 25, 1948. An automobile filled with explosives blew up in front of Nahas' home in Cairo.

- **Jan Masaryk**, a Czechoslovak statesman and diplomat, died on March 10, 1948, from a fall from the window of his room in the Foreign Office. Masaryk was born on September 14, 1886, in Prague. His father was Thomas Masaryk, the first president of the Czechoslovak Republic. Jan Masaryk joined the Czechoslovak Foreign Office in 1919, and in 1925 was appointed minister to London. He served at that post until 1938, when he resigned in protest of the Munich Pact, which resulted in the dismemberment of Czechoslovakia. From 1941 until 1945 Masaryk served as foreign minister and deputy prime minister in the Czechoslovak government-in-exile in London. He remained foreign minister in the post-war government, and stayed in office following the Communist-led coup on February 25, 1948. His death was announced by the Czech government as a suicide, but speculation exists that it was likely that Masaryk was pushed or thrown from his third-story office in the Czernin Palace in Prague.

- **Christop Ladas** (1891–1948), the Greek minister of justice and Liberal party secretary, was killed in a grenade attack on his car in Athens on May 1, 1948. The assassin was identified as Eustratos Moutosyannis, a member of a Communist terrorist group.

- **Maj. Augustin Sram**, a Czechoslovak Communist leader, was assassinated in Prague, Czechoslovakia, on May 27, 1948.

- Seven S.S. and concentration camp officials who had been convicted by the United States military tribunal at Nuremberg of war crimes in the "Doctors' Trial" on August 20, 1947, were hanged on June 2, 1948, at Landsberg Prison. The seven included S.S. **Gen. Karl Brandt** (1904–48), Adolf Hitler's personal physician and leading medical officer for Nazi Germany; **Viktor Brack** (1903–48), the chief S.S. administrative officer, who was personally responsible for the euthanasia program used against German "undesirables" and the construction of death camps in Poland

and the Soviet Union; **Joachim Murgow-sky** (1905–48), the chief S.S. hygienist; **Prof. Karl Gebhardt** (1897–1948), the head S.S. surgeon; **Wolfram Sievers**, an ex–Military Research Institute director; **Waldemar Hoven**, the chief medical officer at Buchen-wald; and **Rudolf Brandt**, the chief of the S.S. Hygienic Institute.

• On August 22, 1948, **Dr. Joseph F. Buehler**, the former state secretary of Poland during the Nazi occupation, was hanged for war crimes in Cracow, Poland.

• On September 1, 1948, **Juan Arevalo y Veitia**, a 56-year-old Cuban anti–Commu-nist labor leader, was shot to death by assas-sins in Havana, Cuba.

• **Count Folke Bernadotte of Wis-borg**, a Swedish diplomat representing the United Nations in Palestine, was assassinated in Jerusalem by three Jewish terrorists on Sep-tember 17, 1948. **Andre Serot**, a French colonel who was accompanying the count, was also killed in the attack.

Bernadotte was born in Sweden on Jan-uary 2, 1895, the nephew of King Gustavus V. He became a leading international statesman through his work with the Swedish Red Cross and the International Boy Scouts. During World War II he was active in attempting to insure the proper treatment of captured sol-diers from both sides of the conflict. Near the end of the war he became directly involved in negotiations instigated by leading Nazis, in-cluding Heinrich Himmler, to reach a peace settlement with the Allies, excluding the So-viet Union. Though this plan proved unac-ceptable, Bernadotte's reputation as a media-tor remained untarnished. Following the outbreak of hostilities in the Middle East dur-ing 1948, Bernadotte was called upon by the United Nations Security Council to serve as their mediator in the conflict on May 20, 1948. He succeeded in negotiating a cease-fire, but was slain by members of the Stern Gang, a Jewish terrorist organization, before he could complete his mission. Two members of the Stern Gang, Yehoshua Zeitler and Meshulam Markover, acknowledged in 1988

that they had been part of the team that mur-dered Bernadotte, and that Yehoshua Cohen had shot both men. Yitzhak Shamir, who later served as prime minister of Israel, was the leader of the Stern Gang, though he denied al-legations that he was involved with the assas-sination.

• On September 17, 1948, **U Tin Tun**, the former foreign minister of Burma and the leader of the Anti-Fascist People's Freedom League, was seriously injured in a car bomb-ing in Rangoon. The 53-year-old Burmese politician died the following day.

• **Amir Sjarifuddin**, the Indonesian na-tionalist leader who served as the second prime minister of the Republic of Indonesia, was executed in December of 1948 following his participation in a Communist uprising. Amir Sjarifuddin was a co-founder of the left-wing Gerino party (Indonesian People's Movement) in 1947. He served in that posi-tion until January of 1948. He lent his support to the abortive Communist rebellion later in the year. Following the army's suppression of the coup, Sjarifuddin was captured and sub-sequently executed.

• **R.M. Suripino**, the former Indonesian Republican envoy to Central Europe, and **Hadjono**, the secretary of the Indonesian Communist party, were also executed in De-cember of 1948 for their role in the rebellion.

• **Selim Zaki Pasha**, the chief of the Cairo city police in Egypt, was assassinated on December 8, 1948, by a member of the Mus-lim Brotherhood, a nationalist organization.

• The major Japanese war crimes trial was held during 1948 at the Tokyo International Military Tribunal. Twenty-seven Japanese criminals were to be tried at that time. Of that number, seven received the death penalty and were executed on December 23, 1948. They included **Gen. Hideki Tojo**, Japan's war-time premier; **Gen. Kenji Doihara** (1883–1948), who was responsible for the Mukden incident in 1931 which led to Japan's attack on Manchuria and who served as commander of Japanese forces in Malaya, Sumatra, and Java during World War II; **Gen. Heitaro Kimura** (1888–1948), Japan's vice minister of war under Premier Tojo; **Gen. Iwame Matsui** (1878–1948), who commanded the Japanese forces during the destruction of Nanking; **Gen. Akira Muto** (1883–1948), who served as the Japanese army's chief of staff in the Philippine campaign; **Koki Hirota** (1878–1948), Japan's premier from 1936 to 1937; and **Seishiro Itagaki** (1885–1948), who served as Japan's minister of war during much of World War II. Gen. Sadao Araki (1877–1966), Gen. Kuniaki Koiso (1880–1950), Gen. Jiro Minami (1874–1955), Gen. Kenryo Sato, Gen. Teichi Suzuki (1889–1989), Gen. Yoshijiro Umezu (1882–1949), Marshal Shunroku Hata (1879–1962), Col. Kingoro Hashimoto (1890–1957), Adm. Takasumi Oka, Adm. Shigetaro Shimada (1883–1976), Baron Kiichiro Hiranuma (1867–1952), Haoki Hoshino (1892–1978), Okinori Kaya (1889–1977), Loichi Kido (1889–1977), Hiroshi Oshima (1886–1975), and Toshio Shiratori (1887–1949) all received terms of life imprisonment. Foreign Minister Mamoru Shigemitsu (1887–1957) was sentenced to seven years' imprisonment. Yosuke Matsuoka (1880–1946) and Osami Nagano (1888–1947) both died before the trials began, and Shumei Okawa (1886–1957) was removed from the trial due to mental illness.

Hideki Tojo, who was born on December 30, 1884, was a graduate of the Tokyo Imperial Military Academy. After serving as military attaché at the Japanese Embassy in Berlin, Tojo served in various positions in the Japanese War Office in Tokyo. In 1937 he was named chief of staff of the Kwantung army in Manchuria, and the following year he was named vice minister of war. He was appointed minister of war in July of 1940 and, on October 16, 1941, became Japan's premier as well. He remained as leader of Japan during much of the war period, also assuming the post of chief of the general staff. In July of 1944 Tojo was forced to resign following major setbacks by the Japanese forces, including the successful invasion of the Mariana Islands by the United States. Tojo made an unsuccessful sui-cide attempt following Japan's surrender on September 11, 1945, but recovered and was subsequently arrested as a war criminal.

Koki Hirota was a leading nationalist and a respected member of the Japanese diplomatic corps. He served as Japan's ambassador to the Soviet Union from 1930 until 1932. In 1933 he was named foreign minister, a position he held until March of 1936, when he was named premier. He served as premier until June of 1937, when he again became foreign minister until 1938. Hirota was a supporter of Japanese expansion, and implemented the Anti-Comintern Pact, which linked Japanese policy with that of Germany and Italy, during his term of office. He was arrested after the United States occupation of Japan and tried as a war criminal.

• **Mahmoud Fahmy El-Nokrashy Pasha** (1888–1948), the prime minister of Egypt, was assassinated by a member of the Moslem Brotherhood on December 28, 1948. Nokrashy Pasha, a former teacher, had joined the Egyptian government in 1920 and had served in various posts during the 1920s and 1930s. He was Egyptian minister of the interior, education, and finance from 1938 to 1940. In 1945 he was elected president of the Saadist party and became prime minister of Egypt on February 25, 1945, following the assassination of Ahmed Maher Pasha (q.v.). He was force to resign on February 15, 1946, but was again appointed prime minister in December of 1946. Nokrashy Pasha was named Egypt's military government following Egypt's invasion of Palestine on May 14, 1948. He was a supporter of Egypt's policy advocating the elimination of the state of Israel, and was a proponent of the withdrawal of English forces from the Anglo-Egyptian Sudan. Nokrashy Pasha's assassin, Abdel Hamid Ahmed Hassan (1927–48), was a member of the Moslem Brotherhood, an extremist organization the prime minister had outlawed earlier in the month. The Brotherhood was critical of Nokrashy Pasha's inability to produce a military victory against Israel. Hassan was tried and executed for the murder soon after, and numerous members of the Brotherhood were arrested as a result of the murder.

# 1949

• Mohammad Reza Pahlavi (1919–80), the shah of Iran, was shot and wounded in Teheran on February 4, 1949. The Shah recovered from his injuries and his attempted assassin, Fakhr Rai, a member of the leftist Tudeh party, was killed by an angry mob.

• **Sheikh Hasan Al-Banna**, the leader of the nationalist Egyptian Moslem Brotherhood, was murdered in the streets of Cairo by government agents on February 13, 1949. Banna was born in Mahmudiyya, near Alexandria, in October of 1906. He was trained as a teacher, and taught Islamic principles in Ismailia and other cities. He formed the Society of Muslim Brothers in 1928 and a teaching society, but it evolved into a political organization after its headquarters moved to Cairo in 1932. Banna gained numerous followers in his attempt to transform Egypt into an Islamic state. He started the daily newspaper *al-Ikhwan al-Muslimun* and backed a slate of candidates for the Chamber of Deputies. His organization was militantly opposed to the United Nations' decision to partition Palestine and often came into conflict with the Egyptian government. Prime Minister Mahmoud Fahmy El-Nokrashy's (q.v.) assassination by a Muslim Brotherhood student in 1948 preceded Banna's own murder the following year.

• Four Iraqi Communist leaders, **Yusuf Salman Yusuf** (known as Fahd), who served as secretary general of the Iraqi Communist Party from 1941 to 1949, Politboro members **Saki Muhammad Basim** and **Husain Muhammad Al-Shabibi**, and **Yahuda Ibrahim Siddiq** were arrested and charged with taking part in a Communist uprising in 1948. They were sentenced to death and publicly hanged on February 13, 1949.

• **Tan Malaka**, a founder and leader of the Indonesian Communist party, was executed by the Indonesian army on April 16, 1949. Tan Malaka, who had led the Indonesian Communist Party (PKI) in the 1920s, had been exiled by the Dutch colonial government in 1922. In 1927 he organized the Indonesian Republican party (PARI) while in exile in Siam. During his years in exile he helped organize Communist groups in the Philippines, Malaya and Singapore. He returned to Indonesia in 1942 and collaborated with the Japanese during World War II. In 1946 he led an unsuccessful coup against the Indonesian government. The Indonesian army suppressed the attempted overthrow and captured Tan Malaka and many of his supporters Tan Malaka was released from prison in 1948, shortly before the start of an uprising led by Musso, the Russian-backed leader of the Indonesian Communist party. Tan Malaka, a nationalist Communist, took no part in this coup attempt, and Musso was subsequently killed in battle. Tan Malaka then formed the Parta Murba (Proletarian party). His ambition to govern Indonesia was cut short in April of 1949, when he was captured by the army and executed.

• On June 11, 1949, **Gen. Koci Xoxe** (Kochi Rodze), the former leader of the Albanian Communist party, was shot following his trial and conviction for anti–Soviet tendencies. Xoxe was born in Korce on May 1, 1911. He became active in political opposition to King Zog I and was imprisoned on several occasions. In 1941, during the Italian occupation of Albania, Xoxe founded the Albanian Communist party and, in 1943, organized the Albanian Liberation party. In March of 1946 he also became minister of the interior and deputy prime minister. As the virtual leader of Albania from 1946 through 1948, Xoxe was active in planning the unification of Albania with Yugoslavia. The break by Marshal Tito of Yugoslavia with the Soviet Union, and Tito's subsequent expulsion from the Cominform, put an end to this plan and resulted in Xoxe's own fall from power. He was dismissed from his positions and arrested on October 6, 1948. He was tried by the Albanian Supreme Court in Tirane and executed following his conviction.

• **Gen. Heliodor Pika** (1897–1949), a former Czechoslovak deputy chief of staff, was executed by hanging for treason in Bory prison in Pizen by the Communist government on June 21, 1949.

• **Kim Koo** (1876–1949), a Korean rightist revolutionary and the leader of the Korean Independence party, was assassinated at his home in Seoul, South Korea, on June 26, 1949. Kim Koo was a former president of the Korean provisional government and had been head of the exiled Korean government in China before he split with President Syngman Rhee. He was also a bitter opponent of the division of Korea. Kim Koo was shot to death by Lt. Ahn Doo-Hee, a Korean army officer, following a political quarrel at his home. Convicted of the killing, Ahn was sentenced to prison for life, but was released several months later. It was speculated that Ahn had acted at the behest of the United States Counter-Intelligence Corps. He returned to the army and was promoted to captain in 1951. 47 years later Ahn was beaten to death at his Seoul home on October 23, 1996, allegedly by members of a militant group seeking revenge for the slaying of Kim Koo.

• **Col. Francisco Javier Arana**, the chief of the Guatemalan armed forces, was assassinated near Lake Amatitlan outside of Guatemala City on July 18, 1949. Arana was the military leader of the revolution in 1944 and a leading potential candidate to succeed president Juan Jose Arevelo of Guatemala. The Guardia de Honor army garrison briefly revolted in the wake of the assassination, but the rebellion was quickly quelled.

• On August 14, 1949, a coup by army officers in Syria resulted in the death of the President, **Husni al-Zaim**, and his prime minister, **Mushin Barazi**. Zaim and Barazi were seized in Damascus by rebellious army officers led by Col. Sami Hinnawi (q.v.), who were distressed by the government's aim of

cutting down the size of the armed forces. Both leaders were tried and quickly executed.

Husni al-Zaim was born in Aleppo in 1897. He served in the Ottoman army and fought against the Arabians during World War I. He joined the French army in Syria in 1920. During World War II Zaim fought against the Allies as part of the Vichy controlled forces. He was briefly imprisoned by the Allies following the conclusion of the war. After his release he was appointed inspector-general of the Syrian police. Zaim was promoted to colonel in May of 1948 and was appointed chief of staff of the Syrian army after the Palestine War. He led a military coup against the government of Shukri el-Kuwatli on March 30, 1949. The following week he took control of the government as prime minister, minister of defense and minister of the interior. In June of 1949 he sponsored a referendum that elected him president of the Syrian Republic. He began a number of reforms which were initially popular. Zaim was forced to deal with Syria's troubled financial situation by increasing taxation, however. He tried to model his regime on Kemal Ataturk's of Turkey and this offended Muslim fundamentalists in the country. He also lost much of his support in the military, which eventually led to his ouster and execution.

Mushin Barazi was born in Hama in 1893. He entered politics and served in several cabinets during the 1940s. He served as a person assistant to President Shukri el-Kuwatli in the late 1940s. Barazi was appointed prime minister on June 26, 1949, following the ouster of Kuwatli and the selection of Husni al-Zaim as president. He suffered the same fate as Zaim as the two men were ousted and summarily executed in August of 1949.

• **Laszlo Rajk** (1909–49), a leading Hungarian Communist politician, was hanged on October 15, 1949, after having been found guilty of charges of plotting against the state. Also tried and hanged with Rajk were **Tibor Szonyi** (1903–49), the former head of the Communist party's cadres section, and **Andras Szalai** (1917–49), a deputy of Szonyi.

Laszlo Rajk joined the Hungarian Communist party in 1930 and fought during the Spanish Civil War. He was arrested by the Germans on several occasions during World War II. Following the conclusion of the war Rajk was named minister of the interior in February of 1946. In December of 1948 he was appointed minister of foreign affairs, and the following year he became secretary general of the People's Independence party. On May 16, 1949, Rajk was arrested for treason. He was tried on September 16, 1949, and convicted of anti-state activities. He was executed the following month.

- **Abdul Hussein Hajir** (1897–1949), a former prime minister of Iran, was shot and mortally wounded on November 4, 1949. Hajir served in the Iranian cabinet as minister of the interior, and of commerce and industry during the early 1940s. In 1946 he was appointed finance minister and, on June 13, 1948, he became Iran's prime minister. He served in that position until his resignation on November 9, 1948. He was shot in a Teheran mosque on November 4, 1949, and died of his wounds the following day. His assassin, identified as Hussein Immami, was executed for the murder on November 9, 1949.

- **Duncan George Stewart**, the British colonial governor of Sarawak, was seriously wounded in an assassination attempt on December 3, 1949. He died of his wounds on December 10. Stewart was born on October 22, 1904, and joined the British colonial office in 1928. He was stationed in Nigeria until 1944, when he was named colonial secretary of the Bahamas. In 1947 he was named to the financial staff of the colonial office in Palestine, and two years later was appointed governor of Sarawak. Less than a month after his arrival at his post, Stewart was attacked by a young Malay, identified as Rosli Bin Dobie (1931–1950), who was charged with the murder. More than a dozen other Malay nationalists were also charged with conspiracy in the assassination.

- Bulgarian Communist leader **Traicho Kostov** was tried for treason and executed on December 16, 1949, in Sofia. Kostov was born on June 17, 1897, and joined the Communist party in his youth. He was involved in a workers' uprising in September of 1923 and, following a period of imprisonment, he went to Moscow for several years. He returned to Bulgaria in 1931 and was again active in the Communist party. He fought with the Resistance during World War II and, following the war, was named a member of the ruling Politburo. On March 31, 1946, Kostov was named deputy prime minister of Bulgaria. The following year he also served as the chairman of the economic and financial committee in the Bulgarian cabinet. On April 4, 1949, Kostov was removed from the Politburo, and two months later was expelled from the Communist party. He was arrested on June 25, 1949, as an anti–Soviet agent, and tried for treason and espionage on December 7, 1949. He was convicted and executed the following week.

# 1950

- **Roman Shukhevych**, known as Lt. Gen. Tara Chuprynka, the chief of the Ukrainian Military Organization (UVO) and founder of the Ukrainian Insurgent Army (UPA), was killed in an ambush by Soviet security forces at Bilohorshca, near Lwow, on March 4, 1950. Shukhevych had remained in the Polish Ukraine after the Soviet Union had occupied the area, and was active in the campaign for Ukrainian independence.

- **Sami al-Hinnawi**, a Syrian military officer who had led the military coup that ousted and executed President Husni al-Zaim (q.v.) and Prime Minister Mushin Barazi (q.v.) in August of 1949, was shot and killed by, Ahmad al-Barazi, a relative of Mushin Barazi, on October 31, 1950. Hinnawi was born in Idlib, near Aleppo, in 1898. He joined the Ottoman army during World War I. He later served in the Syrian army formed by the French and rose to the rank of colonel. Hinnawi ousted the Zaim regime on August 14, 1949 and declared himself president of the Supreme War Council and head of the Syrian army. He asked Hashim el-Atassi to form a government as prime minister the following day. Hinnawi attempted to forge close ties between Syria and Iraq. He was ousted in another military coup led by Abid es-Shishakli (q.v.) on December 19, 1949. He was arrested by the new government and imprisoned until September 8, 1950, when he was released in an amnesty. Hinnawi went into exile in Beirut, Lebanon where he was assassinated.

• On November 1, 1950, two Puerto Rican Nationalists made an unsuccessful attempt to assassinate President Harry Truman in Washington, D.C. Griselio Torresola (1925–50) and Oscar Collazo (1913–94), the would-be assassins, approached Blair House, where Truman was staying, and engaged White House guards Pvt. Joseph O. Davidson, Pvt. Leslie W. Coffelt (1910–50), Pvt. Donald T. Birdzell (1909–91), and Pvt. Joseph Downs, and Secret Service agent Floyd M. Boring in a gun battle. Pvt. Coffelt and Torresola were killed during the exchange, and Pvt. Downs, Pvt. Birdzell and Collazo were injured. The president, who was awakened by the shooting, had rushed to an open window and was told to get back. He complied and was uninjured in the attempt on his life. Collazo, a member of the Nationalist party of Puerto Rico, was sentenced to life imprisonment. He was released from prison in September of 1979 by the president Jimmy Carter.

• **Lt. Col. C. Delgado Chalbaud**, the president of Venezuela, was shot and beaten to death by a group of men on November 13, 1950, in Caracas. Chalbaud, who was born in 1909, had served as president of the three-man military junta that had ruled Venezuela since November of 1948. Police arrested most of the group responsible for the killing. Rafael Simon Urbina, the alleged leader of the assassination, was killed during an attempt to escape from a prison guard on November 14. The military junta remained in control of the country following the assassination, with Lt.

Col. Marcos Perez Jimenez assuming the presidency.

# 1951

• **Ali Razmara**, who had served as prime minister of Iran from June 1950, was assassinated on March 7, 1951, outside the Maschede Soltaneh mosque in Teheran, by a member of the Moslem extremist group Fidaya-i Islam. His assassin, Abdullah Rastigar, was executed in January of 1956. Haji Ali Razmara was born in Teheran in 1901. He graduated from the French military academy of Saint-Cyr in 1925. He became director of the Teheran Military Cadet College in 1938, where he wrote a history of the Persian military. Razmara was promoted to general by the shah during the Allied occupation of Iran in 1944 and was ordered to reorganize the military. He led government troops during the ouster of the Soviet-sponsored Communist Tudeh government in Azerbaijan in December of 1946. Razmara was promoted to chief of staff in 1948, and on June 26, 1950, he was named prime minister by the shah. Razmara, a moderate with little political following, was a strong supporter of the shah. He opposed the nationalization of the oil industry, as he felt that the Iranians would be unable to run the industry without foreign technicians. He also attempted to institute land reform measures, but was blocked by the powerful landowners in the Parliament. Razmara remained head of the Iranian government until his assassination in March of 1951.

• On March 19, 1951, **Abdul Hami Zanganeh**, the former Iranian minister of education and an ally of the slain prime minister Ali Razmara (q.v.), was critically wounded in a shooting by a Teheran University student. He died of his wounds on March 25, 1951.

• On June 7, 1951, seven Nazis convicted in 1946 and 1947 of war crimes were hanged in Landsberg Prison, following the refusal of the

United States Supreme Court to allow another stay of execution. These were the last war criminals sentenced to be executed by the International Military Tribunal at Nuremberg. They included **S.S. Gen. Oswald Pohl**, who destroyed the Warsaw ghetto and supervised extermination systems in occupied countries; **S.S. Gen. Otto Ohlendorf**, who organized mass murders in the southern Ukraine; **S.S. Gen. Erich Naumann**, who massacred Jews and gypsies in the Soviet Union; **S.S. Col. Werner Braune**, who was responsible for mass murders in the Crimea; **S.S. Col. Paul Blobel**, who was responsible for the Kiev massacre in 1941; **S.S. Lt. Hans Schmidt**, the adjutant at Buchenwald concentration camp; and **S.S. Sgt. Georg Schallermair**, the Muehlendorf concentration camp roll call leader who personally beat inmates to death.

Otto Ohlendorf was born in Hoheneggelsen on February 4, 1907. He studied law and, in 1926, joined the Nazi movement as a member of the S.S. He later joined Reinhard Heydrich's (q.v.) intelligence service. In 1941 Ohlendorf was made commander of the S.S. Action Group D. (Einsatzgruppe D), which was in charge of locating and exterminating Russian Jews in the Ukraine. In 1943 he was assigned to the Reich Economic Ministry and, in November of 1944, was promoted to lieutenant general of the S.S. After Germany's defeat in World War II Ohlendorf was arrested by the Allies and tried at Nuremberg in April of 1948 with other Action Group leaders. He was convicted of war crimes and sentenced to death, with his execution coming nearly three years later.

Oswald Pohl was born in Duisberg on June 30, 1892. He served in the army during World War I and joined the Nazi party in 1922. He rose in the ranks of the S.S. and, in February of 1934, he was appointed chief administrative officer in the Reich Security Office. His close association with Heinrich Himmler resulted in further promotions and, in June of 1939, he was named a director in the Reich Interior Ministry. Pohl's major duties included the acquisition for the S.S. of the wealth and valuables of liquidated concentration camp inmates. Following Germany's defeat in World War II, Pohl went into hiding, but was arrested by the Allies in May of 1946. He was tried at Nuremberg on November 3, 1947, by a military tribunal, and was sentenced to death for war crimes. His execution was carried out more than three years later.

• **Riad Es-Solh**, the Lebanese statesman and former prime minister, was assassinated in Amman, Jordan, on July 16, 1951. He was shot to death by three members of the Syrian Nationalist Socialist party while en route to the Amman, Jordan, airport after paying a state visit to King Abdullah (q.v.) of Jordan. Riad es-Solh was born in Saida in 1894. He was active in the Arab nationalist movement and was arrested by the Turkish authorities during World War I. He was sentenced to death, but the sentence was commuted to deportation. Following World War I, he returned to Lebanon where he fought against the French mandate. Solh was again sentenced to death by a French court-martial, but was pardoned in 1924. He continued his opposition to French rule and opposed the Franco-Lebanese treaty of November 13, 1936. He was exiled by the French government, but again returned to Lebanon to form a government as prime minister on August 29, 1943. His government amended the constitution to remove the legal right of the French to administer Lebanon under a League of Nations mandate. Solh and his cabinet were arrested by French forces in Lebanon. When widespread demonstrations against the French occurred, the British stepped in to demand that Lebanon be granted full independence. Solh remained as the first prime minister of independent Lebanon until January 1, 1945. He was again asked to form a government on December 14, 1946. An attempt was made by the Syrian National Socialist party to overthrown the Lebanese government in 1948. The leader of the attempt, Anton Sa'adeh, was sentenced to death and executed in 1949. His supporters vowed to seek revenge against Solh, whom they held responsible for Sa'adeh's death. An attempt was made to assassinate Solh in March of 1950. He stepped down as prime Minister on February 13, 1951, and paid a state visit to King Abdullah of Jordan in July of 1951. He was assassinated en route to the airport to return to Lebanon.

• **King Abdullah Ibn Hussein**, the king of Jordan, was shot to death on July 20, 1951, as he visited the tomb of his father in the Mosque of Omar in the Old City of Jerusalem. His assassin, Mustafa Ashu, who was identified as a follower of the exiled Mufti of Jerusalem, was killed by the king's guards. Abdullah was born in Mecca in 1882, the son of King Hussein of the Hejaz. Abdullah was raised in Turkey and served in the Ottoman parliament in 1908. During World War I Abdullah joined with his older brother, Feisal, and T.E. Lawrence, better known as Lawrence of Arabia, in the Arab rebellion against the Turks. After the war Abdullah joined with his father and brother in a war against King Ibn Saud of Saudi Arabia. After the defeat of his forces Abdullah was persuaded by British colonial secretary Winston Churchill to become emir of Trans-Jordan in 1921. Abdullah remained a close ally of Great Britain, and his army, known as the Arab Legion, was trained and commanded by British Brig. John Glubb. On May 25, 1946, Abdullah was crowned king of independent Trans-Jordan.

In May of 1948 Jordan, in unison with other Arab nations, declared war on Israel. The Arab armies met with greater resistance than expected from the Israeli army, and open hostilities ceased the following year. In April of 1950 Abdullah annexed Arab Palestine, changing the name of his enlarged nation to the Hashemite Kingdom of Jordan. Abdullah envisioned a union between Jordan, Syria, Iraq, and Lebanon under a Hashemite ruler. He was slain by his political enemies before his plans could be put into effect. Abdullah was succeeded by his son, Talal, who abdicated the following year due to illness. Talal was in turn succeeded by Abdullah's grandson, Hussein.

• On July 31, 1951, **Brig. Gen. Charles M. Chamson** (1902–1951), the French commissioner for South Vietnam, and **Gov. Lap Thanh** (1896–1951) of South Vietnam, were killed in a suicide grenade attack in Sadec, near Saigon, by a Communist rebel.

• **S.S. Gen. Jurgen Stroop** (1901–1951), the Nazi officer who suppressed the Warsaw ghetto uprising in 1943, was hanged in Warsaw, Poland, on September 8, 1951, as a war criminal. Stroop was captured by the Allies after Germany's defeat in 1945, and was sentenced to death by an American military tribunal on March 22, 1947, for ordering the execution of American pilots in Greece during the war. He was subsequently extradited to Poland to stand trial for war crimes committed there, and was again sentenced to death.

• **Henry Lovell Goldworth Gurney** (1895–1951), the British high commissioner of Malaya, was assassinated by Communist guerrillas near Kuala Lumpur, in Malaysia, on October 6, 1951. Gurney had served as an official in the British Colonial Office for nearly thirty years and had accepted the position in Malaya on October 6, 1948. He was ambushed and killed in the midst of his campaign to eliminate Communist terrorist activities.

• **Liaquat Ali Khan**, the first prime minister of Pakistan, was assassinated on October 16, 1951, while addressing a public meeting in Rawalpindi. His assassin, Said Akbar, was identified as a member of the Khaksar semi-military. Liaquat was born on October 1, 1895, in Karnal. He received a degree in law from Exeter College in Oxford, England, and returned to India to practice law. He entered politics in 1923, joining the All-India Moslem League led by Mohammad Ali Jinnah. Liaquat served in the United Provinces Legislative Council from 1926 until his election, in 1940, to the Central Legislative Assembly. In 1936 Liaquat was elected secretary general of the Moslem League and, shortly thereafter, became Jinnah's deputy leader of the party. Following the establishment of independent Pakistan in August of 1947 Liaquat was appointed the first prime minister. After Jinnah's death the following year Liaquat assumed complete responsibility for the governing of Pakistan. The territorial dispute with India over Kashmir was the major issue facing Liaquat's government. His negotiations with Prime Minister Nehru of India and his refusal to consider a war with India led to his assassination by a Moslem fanatic. His assassin was killed by a mob immediately after murdering Liaquat.

• **Jean De Raymond** (1907–51), the French commissioner for Cambodia, was stabbed to death by his Vietnamese servant on October 29, 1951. The assailant was identified as Pham Ngoc Lam, an alleged Communist terrorist.

• **Cyril Ousman**, the British vice consul, was assassinated in Jidda, Saudi Arabia, on November 16, 1951. His assassin was Prince Mishari ibn Abdul Aziz ibn Saud (1932–2000), a son of King Ibn Saud. Prince Mishari spent many years in prison for the murder.

# 1952

• On December 3, 1952, eleven Communist politicians in Czechoslovakia were executed for treason. They were arrested in November of 1951, and following a trial before the People's Court in Prague, were found guilty and sentenced to be hanged. Those executed included **Rudolf Slansky**, the former vice premier; **Vladimir Clementis**, the former foreign minister; **Otto Fischl**, the former deputy finance minister; **Josef Frank**, the former Communist party acting secretary; **Ludvik Frejka**, the former chief of the economic section of the president's office; **Bedrich Geminder**, the former head of the Czech Communist party International Section; **Richard Margolius**, the former deputy foreign trade minister; **Bedrich Reicin**, the former deputy defense minister; **Karel Svab**, the former deputy security

minister; **Otto Sling**, the former Brno district Communist party secretary; and **Andre Simon**, the former editor of *Rude Pravo*, the Czech Communist newspaper.

Rudolf Salzmann Slansky was born on July 31, 1901. He joined the Czechoslovak Communist party and, in 1929, was elected to the Central Committee of the party. He served in the Czech national assembly from 1935 until 1936, and in 1945 he was elected secretary general of the Communist party. In 1951 Slansky was named to the position of vice premier of Czechoslovakia. Several months later he was arrested on charges of leading an attempt to overthrow the Communist government, resulting in his trial and execution.

Vladimir Clementis was born in Slovakia on September 20, 1902. He served in the Czechoslovak parliament as a Communist deputy during the 1930s, and served as a legal council to the Czech government in exile in London during World War II. He was appointed undersecretary of state for foreign affairs following his return to Czechoslovakia after the war and, in 1938, was appointed foreign minister. He served in this position until March of 1950, and the following year he was expelled from the Communist party and arrested for subversion. He was subsequently tried and executed.

• **Farhat Hached** (1913–1952), the secretary general of the Tunisian Labor Federation, was shot to death with machine guns outside of Tunis on December 5, 1952. Nationalist leaders blamed the killing on members of a secret society of French colonial groups called the Red Hand. Rioting and violence ensued throughout French North Africa as a result of Hached's murder.

# 1953

• **Brig. Gen. Mohammed Afshartus** (1908–53), the Iranian National Police chief, was found strangled to death near Teheran on

April 20, 1953. Afshartus was an ally of Premier Mohammed Mossadegh.

• **Shedli Kastalli**, the vice president of the municipal council of Tunis, Tunisia, was shot and killed by terrorists on May 2, 1953.

• On June 19, 1953, **Julius** (1918–53) and **Ethel** (1915–53) **Rosenberg** were executed at Sing Sing Prison in New York, following their conviction on charges of conspiracy to transmit atomic secrets to the Soviet Union. The Rosenbergs had been arrested in the summer of 1950 after the United States government learned that Julius Rosenberg had acquired information from his wife's brother, David Greenglass (b. 1922), concerning the atomic bomb project during World War II. The Rosenbergs were sentenced to death for treason by Judge Irving Kaufman (1910–92) in a trial which began in March of 1951 in New York. Greenglass, who served as the government's chief witness at the trial, was sentenced to fifteen years' imprisonment, and two other associates, Harry Gold (1910–72) and Morton Sobell, were sentenced to thirty years in prison.

• **Prince Ezzedine Bey** (1881–1953), the heir to the throne of Tunisia, was assassinated in his palace in Tunis on July 1, 1953. Prince Ezzedine, who was known for his pro–French views, was a cousin of the bey of Tunisia. He was killed by Hei Ben Brahim Ben Ejebala Djeridi, an ex-convict who claimed to have been hired to kill the prince.

• **Hedi Shaker**, the leader of the autonomous Tunisian Neo-Destour party, was assassinated in Tunis on September 12, 1953.

• **Wilhelm Stuckart** (1902–53), the Nazi jurist was drafted the Nuremberg anti–Jewish racial laws of 1935, died in a suspicious car crash near Hanover in December of 1953. It was likely that Stuckart had been killed by members of a Jewish revenge squad organized to hunt down Nazi war criminals. Stuckart had been tried as a war criminal at Nuremberg in 1949, and was sentenced to four years' imprisonment. He was released soon after and settled in West Berlin.

• **Lavrenti P. Beria**, the former head of the Soviet secret police and a close associate of Joseph Stalin, was executed in Moscow as a traitor. During a secret trial presided over by Marshal Ivan S. Konev (1897–1973), Beria and six others were sentenced to be executed. On December 23, 1953, they were executed by a firing squad. The other defendants included **Vsevolod N. Merkulov**, Beria's right-hand man and the former state security and state control minister; **Vladimir G. Dekanozov**, the former Georgian internal affairs minister who had served as deputy foreign minister and was the Soviet Union's ambassador to Berlin at the time of the German invasion during World War II; **P.V. Meshik**, the former Ukrainian internal affairs minister; and **S.A. Goglidze** and **L.E. Vlodimirsky**, two former high-ranking police officials.

Lavrenti Pavlovich Beria was born in Soviet Georgia on March 29, 1899. He became a member of the Communist party in 1917 and, in 1921, joined the Soviet secret police. He was elected first secretary of the Georgian Communist party in November of 1931, and was an active participant in the Stalin purges in Georgia, Azerbaijan, and Armenia. He succeeded Nikolai Yezhov (q.v.) as commissar for internal affairs on December 8, 1938, and, in February of 1941, was named deputy prime minister of the Soviet Union. He served on the State Defense Committee during World War II and, in Mach of 1946, was named to the Politburo. After the death of Joseph Stalin in March of 1953, Beria became the first of four deputy prime ministers. He was well position to succeed Stalin as leader of the Soviet Communist party, but, on July 10, 1953, he was removed from his posts, expelled from the party, and arrested on charges of treason. He was subsequently tried and executed with several of his aides.

# 1954

• **Amir Ahmad Mohamed Amin Didi** (1912–54), the first president of the Maldive Island Republic, died on January 19, 1954, from injuries received from an angry crowd of demonstrators. Amin Didi had served as prime minister of the Maldives since 1945. He became president when the country abolished the sultanate and instituted a republican form of government on January 1, 1953. Maldives went into turmoil on August 21, 1953, when a food crisis resulted in massive demonstrations against the government. Amin Didi was ousted on September 3, 1953, and charged with food offenses. Didi had been living in exile on Male Atoll at the time of his death.

• On March 1, 1954, five members of the United States Congress were wounded when four Puerto Rican Nationalists fired indiscriminately at the floor of the House of Representatives from the spectator's gallery. Bullets struck the table of the majority leader and the surrounding chairs. Rep. Alvin M. Bentley (1918–69) of Michigan, hit in the lung, liver, and stomach, was the most seriously injured. Rep. Ben. F. Jensen (1892–1970) from Iowa, was wounded in the back. Rep. Clifford Davis (1897–1970) from Tennessee, Rep. George H. Fallon (1902–80) from Maryland, and Rep. Kenneth A. Roberts (1912–89) from Alabama all suffered leg wounds. All five recovered and continued serving in the Congress. Four Puerto Rican nationalists were charged, tried, and convicted of assault with intent to kill. They were Rafael Cancel-Miranda (b. 1930), Irving Flores Rodriguez (b. 1926), Andres Figueroa Cordero (1919–79) and Lolita Lebron (b. 1920). Figueroa Cordero was released in 1978 for health reasons and died the following year. The other three were released from prison by President Jimmy Carter in September of 1979.

• **Lucretiu Patrascanu** (1900–54), the former Romanian minister of justice, and **Remus Koppler** were tried for treason as United States sympathizers. They were both executed in Romania on April 18, 1954.

• **Viktor Semyonovich Abakumov** (1894–1954), a leading figure in the Soviet state security system, NKVD, was executed in 1954 in a work camp. Abakumov joined the NKVD in 1935, become a deputy to Lavrenti Beria (q.v.). Abakumov became minister of state security in 1951, and was viewed by Beria as a rival for power. Beria orchestrated his arrest and sentence to a work camp in 1951. Abakumov was executed after Beria's own fall and execution in 1953.

• **Albert L. Patterson** (1895–1954), the Democratic nominee for attorney general for the state of Alabama, was shot to death in Phenix City, Alabama, on June 18, 1954. Patterson, a leading crusader against vice, was presumed murdered by gambling interests in Phenix City. Albert Fuller (1918–69), a former chief deputy sheriff, was sentenced to life in prison for Patterson's murder.

• On August 4, 1954, Brazilian air force major **Ruben Florentino Vaz** was shot and killed in a car at the home of Brazilian opposition leader and journalist Carlos Lacerda (1914–77) in Rua Toneleros, Copacabana, Brazil. Lacerda, who was believed to be the target of the assassination attempt, was only slightly injured. The government of President Getulio Vargas was implicated in the shooting, and Vargas was asked to resign. Vargas committed suicide three weeks later on August 24, 1954.

• **Kou Voravong** (1914–54), the defense minister of Laos, was shot and killed on September 18, 1954, by terrorists while attending a dinner party at the home of Deputy Premier Phouy Sananikone in Vientiane, Laos.

• On October 5, 1954, **Ibrahim El-Shalhi** (1894–1954), the Libyan palace affairs minister, was assassinated by El-Sherif Mohieddin El-Sinussi (b. 1934), a nephew of Queen Fatima of Libya. The shooting resulted in the exile of several members of the imperial family.

• On October 26, 1954, President Gamal Abdel Nasser (1918–70) of Egypt escaped injury when several shots were fired at him in an assassination attempt. Mahmoud Abdel Latif, a member of the outlawed Moslem Brotherhood, was charged with the attempt. Latif and other Moslem Brotherhood leaders, including Youssef Talaat, Sheik Mohammed Farghali, Ibrahim Tayeb, Hindawi Duweir, and Abdel Kader Oda, were executed by hanging on December 7, 1954.

• **Ramdane Ben Abdel Malek**, an Algerian nationalist leader, was killed by French troops near Cassaigne, Algeria, on November 1, 1954, on the outbreak of Algeria's war of independence. Ben Abdel Malek was second-in-command under Ben M'Itidi in the Oran region at the start of the war. **Belkacem Grine**, a rebel leader in the Aures region, was also killed by French forces during the first month of fighting.

• **Hossein Fatemi** (1918–54), the former Iranian minister of foreign affairs, was executed by a firing squad on November 10, 1954. Fatemi, an ally of Mohammed Mossadegh, was the founder of the newspaper *Bakhtar-i-Inruz* in 1949, and was a leading proponent of the nationalization of the Iranian oil industry. When Mossadegh assumed power as premier on April 29, 1951, Fatemi became his personal assistant, and was appointed minister of foreign affairs on October 11, 1952. Following Gen. Fazlollah Zahedi's successful Royalist rebellion on August 19, 1953, Fatemi was forced into hiding. He was located in March of 1954 and arrested. He was tried for treason against the monarchy and sentenced to death.

# 1955

• **Jose Antonio Remon**, the president of Panama, was shot and killed by machine gun fire on January 2, 1955, while at a Panama City racetrack. Remon, who was born in 1908, joined the Panamanian National Police in 1931, and in 1947 was elevated to the position of first commandant of the police. This position gave him much power in the affairs of state and enabled him to become president in 1952. Remon's administration was noted for its seeming lack of corruption and sound fiscal policies. Jose Ramon Guizado (1899–1964), the first vice president of Panama, assumed office after the slaying, but was removed from his position by the Panamanian national assembly two weeks later after having been implicated in the assassination of Remon. Ruben Miro (b. 1912) confessed to having shot Remon after plotting the killing with Guizado and several others. The plotters hoped that Guizado, as president, could help relieve the personal financial difficulties they were then experiencing.

• **Mourad Didouche**, one of the leader of the Algerian nationalist movement, was killed in combat against French colonial troops in January of 1955 while leading a retreat of the armed guerrillas under his command. Didouche was born in 1922 and became involved with the independence movement in the mid–1940s. Didouche was wanted by the colonial police from 1950. He was a leading organizer of Algerian workers for the nationalist movement and commander of revolutionary forces in the Contantine region after the outbreak of the Algerian war for independence.

• In April of 1955 Ahmed ibn Yahya Hamid al-Din (q.v.), the Imam of Yemen, was forced to abdicate following a revolt led by his brothers, **Abdullah** and **Abbas**. Ahmed was imprisoned, but escaped for his captors and was reinstated as imam by loyalist forces. Abdullah, who had proclaimed himself imam, and Abbas were subsequently captured and executed for participating in the revolt. Abdullah had previously served as governor of Hodeida and was Yemen's foreign minister under Ahmed.

• **Col. Adnan al-Malki** (1918–1955), the Syrian deputy army chief of staff, was assassinated while attending a soccer match on April 22, 1955. Malki was the leader of an unsuccessful coup attempt against the regime of Adib al-Shishakli (q.v.) in December of 1952. He was imprisoned until Shishakli's ouster in February of 1954. An opponent of the Baghdad Pact, Malki was a leading political figure in the Syrian army. His assassin, an army sergeant, committed suicide immediately after Malki's murder.

• **John E. Peurifoy** (1907–55), the United States ambassador to Thailand, was killed in an automobile accident outside of the capital of Bangkok on August 12, 1955. One of Peurifoy's sons was also killed in the crash. Peurifoy, a former deputy undersecretary of state, was known as an anti–Communist diplomatic trouble shooter for the State Department. He had served as ambassador to Greece during the Civil War of the late 1940s. He was also instrumental in the deposing of left-wing president Jacobo Arbenz Guzman (q.v.) of Guatemala while Peurifoy was serving as United States ambassador to that country in 1954. His reputation and somewhat mysterious demise fueled speculation that his death may have been caused by leftist sympathizers.

• **Bachir Chichani**, a leading Algerian nationalist during the war of independence, was assassinated on November 1, 1955, by his colleague and successor as commander of forces in the Aures region, Laghrour Abbes. Chichani was an associated of Mostefa Ben Boulaid (q.v.), and had led the Aures Wilaya forces after his arrest earlier in the year.

• **Ali Sultan Mugheiry**, a member of the Arab Association executive committee who served on the Zanzibari Legislative Council, was murdered by Mohamed Hamoud Barwani in 1955. Mugheiry had defied the Arab boycott of the council. His assassin received a sentence of death, which was later commuted to ten years. He was killed in detention during the early months of the 1964 revolution that installed Abeid Karume (q.v.) as president. Hamoud's son assassinated Karume in revenge eight years later.

• **Caliph Mohammed Berdadi**, a leading supporter of the deposed sultan of Morocco, Sidi Mohammed ben Moulay Arafa, was stoned to death by an angry mob in Rabat on November 19, 1955.

# 1956

• **Jesus De Galindez** (1915–1956), a lawyer, writer and leading foe of Dominican dictator Rafael L. Trujillo (q.v.), disappeared from New York on March 12, 1956. As he was never found, it was believed the exiled Galindez had been abducted and flown to the Dominican Republic on Trujillo's orders, and murdered following his arrival. Born in Spain, De Galindez went to the Dominican Republic as an exile during the Spanish Civil War. He worked for the Trujillo regime as a legal advisor for nearly a decade before fleeing that country in 1946. He became an outspoken critic of Trujillo, lecturing throughout the United States.

• **Mostefa Ben Boulaid**, a leader of the Algerian nationalists in their war for independence from the French, was killed on March 27, 1956, by a bomb in a booby-trapped field radio set by the French army's special services. Ben Boulaid was born in Arris in 1917. He became active in the nationalist movement in the late 1940s, and was a candidate for the Algerian Assembly in 1948. He received the majority of votes, but was denied a seat in the assembly. He became a leading rebel commander after the Algerian war for independence, commanding troops in the Aures Wilaya. He was arrested by the French authorities in 1955, but managed to escape later in the year. He continued to lead rebel forces until his death in March of 1956.

• **Gen. Juan Jose Valle**, a leading Argentine army officer during the administration of deposed president Juan Peron, was executed following an attempted revolt against the provisional government in June of 1956.

• **Abbas Mass'udi**, a leading Moroccan independence fighter, was reportedly executed in Fez by order of Medhi Ben Barka (q.v.) on June 27, 1956. Abbas commanded troops in northern Morocco for the Liberation Army. He had been an impediment to Ben Barka's establishment of political offices in the region.

• **Anastasio Somoza Garcia**, the long-time president of Nicaragua, was shot four times and seriously wounded in Leon on September 21, 1956. He died of his injuries on September 29, 1956. His assailant, identified as Rigoberto Lopez Perez (1929–56), was immediately shot to death by Somoza's guards. Somoza was born in San Marcos on February 1, 1896. He was educated in Nicaragua and at Pierce Commercial College in Philadelphia, Pennsylvania. He worked with the Paige Motor Company before returning to Nicaragua. Somoza joined the Liberal Party and gained influence by serving as an interpreter during the intervention of United States Marines in Nicaragua from 1927. Liberal Party candidate Jose M. Moncada was elected president in November of 1928, and Somoza was appointed governor of Leon. He also achieved prominence in the Civil Guard, where he rose to the rank of general. Juan B. Sacasa, the uncle of Somoza's wife, was elected president in 1932, and Somoza was named minister of war. The Nicaraguan army and United States Marines continued to battle insurgents led by Cesar Sandino. Sandino accepted an armistice with the Nicaraguan government and attended a dinner meeting with President Sacasa on February 21, 1934, under a promise of safe conduct. He was arrested by officers of Somoza's National Guard following the meeting, however, and was summarily executed. Somoza became the leading figure in the Nicaraguan government and ousted Sacasa in 1936. He installed Carlos Brenes Jarquin as interim president. Somoza was unopposed for the presidency in elections in December of 1936 and was sworn into office on January 1, 1937. He was reelected president in 1942. He declined to be a candidate in the presidential election in 1947 and relinquished office to his hand-picked successor, Leonardo Arguello, on May 1, 1947.

Arguello attempted to govern without consulting Somoza and was ousted by a military coup later in the month. Somoza installed Victor Roman y Reyes as president in August of 1947. Somoza was again elected president by congress on May 7, 1950, following the death of Roman y Reyes. He was reelected in government-controlled elections in May of 1951. During Somoza's reign the economic situation of Nicaragua greatly improved due to the president's rigid control over the country. Somoza's personal wealth and that of his family also greatly increased. Nicaragua engaged in a brief border war with Costa Rica in January of 1955. Somoza challenged Costa Rican president Jose Figueres Ferrer to a duel before the Organization of American States negotiated an end to the fighting. After Somoza's death he was eventually succeeded by his son, Luis Somoza Debayle (1922–67). Another son, Anastasio Somoza Debayle (1925–80) (q.v.), served as Nicaragua's president from 1967 until 1979.

# 1957

• **Muhammad Larbi Ben M'Hidi**, a leading Algerian rebel commander, was tortured to death in prison by French colonial authorities in February of 1957, refusing to give any information to his captors. Ben M'Hidi was born in 1923 in Ain M'Lila, Constantine province. He became involved in nationalist activities in the early 1940s and was arrested by the French authorities on several occasions. He served as a commander in the Oran wilaya after the start of the Algerian war of independence. He led armed guerrilla forces during the Battle of Algiers until his capture by the French and his death at their hands.

• **Dedan Kimathi**, a leader of the Kenyan nationalist terrorists known as the "Mau Mau" during the 1950s, was captured and executed in a Nairobi prison on February 18,

1957. Kimathi, a Kikuyu tribesman, was born in Nyeri on October 31, 1920. He joined the Kenya African Union (KAU) in the mid–1940s, serving as a leading organizer in the early 1950s. Kimathi was suspected of being involved in the murder of Senior Chief Nderi Wangombe of Thegenge, Nyeri, on October 22, 1952. He was arrested but soon escaped and became a leader of the forest fighters, or Mau Mau. He was a leading figure in uniting the various nationalist and insurgent groups in the country. Before his arrest he and his followers waged a number of guerrilla campaigns against the British in an attempt to win independence for Kenya. Kimathi was captured on November 19, 1956, and convicted of unlawful possession of firearms six days later. He was sentenced to death and executed the following February.

• Guatemalan president **Carlos Castillo Armas** (1914–57), was shot to death in the Presidential Palace in Guatemala City on July 26, 1957. His assailant, Romero Vasquez Sanchez (1937–57), killed himself immediately following the murder of the president. Castillo Armas was a Guatemalan army officer when, in June of 1954, he led a military uprising against the leftist government of Jacobo Arbenz Guzman (q.v.), forcing his resignation. Castillo Armas became provisional president and was elected to a full term the following year. He was a vehement anti–Communist and purged the government and unions of those suspected of leftist sympathies. He also redesigned the agrarian reform programs of his predecessor, returning much of the land to the original owners. His assassin had been discharged from the army for Communist sympathies the previous year, and presumably killed Castillo Armas for his rightist policies.

• **Lev Rebet**, an exiled Ukranian nationalist political leader, was assassinated by Soviet agents in Munich, Germany, in 1957.

# 1958

• On April 28, 1958, **Ducasse Jumelle** (1899–1958), the Haitian minister of interior under President Paul Magloire, and **Charles Jumelle**, both brothers of Clement Jumelle, presidential candidate against Francois Duvalier in 1957, were killed in their home on the orders of President Duvalier. Clement Jumelle died in hiding later in the year.

• **Otto Abetz**, the German ambassador to Vichy France during World War II, died in an automobile accident on May 5, 1958, when his steering mechanism failed. It was speculated that his car may have been sabotaged in revenge for his role in persecuting French Jews during the war. Abetz was born on May 26, 1903, and entered the German Foreign Service in 1935. He served as Germany's ambassador to France during the occupation from 1940 until 1944. Following the war he was arrested as a war criminal and, in 1949, sentenced to twenty years' imprisonment. He was released in the early 1950s and died shortly afterward when his car malfunctioned on the Cologne-Ruhr autobahn in Dusseldorf, Germany.

• **Nasib al-Matni**, a leading Lebanese journalist, was murdered on May 8, 1958. A Maronite, he was a critic of the government of Camille Chamoun. Matni was the owner and publisher of the journal *At-Telegraph*. The Chamoun administration was widely held responsible for Matni's murder, and his assassination led to riots and demonstrations, and ultimately a civil war.

• **Imre Nagy** (1896–1958), the prime minister of Hungary from 1953 until 1955, was executed on June 17, 1958, following a trial conducted by the Soviet government. Nagy, a Hungarian soldier during World War I, was captured by the Russians and joined the Communist party during his imprisonment. After his release he returned home and became instrumental in the development of the Hungarian Communist party. Nagy returned to the Soviet Union in 1930, and remained there until the end of World War II. He served as minister of agriculture in Hungary's first republican government from 1945 to 1946. He briefly served as minister of interior, and succeeded Matyas Rakosi as prime minister in July of 1953. Nagy was a protégé of Georgi M. Malenkov, prime minister of the Soviet Union, and when Malenkov was forced out of office in February of 1955, Nagy soon followed. At the start of the Hungarian National Rising in October of 1956 Nagy was again named prime minister. One of the first acts of his new government was to announce the withdrawal of Hungary from the Warsaw Pact, and the establishment of Hungary as a neutral nation. The Soviet Union responded by sending in the Soviet army and forcing Nagy's removal from office. Nagy fled to the Yugoslav embassy in November of 1956, but was captured two weeks later when he emerged after being promised safe conduct by the Soviets. He was secretly taken to the Soviet Union, where he was tried and executed.

• **Maj. Gen. Pal Maleter**, a supporter of Nagy and a leader in the 1956 Hungarian revolt against the Soviet Union, and **Miklos Gimes** and **Jozsef Szilagy**, two Hungarian journalists, were also tried by the Soviets and executed with Nagy on June 17, 1958. Maleter had served as minister of defense in Nagy's short-lived government and was leading a delegation to negotiate the Soviets' withdrawal from Hungary when he was seized.

• On July 14, 1958, much of the Iraqi royal family was murdered during an army revolt. **King Feisal II**, along with **Abdul-Ilah**, the former regent, and many members of the king's family, were slaughtered and their butchered bodies dragged through the streets of Baghdad after the king had surrendered the palace on a promise of safe conduct for his family within. **Nuri As-Said**, the premier of Iraq, was captured and killed the following day. The coup, led by Brigadier Abdul Karim Kassem (q.v.), was provoked by nationalist sentiments against the pro–Western Hashemite monarchy, and inspired by the success of the Nasser revolution in Egypt. Brigadier

Kassem assumed leadership of the country following the revolt.

Feisal was born in Baghdad on May 2, 1935. He was the son of King Ghazi, who ruled Iraq from September of 1933. Feisal succeeded his father as Iraq's king when Ghazi was killed in an automobile accident on April 4, 1939. Feisal ruled through the regency of his uncle, Abdul-Ilah, during which time he was educated at Harrow in Great Britain. His classmates included his cousin, Hussein, who was to become King of Jordan. Feisal returned to Iraq on May 2, 1953, after having come of age. He remained close friends with his cousin, King Hussein, and planned to federate their nations in response to the militant nationalist policies of Gamal Nasser's newly formed United Arab Republic. Feisal and Hussein reached an agreement in February of 1958 to unify Iraq and Jordan the following July, with Feisal as head of the federation. The proposed federation was aborted when Feisal was ousted and murdered in the nationalist coup led by Brigadier Abdul Karim Kassem.

Abdul-Ilah was born in Taif on November 14, 1913. He was the son of Ali ibn Husain, who had ruled as king of the Hejaz from 1924 until his defeat and ouster by King Saud of Saudi Arabia in 1925. On the death of King Ghazi in 1939, Abdul-Ilah was named regent of Iraq for Feisal II, his nephew. The regency was briefly deposed by pro–German Rashid Ali Gailani, following Abdul-Ilah's declared support for the Allies in 1941. Abdul-Ilah returned to Baghdad following Gailani's ouster and proceeded to declare war on the Axis powers. He was made crown prince in 1943, and following the assassination of Jordan's King Abdullah (q.v.), he was recognized as head of the Hashemite royal family. Abdul-Ilah's moderate pro–Western policies brought him into conflict with some of the more militant Arab nationalists in the region. After Feisal came of age, Abdul-Ilah continued to serve as the King's close advisor until his murder during the nationalist coup.

Nuri al-Said was born in Baghdad in 1888. He attended the Military Academy in Istanbul in 1903 and joined the Iraqi army as an officer in 1908. He was an early Arab nationalist and joined the Arab Revolt during World War I. He was a close advisor to Emir Feisal, and served as his chief of staff during the Arab Revolt led by Lawrence of Arabia. Nuri remained with Emir Feisal during his rule in Syria in 1920 and accompanied him the following year when Feisal was named the first king of Iraq. He was named to the cabinet as minister of defense in November of 1922 and again served in that position during three cabinets between 1923 and 1928. During the next twenty-five years, he remained a major political figure in Iraq and served as prime minister from March 23, 1930, until October 27, 1932, during which time he signed the Anglo-Iraqi Treaty of 1930. Nuri served as foreign minister in several cabinets during the early 1930s. He was forced to flee the country following the coup led by General Bakr Sidqi Al-'Askari (q.v.) in October of 1936. He returned to Iraq following Sidqi's assassination in August of 1937. Nuri served in several diplomatic positions abroad before again serving as prime minister from December 26, 1938, until March 31, 1940. He again fled Iraq following the pro–German coup led by Rashid Ali Gailani. He returned to Iraq following Gailani's ouster and was again named prime Minister on October 19, 1941. Nuri led the Iraqi government in declaring war on the Axis powers during World War II. He retained office until June 4, 1944. He was a leading proponent of Arab unity and a founder of the Arab League. Nuri again formed a government on November 21, 1946, serving until March 30, 1947. He was again prime Minister from January 6 until November 7 of 1949 and founded the Constitutional Union Party. He served as head of government again from September 16, 1950, until July 9, 1952, when he was forced to resign following student rioting. Nuri remained in the government as minister of defense. He was again named prime minister of August 4, 1954. During this term of office, Iraq broke off diplomatic relations with the Soviet Union and signed the Baghdad Pact with Turkey, Pakistan, Iran and Great Britain. His opposi-

tion to Egypt's President Gamal Abdel Nasser, along with his moderate pro–Western policies, met with opposition from nationalists. He stepped down on June 16, 1957, for reasons of health. Nuri's last term as prime minister was from March 3 until May 13, of 1958, when he resigned in preparation to become prime minister of the newly formed federation between Iraq and Jordan. Following the ouster of Feisal II, Nuri was captured and brutally killed on July 14, 1958, when he tried to escape from Baghdad dressed as a woman. His body was reportedly dismembered by an angry mob.

Also killed during the revolt was **Suleiman Toukan** (1892–1958), the Jordanian defense minister, who was in Iraq to help administer the union between the two countries. Toukan had served as mayor of Nablus in the early 1940s and was a member of several Jordanian cabinets in the 1950s. Others killed included **Col. Graham**, the ambassadorial controller at the British Embassy in Baghdad. Two United States citizens, **Eugene Burns**, a newsman, and **George Colley**, the executive vice president of the Pacific Bechtel Corporation, were also murdered by a mob.

Following the Kassim revolt, numerous officials in the deposed government were tried by a People's Court. Among those convicted and sentenced to death were former Iraqi prime ministers Ahmed Mukhtar Baban, Fadhil al-Jamali (1903–97), and Rashid Ali el-Gailani (1890–1965); ex–foreign minister Burhanuddin Bashayan; Gen. Mohammed Rafiq Aref, the former chief of staff of the Iraqi army; and Gen. Ghazi el-Daghistani, the former deputy chief of staff. While most were sentenced to be executed, it appears that the sentences of many were later commuted and the prisoners were eventually released.

• **Reuben Um Nyobe** (1913–58), a Cameroon nationalist leader, was shot to death by a government policeman while in hiding on September 13, 1958. A leader of the Union des Populations du Cameroun (UPC), he supported independence from the French and unification of French and British Cameroons. Um Nyobe went into hiding in 1955 following an unsuccessful revolt against the French colonial authorities. He continued to agitate for Cameroon independence until his death in September of 1958.

# 1959

• In January of 1959 Cuban rebel leader Fidel Castro overthrew the government of Fulgencio Batista. While Batista was able to flee the country, many of his aides and advisors were not so fortunate. Many of the deposed president's followers were tried and executed for "war crimes" during the year. In early January **Gen. Joaquin Casillas Lumpuy**, the commander of Las Villas Province, and **Col. Cornelio Rojas** were executed by a firing squad in Santa Clara. **Capt. Pedro Morejon Caldes** (1921–59) was executed on January 31, and **Maj. Jesus Sosa Blanco** (1908–59), the leader of the Batista government's operations against the rebels in Oriente Province, was executed on February 18. On February 23, **Lt. Col. Ricardo Luis Grao** was executed. During the remainder of the year nearly 600 more former officials met the same fate.

• **Kamil Qazanchi**, an Iraqi Communist leader, was shot and killed in a Mosul prison on March 8, 1959. He was a leader of the Peace Partisan group and a respected lawyer and poet. His death came during a rebellion by soldiers under the command of **Col. 'Abd al-Wahhab Shawwaf**, head of the Mosul garrison. The rebellion proved unsuccessful and Col. Shawaf was reported killed the following day. **'Abdullah al-Shawi**, the commander of the Engineering Regiment, also died during the fighting. **Brig. Nadhem Tabaqchali**, the former commander of the Iraqi army, **Rif'at al-Hajj Sirri**, the head of military intelligence in Baghdad, and four other officers were arrested for complicity in the revolt and executed on September 20,

1959. Four members King Feisal's (q.v.) regime, former interior minister **Sa'id Qazzaz**, former security chief **Bahjat al-'Atiyah**, former Iraqi director of prisons **'Abd al-Jabbar 'Ayyub**, and ex-governor **'Abd al-Jabbar Fahmi** of Baghdad, were also executed at that time.

• **Abdel Aziz Ben Dris**, a leading figure in the ruling Moroccan Independence party and a member of the National Assembly, was murdered on April 24, 1959.

• **Naim Moghabghab**, a member of the Lebanese parliament and a former minister of public works, was attacked and beaten to death on July 28, 1959, near Beirut. Moghabghab was a prominent supporter of former Lebanese president Camille Chamoun.

• **Cho Bong Am** (1899–1959), who twice ran for the presidency of South Korea as the Progressive party's candidate, was hanged for treason in Seoul on July 31, 1959. Cho, a leftist member of the National Assembly, had been defeated by Korean strongman Sygman Rhee in elections in 1952 and 1956. His proposals advocating closer ties between North and South Korea led to his arrest and execution.

• **Solomon W.R.D. Bandaranaike**, the prime minister of Ceylon, was shot by Talduwe Somarama Thero, a Buddhist monk, on September 25, 1959. Bandaranaike died of his injuries the following day. Bandaranaike was born on January 8,, 1899, in Colombo, Ceylon. He entered politics in the late 1920s and joined the United National party. He served as Ceylon's minister of health following independence in 1948 until 1951. He was a leading spokesman for the Buddhist Sinhalese in Ceylon and, in 1951, he founded the socialist Sri Lanka Freedom party. Following the unification of several of Ceylon's leftist parties with his own, Bandaranaike was elected prime minister in April of 1956. His pro–Sinhalese policies alienated the Indian Tamils in Ceylon and caused widespread rioting and violence, culminating in the prime minister's assassination. The assassin was convicted of the murder and hanged on July 6,

1962. Bandaranaike's widow, Sirimavo, became Ceylon's prime minister the following year, serving until 1965, and again from 1970 until 1972.

• **Stefan Bandera** (1909–1959), a Ukrainian nationalist leader, died in exile in Germany in 1959 of poisoning. The death was officially ruled a suicide, but there was much speculation that Soviet agents had murdered him. Bandera fought against both the Germans and the Soviets during World War II in an attempt to secure independence for the Ukraine. He was the leader of the Organization of Ukrainian Nationalist (OUN).

# 1960

• In Caracas, Venezuela, on June 24, 1960, a bomb exploded in a car containing Venezuelan president Romulo Betancourt (1908–81). The president and the defense minister, Gen. Josue Lopez Henriquez, were slightly injured in the explosion. **Col. Ramon Armas Perez**, the chief aide-de-camp to the president, was killed in the explosion. Rafael Trujillo (q.v.), the leader of the Dominican Republic, was believed to have been behind the assassination attempt.

• On July 14, 1960, Nobosuke Kishi (1896–1987), the prime minister of Japan, was stabbed in the leg by an ultra-nationalist who was opposed to the prime minister's support for a new mutual security pact between the United States and Japan. Kishi recovered from his wounds but resigned his office four days later.

• **Hazzaa Majali** (1916–60), the premier of Jordan from 1959, was killed in a bomb explosion in his office in Amman on August 29, 1960. Majali, a close advisor of King Hussein, and ten others, including **Suha Iddin Hammoud**, the foreign affairs undersecretary, and **Assem Taijo**, the tourism department director, were killed in the explosion. Hazzaa Majali was born in the village of Kerak

in 1916. He received a degree in law from Damascus University and practiced law until 1947. He then entered royal service as chief of protocol to the Royal Palace. Majali subsequently was elected mayor of Amman in 1948 and served until the following year. In 1950 he was appointed minister of agriculture, and he served briefly as minister of justice and defense. He was an ardent supporter of King Hussein and was pro–Western in his outlook. Majali was appointed prime minister on December 14, 1955, but was forced to resign five days later following widespread strikes and riots opposing his support for Jordan joining the Baghdad Pact. He was subsequently appointed chairman of Jordan's Development Board, where he remained until his appointment as minister of the Royal Court. He was again named prime minister on May 5, 1959. In March of 1960 Jordanian authorities uncovered a conspiracy to assassinate Majali that implicated Egyptian interests. The prime minister was killed in August of 1960 when two time bombs exploded in the government building that housed his office and buried him under the rubble.

• On October 23, 1960, **Inejiro Asanuma** (1899–1960), the chairman of Japan's Socialist party, was stabbed to death by Otoya Yamaguchi, a seventeen-year-old nationalist student. Asanuma, who was a leading supporter of the United States–Japanese Security Pact, was addressing a political rally in Tokyo at the time of the attack. The assassin committed suicide in jail three weeks after the attack.

• **Enrico Mattei** (1906–62), a leading Italian industrialist, was killed in a plane crash in south Milan on October 27, 1962. **William McHale** (1920–62), the manager of the Time-Life Rome bureau, also perished in the crash. While the crash was initially reported as due to mechanical failure, a judicial panel ruled in November of 1997 that a bomb explosion had brought down the plane. The Sicilian Mafia was alleged to have been responsible. Mattei was head of Ente Nazionale di Idrocarburi (ENI), Italy's oil and gas agency. He had been an aggressive champion of Italy's oil and gas interests, utilizing Italian methane reserves and expanding the nation's oil interests. He was also a leading financial contributor to the Christian Democratic and Socialist parties in Italy.

• **Yvon Emmanuel Moreau** (1922–60), a Haitian senator and Episcopalian minister, was arrested on charges of plotting against President Francois Duvalier. He disappeared in November of 1960 and was presumed killed.

• **Felix-Roland Moumie** (1924–60), the leader of the anti–French Union of Cameroons Populations in the Cameroon Republic, died of thallium poisoning on November 3, 1960, in Geneva, Switzerland. Moumie had entered a hospital two weeks earlier, claiming to have been poisoned by political opponents. French security agents were believed to have been responsible for his murder.

• On December 13, 1960, **Germame Neway** and his brother, Imperial Guard commander **Major Mengestu Neway**, led a coup d'etat against Emperor Haile Selassie while the emperor was out of the country. The revolutionary group seized the Crown Prince Asfa Wossen and other important political figures, and took over various government agencies. Forces loyal to the emperor remained at large and began plans for a countercoup. The rebels came under fire from the loyalist military on December 15, 1960, and numerous civilians were killed when planes bombed Addis Ababa. Germame Neway opened fire on captured political detainees, killing or seriously injuring approximately eighteen leading figures of the nobility and the government. The dead included **Abebe Aragai**, the chairman of the council of ministers; **Lt. Gen. Mulugueta Bulli**, the commander of the Imperial Guard before he was replaced by Mengistu Neway in 1956; **Ras Seyum Mengasha** (1887–60), the Governor of Tigre from 1947; **Makonnen Haptewold**, the former director of commerce; and **Dejaz Latibelu Gabre**, a senator. The Emperor returned to the capital to

resume power two days later and the rebels fled into the countryside. The coup leader evaded capture for a week, until soldiers closed in on their position. Germane Neway shot his brother and committed suicide. Mengestu survived his injuries and was tried for treason. He was executed by hanging on March 31, 1961.

Abebe Aragai was born to a noble family in Salale on August 18, 1903. He served as a bodyguard for Emperor Haile Selassie until the early 1930s, when he was appointed chief of police of Addis Ababa. Following the occupation of Ethiopia by the Italians in 1936, Abebe returned to his hometown, where he led the guerrilla warfare resistance to the occupying forces. Following the liberation of Ethiopia and the return of the emperor in 1951, Abebe was appointed mayor of Addis Ababa. From 1941 until 1942, he served as governor of Sidamo, and from 1943 until 1947 he was governor of Tegre. He was appointed minister of the interior in 1949 and served until April 3, 1958, when he was named minister of defense and chairman of the council of ministers. Abebe was one of the influential government leaders who was detained by rebels during the abortive coup attempt in December of 1960s. He was among those killed when the coup leader opened fire on the detainees after the military began a countercoup on December 15, 1960.

# 1961

On January 17, 1961, **Patrice Lumumba** (1926–61), who served as the first prime minister of the Congo Republic for eleven weeks, was murdered by Congolese soldiers loyal to the government of Joseph Mobutu (1930–97). Lumumba was the founder of the Congolese National Movement (M.N.C.) in 1957 and a leader of left-wing anti-colonialism. He became Congo's prime minister following that nation's independence in July of 1960. One of the first problems of his administration was the secession of the Katanga province under Moise Tshombe (q.v.). Lumumba's inability to control the separatists, and his unpopularity with the army in Leopoldville, resulted in a military coup led by Col. Joseph Mobutu in September of 1960. Lumumba was fleeing to his hometown in Stanleyville when he was captured by Mobutu's troops. **Maurice Mpolo**, the former youth minister, and **Joseph Okito**, the vice president of the Senate, were also taken prisoner, and were killed with Lumumba.

On February 19, 1961, a group of Congolese politicians who had been allies of Patrice Lumumba was executed in Bakwanga, the Congo. **Jean-Pierre Finant**, the president of Oriental Province from June until October of 1960; **Maj. Jacques Fataki**, the former chief of the Stanleyville Military Police; **Gilbert Nzuzi**, Congolese National Movement youth leader; and **Pierre Elengesa**, a leader of the Leopoldville Liberal Circle, had been held captive for several months prior to their execution.

• **Ait Izday** of the Ait Yaflman confederation was executed following an unsuccessful coup attempt against King Mohammed V of Morocco in January of 1961. Ait Izday served as the first governor of Tafilalt from 1956. He began his revolt while the king was out of the country, but it was quickly crushed by the crown prince, Hassan II. Ait Izday was captured and sentenced to death for treason.

• On April 22, 1961, **Jacques Alexis** (1922–61), a Haitian poet and author, and the founder of the Party of Popular Accord in 1959 in opposition to Francois Duvalier, was killed. He had returned to Haiti from exile in April of 1961 and was captured near Mole Saint Nicolason on April 22, where he was bound and stoned to death by a crowd.

• **Rafael Leonidas Trujillo y Molina** (1891–1961), the dictator of the Dominican Republic for over thirty years, was assassinated on May 30, 1961, by machine gun fire while he was driving outside the capital. Trujillo was born in San Cristobal on October 24, 1891.

He joined the Dominican National Guard in 1918, following the United States occupation. He rose through the ranks, becoming chief of staff in 1928. Trujillo seized power in February of 1930 when President Horacio Vasquez was ousted in a revolt. He was a candidate for the presidency in subsequent elections, and was victorious when the opposition candidate withdrew from the election under duress. Trujillo took office on August 16, 1930, and ruled the country in a ruthless fashion, eliminating civil and political rights. Numerous political opponents were arrested or murdered during his regime. Trujillo ordered the slaughter of over 15,000 Haitian immigrant workers in 1937. He stepped down as president on August 16, 1938, and allowed his hand-picked candidate, Jacinto Peynado, to take office. Trujillo remained firmly in control of the country as commander of the army during the presidency of Peynado and Manuel de Jesus Troncoso. Trujillo again became president on May 18, 1942. He was a competent administrator who brought prosperity to the Dominican Republic despite the corruption and brutality of his government. His administration built hospitals, schools and roads throughout the country. He again stepped down as president on May 16, 1952, and allowed his younger brother, Hector Trujillo, to take office. Rafael Trujillo retained power in the country despite growing opposition to his regime. The Organization of American States imposed economic sanctions and severed diplomatic relations with the Dominican Republic in August of 1960 after Trujillo was implicated in an assassination attempt against Venezuelan president Romulo Betancourt. Trujillo retained absolute control of the country until his assassination. Several of his alleged assassins, including Gen. J.T. Diaz, were captured and executed, but many involved in the conspiracy remained active in Dominican politics.

• **Salah Ben Youssef** (1910–1961), the secretary general of the Neo-Destour party during Tunisia's bid for independence, was assassinated while in exile in Frankfurt, West

Germany, on August 14, 1961. Ben Youssef was a militant Arab nationalist and an opponent of Tunisian President Habib Bourguiba. He had been in exile from Tunisia since 1955.

• **Dr. Inkongliba Ao** (1903–61), the leader of the Naga State in India, was shot on August 24, 1961. He died of his injuries the following day. His assassin was a fanatic nationalist who objected to Nagaland becoming an Indian state.

• **Adnan Menderes**, the premier of Turkey from 1950 to 1960, was executed by hanging on September 17, 1961, on Imrali Island in Turkey. Menderes had been ousted from office the previous year and was charged with treason. Two of his former aides, **Fatin Rustu Zorlu** (1910–61), the former foreign minister, and **Hassan Polatkan** (1915–61), the former finance minister, had been hanged the previous day.

Menderes was born in Aydin, near Smyrna, Turkey, in 1899. A member of the Republican People's party, he was elected to the National Assembly in 1930. He resigned from parliament in 1945 to form the Turkish Democratic party, becoming the leader of the opposition to the Republican People's Party's government. Menderes led the Democratic party to victory in the 1950 general elections and was selected as prime minister on May 22, 1950. His government led Turkey into joining the North Atlantic Treaty Organization (NATO) and served as a sponsor of the Baghdad Pact. The Democratic party retained power in the elections of 1954 and 1957. Menderes introduced legislation to control the opposition and the press. The increasingly authoritarian nature of his government led to a military coup on May 27, 1960, and Menderes was deposed. He was charged with crimes against the Turkish constitution, including corruption and extravagance, and was convicted and sentenced to death. Menderes attempted suicide by taking an overdose of sleeping pills after hearing the verdict. He recovered and was executed on September 17, 1961.

• **Dag Hammarskjold**, the secretary general of the United Nations, perished in an airplane crash while en route to a peace mission in the Congo Republic on September 18, 1961. Hammarskjold was born on July 29, 1905, in Jonkoping, Sweden. He entered the Swedish civil service in his youth, serving in the Minister of Finance as an undersecretary. In 1947 he was named to the Foreign Ministry and, four years later, was appointed to the Swedish cabinet as minister of state and deputy foreign minister. In 1951 Hammarskjold was also named to Sweden's delegation o the United Nations, becoming chairman of the delegation the following year He was elected secretary general of the United Nations in April of 1953, succeeding Trygvie Lie. He was an internationally respected statesman who performed his duties at the United Nations fairly and without political bias. He was re-elected to a second turn in 1957. During his terms of office he was active in attempting to settle the many disputes in the Middle East, particularly the Suez Canal crisis. In 1960 the United Nations became involved in the civil war in the Belgian Congo, which had recently gained independence. Hammarskjold authorized the use of United Nations troops in an attempt to restore order in the area, an action which met with the disapproval of the Soviet bloc nations. It was during this conflict that Hammarskjold was killed, while making a personal mission of peace to the Congo. The plane in which he was traveling crashed in Northern Rhodesia while en route to a meeting with warring factions. The circumstances behind the crash remain uncertain, but much speculation exists that sabotage was involved. Hammarskjold became the first, and only, posthumous recipient of a Nobel Peace prize when he was awarded it several months after his death.

• **Prince Louis Rwagasore**, the prime minister of Burundi, was shot and killed in a local restaurant in the capital on October 13, 1961. Prince Rwagasore was born in Gita on January 10, 1929, the eldest son of Mwami Mwambutsa of Burundi. He was educated locally and in Belgium and entered politics upon his return to Burundi in 1956. He founded the Union and National Progress party (UPRONA). His father objected to Rwagasore's political career, as his popularity threatened the Mwami's rule. Rwagasore espoused a nationalist policy that favored independence. His party was victorious in elections for the provisional government, and Rwagasore took office as prime minister on September 29, 1961. He was assassinated two weeks later. Jean Kageorgis, a Greek, was arrested for the murder, and was convicted and executed by a Belgian firing squad on June 30, 1962. **Nicodeme Kaja**, who served as secretary of state in the provisional government in 1961, was also executed for his role in Rwagasore's assassination.

# 1962

• Indonesian President Sukarno (1901–70) was uninjured in an assassination attempt on January 8, 1962. A bomb exploded in the path of the president's car while he was traveling in a motorcade in Macassar.

• **Adolf Eichmann** (1906–62), who was in charge of the deportation of Jews to extermination centers during World War II, was executed in Ramleh Prison in Israel on May 31, 1962. Eichmann, who had disappeared following the end of the war, was tracked down in Argentina by Israeli agents in May of 1960 and secretly captured and brought to Israel. He was tried between April 2 and August 14 of 1961, and was sentenced to death for crimes against humanity.

Eichmann was born on March 19, 1906, and joined the Austrian Nazi Party in 1932. He joined Heinrich Himmler's Security Service (S.D.) in 1934 and, in 1938, was put in charge of the Office of Jewish Emigration. He was personally in charge of the killing of millions of Jews throughout Europe before and during World War II. Following the end of the war Eichmann escaped trial as a war criminal and fled to Argentina. He was not located and brought to justice until fifteen years later.

• President Kwame Nkrumah (1909–72) of Ghana was the target of an assassination attempt on August 1, 1962. Nkrumah was uninjured by a bomb tossed at his car while he was riding through Kulungugu, Ghana.

• On August 22, 1962, French president Charles de Gaulle (1890–1970) was the target of an assassination attempt. The car in which he and his wife were riding near Petit-Clamart was barraged with gunfire, but de Gaulle and the other occupants were uninjured. The Organisation de l'Arme Secret (OAS), a rebel military organization that blamed de Gaulle for the loss of Algeria, was responsible for the attempt on his life. Several conspirators were tried and, on March 11, 1963, Lt. Col. Jean-Marie Bastien-Thiry (1926–63) was executed by a firing squad in Paris for his role in the assassination attempt.

De Gaulle had survived a previous attempt on his life on September 9, 1961, when a bomb was set in the path of his car on a road leading from Paris. De Gaulle was uninjured in that attempt as well, when the bomb failed to detonate properly. It was believed the OAS was also responsible for that attack.

• **Ahmed ibn Yahya Hamid al-Din**, the imam of Yemen, was reported to have died of natural causes on September 18, 1962. Ahmed was born in San'a in 1891, the son of Imam Yahya (q.v.). He was proclaimed crown prince in 1927. Imam Yahya was assassinated in February of 1948, and a reformist government under Abdullah al-Wazir was proclaimed. Ahmed joined with his brothers to lead an army of tribesmen against Abdullah and took control of the government on March 13, 1948. Ahmed approved some reforms in the country and continued to claim that the British Protectorate of Aden was a legal part of Yemen. Ahmed's brothers, Abdullah and Abbas (q.v.), led a revolt against the government in April of 1955. Ahmed was imprisoned and forced to abdicate. He escaped his captors, however, and was reinstated as imam by loyalist forces. Both brothers were imprisoned and executed. Imam Ahmed suffered from poor health during the late 1950s. He was shot and seriously wounded in an assassination attempt on March 27, 1961. Ahmed's injuries and failing health led to his death. He was succeeded by his son, Mohammed al-Badr (1928–96). Imam Mohammed was deposed during a revolution the following week on September 26, 1962. He was originally reported slain, but this proved untrue. **Hasan Bin Abrahin**, the Yemini foreign minister, and ten other officers were summarily executed on September 28, 1962, following the revolution.

• **Pierre Kamdem-Ninyim** (1936–62), a political leader in East Cameroon, was executed by firing squad in 1962 after he was implicated in the killing of a deputy. Kamdem-Ninyim was the traditional chief of the Baham and a member of the Union des Populations du Cameroun (UPC). He was elected to the national assembly in 1960 and served in the cabinet as minister of health until June of 1961.

• **Haylu Kebret**, a leader of the Ethiopian resistance against Italian occupation forces in the 1930s, was arrested for plotting against the government of Haile Selassie. Kebret was executed by hanging in 1962.

# 1963

• **Sylvanus Olympio**, the first president of Togo, was shot and killed near the United States embassy in the capital city of Lome on January 13, 1963. Olympio was born in Agoue, Dahomey, on September 6, 1902. He was educated at the London School of Economics and was employed by the United African Company in 1926. He entered politics as the leader of the Togolese Unity Committee and was a leading spokesman of the Ewe tribe in French Togoland. Olympio supported the reunification of French and British Togoland and was elected president of the Territorial Assembly in 1946. He was also a proponent of autonomy for French Togoland and was opposed by the French colonial government. The French actively supported Nicolas Grunitzky in elections to the Territorial Assembly in 1955, and Olympio's Togolese Unity Committee boycotted the elections. Olympio's supporters continued to advocate autonomy, and France was forced to grant Togo the status of a republic within the French community in 1956. British Togoland was incorporated into Ghana following a referendum later in the year. Olympio's party was victorious in elections in 1958, and he became prime minister on May 16, 1958. He led his country to complete independence on April 27, 1960, and became the nation's first president. Olympio established Togo as a single-party state the following year. He faced opposition from radicals and was the target of three assassination attempts in 1961. Olympio lost the support of elements of the army be denying entry into the Togo army of veterans of the French military. His administration was also marked by tension with Kwame Nkrumah's government of neighboring Ghana. Olympio was ambushed by a group of ex-soldiers, who pursued the president to the United States Embassy, where he intended to seek asylum. He was shot to death by his pursuers at the gates of the embassy on January 13, 1963.

• **Abdul Karim Kassem** (1914–63), the premier of Iraq from 1958, was executed on February 8, 1963, following a military coup against his government in Baghdad. Kassem had led the army in revolt against King Feisal II (q.v.) in 1958 and had ordered the butchering of the king and his family. He became the first leader of the new republican government. His inability to control the diverse forces in Iraq led to his downfall and death. Several days after the coup the new regime announced that some of Kassem's close advisors were also executed, including **Brig. Mahawdi**, the president of the former people's court, **Brig. Abdul Majid Jamil**, **Brig. Daoud Jannasi**, **Col. Ibrahm Kazim Moussawi**, and **Col. Hosni Dhidr Douri**. Following the coup many members of the Iraqi Communist Party were also arrested and murdered, including **Salam 'Adil**, the first secretary of the Party.

Abdul Karim Kassem was born in Baghdad on November 21, 1914. He attended the Iraq Military Academy before joining the Iraqi army in 1934. He rose through the ranks and served as a commander during the Palestine campaign. In 1955 he was promoted to brigadier. Kassem was an Arab nationalist and, with Abdul Salam Arif, led an army uprising against the government of King Feisal II in July of 1958. Following the overthrow and murder of Feisal, Kassem became prime minister on July 14, 1958. He instituted a series of agrarian reform measures later in the year. He broke with Abdul Salam Arif over his support of Egyptian president Gamal Abdel Nasser and imprisoned Arif. Kassem was wounded in an assassination attempt in October of 1959, but recovered after several months of hospitalization. Future Iraqi leader Saddam Hussein was one of the gunmen involved in the attempt. In June of 1961 Kassem declared that Kuwait was an integral part of Iraq. The British army mobilized to protect the sheikdom. Though Iraq made no military move toward Kuwait, Kassem continued to insist that the countries should be unified. The Kassem regime was also faced with a rebellion by the Kurds in northeast Iraq. Abdul Salam Arif organized a military uprising against Kassem on February 8, 1963 and ousted him as leader of the government. He was tried and convicted by the revolutionary court and executed the following day.

• **Henri Lafond** (1895–1963), the president of the Banque de l'Union Parisienne and a member of the French Atomic Energy Commission, was assassinated on March 6, 1963, while driving his automobile in Neuilly, France.

• **Quinim Pholsena** (1915–63), the foreign minister of Laos, was shot and killed on April 1, 1963, by soldiers guarding his home in Vientiane. Quinim Pholsena was an associate of the Pathet Lao, a left-wing, pro–Communist party. He had been active in the Laotian Civil War in 1960, serving as an advisor to Capt. Kon Le in his fight against the pro–Western government. Quinim Pholsena had joined the coalition government after the conclusion of the Civil War.

• **Mohammed Khemisti**, the foreign minister of Algeria, was shot by a Moslem fanatic on April 11, 1963. He died several days later. Khemisti was born in Maghnia in 1930. He became secretary to Abdel Fares, leader of the Provisional Executive, in the early 1960s. He was instrumental in transferring powers from the Provisional Executive to Ahmed Ben Bella, and became Algeria's foreign minister when the country gained its independence from France in 1962.

• **Grigoris Lambrakis** (1917–63), a Greek left-wing deputy and vice president of the Peace Committee, was murdered on May 22, 1963, when he was hit by a van driven by members of an extreme right-wing organization while attending a rally in Salonika. It was later determined that the murder had occurred with the knowledge and sanction of the local police. Lambrakis' murder was the basis for Costa-Gavras' 1969 film Z.

• **Medgar W. Evers**, the Mississippi field secretary of the National Association for the Advancement of Colored People (NAACP) for nine years, was shot in the back upon arriving home shortly before midnight on June 11, 1963, and died minutes later. Byron De la Beckwith (1921–2001) was accused of the murder, but two subsequent trials resulted in no conviction. Beckwith was finally convicted of the crime and sentenced to prison in a retrial in 1994.

Medgar Wylie Evers was born in Decatur, Mississippi, on July 2, 1925. He served in the U.S. Army during World War II and attended Alcorn A & M College after his military service. Following graduation Evers was employed by Magnolia Mutual Insurance, a black-owned Mississippi business. He soon became involved with the NAACP and was hired as a full-time field worker for the organization in Jackson, Mississippi, in 1954. His work included enrolling new members in the NAACP and to expose the racist violence that plagued blacks in Mississippi. Evers led a series of protests and boycotts against segregation in the early 1960s and was subjected to numerous threats of violence by radical racist groups. In May of 1963 a bomb was thrown into his garage and, the following month, an assassin took his life.

• **Clement Barbot**, the chief of Haitian president Francois Duvalier's secret police, the Tontons Macoutes, until his arrest in July of 1960, was killed with his brother, **Harry Barbot**, by Haitian troops in a sugar cane field on July 14, 1963. Barbot had led an unsuccessful insurrection against Duvalier earlier in the year.

• **Ngo Dinh Diem** (1901–63), the first president of South Vietnam, was killed following a military coup in Saigon on November 2, 1963. **Ngo Dinh Nhu** (1910–63), the head of South Vietnam's secret police and Ngo Dinh Diem's brother, was also killed.

Ngo Dinh Diem was born in Hue in 1901. He served as provincial governor in Emperor Bao Dai's government in French Indo-China in the early 1930s, but subsequently gained anti–French views and abandoned politics. He reentered politics in 1947 and formed the National Union Front, an anti–Communist, pro-independence party. In October of 1955 Ngo Dinh Diem, under the patronage of French and American interests in the area, was elected the first president of the Republic of South Vietnam. His rule was endangered by increasing Communist rebel activity sponsored by North Vietnam. Ngo Dinh Diem, a devout Catholic, was also beset by the opposition of Vietnamese Buddhists. Ngo Dinh Diem was ousted and killed by members of the Vietnamese army led by Gen. Duong Van Minh, with the apparent support of the United States government.

Ngo Dinh Nhu, the president's brother, was also an extremely powerful figure in South Vietnam. He was officially the supreme adviser to the president, but also controlled the secret police and the ruling national revolutionary movement. His wife, Madame Nhu, was the official "first lady" of South Vietnam, as the president was a bachelor.

A third brother, **Ngo Dinh Canh**, was the despotic governor of the northern part of South Vietnam. He was arrested by the new military regime following the ouster of his brother. Ngo Dinh Canh was tried for extortion and murder and, on May 9, 1964, was executed.

• **John F. Kennedy**, the thirty-fifth president of the United States of America, was assassinated while riding in a motorcade in Dallas, Texas, on November 22, 1963. John Fitzgerald Kennedy was born in Brookline, Massachusetts, on May 29, 1917. He was the son of Joseph P. Kennedy, a millionaire businessman who served as ambassador to Great Britain during the administration of President Franklin Roosevelt. John Kennedy served in the United States Navy as a P.T.–boat commander during World War II. He was decorated for heroism following the sinking by the Japanese of P.T.–boat 109 in August of 1943. Following his discharge from the navy in 1945, Kennedy began his political career. He was elected to the United States Congress in 1946, representing the 11th congressional district in Massachusetts. In 1952 he defeated Republican incumbent Henry Cabot Lodge for a seat in the United States Senate, and shortly after his inauguration married Jacqueline Lee Bouvier. In 1956 he authored *Profiles in Courage*, a study of his personal political heroes, and was awarded the 1957 Pulitzer Prize for Biography for his efforts. Kennedy was narrowly defeated for the 1956 Democratic nomination for vice president, but was easily reelected to the Senate two years later. He received the Democratic nomination for the presidency in 1960 and went on to defeat Richard M. Nixon in the general election later in the year.

John Kennedy was sworn in as president of the United States on January 20, 1961. His administration was noted for its support for civil rights legislation and the establishment of the Peace Corps. Kennedy's term of office was also marked by difficulties with the Communist-led government of Fidel Castro in Cuba. In 1961 a C.I.A.–sponsored attempt by Cuban exiles to overthrow the Castor regime met with failure in the "Bay of Pigs" incident. The following year Cuba became the base of Soviet nuclear missiles. In a confrontation known as the Cuban Missile Crisis, Kennedy threatened to blockade the island nation unless the Soviet offensive weapons were removed. Soviet Premier Nikita Khruschev agreed to their removal following a period of international tension.

President Kennedy's term of office was cut short on November 22, 1963, when he was shot and killed by a sniper while traveling in a motorcade in downtown Dallas, Texas. He was struck by two bullets and was pronounced dead shortly after his arrival at a Dallas hospital. Texas Governor John B. Connally (1917–93), who was riding with the president, was seriously injured in the shooting, but subsequently recovered. Lee Harvey Oswald, a twenty-four-year-old drifter, was arrested for the murder. On November 24, 1963, Oswald was himself shot and killed by Jack Ruby (1911–67), a Dallas nightclub owner, while being transferred from the Dallas police department.

Kennedy was succeeded by his vice president, Lyndon B. Johnson. The new president appointed a commission, chaired by United States Chief Justice Earl Warren, to investigate the president's killing. The Warren Commission ruled in 1964 that Oswald had fired the fatal shots from a window in the sixth floor of the Texas School Book Depository. The commission also reported that Oswald had acted alone in the planning and execution of the assassination and that there was no evidence of a conspiracy in either the slaying of President Kennedy or of Oswald. Subsequent investigations of the assassination have attempted to show that a conspiracy did exist, with such culprits as agents of Cuban President Castro, disgruntled former C.I.A. agents, and members of organized crime often cited as possible suspects. None of these allegations have been substantiated.

• Brazilian federal senator **Jose Cairala** was shot to death during a gunfight between Senators Arnon de Melo and Silvestre Pericles on the floor of the Senate on December 4, 1963. De Melo and Pericles both were representatives of Brazil's northeast region of Alagoas. The rival senators exchanged shots when de Melo began addressing the Senate and Cairala, a representative of Acre State, was wounded in the abdomen when a stray bullet struck him. He died shortly afterwards during surgery.

# 1964

• Edwin O. Reischauer (1911–90), the United States ambassador to Japan, was stabbed in the thigh by a deranged Japanese youth on March 24, 1964. Reischauer was leaving the United States Embassy in Tokyo at the time of the attack. He recovered from his wounds and continued to represent the United States in Japan.

• **Jigme P. Dorji** (1919–64), the premier of Bhutan, was shot and killed in Punchholing, near the Indian border, on April 5, 1964, by a Bhutanese soldier. It was believed that the assassination of Dorji, an anti–Communist, had been encouraged by the People's Republic of China. Naik Jambey, the alleged assassin, and Gen. Chapda Namgyal Bahadur and Lt. Col. Sangyal Dorji were executed on July 9, 1964, for complicity in the murder.

Jigme Polden Dorji was born in 1919. He was appointed premier in 1955. With his brother-in-law, King Jigme Dorji Wangchuck, he succeeded in abolishing slavery and polyandry and increased Bhutan's contacts with the outside world. His assassination came shortly after Bhutan had sealed off its northern border with Tibet, which was dominated by Communist China.

• On July 27, 1964, several Congolese political leaders were murdered by Communist rebel followers of Pierre Mulele (q.v.) in

Albertville, the capital of the North Katanga province. **Jason Sendwe**, the provisional president of the province; **Fortunat Kabange Numbi**, the former provisional vice president; and **Saloman Ilunga** and **Luther Kabila**, both former cabinet ministers, were among the politicians killed.

• **Abid Es-Shishakli** (1909–64), the former president of Syria, was assassinated while in exile in Brazil on September 28, 1964. Shishakli was born in Hama in 1909. He served in the French army while France ruled Syria under a League of Nations mandate, and deserted to the Syrian army in 1945. Shishakli supported Husni Zaim's (q.v.) military coup in June of 1949, but subsequently broke with Zaim. He was dismissed from the army, but was reinstated following Zaim's ouster by Sami Hinnawi (q.v.) in August of 1949. Shishakli then ousted Hinnawi on December 19, 1949. He allowed the restoration of democratic institutions for several years and took the title of deputy chief of state. When the elected government appeared unable to rule, Shishakli again seized power in a coup. He suspended the Chamber of Deputies and dissolved all political parties in December of 1951. He appointed a supporter, Colonel Fawzi Silo, as chief of state and prime minister, but Shishakli wielded most of the power as deputy prime minister and minister of state. He promoted a new constitution in July of 1953. He formed the Arab Liberation Movement and ran unopposed for the presidency. Shishakli took office on July 11, 1953. He also took the position of prime minister on July 20, 1953. Shishakli became increasingly dictatorial as opposition mounted against his rule. He was ousted by a military coup on February 25, 1954. He fled to Paris and subsequently went into exile in Brazil. Shishakli was convicted in absentia of torture, conspiracy, and treason and sentenced to life imprisonment. He was shot to death on a street in Ceres, Brazil, on September 28, 1964, by a Druze avenging the bombing of the Druze Mountain during his rule.

# 1965

• **Pierre Ngendamdumwe** (1930–65), the premier of Burundi, was assassinated in the capital city of Bujumbura on January 15, 1965. Ngendamdumwe, a member of the Hutu tribe, was a supporter of Prince Louis Rwagasore (q.v.) and had served as minister of finance in the provisional government in 1961. He was selected to replace Andre Muhirwa as prime minister on June 17, 1963. Ngendamdumwe displeased Mwami Mwambutsa by establishing diplomatic relations with the People's Republic of China and was dismissed as prime minister on April 1, 1964. Ngendamdumwe was called upon to form another government by the Mwami shortly before his murder on January 7, 1965. Several former Burundian officials, including ex-premier Abin Nyamoya, were arrested for possible complicity in the murder. Ngendamdumwe's moderate policies were thought to have been the motive behind the assassination by Tutsi extremists.

• **Hassan Ali Mansour** (1923–65), the premier of Iran, was shot in Teheran while entering a government building on January 21, 1965. He died of two gunshot wounds on January 26, 1965. The assassin was identified as Mohammed Bakaril, a twenty-one-year-old Moslem fanatic. Bakaril and three other plotters were executed on June 16, 1965.

Mansour was born in Teheran in 1923, the son of Ali Mansour, who had served as Iran's prime minister in 1950. Hassan Ali Mansour was educated in Teheran and Paris. He returned to Iran to join the diplomatic corps and was named deputy prime minister in 1959. He subsequently served as minister of labor and minister of commerce. He formed the Progressive Center, a political advisor group, in 1961. He was a leader of the group during the elections in 1963 and subsequently became leader of the newly formed New Iran party. He was selected to become Iran's prime minister on March 7, 1964. Mansour was an advocate of the shah's modernization plans and ran afoul of conservative Muslim leaders while carrying out his reforms. He retained office until his assassination on January 21, 1965.

• **Pratap Singh Kairon** (1901–65), the former chief minister of the Punjab region of India, was assassinated on February 6, 1965, while driving near New Delhi. Kairon had served as chief minister from 1956 until his resignation in 1965.

• **Lt. Gen. Humberto Delgado** (1906–65), a leading opposition politician to Portuguese dictator Antonio De Oliveira Salazar (1889–1970), and an unsuccessful candidate for the presidency of Portugal in 1958, was reported missing from his home in exile in Algiers on February 13, 1965. He had reportedly been on his way to meet with anti–Salazar conspirators in Spain. In April of 1965 his body and that of his secretary, Arajarir Campos, were found in a shallow grave near the Spanish town of Badajoz on the Portuguese border. Both had been murdered by heavy blows to the skull, presumably by agents of Salazar's regime.

• On February 17, 1965, the government of Alphonse Massamba-Debat (q.v.) in Brazzaville, the Congo, announced the assassination of **Lazare Matsokota** (1931–65), the attorney general; **Joseph Pouabou**, the president of the Supreme Court; and **Anselme Massouemi**, the information agency director. Other sources indicated that the three men, all leading Lari politicians, had been arrested by government troops shortly before their alleged assassination.

• **Malcolm X**, an American black nationalist leader, was shot to death while addressing a crowd at the Aubudon Ballroom in New York City on February 21, 1965. Thalmadge Hayer (Thomas Hagan) (b.1943), Norman 3X (Norman Butler) (b.1938), and Thomas 15X (Thomas Johnson) (b.1935), all followers of Black Muslim leader Elijah Muhammad (1897–1975), were charged with the assassination. They were convicted of first-degree murder in March of 1966.

Malcolm X was born Malcolm Little in Omaha, Nebraska, on May 19, 1925. His father, Earl Little, was a Baptist minister and supporter of Marcus Garvey's Black Nationalist movement. When Malcolm was a child the family was terrorized by white supremacists seeking to silence his father's activism. Earl Little was found dead on the Lansing, Michigan, trolley tracks. His death was ruled an accident, though it was believed he had been a victim of racial hatred. The family became separated after Malcolm's father's death. Malcolm left school and, in the early 1940s, became involved with various criminal activities in New York's Harlem. Arrested for burglary in Boston in 1946, he spent seven years imprisoned. During his confinement he continued his education and became interested in Elijah Muhammad's Muslim religious organization, the Nation of Islam. Following his parole in 1952, he joined the Nation of Islam and changed his name to Malcolm X, to symbolize his lost tribal name. Malcolm became a leading figure in the Nation of Islam, establishing mosques in Detroit, Harlem and Michigan. He married Betty Shabazz in 1958, and was active in the early days of the civil rights movement. Malcolm broke with Elijah Muhammad in March of 1964 to form his own Muslim Mosque, Inc., and the Organization for Afro-American Unity The break with the Nation of Islam resulted in several threats against Malcolm's life. He escaped a firebombing of his home in East Elmhurst, New York, on February 14, 1965. The following week Malcolm was shot to death.

Malcolm X was the subject of much interest during his life and after his death. Numerous books and documentaries focused on his career and, in 1992, Spike Lee filmed a critically acclaimed biography. Questions lingered about his assassination, with members of his family accusing Elijah Muhammad's successor, Nation of Islam leader Louis Farrakhan, of complicity in the murder. In January of 1995, Qubilah Shabazz (b.1961), one of Malcolm's daughters, was charged with attempting to hire a hitman to murder Farrakhan. Tragedy continued to plague the family when Malcolm's widow, Dr. Betty Shabazz

(1936–97), died on June 23, 1997, of injuries received in a fire in her home in Yonkers, New York, three weeks earlier. The fire had allegedly been started by her 12-year-old grandson.

• **Pio Gama Pinto**, a supporter of Kenyan independence and leading journalist, was assassinated in Nairobi on February 24, 1965. Pinto was born in Nairobi on March 31, 1927. He was educated in India and briefly served in the Indian Air Force during World War II. He became involved with the Goa independence movement from Portugal, co-founding the Goa National Congress. He returned to Kenya in 1949 to avoid arrest by the Portuguese authorities. Pinto immediately became involved with the Kenyan nationalist movement, working as a journalist for several newspapers. In 1954 he was arrested by the colonial authorities for his support of the Mau Mau movement. He was released from detention on Manda Island in 1958 and spent another year restricted in Kabernet. He returned to the independence movement after his release, founding the Kenyan African National Union (KANU) newspaper, *Sauti ya Kanu*, and the Pan African Press. He was elected to the East African Central Legislative Assembly in 1963 and served in the Kenyan Parliament from 1964. He was also a founder of the Lumumba Institute in 1964, and continued to support independence for Portuguese colonies. The following year he was assassinated by unknown gunmen.

• On March 21, 1965, Lt. Gen. Rene Barrientos Ortuno, the president of Bolivia, was shot and injured in an assassination attempt as he was driving on a road near Cochbamba, Bolivia. Barrientos recovered from his injuries and remained president of Bolivia until his death in an airplane crash on April 27, 1969.

• **Mohammed Al-Zubairy**, the former deputy premier and minister of information and education in Yemen, was assassinated on April 1, 1965. Zubairy had been instrumental in arranging a cease-fire between the Royalist and Republican forces in Yemen in late 1964. He had resigned his offices after the cease-fire was broken.

• **Col. Ernesto Molina Arreaga** (1901–65), Guatemala's deputy defense minister, was shot to death in front of his home in Guatemala City on May 21, 1965. His assassins were believed to be left-wing terrorists.

• **Lt. Gen. Achmad Jani**, the Indonesian army chief of staff, and five other army generals were found shot to death near the Halim air base on October 4, 1965. The generals had been kidnapped on September 30, 1965, following the start of a Communist uprising in Indonesia. The murdered generals included **General Suparman**, **General M.T. Harjono**, **General Suprapto**, **General Sutojo** and **General Pandjaitan**. The uprising was crushed by the army led by right-wing Generals Suharto (b. 1921) and Nasution (1919–2000) and led to the ouster of President Sukarno (1901–70) and the establishment of a military government under Suharto. Hundreds of thousands of leftist sympathizers were reported to have been summarily executed over the next seven months.

• **Mehdi Ben Barka** (1920–65), a leading Moroccan opposition politician and internationally known leftist figure, was abducted from a Paris restaurant and presumed murdered in October of 1965. Ben Barka served as president of the National Consultative Assembly from 1956 to 1959. He was accused of subversion by King Hassan II in 1961, and went into exile in France. He returned to Morocco in 1962, and served briefly in the National Assembly. He was again exiled the following year for plotting against the government. He had been condemned to death in absentia before being abducted by members of the Moroccan secret service. Ben Barka's disappearance was responsible for a major rift between the Moroccan and French governments. Several leading Moroccan politicians, including Interior Minister Gen. Mohammed Oufkir (q.v.) and Moroccan security chief Ahmed Dlimi (q.v.) were charged in absentia with the kidnapping by a French court. Dlimi arrived in France near the end of the trial and was arrested. After the trial was resumed Dlimi was acquitted of the charges against him, though Gen. Oufkir was convicted and sentenced to life imprisonment in absentia. Rene Thorp, Pierre Stibbe, and Michel Bruguier, who had served as counsels for the family of Ben Barka, all died several weeks apart between the first and second hearings of the case. Their deaths were presumably of natural causes.

• On October 19, 1965, Leopold Biha, the premier of Burundi, was seriously injured when he was shot at his home in Bujumbura, the capital, during a coup attempt. The coup was unsuccessful and Biha recovered from his injuries the following year. He remained Burundi's premier until his ouster on July 8, 1966, following another coup.

• **Khalid ibn Musai'id Al Sa'ud**, a member of the Saudi ruling family was shot to death by police in 1965 after leader a group protesting the introduction of television into Saudi Arabi by King Faisal (q.v.). Khalid had studied in the West and returned to Saudi Arabia as a religious zealot. He was active in several protests before his death. His brother, Prince Faisal Ibn Musad Ibn Abdel Aziz, assassinated the king ten years later.

• **Dipa Nusantara Aidit**, the leader of the Communist party of Indonesia (PKI), was shot to death by the Indonesian army following a military coup in 1965. Aidit was born in North Sumatra in 1923 and served as the leader of the Indonesian Communist party from 1954 until his death. He was a nationalist as well as a Communist, and his party received some support from Sukarno, the Indonesian president. Aidit, **M.H. Lukman**, the deputy leader, and many other Communist politicians were captured and summarily executed following an abortive coup attempt by the communists, which was followed by a military uprising in opposition.

• **Joseph Bamina**, the former prime minister of Burundi, was executed in Muramvya on December 15, 1965, following an attempted Hutu coup the previous October. Bamina was born in 1925. He belonged to the Hutu tribe and attended Lovanium University. He was a member of the United and National Progress party (UPRONA) and was elected to the National Assembly in 1961. Bamina was elected to the Senate and became its president in 1965. He was selected as prime minister to succeed the assassinated Pierre Ngendamdumwe (q.v.) on January 25, 1965. An advocate of Hutu rights, Bamina was dismissed as prime minister on March 30, 1965, but remained head of a caretaker government until September 30, 1965. He returned to the Senate to serve as president until his arrest following the abortive Hutu revolt in October of 1965. He was condemned in a mass trial and executed along with over 1,500 Hutus. Other prominent Hutu leaders that perished at this time include **Emile Bucumi** (1930–65), a former National Assembly president; **Paul Mirerekano** and **Louis Bucumi** (1940–65), leaders of the Ngendendumwe youth movement; **Ignace Ndimanya**, the former minister of public works; **Gervais Nyangoma**, Burundi's former ambassador to the United Nations; **Pierre Burarame**, the former minister of economics; **Paul Nibirantiza**, a former National Assemblyman; and **Patrice Mayondo**, a former vice-president of the national assembly.

# 1966

• **Abubaker Tafawa Balewa** (1912–66), who had served as Nigeria's prime minister since that nation's independence on October 1, 1960, was murdered during an uprising on January 15, 1966. Northern Regional Premier **Sir Ajhaji Ahmadu Bello**, the sarduana of Sokoto, Western Regional Premier **Chief Samuel Ladoke Akintola**, and Finance Minister **Festus Sam Okotie-Eboh** were also killed during the revolt. The uprising was led by members of the military from Nigeria's Eastern region who were predominantly members of the Ibo tribe. The revolt was carried out by them in the hopes of breaking the hold that the Northern regime's politicians had established in Nigeria, and in an attempt to eliminate the widespread corruption of the civilian government. Gen. Johnson Aguiyi-Ironsi (q.v.), the commander of the army, quickly moved to seize power in Nigeria, and successfully gained control of the country from the rebels. The leader of the rebellion, **Maj. Patrick Chukwuma Kaduna Nzeogwu**, subsequently joined the Biafran successionist movement and was killed in battle with Nigerian troops the following year on July 26, 1967.

Abubaker Tafawa Balewa was born in Bauchi, Northern Nigeria, in December of 1912. He was educated locally and became a teacher in 1944. He continued his education at London University's Institute of Education and returned to Nigeria in 1946. He subsequently entered politics and was elected to the Northern House of Assembly. He became a representative on the Legislative Council the following year. Balewa was a founder of the Northern People's Congress (NPC) with Ajhaji Ahmadu Bello in 1951. Balewa became minister of works in the government in 1952 and minister of transport the following year. He was elected chief minister in September of 1957 and formed a coalition government with Nnamdi Azikiwe's National Council of Nigeria and the Cameroons following parliamentary elections in December of 1959. Nigeria was granted independence from Great Britain on October 1, 1960, and Balewa remained prime minister in the independent government. Political unrest and regional factionalism plagued his government. Balewa remained prime minister following general elections in December of 1964. He was kidnapped during a coup led by rebels on January 15, 1966, and was killed during the early hours of the coup. His body was found on a road near Lago on January 21, 1966.

Festus Samuel Okotie-Eboh was born in Jakpa, Delta State, in July of 1912. A wealthy businessman, he served as first secretary of the Warri National Union. He was elected to the Western Regional Assembly in 1951 and was elected to the federal House of Representatives three years later. The leader of the Na-

tional Council of Nigeria and the Cameroons party, he became minister of labor in 1958. He was also named minister of finance in the national government, a position he held until his murder in January of 1966.

- **Abdullah El-Airiny** (1919–66), the Yemini administration minister, was shot and killed while in his office in Sana on April 13, 1966. Airiny had served as acting president of Yemen since March of 1966. His assassin committed suicide shortly after the shooting.

- **Kamil Muruwwah**, a leading Lebanese journalist was assassinated on May 15, 1966. Muruwwah was born near Sidon, Lebanon, in 1915. A Shi'ite Muslim, he attended the American University of Beirut and subsequently worked as a journalist. Muruwwah founded *Al-Hayat*, a daily newspaper, in 1946 and during the 1950s became an outspoken opponent of Egyptian President Gamal Nasser's ambitions in the Arab world. He also founded the English-language daily newspaper *Daily Star* in 1952. His murder was believed to have been orchestrated by Lebanese supporters of Nasser.

- **Evariste Kimba** (1926–66), the former prime minister of the Congo (Zaire), was hanged in Kinshasa with three former cabinet members on June 2, 1966, after having been convicted on charges of conspiring to assassinate President Joseph Mobutu. The other executed politicians who had all served in the cabinet of ex-premier Cyrille Adoula during the early 1960s were **Sen. Emmanuel Bamba**, the former finance minister; **Jerome Anany**, the former defense minister; and **Alexander Mahamba**.

Evariste Kimba was born in Katanga on July 16, 1926. He was a supporter of Moise Tshombe (q.v.) and served as foreign minister in Tshombe's secessionist Katanga Republic from 1960 until 1963. He was named by Joseph Kasavubu to succeed Tshombe as prime minister of the Democratic Republic of the Congo on October 13, 1965. Tshombe's supporters in the Parliament prevented Kimba from forming a government. Joseph Mobutu led a military coup in November of 1965 and ousted the civilian government. Kimba was subsequently arrested in May of 1966 on charges of plotting against Mobutu's government in what was called the "Pentecost Plot."

• **Johnson T.U. Aguiyi-Ironsi** (1924–66), the head of state of Nigeria, was kidnapped and murdered in Northern Nigeria by army officers on July 29, 1966. Aguiyi-Ironsi, who had come to power during a military revolt on January 15, 1966, was shot and killed with **Lt. Col. Adekunle Faguiyi** (1926–66), the military governor of the Western Region of Nigeria, during another army revolt.

Johnson T.U. Aguiyi-Ironsi was born on March 3, 1924. He was a member of the Ibo tribe and served in the Nigerian army, rising to the rank of major general. He commanded United Nations forces in the former Belgian Congo in the early 1960s and became head of the Nigerian army following the country's independence. Junior officers led a coup against the government of Sir Abubakar Tafawa Balewa (q.v.) in January of 1966. While other members of the government were murdered during the attempt, Aguiyi-Ironsi escaped assassination by the rebels and rallied the army to put down the coup. He subsequently became head of state, though Northern Nigerian leaders distrusted his government and riots against Ibo control of the government took place throughout the North. Continued rebel activity led to Aguiyi-Ironsi's death by insurgents.

• **Ahmed Bassendawah**, a member of the Supreme Council of Yemen, was assassinated in Aden in August of 1966.

• Dr. S.E. Subandrio (b.1914), Indonesia's former foreign minister, was sentenced to be executed in September of 1966. Dr. Subandrio, who had served as a close advisor to Indonesian president Sukarno, was also the former director of the Indonesia Central Intelligence Bureau. He was appointed foreign minister in the 1950s and had served in that position until his ouster in May of 1966. He had been tried for complicity in the unsuccessful Communist uprising the previous year. Jusuf Muda Dalam, the leftist former minis-

ter of central banking, and Gen. Omar Dani (b.1924), the air force commander who had taken part in the rebellion, were also sentenced to death at this time. The executions were not carried out and their death sentences were reduced to life in prison by President Suharto in 1980. **Soumokil**, the former Republik Maluku Selatan leader, was executed in December of 1966. Moluccans in the Netherlands burned down the Indonesian embassy there in protest.

• **Sayyid Qutb**, a leading Muslim philosopher and writer, was hanged for treason in Egypt in September of 1966. He was born in Musha in 1903 and educated in Cairo. He began writing for the publications *al-Ahram* and *al-Risala* in the mid–1930s. Working with the education ministry in the 1940s, Qutb was sent to the United States to study educational systems. He became disdainful of the west and on his return to Egypt he favored increased Islamic teachings in the schools. Qutb resigned his government post in 1953 to join the Muslim Brotherhood. He was imprisoned by the Nasser government on several occasions and began writing books while incarcerated. He became an outspoken critic of the Nasser regime. Qutb was released from prison in 1964, but rearrested the following year. He was hanged for treason in September of 1966.

• **Hendrik F. Verwoerd**, the prime minister of South Africa, was stabbed to death during a session of Parliament in Capetown on September 6, 1966. Verwoerd had previously been shot twice in the head and seriously injured on April 9, 1960, following the Sharpeville shootings. His assailant, David Pratt, was a white farmer who was sentenced to an asylum. Pratt committed suicide in 1961. Verwoerd was not as fortunate on the second attempt on his life. Dimitrios Tsafendas (1918–99), a parliamentary messenger, stabbed the prime minister in the neck and chest while he was attending a session of Parliament. Verwoerd was pronounced dead when he arrived at a Capetown hospital. Tsafendas was declared mentally deranged and sentenced to a mental institution, where he remained until his death in 1999.

Hendrik Frensch Verwoerd was born in Amsterdam, Holland, on September 8, 1901. He accompanied his parents to South Africa as an infant. He was educated at the University of Stellenbosch and attended several universities in Germany. He returned to South Africa to serve as a member of the faculty at the University of Stellenbosch as a professor of psychology in 1928. He became active in right-wing politics, and in 1937 he became editor of *Die Transvaler*, the Nationalist newspaper in Johannesburg. The newspaper was considered pro–Nazi and anti–British during World War II. The Nationalist party was successful in elections of 1948, though Verwoerd was defeated for a seat in Parliament. He was elected to the Senate later in the year and became minister of native affairs in the cabinet of Prime Minister Daniel Malan in 1950. In that position he served as the leading planner and enforcer of apartheid. He left the cabinet in April of 1958 and ran successfully for election to the Assembly Verwoerd, who was known as Oom (Uncle) Henk to his supporters was selected by the National caucus to serve as prime minister following the death of Johannes Strijdom in August of 1958. He took office on September 3, 1958. The continued suppression of the rights of native South Africans resulted in a series of demonstrations in 1960. At a demonstration in Sharpeville, police fired on the protestors, killing 67 and wounding nearly 2000. After recovering from injuries suffered in an assassination attempt, Verwoerd removed South Africa from the British Commonwealth in 1961, and South African became a republic on May 31, 1961. Verwoerd proceeded with his segregation policies, which included the creation of native homelands that would isolate the majority black South Africans on a small percentage of land. He remained prime minister until his assassination in September of 1966.

• **Tran Van Van**, a member of the South Vietnamese Constituent Assembly, was assassinated by Communist terrorists on December 7, 1966. Tran Van Van had been expected to be a candidate for the presidency of South Vietnam.

# 1967

• **Mohammed Khider** (1914–67), the former secretary general of the Algerian National Liberation Front, was shot to death in front of his home in exile in Madrid, Spain, on January 3, 1967. Mohammed Ben Youssef Khider was born in Algiers in 1912. He became involved in the Algerian nationalist movement in the 1940s and was elected deputy for Algiers in 1946. Khider spent several years in exile in Egypt in the early 1950s when his car was used in a terrorist act in Oran. He was arrested by the French authorities in October of 1956, and remained imprisoned during the war for independence. Khider was released following independence and was a supporter of Ahmed Ben Bella's government. He became secretary general of the Front de Liberation Nationale (FLN), Algeria's only legal political party, in 1962. He came into conflict with Ben Bella soon afterwards over the role of the party in Algeria's government. Khider resigned his leadership and left Algeria in 1964. He had remained active in Algerian exile circles and was a critic of Ben Bella and his successor, Houari Boumedienne. Associates of the slain exile leader blamed the regime of President Boumedienne for complicity in the assassination.

• **Hippolyte Kouavi**, the former vice president of Togo under deposed president Nicolas Grunitzky, was tortured to death in prison shortly after Grunitzky's ouster in January of 1967.

• **Julio Iribarren Borges** was found dead on March 3, 1967, near Caracas, Venezuela. He had been shot three times in the back, allegedly by a leftist terrorist group. Iribarren, the brother of Venezuelan Foreign Minister Ignacio Iribarren Borges, had been missing since March 1, 1967. He was Venezuela's social security chief until late 1966, and was responsible for raising an unpopular social security tax.

- **Gen. Emmanuel K. Kotoka** (1926–67), a close associate of Gen. J.A. Ankrah, the military ruler of Ghana who had ousted President Kwame Nkrumah the previous year, was slain during a military revolt on April 17, 1967. The coup attempt was unsuccessful and Gen. Ankrah remained in power. Emmanuel Kwasi Kotoka was born in Alakple, Fiahor, Volta Region, on October 26, 1926. He was educated locally and joined the military in 1947. He studied military training in England, returning to the Gold Coast in 1955. Kotoka saw action in the Congo in 1960. The following year he was promoted to Lieutenant Colonel. Kotoka plotted the coup that ousted Nkrumah in February of 1966. He served as a member of the ruling National Liberation Council and was commissioner in charge of health and commander of the Ghana armed forces. Kotoka was killed during heavy fighting by Lt. Moses Yeboah during a counter coup in April of 1967. The Ghana International Airport was renamed Kotoka International Airport in his memory.

- **George Lincoln Rockwell** (1918–67), the founder and leader of the American Nazi Party, was shot and killed in an Arlington, Virginia, shopping center on August 24, 1967. Rockwell, who founded the American Nazi Party in 1958, was a great admirer of Adolf Hitler. John C. Patler, a twenty-nine-year-old member of Rockwell's organization who had been expelled earlier for extremism, was arrested for the murder. He was tried and convicted and served several years in prison for the crime.

- **Demba Diop**, a Senegalese deputy and leading member of the Union Progressiste Senegalaise, was assassinated in 1967. The murder was believed to have been due to rivalry within the party and two other deputies were imprisoned for the crime.

- **Abdel Hakim Amer**, the former Egyptian defense minister and army chief of staff, reportedly committed suicide on September 14, 1967, a month after having been arrested on charges of plotting a military coup. It was suspected that his death was caused by agents of the Egyptian secret police. Amer was born in 1919 and attended the Military Academy. He fought in the Palestine War in 1948 and was a founder of the Free Officers in the early 1950s. After the ouster of King Farouk Amer served on the revolutionary council, becoming minister of war in 1954. He served as vice president and minister of war of the United Arab Republic from 1958, until Syria withdrew from the union in 1961. He subsequently served on the Presidential Council and as minister of defense. Amer was widely blamed for Egypt's defeat by Israel in the 1967 war and was dismissed from his duties. He was arrested in August of 1967 on charges of plotting against the government and died the following month.

- **Maj. Ernesto "Che" Guevara De la Serna**, the Argentine-born Cuban revolutionary leader, was killed by government troops in Bolivia on October 9, 1967. Guevara was born in Rosario, Argentina, on June 14, 1928. He joined the Communist party in Argentina and took part in revolutionary activities there. In the late 1950s Guevara joined the Cuban revolutionary movement and took part in the guerrilla war against the regime of Fulgencio Batista. He became a close aide to Fidel Castro and served as minister of industries after President Batista was ousted from power. In 1965 Guevara left Cuba and returned to revolutionary activities in South and Central America. At the time of his capture and death, Guevara was leading a band of guerrilla fighters in the mountains of Bolivia. While it was initially announced by the regime of President Rene Barrientos Ortuna that Guevara had been killed during a gun battle with members of the Fourth Bolivian Rangers Division, commanded by Gen. Joaquin Zenteno Anaya (q.v.), it appears likely that he was captured and summarily executed by the Bolivian army.

# 1968

• **Deendayal Upadhyaya**, the president of Jana Sangh, the second largest political party in India, was killed when he was shoved from a moving train while en route to New Delhi on February 11, 1968. Pandit Deendayal Upadhyaya was born in the village of Rajasthan on September 12, 1916. Upadhyaya became involved in politics in the late 1930s, joining the Rashtriya Swayamsevak Sangh (RSS) in 1937. He joined the Jana Sangh in 1952, becoming General Secretary. He succeeded Syama Prasad Mookherji as president of the party in 1967. Upadhyaya was also a noted journalist and author.

• **The Rev. Dr. Martin Luther King, Jr.**, the leading figure of the civil rights movement in the United States, was shot and killed in Memphis, Tennessee, on April 4, 1968. Dr. King was born on January 15, 1929, in Atlanta, Georgia. He was ordained a minister in 1947 and served as pastor of the Ebenezer Baptist Church in Atlanta. He became nationally identified with the civil rights movement in 1956 by leading a successful boycott of the Montgomery, Alabama, bus system in protest of their policy of racial segregation. King subsequently founded the Southern Christian Leadership Conference to assist him in his pursuit of racial desegregation. He was often imprisoned for his policy of civil disobedience to laws he considered discriminatory. On September 20, 1958, Dr. King was seriously injured by a knife-wielding deranged woman in New York. Following his recovery he organized and led a major civil rights march on Washington, D.C., in 1963 in support of the Civil Rights Act. The act was passed by Congress the following year. In 1964 Dr. King also received the Nobel Prize for Peace for his non-violent advocacy of equal rights for people of all races. Dr. King was shot and fatally wounded by a sniper in April of 1968 while standing on the balcony of the Lorraine Motel in Memphis. He was in the city in support of striking city sanitation department employees. His death brought forth a surge of racial violence in cities throughout the United States. His assassin was identified as James Earl Ray (1928–98), who was captured in London, England, several months later. Ray pleaded guilty to the murder and was sentenced to life imprisonment. Ray later attempted to retract his guilty plea and gain a trial, amidst allegations that the King assassination was the result of a conspiracy. Ray remained imprisoned until his death from liver failure on April 23, 1998.

• On April 11, 1968, Rudi Dutschke (1940–79), a leader of the West German student revolutionary movement, was seriously injured in a shooting incident in West Berlin. Dutschke, who was shot three times by a pro-Nazi youth, survived his injuries but never fully recovered.

• Houari Boumedienne (1927–78), the president of Algeria, was unharmed when two men sprayed his limousine with machine gun fire on April 25, 1968. Boumedienne remained Algeria's leader until his death in 1978.

• Camille Chamoun (1900–86), who served as president of Lebanon from 1952 to 1958, was the target of an assassination attempt on May 31, 1968. Chamoun, the leader of the National Liberal party, was shot at by a young Moslem, but was uninjured in the attempt on his life. Chamoun survived more than five other attacks on his life during his political career.

• Andy Warhol (1927–87), the eccentric pop artist and filmmaker, was shot and seriously wounded at his studio, The Factory, by aspiring writer and feminist Valerie Solanas on June 3, 1968. Though Warhol survived his injuries, he never completely recovered from the shooting. Solanas was sentenced to three years in prison for the assassination attempt and was released in 1971. Warhol died on February 22, 1987, following gall bladder surgery. His assailant died the following year in San Francisco of emphysema and pneumonia on April 26, 1988.

• **Robert F. Kennedy**, a candidate for the Democratic nomination for the presidency of the United States, as assassinated in Los Angeles, California, on June 5, 1968. Kennedy, a Democratic senator from New York since 1965, was the brother of assassinated United States president John F. Kennedy (q.v.) and had served as attorney general during the Kennedy administration. Robert Kennedy was born on November 20, 1925, in Brookline, Massachusetts. He worked in the United States Department of Justice during the early 1950s before managing the United States Senate campaign of his brother, John. Kennedy subsequently served as the chief counsel for the select Senate committee on improper activities of labor from 1957 until 1960. In that year he managed his brother's campaign for the presidency of the United States. Following John Kennedy's election as president Robert was appointed United States attorney general. Bobby Kennedy was a strong proponent of civil rights legislation. He also used his position to seek to eliminate labor union corruption. He remained as attorney general in the cabinet of President Lyndon Johnson following the assassination of President Kennedy in November of 1963. He resigned the following year to run for the United States Senate in New York, and defeated the Republican incumbent, Kenneth Keating, in the general election of that year. His support for social legislation and his outspoken criticism of President Johnson's Vietnam War policies established him as a leader of the Democratic party's liberal wing. Kennedy entered the campaign for the Democratic presidential nomination in March of 1968, and succeeded in winning several primaries during the spring. He was shot by Sirhan B. Sirhan (b.1944), a Jordanian immigrant, in a Los Angeles hotel after winning the important California primary. Senator Kennedy died the following morning. Sirhan was tried and convicted of the murder and sentenced to life imprisonment.

• On August 13, 1968, Georgios Papadopoulos (1909–99), the prime minister of Greece who had seized power in a military coup the previous year, was uninjured when a bomb exploded in the path of his car. The government arrested numerous opposition leaders in the wake of this assassination attempt, charging over twenty people with complicity in the plot. The leader of the plot, Alexandros Panagoulis (q.v.) was sentenced to prison, where he remained until the ouster of the Papadopoulos government in 1973.

• **John Gordon Mein**, the United States ambassador to Guatemala since 1965, was shot to death by machine gun fire while riding in his car in Guatemala City on August 28, 1968. Mein was born on September 10, 1913. He joined the foreign service in 1947 and served in diplomatic positions in Italy, Norway, the Philippines, Indonesia, and Brazil. He was appointed United States ambassador to Guatemala in 1965. Mein was killed while fleeing from a group of urban guerrillas who were attempting to kidnap him. His assassins were believed to be members of the Revolutionary Armed Forces, a left-wing terrorist group. The same group was believed to be responsible for the murders of **Col. John D. Webber**, the chief of the United States military mission, and **Capt. Ernest Munro**, the chief of the United States Embassy naval section, in Guatemala in January of 1968.

• **Pierre Mulele** (1929–68), a Congolese rebel leader who had led a 1963 uprising in Kwilu Province, was executed before a firing squad in Kinshasa on October 9, 1968. Mulele had returned to the Congo (Zaire) earlier in the year under a general amnesty proclaimed by President Joseph Mobutu. He was subsequently arrested and convicted of rebellion and terrorism by a military tribunal. A Maoist trained in guerrilla warfare in China, Mulele was minister of education in the government of Patrice Lumumba (q.v.).

• **Nasir al-Hani**, who had briefly served as Iraq's foreign minister in the cabinet of Abdul Razal al-Naif (q.v.) earlier in the year, was found murdered in November of 1968. Hani was a leading critic of the ruling Ba'thist regime.

# 1969

• **Dr. Le Minh Tri** (1926–69), the South Vietnamese minister of education, was killed in Saigon on January 6, 1969, when a grenade was thrown into a car he was riding in. His assassination was presumed to be the work of Communist guerrillas.

• Following an alleged attempt coup against President Francois Macias Nguema (q.v.) of Equatorial Guinea in January of 1969, several prominent members of the government were arrested and killed. They included **Bonifacio Ondo Edu**, who had served as Equatorial Guinea's premier during the nation's pre-independence days and had been defeated by Macias in the presidential election the previous year; **Saturnino Ibongo Iyanga** (1937–69), the country's ambassador to the United Nations; **Atanasio Ndongo Miyone**, the foreign minister and purported leader of the coup attempt; **Gori Molubuela**, the chief of the cabinet; **Mitogo Osa**, the secretary general of the foreign ministry; **Mariano Mba Micha** (1930–69), former minister of foreign affairs; **Ricardo Maria Bolopa Esape**, former representative to the Spanish Cortes from 1964 to 1968; **Gaspar Coperiate Muebake**, a parliamentary deputy and member of the Union Bubi; **Jesus Eworo Ndongo**, the former minister of justice; **Aurelio Nicolas Itoha Creda**, the former minister of labor; **Gustavo Watson Bueco**, former minister of public health and ambassador to Cameroon; **Ricardo Martinez Pelayo Erimola Yema**, the minister of industries and mines; **Pastor Torao Sikara**, Bubi chief and president of the National Assembly; **Manuel Morgades Besari**, a member of the senate; **Antonio Edongo Engonga**, vice president of Equatorial Guinea; **Asumu Ngomo Ndumu**, governor of Rio Muni province; **Rafael Nsue Nchama**, the former minister of agriculture, and his successor, **Augustin Nve Ondo Nchama**; and **Armando Balboa**, the secretary of the National Assembly.

Bonifacio Ondu Edo was born in Evinayong and was a member of the Fang tribe. He became active in the Equatorial Guinean independence movement in the 1950s and went into exile in Gabon in 1959. Ondu Edo returned to Equatorial Guinea in 1960 to serve as mayor of Evinayong. He was a founder of the Movement for the National Unity of Equatorial Guinea (MUNGE) in 1963. He served as premier of the pre-independence government from December 15, 1963. He was a proponent of a gradual process of independence from Spain. Ondu Edo was promoted by the colonial government to serve as president of an independent Equatorial Guinea. He was defeated by Francisco Macias Nugema in a runoff election in September of 1968. When Equatorial Guinea was granted independence on October 12, 1968, Ondu Edu went into exile in Gabon. He was extradited to Equatorial Guinea in November of 1968 and detained by the Macias Nguema government. Ondu Edo was charged with conspiracy and was murdered with members of his family including his wife, **Edelvina Oyana**, in January of 1969.

• **Eduardo Mondlane** (1920–69), the leader of the Front for the Liberation of Mozambique (FRELIMO), was killed on February 3, 1969, when a bomb exploded in his mail in Dar es Salaam, Tanzania. Mondlane had served as a leader of the guerrilla organization seeking to free Mozambique from Portuguese rule since the mid–1960s.

• **Dr. Tranh Anh**, the acting dean of Saigon University's Medical College and an associate of Dr. Le Minh Tri (q.v.), was shot to death by terrorists in Saigon, South Vietnam, on March 4, 1969.

• **Alexandre Banza**, a leading political figure in the Central African Republican, was tried and executed on April 12, 1969, following an unsuccessful coup attempt against President Jean Bedel Bokassa. Banza had served as the republic's minister of state for public health.

- **Gen. Ngalo**, a leader of the 1964 rebellion in the Congolese region of Kisangani, was captured and executed in the Congo (Zaire) on June 16, 1969.

- **Moise Tshombe**, the former premier of the Congo Republic (Zaire) who had led the successionist Katanga Province during the Congo's civil war in the early 1960s, died while in detention in Algeria on June 29, 1969. Tshombe had been imprisoned in Algeria for the previous two years after his private plane had been hijacked there while en route from his exile in Spain in June of 1965. The Algerian government detained Tshombe while deciding whether to free the ex-premier, or extradite him to the Congo, where he was under a sentence of death in absentia. Tshombe's death was reported to have been from natural causes, according to an autopsy signed by eleven Algerian doctors. While there is no strong evidence to support the likelihood that Tshombe was murdered, his controversial nature and sudden demise led to speculation that there may have been foul play.

Moise-Kapenda Tshombe was born in the Katanga region of the Congo on November 10, 1919. He was active in the political affairs of the pre-independent Congo, and was involved in the planning for Congolese independence from Belgium in 1960. Shortly after the Republic of the Congo was proclaimed on June 30, 1960, the country was beset by domestic turmoil. Tshombe then declared the southern province of Katanga independent from the rest of the country. He utilized European mercenary troops to repel the forces of Patrice Lumumba's (q.v.) central government. The following year Tshombe was held responsible for Lumumba's death when the recently deposed prime minister was captured and killed in Katanga by forces hostile to his government. The United Nations troops were twice repulsed by the Katangan forces and their mercenary allies, but in January of 1963, the United Nations was successful in crushing the Katanga successionists and driving Tshombe into exile in Spain. In July of 1964 Tshombe returned to the Congo's capital and was named prime minister in the government of Joseph Kasavubu. Tshombe was dismissed two years later, in October of 1965, and again went into exile in Spain. Tshombe, while in exile, was tried and condemned for treason and complicity in the death of Patrice Lumumba by the government of Joseph Mobutu, the Congolese army leader who had deposed Kasavubu shortly after Tshombe's ouster. After two years in exile Tshombe was kidnapped and taken to Algeria, where he remained until his death.

- **Augusto Vandor** (1929–69), a leading Argentine labor organizer and president of the Argentine Metal Workers Union, was shot and killed by assassins in his office on June 30, 1969, shortly after his refusal to participate in a general strike against the administration of Gen. Juan Carlos Ongania.

- **Thomas Mboya**, a Kenyan nationalist leader and minister of economic planning, was shot to death in Nairobi on July 5, 1969. Mboya, a member of the Luo tribe, was born in Kenya in 1930. He joined Jomo Kenyatta's Kenya African Union in the early 1950s, becoming treasurer in 1953. He became active in the Kenyan Federation of Labor following the government's suppression of the political party, and became a leading advocate of independence for Kenya. In 1960 he was named general secretary of the Kenyan African Nation Union and served as Kenya's minister of labor from 1962 until 1963. In 1963 he was appointed minister of justice, and the following year he was named minister of economic development and planning. He was a leading presidential candidate when he was shot and killed in Nairobi by Isaac N. Njorage, a member of the Kikuyu tribe. Njorage was convicted of the murder and hanged on November 8, 1969.

- In September of 1969 President Julius Nyerre of Tanzania returned several alleged plotters against the government of Sheikh Abeid Karume (q.v.) of Zanzibar to that island nation. **Abdullah Kassim Hanga**, the former vice president of Zanzibar; **Othman Shariff**, Zanzibar's former ambassador to the

United States; and **Ali Mwange Tambwe**, a former government minister, were arrested and executed on their arrival.

Abdullah Kassim Hanga was born in Zanzibar in 1932. He became active in the Afro-Shirazi party and served as deputy general secretary when Zanzibar was granted independence in December of 1963. Hanga was named prime minister of Zanzibar following the revolution on January 14, 1964. The post was abolished a few hours later, and Hanga remained in the government as vice president of the Zanzibar Republic. He subsequently served in the cabinet as minister of industries, mineral resources, and power. He became minister of state following the merger of Zanzibar with Tanganyika in April of 1964. Hanga subsequently fled Zanzibar when he was charged with plotting against the government of Abeid Amani Karume. He went into exile in Guinea until 1967, when he returned to mainland Tanzania after being given a promise of safety by President Nyerere. Two years later Hanga was arrested and returned to Zanzibar, where he was executed.

• **Abdirashid Ali Shermarke**, the president of Somalia, was shot to death on October 15, 1969. Shermarke had served as his country's first prime minister from 1960 to 1964 and had been elected president in 1967. His regime had been marked largely by a domestic policy that invoked little unrest. Nevertheless, while visiting the rural city of Los Anod, north of the capital of Mogadiscio, Shermarke was shot and killed by Abulkadir Abdi Mohammed, a twenty-two-year-old policeman, who then surrendered to the authorities. The killing appeared to lack a political motive, and may have been the result of a tribal feud, as both the president and his killer were members of the same tribe. The Somalian army seized control of the country shortly after Shermarke's assassination. His assassin was convicted and sentenced to death the following year.

Abdirashid Ali Shermarke was born in Hararardera on October 16, 1919. He attended school locally and joined the British administration civil service. He was active in the Somali Youth League, and continued his studies at Rome University, where he received a degree in political science in 1958. Shermarke was elected to the National Assembly the following year and was chosen as prime minister of independent Somalia on July 12, 1960. The ruling Somali Youth League retained power in general elections in 1964, but President Aden Abdullah Osman replaced Shermarke as prime minister on June 14, 1964. Shermarke was a candidate for the presidency in 1967 and was elected to a six-year term, taking office on July 10, 1967. He was successful in negotiating a settlement for border disputes with neighboring Kenya and Ethiopia. His term of office was cut short by an assassin's bullet.

• **Carlos Marighela**, the leader of the National Liberation Action, a Brazilian guerrilla organization, was killed in Sao Paulo by Brazilian police on November 4, 1969. A leading urban guerrilla theoretician, Marighela's *Minimanual of the Urban Guerrilla* largely influenced such later groups as the Red Brigades and the Red Army Faction.

• **Rt. Rev. Dillard H. Brown**, U.S. Episcopal missionary bishop of Liberia, was murdered on November 19, 1969. His death resulted in a massive crackdown against opponents of Liberian president William Tolbert (q.v.).

• **Jorge Soliz Roman**, a Bolivian peasant leader who had served under President Rene Barrientos as minister of agriculture, was assassinated on November 26, 1969.

• **David Guerra Guzman**, an anti–Communist Guatemalan congressman, was shot to death by left-wing terrorists in Guatemala City on December 17, 1969.

• President Milton Obote (b. 1924) of Uganda was shot and seriously wounded following apolitical rally in Kampala on December 19, 1969. Obote recovered from his injuries and remained his country's president until his overthrow by Idi Amin in 1971. Obote again became head of state of Uganda in 1980, shortly after Amin's ouster, and served until 1985, when he was once again deposed in a coup.

# 1970

• Labor leader **Joseph A. "Jock" Yablonski** was found murdered at his home in Clarksville, Pennsylvania, on January 5, 1970. Yablonski's wife, Margaret, and daughter, Charlotte Joanne, were also found shot to death. It was believed that the three had been killed on New Year's Eve. Yablonski had lost a campaign the previous month against W.A. 'Tony' Boyle (1904–85) for the presidency of the United Mine Workers Union. The campaign had been a particularly brutal one, with Yablonski accusing the incumbent Boyle of corruption and mismanagement.

Yablonski, who was born on March 3, 1910, had long been involved in union activities. He had served as a member of the UMW's international executive board from 1952 to 1958, when he was elected president of the Washington, D.C., district. He was defeated for reelection to that position in 1966. Three men, believed to be hired killers, were arrested and convicted of the murder. In 1973 Boyle was himself indicted, convicted, and sentenced for life for having hired Yablonski's killers. He died while serving his sentence in June of 1985.

• During 1970 terrorists assassinated many prominent political leaders in Guatemala. On January 13, 1970, **Justo Lopez Costanza**, head of Guatemala's intelligence service, was killed in Guatemala City by machine gun fire. **Isidoro Zarco**, associate editor of the pro-government newspaper *Prensa Libre*, was shot to death in Guatemala City on January 28, 1970. On January 30, 1970, **Col. Oscar Giron Perrone**, who had participated in the coup overthrowing President Jacob Arbenz Guzman (q.v.) in 1954, was found shot to death outside of Guatemala City. Giron Perrone was a supporter of Col. Carlos Arana Os-

orio, the presidential candidate supported by the National Liberation Movement and the Institutional democratic party. **Jose Bernabe Linares**, a former Guatemala secret police chief, was shot to death in Guatemala City on March 11, 1970. He had headed the secret police from 1931 to 1944 and from 1954 to 1956.

• **Brig. Gen. Pierino Yere Okoya**, a leading Ugandan military commander and possible rival to Idi Amin, was shot to death at his home near Gulu on January 25, 1970. His wife was also murdered. A member of the Acholi tribe, Okoya had taken charge following the assassination attempt against President Milton Obote in December of 1969, and had criticized the actions of Amin at the time. It was believed the Okoya's murder was directed by Amin, who ousted Obote and became president in a coup exactly a year after Okoya was killed.

• On March 8, 1970, Archbishop Makarios III (1913–77), the president of Cyprus, survived an attempt on his life by right-wing Greek Cypriots. Makarios was not harmed in the attempt and remained the leader of Cyprus until his death in 1977.

• **Polycarpos Georghiades** (1930–70), a former Cypriot minister of interior and defense, was found shot to death in his car on a road near Nicosia, Cyprus, on March 15, 1970. Georghiades, a hero in the Cypriot fight for independence, had served under Archbishop Makarios from 1960 to 1968. He had become an opponent of the president in recent years. Georghiades, with Glafkos Clerides, was a co-founder of the Unified Nationalist party, which was formed to contest future elections promised by Makarios. There was some speculation that Georghiades had been involved in a planned coup against the Makarios government at the time of his death.

• **Iman El Hadi El Mahdi**, a Sudanese rebel leader, was killed while trying to escape to Ethiopia after an unsuccessful right-wing revolt against President Gaafar al-Nimeiry of the Sudan. Mahdi was killed on March 31, 1970, in an exchange of gunfire while he and his supporters were attempting to cross the Sudanese border in two jeeps.

- **Faisal Abdul Latif Al-Shaabi** (1937–70), the premier of South Yemen from April to June of 1969, was shot and killed on April 3, 1970, while trying to escape from a detention camp near Aden. Latif had been under house arrest since his ouster. He was a disciple of Palestinian nationalist leader George Habash and a founder of the National Liberation Front (NLF), the Aden branch of the Arab Nationalist Movement. He had previously worked in the Federal Ministry of Commerce and Industry and served as the leading spokesman for the NLF while his cousin, Qahtan al-Shaabi, remained under house arrest in Egypt in 1966. Following the establishment of the independent People's Republic of South Yemen in November of 1967, al-Latif served in several cabinets. On April 6, 1969, he was named as premier, replacing Qahtan al-Shaabi. One of his first official acts was a state visit to Kuwait, which resulted in aid for South Yemen. He was deposed with his cousin on June 22, 1969, and placed under arrest. Latif remained imprisoned until his death.

- **Count Karl von Spreti** (1907–70), the West German ambassador to Guatemala, was kidnapped and killed by terrorists in Guatemala City. Von Spreti had been kidnapped from his home on March 31, 1970, by a Marxist group in Guatemala called the Rebel Armed Forces (FAR). Following the Guatemalan government's refusal to give in to their demands, the guerrillas killed von Spreti with a single bullet to the left side of his head. His body was found on April 4, 1970, in a mud hut outside of Guatemala City.

- Right-wing terrorists killed several prominent Guatemalan politicians in reprisal for the killing of Ambassador von Spreti. On April 8, 1970, **Cesar Montenegro Paniagua**, a Guatemalan labor leader and congressman during the 1950s, was strangled in Guatemala City. Another left-wing labor leader, **Francisco Barreno** (1930–70), was shot to death on a highway outside of Guate-

mala City after having been kidnapped on April 25, 1970. On April 28, 1970, **Julio Cesar De la Roca** (1932–70), a journalist, was shot and killed outside the capital. **Marco Antonio Marroqui**, the mayor of Jocotan, Chiquimula, Guatemala, was ambushed and killed on May 6, 1970. **Rafael Horacio Sanchez**, a leading supporter of Carlos Arana Osorio, Guatemala's president-elect, was shot to death by machine gun fire in Guatemala City on May 11, 1970. **Victor Rodriguez**, another supporter of Arana, was assassinated in Chiquimula on July 8, 1970, and **Aldana Sanchez**, the mayor of Zacapa, Guatemala, was shot to death by leftists on July 12, 1970.

- **Hector Moran Charquero**, the head of Uruguay's police intelligence, was machine-gunned to death on April 12, 1970, by Tupamaro guerrillas in Montevideo. He had headed a special anti-guerrilla police unit which had been charged with the torturing of political prisoners.

- Chiang Ching-kuo (1910–88), the deputy premier of Taiwan, was uninjured during a shooting attempt on his life on April 24, 1970. Chiang, the son of Nationalist Chinese president Chiang Kai-shek, was attacked by a Taiwanese gunman while on a visit to New York City. Chiang remained a leading political figure in the Nationalist Chinese government in Taiwan, and succeeded his father as head of state in 1975.

- **Brig. Gen. Supardjo**, the highest-ranking army officer to take part in the 1965 Communist coup attempt in Indonesia, was executed by a firing squad in May of 1970.

- **Marco Antonio Yon Sosa**, a Guatemalan guerrilla leader, and two of his followers were killed on May 16, 1970, in a gun battle with Mexican soldiers on the Mexican side of the Guatemalan border. Yon Sosa, a lieutenant in the Guatemalan army until 1960, when he joined the rebellion against President Miguel Ydigoras Fuentes, was head of the Maoist MR-13 guerrilla revolutionary movement in Guatemala.

• **Maj. Robert P. Perry**, the United States Army attaché to the United States embassy staff in Jordan, was shot and killed by Palestinian guerrillas at his home in Amman on June 10, 1970. Perry was born in Chicago on February 1, 1936, and had served as a foreign area specialist in the army. He had served in Jordan from March of 1967, having previously been stationed at the U.S. Embassy in Beirut, Lebanon from 1963 to 1966.

• Former Argentine president **Pedro Aramburo** was kidnapped by members of the Juan Jose Valle (q.v.) Command, a leftist guerrilla group on May 29, 1970. The kidnappers announced his execution on July 1, 1970, and the ex-president's body was found near Buenos Aires on July 16.

Pedro Eugenio Aramburo was born in Rio Curato, Argentina, on May 21, 1903. He attended the Buenos Aires National Military College and subsequently served in the army. He served as an officer on the general staff from 1936 and was named military attaché in Rio de Janeiro, Brazil in 1951. He was also promoted to brigadier general by President Juan Peron. Aramburu returned to Argentina in 1953 to become director general of the Army Medical Corps. Aramburu joined the military rebellion against Peron in September of 1955. He was named army chief of staff in the subsequent provisional government of Eduardo Lonardi. On November 13, 1955, Aramburu and other members of the junta charged Lonardi with appeasing Peronists and forced him from office. Aramburu was selected as the new provisional president. He restored the constitution of 1853, disbanded and outlawed the Peronist party, and allowed for a free press. He also denationalized the national bank and instituted wage controls in an attempt to stabilize the economy. Aramburu was faced with the first major challenge to his regime in June of 1956, when troops led by two former Peronist generals, Juan Jose Valle and Raul Tanco, rebelled against the government. The rebellion was crushed, and General Valle and other plotters were executed by firing squad. Aramburu then made arrange-

ments for democratic elections in which he and other members of the junta were barred from participating. Aramburu relinquished office to the victor, Arturo Frondizi, on May 1, 1958, and subsequently retired from the military. He tried for a political comeback in the presidential elections of 1963, but fared poorly, finishing last in a six-man election. He remained a marginal figure in Argentine politics until his kidnapping and murder by terrorists.

• **Gen. Teymour Bakhtiar** (1914–70), an Iranian army officer and opponent of Shah Mohammed Reza Pahlavi, was assassinated in Iraq, near the Iranian border, on August 8, 1970. His assailant was an aide accompanying him on a hunting trip. Bakhtiar attended the St. Cyr military college in France and served in the Iranian army from the 1930s. He served as military governor of Teheran under the shah and, in 1958, was named the first chief of SAVAK, the Iranian secret police. In the early 1960s, fearing his growing power, the shah removed Bakhtiar from his position. Bakhtiar went into exile, where he became a leading opponent of the Shah's regime. His murder was believed to have been ordered by the Shah.

• On August 8, 1970, a plot against the government of President Gnassingbe Eyadema of Togo was uncovered, resulted in the arrest of twenty-seven plotters. The leader of the plot, former labor minister Noe Kutuklui (1923–88), escaped from the country and went into exile. **Clement Kolor** (Apr. 7, 1929–1970), a member of the National Assembly from 1958 until 1963, was among those arrested. He allegedly died while trying to escape from a police station window, though there were reports he was tortured to death while in custody. Other plotters who were convicted included **Jean-Alexandre Osseyi** (Apr. 22, 1935–1971), a police inspector who was reportedly executed in prison in 1971; **Marc Atipede** (Mar. 12, 1912–1970), a leading physician and critic of the Eyadema regime who perished in prison in 1970; and **Laurent Djagba** (1926–71), the speaker of the National Assembly under President Sylvanus Olympio (q.v.) until his ouster in 1963, who was also executed in prison in early 1971.

• **Daniel A. Mitrione** (1920–70), a U.S. police advisor to the government of Uruguay, was killed by Tupamaro guerrillas in Montevideo following a kidnapping by the left-wing terrorists on July 31, 1970. He was executed following the Uruguayan government's refusal to accede to the guerrillas' demand to release political prisoners. The kidnapping and murder of Mitrione was the basis for *State of Siege*, a 1973 film directed by Costa-Gavras.

• **Jose Varela Alonso** (1913–70), an Argentine labor leader, was shot and killed on August 27, 1970, while driving to his office in Buenos Aires. Alonso, a moderate Peronist leader, was the head of the Argentine Textile Workers' Union. The Montoneros Command of the National Liberation Army, a left-wing terrorist group, claimed responsibility for the killing.

• **Larry N. Kuriyama** (1921–70), a Hawaiian state senator, was shot to death in the garage of his home on October 12, 1970. Kuriyama, a Democrat, had served in the Hawaiian state legislature since 1959. He was the chairman of the Senate Committee on Higher Education, and was unopposed for re-election in his Oahu Senate district.

• **Pedro N. Taruc** (1907–70), the leader of the Communist Hukbalahap agrarian rebel movement in the Philippines, was shot and killed by government soldiers in Angeles City on October 16, 1970. Taruc, who had led the Huks since 1964, was the secretary general of the Philippine Communist Party.

• **Floro Crisologo**, a Philippine congressman from Ilocos Sur Province and an advisor to President Ferdinand Marcos, was shot and killed in Viga, the Philippines, while attending mass on October 18, 1970.

• **Pierre LaPorte** (1921–70), the minister of labor in Quebec, Canada, was killed by strangulation by French separatists in Quebec after having been kidnapped on October 10,

1970. La Porte's body was found in a car near the Canadian military base at Saint-Hubert on October 18, 1970. The kidnappers, members of Chenier cell of Le Front de Liberation de Quebec (FLQ), had previously abducted James R. Cross, the British trade commissioner, on October 5. They had demanded the release of twenty-three "political prisoners" and a ransom of $500,000 in gold for the release of LaPorte and Cross. The government refused to accept the demands and proclaimed a state of emergency. LaPorte was killed shortly after this proclamation. Cross was rescued unharmed several months later.

Pierre LaPorte was born in Montreal in 1921. He worked as a journalist from the mid–1940s until 1961, when he entered politics as a member of the Liberal party in Quebec. He was named to the provincial cabinet in 1962, serving as municipal affairs minister. He also became cultural affairs minister in 1964. After the Liberal party defeat two years later LaPorte remained in the National Assembly. When the Liberals returned to power in 1970, Laporte was named minister of immigration, manpower and labor.

• **Belkacem Krim**, one of the leaders of the Algerian Front for National Liberation (FLN) during Algeria's struggle against France for independence, was found strangled in his Frankfurt, West Germany, hotel room on October 20, 1970. Krim was born near Dra-el-Mizan in 1922. He had become active in the Algerian nationalist movement in 1947 following his assassination of a forest ranger. Krim was sentenced to death in absentia by the French on two occasions in the late 1940s, but eluded capture. He served as vice president and minister of the armed forces in the provisional revolutionary government in 1958 and was minister of foreign affairs for the rebels at the signing of the 1962 agreement with France allowing Algerian independence. He subsequently became involved with a dispute with Ahmed ben Bella, who became Algeria's first president after independence, and Krim retired from active politics. He opposed the regime of ben Bella's successor, Houari

Boumedienne, and founded the Democratic Movement for Algerian Renewal, a Paris-based exile group, in 1967. Krim was condemned to death in absentia in Algeria on charges of attempting to overthrow the Boumedienne government. His death was believed to have been caused by agents of the Algerian government.

• **Gen. Rene Schneider Chereau** (1918–70), the commander-in-chief of the Chilean army from 1969, was shot on October 22, 1970, by right-wing terrorists as he was being driven to work in Santiago. He died on October 25, 1970. Schneider had encouraged the army to avoid political involvement during the administration of President Salvador Allende (q.v.). It was alleged that Schneider's murder was initiated by right-wing forces in Chile, with the support of the United States CIA, to prevent Marxist Salvador Allende (q.v.) from becoming elected president of Chile. A former general, Roberto Viaux, and others were arrested for complicity in the murder, and Viaux was subsequently exiled to Paraguay.

• On November 1, 1970, **Zygfryd Wolniak** (1922–70), the Polish deputy foreign minister; **Chaudhri Mohammed Nazi**, Pakistan's deputy intelligence chief; and **Mohammed Ashraf** and **Mohammed Yasin**, both Pakistani journalists, were killed during an airport reception for Polish president Marian Spychalski in Karachi, Pakistan. The deaths occurred when a truck driven by Feroze Abdulah drove through the crowd at the reception area.

• **Julio Caney Herrera**, a Guatemalan law professor and leftist politician, was murdered on November 16, 1970, while driving to work in Guatemala City. On December 18, 1970, **Arnaldo Otten Prado**, a Guatemalan National Liberation Movement deputy, was also shot to death while driving in Guatemala City. **Jaime Monge Donis**, the secretary general of the Guatemalan Labor Federation, was shot and killed near his home in Guatemala City on December 23, 1970.

• **Maj. Gen. Teshome Erghietu** (1918–70), the commander of the Ethiopian Second Army Division, was killed by rebel guerrillas on November 21, 1970. Teshome Erghietu was on an inspection tour in Northern Ethiopia at the time of the attack.

• On November 27, 1970, Pope Paul VI (1897–1978) escaped serious injury while he was attacked by a man wielding a knife. The pope was on a visit to the Philippines at the time of the assassination attempt. Paul VI remained the leader of the Roman Catholic church until his death in 1978.

---

# 1971

• **Adolfo Mijangos Lopez** (1929–71), a leader of the Guatemalan opposition coalition, was killed by machine gun fire in Guatemala City on January 13, 1971, while his driver was helping him from his wheelchair into his car.

• Three Cameroonian opposition leaders convicted of treason and of plotting the assassination of President Ahmadou Ahidjo were executed on January 15, 1971. They included **Ernest Ouandie** (1924–71), an early anti–French nationalist leader and the president of the banned Union of Cameroonian Peoples; **Gabriel Tabeu**, the head of the Holy Cross for the Liberation of Cameroon; and **Raphael Fotsing**, a member of Ouandie's group. Ouandie had led a guerrilla movement against the Ahidjo regime from 1962 until his capture in August of 1970.

• Several leading Guinean politicians were executed by hanging in Conakry, Guinea, after allegations they were involved in a plot to overthrow Sekou Toure as president. **Ousmane Balde**, the long-time minister of finance and president of the Central Bank, **Ibrahima Barry** (1923–71), the former secretary general of the Mouvement Socialiste Africain and member of Sekou Toure's government in the 1960s, **Keita Kara de**

**Soufiana** (1923–71), the former commissioner of police, and **Magassouba Moriba** (1923–71), the former minister of the interior, were among those executed.

• **Jacobo Arbenz Guzman**, who was president of a Communist-leaning government in Guatemala in the early 1950s, drowned in the bathtub of his home in Mexico City on January 27, 1971. Col. Arbenz served as Guatemala's minister of defense in the government of President Juan Jose Arevalo in the late 1940s. After the assassination of Arbenz's leading rival, Francisco Arana (q.v.), a right-wing Guatemalan politician, Arbenz was elected to the presidency. He began his term of office on March 15, 1951. During his administration he continued the agrarian reform programs of his predecessor and encouraged relations with Communist countries. Guatemala's relationship with the United States deteriorated due to the Arbenz government's appropriation of the United Fruit Company's interests in the country. Arbenz became known as the "Red Colonel," and in June of 1954, he was ousted in a military coup led by right-wing Col. Carlos Castillo Armas (q.v.). The coup was supported by the United States government and the Central Intelligence Agency. John Peurifoy (q.v.), the United States ambassador to Guatemala, was believed to have been a principal architect of the revolt. Arbenz fled the country and spent the remainder of his life in exile. His death in 1971 was attributed to drowning under a stream of scalding tap water after a fall in his bathtub. Arbenz's death was ruled an accident, but the unusual nature of his demise, coupled with his controversial past, led some to question the true cause of death.

• **Hardan Takriti**, the former vice president of Iraq, was shot to death in a hospital courtyard in Kuwait on March 30, 1971. Takriti, who had also served as Iraq's air marshal, had been living in exile in Kuwait since October of 1970, following his ouster as vice president.

• **Azor Adelaide**, a political activist in Mauritius, was assassinated in 1971. Sir Gae-

tain Duval, the deputy prime minister of Mauritius, was arrested in connection with the murder in 1989.

• **Col. Roberto Quintanilla Pereira** (1928–71), the Bolivian consul general to Hamburg, was shot and killed by an unidentified woman in his office in Hamburg on April 1, 1971. Quintanilla was the head of intelligence in Bolivia under former president Rene Barrientos. The Bolivian National Liberation Army (ELN) claimed responsibility for the murder.

• **Gen. Ziadin Farsiou** (1919–71), the chief of the Iranian military court, was shot by terrorists as he was leaving his home in Teheran on April 7, 1971. He died of his wounds on April 11, 1971.

• **Kyin Pe**, the general secretary of the Burmese Karen National Union Front, a Communist insurgent organization, was killed by government troops at his headquarters in Burma in April of 1971.

• **Vladimir Rolovic**, the Yugoslavian ambassador to Sweden, was shot by Croatian separatists on April 7, 1971. He died the following week on April 15, 1971.

• **Alberto Larrea Humerez**, the Bolivian minister of economics under former president Rene Barrientos, was assassinated on April 19, 1971.

• **Pietro Scaglione**, the chief public prosecutor of Palermo, Italy, was shot and killed on May 5, 1971. His assassins were believed to have been members of the Mafia.

• **Ephraim Elrom** (1912–71), the Israeli consul general to Turkey, was murdered in Istanbul on May 22, 1971, by left-wing terrorists who had kidnapped him a week earlier. Elrom, a former Israeli Criminal Investigation Department chief, had interrogated Nazi war criminal Adolf Eichmann (q.v.) before Eichmann's trial and execution in 1962. Elrom had been with the Israeli Foreign Service since 1969.

• **Maximiliano Gomez** (1943–71), the exiled secretary general of the Dominican Popular Movement (MPD), a leftist opposition movement, was murdered in Brussels, Belgium, on May 23, 1971.

• **Edmundo Perez Zukovic** (1912–71), the former minister of the interior in Chile and a leader of the Christian Democratic party, was shot and killed by left-wing terrorists in Santiago on June 8, 1971.

• In June of 1971 leftist army officers launched a coup attempt against Sudanese president Gaafar al-Nimeiry. The revolt was suppressed by forces loyal to President Nimeiry, and most of the coup leaders were seized. Fourteen participants in the rebellion were tried and executed during the month. The dead included **Maj. Hashem Atta** (1935–71), the leader of the coup; **Lt. Col. Babakr Al-Nur Osman**, who had been named president of the revolutionary council; **Maj. Farouk Osman Hamadallah**, an aide to Lt. Col. Nur; **Abdul Khalek Mahjoub**, the leader of the Sudanese Communist party and alleged mastermind of the coup; **Joseph Garang**, a former Communist minister for Sudanese southern affairs; **Shafie Ahmed El-Sheikh**, the leader of the Communist-led Trade Union Federation; **Col. Abdul Moneim Mohammed Ahmed**, the commander of the Third Armored Division; **Lt. Col. Osman Hussein**, commander of the Presidential Guard; and **Maj. Mohammed Ahmad Al-Zein, Lt. Ahmad Osman Abdel Rahman Al Hardale** and **Capt. Muawiya Abdul Hay**, members of the rebel junta.

• **Jose Luis Arriaga Arriola** (1935–71), a Guatemalan congressman and member of the opposition Revolutionary party, was shot to death near his home in Guatemala City on July 6, 1971.

• On July 10, 1971, during an unsuccessful military coup against King Hassan II (1929–99) of Morocco, several guests at a birthday reception for the king were killed at Sikrit Palace outside of Rabat. They included **Marcel Dupret**, the Belgian ambassador to Morocco; former premier **Ahmed Bahnini**, the president of the Moroccan Supreme Court; and several Moroccan generals. **Gen. Ahmed**

**Medbouh** and **Lt Col. Mohammed Ababou** (1936–71), the leaders of the coup, were accidentally shot and killed by their own men. **Gen. Bougrine, Gen. Hamou, Gen. Mustapha Amharache** (1923–71), **Gen. Habibi**, and six colonels were executed on July 12, 1971, for complicity in the coup.

Ahmed Bahnini was born in 1914. He was appointed president of the Supreme Court following morocco's independence in 1956. Bahnini was named to the cabinet as minister of justice in 1963. He was appointed prime minister by King Hassan II on November 13, 1963. His government was threatened by major riots in Casablanca in March of 1965. Bahnini was dismissed on June 7, 1965, when King Hassan declared a state of emergency and became his own prime minister. Bahnini was renamed president of the Supreme Court and retained that position until he was killed by rebel troops during an unsuccessful coup attempt in July of 1971.

• **Mohammed Mustafa Shereim**, known as **Abu Ali Ayad**, a Palestinian guerrilla leader and military aide to Yasir Arafat, was shot to death by Jordanian soldiers near Amman, Jordan, on July 22, 1971.

• **Mahmud Mustafa**, the vice president of Nesame Islam, a rightist party in East Pakistan, was shot and killed while addressing a crowd near Dacca on August 11, 1971.

• **Germain M'Ba**, a leading opponent of Gabon's president Albert Bongo, was assassinated in Libreville, Gabon, in September of 1971.

• On September 12, 1971, **Lin Piao**, the Chinese Communist leader who had been selected to succeed Chairman Mao Tse-tung (Mao Zedong), was reported to have been killed in a plane crash following an alleged coup against Mao. Lin's wife, **Yeh Chun**, a member of the Chinese Communist Politburo, and seven other supporters of Lin were also reported killed in the crash. The plane, which was possibly shot down, was said to have been over Mongolia en route to the

Soviet Union when it crashed. It was also reported from the Soviet Union that the bodies of the passengers were riddled with bullet wounds.

Lin Piao was born in 1908 in the Hupeh Province of China. He had served as a general in Mao's Long March in 1934, and had fought with the Communist insurgents during the Civil War in 1946. He was appointed deputy premier in 1954, and served as a member of the Politburo from 1955. Lin, who had become minister of defense in 1959, was instrumental in organizing the Chinese Cultural revolution of the mid–1960s. He had been named as heir apparent to Chairman Mao as Communist party leader in 1969.

- **Carlos Lamarca** (1938–71), a leading Brazilian terrorist, was shot and killed by military police on September 17, 1971. Lamarca, a former captain in the Brazilian army, had been wanted by the government for acts of political terrorism for the previous three years.

- **Abdul Konem Khan**, the governor of East Pakistan from 1962 to 1969, was assassinated in his home in Dacca on October 14, 1971.

- **Nguyen Van Bong** (1929–71), a founder and leader of the Progressive Nationalist party, a non–Communist opposition group to Vietnamese president Nguyen Van Thieu, was killed in Saigon when a bomb planted in his car exploded on November 10, 1971.

- **Fu'ad al-Rikabi**, who served as the first secretary-general of the Ba'th Party from 1952 to 1959, was murdered in an Iraqi prison in November of 1971. The government alleged that fellow inmates were responsible for the killing, but government security forces were suspected.

- On November 25, 1971, **Yukio Mishima**, an internationally acclaimed Japanese author, led a group of four followers to the headquarters of the Japanese Eastern Regional Command. Once there, Mishima seized Lt. Gen. Kanetoshi Mashita, the regional commander, and demanded that the troops assemble in the courtyard beneath the balcony of Mashita's office. Mishima then delivered a speech criticizing the lack of militarism and discipline in Japanese society. Following his address and a cry of "Long live the Emperor," Mishima returned to Mashita's office where he committed seppuku, a ceremonial ritual disembowelment suicide of ancient Japan. Mishima stabbed himself in the abdomen with a dagger, after which an aide, Masakatsu Morita, decapitated the author. Morita then committed seppuku himself. Mishima's three surviving followers were then taken into custody by Japanese police.

Mishima, who was born in Tokyo in 1925, was considered a leading contender for the Nobel Prize in literature. His first novel, *Confessions of the Mask*, an autobiographical work written when he was nineteen years old, gained him an international reputation. His works, which numbered over 100 novels, short stories and plays, included *Temple of the Golden Pavilion, Patriotism, The Sailor Who Fell from Grace with the Sea*, and *The Sea of Fertility*. Mishima's political philosophy was dominated by militaristic ideals and samurai ethics. In 1968 he founded a right-wing paramilitary organization known as "Tafeno-Kai," or Shield Society, which he hoped to use to return Japan to a militarist state. The four men who accompanied him in his capture of the Eastern Regional Command were members of this organization. Mishima's followers claimed that the author was hoping to inspire a rebellion in the Japanese armed forces with his balcony address, and when that seemed to have failed, he hoped his suicide would encourage a return to militarism.

- **Wasfi al-Tal**, the Jordanian prime minister, joined the many Middle Eastern victims of political assassination when he was shot to death by three gunmen in the lobby of the Sheraton Hotel in Cairo on November 28, 1971, after returning from a meeting of the Arab League being held in Egypt. Jordanian foreign minister Abdullah Salah was slightly wounded in the assault. Two of the assailants were captured near the hotel, and two others were captured later in the day. The assassins claimed to be members of the Black Ilul, or Black September, movement, formed to avenge the deaths of Palestinians during clashes between the Jordanian army and the Palestinians in September of 1970. Tal had been prime minister of Jordan at the time and was held directly responsible for the killing of the radical Palestinians. Tal, a hard-line supporter of the moderate Jordanian monarch, King Hussein, was regarded as one of the Palestinian militants' deadliest foes.

Wasfi al-Tal was born in Irbid in 1920. Educated at the American University in Beirut, he became a teacher upon graduation. He joined the British army in 1942 and served as a liaison officer in London. Tal worked in the Arab Information Office in London from 1945 to 1948 before returning to Palestine to fight in the Arab-Israeli war in 1948. He subsequently worked in various administrative offices in the Jordanian government before being appointed director of the Jordan Government's Press Bureau. Tal's strong support for Jordan's involvement in the Baghdad Pact resulted in his being sent to the West German Embassy as a counselor when demonstrations against the pact brought down the government. He returned to Jordan in 1957, where he again held several positions before being appointed ambassador to Iran in 1961. Tal was recalled to Jordan, and on January 28, 1962, he was named prime minister. His support for the royalist cause during the Yemini civil war brought Jordan into direct conflict with the interests of Gamal Abdel Nasser's Egypt. On March 28, 1963, Tal resigned as prime minister because of widespread criticism of his pro–Western views. He was once again named prime minister on February 13, 1965, and his government generated a climate of improved economic activity. He remained in office until March 4, 1967. In September of 1970 the Jordanian army engaged in an armed conflict with Palestinian guerrilla groups in Jordan. Tal, who had encouraged the army's crackdown on the guerrillas, was appointed prime minister in October 28, 1970. His activities gained him the enmity of the Palestinians, and

led to his assassination the following November.

• **John Barnhill** (1906–71), a militant Protestant member of Northern Ireland's ruling Unionist party, was murdered by members of the Irish Republican Army on December 12, 1971. His assailants shot Barnhill and blew up his mansion in Strabane, near the Irish Republic border.

• **Prince Sisowath Rattasa**, an uncle of former Cambodian chief of state Prince Norodom Sihanouk, was killed by a grenade thrown by a terrorist on a street near the palace in Phnom Penh on December 21, 1971.

# 1972

• **Sheik Khaled bin Mohammed Al Qasimi** (1926–72), the ruler of Sharjah, was killed during an unsuccessful coup attempt led by Sheikh Saqir ben Sultan, the former ruler, on January 24, 1972. Nine members of the sheik's family were also killed. Sheik Sultan, who had been ousted from power six years earlier, was arrested following the coup attempt. Sheik Saqr bin Mohammed al-Qasimi, the youngest brother of the slain ruler, succeeded to the throne.

• A revolt against the government of Congolese president Marien Ngouabi failed on February 22, 1972. The leaders of the rebellion were subsequently killed, including **Elie Theophile Itsomou**, who had served in Ngouabi's cabinet as secretary for health and labor. Another rebel leader, Ange Diawara (q.v.), escaped from the capital but was killed by government troops the following year.

• **Maj. Gen. Mohammed Omran** (1922–72), the former Syrian minister of defense and deputy premier, was shot and killed while in exile in Tripoli, Lebanon, on March 4, 1972. Omran had been active in the 1963 Baathist coup in Syria and served in his posts until 1964, when he went into exile in Lebanon.

• **Sheik Abeid Karume** (1906–72), who had seized power in Zanzibar during a bloody coup in January of 1964, met his own end in a violent fashion on April 7, 1972. Karume died of gunshot wounds when gunmen burst into a meeting of his ruling Afro-Shirazi party. Sheikh Tabit Kombo, the secretary general of the party, was critically wounded. Two of the gunmen were killed during the assault, and a third was later found dead, a presumed suicide. The leader of the assassins was Lt. Hamoud, who blamed Karume for the death of his father while in detention during the 1964 revolution.

Abeid Amani Karume worked as a sailor on cargo boats while in his teens. He returned to Zanzibar in 1938 and founded a shore launch service. Karume became active in politics and was elected to the town council in 1954. He led the African Association into a merger with the Shirazi Association to form the Afro-Shirazi party in 1957. Karume led the party in subsequent elections, but although he received a slight plurality, he was unable to form a government. A violent revolution led by John Okello overthrew the monarchy and ousted the government on January 12, 1964. Karume was selected as head of state. Relations between the new government and Okello deteriorated, and he was expelled from Zanzibar several months after leading the revolution. Karume negotiated a union between the island of Zanzibar and its neighbor on the mainland, Tanganyika, and the two nations merged to form Tanzania on April 26, 1964. Karume became first vice president of the United Republic of Tanzania and retained power on Zanzibar. He was regarded as a despot and ruled the island as a one-party state. He ruthlessly crushed opposition and eliminated potential rivals from the government. Following his assassination he was succeeded by Aboud Mwinyi Jumbe as Tanzania's first vice president and leader of Zanzibar.

• **Gen. Juan Carlos Sanchez** (1919–72), an Argentine army officer with the Second Army Corps, was shot and killed by terrorists on April 10, 1972, while en route to his headquarters in Buenos Aires.

• **Aberdan Sallustro** (1915–72), an executive with the Argentine Fiat auto company, was murdered by the terrorist group the People's Revolutionary Army of Argentina, on April 10, 1972. He had been kidnapped three weeks earlier on March 21, 1972, in Buenos Aires. Sallustro was killed when police raided the terrorist hideout where he was being held.

• In early April of 1972 **Charles Ndizeye** (1947–72), who had briefly ruled the tiny East African nation of Burundi as **Ntare V** for four months in 1966, was invited to return to his country by Michel Micombero (1939–83), the man who had deposed him in November of 1966. Burundi had a long history of political violence even before its independence in 1962. Ntare's brother, Prince Louis Rwagosore (q.v.), had been assassinated in 1961, and two of the country's first three premiers had also died at the hands of assassins. Ntare himself had led the coup which deposed his father, Mwami Mwambutsa IV, on July 8, 1966. A former resident described the nation as "a country in which *Macbeth* is constantly being reenacted." Ntare, who had been living in exile in West Germany, accepted Micombero's invitation to return after being granted a presidential guarantee of safe conduct. Upon arriving in Bujumbura, the capital, he was seized by government troops and placed under "protective custody." This protection was short lived, as in less than a month Ntare was dead, slain by Burundian troops in Gitega, sixty miles east of the capital, on April 29, 1972. The government claimed the killing came as a result of supporters attempting to free the twenty-five-year-old ex-king during an abortive coup.

• On May 15, 1972, Governor George C. Wallace (1919–98) of Alabama, a candidate for the Democratic nomination for president, was shot and seriously wounded in a Laurel, Maryland, shopping center parking lot during a campaign speech prior to the Maryland primary. His assailant, identified as Arthur Bremer, was arrested and convicted of the crime. Governor Wallace survived his injuries, though he remained partially paralyzed and confined to a wheelchair. He was unsuccessful in his bid for the presidential nomination in that year and again in 1976, although he continued to serve as Alabama's governor until 1979, and again from 1983 until 1987. He died on September 13, 1998.

• **Olivero Castaneda Paiz**, a leader of the National Liberation Movement (MLN) and first vice president of the Guatemalan congress, was shot and killed on June 25, 1972.

• **Ghassan Kanafani**, a leader of the Popular Front for the Liberation of Palestine (PFLP), died in an explosion in his car in Beirut, Lebanon, on July 8, 1972. Kanafani was born in Acre, Palestine, in 1936 and settled in Lebanon after Israel was established in 1948. He was an early Palestinian activist, joining the Movement of Arab Nationalists in 1954. A founder of the Popular Front for the Liberation of Palestine in 1967, he became a leading advisor to George Habash. He served as a leading spokesman for the PLFP and was the founder and editor of *Al Hadaf*, its weekly journal, from 1969. Palestinian sources claimed that the Israeli intelligence service was responsible for the slaying, which also claimed the life of his young niece.

• **Kjell Richard Haeggloef** (1942–72), the first secretary of the Swedish Embassy in Bogota, Colombia, was shot and killed while riding in his car in Bogota on July 17, 1972. Haeggloef had earlier been asked to leave Colombia following reports that he had contacts with guerrilla groups operating in the area. His assassin was identified as Karl Iver Reinhold, a Swedish newsman.

• **Col. Artigas Alvarez**, the chief of Uruguay's civil defense, was shot and killed by Tupamaro guerillas in Montevideo on July 25, 1972.

• On August 16, 1972, King Hassan (1929–99) of Morocco survived a coup attempt when the plane in which he was flying was attacked by fighters of the Royal Moroccan Air Force.

The plane was shot up, but managed to land safely. The alleged leader of the rebellion, **Gen. Muhammad Oufkir** (1920–72), the Moroccan minister of defense, was reported to have committed suicide, from multiple bullet wounds to the body, in the capital on August 17, 1972, following the coup's failure.

Muhammad Oufkir had attended French military schools in Morocco and served in the French army in Indo-China. He had served as France's liaison with Mohammed V, and arranged his return from exile after Morocco's independence. He ruthlessly crushed the Rif rebellion in 1959 and was named minister of interior in 1961. He had been convicted in absentia in a French court of masterminding the abduction and murder of Moroccan opposition leader Medhi Ben Barka (q.v.) in 1965. Seven air force officers were subsequently arrested for complicity in the coup attempt and were executed the following year on January 13, 1973.

• **Phan My Truc**, the publisher of a progovernment newspaper in Saigon, South Vietnam, was shot to death in a Saigon restaurant on August 26, 1972.

• On September 5, 1972, eight terrorists belonging to the Arab Black September guerrilla movement attacked the compound housing Israeli athletes at the Olympic Village in Munich, West Germany. Weight lifter **Yossef Romano** and wrestling coach **Moshe Weinberger** were killed during the initial assault. The terrorists, with their nine remaining hostages, were transported by helicopter to Munich's Furstenfeldbruck airport, where they intended to proceed to Cairo, Egypt, and ransom the captured athletes for the release of fellow terrorists held in Israel and West Germany. The West German authorities opened fire on the guerrillas before they could board the plane designated to carry them to Egypt. During the subsequent gun battle six of the terrorists were slain, and the remaining two were wounded and captured, but not before the nine Israelis were murdered. A terrorist threw a hand grenade into the helicopter containing track coach **Amitzur Shapira**, weight lifter **David Marc Berger**, fencing master **Andrei Spitzer**, wrestler **Mark Slavin**, and rifle coach **Kehat Shorr**, killing all of them in the explosion. The four hostages in the remaining helicopter were then shot to death by two of their captors. They included weight lifter **Zeev Fridman**, weight lifting judge **Yacov Springer**, wrestler **Eliezer Halfin**, and wrestling referee **Yossef Gutfreund**. It was believed that Palestinian leader Ali Hassan Salameh (q.v.) had been the mastermind behind the assault.

• **George Duckett**, Bermuda's commissioner of police, was murdered by unknown assailants at his home in Hamilton, Bermuda, on September 9, 1972.

• **Benedicto Kiwanuka** (1922–72), the chief justice of the Ugandan Supreme Court, who had served as that nation's first prime minister in 1962, was seized and murdered by agents of Ugandan president Idi Amin on September 21, 1972.

Benedicto Kiwanuka was born in Buddu in 1922, a member of the Muganda tribe. He was educated locally and served in the army from 1942 until 1946. He continued his education in Basutoland and attended University College in London, where he received a degree in law in 1956. Kiwanuka was elected to the Uganda Legislative Council in 1961 and served in the government as minister without portfolio. He was elected chief minister on July 2, 1961, and became prime minister on March 1, 1962, when Uganda was granted self-rule. He lost his seat in the assembly the following month when the Uganda People's Congress led by Milton Obote came to power. Kiwanuka relinquished office to Obote on April 25, 1962. He returned to practice law in Kampala. Kiwanuka was detained after an assassination attempt against President Obote in December of 1969. He was released soon afterwards and was named chief justice of the Ugandan Supreme Court. He was considered an opponent of Idi Amin's regime, which led to his murder in 1972.

Idi Amin, who had seized power in Uganda in 1971 and remained president until his own ouster in 1979, orchestrated the political murder of over 100,000 of his countrymen during his eight years in power. Henry Kyemba, who served as a minister in Amin's government until 1977, recorded some of the more prominent victims of Amin's reign. They included Anglican archbishop Janani Luwum (q.v.); **Lt. Col. Michael Ondoga**, the Ugandan ambassador to the Soviet Union from 1971 to 1973 and foreign minister from 1973 until 1974; **Yekosfati Engur**, minister of culture and community development; **Haji Shaban Knuto**, minister of works under Milton Obote, Amin's predecessor; **William Kalema**, former minister of commerce; **Basil Bataringaya** (1927–72), former minister of internal affairs; **John Kakonge**, former minister of agriculture; **Joshua Wakholi**, former minister of public service; **Alex Ojera**, former minister of information; **Haji Ali Kisekka**, former deputy minister for the East African Community; **Frank Kalimuzo**, vice chancellor of Makerere University; **Joseph Mubiru**, governor of the Central Bank; and **Brig. Charles Arube**, chief of staff of the Ugandan Army.

• **Hachem Jawad**, the United Nations Development Program's representative in the Middle East, was killed in his office near Beirut, Lebanon, on October 11, 1972. Jawad, a former Iraqi foreign minister, was shot by Ahmed Mahmoud Jaafry, his former driver, who subsequently committed suicide.

• **Abdel Wael Zuaiter**, a clerk at the Libyan Embassy in Rome, was shot and killed in the lobby of his Rome apartment on October 16, 1972. Zuaiter, a Jordanian, was reportedly the top agent in Italy of the Palestinian organization Al Fatah. His assassins were believed to have been members of the Israeli Secret Service.

• Imelda Marcos (b. 1931), the wife of President Ferdinand Marcos of the Philippines, survived an assassination attempt on December 7, 1972. Mrs. Marcos was injured when she was attacked by a knife-wielding man while addressing a crowd in Manila. The assailant was slain by Mrs. Marcos' guards, and she recovered from her injuries. Mrs. Marcos remained the first lady of the Philippines until the ouster of her husband in early 1986.

• **Mahmoud Hamshari**, a leading Palestinian diplomat in Paris, was fatally injured by a bomb planted in his apartment telephone on December 8, 1972. He died the following month on January 9, 1973. Hamshari, was reputed to be a member of the Black September guerrilla movement, was believed to have been assassinated by members of the Israeli Secret Service.

• Rwanda experienced another round of political violence following a Huto revolt. Numerous Hutu political figures were arrested and executed. **Jean Chrisostome Bandyambona**, a former minister of education and minister of social affairs, was killed in May of 1972. Other victims included **Joachim Baribwegure** (1923–72), another former social affairs minister and militant Hutu; **Amedee Kabugubugu** (1934–72), the former minister of education; **Marcien Burasekuye**, the former minister of post, telegraph and telecommunications; **Abraham Boyayo**, the former director general of the ministry of national education and culture; **Pascal Bubiriza** (1932–72), a former ambassador to Ethiopia and minister of communications; and **Marc Ndayiziga**, a former minister of public works.

# 1973

• **Amilcar Cabral** (1926–73), the secretary general of the African Party for the Independence of Guinea and Cape Verde (PAIGC), was shot to death near his home in Conakry, Guinea, on January 20, 1973. His assailants were believed to be rival members of Cabral's independence movement. Cabral was born in Bafata, Guinea-Bissau, on September

12, 1924. A graduate of the University of Lisbon Institute of Agronomy, he became involved in the nationalist movement in the early 1950s. He founded the pro-independence party PAIGC in 1956, and had led a guerrilla campaign to free Guinea-Bissau from Portugal's colonial empire. He had conducted his campaign against the Portuguese from the neighboring Republic of Guinea. He was widely respected throughout Africa as a leading nationalist statesman, and his death cost the Guinean independence movement its most able leader. Guinea-Bissau achieved independence from Portugal the following year, with Amilcar Cabral's brother, Luis, serving as the nation's first president.

• Palestinian leader **Hussein Abad Al-Chir** was killed in an explosion in his hotel room in Nicosia, Cyprus, on January 24, 1973. Al-Chir, reportedly a liaison between the Palestinians and the Soviets, was believed to have been a victim of Israel's Secret Service.

• In February of 1973 **Col. Francisco Alberto Caamano Deno**, who was a leader of the anti-government troops during the Dominican Republic's 1965 Civil War, was shot and killed in the central mountains area. Caamano Deno, a leftist who had been living in exile in Cuba, had reportedly led a small group of guerrillas in an attempt to overthrow the government of President Joaquin Belaquer.

• On March 1, 1973, an armed band of Palestinian guerrillas stormed the Saudi Arabian Embassy in the Sudan during a party given in honor of departing United States charge d'affaires **George Curtis Moore** (1926–73). Several diplomas in attendance were wounded during the attack. Following the failure of the Sudanese government to negotiate with the guerrillas, members of the Black September movement, the attackers killed Moore, United States ambassador **Cleo A. Noel, Jr.** (1919–73) and Belgian charge d'affaires **Guy Eid**.

Cleo Noel was born in Oklahoma City, Oklahoma, on August 6, 1918. He had served in the State Department from 1949 and was a veteran specialist in Middle Eastern affairs. He had served in diplomatic positions in Lebanon and Saudi Arabia, and had been stationed in Khartoum twice previously, in 1961 as vice consul and in 1966 as deputy chief of mission. He was appointed United States ambassador several months earlier, following the restoration of diplomatic relations between the United States and the Sudan.

George Curtis Moore had joined the Foreign Service in 1950, serving as a resident officer in Frankfurt, Germany. In 1953 he was stationed in Cairo and subsequently served in other embassies in the Middle East. In 1969 Moore was sent to Khartoum as counselor and charge d'affaires, serving as the head of the Embassy there in the absence of an ambassador. He was scheduled to leave the Sudan the week following his murder.

• **Theophile Mally** (1913–73), the former Togolese minister of the interior, reportedly died in prison in March of 1973 after having been arrested for passing a bad check the previous month. Mally was a member of the Comite de l'Unite Togolaise from the mid–1940s. He was named minister of the interior in the government of President Sylvanius Olympio (q.v.) in May of 1960, retaining office until Olympio's ouster and murder in 1963. He spent several years in exile until returning to Togo in 1967. He held several minor positions in the government of President Gnassingbe Eyadema, before his arrest.

• **Sir Richard Christopher Sharples** (1916–73), the British governor of Bermuda, was murdered on the grounds of the Government House in the capital of Hamilton on March 10, 1973. Sharples had served in the British army during World War II and was Field Marshal Montgomery's military assistant in the early 1950s. He was elected to Parliament in 1954. A member of the Conservative party, he served as minister of state for home affairs in the government of Edward Heath from 1970 until 1972. He was appointed governor of Bermuda in October of 1972. Sharples' chief aide, **Capt. Hugh**

**Sayers**, was killed with the governor. The murder remained unsolved but seemed related to the killing six months earlier of George Duckett (q.v.), the Bermudan police commissioner.

• **Col. Hector J. Irabarren**, the chief of military intelligence for the Argentine Third Army in Cordoba province, was assassinated on April 3, 1973, by leftist terrorists.

• **Basil Al-Kubaisi**, a Palestinian law professor affiliated with the Popular Front for the Liberation of Palestine, was shot and killed in the streets of Paris on April 6, 1973. His assassination was believed to have been arranged by members of the Israeli Secret Service.

• **Mohammed Yussef Najjar ("Abu Yussef")**, a leader and one of the founders of Al Fatah; **Kamal Adwan**, a Palestinian guerrilla who was reportedly in command of guerrilla operations in Israeli occupied territories in the 1967 war; and **Kamal Nasser** (1928–73), a leading Arab poet and spokesman for the Palestine Liberation Organization, where shot to death by Israeli soldiers on April 10, 1973, when their guerrilla headquarters in Beirut, Lebanon, were raided in a surprise attack.

• **Zaid Muchassi**, a Palestinian leader, was killed in an explosion in his hotel room in Athens, Greece, on April 12, 1973.

• **Ange Diawara** (1941–73), a Congolese leftist leader, was killed by government troops on April 23, 1973, after having been accused of leading a rebellion against President Marien Ngouabi (q.v.) of the Congo. Diawara had been a member of the Politburo of the Congolese Worker's Party. He had also served in President Ngouabi's cabinet as secretary of state for defense from October of 1968 until December of 1971. He led an unsuccessful revolt against the government in February of 1972.

• **Sheik Mohammed Ali Othman** (1910–73), a member of the three-man ruling council of North Yemen, was ambushed and killed by bazooka fire near his home on May 29, 1973. Othman was the leader of the ruling faction in Ta'izz, the second largest city in North Yemen.

- **Lt. Col. Lewis L. Hawkins** (1931–73), a United States army colonel stationed in Teheran as an advisor to the Iranian armed forces, was shot to death by two gunmen on June 1, 1973.

- **Mohammed Boudia**, an Algerian who was reportedly active in the Palestinian terrorist network, was killed when a bomb exploded in his car in Paris, France on June 28, 1973. Boudia was believed to have been the victim of the Israeli Secret Service.

- **Gen. Hammad Chehab** (1922–73), the defense minister of Iraq, was assassinated during an abortive coup attempt on June 30, 1973. Chehab and Lt. Gen. Saadoun Gheidan, the interior minister, were kidnapped from a state banquet by **Nazim Kazzar** (1938–73), the Iraqi security chief and leader of the coup attempt. Chehab was killed and Gheidan wounded after Iraqi troops attempted to apprehend the plotters. Kazzar and twenty-one other conspirators were arrested and found guilty of treason. The were executive on July 7, 1973. Fourteen others were convicted and executed the following day, including **Muhammad Fadhil**, head of the Ba'th military bureau.

- **Col. Yosef Alon** (1927–73), the deputy military attache of the Israeli Embassy in Washington, D.C., was murdered at his home in Chevy Chase, Maryland, on July 1, 1973.

- **Capt. Arturo Araya** (1928–73), a naval aide to Chilean president Salvador Allende (q.v.), was killed on July 27, 1973, by machine gun fire while standing on the balcony of his home in Santiago, Chile.

- On August 20, 1973, right-wing Laotian air force **Gen. Thoa Ma** (1930–73), was killed while leading an unsuccessful coup attempt against the Laotian coalition government. Thoa Ma died when his plane was shot down at the Vientiane airport. He had been living in exile in Thailand since 1966, when he had fled Laos after leading a previous unsuccessful coup attempt.

- **Outel Bono** (1934–73), an exiled opponent of President Francois Tombalbaye (q.v.) of Chad, was assassinated in the streets of Paris, France, on August 26, 1973. Bono, a former director of health services, had been in the process of creating a Chadian opposition party at the time of his murder. A physician, Bono had been active in the independence movement and was a critic of President Tombalbaye. He was arrested in March 1963 and sentenced to death on charges of conspiring against the government. He was later amnestied and released from prison in 1965. Bono was again arrested in 1969, and held in prison for a brief time. Bono remained under police observation until he left Chad in July of 1972. His killing came a day before he was scheduled to announce the formation of an opposition party to Tombalbaye.

- **James Shebazz** (1921–73), a leader of the Black Muslims, was shot and killed in front of his home in Newark, New Jersey, on September 5, 1973. Shebazz was a close associate of Malcolm X (q.v.) and had become the leader of his New York mosque following Malcolm X's assassination in 1965.

- **Mohammed Hashim Maiwandwal**, who had served as prime minister of Afghanistan from 1965 until 1967, was reported to have hanged himself by his necktie in a prison cell on October 1, 1973. Maiwandwal had been arrested earlier in the month and charged with involvement in a coup attempt against the government of President Mohammed Daud Khan (q.v.). Maiwandwal was born on March 12, 1921. He edited and wrote for several Afghanistani newspapers in the 1940s and became press secretary to the Afghan government in 1949. The following year he was appointed advisor to King Mohammed Zahir Shah. During the 1950s Maiwandwal served as ambassador to Great Britain and to Pakistan, and from 1958 to 1963, he was ambassador to the United States. He became Afghanistan's prime minister on November 1, 1965. During his tenure in office, he was noted for his policies of modernization and liberalization of the government. He had completed a second five-year plan of development and had started a third when he resigned for reasons of health on November 1, 1967. Maiwandwal was the leader of the Progressive Democracy movement when he was arrested on September 20, 1973, on charges of conspiring to overthrow the government.

• **Salvador Allende Gossens**, the Marxist president of Chile, was killed during a military coup on September 11, 1973. Allende was born in Valparaiso, Chile, on July 26, 1908. He was a founder of the Chilean Socialist party in 1933 and served as a deputy in the Chilean Congress. He was named minister of health in 1939 and helped organize relief efforts following a massive earthquake later that year. Allende was elected to the Senate in 1945 and, in 1952, made his first race for the presidency of Chile. He was defeated in that campaign as well as in two subsequent races in 1958 and 1964. Allende again ran for president in 1970 and received a plurality in the general elections held on September 4 of that year. The following month he was officially elected president by a vote of a joint session of Congress and, on November 4, 1970, he was sworn in to head the first freely elected Marxist government in South America. Allende's term of office was marked by civil disorders and a failing economy. The Chilean government was near collapse when a military uprising, presumably with the assistance of the United States Central Intelligence Agency, launched an attack on the Presidential Palace. Allende was killed during the assault, though officially his death was reported as a suicide. He was replaced by a military junta led by Gen. Augusto Pinochet.

• **Tommy Herron** (1937–73), an Irish Protestant leader, was shot and killed by assassins near Lisburn, Northern Ireland, on September 15, 1973. Herron had been the deputy leader of the militant Ulster Defense Association.

• **Jose Rucci**, a leader of the Argentine labor movement, was assassinated by machine gun fire at his home in Buenos Aires on September 24, 1973. Rucci, a moderate ally of Juan Peron, served as secretary general of the Confederacion Geneal de Trabajo, the leading Argentine labor union. His assassination was believed to have been the work of the leftist Marxist People's Revolutionary Army. Several days later, leftist guerrillas were responsible for the slaying of **Enrique Grinberg**, another moderate labor leader.

• **German Castros Rojas**, the former governor of Talca, Chile, was executed in Quillota on September 25, 1973, on charges of killing a policeman while trying to blow up a dam. Castros Rojas was a leading leftist in the area and had been a supporter of deposed Chilean president Salvador Allende (q.v.).

• **Marcus A. Foster** (1923–73), the superintendent of the Oakland, California, city school system, was shot and killed on November 6, 1973, while walking to his car at his office parking lot following a school board meeting. Robert Blackburn, Foster's assistant superintendent, was also shot and critically injured at that time. Foster had formerly served as associate superintendent of community affairs for the Philadelphia School District before his appointment by the Oakland Board of Education in 1970.

Russell Little (b.1949) and Joseph Remiro (b.1946) were subsequently arrested and charged with Foster's murder. They were tried and convicted of the killing, but the convictions were later overturned. Little was acquitted in a retrial and Remiro was sentenced to life imprisonment. Remiro and Little were members of the Symbionese Liberation Army (SLA), a terrorist organization that also kidnapped newspaper heiress Patricia Hearst on February 4, 1974. Six members of the SLA, including Donald "Field Marshal Cinque" DeFreeze (1944–74), the leader of the group, were killed in a shootout with Los Angeles police on May 17, 1974. The other SLA members killed at that time were Nancy Ling Perry (1948–74), the group's spokesperson, who had written a letter claiming the SLA's responsibility for Marcus Foster's assassination; Patricia "Mizmoon" Soltysik

(1950–74); Camilla "Gabi" Hall (1945–74); William "Cujo" Wolfe (1951–74) and Angela "Gelina" Atwood (1949–74).

Patty Hearst, who was believed to have been indoctrinated by the SLA following her abduction, was subsequently charged with armed robbery, kidnapping and other felonies. She was arrested on September 18, 1974, along with William and Emily Harris, two other surviving members of the SLA. Ms. Hearst and the Harrises were tried the following year and convicted on most charges. Hearst served two years of a seven year sentence before President Jimmy Carter commuted her sentence. Bill and Emily Harris served 8½ years in prison before their release.

• **John A. Swint** (1917–73), the general manager of Transax, a Ford Motor Company–owned manufacturing plant, was assassinated by leftist guerrillas while en route to Cordoba, Argentina, on November 22, 1973.

• **Abdus Samad Khan Achakzai** (1907–73), the leader of the Pathan Khawa National Awami party and a member of the Legislative Assembly in Baluchistan, Pakistan, was murdered on December 2, 1973, during a grenade attack on his home in Quetta, Pakistan.

• **Adm. Luis Carrero Blanco**, the premier of Spain, was killed on December 20, 1973, when a bomb planted underneath his car exploded in front of a church in Madrid. Carrero Blanco was born on March 4, 1903, in Santona, Spain. He graduated from the Spanish naval academy and was commissioned an ensign in 1922. He saw active duty in Spain's colonies in North Africa in the early 1920s. Carrero Blanco was promoted to lieutenant in 1926 and was later given command of a submarine. He returned from sea after five years and continued his studies in naval warfare. He was named to the staff of the Spanish naval academy in 1934. Carrero Blanco joined the Nationalist navy during the Spanish Civil War, and following Francisco Franco's victory in 1939, he was named chief of naval operations. He became a close associate of Franco and was appointed undersec-

retary to the presidency of the government in 1941. He was appointed to the Spanish Parliament, the Cortes, the following year. Carrero Blanco also became vice president of the Cortes in 1942. He joined Franco's cabinet in 1951 and remained a key advisor throughout the 1950s and 1960s. He also rose through the ranks of the navy and was promoted to admiral in 1966. Franco appointed Carrero Blanco as vice premier in September of 1967. Franco relinquished his duties as head of government, while retaining the presidency, under a new constitution in June of 1973. Carrero Blanco was appointed premier in the new government on June 8, 1973. He was killed six months later when an explosion hurled the limousine in which he had been a passenger onto the roof of the Madrid church where he had just attended services. The assassination was believed to have been carried out by members of a Basque separatist organization retaliating for the government's killing of nine Basque militants. Fourteen people were arrested in connection with Carrero Blanco's murder, but all were amnestied by King Juan Carlos in 1978.

# 1974

• On February 22, 1974, a plot to assassinate United States President Richard M. Nixon (1913–94) using a commercial airliner was foiled before it got off the ground. Samuel J. Byck (Jan. 30, 1930–1974), an unemployed salesman from Philadelphia, planned to hijack a commercial airplane and crash it into the White House. Arriving at the Baltimore-Washington International Airport armed with a pistol and a gasoline bomb, he forced his way aboard Delta Flight 523, shooting and killing an airport guard. He seized control of the cockpit of the plane, shooting the co-pilot in the stomach when the pilot refused take off. He subsequently shot the pilot in the shoulder and fired a second fatal bullet into the co-pilot before snipers opened fire on the plane. Byck was hit by several shots before placing his gun to his right temple and taking his own life.

• **Billy Fox** (1937–74), a senator from the Republic of Ireland, was ambushed and slain by a gang of assassins in County Monaghan on March 13, 1974. Fox, a Protestant member of the Fine Gael party, was an outspoken critic of British military actions in Northern Ireland. A Protestant extremist organization, The Ulster Freedom Fighters (UFF), claimed credit for the killing and five men, Sean McGettiaan, George McDermott, James McPhillips, Sean Kinsella and Michael Kinsella, were arrested three months later and sentenced to life imprisonment for Fox's murder.

• **Jose De la Torriente** (1904–74), a former Cuban agriculture minister, was shot and killed by a sniper at his home in Coral Gables, Florida, on April 13, 1974. De la Torriente had served as a leader of exile Cubans hoping to overthrow Fidel Castro.

• **Aisa Diori** (1928–74), the wife of Niger's President Hamani Diori (1916–89), was killed during a military coup against her husband in the capital on April 15, 1974. The coup, led by Col. Seyni Kountche (1931–87), removed Diori from power. His wife was killed while urging the Taureg Presidential Guard to resist the rebels.

• **Judge James Lawless** (1923–74) of the Washington (state) Superior Court was killed when a mail bomb delivered to the county courthouse in southeastern Washington exploded on June 3, 1974. Lawless had served on the superior court for the previous sixteen years.

• **Kungu wa Karumba** (1895–1975), an early proponent of Kenyan independence, vanished in June of 1974. He was believed to have been killed either in Kenya or Uganda. He became involved in political affairs in the early 1920s and entered the Kikuya Central Association in 1935. He joined Jomo Kenyatta's Kenya African Union in the late 1940s. Karumba was arrested in October of 1952 and was detained by the colonial authorities for the next eight years. After his release he became a leading businessman in Kenya, founding the Wanainchi Transport Company. He remained a leading figure in Kenya until his presumed murder in 1974.

• **Walter Hildebrand**, the president of the Supreme Court of Liechtenstein, was shot to death on June 20, 1974, during a court session. His assassin was identified as Reinhold Glatt, a Swiss national.

• A coup attempt against the government of President Francisco Macias Nguema (q.v.) of Equatorial Guinea failed in June of 1974. Numerous conspirators were arrested and executed on June 26, 1974. They included **Roman Boricho Toichoa**, the former minister of labor; **Felipe Esono Nsue**, the chief of the Oyek tribe and former mayor of Evinayong; **Manuel Kombe Madje**, an official with the Ministry of Health; **Ekong Andeme**, the minister of mines and industry; **Lucas Ondo Micha**, an education ministry official; **Marcos Ropo Uri**, former minister of finance; and **Expedito Rafael Momo Bokara**, the minister of justice.

• **Mohammed Ahmed Noman**, a former foreign minister of North Yemen, was shot and killed on June 28, 1974, in Beirut, Lebanon. Noman had served as foreign minister prior to his ouster during a military coup two weeks before his assassination.

• **Arturo Mor Roig** (1915–74), a former Argentine interior minister, was shot and killed in Buenos Aires on July 15, 1974. Mor Roig served as the president of the Argentine chamber of deputies from 1963 until 1966. In March of 1971 he was named minister of the interior by the military government of Gen. Lanusse. While serving in that office Mor Roig was responsible for implementing the election procedures which were to return Argentina to civilian rule. He was widely praised for his role in insuring that the Argentine elections in March of 1973 were conducted in a fair and honest manner. Mor Roig retired from political activities following the establishment of the new government. He was ambushed and murdered by four unidentified assailants while having lunch near the metal-lurgical company at which he was employed.

• **Madame Park Chung Hee**, the wife of the president of South Korea, was struck and killed by a bullet aimed at her husband on August 15, 1974, while attending a speech given by President Chung Hee Park (q.v.) at the National Theater in Seoul. The president was uninjured in the assault. Madame Park, who was born Yook Young Soo in 1926, was a popular figure in South Korea and was known for her charitable activities. The as-sassin, identified as Mun Se Kwang, was tried and, on December 20, executed for the mur-der.

• **Rodger P. Davies**, the United States ambassador to Cyprus, was fatally injured in Nicosia when a Greek Cypriot sniper fired bullets into the American Embassy there on August 19, 1974. Davies was born in Berkeley, California, on May 7, 1921. He served in the U.S. Army during World War II and joined the Foreign Service in 1946. He served in var-ious diplomatic positions throughout the Middle East and, in 1962, was named deputy director of the Office of Near Eastern Affairs. In 1965 he was named deputy assistant secre-tary of state. Davies was appointed ambas-sador to Cyprus in May of 1974.

• **Gen. Carlos Prats** (1915–74), the for-mer leader of the Chilean army during the ad-ministration of President Salvador Allende (q.v.), died with his wife, Sofia Cuthbert, when a bomb exploded in the car in which they were riding on September 30, 1974. Prats was living in Buenos Aires, Argentina, at the time, having fled Chile after the overthrow of Allende in 1973. An Argentine court found an alleged former Chilean spy, Arancibia Clavel, guilty of the killing in November of 2000. He was sentenced to life imprisonment.

• **Alberto Villar** (1923–74), the federal police chief of Argentina, died in a bomb ex-plosion aboard his cabin cruiser in Buenos Aires on October 31, 1974.

• **Guenter Drenkman**, the president of the West German Supreme Court, was shot and killed by members of the Baader-Mein-hof guerrilla movement while at his home in Bonn on November 9, 1974.

• Sixty former officials of the Ethiopian government, including eighteen generals and fourteen other military officers, as well as leading aristocrats, former cabinet ministers, and provincial governors, were executed in Addis Adaba on November 23, 1974. The dead included **Lt. Gen. Aman Michael Andom** (1924–74), chairman of the ruling military council of Ethiopia, who was killed at his home when he resisted arrest following his ouster. Others executed include **Akililu Habte-Wold** (1908–74), the prime minis-ter of Ethiopia from 1961 until 1974; **En-dalkachew Makonnen** (1926–74), an Ethiopian diplomat who served as prime min-ister in 1974; **Rear Admiral Alexander (Eskender) Desta**, grandson of Emperor Haile Selassie and commander of the Ethiopian navy from 1955; **Ras Asrate Kasa**, the former head of the Crown Coun-cil; **Yelma Deresa**, the former ambassador to the United States and foreign minister; **Ras Mesfin Sileshi**, the former governor of Shoa Province; **Col. Solomon Kedir**, the former chief of security; **Lt. Gen. Abiye Abebe** (1918–74), the former defense minister who served as president of the senate in 1964; **Lt. Gen. Yilma Shibeshi**, the former police commissioner; **Lt. Gen. Haile Baike-dagne**, the former deputy armed forces chief of staff; **Lt. Gen. Essayas Gabre Se-lassie**, a former member of the senate; and **Assefa Ayene**, the former communications minister and armed forces chief of staff.

Aman Michael Andom was born in Eri-trea in 1924. He served with the Resistance in fighting the Italian occupation forces in the 1930 and, after the liberation of Ethiopia, joined the regular army. Andom was stationed in Korea as part of the United States troops serving there. Soon afterwards he was named commandant of the Harar Military College. He was active in the border dispute with So-malia and earned the nickname of "the Desert Lion." Andom became a leading proponent of political reforms in Ethiopia and earned the displeasure of the Emperor. He was moved from the army and served in the Ethiopian Senate. When young army officers took over the government in 1974, Andom was named chief of staff and defense minister. Following the ouster of the emperor in September of 1974, Andom served as chairman of the Provisional Military Administrative Committee. He was ousted by more revolutionary members of the government on November 24, 1974, and was killed in a gun battle with soldiers sent to arrest him.

Akilu Habte-Wold was born in Addis Ababa in 1908. He was educated in Alexandria, Egypt, and the University of Paris. He completed his education in 1936, but remained in Europe during the Italian occupation. Akilu returned to Ethiopia in 1941 and was appointed vice minister of foreign affairs in October of 1943. He was Ethiopia's representative to the United Nations Charter session in San Francisco in 1945. He became minister of foreign affairs in 1949 and was appointed deputy prime minister in 1957. The following year he stepped down as foreign minister. Akilu returned to the Foreign Ministry in 1960, while remaining deputy prime minister. He was abroad with Emperor Haile Selassie when a coup attempt took place in the capital. Akilu's brother, Makonnen Habte-Wold (q.v.), and other government leaders were killed by the insurgents. The coup was crushed, and Akilu was appointed prime minister on March 29, 1961. He remained head of the government and a leading advisor to the emperor throughout the 1960s. He was granted the right to appoint his own cabinet members in a reorganization of the government in March of 1966. Akilu supported the emperor's land taxation and reform policies and halted a revolt against the land tax in Gojam Province in 1969. Ethiopia experienced a famine in the early 1970s, and the government's inability to cope with the crisis caused widespread dissent. The Ethiopian military mutinied for higher pay in February of 1974. The emperor dismissed Akilu on February 28, 1974, in the hopes of appeasing critics of the government. Akilu was arrested shortly after his ouster. The emperor was dethroned in September of 1974, and Akilu joined many other members of Haile Selassie's government in being executed on November 24, 1974.

Endalkatchew Makonnen was born in Addis Ababa in 1926, the son of former Prime Minister Makonnen Endalkatchew. He was educated at Oxford University in Great Britain. Makonnen was subsequently appointed Ethiopia's ambassador to Great Britain, where he remained until 1961. He returned to Ethiopia to serve in the government as minister of commerce and industry. He was appointed Ethiopia's representative to the United Nations in 1966, where he served until 1969. Makonnen returned to the cabinet as minister of communications until his appointment as prime minister on February 28, 1974. He tried to restore order in the country, but could not stop the growing tide of discontent against the regime of Haile Selassie. Makonnen was forced to resign on July 22, 1974, and was arrested shortly thereafter. Makonnen was executed with many other members of his former government on November 24, 1974.

Ras Asrate Kasa was born in 1918, a descendant of the Shewan royal family. He was named governor of Begemder in 1942, and subsequently served as governor of Wellega from 1944 to 1946, and Arussi from 1946 to 1952. He returned to govern Begemder in 1952 and became governor of Shewa in 1956. The following year he became vice-president of the Senate. He was a leader of the countercoup that crushed the rebellion against the emperor in December of 1960. Asrate Kasa served as senate president from 1961 until 1964. He subsequently served the emperor as his representative in Eritrea. He remained a leading advisor to the emperor and he and his family were among those seized by the Derg following the ouster of Haile Selassie.

Yelma Deresa (1907–74) studied economics in England. He was detained in Italy during the occupation but returned to Ethiopia in 1941 to serve as minister of finance. He remained in the cabinet as minister of commerce from 1949 until 1953, when he was appointed ambassador to the United States. He returned to Ethiopia to serve as minister of foreign affairs in 1958. Yelma Deresa again served as minister of finance from 1960 until 1969. He was arrested by the Derg and executed following after the uprising of 1974.

Haile Selassie was born Lij Tafari Makonnen on July 23, 1892, at Ejarsa Gora in Harar. He was the son of Ras Makonnen, a leading advisor of Emperor Menelik II. He was named by the emperor as governor of the Sidamo province in southern Ethiopia in 1908. His success in the region led to his subsequent appointment as governor of Harar. Haile Selassie was named regent and heir apparent when Emperor Menelik's daughter, Princess Zauditu, assumed the throne following the ouster of Menelik's successor, his grandson Lej Iyasu. Haile Selassie was a powerful influence during Zauditu's reign, and assumed the throne upon her death on November 2, 1930. Ethiopia was invaded by Italy in October of 1934 and Haile Selassie led the army against the Italians. He was forced to flee the country when the invaders seized the capital in May of 1936. He appealed to the League of Nations for assistance and worked for foreign intervention to reclaim his country. Following the liberation of Ethiopia by British troops in May of 1941, Haile Selassie returned to Addis Ababa. Haile Selassie faced several challenges to his regime in the 1950s and survived a coup attempt by members of the Imperial Guard to declare his son, Asfa Wossen, as emperor in December of 1960. Despite granting some political reforms, Haile Selassie's regime came under increasing pressure from insurgents, which worsened following a severe drought in 1973. Haile Selassie was forced to name a reformist government, but the reforms were unable to curb the unrest in the country. The Emperor was deposed by a coup led by junior military officers on September 13, 1974. Two months later over 60 of his closest aides and advisors were executed. Haile Selassie was placed under house arrest, and the harsh conditions of his imprisonment led to his death on August 27, 1975. Some reports indicate that the former emperor was strangled in his bed by agents of the Mengistu government.

# 1975

- **Lalit Narayan Mishra**, the Indian minister of railways, was killed in a bomb explosion in Samastipur Bihar, India, on January 2, 1975. His assassins were believed to be Anand Marg terrorists.

- **Hayat Mohammad Khan Sherpao**, the senior minister of Pakistan's Northwest Frontier province, was killed in a bomb explosion at Peshaward University on February 7, 1975. Sherpao was a close ally of Pakistan's prime minister, Zulfikar Ali Bhutto (q.v.).

- **Edmundo Bosio Dioco** (1923–75), the former vice president of Equatorial Guinea, was arrested and executed on February 9, 1975. The government announced that he had committed suicide in prison. Bosio Dioco was a school teacher who served as Equatorial Guinea's representative to the Spanish Cortes from 1964 to 1968. He was a candidate for president in 1968 and became vice president of Equatorial Guinea after Francisco Macias Nguema's election. He also served in the government as minister of commerce before his arrest and murder.

- **Col. Richard Ratsimandrava** (1931–75) was selected as president of the Malagasy Republic (Madagascar) by the ruling military government on February 5, 1975. Six days later, on February 11, he was dead, the victim of an assassin's bullets. Ratsimandrava was shot and killed while en route from the presidential palace to his residence in Tananrive. Two of the president's bodyguards were also killed, and it was reported that two of the assassins perished in the subsequent gunfight. The military leadership remained in power, selecting Gen. Gilles Andrinmazo as the new head of state.

Richard Ratsimandrava was born on March 21, 1931. He attended the French Military College in St. Cyr and served in the French gendarmerie. He was stationed in France, Morocco, and Algeria until he returned to Madagascar following independence in 1960. Ratsimandrava became a leader in the Madagascan army, where he rose to lieutenant colonel in 1968. He was appointed minister of the interior in the military government under President Gabriel Ramanantsoa. He orchestrated the ouster of Ramanantsoa and became his successor. His rule ended six days later with his assassination.

• Lebanese political leader **Ma'ruf Sa'd** (1910–75) was shot to death by an army sniper on February 26, 1975. He died of his wounds the following month. Sa'd was active in the Palestinian nationalist movement from the 1930s. He entered the Lebanese parliament in 1957 and was a leader in the 1958 rebellion. He founded the Popular Nasserist Organization in 1972, but lost his seat in the parliament two years later. His assassination in February of 1975 was viewed as one of the leading causes of the civil war in Lebanon that broke out later in the year.

• **John P. Egan** (1913–75), the United States honorary consul in Cordoba, Argentina, was murdered by Montoneros guerrillas, and his body was dumped on a roadside near Cordoba on February 27, 1975. Egan had been kidnapped by the leftist terrorists two days earlier.

• **J.M. Kariuki**, a leading critic of the Kenyan government and member of parliament, was found shot to death in the Ngong Hills near Nairobi on March 10, 1975. Kariuki was reported missing on March 2. Josiah Mwangi Kariuki was born in the Rift Valley Province of Kenya on March 21, 1929. Educated locally and at King's College in Uganda, he became involved with the Kenya African Union (KAU) in the early 1950s. Kariuki was detained in 1953 and held for the next seven years. After his release Kariuki authored the biographical work, *Mau Mau Detainee*, at Oxford University. He returned to Kenya in 1963 and won an election for the Aberdare's Constituency. He became leader of the National Youth Service the following year. Kariuki was named assistant minister for agriculture in July of 1968 and assistant minister for tourism and wildlife the following year. He was dismissed from the government in 1974, but remained a popular political figure and potential challenger to Kenyan President Jomo Kenyatta. The following year was abducted and brutally murdered. His assassins were never found, though the Kenyan government was implicated in the killing.

• **Herbert W.T. Chitepo**, a Rhodesian black nationalist leader and outspoken critic of the white Rhodesian government, died in a car bomb explosion in Lusaka, Zambia, on March 18, 1975. Chitepo was born on June 5, 1923, and was the first black lawyer to practice in Rhodesia. In the early 1960s Chitepo went into exile in Tanganyika and was elected chairman of the Zimbabwe African Nation Union. He later moved to Zambia, where he retained his leadership of the black nationalist organization until his death.

• **Faisal**, the king of Saudi Arabia, was assassinated on March 25, 1975, in Riyadh, the capital, during an audience with the oil minister of Kuwait. He was shot to death by Prince Faisal Ibn Musad Ibn Abdel Aziz, a nephew, who was beheaded for the killing three months later. The king was succeeded by his brother, Crown Prince Khalid.

Faisal ibn Abdul-Aziz al Saud was born in Riyadh in 1905. He was the son of King Ibn Saud and commanded his father's troops in a battle for the Hejaz against Hashemite King Hussein Ibn-Ali in 1925. Faisal was subsequently appointed viceroy of the Hejaz by his father. Faisal was named foreign minister in his father's government in 1932. He represented Saudi Arabia at numerous international conferences and served as his country's representative to the United Nations Charter Conference in San Francisco in 1945. Faisal's older brother, Saud, succeeded to the throne in November of 1953 following the death of Ibn Saud. Faisal was named crown prince and also served in the government as Saudi Arabia's first prime minister. Faisal attempted to control his brother's extravagant financial habits which had brought Saudi Arabia close to bankruptcy. A dispute between the brothers led to Faisal's resignation as prime minister in 1960. He continued to serve as foreign minister, however. Faisal supported the Royal Council's decision to force the abdication of King Saud on November 2, 1964, and he succeeded his brother to the throne. In the fall of 1973, Faisal was the first Arabian monarch to use his oil-rich country's leading export as a weapon against Western countries in an attempt to sway their Middle Eastern policies. He remained on the Saudi throne until his murder in March of 1975.

• On April 13, 1975, luck ran out for **N'Garte Tombalbaye**, the first president of the landlocked and poverty stricken African nation of Chad. Tombalbaye, who had ruled Chad since its independence from France in 1960, had survived eight previous assassination attempts. Earlier in the year, Kattouma Guembang, the former head of the Progressive party's women's wing, was tried for attempting to kill Tombalbaye with witchcraft, in which she had hired several wizards to pierce the eyes of a black sheep, representing the president, and bury it alive. Tombalbaye's demise came in a less esoteric manner. He was mortally wounded by machine gun and mortar fire directed at his official residence during an army revolt against his despotic administration. The dictator died of his wounds later in the day. The coup was led by Gen. Mbaila Odingar and resulted in the freeing of Gen. Felix Malloum, who had been imprisoned since 1973 for allegedly conspiring to overthrow the government during a previous coup attempt. Malloum was himself named Chad's head of state as Tombalbaye's successor.

Francoise Tombalbaye was born in Badaya in southern Chad on June 15, 1918. He worked as a school teacher and became a leader of the Chad trade union movement in 1946. He was active in the establishment of the Chad Progressive party (PPT) in 1947. Tombalbaye was elected to the Territorial Assembly in March of 1952, though the Progressive party was defeated. The PPT received a majority of votes in the Assembly in elections in March of 1957, and Chad was granted self-government on November 28, 1958. Tombalbaye replaced Gabrielle Lissette as Progressive party leader and was selected as prime minister on March 24, 1959. He also became head of state when Chad received full independence on August 11, 1960. Tombalbaye consolidated his power and banned all opposition parties in January of 1962. His regime was faced with numerous coup attempts and rebellions. Violence erupted between the Sudanic Muslims of northern Chad and the Bantus of the south. The Chad National Liberation Front (FROLINAT) was founded in June of 1966 to unite Muslim opposition to Tombalbaye's government. Tombalbaye also faced opposition from elements of the military, which ultimately led to his death in a military revolt in April of 1975.

• **Mujibur Rahman**, the founder and president of Bangladesh, was killed during an army coup on April 15, 1975. Sheik Mujibur Rahman was born in Tungipara, in the Faridpur District of India, on March 17, 1920. He was the founder of the East Pakistan Muslim Students' League in the 1950s. In 1959 he was the co-founder of the Awami League, a political organization advocating autonomy for East Pakistan. Sheikh Mujib was imprisoned on several occasions during the administration of Gen. Mohammed Ayub Khan of Pakistan. In the 1970 general election, the Awami League received an overwhelming majority of votes in East Pakistan. Sheikh Mujib was arrested the following year after he initiated a campaign of noncooperation with West Pakistan. Violence erupted in East Pakistan when government troops tried to enforce martial law. At the end of the year, East Pakistan, with the assistance of India, emerged victorious in what had become a civil war. The independent nation of Bangladesh was proclaimed, and on January 12, 1972, Mujib became the first prime minister. He had great difficulty restoring order and economic stability in the war-torn country. Mujib took the office of president and began government by executive decree in January of 1975. Four months later, on August 15, 1975, he and several members of his family were killed in a military coup. Khondkar Mushtaque Ahmed, a former close associate of the slain president, was chosen by the leaders of the cup as Sheikh Mujib's successor.

- **Lt. Col. Andreas Baron von Mirbach**, the military attaché at the West German Embassy in Stockholm, Sweden, was killed by terrorists during an assault on the Embassy. During a subsequent shootout with the police, much of the Embassy was destroyed and seven of the terrorists were captured.

- **Col. Paul R. Shafer, Jr.**, and **Lt. Col. John H. Turner**, military officers stationed at the United States Embassy in Teheran, Iran, were shot to death by three Iranian terrorists on May 21, 1975.

- Chicago crime boss **Sam Giancana** (1908–75) was shot to death in the basement kitchen of his home in Oak Park, Illinois, on June 19, 1975. A member of the Chicago mob from the days of Al Capone in the 1920s, he took control of the mob in the mid–1950s. It was believed that Giancana, along with his associate Johnny Roselli (q.v.), was involved in several CIA plots against the life of Cuban dictator Fidel Castro in the early 1960s. Giancana had been called to testify before the Senate Intelligence Committee investigating CIA activities shortly before his murder. Both the CIA and the mob denied a role in Giancana's murder.

- **Maj. Michel Aikpe** (1942–75), a former minister of the interior in Benin, was assassinated on June 25, 1975. Aikpe was a member of the Comite Militaire Revolutionnaire that oversaw the government of Benin under Gen. Christophe Soglo. Aikpe also briefly served as minister of the interior in 1968. He was instrumental in orchestrating the coup in October of 1972 that brought

Major Mathieu Kerekou to power. Aikpe subsequently served as minister of the interior and security under Kerekou. He was sent to Borgou as a prefect in 1975, where he was murdered.

- **Alfred Duraiyappah**, a Tamil political leader in Sri Lanka who served as mayor of Faffna and a member of the Sri Lankan parliament, was assassinated by Tamil extremists on July 27, 1975.

- On July 30, 1975, **James R. Hoffa** (1913–75), the former president of the International Brotherhood of Teamsters, was reported missing. Hoffa was elected to the presidency of the Teamsters union in 1957. He remained in office through his 1967 conviction on charges of fraud, conspiracy, and jury tampering. He resigned the presidency in June of 1971 and was subsequently released from prison when his twelve-year sentence was commuted by President Richard Nixon. A condition of his release was that he not take part in any union activities until 1980. Hoffa was challenging that stipulation in court at the time of his disappearance. Hoffa was last seen on the evening of July 30, 1975, at a restaurant in Bloomfield Township, Michigan. It was suspected that Hoffa had been killed by organized crime figures and rival union associates. His body was never recovered.

- On September 5, 1975, United States president Gerald R. Ford (b.1913) was assaulted by a young woman with a pistol in Sacramento, California. The weapon was wrestled away from the woman by a Secret Service agent before a shot could be fired. The assailant was identified as Lynette "Squeaky" Fromme, a 26-year-old follower of mass murderer Charles Manson. She was tried and convicted of the attempt on the president's life and sentenced to prison.

Several weeks later, on September 22, 1975, another attempt was made on the life of President Ford, when a woman fired a pistol shot at the president as he left his hotel in San Francisco. The bullet missed its target, and the president was again uninjured in the assassination attempt. The second would-be assassin was identified as Sara Jane Moore, a 45-year-old civil rights activist. She was tried and convicted of the crime.

• **Bernardo Leighton**, the vice president of Chile's Christian Democratic party in exile, was shot and killed in Rome, Italy, on October 6, 1974.

• **Gen. Ramon Arthur Rincon Quinones**, the inspector general of the Colombian army, was shot to death while driving to the Ministry of Defense in Bogota on October 6, 1975. Rincon Quinones had been active in suppressing leftist terrorists in Colombia, and was believed to have been a victim of them.

• **Danis Tunaligil** (1915–75), the Turkish ambassador to Austria, was shot and killed in his office at the Turkish embassy in Vienna on October 22, 1975. The Armenian Liberation Organization claimed responsibility for the assassination. **Ismail Erez** (1919–75), the Turkish ambassador to France, was shot and killed two days later, on October 24, 1975, by Armenian terrorists while riding in his car through the streets of Paris.

• **Prof. Gordon Hamilton Fairley** (1930–75), a leading British cancer researcher who was responsible for the tumor research unit at St. Bartholomew's Hospital in London, was killed in a bomb explosion. The bomb was planted under the car of Hugh Fraser (1937–87), a Conservative party member of Parliament, by members of the Irish Republican Army. Caroline Kennedy, the daughter of slain United States president John F. Kennedy (q.v.), was Fraser's house guest at the time of the attempt on his life and had been planning to use the automobile when the bomb went off. Fraser and Ms. Kennedy were uninjured in the blast that killed Prof. Fairley, who was walking past the car when the explosion occurred.

• **Guillermo De Vega** (1932–75), an aide of Philippines president Ferdinand Marcos, was shot and killed in his office near the Presidential Palace in Manila on October 27, 1975.

• **Mohammed Mansoor Ali** and **Tajuddin Ahmed**, two former prime ministers of Bangladesh, were killed in a Dacca jail on November 3, 1975, after having been imprisoned for three months following the army coup that deposed and killed President Mujibur Rahman (q.v.). **Syed Nazrul Islam**, the former vice president, and **A.H.M. Kamuruzzaman**, the former commerce minister, were also slain at that time.

Tajuddin Ahmed was born in 1922. He was a close associate of Sheikh Mujibur Rahman prior to Bangladesh's independence. He served as prime minister of Bangladesh's first provisional government from December 1, 1971, until January 12, 1972. Ahmed was a proponent of closer ties with the Soviet Union. He fell out of favor when Sheikh Mujibur began a policy favoring the United States. Ahmed was arrested in August of 1975 and murdered along with other high-ranking officials in a Dacca jail on November 3, 1975.

Mohammed Mansoor Ali was born in 1919. He was educated as a lawyer and served as president of the Pabna Lawyers Association. From 1946 until 1950 he was vice president of the Pabna District Muslim League. He joined the Awami League in 1951 and was named to the cabinet of Ataur Rahman Khan in 1956. Mansoor Ali served as the Awami League's vice president from 1969 and subsequently served in Bangladesh's government-in-exile as finance minister. He served in various cabinet positions following Bangladesh's independence in 1971. He was named prime minister in the government of Sheikh Mujibur Rahman on January 26, 1975. Mansoor Ali was deposed with Sheikh Mujibur in a coup on August 15, 1975. He was imprisoned in a Dacca jail, where he was murdered on November 3, 1975.

Syed Nazrul Islam was born in 1925. He joined the Awami League in 1953 and became a leading advisor to Sheikh Mujibur Rahman. He served as senior vice president of the Awami League and was acting president of the Bangladesh government in exile during Mujib's imprisonment from April of 1971. Nazrul Islam served as minister of industry in the subsequent Mujib government. He was named vice president of Bangladesh in January of 1975. He was removed from office and imprisoned following the ouster of Mujib in August of 1975, and murdered three months later with other prominent political leaders.

- **Brig. Khaled Mosharraf**, a leader of the army dissidents who had overthrown President Mujibur Rahman (q.v.) of Bangladesh earlier in the year, was assassinated in November of 1975, in Dacca.

- **Ross McWhirter** (1925–75), the co-editor of the *Guinness Book of World Records*, was shot to death in front of his home in London on November 27, 1975. Ross McWhirter and his twin brother, Norris, were British sportswriters and television personalities before they began editing the best-selling trivia books. The McWhirters were also strong proponents of civil liberties and outspoken critics of terrorist activities. Ross McWhirter had recently offered a cash reward for information that could be used to track down terrorists. It was believed his assassination was the work of agents of the Irish Republican Army.

- **Umar Ben Jelloun** (1933–75), a leading Moroccan political activist, was murdered in Casablanca on December 18, 1975. Ben Jelloun had been an ally of Mehdi Ben Barka (q.v.) in the 1950s, joining with him to form the Union Nationale des Forces Populaires (UNFP). He had been imprisoned on several occasions during the 1960s and early 1970s on charges of conspiring against the government.

- **Sheikh Kassem Imad** (1922–75), the Muslim governor of North Lebanon, was killed in a barrage of machine gun fire near his home in Tripoli on December 20, 1975.

- **Richard S. Welch** (1929–75), the chief of the United States Central Intelligence Agency in Greece, was shot and killed in front of his Athens residence on December 23, 1975. Welch had previously been stationed in Greece in the 1950s and had also served in the intelligence field in Cyprus and Central America. His death was believed to have been caused by left-wing terrorists who were aware

that his official listing as a special assistant to the ambassador was a cover for his CIA affiliation.

# 1976

- **Murtala Ramat Mohammed**, the leader of the Nigerian military government was killed during an unsuccessful coup attempt on February 13, 1976. Mohammed was shot and killed by dissident army officers during the early stages of the coup. His assailants shot and killed him when his limousine was caught in a traffic jam in Lagos. The rebel officers, led by **Lt. Col. Bukar S. Dimka**, were subsequently arrested by government troops. Thirty-seven participants in the planned overthrow, including Dimka and **Joseph Deshi Gomwalk** (1935–76), the former governor of Benue-Plateau State, were executed between March 11 and 15. Mohammed was succeeded as Nigeria's head of state by Olusegun Obasanjo.

Murtala Ramat Mohammed was born in Kano, in Northern Nigeria, on November 8, 1938. He was educated in Nigeria and at the Royal Military Academy at Sandhurst in Great Britain. He entered the Nigerian army in 1960 and served with the United Nations' peace-keeping troops in the Congo in 1962. Mohammed became commander of the Army Signals in November of 1965. He was promoted to lieutenant colonel in April of 1966. He was a leader of the military coup in July of 1966 that resulted in General Yakubu Gowon becoming Nigeria's head of state. Mohammed was a military leader during the civil war against Biafran secessionists in the late 1960s. He led a military coup against the government of Gowon on July 29, 1975, and assumed the presidency. He attempted to eliminate corruption in the government, but was unsuccessful in halting economic inflation. Mohammed was ambushed during an unsuccessful coup attempt in February of 1976.

- **Boonsanong Punyodyana**, the secretary general of the Thailand Socialist party, was shot to death in Bangkok on February 28, 1976.

- On March 15, 1976, **Captain Muhamad Sidi** and **Major Moussa Bayere** (1936–76) led a coup attempt against the military regime of Gen. Seyni Kountche (1931–87). The rebels assault on the Presidential Palace failed and the coup was crushed. The leaders of the coup were arrested and convicted of plotting against the government. **Ahmed Mouddour** (1941–76), the former director of the Union Nigerienne de Credit et de Cooperation, was considered the political mastermind behind the coup. He was executed along with Captain Sidi, Major Bayere and **Idrissa Boube** (1938–76), the former director of the Surete Nationale, for their participation in the rebellion on April 21, 1976.

- On April 13, 1976, Brig. Gen. Felix Malloum (b. 1932), the president of Chad, was uninjured in an assassination attempt. Shots were fired at President Malloum during a parade marking the first anniversary of the coup that deposed former President Francois Tombalbaye (q.v.) and installed Malloum in power.

- **Alexandros Panagoulis**, a deputy in the Greek Parliament, was killed in an automobile accident on May 1, 1976, that was suspected of having been a planned political assassination. Panagoulis, who was born on July 2, 1939, had made an unsuccessful attempt to assassinate Georgios Papadopoulos, the former head of state of Greece, on August 13, 1968. He was imprisoned until 1973 and returned to Greece following the overthrow of the Papadopoulos government in 1974.

- **Gen. Joaquin Zenteno Anaya** (1923–76), the Bolivian ambassador to France, was shot to death in Paris on May 11, 1976. Gen. Zenteno had served as Bolivia's foreign minister from 1964 to 1966. He had also led the army's campaign against the guerilla forces of Che Guevara (q.v.), which culminated in Guevara's death in 1967. Gen. Zenteno was named army chief of staff in 1971. He remained in that position until 1973, when he was appointed to the French diplomatic post. His assassins claimed to be members of the "International Che Guevara Brigade," and said the murder was in retaliation for the killing of Guevara nine years earlier.

- On May 16, 1976, **Zelmar Michelini** and **Hector Gutierre Ruiz**, two former members of the Uruguayan Senate, were kidnapped and murdered by right-wing terrorists in Buenos Aires, Argentina. Michelini and Gutierre Ruiz had been living exile in Argentina for several years.

- **Juan Jose Torres Gonzales**, the former president of Bolivia, was reported kidnapped from his home in exile in Buenos Aires, Argentina, on June 1, 1976. Two days after Torres' kidnapping, police reported finding his body, blindfolded and shot three times in the head, beside a bridge sixty miles from Buenos Aires. Thus, a Bolivian refugee became the most prominent exiled leftist to meet death at the hands of right-wing extremists in Argentina, joining over 300 others at the time of his death.

  Juan Jose Torres Gonzales was born in Cochambamba on March 5, 1921. He was educated at the Bolivian Military Academy and served in the Bolivian army. He was active in the military coup that gave Victor Paz Estenssoro the presidency in 1952, and he rose to the rank of colonel during his administration. Torres was named ambassador to Uruguay by Paz's successor, Rene Barrientos. He later served as minister of labor and social security in Barrientos' military cabinet. Torres was promoted to general and named chief of staff of the armed forced by Barrientos in 1967. He remained in the government as secretary-general of the Supreme Council of National Defense following Barrientos' death in a helicopter crash in 1969. He assisted General Alfred Ovando Candia in ousting the civilian government of Luis Siles Salinas in September of 1969 and was appointed chief of the armed forces by the subsequent Ovando administration. When Ovando was forced to resign on October 6, 1970, under the threat of a right-wing military coup, Torres led a left-wing countercoup with the support of workers and students and was sworn in as president the following day. He continued the policy of nationalizing foreign businesses and supported the labor unions' call for higher wages. Torres also expelled the Peace Corps from Bolivia and had strained relations with the United States. He retained office until August 22, 1971, when his government was ousted by another right-wing military coup led by Hugo Banzer Suarez. Torres went into exile in Peru and moved to Argentina in 1973, where he was kidnapped and murdered three years later.

• **Carlos Abdala**, the Uruguayan ambassador to Paraguay, was mortally wounded in Asuncion, Paraguay, on June 7, 1976. His assassin, Danziv Danjanovic, was intending to murder the Yugoslav ambassador and shot Abdala by mistake. Abdala died of his wounds the following day.

• On June 16, 1976, **Francis E. Meloy, Jr.**, the United States ambassador to Lebanon, and **Robert O. Waring**, the United States economic counselor, were shot and killed in Beirut. The two men were en route to a meeting with warring Moslem and Christian factions in Beirut in the hopes of establishing a truce.

Francis Meloy was born in Washington on March 28, 1917. He served in the U.. Navy during World War II. Meloy joined the diplomatic corps and, in 1946, was stationed in Saudi Arabia as a vice consul. During the Truman administration Meloy served as Secretary of State Dean Acheson's personal assistant. From 1962 until 1964 he served as director of the Office of Western European Affairs. In 1964 he was appointed the deputy chief of missions in Rome, and in 1969 was named United States ambassador to the Dominican Republic. In April of 1976 he arrived in Lebanon as United States ambassador.

Robert O. Waring was born in New York in 1920. He joined the State Department in 1933 and became a leading economic advisor at various United States embassies. He served as economic counselor at the embassies in Austria and West Germany from 1961 until 1966. He was sent to Beirut in June of 1972 and became the senior member of the Embassy staff there.

• **Gen. Cesareo Cardozo** (1926–76), the federal police chief of Argentina, was killed when a bomb exploded under his bed in Buenos Aires on June 18, 1976.

• On July 7, 1976, a number of high ranking officials in Equatorial Guinea were executed by the government of Francisco Macias Nguema (q.v.). They included **Miguel Eyegue Ntutumu**, the former governor of Rio Muni and vice president of Equatorial Guinea; **Andres Nko Ibassa**, the former economic minister; **Norberto Nsue Micha**, the former director of national security; **Jesus Alfonso Oyono Alogo**, the minister of public works and secretary to the presidency; and **Job Obiang Mba** and **Buenaventura Ochago Ngomo Abeso**, former ministers of education.

• In late July of 1976 Chicago mobster **Johnny Roselli** (1905–76) was murdered. His body was placed in an oil drum and sunk in the ocean near Florida, but Roselli's decomposing body caused the drum to surface to be discovered by the police. A leading figure in the Chicago mob from the 1930s, he had represented the mob's interest in Hollywood, where he produced several crime films. A top associate of Chicago boss Sam Giancana (q.v.), Roselli became involved with the CIA's plot to assassinate Cuban leader Fidel Castro in the early 1960s. Known as Operation Mongoose, the plan included several outlandish schemes including poisoning the Communist dictator's cigars. Roselli testified at the Senate Intelligence Committee hearings on the Castro plot in 1975. It was not known if his murder the following year was related to his mob activities or to his knowledge of about CIA plotting.

• **Christopher Ewart-Biggs**, the British ambassador to Ireland, was killed in an explosion of a land mine in the Dublin Mountains on July 21, 1976. Ewart-Biggs was born on August 5, 1921. He served in the British Foreign Service from 1949 and had held diplomatic positions in the Middle East, the Philippines, Belgium, and France. He was appointed ambassador to Ireland on July 8, 1976. His death three weeks later was believed to have been the work of Irish Republican Army members.

• On July 25, 1976, Ethiopian army officers **Lt. Col. Berhanu Haile** and **Lt. Haile Marian Hassan** were executed at Assab on the Red Sea by the ruling military government of Ethiopia. **Lt. Bewookau Kassa** and **Lt. Seleshi Beyene**, former members of the Ethiopian Dergue, were executed on August 10, 1976.

• **Orlando Letelier** (1932–76), the foreign minister of Chile during the presidency of Salvador Allende (q.v.), was killed in Washington, D.C., when a bomb exploded in his car on September 21, 1976. **Ronnie Karen Moffit** (1951–76), who assisted Letelier at the Institute for Policy Studies in Washington, was also killed in the explosion. Letelier had also served as Chile's ambassador to the United States from 1971 until May of 1973. Following the overthrow of President Allende, Letelier had been an outspoken critic of the regime of Gen. Augusto Pinochet. The Chilean secret police (DINA) were believed responsible for the murder. American-born Michael V. Townley confessed to having planted the bomb and served five years in prison. Brig. Pedro Espinoza and Gen. Manuel Contreras were charged and convicted of participation in the murder in 1993.

• **Fikre Merid**, an Ethiopian politician and leading advisor to the Dergue, was shot and killed while driving his car in Addis Adaba, on October 1, 1976.

• **Juan Maria De Araluce y Villar** (1917–76), an advisor to King Juan Carlos of Spain, was assassinated by machine gun fire on October 4, 1976, at his home in San Sebastian. His assailants were believed to have been members of a Basque separatist group.

• **Marie Drumm** (1920–76), a leading political organizer of the Irish Republican Army, was assassinated in her hospital bed on October 28, 1976. Mrs. Drumm had served as vice president for the Provisional Sinn Fein, the legal political wing of the IRA, until her resignation several weeks earlier for reasons of health.

• **Guetenet Zewed**, the Ethiopian permanent secretary in the Ministry of Labor and Social Affairs, was shot and killed in Addis Adaba, on November 9, 1976.

• **Prince Jean De Broglie** (1921–76), a former French deputy foreign minister, was shot and killed on the streets of Paris on December 24, 1977. De Broglie had been a Conservative member of the French National Assembly since 1958. As the French state secretary for the French Sahara in 1961, he was instrumental in negotiating the treaty for Algerian independence. De Broglie's murder appeared to lack a political motive and was more likely due to his private business dealings.

# 1977

• **Diallo Telli**, the former national minister of Guinea and secretary general of the Organization of African Unity from 1964 until 1972, died in a Guinean prison in 1977. Telli had been imprisoned by the government of President Sekou Toure on charges of attempting to overthrow the Guinean government. His death was not announced until November of 1978.

• **Ato Tsegaye Debalke**, a leading figure in the Ethiopian Ministry of Culture, was shot to death at his home in Addis Adaba on February 2, 1977.

• **Brig. Gen. Teferi Benti** (1921–77), who had served as head of state and chairman of the provisional military administrative council of Ethiopia since 1974, was killed during a gun battle at the headquarters of the governing council on February 3, 1977. The gun battle was a result of a clash between supporters of Brig. Gen. Benti and those members loyal to Lt. Col. Mengistu Haile Mariam. Six of Benti's followers were either slain during the battle or summarily executed shortly afterwards. They included **Capt. Alemayehu Haile**, **Capt. Mogus Wolde-Michael**, **Lt. Col. Asrat Desta**, **Lt. Col. Hiruy Haile Selassie**, **Capt. Tefera Deneke**, and **Corporal Halu Belay**. **Lt. Col. Daniel Asfaw**, a council member loyal to Lt. Col. Mengistu, was also slain during the fighting. Benti had joined the Ethiopian army in the mid–1950s. He had served as Ethiopia's military attaché in Washington and had taken part in the military coup that ousted Emperor Haile Selassie in 1974. Benti was named chairman of the council on November 28, 1974, following the murder of Lt. Gen. Aman Michael Andom (q.v.) several days earlier. Benti was succeeded by Lt. Col. Mengistu.

• **Janani Luwum** (1925–77), the Anglican archbishop of Uganda and a leading critic of President Idi Amin, was killed after having been arrested by Ugandan police on February 16, 1977. **Lt. Col. Erinaya Oryema**, the minister of land and water resources, and **Charles Oboth-Ofumbi**, the minister of internal affairs, were also killed. The Ugandan government officially announced the deaths as being the result of an automobile accident, but it was far more likely that they were murdered on orders from President Amin.

• On February 18, 1977, Gen. Jorge Rafael Videla (b. 1925), the president of Argentina, was uninjured in an assassination attempt in Buenos Aires. This incident marked the third unsuccessful attempt on Gen. Videla's life within a year.

• **Dr. Muhammed Al-Fadel** (1919–77), the president of Damascus University, was shot and killed near his office in Damascus, Syria, on February 22, 1977. Dr. Fadel had previously served as Syria's minister of justice in 1966.

• **Kamal Jumblatt**, a Lebanese Moslem leftist leader, was shot to death by machine gun-wielding terrorists on a mountain road near Beirut on March 16, 1977. Jumblatt was born on December 6, 1917, in Mukhtara, a village near Beirut. He was the hereditary chieftain of the Jumblatist Druse clan and, in 1940, he assumed leadership. He was elected to the Lebanese Parliament in 1947 and, two years later, founded the Progressive Socialist party. He remained an important figure in Lebanese political circles and was responsible for the rise and fall of several Lebanese presidents. Although he was a Socialist and greatly admired in the Soviet Union, having received the Lenin Peace Prize in 1973, he was opposed to Communism. Political violence was not unusual to the Jumblatt family. Kamal Jumblatt's father was murdered in the 1920s and his sister Linda Atrash, was assassinated in Beirut on May 27, 1975. The killing of Kamal Jumblatt was a serious blow to the stability of Lebanon and a major factor in reopening the ongoing Civil War there.

• **Marien Ngouabi** (1938–77), the president of the Democratic Republic of the Congo, was shot and killed in his living quarters at his general staff headquarters in Brazzaville on March 18, 1977. The coup attempt was led by Capt. Barthelemy Kikadidi and was reportedly organized by former President Alphonse Massamba-Debat (q.v.). Ngouabi was succeeded by Joachim Yhombi-Opango as leader of the military government.

Marien Ngouabi was born in the northern Koyoyu tribe in Ombele in 1938. He was educated locally and at the military academies in France. He returned to the Congo in 1962 and helped to form a paratroop corps in Brazzaville. Ngouabi had risen to the rank of captain when he led a mutiny in 1966 against the plans of Alphonse Massamba-Debat's government to incorporate the army into the national militia. Ngouabi was demoted, but the government's plan was scrapped. He was subsequently posted to the general staff headquarters. In July of 1968 he was arrested, but he was freed by his supporters in the military. Massamba-Debat was forced to name Ngouabi as chief of staff. Ngouabi also served as president of the National Revolutionary Council. Massamba-Debat was forced from Office on September 4, 1968, and Captain Alfred Raoul was named leader of the provisional government. Ngouabi remained leader of the Revolutionary Council and replaced Raoul as president on January 1, 1969. Ngouabi formed the Congolese Workers' party (PCT) in January of 1970. His government survived a right-wing coup attempt two months later. Ngouabi was also challenged by an abortive coup attempt from the left in February of 1972. He established the Congo as a people's republic and maintained close relations with the Soviet Union and Cuba. He retained power until his assassination during a coup attempt in March of 1977.

• **Emile Cardinal Biayenda**, the Roman Catholic archbishop of Brazzaville, was kidnapped and murdered on March 22, 1977, four days after the murder of the Congo's president, Marien Ngouabi (q.v.). Biayenda had been a supporter of Ngouabi's socialist regime. The Congolese government announced that both murders had been accomplished under the direction of former President Alphonse Massamba-Debat (q.v.), who was subsequently executed.

Emile Biayenda was born in Mpongala, the Congo, in 1927. He studied at the Seminary of Brazzaville in the Congo and the Catholic University of Lyon in France. He was ordained a priest in October of 1958. He performed pastoral duties in the Brazzaville archdiocese until 1964, when he was placed under house arrest by the government. He was acquitted of charges and released. Biayenda subsequently continued his studies, returning to Brazzaville in 1969. He was named titular Archbishop of Garba and coadjutor of Brazzaville in March of 1970. He was elevated to Archbishop of Brazzaville in June of 1971. He was created a cardinal priest by Pope Paul VI on March 5, 1973, becoming the first Congolese to serve in the College of Cardinals.

• **Alphonse Massamba-Debat**, the former president of the Congo, was executed on March 25, 1977, for complicity in the murder of Congolese president Marien Ngouabi (q.v.) the previous week.

Alphonse Massamba-Debat was born to the southern Lari tribe in Nkolo in 1921. He was educated locally before attending civil service training school in Brazzaville. He worked as a teacher in Fort Lamy from 1940, and joined the Chad Progressive party. In 1947 he returned to the Congo, where he continued to work as a teacher. He also remained involved in politics and joined Fulbert Youlou's Democratic Union for the Defense of African Interests (UDDIA) in 1956. Following elections in 1957, he served as a secretary to the minister of education. Massamba-Debat was elected to the National Assembly in 1959 and served as president of the Assembly. He was named minister of state in 1961 and was appointed minister of planning and equipment in Youlou's cabinet shortly thereafter. He became a critic of Youlou's policies and resigned from the government in May of 1963. Youlou was ousted on August 15, 1963, and Massamba-Debat was named president of the provisional government the following day. He was elected president in December of 1963. Massamba-Debat's government was under immediate pressure from leftist agitation. The Congolese government strengthened its ties with the Soviet Union and the People's Republic of China, and diplomatic relations with the United States were severed in 1965. Massamba Debat survived a mutiny of the military in June of 1966. The political situation in the Congo deteriorated in 1968, and Massamba-Debat was forced to resign on September 4, 1968, following a military coup. He retired to live in seclusion in his native village of Boko. He was arrested on March 18, 1977, following the assassination of President Ngouabi, and executed several days later.

• **Rodolfo Jorge Walsh**, a leading Argentine playwright and novelist, disappeared from his home on March 24, 1977, after publishing a letter critical of the ruling military government of Argentina. He was reportedly abducted by agents of the government and summarily executed. Walsh was born in

Choele-Choel, Rio Negro Province, in 1927, of Irish descent. He began writing in the early 1950s and, in 1957, authored articles with political overtones, becoming one of the first investigative journalists in Argentina. His better known works include the story *Operacion Masacre*, and the plays *La Granada* and *La Batalla*. Walsh was an early opponent of the military regime that seized power in Argentina in 1976, forming the underground news service Agencia de Noticia Clandestine (ANCLA) to document excesses of the government. Walsh soon became a target of the repressive regime. His daughter, Vicki (1950–76), was kidnapped and murdered on September 29, 1976. The following March, Walsh himself became a victim of the repression.

• **Chalard Hiranyasiri**, a former Thai general, was executed in April of 1977 for complicity in an attempted coup the previous month. Chalard had been ousted from the army in October of the previous year following a military coup. He subsequently became a Buddhist monk, but left the monastery to help organize a coup against the regime that had ousted him.

• **Siefried Buback** (1920–77), a federal attorney general in West Germany, was shot and killed while riding in an automobile in Karlsruhe, West Germany, on April 7, 1977. Buback had been involved in the 1975 trial of members of the Baader-Meinhof gang, and his assassination was thought to be a revenge killing by surviving members of that organization.

• **Kadhi Abdullah Al-Hagri**, a former premier of the Yemen Arab Republic, was shot and killed by an unknown assassin outside the Hyde Park Hotel in London, England, on April 10, 1977. Hagri's wife, **Fatimah**, and **Abdulla Ali Al-Hammami** (1932–77), minister and plenipotentiary of the Yemen Arab Republic Embassy, were also killed in the attack.

Kadhi Abdullah al-Hagri was born in 1912. He served as minister in Iman Ahmed's government in the 1950s. He remained a royalist and was a personal friend of King Faisal

of Saudi Arabia. Hagri was named premier of a conservative cabinet on December 30, 1972. He retained office until March 3, 1974, when he stepped down for reasons of health. Hagri was subsequently appointed deputy chief of Yemen's Supreme Court. He had accompanied his wife to London for medical treatment in February of 1977, where they both met their death by an assassin's bullet.

• **Mauricio Borgonovo Pohl** (1940–77), the foreign minister of El Salvador, was kidnapped on April 19, 1977, by leftist terrorists. He was murdered on May 10, 1977, after the government refused to meet the kidnappers' demands to release various political prisoners.

• **Taha Carim**, the Turkish ambassador to the Vatican, was shot and killed near his resident in Rome on June 9, 1977. Carim was believed to have been the victim of an Armenian terrorist organization.

• **Major Sani Souna Sido** (1933–77) was executed while imprisoned in Agadez, Niger, in June of 1977. Major Sido had led a conspiracy against the military government of Gen. Seyni Kountche in August of 1975. Sido had served as minister of the interior, mines and geology in Kountche's regime briefly in 1974. He was arrested after the failure of the coup attempt and imprisoned in Agadez. His death was originally announced as due to natural causes, but it was later revealed that he was murdered by the Agadez commander, Lt. Col. Bagna Beidou.

• **Brig. Gen. Abdul Hami Razouk**, the commander of the Syrian army's missile corps, was killed by assassins at his home in Damascus, Syria, on June 18, 1977.

• **Dr. Mohammed Hussein Al-Zahabi** (1913–77), the former Egyptian minister of religious endowments and Al Azhar affairs, was kidnapped on July 3, 1977, by members of a Moslem cult of fanatics called the "Jamaat al-Tafkeer wal-Hija" ("Society for Atonement and Flight"). Dr. Zahabi had attempted to eliminate the cult during his term as minister from May of 1975 until November of 1976. His body was found on July 6, 1977, near the Giza pyramids. The cult's leader, Shukri Ahmed Mustafa, and many other members were arrested for the murder.

• **Osmin Aguirre Salinas**, the former president of El Salvador, was shot to death near his home in San Salvador on July 12, 1977. The 88-year-old former politician was presumed to have been murdered by members of the leftist terrorist organization, the Farabundo Marti Popular Liberation Front, for stopping a land reform program over forty years earlier.

Osmin Aguirre y Salinas was born in 1889. He served in the Salvadorian military, where he rose to the rank of colonel and served as chief of police. Aguirre was a leader of the coup that forced the resignation of Salvadorean leader Maximiliano Hernandez Martinez in May of 1944. Aguirre led another coup against Hernandez's vice president and successor Andres Ignacio Menendez on October 21, 1944. Aguirre served as president of the subsequent military regime. He presided over new elections and relinquished office to the victor, Salvador Castaneda Castro, on February 28, 1945. Aguirre subsequently retired from politics and lived in relative obscurity until his murder in July of 1977.

• **Delorme Mehu**, Haiti's ambassador to Brazil, was shot to death in Salvador, Brazil, by a hired assassin on July 13, 1977.

• **Abdullah Yousuf**, a leading Ethiopian politician in the Harar Province, was assassinated on July 30, 1977. The head of the Ethiopian Security Police, **Lt. Col. Mulugetta Alemu**, was shot and killed on August 3, 1977.

• **Stephen B. Biko** (1947–77), a South African black student leader, died of head wounds on September 12, 1977, while being held in police custody. Biko was the founder of the Black Consciousness Movement, the South African Students' Organization, and other groups whose purpose was to bring nonviolent pressure on the South African authorities to eliminate the apartheid system. He was arrested by South African police for violating

apartheid rules. An inquest into Biko's death acquitted the authorities involved of responsibility, but world opinion placed the blame on the South African government. In January of 1997 five police officers admitted to the beating murder of Biko while he was in custody.

• **Carlos Alfaro Castillo** (1925–77), the rector of the University of El Salvador, was shot and killed by a band of assassins in San Salvador on September 16, 1977.

• **Seamus Costello** (1939–77), a leader of the Marxist Irish Republican Socialist party, was shot and killed in the streets of Dublin on October 5, 1977. Costello had broken with the Irish Republican Army in 1974, forming the more radical group he led. The rival organizations had been engaged in a bloody battle for several years and it was believed Costello's murder was in retaliation for the killing of Belfast IRA leader Billy McMillan in 1975.

• **Augusto Unceta Barrenechea**, the president of the provincial council of Vizcaya, in the Basque province of Spain, was shot and killed by militant Basque separatists on October 8, 1977.

• **Col. Ibrahim Al-Hamdi**, the head of state of the Yemen Arab Republic, was assassinated at the home of his brother in Sana on October 11, 1977. Hamdi's brother, **Lt. Col. Abdullah Mohammed al-Hamdi**, and **Col. Ali Kannas Zahra**, the commander of the North Yemeni armed forces, were also killed in the attack. Hamdi was scheduled to make a state visit to Marxist South Yemen later in the week. His assassination was suspected of having been carried out to prevent discussions of a union between the two Yemens. Hamdi was succeeded by Ahmed al-Ghashmi (q.v.).

Ibrahim Muhammad al-Hamdi was born in 1943. He served in the Yemini military, where he rose to the rank of lieutenant colonel. He was a leader of the military coup that ousted the government of Sheikh Abdul Rahman al-Iyani on June 13, 1974. Hamdi led the ruling Military Command Council. He established a strong central government and led Yemen to close relations with Saudi Arabia. He also improved ties with the United States until his assassination by unknown gunmen in October of 1977.

• **Hans-Martin Schleyer**, a West German industrialist and a leader of the West German employers' association, was kidnapped by leftist terrorists in Cologne on September 5, 1977. His body was found on October 19, 1977, in the eastern section of France. Schleyer was born on May 1, 1915, and was active in the Nazi party during World War II. He had become a major figure in the reemergence of the West German automobile industry during the post-war period and served as the director of the Daimler-Benz Automobile Company.

Schleyer's kidnapping and murder were carried out by members of the Red Army Faction, an off-shoot of the anarchist terrorist group the Baader-Meinhof Gang. Schleyer was killed the day after the Baader-Meinhof cofounder, Andreas Baader, and Jan-Carl Raspe, a member of the gang, had shot and killed themselves with guns that had been smuggled into their cells in a maximum security prison in Stuttgart, West Germany. Gudrun Ensslin, another imprisoned terrorist, hanged herself in the same prison, and Irmgard Moller stabbed herself with a butter knife, but survived. Those four had been among the eleven imprisoned terrorists whose release was demanded by four hijackers of a Lufthansa airliner. The suicides followed a successful West German commando raid at Mogadishu, Somalia, in which three of the four hijackers were killed and the passengers freed. Ingrid Schubert, another of the eleven terrorists the hijackers were hoping to release, hanged herself in Munich's Stadelheim Prison on November 11, 1977. Baader, Raspe and Ensslin had all been imprisoned since 1972 and Schubert had been arrested in 1970. The other Baader-Meinhof co-founder, Ulrike Meinhof, had hanged herself the previous year, on May 9, 1976, in Stammheim Prison in Stuttgart, while being tried for terrorist activities.

Gang member Holger Meins had died in November of 1974 following a hunger strike. The anarchist Baader-Meinhof Gang had been responsible for numerous terrorist activities since it was founded in the late 1960s. They were also believed responsible for the murders of Siefried Buback (q.v.), a West German federal prosecutor, and Jurgen Ponto (q.v.), a prominent banker, earlier in the year. Terrorists Christoph Wackernage, who was believed involved in Schleyer's kidnapping, and Gerd Richart Schneider were wounded and captured by Dutch police on November 11, 1977. Willy Peter Stoll, who was believed to have organized the kidnapping of Schleyer, was shot and killed by German police in Dusseldorf on September 6, 1978.

• **Saif Ibn Said Al-Ghubash** (1937–77), the state minister for foreign affairs for the United Arab Emirates since 1973, was shot to death on October 25, 1977. Ghubash was killed during an unsuccessful assassination attempt on Syrian foreign minister Abdal Halim Khaddam.

• **Lt. Gizew Temesgen**, the information minister of the Ethiopian Dergue, was assassinated on November 2, 1977. In a separate incident on the same day, **Guta Sernesa**, a member of the governing assembly in Addis Adaba, Ethiopia, was shot and killed. **Lt. Solomon Gesesse**, another member of the Ethiopian Dergue, was assassinated on November 13, 1977.

• **Lt. Col. Atnafu Abate** (1937–77), the vice chairman of the ruling revolutionary council of Ethiopia, was executed by the military regime on November 12, 1977. **Haile Frida**, the principal Marxist theoretician of Ethiopia, was also executed at that time.

• **Dr. Avi Ahmad Khoram**, the minister of planning of Afghanistan from 1974, was shot and killed near his office in Kabul on November 16, 1977.

• **Robert Smit** (1933–77), a leading South African economist and a former director of the International Monetary Fund, was found murdered with his wife at their home in Johannesburg, South Africa, on November 23, 1977. Smit, who was a National party candidate for Parliament, was considered a leading candidate to become South Africa's next minister of finance.

# 1978

- **Innocent Belmar**, a member of the Grenadan cabinet, was shot and killed on January 4, 1978.

- **Said Hammami** (1941–78), the London representative of the Palestine Liberation Organization, was shot to death by assassins on January 4, 1978, in London. Hammami was a moderate Palestinian nationalist and a critic of terrorist activities. He had served in his position in London since 1972. His assassin was believed to be a member of an extremist Palestinian organization

- **Pedro Joaquin Chamorro Cardenal** (1920–78), the editor of the leading Nicaraguan opposition newspaper to the Somoza regime, was shot and killed in Managua on January 10, 1978. Chamorro was the editor and publisher of *La Prensa* and the founder of the Democratic Union of Liberation, a coalition of opposition parties. Chamorro had been arrested in the early 1940s during the administration of President Anastasio Somoza Garcia (q.v.). He had remained an outspoken critic of the Somoza family during the administrations of the elder Somoza's two sons, Luis and Anastasio Somoza Debayle (q.v.). His death was attributed to supporters of the Somoza regime, and widespread civil unrest followed his funeral. Somoza was forced to flee the country the following year and, after a period of rule by a Sandinista government, Chamorro's widow, Violeta Barrios de Chamorro, was elected president of Nicaragua in 1990, serving until 1997.

- **Joaquin Viola Sauret**, the former mayor of Barcelona, Spain, died in his home on January 25, 1978, when a bomb strapped to his chest by left-wing terrorists exploded. Sauret had served as Barcelona's mayor from 1975 until 1977. It was believed that Sauret's assassins, members of the International Communist party, had intended to kidnap the former mayor when the bomb detonated accidentally.

- **Toivo Shiyanga**, the South African minister of health for South West Africa (Namibia) and the leader of the Ovambo tribe, was shot to death by Namibian nationalists in February of 1978.

- **Youssef El-Sebai** (1918–78), the editor of the Egyptian newspaper *Al Ahram*, was shot and killed in a hotel lobby in Nicosia, Cyprus, by Palestinian radicals on February 18, 1978. Sebai was a close advisor to Egyptian president Anwar Sadat (q.v.) and had previously served as information minister in the Egyptian government.

- **Gen. Reynaldo Perez Vega** (1925–78), a leading military adviser to Nicaraguan president Anastasio Somoza Debayle (q.v.), was killed by Sandinista guerrillas during a kidnapping attempt on March 8, 1978. Gen. Perez Vega was a former director of the Nicaraguan Immigration Department and had served as a member of the ruling military junta from 1967 until 1974.

- **Jesus Haddad Blanco** (1938–78), the director general of the Spanish prison system, was shot and killed by machine gun fire as he entered his car in Madrid on March 22, 1978. Haddad Blanco had been appointed prison director three months prior to his assassination. His assailants were believed to be members of the leftist First of October Groups of Anti-Fascist Resistance.

- **Clemens Kapuuo** (1923–78), a leading South-West African tribal chief, was assassinated in the black township of Katatura on March 27, 1978. Kapuuo, the chief of the Hereros tribe since 1970, was the leader of the Democratic Turnhalle Alliance, a pro–South African organization in South-West Africa. He was considered a leading candidate to become the first president of the South-West African territory.

• **Miguel Tobias Padilla** (1943–78), the undersecretary of economic coordination in Argentina, was shot to death in Buenos Aires on April 11, 1978. Tobias Padilla was also a leading government advisor on labor affairs.

• **Amir Aqbar Khabir**, the leader of the leftist Parcham (Flag) party of Afghanistan, was assassinated on April 17, 1978, in Kabul. His murder led to widespread civil disorders in Afghanistan against the regime of Mohammad Daud Khan (q.v.).

• **Mohammed Daud Khan**, the president of Afghanistan, was killed following a leftist coup on April 28, 1978. Several thousand other Afghanistani politicians, including President Daud's brother **Mohammed Naeem**, the vice president, and the air force chief of staff, were also killed during the coup.

Mohammed Daud Khan was born in Kabul in 1909. He was educated in Kabul and Paris. In 1932 he was appointed governor of the province of Kandahar by his uncle, King Nadir Shah (q.v.). Following Nadir's assassination in 1933, Daud became governor and commander in chief of Afghanistan's Eastern Province, and in 1937 he became commander in chief of the central armed forces. Daud remained a powerful force in the military until 1946, when he was appointed ambassador to France. Four years later he returned to Kabul as minister of defense. Daud succeeded Shah Mahmud Khan as prime minister on September 7, 1953. As prime minister, Daud actively sought the financial support of the Soviet Union while maintaining Afghan neutrality. For ten years Daud ruled Afghanistan virtually alone, as he reduced King Zahir's role to that of a figurehead. The king was finally able to remove Daud as prime minister on March 10, 1963, by promoting a constitution that made it illegal for a member of the royal family to serve in the government. Daud remained in Kabul, though his relationship with the king was strained. On July 17, 1973, Daud took advantage of the absence of King Zahir from the country for medical reasons and

ousted his cousin in a military coup. Daud abolished the monarchy and assumed the posts of president and prime minister. He successfully put down several coup attempts in 1973 and 1974, though economic difficulties in the country continued to escalate. The president was also faced with opposition from the powerful Muslim Brotherhood. Daud survived another coup led by former military officers in November of 1976. The following year Daud called a meeting of the Grand National Assembly to approve a new constitution granting greater powers to the president. There was an outbreak of domestic violence following the murder of a prominent Afghan Communist leader in April of 1977. Daud began a crackdown on Communists following a period of rioting and demonstrations against his regime. Soon after he was ousted and killed in a coup. Nur Mohammad Taraki (q.v.), a leader of the coup, subsequently assumed the role of chief of state.

• **Henri Curiel** (1914–78), a founder of the Egyptian Communist party, was shot and killed in Paris, France, on May 4, 1978. Curiel, a suspected leader of international terrorism, was believed killed by Organization Delta, a right-wing terrorist organization.

• **Aldo Moro**, a former Italian premier who had been kidnapped by leftist Red Brigade terrorists, was murdered by his captors on May 9, 1978. Moro, who was president of the Christian Democratic party and a likely candidate for the Italian presidency, was kidnapped on March 16, 1978. His kidnappers demanded the release of thirteen of their fellow Red Brigade members held in prison, and murdered Moro when the Italian government refused to accede to their demands. Moro's body was found in a parked car near the center of Rome.

Aldo Moro was born in Maglie, in southern Italy, on September 23, 1916. He was educated at the University of Bari, where he became involved in a Catholic student organization. He graduated from the university with a doctorate in law in 1940. Moro joined the Christian Democratic party after World

War II and was elected to the Constituent Assembly in 1946. He served on the committee that drafted the constitution that created the Republic of Italy in June of 1946. He was elected to the Chamber of Deputies in April of 1948 and became an influential member of the Christian Democratic parliamentary group. Moro was appointed undersecretary of state in the government of Alcide de Gasperi in May of 1948. He was named to the cabinet as minister of justice in July of 1955 and was instrumental in reforming the Italian prison system. He was shifted to the Ministry of Education in May of 1957 and became the leader of the Christian Democrats in March of 1959. Moro supported a coalition between the Christian Democrats and the Socialists and became premier of a center-left government in December of 1963. He remained premier until June of 1968, when the Socialists refused to participate in a new government. Moro subsequently served as foreign minister until November of 1974, when he formed a coalition government with the Republican party. He remained premier of a minority government from February of 1976 until July of 1976. Moro was then elected president of the Christian Democrats, and remained a leading figure in Italian politics until his kidnap and murder.

• **Bruce McKenzie**, a former Kenyan minister of agriculture, was killed on May 24, 1978, when a bomb exploded as the airplane in which he was flying took off from Uganda's Entebbe Airport.

• **Ali Soilih**, the deposed president of the Comoro Islands, was shot and killed, allegedly while trying to escape captivity, on May 29, 1978. Ali Soilih had been overthrown during a coup led by Robert Denard, a former French mercenary, on May 13, 1978, and was succeeded as president by Ahmed Abdallah.

Ali Soilih was born on Grande Comoro Island in 1937. He was educated in Madagascar and France, where he studied agriculture. In 1964 he returned to the Comoros to serve as president of the Economic Development Society. He was elected to the Territorial Assembly in 1968. Soilih served in the cabinet of Prince Said Ibrahim as minister of public works from 1970 until 1972. He was the leader of the People's party and was an advocate of a gradual process of independence. He opposed Ahmed Abdallah's unilateral declaration of independence from France in July of 1975. Soilih led a coup to oust Abdallah on August 3, 1975. Soilih was chosen to be president of the Comoros by the National Council of the Revolution on January 3, 1976. He attempted to establish a leftist people's republic and abolish the feudal institutions in the Comoros. He banned political activity in the country and survived several coup attempts until his ouster in May of 1978.

• **Lt. Gen. Ari Nazar Geidarov** (1926–78), the interior minister of the Soviet Republic of Azerbaijan; **Saladin Kyazimov**, the deputy interior minister; and **Lt. Col. Aziz Saikhanov**, were shot and killed in June of 1978. Geidarov, who had served in his position since 1970, and the others were killed by Muratov, an Azerbaijani prison official who subsequently committed suicide.

• **Tony Franjieh** (Toni Franjiyyah), the son of Christian militia leader and former Lebanese president Suleiman Franjieh, was killed with his family by shellfire directed at his home by rival Falangists on June 13, 1978. He was born in Zgharta in 1941 and educated in Tripoli. A founder of the Zgharta Social Culture Club, he was instrumental in recruiting many young men into joining his family's political faction. He was elected to parliament in 1972 and was a leader there under his father's presidency. He also served in the cabinet under his father. A founder of the Forces of al-Maradah militia, he joined with the right-wing coalition that fought in the civil war of 1975. He came into conflict with rightist leader Bashir Gemayyel (q.v.) during the fighting. The death of Tony Franjieh came after weeks of fighting between the rival factions and precipitated violent acts of retaliation by the Franjieh clan. His son, Suleiman Franjieh, Jr., succeeded him as leader of the Franjieh organization.

• **Ali Yassin**, a moderate Palestine Liberation Organization official in Kuwait, was shot and killed at his home on June 15, 1979.

• **Ahmed Hussein al-Ghashmi**, the head of state of the Yemen Arab Republic, was killed when a bomb exploded in his office in the capital of Sana'a. The bomb was in a briefcase carried by an envoy from President Salem Ali Rubayyi (q.v.), the president of South Yemen. The Rubayyi government denied any knowledge of the assassination plot. Ghashmi was born in 1939. He served in the Yemeni military, rising to the rank of lieutenant colonel. He served as commander of the armed forces and became chairman of the Military Command Council following Ibrahim al-Hamdi's (q.v.) assassination in October of 1977. Ghashmi was appointed president of the Yemen Arab Republic by the Constituent Assembly in April of 1978, and retained office until his assassination.

• **Salem Ali Rubayyi**, the head of state of the People's Democratic Republic of Yemen, was ousted in a leftist coup and summarily executed by a firing squad in Aden on June 26, 1978. The coup was led by Abdel Fattah Ismail (q.v.), an extreme pro–Soviet member of the Presidency Council. President Rubayyi had attempted to have Ismail arrested for complicity in the assassination of North Yemen's president Ahmad Al-Ghasmi (q.v.) several days earlier. Ismail's militia defeated troops loyal to Rubayyi after a day of heavy fighting. Executed with Rubayyi were **Jassem Saleh** and **Salem Al-Aouar**, two of the deposed president's leading advisers.

Salem Ali Rubayyi was born in 1934. He was employed as a school teacher and became active in the Front for the Liberation of South Yemen (FLOSY) in 1963. He was involved in a revolt against President Qahtan Muhammad al-Shaabi in 1967 and was sent into exile. Rubayyi returned following Shaabi's ouster and took office as chairman of the Presidential Council on June 22, 1969. He also served as commander of the armed forces. He was the leader of the pro–Chinese faction on the council. Rubayyi initiated negotiations to discuss the unification of North and South Yemen. He also attempted to improve South Yemen's relations with Saudi Arabia and the United States. He retained power until his ouster and execution during a brief civil war.

• **Abdul Razzak Al-Naif**, a former premier of Iraq, was shot and mortally wounded on July 9, 1978. He was struck twice in the head while standing in front of the Inter-Continental Hotel in London, England. He died the following day. Naif was the target of a previous assassination attempt in 1972.

Abdul Razzak al-Naif was born in 1933. He served in the Iraqi military, where he rose to the rank of colonel. He served as deputy director of the Iraqi military intelligence system and masterminded the bloodless coup that ousted President Abdul Rahman Arif in July of 1968. Naif was named prime minister in the new government. He was in turn ousted several weeks later on July 30, 1968, by President Ahmed Hassan al-Bakr. Naif subsequently fled Iraq and was sentenced to death in absentia. He went into exile in London, where he was assassinated.

• **Brig. Gen. Juan Sanchez Ramos** (1914–78), a Spanish artillery officer in charge of military supplies, and **Lt. Col. Juan Perez Rodriguez**, his aide, were shot and killed by left-wing terrorists in Madrid on July 21, 1978.

• **Ezzedine Kalak** (1948–78), the chief representative of the Palestine Liberation Organization in Paris, was assassinated with his aide, **Hammad Adnan**, in their Paris office on August 3, 1978. Kalak, a leading supporter of PLO chief Yassir Arafat, was thought to have been the victim of Palestinian extremists backed by Iraq.

• **Georgi Markov** (1929–78), a Bulgarian writer who had defected in June of 1969, died on September 11, 1978, after having a poison contained in an alloy ball injected into his leg by the point of an umbrella. Markov was a successful author and playwright in Bulgaria. He defected to Italy in 1969 and, in 1971, moved to London. He joined the British Broadcasting Corporation's Bulgarian Service, and became a broadcaster for Radio Free Europe. Markov, who had reported receiving death threats, was jabbed in the thigh by an umbrella while walking past a London bus stop on September 7, 1978. Four days later Markov died. A small ball, thought to have contained a poison, was found in Markov's leg following an autopsy. Markov's mysterious death was presumed to have been the work of Bulgarian agents.

• **Rafael Pardo Buelvas** (1928–78), a former Colombian minister of the interior, was shot and killed in Bogota on September 12, 1978, by a member of the leftist M-19 terrorist group.

• **Capt. Francisco De Asis Liesa** (1922–78), who was second in command of the Spanish naval base at Boilboa, was shot to death by terrorists during a kidnapping attempt near his home on October 3, 1978.

• **Fedele Calvosa**, the public prosecutor of Frosinone, Italy, was shot and killed by terrorists on November 8, 1978.

• **Jose Franciso Mateu Canovas** (1920–78), a Spanish jurist who had headed Gen. Francisco Franco's Court of Public Order from 1968 until 1975, was assassinated by gunmen near his home in Madrid on November 16, 1978. Mateu had been a substitute of the Spanish supreme court following the dissolution of the Court of Public Order in 1975.

• On November 18, 1978, United States Representative **Leo Ryan** was killed with four members of his party while departing from a meeting with leaders of the People's Temple commune in Guyana. Ryan was born in Lincoln, Nebraska, on May 5, 1925. He served in the U.S. Navy during World War II. Ryan entered politics and was mayor of South San Francisco in 1962. He served in the California state assembly from 1963 to 1973. Ryan, a Democrat, was elected to the U.S. Congress from California's 11th District in 1973. He had been in Guyana to investigate allegations that the Reverend Jim Jones (1931–78) was holding members of his cult against their will at the People's Temple headquarters in Jonestown, Guyana. As Ryan was preparing to depart from the Port Katiuma airstrip, he and his party were attacked by armed members of the commune. Ryan, three newsmen — NBC-TV reporter **Don Harris**, *San Francisco Examiner* photographer **Gregory Robinson** and NBC cameraman **Robert Brown** — and another passenger were shot and killed in the assault.

Jones, who had moved his commune from San Francisco earlier in the year, ordered his followers to take cyanide-laced Kool-Aid drinks following the attack on the visiting party. Jones and his mistress, Maria Katsaris, then shot themselves to death. When Guyanan troops arrived at Jonestown on November 19, 1978, they found the dead bodies of Jones and over 900 (nearly 300 of them children) of his followers.

• **George Moscone** (1929–78), the mayor of San Francisco, and **Harvey Milk** (1931–78), a member of the San Francisco board of supervisors, were shot and killed in their offices by Dan White (1946–85), a former supervisor, on November 27, 1978.

George Moscone was born in San Francisco on November 24, 1929. A Democrat, he was elected to the San Francisco board of supervisors in 1963. In 1966 he was elected to the California state senate and served as floor leader from 1967 to 1976. In December of 1975 he was elected mayor of San Francisco and was sworn in the following January.

Harvey Milk had been elected to the board of supervisors in November of 1977. He was an avowed homosexual and an outspoken leader in the fight for homosexual rights.

Dan White was elected to the board of supervisors at the same time as Harvey Milk. He was a conservative and often at odds with Milk and Mayor Moscone. White had resigned his office for personal reasons earlier in the month. He changed his mind and requested that Mayor Moscone reappoint him to the position he had vacated. When the mayor rejected his appeal, White fired four bullets into him. He then found Supervisor

Milk and shot him five times. White was arrested and charged with the murders, but was found guilty of voluntary manslaughter. His defense claimed that he was not responsible for his actions due to a temporary deranged condition caused by overindulging in junk food. White was sentenced to seven years and eight months in prison, and was paroled in 1984. He committed suicide the following year on October 21, 1985.

# 1979

• **Maj. Gen. Constantine Ortin Gil** (1915–79), was shot to death outside his apartment in Madrid, Spain on January 3, 1979. Gen. Ortin was the military governor of Madrid and a veteran of the Spanish Civil War from 1936 to 1939. His assassination was believed to have been carried out by Basque separatists.

• **Ali Hassan Salameh** (1943–79), a Palestinian guerrilla leader known as **Abu Hassan**, was killed in a car bomb blast in front of his home in Beirut, Lebanon, on January 22, 1979. Abu Hassan was believed to have been the mastermind behind the massacre of Israeli athletes at the 1972 Munich Olympics (q.v.). He had survived several previous attempts on his life. At the time of his death he was serving as chief bodyguard to Palestinian leader Yasir Arafat.

• **Alberto Fuentes Mohr** (1928–79), a former Guatemalan minister of finance and foreign affairs, was shot to death by submachine gun fire on January 25, 1979. Mohr had been kidnapped by leftist guerrillas in 1970 while serving as foreign minister. He was subsequently exchanged for the release of a jailed guerrilla. As an opposition member of Congress, Fuentes Mohr was a leading critic of extremism on both the left and the right.

• Magistrate **Emilio Alessandrini**, the public prosecutor of Milan, was shot and killed by an unknown assassin on January 29, 1979.

• **Adolph Dubs**, the United States ambassador to Afghanistan, was shot to death on February 14, 1979, after being abducted by Moslem terrorists en route to the United States Embassy. He was reportedly killed by police, who were allegedly trying to free him. Dubs, known as "Spike," was born in Chicago on August 4, 1920. He served in the U.S. Navy during World War II. A thirty-year veteran of the diplomatic corps, he had served as a foreign service officer in West Germany, Liberia, Canada, the Soviet Union, and Yugoslavia. He was acting chief of the United States mission to the Soviet Union from 1972 until 1974, and in 1975 was named deputy assistant secretary of state for Near Eastern and South Asian affairs. In 1978 he was appointed ambassador to Afghanistan. His death had a serious negative effect on United States and Afghanistani relations.

• **Brig. Gen. Agustin Munoz Vazquez** (1913–79), a retired Spanish general, was shot to death en route to his daughter's home in northern Madrid on March 5, 1979. His alleged killers were the First of October Anti-Fascist Revolutionary Group. Gen. Munoz Vazquez was a quartermaster officer who had last served in the Spanish enclave of Ceuta in North Africa. He had been semi-retired since 1977.

• **Andre Michaux** (1931–79), a Belgian national bank official, was shot to death by two men in front of his Brussels home as he was parking his car on March 21, 1979. Michaux was believed to have been shot by mistake, as his residence was near that of a British diplomat.

• **Manuel Colon Argueta** (1931–79), a former mayor of Guatemala City from 1970 to 1974, and leader of the United Front of the Revolution, was killed by machine gun fire while driving to work in Guatemala City on March 22, 1979. Colon had gained popularity as a strong critic of the military regimes that have ruled Guatemala, and was one of the most popular leftist leaders in that country.

• **Muazzam Zaki**, a high-ranking Palestine Liberation Organization official in Pakistan, was shot and killed at his home in Islamabad by an unknown assassin on March 22, 1979.

• **Sir Richard Sykes** (1920–79), the British ambassador to the Netherlands, was killed by two gunmen outside his home in the Hague as he was leaving for the Embassy on March 22, 1979. The provisional wing of the Irish Republican Army was thought to have gunned down the British ambassador. Sykes had joined the Foreign Office in 1947 and served in Peking, Brussels, Santiago, Athens, and London before being appointed as ambassador to Cuba in 1970. He served there for two years. Sir Richard was then sent to Washington as deputy chief of mission to Ambassador Sir Peter Ramsbotham. He gained a reputation for his keen grasp of military and defense issues. He was knighted in 1977. Before being sent to his post at the Hague, in June of 1977, he had been the chief investigator of the bomb murder of Christopher Ewart-Biggs (q.v.), Britain's ambassador to Ireland, in July of 1976. Sir Richard, who was deputy undersecretary of state at the British Foreign Office at that time, recommended tighter security at all British diplomatic missions.

• **Airey Middleton Sheffield Neave**, a leading British Conservative politician, was killed when a bomb placed in his car exploded outside of the House of Commons garage on March 30, 1979. Neave was born in London on January 23, 1916. He served in the army during World War II and was a member of the British prosecution team at the Nuremberg trials. He was first elected to the House of Commons in 1953. He was an early supporter of Margaret Thatcher and was instrumental in her selection as Conservative party leader, and later prime minister. In 1975 Neave became the Conservative party's parliamentary spokesman on Northern Ireland, which made him an important target for Irish Republican Army terrorists.

• **Abune Tewoflos Woldemariam**, the former Patriarch of the Ethiopian Orthodox Church, vanished and was presumed murdered in 1979. His body was later found. Tewoflos succeeded Abune Baselyos in 1974 after Baselyos was ousted and arrested by the Derg. Tewoflos was removed from his position and imprisoned in 1976.

• **Zulfikar Ali Bhutto**, the former prime minister of Pakistan, was hanged on April 4, 1979. Bhutto, who had been ousted from power by Gen. Mohammad Zia-ul-Haq in July of 1977, was arrested and charged with the murder of a political opponent. He was convicted of the murder and sentenced to death on March 18, 1978. Despite pleas for clemency, the Pakistani government proceeded with the execution, and Bhutto was hanged, on April 4, 1978, in Rawalpindi Jail.

Zulfikar Ali Bhutto was born to a wealthy family near Larkana, in the Sind Province, on January 5, 1928. He attended the University of California at Berkeley, where he graduated with a degree in political science in 1950. He then attended Oxford University in Great Britain, where he received a degree in law. Bhutto returned to Pakistan to practice law in Karachi in 1953. He served as a member of the Pakistani delegation to the United Nations in 1957 and represented Pakistan at a UN conference in Geneva the following year. He was named to the cabinet of Mohammed Ayub Khan as minister of commerce in 1958. Bhutto was shifted to the Ministry of Information and National Reconstruction in January of 1960. He headed several other ministries in Ayub Khan's government and was elected to the restored National Assembly in June of 1962. He was appointed foreign minister in January of 1963. Bhutto came into disagreement with the Ayub Khan government over Pakistan's relationship with the United States. Bhutto advocated closer ties with the People's Republic of China and condemned United States pressure that led to the peace settlement between Pakistan and India in January of 1966. He was dismissed from the government in July of 1966 and became a leading spokesman of dissent to Ayub Khan's rule. Bhutto founded the Pakistan People's party in December of 1967. He was arrested for anti-government activities in November of 1968, and he became the central figure in the opposition by the time of his release in February of 1969. Ayub Khan was replaced the following month by General Mohammed Yahya Khan, who allowed a national election to take place in 1970. Bhutto's party won a victory in West Pakistan, and Sheikh Mujibur Rahman's (q.v.) Awami League received a vast majority in East Pakistan. Sheikh Mujibur, who advocated autonomy for East Pakistan, would have become prime minister because East Pakistan had the largest delegation in the National Assembly. Bhutto announced plans to boycott the assembly, and Yahya annulled the election. A civil war developed in East Pakistan when supporters of Sheikh Mujibur proclaimed the region the independent nation of Bangladesh. Yahya Khan appointed Bhutto as deputy prime minister and foreign minister in December of 1971, following India's involvement in the conflict. The government was forced to accept a cease-fire later in the month, and Yahya resigned as president on December 20, 1971. Bhutto was placed in charge of the government. He returned the country to civilian rule and also served in the government as minister of defense, the interior, and foreign affairs. He promoted a new constitution in August of 1973 that reduced the presidency to a ceremonial position. Bhutto stepped down as president on August 14, 1973, but remained head of government as prime minister. He was successful in improving Pakistan's economic stability and helped to restore his nation's self-esteem that had been damaged by the war with Bangladesh and India. The Pakistan People's party won a major victory in elections to the National Assembly in March of 1977. The opposition Pakistan National Alliance claimed electoral fraud, and strikes and demonstrations took place throughout the country. The army staged a coup and ousted Bhutto as prime minister on July 5, 1977. General Mohammed Zia ul-Haq imposed martial law and ordered Bhutto's imprisonment the following September. Bhutto was charged with having or-

dered the assassination of Ahmed Raza Kasuri, a political opponent, in 1974. Kasuri's father, Nawab Mohammed Ahmed Khan, was killed in the attempted assassination. He was convicted and hanged in April of 1979.

• **Amir Abbas Hoveida**, a former prime minister of Iran, was executed by the Iranian revolutionary government on April 7, 1979. Hoveida was born in Teheran on February 18, 1919. He was educated in Belgium and France and then returned to Teheran to join the Iranian Foreign Office. He was stationed in various overseas embassies, including Paris and Bonn, and also served at the United Nations in New York. Hoveida returned to Teheran to serve on the board of the National Iranian Oil Company in 1958. He was named minister of finance in the government of Hassan Ali Mansour (q.v.) and was appointed to replace Mansour as prime minister when he was assassinated on January 26, 1965. He also became leader of the New Iran party and led the party to victory in the elections of 191. Iran's economic prosperity secured Hoveida's position during the early 1970s, though the nation continued to be plagued by Islamic fundamentalists who opposed the shah's rule. Hoveida was replaced as prime minister in August of 1977 following criticism of his government's handling of public services. He remained in the government as minister of the royal court until September of 1978. He was briefly detained by the military government installed by the shah in November of 1978. Hoveida was arrested following the ouster of the shah in February of 1979. He was charged with crimes against the nation and sentenced to death. He was executed by a firing squad in Teheran on April 7, 1979.

• **Adel Mini**, the attorney general of the Syrian State Security Court, was assassinated on April 11, 1979. Mini was an aide to Syrian president Hafez Assad. Mini's death came amid rising violence between the Alawite Moslem sect, of which Mini was a member, and the majority Sunni Moslems of Syria.

• **Gen. Vali Ullah Gharani**. a leading Iranian army officer, was shot and killed by three gunmen in the back yard of his Teheran home on April 23, 1979. Gharani had served as the first chief of staff of the Iranian army following the revolution that deposed the shah of Iran in February of 1979. He had resigned his position on March 27, 1979, after he had ordered the army to put down a rebellion in Kurdistan. Gharani had served as head of the Army Intelligence Service in the 1950s until his dismissal by the shah in 1957. He had remained in retirement until his appointment as army leader on February 15, 1979.

- **Ayatollah Morteza Motahari**, a leading member of the ruling Iranian Revolutionary Council, was shot and killed while leaving a meeting with Prime Minister Mehdi Bazargan in Teheran on May 1, 1979. Motahari's assassins were reported to be members of the Forghan Fighters, an underground revolutionary group who also claimed responsibility for the assassination of Gen. Vali Ullah Gharani (q.v.) the previous month. Motahari was born in Mashhad in 1919 and studied in Qom under the Ayatollah Khomeini. He later taught theology at Tehran University, where his criticism of the Shah led to his arrest in 1964. Motahari was again arrested and imprisoned in 1975. He remained a leader of the Islamic movement to oust the Shah's regime and headed the Revolutionary Council from February of 1979. His role in the formation of a new government was cut short by his murder three months later.

- **Carlos Antonio Herrera Rebollo**, the minister of education in El Salvador, was shot and killed while driving to his office in San Salvador on May 23, 1979. Herrera Rebollo had previously served as mayor of San Salvador, and was a member of the Christian Democratic party. His assassins were believed to be members of the Popular Liberation Group, a left-wing terrorist organization.

- On May 25, 1979, Ayatollah Hashemi Rafsanjani, a leading Iranian political and religious figure, was injured in an assassination attempt. Rafsanjani recovered from his wounds.

- **Lt. Gen. Luis Gomez Hortiguela** (1910–79), a leader of the Spanish army's personnel department, was assassinated by machine gun fire on May 25, 1979, while driving in Madrid. **Col. Agustin Laso**, and aide; **Col. Juan Avalos Gomariz**, the general's secretary; and **Luis Gomez Borrego**, the general's chauffeur, were also killed in the attack. The killings were believed to have been the work of a Basque separatist group.

- **John Howland Wood, Jr.**, judge of the United States District Court for the Western District, was shot by a single bullet to his back while leaving his home in San Antonio, Texas, on May 29, 1979. Wood was born in Rockport, Texas, on March 31, 1916, and attended the University of Texas. He began practicing law after serving in the U.S. Navy during World War II. He was appointed a federal judge in 1970 and became known as "Maximum John" for applying maximum sentences to drug traffickers who came before his court. It was believed that an El Paso drug lord had ordered his killing. The hired gunman was identified as Charles Harrelson, the father of movie star Woody Harrelson. He was convicted and sentenced to life imprisonment for the murder.

- **Hugo Wey** (1930–79), the Swiss charge d'affaires in San Salvador, was killed during a kidnapping attempt by leftist terrorists on May 30, 1979.

- **Gen. Jose Cansino** (1927–79), the chief of staff of the Guatemalan army, was assassinated by terrorists on June 10, 1979, while riding through Guatemala City. Gen. Cansino was the third-ranking member of the ruling Guatemalan military government.

- **Lt. Gen. Fred W.K. Akuffo**, the military head of state of Ghana was overthrown during a coup led by Flight L. Jerry Rawlings (b.1947) on June 4, 1979. The new government accused Akuffo and other high-ranking officials of corruption. On June 16, 1979, **Gen. Ignatius Kutu Achaempong** and **Lt. Gen. Akwasi Afrifa**, Akuffo's predecessors as head of state of Ghana's military government, were executed. Lt. Gen. Akuffo was himself executed on June 26, 1979.

Akwasi Amankwa Afrifa was born to an

Ashanti family in Mampong on April 24, 1936. He attended mission schools locally and received a scholarship to Cape Coast's Adisadel College. He was expelled from college and entered the army. Afrifa attended officers training school and graduated from Sandhurst in 1960. He saw duty as part of the United Nations Peacekeeping Forces in the Congo in the early 1960s. On his return to Ghana, he began making plans for a coup against the Nkrumah regime, which he took part in on February 24, 1966. Following the ouster of Nkrumah, he served on the National Liberation Council, as minister of finance and economic affairs. When J.A. Ankrah was forced to resign on April 2, 1969, Afrifa replaced him as chairman. He supervised a return to civilian rule by allowing an election in August of 1969. He remained a member of the supervisory Presidential Commission until the following year. From December of 1970 he served as a member of the Council of State under President Akufo-Addo. When another military coup ousted the civilian government, Afrifa's resistance to the coup leaders resulted in his arrest and detention until July 3, 1973. He remained in political retirement until 1978, when he became an active member of the People's Movement for Freedom and Justice. He was elected to Parliament in June of 1979. Afrifa was arrested following the coup of June 1979 and charged with abuse of power and misuse of state funds. He was executed near Accra on June 26, 1979.

Ignatius Kuti Achaempong was born in Kumasi on September 23, 1931. He was educated at local mission schools and at the Central College of Commerce in Agona Swedru. He worked as a teacher until the early 1950s, when he joined the army. Achaempong was commissioned as an officer in 1959 and attended military training schools in Great Britain and the United States. He continued to serve in the army following Ghanaian independence and served in the United Nations peacekeeping force in the former Belgian Congo in 1962. Achaempong was promoted to the rank of colonel and was named commander of the 1st Infantry Brigade in Accra in No-

vember of 1971. He led the military coup that ousted the elected government on January 13, 1972. Achaempong served as head of state and chairman of the National Redemption Council. His military government suspended the constitution and dissolved the National Assembly. He continued to serve as head of the ruling Supreme Military Council until he was ousted by other members of the council on July 5, 1978. He was detained by the new government and was dismissed from the army following his release. Achaempong was again arrested following the coup of June 1979. He was tried on charges of corruption and executed near Accra on June 16, 1979.

Fred W.K. Akuffo was born in Akuropon on March 21, 1937. He was educated at local missionary schools and entered the army in 1957. He was sent to the British Royal Military Academy at Sandhurst for training and was commissioned in 1960. Akuffo served on the United Nations peacekeeping force in the former Belgian Congo in the early 1960s. He was given command of the Ghana Parachute Battalion and rose to the rank of colonel. He became a member of the ruling Supreme Military Council under Ignatius Achaempong in 1975, and served as chief of the defense staff. Akuffo joined with other members of the council to oust Achaempong on July 5, 1978, and he became Ghana's head of state. He vowed to restore Ghana to a parliamentary democracy and freed many political prisoners. He instituted austerity measures to improve Ghana's sinking economy. Akuffo's insistence on an amnesty for himself and other members of the military government before he would allow a return to civilian rule sparked a coup by junior officers. He was ousted by Flight Lt. Jerry Rawlings on June 5, 1979. He was arrested and charged with abuse of power and misuse of state funds and was executed near Accra on June 26, 1979.

• On June 25, 1979, United States Gen. Alexander Haig (b. 1924), the supreme commander of the Allied forces in NATO, was uninjured when a land mine exploded in his car's path in Belgium. It was believed that the attempt on Gen. Haig's life was organized by West German Red Brigade terrorists.

- **Police Col. Antonio Varisco** was murdered by terrorists in Rome on July 13, 1979. Col. Varisco was the director of security of the central courts in Rome.

- **Zuheir Mohsen** (1936–79), the leader of the Saiqa, a pro–Syrian Palestinian guerrilla organization, was assassinated in Nice, France, on July 24, 1979. Mohsen, who was also the leader of the Palestinian Liberation Organization's military department, had led the Saiqa since 1971. His murder was believed to have been orchestrated by Israeli agents.

- On July 28, 1979, a coup attempt, supposedly orchestrated by Syria, was uncovered in Iraq against the regime of Saddam Husain. Over twenty people were subsequently executed including RCC secretary **Muhi 'Abd al-Husain Mashhadi**, and his colleagues **'Adnan Hamdani, Muhammad 'Ayish, Muhammad Mahjub**, and **Ghanim 'Abd al-Jalil**. 'Abd al-Khaliq al-Samarra'i, who had been imprisoned because of his alleged involvement in an attempted coup in July of 1973, was also executed at that time.

- **Louis Mountbatten, Earl of Burma**, was killed in a bomb blast aboard his fishing boat off the coast of County Sligo, Ireland, on August 27, 1979. Also killed in the explosion were Nicholas Knatchbull, Mountbatten's fourteen-year-old grandson, and Paul Maxwell, a local crew member.

Prince Louis Francis Albert Victor Nicholas of Battenberg was born in Windsor, England, on June 25, 1900. He was the son of Prince Louis of Battenberg and Princess Victoria. He served in the Royal Navy during World War I. The family name of Battenberg was changed to Mountbatten in 1917 as a result of anti–German feelings. Mountbatten rose to the rank of captain prior to World War II. He commanded a destroyer flotilla in the early months of the war. He was made chief of combined operations in 1941 and planned the invasion of Europe. Mountbatten was named supreme allied commander for Southeast Asia in 1943. He led the recapture of

Burma from Japanese control in 1945. Mountbatten was created a viscount in 1946 and became earl of Burma in 1947. He was named the last British viceroy of India on February 20, 1947. He presided over the end of British rule in India and served as India's first governor-general after independence on August 15, 1947. Mountbatten relinquished his position on June 21, 1948, and returned to Great Britain. He returned to the Royal Navy as a rear admiral and became commander in chief of the Mediterranean fleet in 1952. He served as first sea lord from 1955 until 1959. Mountbatten was the first chief of the British Defense Staff from 1959 until his retirement in 1965, and reorganized Britain's defense forces. His assassination fourteen years later was attributed to the Provisional Irish Republican Army. Thomas McMahon, an explosives expert in the IRA, was tried for the killings. He was convicted and sentenced to life imprisonment.

- **Jose Javier Romero Mena**, an educator and the brother of President Carlos Romero of El Salvador, was killed by leftist guerrillas near his home in Apopo, El Salvador, on September 6, 1979.

- **Nur Mohammad Taraki**, the head of state of Afghanistan, was ousted and killed in a coup on September 16, 1979. Taraki was born in 1917 in the Ghazni Province of Afghanistan. He worked in Bombay, India, in the late 1930s, where he became a follower of Mahatma Gandhi (q.v.). In the late 1940s he began working in minor positions for the Afghan government and was stationed at Afghanistan's embassy in the United States in the early 1950s. Taraki, a noted writer and Marxist intellectual, founded the Maoist Khalq, or Masses, party in 1963 in opposition to King Zahir Shah. The party divided with the ascension of the Mohammed Daud Khan (q.v.) regime in 1973, with the pro–Soviet Parcham, or Banner, party faction supporting Daud. Taraki remained a leading opponent of the Daud regime and served several jail sentences for his views. He became secretary-general of the People's Democratic party when the two rival factions of the Khalq re-united in 1977. On April 27, 1978, Taraki was a leader of a bloody coup which overthrew and killed President Daud. Three days later Taraki was named president and prime minister of the new Soviet-backed government. Taraki relinquished the post of prime minister of Hafizullah Amin (q.v.) on March 27, 1979, following a major revolt by conservative Muslim tribesmen opposed to the Marxist regime. Taraki's Soviet advisors favored the ouster of the brutal Amin as prime minister, but their plan backfired when Amin instead overthrew Taraki on September 16, 1979. The new government announced that Taraki died of an undisclosed illness on October 9, 1979, though it was later revealed that Taraki had died of gunshot wounds at the time of his ouster.

• **Carlo Ghiglieno**, an executive of the Fiat Automobile Company, was shot and killed by Red Brigade terrorists in Turin, Italy, on September 21, 1979.

• **Gen. Lorenzo Gonzalez-Valles Sanchez** (1920–79), the military governor of the Guipuzcoa province in Spain, was assassinated by Basque separatists while he was walking along a seaside boardwalk in San Sebastian on September 23, 1979.

• **Cesare Terranova**, a Sicilian judge, was assassinated by terrorists in Palermo, Italy, on September 25, 1979.

• **Francisco Macias Nguema**, the dictatorial ruler of Equatorial Guinea until his ouster on August 3, 1979, was executed by the new government on September 29, 1979. Francisco Macias Nguema Biyogo Negue Ndong was born in Nfenga on January 1, 1924. He was a member of the Fang tribe and was educated at local mission schools. He began work in the Spanish colonial government as a clerk in 1944. After serving in various administrative positions, he was appointed mayor of Mongomo in the late 1950s. Macias Nguema entered the pre-independence government of Bonifacio Ondo Edu (q.v.) as vice president of the Government Council in 1964. Macias Nguema challenged

Ondu Edu for Equatorial Guinea's presidency in elections held in September of 1968. When Equatorial Guinea was granted independence from Spain on October 12, 1968, Macias Nguema established a government with himself as minister of defense. He began a campaign to force Spanish troops from the country in 1969. Spanish residents were threatened and attacked by supporters of the government. Foreign Minister Atanasio Ndongo (q.v.) and Saturnino Ibongo (q.v.), Equatorial Guinea's representative to the United Nations, attempted to negotiate a political settlement with the Spanish government. Macias Nguema charged that Ndongo and Ibongo were part of a Spanish plot to oust the government and had the two men arrested and murdered in prison. Macias Nguema instituted a reign of terror that was one of the most brutal in the world. Numerous real or supposed opponents of the regime were arrested and summarily executed by the government. Examples of Nguema's exploits include reports that he had several hundred political prisoners executed in a stadium on Christmas Eve while loudspeakers blared the song "Those Were the Days, My Friend." Macias Nguema became president for life in 1972. He also introduced a new constitution the following year and Africanized Spanish names within the country, including his own. Leading a brutal campaign against intellectuals in the country, he killed or drove thousands into exile. Macias Nguema's government reportedly killed in excess of 50,000 people during his reign. The economy of Equatorial Guinea also suffered under Macias Nguema, and the country was bankrupt by the late 1970s. He was widely considered mentally unbalanced, but survived numerous plots to oust his government during his rule. He uncovered an army plot against him in June of 1979 and had the organizers summarily executed. Another military coup, led by Macias Nguema's nephew, Teodoro Obiang Nguema Mbasongo, succeeded in ousting the president on August 3, 1979. Macias Nguema went into hiding in his home village, but was captured by government troops on August 18, 1979. He was sent to Bata prison to await trial. Macias Nguema was convicted on charges of murder and corruption, and was executed on September 29, 1979.

• **Vincent Teekah** (1941–79), who had served as minister of education in Guyana from 1977, was shot and killed while driving in Georgetown, Guyana, on October 25, 1979.

• **Chung Hee Park**, the president of South Korea, was assassinated while dining in a Seoul restaurant on October 26, 1979. Chung Hee Park was born in Sangmo-ri, Kyongsang-pukdo Province, on September 30, 1917. He was educated in Korea and worked as a teacher after his graduation in 1937. Park entered the Manchukuo Military Academy under the Japanese administration of Korea in 1940. He entered the Japanese Imperial Military Academy two years later and graduated in 1944. Park served in the Japanese army as a lieutenant in Manchuria during World War II. He returned to Korea following Japan's defeat in August of 1945. He entered the Korean Military Academy and was commissioned as a captain in the Korean army in December of 1946. Park was arrested and court-martialed on charges of conspiring against the government in 1948. He was spared from prosecution by serving as a witness against the other conspirators. Park returned to the army and rose to the rank of brigadier general during the Korean War. He served in various military positions during the 1950s and was promoted to major general in 1958. He was also given command of the First Army in 1958. President Syngman Rhee was forced to resign from office in April of 1960. Park led a military coup to overthrow the subsequent government of Premier John Myun Chang in May of 1961. Park served as vice-chairman of the ruling Supreme Council for National Reconstruction. He replaced Chang Do Young as chairman of the ruling military junta in July of 1961. Park became acting president of the Republic of Korea on March 24, 1962. He retired from the army as a full general in August of 1963 to be the government-

sponsored Democratic Republican party candidate in the presidential elections the following October. He narrowly defeated Yun Po Sun and was sworn into office in December of 1963. He led the government in establishing diplomatic and trade relations with Japan in August of 1965, despite demonstrations against his policy. He was also successful in leading Korea to economic prosperity. Park again defeated Yun Po Sun in presidential elections in May of 1967. Park was a supporter of the United States policy in Vietnam and committed Korean troops to the military action there. He was the target of an unsuccessful North Korean assassination plot in January of 1968. A referendum was passed in October of 1969 to allow Park to run for a third term in office. He defeated Kim Dae Jung in a close contest in 1971. Park declared martial law in October of 1972 and amended the constitution to grant himself near dictatorial powers. Park jailed opposition political leaders as dissent to his rule continued to grow. Park's wife, Yook Young Soo (q.v.), was killed in an unsuccessful assassination attempt against him on August 15, 1974. He was also faced with international criticism for human rights abuses in the country. Park was assassinated by South Korean intelligence chief Kim Jae Kyu while at a dinner party in Seoul on October 26, 1979. **Cha Choi Chol**, a leading advisor and chief bodyguard of the president, and four other aides were also slain in the attack. It was believed that Kim Jae Kyu planned a coup attempt against Park. Kim and four associates were arrested for the murders and hanged on May 24, 1980.

• **Mohammed Mofatteh**, a close aide to Iranian leader Ayatollah Khomeini, was shot and killed near the Islamic College in Teheran on December 17, 1979. Mofatteh was a leader of the anti-shah movement before Khomeini's return from exile, and was the director of the leading Islamic religious school in Teheran.

• **Hafizullah Amin**, who had become president of Afghanistan during a coup three months earlier, was overthrown and killed on December 27, 1979. Hafizullah Amin was born on August 1, 1929, in Paghman, Afghanistan. Amin reportedly attended Columbia in the United States. He later joined Nur Mohammad Taraki's (q.v.) Khalq party in the 1960s and was active in the coup which overthrew the regime of Mohammed Daud Khan (q.v.) in April of 1978. Amin was named foreign minister in Taraki's new Marxist government. On March 27, 1979, Amin became Taraki's prime minister and was responsible for the brutal repression of Muslim insurgents in the provincial Afghan capital of Herat. Continuing religious and civil disorders in Afghanistan resulted in a buildup of Soviet military support for the besieged Afghan regime. Amin ousted and killed Taraki on September 16, 1979, and took control of the government. The Amin government proved even more unpopular than its predecessor as rebels advanced throughout the country. Amin survived as president for a little over three months. He was ousted and killed on December 27, 1979, in a Soviet-backed coup which installed Babrak Karmal as the new Afghan leader.

• **Viktor S. Paputin** (1926–79), the Soviet deputy interior minister, was also reported killed during the Afghanistani coup on December 27, 1979, which deposed Hafizullah Amin (q.v.). Paputin was allegedly the architect of the Soviet-backed coup.

# 1980

• On January 31, 1980, thirty-nine people were killed in a fire at the Spanish Embassy in Guatemala City. The Embassy building had been seized by Guatemalan Indian peasants during the week, and most of the people inside died in the flames. The dead included **Eduardo Caceras Lehnhoff**, a former vice president of Guatemala, and **Adolfo Molina Orantes**, Guatemala's foreign minister.

• **Mario Zamora Rivas**, the attorney general of El Salvador, was shot and killed by right-wing gunmen in San Salvador on February 23, 1980. He was a prominent moderate leader and a member of the Christian Democratic party.

• Former United States Representative **Allard K. Lowenstein** of New York was shot and killed on March 14, 1980, in his New York law office. Dennis Sweeney, a former associate of Lowenstein, was charged with the murder. Lowenstein was born in Newark, New Jersey, on January 16, 1929, and was a teacher at Stanford University. He was an early supporter of the civil rights movement in the 1960s and an opponent of American involvement in the war in Vietnam. In 1968 Lowenstein was a leader of the "Dump Johnson" movement, and succeeded in persuading Sen. Eugene McCarthy of Minnesota to run for the Democrat nomination for the presidency that year. McCarthy's early primary showings as a peace candidate eventually resulted in the withdrawal of President Lyndon Johnson from the race. In 1968 Lowenstein was elected to Congress from the Fifth Congressional District in New York, representing Long Island. He served only one term, being defeated in six later bids for the office. In 1977 he was appointed as the United States representative to the United Nations Commission on Human Rights.

• **Russell G. Lloyd** (1932–80), the former mayor of Evansville, Indiana, died on March 21, 1980, of gunshot wounds he received in a shooting incident earlier in the week. Lloyd, who had stepped down as mayor three months earlier, was shot by Julie Van Orden, who claimed that city inspectors were harassing her about the condition of her home. It was believed that Lloyd's assailant was not aware that he was no longer Evansville's mayor.

• **Oscar Arnulfo Romero y Galdames**, the Salvadoran Roman Catholic archbishop was shot and killed by an unknown gunman in San Salvador on March 24, 1980. Archbishop Romero was born in El Salvador on August 15, 1917. He was appointed the Roman Catholic archbishop of El Salvador in 1977. While he was previously considered a conservative, he became a leading critic of the regime of Gen. Carlos Humberto Romero and of human rights violations in El Salvador. In 1979 he was nominated for the Nobel Peace Prize for his attempts to better the life of the poor people of his nation. He had received numerous threats from right-wing factions in El Salvador before his death.

• On April 12, 1980, President **William R. Tolbert, Jr.** of Liberia was shot and killed during a coup led by Master Sgt. Samuel Doe. More than twenty-five other prominent Liberian political figures died during the coup or were executed shortly afterward. On April 22 the new military government put to death by firing squad President Tolbert's brother **Frank Tolbert**, the president of the Senate; **Reginald Townsend**, the leader of the ruling True Whig party; **Cecil Dennis**, the foreign minister; **James Phillips**, the finance minister; **Cyril Bright**, the agriculture minister; **John Sherman**, the commerce minister; **James Pierre**, the chief justice of the Liberian supreme court; **Joseph Chesson**, a jurist; **Frank Stewart**, the budget director; **Richard Heneries**, the speaker of the House of Representatives; Congressman **Charles King**; and **Clarence Parker**, the treasurer of the True Whig party.

William Richard Tolbert, Jr., was born in Bensonville on May 13, 1913. He was educated locally and received a degree from Liberia College in 1934. He was employed in the Liberian civil service the following year. Tolbert entered politics and was elected to the House of Representatives as a member of the True Whig party in 1943. He was elected vice president under William V.S. Tubman in 1955. Tolbert exercised little power during Tubman's administration, though he continued to serve as Tubman's running mate in subsequent elections. Tolbert succeeded to the presidency when Tubman died in office on July 23, 1971. Tolbert sponsored some liberal reforms in the country and allowed the formation of the opposition Progressive Alliance of Liberia in 1973. He was reelected with little opposition in 1975. His government faced increasing criticism for the economic disparity in the country, however. The army fired upon a large group of demonstrators protesting the increase in the price of rice in April of 1979 and killed over 70 of the protestors. This action set off a wave of anti-government rioting throughout the country. Tolbert ordered the arrest of leaders of the opposition in March of 1980. He was ousted and killed the following month during a military coup.

• **Gurbachan Singh**, an Indian religious leader who was regarded by several hundred thousand followers of the Nirankari Sect as a living saint, was shot and killed near his New Delhi home by two assassins on April 24, 1980.

• **Farrokhrou Parsa**, the minister of education in the government of the deposed shah of Iran, was executed by a firing squad on May 8, 1980. Mrs. Parsa had also served as the first female member of the Iranian parliament. She had been arrested following the overthrow of the shah and was tried and condemned by a revolutionary court.

• On June 2, 1980, Bassam al-Shaka, the Palestinian mayor of the West Bank city of Nablus, and Karim Khalef, the mayor of Ramallah, were seriously injured in separate car bombings. Shaka lost both legs in the explosion. An attempt was made on the life of another West Bank mayor, Ibrahim Tawil of Bireh, on the same day. A Jewish terrorist organization claimed responsibility for the bombings.

• Guyanan historian **Walter Rodney** was killed in June of 1980 in an explosion in Guyana. Rodney was also a member of the opposition party Working People's Alliance (WPA).

• **Gun Tazak** (1931–80), the deputy chairman of the Turkish right-wing National Action party, was shot to death at his home in Ankara in June of 1980.

• **Lt. Col. Roger Vergara Campos** (1937–80), the director of Chile's army intelligence school, was assassinated by four leftist gunmen in Santiago on July 15, 1980.

- **Nihat Erim**, a former prime minister of Turkey, was shot and killed at his summer home in Kartal, near Istanbul, by left-wing gunmen on July 18, 1980. Erim was born in Kandira in 1912. He attended the University of Istanbul and the University of Paris and received a degree in law. He returned to Turkey to serve as a law professor at Ankara University. Erim was appointed to the Ministry of Foreign Affairs as a legal advisor in 1942. He joined the Republican People's party and was elected the National Assembly in 1945. He served as minister of public works and deputy prime minister from 1948 until 1950. Erim retired from politics in 1950 following the rise of the Democratic party to power. He was again elected to the National Assembly in 1961 and represented the Turkish Parliament at the European Council until 1970. Erim was named prime minister on March 19, 1971, and served as head of a coalition government while Turkey was under martial law. His government outlawed extremist parties on the left and the right and banned poppy-growing in Turkey. He resigned from office on April 17, 1972, when the National Assembly refused his request for extraordinary powers to combat terrorism. Erim subsequently served in the Turkish Senate until his murder in July of 1980.

- Former Iranian premier Shahpur Bakhtiar (b. 1916), was attacked by three gunmen at his home in Paris on June 18, 1980. Bakhtiar, who had served as the last prime minister of the deposed shah of Iran, was uninjured in the shooting, which claimed the lives of two people. Bakhtiar was a leading exiled opponent of the regime of the Ayatollah Khomeini.

- **Salah al-Din Bitar**, a former Syrian premier, was shot and killed by an assassin as he entered his magazine office while in exile in Paris on July 21, 1980. Bitar was born in Damascus in 1912. He was educated in Damascus and at the Sorbonne in Paris, where he received a degree in science. He returned to Syria and became a teacher in 1934. Bitar entered politics in 1942 in opposition to the French mandate in Syria. He co-founded the Arab Renaissance, or Ba'ath, party with Michael Aflaq in 1942. He started the party newspaper, *al-Ba'ath*, in 1946 and served as editor. Bitar went into exile in Lebanon in 1953 after being accused of plotting against the government of Abid es-Shishakli (q.v.). He returned to Syria to organize the merger of the Ba'ath and Socialist parties. Bitar was elected to Parliament following the ouster of the Shishakli government in February of 1954. He was named foreign minister in the government of Sabri el-Assali in June of 1956. He was instrumental in negotiating the merger between Syria and Egypt to form the United Arab Republic in 1958. Bitar subsequently served as minister of state for Arab affairs in the United Arab Republic government. He resigned near the end of 1959 in opposition to President Gamal Abdel Nasser's curtailing of Ba'athist influence on the government. A group of rightist army officers led a military coup against the Egyptian-dominated government and withdrew Syria from the United Arab Republic in September of 1961. Bitar fled the country, and went into exile in Beirut, Lebanon. He returned to Damascus and became prime minister in March of 1963, following the Ba'athist coup that ousted President Nazim el-Kudsi. Bitar stepped down as prime minister in November of 1963, to become vice president of the Revolutionary Council. He was again named prime minister by President Amin al-Hafiz in May of 1964 and served until the following October. He was once again asked to form a government in December of 1965. Bitar retained office until February of 1966, when the extremist faction of the Ba'ath party ousted the government of al-hafiz. Bitar was arrested following the coup, but escaped and fled to Lebanon. He was tried in absentia for conspiring against the Syrian government in January of 1969 and sentenced to life imprisonment. He settled in exile in France in 1970, where he served as editor of *Arab Renaissance*, a political journal, until his murder in July of 1980.

- **Ali Akbar Tabatabai** (1931–80), the former spokesman and press attaché for the Iranian Embassy in Washington, was shot and killed at his home in Washington, D.C., on July 22, 1980. Before coming to the United States, Tabatabai had served as the director general of foreign information at the Iranian Information Ministry in Teheran under the shah. He was also the founder of the Iranian Freedom Foundation and a leading critic of the regime of the Ayatollah Khomeini.

- **Riyad Taya** (1926–80), the president of the Lebanese publisher's syndicate since 1967, was shot to death on July 23, 1980, while en route to his office in Moslem West Beirut.

- **Musa Shaib** (1938–80), the secretary of the Ba'ath party in Lebanon, was shot to death by machine gun fire near the Beirut International Airport on July 28, 1980.

- **Galip Ozmel**, the Turkish attaché in Athens since 1977, was shot and killed in the Athens suburb of Pangrati on July 30, 1980.

- **Gen. Enrique Briz Armengol** (1916–80), a Spanish logistics officer was shot and killed on September 2, 1980, by gunmen in Barcelona, Spain. His assassins were thought to be members of the October First Revolutionary Antifascist Group (GRAPO), a left-wing terrorist organization.

- **Felix Garcia Rodgiruez**, a Cuban attaché at the United Nations, was shot and killed in New York City while driving in his car on September 11, 1980. An anti–Castro terrorist group was believed responsible for the murder.

- **Anastasio Somoza Debayle**, the deposed ruler of Nicaragua, was killed by bazooka and machine gun fire while in exile in Asuncion, Paraguay, on September 17, 1980. Somoza was born in Leon, Nicaragua, on December 5, 1925. He was the son of Anastasio Somoza Garcia (q.v.), who ruled Nicaragua from 1937. he younger Somoza was educated at military schools in Nicaragua and the United States, where he graduated from West Point in 1946. He returned to Nicaragua to serve in the National Guard. He had risen to the rank of colonel by the time of his father's assassination in 1956. His brother, Luis Somoza, succeeded to the presidency in 1956, and Anastasio became commander of the National Guard. Luis Somoza relinquished office to Rene Schick Gutierrez in May of 1963, and Anastasio Somoza began making plans for obtaining the presidency for himself. He received the nomination of the Liberal party in August of 1966 and defeated Conservative leader Fernando Aguero Rocha in February of 1967. He was sworn into office on May 1, 1967. Somoza attempted to modernize the country and invoked austerity measures on the economy to provide funds for education and health programs. Somoza reached an agreement with leaders of the Conservative opposition to draft a new constitution and provide free elections. He turned over the presidency to a civilian triumvirate on May 1, 1972, in order to prepare for democratic elections. Somoza was reelected in September of 1974, though critics accused the government of electoral fraud. Somoza again took office the following December. His later regime was marked for its corruption and human rights abuses. The Sandinista National Liberation Front launched an attack on the government in October of 1977. A bloody civil war ensued that resulted in Somoza's ouster by the Sandinistas on July 17, 1979. Somoza went into exile in Paraguay, which became the scene of his assassination in September of 1980.

- Political violence from the left and the right resulted in the death of many prominent El Salvadorans during 1980. **Maria Magdalena Henriquez**, the Salvadoran Human Rights Commission's spokeswoman, was found murdered near San Salvador on October 7, 1980. She had been kidnapped in downtown San Salvador on October 3 by right-wing gunmen.

**Archibald Gardner Dunn**, the South African ambassador to El Salvador, was executed by leftist terrorists on October 9, 1980. Dunn had been kidnapped on November 28, 1979, by members of the Popular Liberation Forces guerrilla group, and was killed following the El Salvadoran government's refusal to negotiate with the kidnappers.

**Melvin Rigoberto Orellana**, the El Salvadoran Christian Democratic party's chief spokesman, was shot and killed by the leftist Popular Liberation Forces on October 10, 1980, near his home in the capital. Rightwing gunmen shot and killed **Ramon Valladares**, the administrator of El Salvador's Human Right's Commission, on October 26, 1980, in San Salvador, and **Felix Antonio Ulloa**, the rector of the University of El Salvador, was shot and killed on October 29, 1980. **Manuel De Jesus Rivas Rodriguez**, El Salvadoran business leader and director of El Salvador's International Trade Fair, was assassinated on November 3, 1980.

On November 27, 1980, the bodies of six prominent El Salvadoran leftists were found near the capital following their kidnapping during a meeting. The dead included **Enrique Alvarez Cordoba**, the leader of the Democratic Revolutionary Front (FDR); **Juan Chacon**, the leader of the Popular Revolutionary Bloc; **Manuel Franco** of the Communist National Democratic Union; **Enrique Barrera**, a member of the National Revolutionary Movement; **Humberto Mendoza**, a member of the Popular Liberation Movement; and **Donoteo Hernandez**, a labor union leader. The Maximilian Hernandez Brigade, a right-wing terrorist organization, claimed responsibility for the killings.

On December 4, 1980, the bodies of three American Roman Catholic nuns and one lay worker were found outside of San Salvador. The dead included **Sister Dorothy Kazel** (1940–80), **Sister Ita Ford** (1940–80), **Sister Maura Clarke** (1934–80); and **Jean Donovan** (1953–80). The four had been shot and strangled. The murderers were thought to be right-wing extremist members of the El Salvadoran army.

• **Eduardo Garcia**, the Dominican Republic's ambassador to Colombia, was shot to death in Bogota by Rafael Sanchez, the Dominican consul, on November 16, 1980. The Colombian police indicated that the killing was not politically motivated.

• **Francisco Sa Carneiro**, the prime minister of Portugal, was killed when his light plane crashed shortly after taking off from Lisbon airport on December 4, 1980. The crash was initially attributed to mechanical failure, but further investigations twenty years later led to much speculation that the crash could have been caused by sabotage. Six other people died in the crash while Sa Carneiro was en route to a campaign rally in northern Portugal. Francisco Lumbrales de Sa Carneiro was born in Oporto on July 19, 1934. He graduated from law school and worked as a lawyer in Oporto. He was elected to the National Assembly in 1969. He was active in attempting to liberalize the authoritarian regime of Premier Marcello Caetano and resigned from the Assembly in 1973. Following the military coup that ousted the Caetano government in April of 1974, Sa Carneiro founded the Popular Democratic party. He served in the cabinet of Adelino de Palma Carlos as minister without portfolio, but resigned in protest of the government's nationalization policies. In the elections of December of 1979, Sa Carneiro led the Democratic Alliance to victory. He became premier on January 3, 1980, and began plans for the reduction of nationalization of industry and for seeking Portugal's admission to the European Economic Community. Sa Carneiro remained premier until his death.

• **Sultan Ibraimov** (1927–80), the premier of the Khirgiz Soviet Socialist Republic in the Soviet Union, was killed while sleeping at a sanatorium near the capital city of Frunz on December 4, 1980.

• **John Lennon**, a British composer, musician and a founding member of the Beatles, was shot to death in front of his New York apartment by Mark David Chapman on December 8, 1980. Lennon was born in Liverpool, England, on October 9, 1940. When he was seventeen he organized the Quarrymen, his first rock group. In the late 1950s he joined with Paul McCartney, George Harrison, and eventually Ringo Starr to form the Beatles. In the early 1960s these four musicians became one of the most popular musical phenomena of all time. Lennon was lead singer, lyricist and composer for the group and was known as a social and political activist during the late 1960s. He was also an outspoken proponent of the peace movement. In 1970 the Beatles disbanded but Lennon continued to write and record music until 1975. He then spent five years in retirement to be with his wife, Japanese artist and musician Yoko Ono, and their son, Sean. In 1980 he began recording again, only to have his career cut short by his murder.

• **Sarik Ariyak**, the Turkish consul general in Sydney, Australia, was shot to death in his car on December 17, 1980. The shooting was believed to be the work of Armenian terrorists.

• **Darwich El-Zouni** (1924–80), an associate of Syrian President Hafez al-Assad, was assassinated in Damascus on December 27, 1980. El-Zouni was a leading member of the Unionist Socialist party of Syria.

• **Gen. Enrico Calvaligi** (1919–80), the deputy commander of northern Italy's Carabinieri anti-terrorist force, was shot to death in Rome on December 31, 1980. Calvaligi was also the security director of the maximum security prison where most convicted terrorists were being held.

# 1981

• On January 3, 1981, two Americans involved in El Salvador's land redistribution program and the head of the country's agrarian program were shot to death by gunmen in a hotel coffee shop in San Salvador. **Michael P. Hammer** (1938–81), of Potomac, Maryland; **Mark David Pearlman** (1944–81), of Seattle, Washington; and **Jose Rodolfo Viera** (1945–81), the president of El Sal-

vador's Institute for Agrarian Transformation, were the victims. Hammer and Pearlman were affiliated with the American Institute for Free Labor Development in Washington, D.C. Hammer had been involved with the institute for seventeen years and was regarded as an expert on agrarian affairs in South and Central America. Pearlman had spent the previous seven months in El Salvador in an attempt to design a workable land redistribution program. The assassinations were thought to be the work of right wing death squads who were in violent opposition to land redistribution.

• **Hammad Abu Rabia** (1929–81), a Bedouin member of the Israeli Knesset, was assassinated in Jerusalem on January 12, 1981. Rabia had been a member of the Knesset since 1974.

• **Artemio Camargo**, a leader of the Bolivian Tin Miners Union; **Jose Reyes Carvajal** and **Arcil Menacho**, both former Bolivian national deputies; and four university professors were found dead on January 15, 1981, after having been arrested by Bolivian police in La Paz. The slain leftist leaders were thought to have been executed by the Bolivian police under the command of Col. Luis Arce Gomez, the interior minister.

• Bernadette Devlin McAliskey (b.1947), a militant Irish political activist, was seriously wounded in an assassination attempt on January 16, 1981. Mrs. McAliskey and her husband, Michael, were shot by militant Protestant terrorists at their home in County Tyrone, Ireland.

• **Sir Norman Stronge** (1895–1981), a leading Protestant and former speaker of the Stormont, Northern Ireland's parliament, was shot to death with his son, **James Stronge**, at his home in Tynan Abbey castle in South Armagh on January 21, 1981. The killings were thought to be the work of the Irish Republican Army, who destroyed the castle with explosives. Stronge had been speaker of the Stormont from 1945 to 1969.

• President Ahmed Sekou Toure (1922–84) of Guinea was the target of an unsuccessful assassination attempt at the Conakry airport on February 20, 1981.

• **Tariq Rahim**, a Pakistani diplomat, was shot and killed while aboard a Pakistan International Airlines plane that was hijacked by a terrorist group led by the son of Zulfikar Ali Bhutto (q.v.), Pakistan's executed former president, on March 2, 1981. The plane was taken to Kabul, Afghanistan, where the remaining passengers were released following negotiations with the Pakistani government.

• Two Turkish diplomats, **Tecelli Ari** and **Resat Morali**, were shot by Armenian terrorists in Paris on March 4, 1981, as they were leaving the Turkish Embassy there. Ari was killed instantly in the attack, and Morali died a short time later.

• The wife of Isam al-Attar, the leader of Syria's Muslim Brothers, was murdered by agents of the Syrian government in Germany in March of 1981. Attar, who led the Muslim Brothers from 1957 until going into exile in 1963 was a leading critic of Syria's Ba'thist regime and an advocate of its violent overthrow.

• **Chester Bitterman**, a United States Bible translator working with the Summer Institute of Linguistics, was murdered by leftist guerrillas in Bogota, Colombia, on March 7, 1981. Bitterman, who had been kidnapped in January, was accused of being a United States Central Intelligence Agency agent.

• President Ronald Reagan (b.1911) of the United States was shot in the chest on March 30, 1981, outside of the Washington Hilton Hotel after giving an address to a labor group. He was immediately rushed to a hospital and, after undergoing surgery, recovered from his injuries. The attempted assassin was identified as John W. Hinckley, Jr., twenty-five. Presidential press secretary James S. Brady was critically injured in the attack, and Secret Service agent Timothy J. McCarthy and District of Columbia police officer Thomas Delahanty were also seriously wounded. All of the victims survived the assault. Hinckley was tried for the assassination attempt but found not guilty due to insanity. It appeared that he had

shot the president in an attempt to impress actress Jodie Foster, with whom he was obsessed. The court ordered him committed to a mental institution.

• **Muhammad Baqir al-Sadr**, an Iraqi Shiite leader and a founder of the political association the Islamic Call in the late 1950s was arrested with his sister **Bint Huda**. They were imprisoned in Baghdad until their execution on April 9, 1980.

• **A. Thiagarajh**, a Tamil member of the Sri Lankan parliament representing Vadukkoddai, was assassinated by Tamil terrorists on April 24, 1981.

• **Heinz Nittel** (1931–81), a leader of the Austrian Socialist party and the president of the Austrian-Israeli Friendship League, was shot to death on May 1, 1981, outside his Vienna home. Nittel was the transportation minister for the regional government in Vienna.

• **Brig. Gen. Andres Gonzalez De Suso** was shot to death outside of his apartment in Madrid on May 4, 1981. The assassins were thought to be members of GRAPO, a Maoist terrorist group.

• **Heinz Herbert Karry** (1920–81), the minister of economic affairs in Hesse, West Germany, and the state deputy prime minister, was shot to death while sleeping at his home in Frankfurt on May 11, 1981. Karry was a member of the Free Democratic party and had recently been involved in supporting the construction of new atomic power plants.

• Pope John Paul II (b.1920) was shot and seriously wounded on May 13, 1981, in Rome The pope was struck by two bullets which were fired at him as he was being driven through a crowd in St. Peters' Square. He was immediately rushed to the hospital, where he underwent surgery for the partial removal of his intestines. Following a long hospital stay the pope eventually recovered. The assassin was identified as Mehmet Ali Agca (b.1958), a Turk, who was convicted of the crime and sentenced to life imprisonment. Ali Agca had previously been convicted of the murder of a moderate Turkish newspaper editor, Abdi Ipekci, on February 1, 1979. There was much speculation that a wider conspiracy involving the Bulgarian Secret Service existed. Several Bulgarians were indicted in that regard, and tried for complicity in the shooting.

• **Ziaur Rahman**, the president of Bangladesh, was murdered on May 30, 1981, during an unsuccessful coup attempt. President Zia, two aides, and several bodyguards were shot to death while sleeping in a guest house in Chittagong. Ziaur Rahman was born in Bogra on January 19, 1936. He joined the Pakistani army in 1953 and was commissioned two years later. He fought in the Indo-Pakistan War in 1965 and taught at the Pakistan Military Academy from 1966 until 1969. Zia soon became a supporter of the Bengali nationalist movement. He had been promoted to major at the time of East Pakistan's war for independence. He led his forces into rebellion, and in March of 1971, he proclaimed the independence of Bangladesh on a radio broadcast. He organized the First Brigade of the Bangladesh army in the fall of 1971. Following Bangladesh's independence, Zia was named army deputy chief of staff in June of 1972. He was named army chief of staff after the ouster of President Mujibur Rahman (q.v.) in August of 1975. He was subsequently named deputy chief martial law administrator in November of 1975. He became chief martial law administrator in November of 1976. Zia became president of Bangladesh on April 21, 1977, following the resignation of Abu Sadat Mohammed Sayem. He announced plans to hold democratic elections, but was slow to fulfill his promises. He survived a coup attempt in November of 1977. In June of 1978 Bangladesh held a presidential election, and Zia retained office by a wide margin. Though Bangladesh remained one of the world's poorest nations, Zia was given credit for having brought some reforms and stability to the nation. Following his murder Vice President Abdus Sattar took office as president and succeeded in putting down the revolt. On June 2, 1981, it was reported that

**Maj. Gen. Manzur Ahmed**, the leader of the coup, and two other high-ranking officers were killed by enraged guards following their arrest.

• **Naim Khader**, an official of the Palestine Liberation Organization, was shot to death in Brussels, Belgium, on June 1, 1981, while on his way to work. Khader had been working in the PLO's Brussels office since 1976 as a lobbyist for the PLO in the Common Market. Khader, a moderate, was killed by a lone gunman who shot him at close range. The assassination was speculated to be the work of either the Israeli Secret Service or Arab extremists.

• On June 22, 1981, following the ouster of Abolhassan Bani-Sadr as president of Iran, a number of his supporters were executed as "counter-revolutionaries." Among the thirty-two people shot by a firing squad were **Saeed Soltanpur**, a poet and playwright; **Ali-Ashghar Amirani**, editor and publisher of a biweekly news magazine critical of the government; and **Borzu Abbasi Shirin-Abadai**, who was said to have been the head of Savak, the deposed shah's secret police. Shirin-Abadai was thought to have participated in the 1954 coup that had returned the shah to the throne. Between June and October over 2,000 more executions took place in Iran.

• Hojatolislam Mohammed Ali Khameini, a leading Iranian defense adviser to the Ayatollah Khomeini, was seriously injured in a bomb blast while he was addressing a crowd in a Teheran mosque on June 27, 1981. Khameini recovered from his injuries.

Other Iranian leaders were less fortunate on the following day as an explosion on June 28, 1981, ripped the offices of the Islamic Republican party in Teheran, resulting in the deaths of over thirty people. Included among the dead were chief justice **Ayatollah Mohammed Beheshti**, environmental minister **Dr. Mohammed Ali Fayazbaksh**, deputy commerce minister **Assadolah Zadeh**, transport minister **Musa Kalantari**, and **Hojatoleslam Mohammed Montazeri**, a Teheran prayer leader and member of the Iranian parliament. Other victims included two other members of the Iranian cabinet, eight deputy ministers and nearly two dozen members of he Majlis (parliament). More than seventy other party members were injured in the bomb blast that occurred while Beheshti, the party leader, was addressing the assembly. The explosive device was placed near the speaker's podium during a meeting called to select a new Iranian president following the ouster of Abolhassan Bani-Sadr.

Ayatollah Mohammad Hossein Beheshti was born in 1929 in Isfahan, Iran. Beheshti had served as a member of Iran's ruling Islamic Revolutionary Council since February 3, 1979, and became the first secretary of the Council shortly thereafter. Beheshti was a close advisor to Ayatollah Ruhollah Khomeini and had played a leading role during the seizure of the American Embassy in Teheran and the subsequent hostage crisis. Shortly before his death Beheshti had orchestrated the ouster of Iranian president Abolhassan Bani-Sadr. He was in the process of selecting Bani-Sadr's replacement at the time of his death.

• Political violence continued in Iran throughout the remainder of the year. During the period of July 8–15, 1981, over forty leftists and supporters of deposed president Bani-Sadr were executed. The slain included **Karim Dastmalchi** and **Ahmad Javameriyan**, both prominent Teheran businessmen and members of the Teheran Bazaar, a group of merchants who had helped finance the ouster of the shah in 1979.

• On July 23, 1981, **Hojatolislam Seyyed Hassan Beheshti**, the nephew of the assassinated Ayatollah Beheshti (q.v.), was himself killed at his home in Isfahan. The younger Beheshti was a candidate for the Majlis at the time of his death. **Hassan Ayat**, a member of the ruling Islamic Republic party and one of its leading theoreticians, was shot and killed in Teheran on August 5, 1981. **Saleh Khosravi**, a mullah from Sanandaj, Iran, was assassinated with his son while leaving a mosque on August 16, 1981.

• The rash of assassinations and political killing culminated on August 30, 1981, when a bomb exploded in the office of Iranian premier **Mohammed Jad Bahonar**. Bahonar, President **Mohammed Ali Raja'i, Col. Houshang Dastgerdi** of the national police, and five others died as a result of the explosion. The Mujahedeen-i-Khaq, a leftist guerrilla group and the leading opposition front to the Ayatollah Khomeini's regime, was considered to be responsible for this and other attacks on the Iranian leadership. It was later announced by Teheran radio that **Massoud Kashmiri**, a secretary to Prime Minister Bahonar, was directly involved in the placing of the bomb. Kashmiri had also died in the explosion.

Mohammed Ali Raja'i was born in Kazvin in 1933. He was educated at the Graduate Teachers College in Teheran, where he received a degree in 1960. He became involved in anti-government activities in the 1960s and was arrested and tortured on several occasions. Following the overthrow of the shah in January of 1979, he became a leader of the Association of Islamic Teachers. He was subsequently named to the cabinet as minister of education. Raja'i was nominated under duress by President Abolhassan Bani-Sadr to succeed Medhi Bazargan as prime minister on August 12, 1980. When Bani-Sadr was forced out of the presidency the following year, Raja'i was elected to succeed him on June 24, 1981. His term of office was cut short when he was killed along with other Iranian politicians in a bomb blast in the prime minister's office on August 30, 1981.

Mohammed Javad Bahonar was born in Kerman in 1934. He studied theology under the Ayatollah Khomeini in Qoom and was active in the opposition movement to the shah's regime. He was arrested in the early 1960s for his activities, and in 1962 he was a founder of an underground political organization with Mohammed Ali Raja'i (q.v.). He was a follower of Khomeini while the Ayatollah was in exile and was instrumental in organizing strikes and demonstrations against the shah. Following the ouster of the shah in January of

1979, Bahonar served as a member of the Revolutionary Council. He was also involved in the drafting of the new Iranian constitution. He was named to Raja'i's cabinet as minister of education in March of 1981. He was also elected leader of the Islamic Republic party following the death of Ayatollah Mohammed Beheshti (q.v.) in a bomb explosion in June of 1981. When Prime Minister Raja'i was selected to replace Abolhassan Bani-Sadr as president, Bahonar was named prime minister. He took office on August 4, 1981. He was killed with Raja'i and other leading Iranian officials when a bomb exploded in his office on August 30, 1981.

• **Hojatolislam Nasser Jamali**, a court officer in Teheran, and clergyman **Hojatolislam Mortraza Ayatollahi Tabataba Yazdi** were assassinated in Teheran on August 31, 1981. On September 5, another bomb explosion killed **Hojatolislam Ali Qoddousi**, the Iranian revolutionary prosecutor general. On September 11 **Ayatollah Assadollah Madani**, a leading advisor to Ayatollah Khomeini, was assassinated during a grenade attack in Tabriz, the capital of the Iranian East Azerbaijan province. Seven others were killed during the attack, including the assassin, who had rushed Madani while holding a hand grenade. **Hojatolislam Abdulkarim Hashemi Nejad**, an Iranian parliament member, was also killed in a suicide grenade attack on September 29. Nejad was the Islamic Republic party's secretary general in Meshed Iran.

• **Chen Wen-Cheng**, a professor at Carnegie-Mellon University in Pittsburgh, was found dead on the campus of the National Taiwan University on July 3, 1981. Chen's death occurred following an interrogation by Taiwan security forces regarding his association with a Taiwan independence movement in the United States. The United States State Department requested a full investigation of Chen's death.

• On July 6, 1981, the body of **Giuseppe Taliercio**, an Italian executive of the Montredison petrochemical works, was found in the trunk of an automobile near his business. Taliercio had been kidnapped by Red Brigade terrorists in May of 1981.

• **Thomas Weh Syen**, Liberia's deputy head of state, and four other members of the ruling People's Redemption Council were executed on August 14, 1981, following an unsuccessful coup attempt against Samuel Doe (q.v.), the nation's leader. The executed men had all been supporters of Doe when he seized power in the 1980 coup that deposed President William Tolbert (q.v.).

• **Louis Delamare** (1922–81), the French ambassador to Lebanon, was shot and killed while driving in West Beirut on September 4, 1981. Delamare had served in Lebanon since 1979, and had previously held diplomatic positions in Romania, Turkey and Tunisia. He had served as France's ambassador to Dahomey (Benim) from 1969 to 1975, and was the French Foreign Ministry's director of press information from 1975 until assuming his post in Lebanon.

• On September 15, 1981, Gen. Frederick Kroesen, the commander-in-chief of United States forces in Europe, was slightly injured when an anti-tank grenade struck the car he was riding in near his Heidelberg, West Germany, headquarters.

• **Anwar al-Sadat**, the president of Egypt, was assassinated during a military parade in Nasr City, near Cairo, on October 6, 1981, by a group of commandos who charged the reviewing stand with grenades and machine guns. At least eight other members of Sadat's party were killed, including the president's private secretary, chief chamberlain, and official photographer. A delegate from Oman was also slain. The Belgian and Irish ambassadors to Egypt, leading Coptic clergyman Bishop Samuel, and three American military observers were among the dozens injured. The attack was led by Lt. Khaled Ahmed al-Istambouly (1957–82). Though several attackers were killed by presidential guards, Istambouly and four others survived and were indicted and convicted of direct participation in the attack. Twenty other Egyptians were also indicted for conspiracy, including Aboud el-Zoumar, who was considered the leader of the conspiracy, and Sheik Omar Abdel Rahman, a mufti from Asyut, Egypt. The assassination was intended to install a Moslem religious government with Sheik Rahman as head of state. Sadat was succeeded by his vice president, Hosni Mubarak, who vowed to continue Sadat's domestic and foreign policies.

Anwar al-Sadat was born in Talah Monufiya on December 25, 1918. He was educated in Cairo and entered the Royal Military Academy in 1936. He met Gamal Abdel Nasser at the Academy and, after his graduation in 1938, participated in the formation of the Free Officers Group dedicated to the ousting of the Egyptian monarchy. Sadat's hatred of the British resulted in his collaboration with the Germans during World War II. He was arrested and court-martialed for his activities in October of 1942. He was dismissed from the army and imprisoned in a detention camp, but he escaped in November of 1944 and went into hiding. Sadat engaged in revolutionary activities and was again arrested on charges of terrorism in 1946. In 1949 he was released and he was allowed to resume his career in the army the following year. Sadat was involved in Nasser's conspiracy to overthrow King Farouk in July of 1952. He served as a member of the ruling Revolutionary Command Council and served as Nasser's minister of state from 1954 to 1956. The following year he became secretary-general of the National Union, Egypt's only legal political party. He was elected president of the National Assembly in 1961 and also served as one of Nasser's four vice presidents from 1964 until Nasser restructured the government after the Six Day War in 1967. Nasser named Sadat his vice president in December of 1969, and Sadat succeeded to the presidency when Nasser died of a heart attack on September 28, 1970. The National Assembly confirmed his succession the following month. Sadat vowed to continue Nasser's policies and extended the truce agreement with Israel that Nasser had negotiated. He also dedicated the Aswan Dam in January

of 1971, a project that had been initiated by Nasser a decade earlier. Sadat also negotiated the creation of the Federation of Arab Republics with Libya and Syria in 1971. He expelled Soviet military personnel from Egypt in July of 1972 when he was denied an increase in military assistance. Sadat also took the post of prime minister in March of 1973. He abrogated the 1967 cease-fire agreement with Israel on October 6, 1973, and launched an attack across the Suez Canal. Egyptian forces gained ground in the Sinai Peninsula before agreeing to another cease-fire. Egypt also reestablished diplomatic relations with the United States in November of 1973. The slow process of peace negotiations in the Middle East led Sadat to begin an independent initiative in 1977. In a daring attempt to break the stalemate, Sadat offered to go to Israel to present his views to the Israeli government. Israeli prime minister Menachem Begin issued an invitation, and Sadat visited Jerusalem on November 19, 1977. Negotiations between Egypt and Israel continued with the support of the United States at Camp David, Maryland. This led to the signing of an Israeli-Egyptian peace treaty in March of 1979. Though Sadat and Begin were awarded the Nobel Peace Prize in 1978, Sadat was vilified throughout most of the Arab world for what was considered his betrayal of the long-standing goal to destroy Israel. Sadat initially remained popular in Egypt, but was threatened with domestic unrest when the Egyptian economy failed to improve. Sadat gained the antipathy of Iran when he offered asylum to the exiled shah in July of 1980. Sadat also initiated a crackdown on Muslim fundamentalists who were involved in civil unrest against the government. These actions led to his assassination during a military parade on October 6, 1981.

• **Majed Abu Shrar**, a leading member of the Palestine Liberation Organization, died in a bomb explosion in his hotel room in Rome Italy, on October 9, 1981.

• **Mohinder Paul**, the leader of the opposition Janata party in India, was assassinated by Sikh assassins in Punjab on October 23, 1981.

• **The Rev. Robert John Bradford** (1941–81), a Northern Ireland politician and Methodist clergyman, was shot and killed by Irish Republican Army gunmen in Belfast on November 14, 1981. He became the first member of the United Kingdom Parliament from Northern Ireland to be assassinated. The Rev. Bradford was a leading Protestant politician in Northern Ireland. He was first elected to the Northern Ireland Assembly in 1973 and served as a member of the Official Unionist party from South Belfast in the United Kingdom Parliament from 1975. He was an outspoken opponent of the Irish Republican Army and an advocate of the death sentence for convicted terrorists.

• On December 11, 1981, **Ayatollah Abdol-Hossein Dastgheib** (1912–81), the Ayatollah Khomeini's representative in Shiraz, was killed with seven others during a bomb attack at his home. Two other supporters of the Ayatollah Khomeini, **Mojtaba Ozbaki**, a member of the Iranian parliament from Shahr-I-Kourd in central Iran, and **Gholamali Jaaffarzzadeh**, the governor of Meshed, were slain by grenades in Meshed on December 22, 1981. The two were traveling in a motorcade toward a Shiite Moslem holy shrine when they were attacked by two grenade-wielding men on a motorcycle.

• **Mehmet Shehu**, the premier of Albania, who was considered to be a potential successor to Albanian Communist party chairman Enver Hoxha, was reported to have committed suicide on December 18, 1981. Speculation indicated that Shehu may have been executed instead due to his failing relationship with Hoxha. Mehmet Shehu was born in Corush on January 10, 1913. He joined the Communist party in the 1930s and fought against the Fascists in the Spanish Civil War. Shehu fought against the Italian and German occupation forces during World War II. He became army chief of staff following the war. Shehu was an ally of Enver Hoxha, and he opposed a proposed federation between Al-

bania and Yugoslavia. He succeeded Koci Xoxe (q.v.) as minister of the interior in 1948 when Xoxe was ousted following a purge of pro–Tito sympathizers in Albania. Shehu was also appointed to the Politburo and became deputy premier. When Hoxha relinquished the position of prime minister, Shehu succeeded him in July of 1954. He attempted to promote industry and agriculture in Albania, but the Albanian economy continued to falter after the Soviet Union, and later China, cut off economic aid. Viewed as a likely successor to Hoxha as leader of the Communist Party, Shehu came into conflict with his longtime ally when he began advocating an opening of relations with the West. Shehu resigned as Albania's defense minister early in 1981, and his death on December 18, 1981, was reported by the Albanian government that he had committed suicide "at a moment of nervous distress." The absence of a state funeral indicated that Shehu's cause of death may have been the result of an execution following his fall from power rather than suicide.

# 1982

• **Lt. Col. Charles Robert Ray** (1939–82), a United States military attaché to the American Embassy in Paris, was shot dead outside his home on January 18, 1982, by a lone gunman. A Beirut terrorist organization called the Lebanese Armed Revolutionary Faction claimed responsibility for the assassination.

• **Kemal Arikan** (1928–82), the Turkish consul general in Los Angeles, was assassinated by two gunmen while he sat in his car at a busy intersection on January 28, 1982. An Armenian terrorist group, the Justice Commandos of the Armenian Genocide, claimed responsibility for the killing. Arikan was the twentieth Turkish diplomat slain by Armenian terrorists in ten years.

- **Sgt. Maj. Willem Hawker**, the leader of an unsuccessful rebellion in Suriname in 1981, was executed by the ruling national military council on March 12, 1982.

- **Ali Hajem Sultan**, the third secretary of the Iraqi Embassy in Beirut, Lebanon, was assassinated by three gunmen in the Lebanese Christian-dominated suburb of Hazmiye on March 22, 1982.

- **Benedicto Santos**, the chief of the Guatemalan National Police Command Six, was shot and killed by leftist rebels while driving near the capital of Guatemala on March 28, 1982.

- **Datuk Mohammad Taha Abdul Talib**, the speaker of the Negri Sembilan State Assembly in Malaysia, was assassinated on April 14, 1982. Talib was a United Malays National Organization candidate for the National Assembly at the time of his murder. **Datuk Mokhtar Bin Haji Hashim**, the Malaysian federal minister of culture, youth, and sports, was charged with the killing and executed in April of 1983.

- **Sheik Ahmed Assaf**, a Lebanese Moslem religious leader, was shot to death in Moslem West Beirut on April 26, 1982.

- **Pio La Torre** (1927–82), a leading Italian Communist politician in Sicily, was shot to death with his driver near the Communist Party headquarters in Palermo on April 30, 1982. La Torre was a member of the Italian Parliament and an outspoken opponent of the Italian Mafia. He served on the Anti-Mafia Commission in parliament and had sponsored legislation to give the police more powers to combat organized crime.

- **Muhammad Seddik Ben Yahia**, the foreign minister of Algeria, died in a mysterious plane crash on May 3, 1982. Ben Yahia, who had been instrumental in negotiating the release of American hostages from Iran in 1981, was on a diplomatic mission to seek a solution to the war between Iraq and Iran. It was speculated that Ben Yahia's plane may have been deliberately shot down by a faction in Iran which did not want his peace initiatives to take place. Ben Yahia was born in Djidjelli, lower Kabylia, in 1932. He studied law and became involved with the Algerian nationalist movement in the 1950s. He served in the Algerian government after independence, becoming ambassador to Moscow in 1963. He was named to Houari Boumedienne's cabinet as minister of information in 1966 and, in 1971, became minister of higher education and scientific research. Ben Yahia had served as Foreign Minister since January of 1979.

- **Orham Gunduzi**, the honorary Turkish consul general in New England, was shot to death in Somerville, Massachusetts, on May 4, 1982. His assailant was believed to be an Armenian terrorist.

- **Angel Pascual Mugica**, the director of Spain's Lemoniz Nuclear Power Plant, was shot to death by Basque terrorists while driving to work on May 5, 1982.

- On June 3, 1982, Shlomo Argov, Israel's ambassador to Great Britain, was seriously injured in an assassination attempt in London. Black June, a militant Palestinian terrorist group led by Abu Nidal, claimed responsibility for the attack.

- **Erkut Akbay**, an attaché at the Turkish embassy in Portugal, was shot and killed by Armenian terrorists on June 7, 1982, outside his home in Lisbon.

- **Kamal Hussein**, a Palestine Liberation Organization official in Rome, Italy was killed in a car bomb explosion near his office on June 17, 1982. It was believed that Hussein's killers were members of a Jewish terrorist organization.

- **Koenyame Chakela**, the secretary general of the outlawed Basotho Congress party of Lesotho, was shot and killed in July of 1982.

- **Fadel el-Dani** (1944–82), the deputy director of the Palestine Liberation Organization's office in Paris, was killed by a bomb blast outside his Paris home on July 23, 1982.

- **Romiro Ponce**, the mayor of San Lorenzo, El Salvador, was killed by leftist guerrillas on August 4, 1982.

• **Ruth First** (1925–82), a South African political activist and writer, was killed on August 17, 1982, by a letter bomb sent to her office at the Centre for African Studies in Maputo, Mozambique. First had been a leading opponent of South Africa's apartheid system, and was a member of the banned Revolutionary Council of the African National Congress. She had been imprisoned by the South African government in the early 1960s, and had lived in exile in Mozambique since 1978.

• **Col. Atilla Altikat**, a Turkish military attaché in Ottawa, Canada, was shot and killed by Armenian terrorists while driving to work on August 27, 1982.

• **Gen. Carlos Alberto Dalla Chiesa**, one of Italy's highest ranking police officers, was shot and killed in Palermo, Sicily, on September 3, 1982. Dalla Chiesa, as prefect of police for Palermo, was a leading figure in the fight against the Mafia in Italy. His wife and bodyguard were also killed in the attack, which was presumed to have been initiated by the Italian Mafia.

• **Zahoorul Hasan Bhopali**, a member of the Pakistani Federal Council, was slain by gunmen at his office on September 13, 1982.

• **Bashir Gemayel**, the president-elect of Lebanon, was killed in a bomb blast which leveled the headquarters of his Lebanese Christian Phalangist party in Beirut on September 14, 1982. Bashir Gemayel was born on November 10, 1947, in Beirut. He was the sixth son of Pierre Gemayel, the leader and founder of the Phalangist party. He studied law in the United States and became active in politics on his return to Lebanon. During the Lebanese Civil War of 1975–76, Gemayel became known as a fierce and ruthless leader of the Christian militias in the fight against Palestinians and Moslems. In the following years Gemayel continued conducting an armed struggle against his foes, as well as against fellow Christian militia rivals. He had twice before been the target of assassination attempts. The second attempt, on February 23, 1980, resulted in the death of his eighteen-month-old daughter, Maya, in a car bombing.

When Lebanese president Elias Sarkis announced his retirement in mid–1982, Gemayel became a candidate for the presidency. With the tacit support of Israel, Gemayel was elected by the Lebanese parliament on August 12, 1982. At 34 he would have become Lebanon's youngest president had he survived until his inauguration later in the month. Amid the continuing deterioration of the political situation in Lebanon, the parliament selected Gemayel's older brother, Amin, as the new president. Habib Shartuni, the man who planted the bomb that killed Gemayel, was captured and imprisoned. He was released in the mid–1980s, when the Lebanese state collapsed.

• **Brig. Saad Sayel** (1929–82), known as **Abu Walid**, was killed by gunmen near Beirut, Lebanon, on September 28, 1982. Walid was a leading military strategist for the PLO and had organized resistance to the Israeli siege of Lebanon.

• **Ayatollah Ashrafi Isfahani** (1899–1982) was killed by a grenade blast in Bahtaran, Iran, on October 15, 1982. Isfahani was the Ayatollah Khomeini's special representative in the Bahtaran Province. The attacker, who was also killed in the blast, was thought to be a member of the underground People's Mujahedeen guerrillas.

• **Gen. Victor Lago Roman** (1919–82), the Spanish commander of the elite Brunete First Armored Division in Madrid, was shot to death by machine gun fire on November 4, 1982.

# 1983

• **William Doyle**, a Catholic judge in Northern Ireland, was shot to death in front of St. Bridget's Church in South Belfast on January 16, 1983. The Provisional Irish Republican Army claimed responsibility for the murder.

• **Ahmed Dlimi** (1931–83), a leading military advisor to King Hassan II of Morocco, was killed in a car crash on January 25, 1983, in Marrakesh. Dlimi was in charge of the Moroccan army's operation against the Polisario Front in the Western Sahara at the time of his death. While serving as Morocco's security chief in the 1960s, Dlimi had been tried and acquitted by a French court for the abduction of Moroccan exile leader Mehdi Ben Barka (q.v.) in Paris in 1965. It was speculated that Dlimi may have been involved in a conspiracy against King Hassan, and that he may have been assassinated.

• **Attati Mpakati**, an opponent of Malawi president Hastings Banda, was assassinated by a letter bomb in Zimbabwe on March 28, 1983.

• **Issam Sartawi**, a moderate leader of the Palestine Liberation Organization, was shot to death in his hotel lobby on April 10, 1983, while attending a meeting of the Socialist International in Portugal. Sartawi was born in Palestine in 1935. He was a heart surgeon working in the United States in 1967, but following the Arab-Israeli War, he returned to the Middle East to join the Palestine Liberation Organization's guerrilla wing, Al-Fatah. His militancy toward Israel declined over the years, and Sartawi became one of the leading voices of moderation in the PLO. A close adviser to PLO chairman Yasir Arafat, Sartawi was one of the few Palestinian leaders to openly advocate Palestinian coexistence with Israel. The Revolutionary Council of the Fatah (or Black June group), led by terrorist leader Abu Nidal, claimed responsibility for the killing.

• **Dick Matenje**, the secretary general of the Malawi Congress party, was killed with three other political leaders in an automobile accident on May 22, 1983. **Aaron Gadama**, the minister of the central region; **John Sangala**, a former minister of health; and **David Chiwanga**, a former member of the Parliament, were also killed. Matenje was thought to be a potential rival to President Hastings K. Banda, and some claimed that Matenje and

the others had been killed following an unsuccessful coup attempt.

• **Benigno Aquino, Jr.**, a leading opponent of President Ferdinand Marcos of the Philippines, was shot and killed as he was debarking an airplane at the Manila airport on August 21, 1983. Benigno Simeon Aquino, Jr. was born in Tarlac, the Philippines, on November 27, 1932. In 1955, following a career as a journalist, Aquino was elected mayor of Concepcion. He became governor of Tarlac Province in 1961, following two years as vice governor. In 1966 he became the secretary general of the Liberal party, and the following year he became the only member of his party to win a seat in the Senate. Aquino was viewed as a potential rival to the presidency of Ferdinand Marcos, but was imprisoned following Marcos' declaration of martial law in September of 1972. Aquino was sentenced to death and served eight years in prison. In 1980 he was allowed to travel to the United States for open-heart surgery. He remained in the United States for the next three years, until deciding to return to the Philippines in the summer of 1983. Aquino, who had received death threats prior to his arrival, was shot and killed on the heavily guarded tarmac as he left the plane at Manila Airport. His alleged assassin, Roland Galman, was immediately killed by security guards. A number of high-ranking army officers were subsequently implicated for complicity in the assassination of Aquino, including armed forces chief of staff Gen. Fabian Ver and airport security chief Brig. Gen. Luther Custodio, but charges were never substantiated. The killing of Aquino led to increased pressure on the government of Ferdinand Marcos, culminating in his defeat as president by Aquino's widow, Corazon, in early 1985. In September of 1990 a Filipino general and fifteen soldiers were convicted of Aquino's murder and sentenced to life in prison.

• On September 1, 1983, Korean Airlines flight 007 was shot down over the Sea of Japan by the Soviet military after allegedly crossing over into Soviet air space. Among those who perished aboard the downed airliner was **Lawrence P. "Larry" McDonald**, a conservative Democratic Congressman from Georgia. McDonald was born in Atlanta, Georgia, on April 1, 1935. He had served as U.S. Representative from Georgia's 7th District since 1975. His remains were never recovered.

• A bomb attack in Burma on October 9, 1983, killed nineteen people, including six top aides to South Korean president Chun Doo Hwan. The bomb exploded when South Korean officials, on a state visit to Burma, were lined up at Rangoon's national cemetery. Chun escaped death in the blast due to his motorcade's delay in traffic. Among the killed were **Lee Bum-Suk** (1925–83), South Korean foreign minister and a former ambassador to Tunisia and India; **Kim Jae-Ik** (1938–83), a senior presidential economic adviser who was the architect of South Korea's economic liberalism; **Kim Dong-Whie** (1932–83), South Korean minister of commerce and industry and former ambassador to Iran; **Suh Sang Chul** (1935–83), the minister of energy and resources; **Suh Suk-Joon** (1938–83), deputy premier and economic planning minister; and **Hahm Pyong-Choon** (1932–83), chief secretary. The South Korean ambassador to Burma was also among the dead. The seriously injured included Lee Kee-Baek, chairman of the joint chiefs of staff, and Lee Ki-uk, the vice finance minister. The South Korean government blamed the attack on North Korean terrorists.

• Political violence in El Salvador escalated on October 10, 1983, with the murder of **Victor Manuel Quintanilla**, a leftist politician in El Salvador and mayor of Usulutan from 1979 to 1980. Also killed at this time were **Jose Antonio Garcia Vasquez**, a member of the Democratic Revolutionary Front; **Santiago Hernandez**, secretary general of the Unified Labor Federation; and **Prof. Doira Munoz Castillo**, a chemistry professor at the National University. Fifteen other labor activists and three other professors had been kidnapped or killed during the previous six weeks. The Maximiliano Hernandez Martinez Anti-Communist Brigade, a rightist death squad, claimed it carried out the killings. The bodies were dumped along a highway north of San Salvador.

Another victim of right-wing violence was **Marianella Garcia Villas**, a founder of the Salvadoran Commission for Human Rights, who was murdered on March 14, 1983.

• **Maurice Bishop**, prime minister of Grenada since 1979, was executed on October 19, 1983, after his removal from office in a coup. Others shot following the coup were foreign affairs minister **Unison Whiteman**, education minister **Jacqueline Creft**, housing minister **Norris Bain**, **Cecil Maitland**, and **Keith Hayling**. An estimated sixty other people also died during and after the coup.

Bishop was born in Grenada on May 29, 1944. While practicing law in Great Britain, Bishop became interested in the black militancy movement and returned to Grenada in 1970. He was a founder of the left-wing New Jewel Movement in 1972 along with his law partner, Bernard Coard. Bishop's group was a leading voice of opposition to Prime Minister Eric Gairy and was thus a prime target of the political violence unleashed by Gairy's secret police, called the Mongoose Gang. Bishop was beaten on several occasions, and in 1974, his father, Rupert, was murdered. In 1976 Bishop was elected to the Grenada parliament, and in March of 1979, he seized power while Gairy was out of the country. Bishop was an avowed Marxist and gained financial assistance for his country from Cuba and the Soviet Union. Following an attempt by Bishop to improve relations with the United States, the more radical members of his government, including Coard and Gen. Hudson Austin, seized power and arrested Bishop and several of his aides. It was reported that Bishop was freed from house arrest by a mob of supporters, but was subsequently recaptured by the army and executed within Fort Rupert. Following the overthrow of the new government by direct American military intervention, the coup leaders were arrested. In February of 1984 eleven people were accused in Magistrates Court of conspiracy to commit an act of terrorism and causing the deaths of Bishop and the others. The accused included Bernard Coard, the Marxist deputy prime minister who led the coup attempt; his wife, Phyllis; Gen. Hudson Austin, head of the military junta; Selwyn Strachan, Bishop's minister of national mobilization, and Leon Cornwall, Grenada's ambassador to Cuba under Bishop.

- **Sheik Halim Takieddine** (1923–83), a moderate Druze religious judge in West Beirut, Lebanon, was shot to death on December 1, 1983, by a lone assassin.

# 1984

- **Giuseppe Fava** (1925–84), an Italian novelist and journalist who was a prominent critic of organized crime, was found murdered in his car in Catania, Sicily, on January 5, 1984.
- **Malcolm H. Kerr** (1932–84), the president of the American University of Beirut, Lebanon, was shot and killed by two gunmen on January 18, 1984. Dr. Kerr, a scholar in Middle Eastern affairs, was ambushed as he stepped from an elevator leading to his office at the university.
- **Amar Tagazy**, the Libyan ambassador to Italy, was shot and mortally wounded by two gunmen near his home in Rome on January 21, 1984. Tagazy died of his injuries on February 10, 1984.
- **Ricardo Arnold Pohl**, a member of El Salvador's Constituent Assembly, was shot to death on January 27, 1984. Pohl, a rightist, was ambushed by two gunmen while driving in San Salvador.
- **Lt. Gen. Guillermo Quintana Lacaci** (1917–84) of Spain, the retired military

commander of Madrid, was shot and killed by two Basque terrorists near his home in Madrid on January 29, 1984.

- **Ravindra Mhatre**, the assistant Indian high commissioner in Birmingham, England, was kidnapped on February 3, 1984, by members of the Kashmir Liberation Army. Mhatre's abductors demanded the release of condemned Kashmiri separatist leader **Magbool Butt**. When the demands were not met, Mhatre was murdered by his kidnappers on February 5. Butt was the founder of the Jammu-Kashmir Liberation Front and had been convicted of the murder of an Indian intelligence agent in Kashmir in 1965. He was under a sentence of death in New Delhi, and was subsequently hanged on February 11.

- **Gen. Gholam Ali Oveisi**, an exiled Iranian army officer, was shot to death on a Paris street on February 7, 1984, by an unidentified gunman. Oveisi, who had served as a leading military adviser to the deposed shah of Iran, was the head of an exile organization hostile to the government of the Ayatollah Khomeini.

- **Khalifa Ahmed Abdel Aziz Al-Mubarak** (1944–84), the United Arab Emirates ambassador to France since 1980, was shot and killed near his apartment in Paris on February 8, 1984. The Arab Revolutionary Brigade claimed responsibility for the assassination.

- **Enrique Casas Vila**, a Basque Socialist party senator in Spain, was murdered on February 23, 1984. The killing was thought to be the work of an extreme faction of Basque terrorists.

- **Antoine Indrissou Meatchi**, the former vice president of Togo, was reportedly tortured to death in prison in March of 1984. Meatchi was born in Lama Kara on September 23, 1925. He studied tropical agriculture in Africa and France. He entered the civil service in the early 1950s and was selected by Nicolas Grunitzky to serve as minister of agriculture in 1956. He was also named minister of finance the following year. A member of the

National Assembly, he led Grunitzky's Parti Togolais du Progres after Grunitzky lost office in 1958. Meatchi went into exile after his arrest for plotting against the government of President Sylvanio Olympio (q.v.) in 1961. He returned to Togo after Olympio was ousted and killed in January of 1963. Grunitzky and Meatchi returned from exile, serving as president and vice-president of the new government, respectively. Meatchi was dropped from the government in 1966 after leading an abortive coup against Grunitzky. He briefly served as minister of public works from December of 1966 until Grunitzky's ouster the following month. Under the new government of Gnassingbe Eyadema Meatchi served as director of agricultural services until 1978. He was arrested and imprisoned in 1982 on charges of corruption in office. It was reported that he had died in prison of a heart attack in 1987, but reports indicate that he had died due to torture and maltreatment in prison in March of 1984.

- **Kenneth Whitty** (1939–84), the British consul's assistant cultural representative in Athens, Greece, was shot to death on March 28, 1984, while driving in downtown Athens. His lone assailant was thought to be an Arab.

- A coup attempt against the government of Cameroon was launched on April 6, 1984. The coup failed when loyalist troops retained control of the military. **Issa Adoum**, a leading banker and civil servant, was considered the civilian leader of the coup. He was arrested soon after the coup's failure and executed on May 2, 1984.

- U.S. diplomat **Dennis Keough** and **Lt. Col. Ken Crabtree** were killed by a bomb booby trap at a gas station near Oshakati, Namibia, on April 14, 1984. The two men were part of a team to observe the withdrawal of South African troops in the area. The bombing was believed to have been orchestrated by SWAPO guerrillas.

- **Joaquim Alfredo Zapata Romero** (1925–84), the highest ranking Salvadoran employee at the United States Embassy in El Salvador, was shot and killed by leftist rebels near San Salvador on April 16, 1984. The rebel group RPB claimed that Zapata was the chieftain of right-wing death squads which acted in conjunction with the United States Embassy.

- **Rodrigo Lara Bonilla**, the Colombian Minister of Justice, was shot and killed on April 30, 1984, in northern Bogota. His assassination was believed to be the result of his efforts to eradicate the drug traffic in Colombia.

- **Hanna Moqbell** (1942–84), the secretary general of the Arab Journalists Union, was shot and killed in Nicosia, Cyprus, on May 3, 1984. Moqbell was a prominent opponent of PLO leader Yasir Arafat.

- **Manuel Buendia Tellez Giron** (1926–84), a prominent Mexican journalist, was shot to death on May 30, 1981, in Mexico City on the way home from his office. Buendia was the author of *Red Privada* (Private Network) in the Mexican daily *Excelsior*. He had frequently been responsible for exposure of corruption in politics, labor and business during his thirty-five-year career. At the time of his assassination he was engaged in writing a series of articles on Mexico's oil industry.

- **Jarnail Singh Bhindranwale**, a Sikh extremist leader, was killed during an Indian army attack on the Golden Temple, the holiest of Sikh shrines, in Amritsar, Punjab, on June 6, 1984. Jarnail Singh Bhindranwale was born in the Faridkot District of Punjab, India, in 1946, and began his religious education at an early age. He was adopted by Kartar Singh Bhindranwale, a Sikh leader, and assumed his name and title when he died in 1977. Bhindranwale became actively involved in Sikh extremism in 1980 and was charged in connection with the murder of moderate Sikhs. After his surrender to Indian authorities, and subsequent release three weeks later, Bhindranwale challenged the Indian government to grant autonomy to the Punjab region. On May 31, 1984, he openly rebelled against the government by threatening to withhold food and power produced in the Punjab from the rest of India. The Indian army was sent by Prime Minister Indira Gandhi (q.v.) to crush the uprising. Bhindranwale was killed with hundreds of his followers when the army entered the Golden Temple at Amritsar.

• **Brig. R.S. Puri**, a leading Indian army commander, was shot and killed in the northeastern state of Bihar on June 9, 1984. Suspected Sikh extremists assassinated **Hardyal Singh**, acting president of Indira Gandhi's Congress party, in the Punjab's Jullundur district, on June 16, 1984.

• **Alan Berg** (1934–84), a radio talk show host, was shot and killed outside his home in Denver, Colorado, on June 18, 1984. Berg was a former criminal lawyer who had gained a large following as a controversial host of a radio call-in program. Berg's murder was perpetrated by a member of an extremist anti–Semitic group.

• The violence in India culminated on October 31, 1984, with the assassination of Prime Minister **Indira Gandhi**. She was shot and killed near her New Delhi office by her Sikh bodyguards. Indira Priyadarshina Gandhi was born in Allahabad, India, on November 19, 1917. She was the only child of Jawaharlal Nehru, India's first prime minister. In 1942, after studying in England, she married Feroze Gandhi, against her father's wishes. This marriage later ended in divorce. In 1959 she first became prominent in political affairs with her election as president of the ruling Congress party. Following the death of her father in 1964, Mrs. Gandhi served as minister of information in the government of his successor, Lal Bahadur Shastri. When Shastri died in 1966, she became prime minister.

Mrs. Gandhi proved to be a capable and forceful politician at home and abroad. In 1971 she joined India in a successful war for independence of Bangladesh (formerly East Pakistan) from West Pakistan and, in 1971, incorporated the kingdom of Sikkim into India proper. Following a period of economic and political reversals in 1975, Mrs. Gandhi declared a state of emergency and ruled by de-

cree. During this period she instituted a number of unpopular measures, including sterilization in over-populated areas, and arrested political opponents. In 1977 she was defeated for election and replaced by the opposition Janata party. Following her defeat she was arrested on two occasions on charges of abuse of authority. In 1980 Mrs. Gandhi again became prime minister as her Congress (I) party defeated the Janata party. That same year saw the death of her elder son and potential successor, Sanjay Gandhi, in an aircraft accident.

Her greatest threat during her later years in office came from the Punjab region, where militant Sikhs agitated for an autonomous state. The unrest culminated in an attack by the Indian army on the Golden Temple, the Sikhs' holiest shrine, in Amritsar, resulting in the death of Sikh extremist leader Sant Jarnail Sing Bhindranwale (q.v.) and many of his followers. Several months later, Mrs. Gandhi was assassinated by her two Sikh bodyguards while walking to her office in New Delhi. The assassins were identified as Beant Singh and Satwant Singh (1963–89). Beant Singh was killed during a subsequent shoot-out with palace guards and, in January of 1986, Satwant Singh was sentenced to death. Two other Sikhs, Kehar Singh (1935–89) and Balbir Singh, were convicted of conspiracy and also received a death sentence. Kehar Singh and Satwant Singh were executed by hanging on January 6, 1989. Mrs. Gandhi was succeeded by her second son, Rajiv Gandhi (q.v.), as prime minister.

• On October 12, 1984, a bomb exploded in the Grand Hotel in Brighton, England, where the Conservative party was holding its annual meeting. British Prime Minister Margaret Thatcher, who was staying in the hotel at the time, was uninjured in the blast, which claimed the lives of **Sir Anthony Berry**, a member of parliament; **Roberta Wakeman**, the wife of Conservative party whip John Wakeman; **Jeanne Shattock**, the wife of the West England Conservative leader; and **Eric Taylor**, a Brighton party official. Over thirty other people at the hotel were injured, including John Wakeman and Norman Tebbit, the trade and industry secretary. The Irish Republican Army claimed responsibility for the attack, citing Mrs. Thatcher's policy on Northern Ireland and the reason.

• **Santos Hernandez** (1928–84), who had served as a member of Guatemala's Constituent Assembly since July as a member of the right-wing Movement of National Liberation party, was shot to death by gunmen as he walked along a street in southern Guatemala City in October of 1984.

• On October 29, 1984, the body of Polish **Rev. Jerzy Popieluszko** (1947–84) was found in the waters of a reservoir, eleven days after he had been kidnapped by secret police officers. Popieluszko had been an active anti–Communist Roman Catholic clergyman in Poland and a strong supporter of the Polish Solidarity labor movement. He was the parish priest at St. Stanislaw Kostka Church in Warsaw, and had gained much attention for his "Masses for the Homeland," which he began in January of 1982. During these services Popieluszko had used his sermon as a forum to denounce the Polish Communist authorities for their imposition of martial law or banning of trade unions. In October of 1984 Popieluszko was abducted near the town of Torun, near Warsaw. Eleven days later his brutally beaten body was found in the Wloclawek reservoir. Three secret police officers, Capt. Grzegorz Piotrowski, Lt. Waldemar Chmielewski and Lt. Leszek Pekala, were charged with the abduction and murder.

• **Jim Ntuta**, a Zimbabwe African People's Union (ZAPU) member of Parliament in Zimbabwe, was shot and killed on his Matabeleland farm in November of 1984. Ntuta was a supporter of Joshua Nkoma.

• **Moven Ndlovu** (1934–84), a senator and member of the Zimbabwe African National Union (ZANU), was assassinated in Beitbridge, Zimbabwe, on November 9, 1984.

• **Evner Ergun** (1932–84), the Turkish deputy director of the United Nations Center for Social Development and Humanitar-

ian Affairs in Vienna, Austria, was assassinated on November 18, 1984, while driving through downtown Vienna. The Armenian Revolutionary Army claimed responsibility for the killing.

• **Fouad Kawashmeh** (1936–84), the former mayor of the Israeli-occupied West Bank town of Hebron, was shot to death in front of his home in Amman, Jordan, on December 29, 1984. Kawashmeh was an Executive Committee member for the Palestine Liberation Organization and a supporter of chairman Yasir Arafat.

---

# 1985

---

• In January of 1985 violence broke out in the French colony of New Caledonia, an island group in the Pacific Ocean. Radical separatist Caledonians, or Kanaks, conducted a series of violent acts to drive the French into granting independence to New Caledonia. **Eloi Machoro**, a Kanak separatist leader, was killed in a shoot-out with police on January 12, 1985, and over a dozen other people died during the upheaval. Machoro was born in a tribe from Nakety in 1945. A teacher, he joined the CPU (Union Caledonienne) in 1977 and became secretary-general of the organization in October of 1981. He served as minister for security in the provisional independent government from November of 1984. His death was viewed as a political assassination by the independence movement and Machoro was regarded as a martyr by the Kanaks.

• **Domingo Aviles** (1929–85), the rightist mayor of Santa Elena, El Salvador, was assassinated by four unidentified gunmen while in his office on January 11, 1985. Aviles was a member of the National Conciliation party in El Salvador. A second rightist El Salvadorean politician was assassinated on January 18, 1985: **Graciela Monico Palma** (1960–85), mayor of San Jorge in eastern El Salvador and a member of the right-wing Nationalist Republican Alliance party, was shot to death in her office. On January 23, 1985, **Medardo Avelar Bonille**, a National Republican Alliance candidate for the National Assembly in El Salvador, was shot to death in San Salvador.

• **Rene Audran** (1930–85), a French Ministry of Defense official, was shot to death near his Paris suburb home on January 25, 1985. Audran was in charge of international arm sales. Direct Action, a left-wing guerrilla group allied with the German Red Army Faction, claimed responsibility for the assassination.

• **Ernst Zimmerman** (1930–85), a West German armaments manufacturer, was shot and killed at his home near Munich on February 1, 1985. Zimmerman was the chief executive of the Motoren und Turbinen Union G.m.b.H., a company which supplied engines for combat planes and tanks used by NATO and the West German military. The Red Army Faction, a left-wing guerrilla organization, claimed responsibility.

• **Leamon Hunt** (1929–85), an American diplomat, was shot and killed near his apartment in Rome on February 14, 1985. Hunt was Director General of the Multinational Observer Force assigned to the Sinai peninsula after the Camp David accords between Egypt and Israel. His apartment had served as the MOF's headquarter. Hunt had served in the Foreign Service for thirty-two years and was formerly assigned as charge d'affaires in Beirut, Lebanon.

• **Lt. Col. Ricardo Aristides Cienfuegos**, the El Salvadoran army's chief spokesman, was shot to death by unidentified gunmen at a private club near San Salvador on March 7, 1985. The assassins were believed to be members of the left-wing Farabundo Marti National Liberation Front (FMLN). This group claimed responsibility for a second high-ranking assassination on March 23, 1985, with the killing of retired **Gen. Jose Alberto Medrano**. Gen. Medrano was a former commander of the National Guard and the founder of the National Intelligence

Agency and the National Democratic Organization (Orden), which had been responsible for the killing of Salvadoran leftists in the 1970s. Medrano, a hero of the border war with Honduras in 1969, had been an unsuccessful presidential candidate in 1972.

• **Valentin Khitrichenko** (1937–85), a Soviet economic attaché stationed in New Delhi, India, was assassinated by a gunman near the Soviet Embassy on March 21, 1985.

• **Gerardo Veracruz Berrocal**, the Peruvian mayor of Pampa Cangallo in the Ayacucho department, was assassinated by left-wing Shining Path guerrillas on March 26, 1985.

• **Prof. Ezio Tarantelli** (1942–85), an Italian labor economist, was assassinated in Rome by Red Brigade terrorists on March 27, 1985. Tarantelli was an advisor to the Italian Federation of Unionized Workers and president of the Institute of Economic Studies at Rome University.

• **William Buckley** (1928–85), who was reportedly the Beirut station chief for the United States Central Intelligence Agency, was kidnapped in Beirut, Lebanon, on March 16, 1984. Buckley, who had been in Lebanon for several months prior to his capture, was presumed to have been in charge of reorganizing the United States' intelligence gathering network in the area. His kidnappers were identified as members of an Iranian-backed extremist group called the Islamic Jihad. On October 14, 1985, the Islamic Jihad announced that Buckley had been executed in retaliation for an Israeli raid against the Palestine Liberation Organization's headquarters in Tunisia. Though Buckley's body was not found, it was later assumed that he had perished in June of 1985, as the result of torture and lack of medical care.

• **Haruo I. Remeliik** (1934–85), the president of the western Pacific island republic of Palau, was shot and killed on June 29, 1985, at his home in the capital city of Koror. Remeliik had become Palau's first president in January of 1981. He had been reelected to a second term in the United States trusteeship in November of 1984. Four men were arrested and charged with the assassination in July. Among those charged were Melwert Tmetuchel, the son of Roman Tmetuchel, a political rival of Remeliik, Leslie Twed, and Anghelio Sabino. All were convicted of murder and sentenced to lengthy prison terms.

• **Ziad J. Sati** (1945–85), the first secretary of the Jordanian Embassy in Turkey, was shot to death by Shiite Moslem assassins while driving a car in Ankara, Turkey, on July 24, 1985.

• **Vice Adm. Fausto Escrigas Estrada** (1926–85) of the Spanish defense ministry was assassinated on July 29, 1985, by suspected Basque guerrillas while driving in downtown Madrid. Escrigas was the fiftieth Spanish military officer killed by Basque terrorists since the assassination of Prime Minister Luis Carrerro Blanco (q.v.) in 1973. Later in the day, **Agustin Ruiz** (1942–85), the deputy police chief of Vitoria, the Basque capital, was shot and killed near police headquarters by a lone gunman.

• **Lalit Maken** (1951–85), a first-term Congress (I) member of the Indian parliament and a prominent labor union leader, was shot and killed near his home in New Delhi on July 31, 1985. His wife, Geetanjali, and a party worker were also slain in the attack.

• **Pierre Mizael Andrianarijoana**, the leader of a Madagascan anti-government kung fu sect, was killed with nineteen of his followers in an attack by a government security force on their Antananarivo headquarters on August 1, 1985.

• **Dev Dutt Khullar** (1923–85), a Congress party member and Hindu village leader, was killed in an attack on the home of Gurdial Saini, the Congress party president, on August 20, 1985. Saini was seriously wounded in the attack, which was believed to have been carried out by Sikh militants.

• **Harchand Singh Longowal**, president of Akali Dal, the leading Sikh moderate party, was shot and killed by militant Sikhs in Punjab, India, on August 30, 1985. The assailants were reported to be Malvinder Singh and Gian Singh, both of whom were arrested and charged in the slaying. Sant Harchant Singh Longowal was born in Laungowal, Punjab, India, in 1928. He had joined the Akali Dal party in 1944 and had been a disciple of Mahatma Gandhi's policy of non-violent civil disobedience. In 1964 he had become president of the local chapter of the party, and in 1980 became president of the party. Longowal had been a moderate voice in the face of Sikh extremism, which culminated in militant Sikhs, under the leadership of Jarnail Singh Bhindranwale (q.v.), barricading themselves in the Golden Temple at Amritsar, and the subsequent storming of that Sikh holy shrine by Indian troops. Longowal's assassination followed the signing of an agreement with Prime Minister Rajiv Gandhi (q.v.) allowing Sikh autonomy for the Punjab, a move supported by the majority of Sikhs, but vehemently opposed by the extremists, who then orchestrated Longowal's assassination.

• **Arjun Dass** (1939–85), another leading Indian political figure, was shot to death on September 4, 1985, in New Delhi. His bodyguard was also killed in the attack and several other people were badly wounded. Dass, a Congress (I) party member of the New Delhi city council and a supporter of Prime Minister Rajiv Gandhi (q.v.), was assassinated by Sikh militants in a raid on his council office. Three Sikhs were arrested for Dass' murder.

• **Albert Atrakchi** (1955–85), an administrative attaché at the Israeli Embassy in Cairo, Egypt, was shot to death by machine gunfire near Cairo on August 20, 1985. His wife, Illana, and another embassy employee, Mazal Menashe, were also wounded in the attack. Atrakchi was the first Israeli diplomat slain in Egypt since diplomatic recognition was established in Egypt in 1979. A radical group called Egypt's Revolution claimed responsibility for the murder.

• **Mustafa Kassem Khalife**, a senior Palestinian guerrilla leader and supporter of Yassir Arafat, was killed at his home in the

Ein el-Hilweh refugee camp in Sidon, Lebanon, on August 29, 1985. Four days earlier, **Mohammed Shikhaani**, another Palestinian leader loyal to Arafat, had also been assassinated.

• Two Tamil members of the Sri Lankan parliament, **V. Dharmalingam** of Manipay and **K. Alalasundaram** of Kopay, were assassinated by Tamil Tiger terrorists on September 2, 1985.

• **Hugo Spadafora**, a leading critic of General Manuel Noriega's regime in Panama, was murdered under Noriega's orders on September 13, 1985. Spadafora's decapitated body was found near the Costa Rican border the following day.

• On October 2, 1985, **Arkady Katkov**, a Soviet diplomat who served as a consular secretary at the Soviet embassy in Beirut, Lebanon, was found shot to death. Katkov and three other Soviets, Oleg Spirin, Valery Mirkov and Dr. Nikolai Svirsky, had been kidnapped in West Beirut by a radical Muslim group, the Islamic Liberation Organization, on September 30, 1985. The Soviet government brought much pressure for the release of the three surviving hostages, who were returned unharmed on October 30, 1985.

• **Gregorio Murillo**, the governor of the southern Philippines province of Surigao del Sur, was shot to death on October 23, 1985, in the capital of Tadag. He was thought to be a victim of Communist insurgents.

• During a seventeen-hour siege on November 6 and 7, 1985, leftist guerrillas of the April 19 Movement took control of the Palace of Justice in Bogota, Colombia, and seized numerous hostages. Colombian soldiers, under orders from President Belisario Betancur, successfully ended the siege on November 7, 1985, by blowing down the walls of the Palace of Justice. Over fifty bodies were found within, including those of ten Supreme Court justices and most of the guerrillas. The dead included Chief Justice **Alfonso Reyes Enchandia**, magistrate **Manuel Gaona**, and auxiliary magistrate **Maria Ines Ramos**.

Also killed were guerrilla leader Andres Almarales and other rebel leaders including Vera Grave, Afranio Para, Antonio Jacquim, Francisco Otero, and Guillermo Eluencio Ruiz.

• **Gen. Thomas Quiwomkpa**, a leader of an unsuccessful coup attempt against President Samuel K. Doe (q.v.) of Liberia on November 12, 1985, was captured by loyalist troops and shot to death on November 15. Quiwomkpa was one of the officers who had aided Doe in seizing power from President William Tolbert (q.v.) in 1980. He had served as Liberia's armed forces commander from 1980 until 1983.

• **Gerard Hoarau**, exiled leader of the opposition to President France-Albert Rene of the Seychelles, was shot to death in front of his home in London on November 29, 1985.

# 1986

• **Ignacio Gonzalez Palacios**, the director of the Guatemalan secret police, was shot and killed while driving in Guatemala City on January 2, 1986.

• On January 13, 1986, **Abd-al Fattah Ismail**, a former president of South Yemen; **Ali Ahmed Nasser Antar**, the vice president and first deputy premier of South Yemen; and **Salih Muslih Qasim**, the defense minister, were killed following a coup attempt against President Ali Nasser Mohammed. Fighting between the factions of Ismail and Nasser developed into a civil war, with the forces loyal to Ismail emerging victorious several weeks later. It was announced in February that Ismail had died in an incinerated armored vehicle that tried to rescue him from Party Headquarters shortly after fighting broke out. Antar and Qasim were both killed during the initial fighting. Abd-al Fattah Ismail was born in 1939. He worked in an oil refinery and became a proponent of Marxism. He became the leader of the pro–Soviet faction of the National Front and served on the three-member Presidential Council from August of 1971. Ismail opposed Salem Ali Rubayi's (q.v.) negotiations with North Yemen over the question of Yemeni unification and was implicated in the bombing assassination of President Ahmed al-Ghashmi (q.v.) of North Yemen. Rubayyi attempted to arrest Ismail for complicity in the murder, and Ismail's supporters ousted Rubayyi as chairman of the Council in June of 1978. Ismail remained on the Presidential Council and succeeded Ali Nassir Muhammad Hussani as head of state as chairman of the newly formed Supreme People's Council on December 27, 1978. He reportedly stepped down from office for reasons of health in April of 1980, and Muhammad again became head of state. He returned to chair the Yemeni Socialist party in February of 1985. President Muhammad purged Ismail's supporters in the government in January of 1986, and Ismail was killed in the subsequent fighting.

• **Rear Adm. Cristobal Colon De Caravajal y Maroto** (1925–86), the seventeenth duke of Veragua and director of the Naval Museum in Madrid, was assassinated in downtown Madrid on February 6, 1986. Caravajal, a direct descendant of Christopher Columbus, was believed to have been a victim of Basque separatist terrorists.

• **Evelio Javier**, the director of Corazon Aquino's presidential campaign in the province of Antique, the Philippines, was ambushed and murdered on February 11, 1986. It was believed that Javier was assassinated by supporters of President Ferdinand Marcos.

• **Olaf Palme**, the prime minister of Sweden, was shot and killed by an unknown assassin on February 2, 1986. Palme was killed as he was walking with his wife down a Stockholm street shortly after having left a movie theatre. Sven Olof Jochim Palme was born in Stockholm on January 30, 1927. He was educated locally and attended Kenyon College, in Ohio, in the United States. He graduated in 1948 and returned to Sweden, where he received a degree in law at Stockholm University in 1951. Palme became active in the So-

cial Democratic party and served as personal secretary and speech writer for Prime Minister Tage Erlander from 1954. Palme was elected to the upper house of the Swedish Parliament in 1956 and was named to Erlander's cabinet as minister without portfolio in 1963. He was appointed minister of communications in 1965 and was named minister of education two years later. He was an opponent of the United States' involvement in Southeast Asia during the Vietnam War and participated in an anti-war demonstration outside the United States Embassy in Stockholm in 1968. Palme was also a critic of the Soviet Union's invasions of Czechoslovakia later in the year. He was chosen to lead the Social Democratic party following Erlander's retirement and became prime minister on October 14, 1969. He continued his predecessor's policies of social and labor reform. The Social Democrats lost support in general elections in 1970 and 1973. Sweden faced a declining economy and increased labor unrest, and the Social Democrats lost control of the government in elections in September of 1976. Palme was replaced as prime minister in October of 1976. He served as leader of the Opposition until October 7, 1982, when he returned to lead a minority Socialist government. He continued to head the government until his murder in February of 1986. An unemployed worker, Carl Gustav Christer Pettersson (b. 1944), was arrested for Palme's murder and tried in 1989. He was convicted by a jury, but released in October of 1989 with an appeals court reversed the verdict due to lack of evidence.

• **Zafir al-Masri**, who had recently been appointed mayor of the occupied West Bank city of Nablus, was shot and killed on March 2, 1986, while walking to work. Al-Masri, a moderate Arab, had replaced the Israeli military administration when he was appointed mayor in December of 1985. His murder was believed to have been the work of Palestinian extremists.

• **Manuel Santan Chiri**, the Peruvian governor of the southern province of Ica, was murdered by assassins near his home on March 24, 1986. Santan Chiri was a leading member of the APRA party in southern Peru.

• **Sant Sing Lidder**, a Congress (I) party member of the assembly in Punjab, was shot and killed in Likhar, India, on April 28, 1986.

• **Rear Adm. Carlos Ponce De Leon Canessa**, a Peruvian naval officer, was killed in a grenade attack launched by leftist guerrillas outside his home in Lima, Peru, on May 5, 1986.

• **Karl Heinz Beckurts** (1930–86), a nuclear physicist who worked with the West German armament firm Siemens AG as chief of research was killed by a bomb while driving to work on July 9, 1986. The leftist terrorist group the Red Army claimed responsibility for the murder.

• **Gustavo Arias Londono**, a founder and second-in-command of the leftist M-19 rebel group in Colombia, was shot to death by the police after being detained at a road block on July 23, 1986.

• **Hernando Baquero Borda**, a Colombian Supreme Court Justice, was shot to death in Bogota on July 31, 1986. Baquero had survived the siege of the Palace of Justice by leftists rebels the previous year. Another Supreme Court Justice, **Gustavo Zuluaga Serna**, was murdered several months later on October 30, 1986. Both justices were believed to have been assassinated by the Colombian drug cartel in an effort to intimidate the government and the judicial system.

• **Gen. Arun S. Vaidya** (1926–86), India's former army chief of staff, was shot to death in the western Indian city of Pune on August 10, 1986. Vaidya, who had retired in January of 1986, had been a prominent target of Sikh extremists for having supervised the Indian army's attack on the Sikh Golden Temple shrine in Amritsar in 1984.

• **R.P. Gaind**, an additional district and sessions judge in Chandigarh, India, was shot to death by Sikh assassins in the northern Indian state of Punjab on September 1, 1986.

• **Nathal Abdul Salam** (1953–86), an Iraqi consular official at embassy in Pakistan, was killed in a car bombing in Karachi, Pakistan, on September 14, 1986.

• **Col. Fedor I. Gorenkov**, the Soviet deputy military attaché for air and naval matters in Pakistan, was shot and killed by a gunman in Islamabad on September 16, 1986. he assailant was identified as Zafar Ahmed, a Pakistani with a history of mental illness.

• **Col. Christian Goutierre** (1926–86), the French military attaché in Beirut, Lebanon, was shot and killed near the French Embassy by a member of a radical Arab organization on September 18, 1986.

• **Gerold von Braunmuehl** (1935–86), an official in the West German Foreign Minister, was shot and killed by leftist terrorists on October 10, 1986. Braunmuehl was an assistant to foreign minister Hans-Dietrich Genscher and served as head of the Foreign Ministry's political department.

• **Samora Machel**, the first president of Mozambique, was killed in a plane crash near Nkomati, South Africa, while returning from a state visit to Zambia to meet with other African leaders on October 19, 1986. While the South African government claimed the crash was an accident, attributable to weather conditions and mechanical failure, some African leaders speculated that the government was responsible for Machel's death. Mozambique was often used as a base by anti-apartheid guerrillas for attacks on South Africa. A number of senior Mozambiquan officials were also killed in the crash, including **Luis Alcantara Santos**, the transport minister; **Jose Carlos**, the deputy foreign minister; and **Fernando Joao**, a senior official in the defense ministry. Samora Moises Machel was born in Xilem'bena, in Gaza Province, on September 29, 1933. He was educated in local mission schools and worked as a nurse. He joined the Mozambique Liberation Front (Frelimo) in Tanzania in 1962 and was sent to Algeria for military training. Machel was placed in charge of Frelimo's guerrilla operations in 1964 and became commander in chief of the organization in 1968. He became leader of Frelimo following the assassination of Eduardo Mondlane (q.v.) on February 3, 1969. Mozambique gained its independence from Portugal on June 25, 1975, and Machel served as the nation's first president. He attempted to establish Mozambique as a Socialist state. He maintained relations with the West and South Africa, which provided financial assistance to Mozambique. His government was threatened by the Mozambique National Resistance (Renamo), which fought a guerrilla rebellion against the government. Machel remained Mozambique's head of state until his death in a plane crash in October of 1986.

- **Dele Giwa**, the editor of the Nigerian publication *Newswatch*, was killed by a letter bomb on October 21, 1986.

- **Onkar Chandh**, the leader of Indian prime minister Rajiv Gandhi's (q.v.) political party in Hajipur, India, was found dead on October 25, 1986. Chandh had been stabbed to death by Sikh terrorists.

- **Gen. Rafael Garrido Gil**, the Spanish military governor of the Basque province of Guipuzcoa, was killed on October 25, 1986, when a bomb placed on top of his car exploded. The general's wife and son were also killed in the attack, which was believed to have been carried out by Basque separatist guerrillas.

- On November 5, 1986, the body of **Ivan Menendez Macin** (1948–86), a prominent Mexican journalist, was found shot to death in the trunk of his car in Mexico City. Menendez, who had served as an economic consultant to the Mexican government from 1970 to 1976, was the director of the Spanish edition of *Le Monde Diplomatique*. he was the fifth Mexican journalist to be murdered in 1986. **Dr. Jorge Brenes** (1940–86), the publisher of *El Rio* in Rio Bravo and *Frontera* in Reynosa, was murdered at his home on June 17, 1986. **Ernesto Flores Torrijos**, the publisher of *El Popular* in Matamoros, and **Norma Moreno Figueroa**, the paper's assignments editor, were shot and killed in July. **Odilon Lopez Urias**, a political columnist

for *La Voz del Agora* in Sinaloa, was abducted and murdered in October.

- **Angelica Quintana**, a candidate for the municipal council in Huancayo, Peru, on the American Popular Revolutionary Alliance (APRA) ticket, was assassinated by the leftist guerrilla group Shining Path on Nov. 8, 1986.

- **Rolando Olalia** (1934–86), a leader of the left-wing People's party in the Philippines and a prominent supporter of President Corazon Aquino, was abducted following a union meeting on November 12, 1986. His bullet-riddled body was found near a Manila highway the following day. Olalia was also the leader of the May First Movement, a leftist trade union, and had threatened to lead a general strike if the Philippine military attempted the ouster of Mrs. Aquino.

- **David Puzon** (1921–86), a former member of the Philippine parliament, was shot to death by gunmen near his factory in Manila on November 19, 1986. Puzon was a leading member of the right-wing business community and a close ally of defense minister Juan Ponce Enrile.

- **Ulbert Ulama Tugong** (1939–86), a leading Moslem politician in the southern region of the Philippines, was shot and killed in downtown Manila on November 22, 1986. Tugong was also an influential supporter of President Corazon Aquino.

- Five people were abducted and murdered in Roma, Lesotho, in November of 1986, including two former cabinet members — Foreign Minister **Vincent Makhele** and Information Minister **Desmond Sixishe**.

- **Georges Besse** (1928–86), the president of the French Renault automobile company, was shot and killed near his home in Paris on November 17, 1986. Besse's assassination was the work of the left-wing French radical group Direct Action.

- In December of 1986 Goukouni Oueddei (b.1944), who served as president of the African nation of Chad from 1979 until 1982, was shot and wounded in the legs by Libyan soldiers in Tripoli. Oueddei, who was being assisted by Libyan president Moammar Gadhafi during a civil war in Chad, had recently begun feuding with the Libyan leader. He was hospitalized following his injury, and subsequently placed under house arrest.

• **Edward King** (1933–86), the mayor of Mount Pleasant, Iowa, was shot and killed during a city council meeting on December 10, 1986. The assassin, Ralph Orin Davis, also critically injured two members of the council, Joann Shankey and Ronald Dupree. Davis, who claimed he shot Mayor King because the city would not pay for repairs on his basement caused by a backup in the sewage system, was charged with murder.

• **Mosbah Mohammed Gharibi**, the financial attaché of the Libyan Embassy in Damascus, Syria, was ambushed and killed by machine gun fire on December 25, 1986, in Taanayel, a small city near Beirut, Lebanon.

# 1987

• **Joginder Pal Pandey**, a leading Hindu political figure who had served as general secretary of the ruling Congress (I) party in Punjab, India, was shot to death by assassins armed with automatic rifles on January 19, 1987. Pandey's murder was allegedly the work of militant Sikh extremists.

• During 1987 leftist Shining Path rebels continued terrorist attacks in Peru against the regime of President Alan Garcia Perez. On January 30, 1987, **Cesar Lopez Silva**, a national executive committee member of the ruling political party, the American Popular Revolutionary Alliance (APRA), was murdered, and **Pedro Moreno**, an APRA official in Lima, was shot to death on February 19. **Rodrigo Franco**, the chairman of Enci, Peru's food and agriculture company, and a close friend of President Garcia, was assassinated on August 29, 1987, joining nearly 250 other APRA members slain in the previous two years.

• **Linda Obasanjo** (1941–87), the wife of former president Olusegun Obasanjo of Nigeria, was shot and killed on February 13, 1987, by a group of armed men in the Nigerian capital of Lagos.

• **Gen. Licio Giorgieri** (1925–97), a senior Italian Air Force officer in charge of air and space weapon research, was slain by two gunmen on March 20, 1987. The Union of Fighting Communists, a left-wing terrorist group connected with the Red Brigade, claimed credit for Giorgieri's assassination.

• **Maurice Gibson** (1913–87), a senior Northern Irish jurist, and his wife, **Cicely**, were killed in a car bomb explosion while driving from Belfast to Dublin on April 25, 1987. The Irish Republican Army claimed responsibility for the murder of Gibson, the Appeal Court Lord Justice of Northern Ireland.

• Hassan Abu Basha (b. 1925), the former interior minister of Egypt who was instrumental in arresting Moslem extremists after the 1981 assassination of President Anwar el-Sadat (q.v.), was seriously injured by a gunman on May 5, 1987, in Cairo.

• **Rashid Karami**, the Prime Minister of Lebanon, was killed aboard his helicopter when an explosive device inside his attaché case blew up shortly after taking off from Kubbeh army base in Tripoli, Lebanon. Karami was born in Miriata on December 30, 1921. His father was Abdel Hamid Karami, the Grand Mufti of Lebanon who had served as prime minister in 1945. Rashid Karami was educated in Cairo, Egypt, and received a degree in law in 1947. He returned to Beirut to practice law and became the political leader of Tripoli following the death of his father in 1950. He was elected to the Parliament in 1951 and served in the cabinet as minister of justice. Karami served as minister of national economy and social affairs from 1953. He was appointed prime minister by President Camille Chamoun in September of 1955, and his government resigned in March of the following year. Karami subsequently broke with the Chamoun presidency and became a leading spokesman of the pro–Egyptian faction in

Lebanon. He was a leader of the civil insurrection that threatened Chamoun's presidency. Following the election of General Fuad Chehab as president, Karami was again named prime minister in September of 1958. He resigned in May of 1960, but again formed a government in October of 1961. Karami remained prime minister until February of 1964, and was reappointed in July of 1965. He stepped down again on March 30, 1966, and was again renamed to the position in December of 1966. His government lasted until February of 1968. He returned to office in January of 1969, and his government was threatened with the presence of Palestinian guerrillas in Lebanon. Karami threatened to resign on several occasions during 1969, but was persuaded to remain in office by President Charles Helou until September of 1970. He went into opposition against President Suleiman Franjieh in 1974. President Franjieh reluctantly agreed to accept Karami as prime minister in May of 1975 in hopes that his support from the Islamic leftist opposition would help settle the civil war that developed in the country. Karami was unsuccessful in his attempts to reach a settlement and resigned in December of 1976. He supported the election of Elias Sarkis as president in 1976 and announced his retirement from politics the following year. He reemerged in 1977 and reconciled his differences with former president Franjieh. Karami was again named prime minister by President Amin Gemayel in April of 1984 as head of a government of national unity. Karami announced his resignation in May of 1987, but Gemayel refused to act upon it. He was killed the following month when a bomb exploded aboard his helicopter.

• **Cassius Make** and **Paul Dikeledi**, two South African anti-apartheid leaders, were murdered by gunmen in Swaziland on July 9, 1987. Make and Dikeledi, both members of the African National Congress (AND), were the latest of eleven murders of ANC members in Swaziland. On July 26, 1987, **Eric Mntonga**, a leading black anti-apartheid activist in South Africa, and the regional coordinator for the Democratic Alternative for South Africa, was found murdered near his home in King William's Town. Mntonga had been stabbed and beaten to death.

• **Naji Al-Ali**, a leading Palestinian cartoonist, was shot by an assassin in London on July 22, 1987. He died of his injuries the following month on August 29, 1987. Al-Ali was born in Galilee in 1938, and was raised in a refugee camp in Lebanon. He began drawing cartoons for a Lebanese newspaper in the early 1970s. He worked for the *Al-Qabas* newspaper in Kuwait from 1982, transferring to their London office soon afterwards.

• During 1987 trials against Nazis accused of war crimes during World War II took place in several countries. **Fyodor Fedorenko** (1907–87), a Ukrainian who served as a concentration camp guard at Treblinka, in Poland, was executed by the Soviet Union on July 27, 1987. Fedorenko, who had lived in the United States since the end of World War II, had been deported to the Soviet Union in 1984, where he was tried and convicted of war crimes. Karl Linnas (1920–87), a Nazi concentration camp commandant in Estonia who had been under a sentence of death in the Soviet Union, was deported from the United States on April 20, 1987. Linnas died in a prison near Leningrad on July 2 while awaiting an appeal.

• **Muhammad Shuqair**, Lebanese President Amin Gemayel's only Muslim advisor, was assassinated on August 2, 1987.

• Political violence erupted during the 1987 presidential election in Haiti. The military junta of Lt. Gen. Henri Namphy, who had ended the 22 year rule of the Duvalier family in 1986, called for a general election to be held in November of 1987. The campaign was marked by charges of corruption and many instances of violence, including the assassination of two presidential candidates. **Louis Eugene Atisse** was hacked to death by a mob of peasants on August 2, 1987. Atisse had been addressing a crowd on the steps of a church in Leogane at the time of the attack. On October 13, 1987, **Yves Volel** (1933–87), the candidate of the Christian Democratic Rally, was shot and killed by Haitian police in front of a Port-au-Prince police station. Volel had been demanding the release of political prisoners held by the Namphy regime prior to his murder. The government alleged Volel was inciting a riot, though Volel's supporters claimed his death was a premeditated act by the government to silence an outspoken critic.

On election day there was widespread rioting and armed attacks on polling places by former Tonton Macoutes, a para-military group which had supported the deposed Duvalier regime. The government postponed the election until 1988 amid charges that the Namphy regime intended to hold power by force of arms.

• **Jaime Ferrer** (1917–87), a leading Filipino politician who served in the cabinet as Secretary of Local Government, was shot to death outside his home in the Manila suburb of Paranque on August 2, 1987. Ferrer, a leading anti–Communist, had served as minister of agriculture in President Ramon Magsaysay's cabinet in the 1950s. The band of assassins were believed to have been members of the communist New People's Army.

• **Pedro Valencia Giraldo** (1939–87), a Colombian senator and leader of the leftist Patriotic Union party, was shot and killed by gunmen who crashed a car into his home on August 14, 1987.

• During 1987 political violence continued in Sri Lanka between Buddhist Sinhalese and Hindu Tamils. On August 18, 1987, President Junius R. Jayewardene (1906–96) was the target of an assassination attempt. A terrorist, believed to be a Sinhalese protesting a proposal granting the Tamil minority autonomy in certain Sri Lankan regions, opened fire with an automatic weapon in the Sri Lankan parliament. The attacker threw a grenade under the table where President Jayewardene was seated. The president was uninjured in the attack, but one legislator was killed and fifteen others, including Prime Minister Ranasinghe Premadasa (q.v.) and National Security Minister Lalith Athulathmudali (q.v.), were injured.

• Jamaican reggae star **Peter Tosh** (1944–87) was killed by three gunmen at his home in Kingston on September 11, 1987. **Wilton "Doc" Brown**, a local health food manufacturer, and **Jeff Dixon**, a Jamaican disc jockey, were also fatally wounded in the assault, and four other friends of Tosh were injured. The gunmen were believed to have been robbers, but Tosh's position of a leading spokesman for social change in Jamaica clouded the circumstances of his death. Tosh was a Rastafarian, a member of a religious sect that revered the late Emperor Haile Selassie (q.v.) of Ethiopia. He was also a founding member of the Wailers, a reggae band led by Bob Marley (1945–81), that received international recognition and popularized reggae music in the United States. Marley himself survived an assassination attempt in December of 1976 when he was wounded by unidentified gunmen prior to giving a free benefit concert for the re-election campaign of former Jamaican Prime Minister Michael Manley.

• **Leandro Alejandro**, a leading Filipino leftist, was shot to death near Manila on September 19, 1987. Alejandro was the secretary-general of the Bayan coalition, a leftist political party.

• **Mehdi Hashemi**, a close aide to Ayatollah Hussein Montazeri, the presumed successor to Iranian strongman Ayatollah Khomeini, was executed by a firing squad in Teheran on September 28, 1987. Hashemi was believed to have been the official responsible for the exposure of the negotiations between former United States national security advisor Robert McFarlane and Iranian Parliament Speaker Hashemi Rafsanjani, which resulted in the Iran-Contra affair following allegations of an arms-for-hostages deal between the United States and Iran. Hashemi was also the leader of the World Islamic Movement, an organization dedicated to the export of Iran's fundamentalist Islamic revolution. He was tried and found guilty of the Islamic crime of "corruption on earth." His execution was believed to have been a blow to Montazeri's leadership struggle against Rafsanjani.

- **Jaime Pardo Leal**, the leader of the leftist Patriotic Union (UP) party in Colombia, and candidate for president in the 1986 elections, was murdered by rightist paramilitary members on October 11, 1987. Pardo was shot and killed in his car near the capital of Bogota. The Patriotic Union, Colombia's largest leftist party, had been beset by numerous acts of violence against its members. Nearly 500 party members, including four members of the Colombian congress, had been assassinated since the 1986 elections. Pardo's murder sparked protests and rioting throughout Colombia.

- **Thomas Sankara**, the president of Burkina Faso, was ousted in a military coup on October 15, 1987. Sankara and twelve of his aides were executed outside of the capital shortly after the coup. Sankara was born in Upper Volta on December 21, 1949. He served as a paratrooper in the Upper Voltan army and took part in the border war with Mali in 1974. He served as secretary of state for information in the government of Saye Zerbo in 1981, but resigned in a dispute with the president. Sankara was instrumental in the coup that ousted Zerbo in November of 1982. He was appointed prime minister of Upper Volta on January 10, 1983, by the ruling People's Salvation Council. He was ousted from that position by President Jean-Baptiste Ouedraogo on May 17, 1983. In May of 1983 Sankara was briefly imprisoned, and he subsequently made plans to overthrow the government. He led a company of paratroopers against Ouedraogo on August 4, 1983, and became president of the ruling National Revolutionary Council. The following year, on August 4, 1984, Sankara changed the name of Upper Volta to Burkina Faso, meaning the country of honest men. He pursued a policy of radical nationalism and sought to reduce government corruption. Sankara was ousted and killed during a coup led by Capt. Blaise Compaore, his second in command, in October of 1987.

- **Herbert Ernesto Anaya** (1955–87), the president of the Salvadoran Human Rights Commission, was shot and killed by two men believed to be members of a right-wing death squad as he left his home in San Salvador on October 26, 1987. The Commission, which had been founded ten years earlier, was instrumental in addressing human rights violations of the Salvadoran government during the on-going civil war against leftist rebels. Six other commission members had been killed or disappeared since 1980, and Anaya had been arrested the previous year for his criticism of the government. His assassination sparked demonstrations against the Salvadoran government.

- **Rene Joaquin Cardenas** (1955–87), a member of the Salvadoran government's human rights commission, was shot to death at his home in San Miguel by three gunmen on December 10, 1987. Cardenas served as a regional delegate on the commission, which was not directly connected to the independent group led by Herbert Anaya, who had been murdered several months earlier.

- **Harsha Abeywardene** (1944–87), the leader of the ruling United National Party in Sri Lanka, was slain by two assassins in the capital of Colombo on December 23, 1987. Abeywardene's bodyguard, chauffeur and aide were also killed in the barrage of automatic weapon fire and hand grenades. The murder of Abeywardene, a close ally of Sri Lankan President Jayewardene, ended a year of political violence on the small island nation that included the massacre of over 127 bus passengers by Tamil guerrillas on April 17.

# 1988

- **Mahdi al-Hakim**, a leading Shiite Muslim active in the Iraqi opposition, was shot and killed in a hotel lobby in Khartoum, Sudan, on January 17, 2001. Agents linked to Iraqi President Saddam Hussein were believed to have been responsible for the killing.

- **Carlos Mauro Hoyos Jimenez**, the attorney general of Colombia, was kidnapped and murdered by drug smugglers near Medellin on January 25, 1988. Hoyos had traveled to Medellin to investigate the release of drug kingpin Jorge Luis Ochoa Vasquez and was en route to the airport when he was captured. His body was found in the village of El Retiro several hours later. The killers also shot to death two of Hoyos' bodyguards during the initial assault.

- **Vijaya Kumaratunga**, a leading Sri Lankan film star and opposition political leader, was shot to death at his home in a Colombo suburb by Sinhalese extremists on February 16, 1988. Kumaratunga, the leader of the leftist People's Party, favored reconciliation with the Tamils. His wife, Chandrika Kumaratunga, the daughter of former Sri Lankan prime ministers S.W.R.D. Bandaranaike (q.v.) and Sirimavo Bandaranaike, became prime minister of Sri Lanka in August of 1994. She was the target of several assassination attempts in the 1990s by the Tamil Tigers.

- **Alexandros Athanasiadis** (1929–88), a leading Greek industrialist, was shot to death in Athens on March 1, 1988. The terrorist group November 17 Revolutionary Organization claimed credit for the assassination.

- **Alfonso Cujavanta**, the Patriotic Union (UP) leader in Colombia's Cordoba Province, was assassinated on March 15, 1988. Political violence in Colombia had claimed the lives of twenty-nine leftist Patriotic Union candidates for local mayors and over one hundred other Patriotic Union candidates for local office during the six months preceding elections in March of 1988.

- **Abu Jihad** (1935–88), a leading Palestine Liberation Organization officer, was assassinated at his home near Tunis, Tunisia, on March 16, 1988. Jihad, originally Khalid al-Wazir, was the PLO's senior military officer and Yasir Arafat's leading advisor. He and Arafat were founders of the Al Fatah faction in the 1960s and he was accused by Israel of orchestrating numerous terrorist attacks in the region. His death was believed to have been orchestrated by the Israeli secret service.

- Mexican journalist **Hector Felix Miranda** was shot to death by a former state policeman on April 20, 1988. Felix Miranda was the editor of the Tijuana magazine *Zeta*.

- **Hagop Hagopian**, the leader of the Armenian Secret Army for the Liberation of Armenia, or the Orly Group, was shot to death at his Athens home by two unidentified gunmen on April 25, 1988. Hagopian's organization made several terrorist attacks in Turkey and Western Europe in the early 1980s. The goal of the group, which was formed in 1975, was to force the Turkish government to acknowledge genocide of Armenians in 1915 and to give territory for an Armenian homeland.

- **Jorge Alberto Serrano**, a Salvadoran military judge, was shot to death in San Salvador on May 11, 1988. Serrano was presiding over the trial of several military officers accused of operating a kidnapping ring at the time of his death.

- **Richard J. Daronco** (1932–88), a Federal District Judge, was shot to death at his home in Pelham, New York, on May 21, 1988. Daronco was slain by a former New York City police officer, Charles L. Koster (1921–88), who was upset over the judge's decision to dismiss a sexual discrimination lawsuit that had been filed by his daughter. Koster committed suicide after killing Judge Daronco.

- **William E. Nordeen** (1937–88), a Navy Captain who served as the U.S. military attaché in Athens, Greece, was killed in a car bomb blast near his home in Kefalari, Greece, on June 28, 1988. The leftist terrorist group November 17 Revolutionary Organization claimed credit for the assassination.

- Haitian human rights advocate and lawyer **Lafontant Joseph** (1934–88) was stabbed and beaten to death in Port-au-Prince on July 11, 1988. His body was found in his jeep near the airport in Port-au-Prince. He was the founder and leader of the Center for Human Rights Education since 1986, and a member of the National Congress of Democratic Movements. Joseph had been imprisoned by the government of Lt. Gen. Henri Namphy for the previous two years. His death came shortly after Namphy returned to power the previous month.

• **Capt. Pierre Anga**, a leading Congolese army officer, was killed in July of 1988 during a battle with government security forces. Anga had led a ten month rebellion in the Congo near Owando in Cuvette Province. Anga had served on the Congolese Labour Party Military Committee that governed the Congo for several weeks after the assassination of President Marien Ngouabi (q.v.) in 1977.

• **Rona y Gonzalez Reyes**, the publisher and editor of the Mexican newspapers *El Mundo* and *El Dia*, was shot to death by gunmen in Comitan, southern Mexico, on July 13, 1988. Television anchorwoman **Linda Bejarano** was assassinated two weeks later on July 23, 1988, in Ciudad Juarez, Mexico. Two other people were killed in the car with Bejarano, who was pregnant. Federal police were charged with the murders, claiming that the journalist and her companions were mistaken for drug traffickers.

• **Sohan Singh**, the high priest of the Golden Temple at Amritsar, India, and moderate Sikh leader **Bhan Singh** were shot to death in Ludhiana, Punjab, on July 25, 1988. The killings were believed to have been carried out by Sikh militants who opposed the attempts by moderates to negotiate a reconciliation with the government of India.

• **Mohammed Zia ul-Haq**, the president of Pakistan, was killed when his aircraft exploded in midair soon after takeoff and crashed near Bahawalupr on August 17, 1988. Twenty-nine other passengers were killed including U.S. Ambassador **Arnold Raphel** (Mar. 16, 1943–88), Chief U.S. Military Attaché **Brig. Gen. Herbert Wassum** (Dec. 20, 1938–1988), and ten senior Pakistani army officers. Raphel had been a officer in the foreign service since 1966 and was appointed ambassador to Pakistan in 1988. The cause of the crash could not be determined, but a terrorist action was suspected.

Mohammed Zia ul-Haq was born in Jullundur, in East Punjab, on August 12, 1924. He attended St. Stephen's College in Delhi and the Royal Indian Military Academy at Dehra Dun. He was commissioned into the British army in May of 1945 and saw action in Burma and Indonesia near the end of World War II. Zia entered the Pakistani army after the partition of India in 1947. He received further military training in Pakistan and the United States. He was promoted to lieutenant colonel in 1964 and participated in the war between Pakistan and India the following year. Zia rose to the rank of brigadier general in 1969 and commanded an armored brigade. He was sent to Jordan later in the year to serve as a military advisor to the Royal Jordanian Army during its conflict with Palestinian guerrillas. He returned to Pakistan in 1971 and served as a deputy division commander in the civil war that resulted in the formation of Bangladesh. Zia was promoted to general in March of 1976 and was named army chief of staff by President Zulfikar Ali Bhutto (q.v.). Riots and civil disorders followed allegations of fraud in general elections held in March of 1977. Fearing civil war, Zia led a military coup to oust Bhutto on July 5, 1977. He took control of the government and declared martial law. He ordered Bhutto's arrest in September of 1977 and clamped down on all political activity in the country. Zia made plans to restore Pakistan to civilian rule in 1978 and appointed a civilian cabinet the following August. He assumed the presidency on September 16, 1978, and introduced an Islamization plan for the country. He continued to face widespread discontent against his rule. Protests against the government escalated following the execution of Bhutto in April of 1979, and Zia restored military rule. Bhutto's daughter, Benazir, became the leader of the Pakistan People's Party, and she was imprisoned and forced into exile by the Zia government. A referendum approved Zia's Islamization plan in December of 1984. He allowed election to the National Assembly in February of 1985 and lifted martial law restrictions later in the year. Zia approved a civilian government in March of 1985. He dismissed the government in May of 1988 and called for new elections. He banned political parties in the elections scheduled for later in the year. He remained Pakistan's head of state until his death in an airplane crash on August 17, 1988.

• **Lazarus Salii** (1934–88), the president of Palau, a republic in the western Pacific, was shot to death in his home in Koror, the capital of Palau, on August 20, 1988. Salli had served as president since October of 1985. He had succeeded President Haruo I. Remeliik (q.v.), following Remeliik's assassination.

• **Inocencio Romero Suarez**, the candidate for mayor of Tezonapa for the Mexican Socialist Party, was murdered on September 10, 1988.

• **Antonia Saetta**, a judge on the Palermo court of appeals in Sicily, was assassinated while driving near the town of Caltanisetta on September 25, 1988. The judge's handicapped son was also killed in the attack. **Mauro Rostagno**, a leftist politician and critic of the Sicilian Mafia, was shot to death the following day. Both killings were believed to have been carried out by the Sicilian mob.

• **Lionel Jayatilleke**, minister of education and reconstruction in J.R. Jayewardene's cabinet in Sri Lanka, was assassinated by the militant Sinhalese group, the People's Liberation Front (JVP) on September 26, 1988.

• **Lucio Salvador**, the mayor of Sociedad, Morazan province, El Salvador, was assassinated by leftists on October 25, 1988. Salvador was a member of the rightist National Republican Alliance (Arena) party.

• **Maj. Gen. B.N. Kumar**, a leading Indian army general, was shot to death by assassins in Chandigarh, Punjab, on November 7, 1988, by militant Sikh separatists. Gen. Kumar had been criticized the previous year when, as head of the Bhakra Beas Management Board, he was said to have mishandled flooding in the Punjab region that claimed the lives of hundreds of people.

• **Napoleon Villafuerte**, the mayor of Sesori in San Miguel province, El Salvador, was abducted by the Farabundo Marti National Liberation Front (FMLN) on November 23, 1988. Villafuerte was found dead two days later.

# 1989

• **Manuel Adan Rugama**, known as Commander Avreliano, was shot to death by gunmen in Tegucigalpa, Honduras, on January 7, 1989. Adan Rugama was an aide to Nicaraguan Contra leader Enrique Bermudez.

• **Anastasios Venarthos** (1937–89), a Supreme Court deputy prosecutor, was shot to death outside his Athens, Greece, home on January 23, 1989. The leftist terrorist group, the May 1 Revolutionary Organization, claimed credit for the murder.

• **Gustavo Alvarez Martinez**, the leader of the Honduran armed forces from 1982 to 1984 and a leading supporter of Nicaragua's contras, was shot to death by six gunmen near his home in Tegucigalpa on January 25, 1989. Alvarez had also served as a leader of Honduras' national police from 1982 to 1984. The leftist Cinchonero Popular Liberation Movement claimed responsibility for the killing.

• **Saul Cantoral Huamani** (1945–1989), the secretary general of the Peruvian Miners' Union, was abducted and shot to death in Peru by rightist terrorists. His body was found in a Lima slum on February 14, 1989. The right-wing militia, Commando Rodrigo Franco, was believed to have been responsible for the murder of Cantoral and social worker **Consuelo Garcia**, whose body was also recovered.

• **Jose Antequera** (1951–1989), a member of the executive board of the Patriotic Union (PU) of Colombia, was shot to death at the Bogota International Airport on March 3, 1989. Liberal Party presidential candidate Senator Ernesto Samper Pizano was also injured in the attack.

• **Abdurrezzak Ceylan**, an opposition party deputy in the Turkish Parliament, was shot and killed in Parliament in Ankara, Turkey, on March 29, 1989. Two fellow deputies also from Ceylan's southern province, Zeki Celiker and Idris Arikan, accused each other of the shooting.

• Muslim cleric **Abdullah al-Ahdal** (1952–89), was shot to death in Brussels, Belgium, on March 29, 1989. Librarian **Salem el-Behir** (1948–89) was also killed in the shooting. Al-Ahdal's assassination came shortly after his criticism of Iran's Ayatollah Khomeini's sentence of death against author Salman Rushdie.

• **Hassan Djamouss** and Idriss Deby, two leading military advisers to President Hissen Habre of Chad, led a coup attempt against the government in April of 1989. The coup was unsuccessful and Djamouss was killed in the attempt. Deby fled the country.

• **Afranio Parra**, a founder of the leftist Colombia April 19 Movement (M-19), was shot to death by three policemen in Colombia on April 7, 1989. Two other M-19 rebels were also killed in the attack.

• **Col. James Rowe**, the chief of the army division at the Joint U.S. Military Assistance Group in the Philippines, was ambushed and killed by gunmen as he left his home in Quezon City on April 21, 1989. Juanito Itaas and Danilo Continente, members of the rebel group the New People's Army, were arrested and convicted of Rowe's murder and sentenced to live imprisonment.

• **David Webster** (1945–89), a leading white anti-apartheid activist in South Africa, was shot to death by unknown assailants in a Johannesburg suburb on May 1, 1989. Webster was an anthropology teacher at Witwa-tersrand University and a member of the opposition United Democratic Front. His death was believed to have been orchestrated by right-wing militias, of whom Webster was an outspoken critic.

• **T. Panchalingam**, a senior representative of the Sri Lankan government, was shot to death in Manipay, Sri Lanka, on May 1, 1989. Tamil Tigers terrorists claimed responsibility for the assassination.

• **Jean-Marie Tjibaou** (1936–89), a leader of the Kanak independence movement in New Caledonia, was assassinated in Wadrilla on May 4, 1989. The group's vice president, **Yeiwene Yeiwene**, was also killed in the assault. Djubeli Wea, a rival Kanak leader and the alleged assassin, was shot to death at the scene. Three other suspects were also arrested. A former Catholic priest, Tjibaou was leader of the fight for Kanak independence from France from 1975. He signed the Matignon Accords with the French government in 1988, which began the process for limited self-government for New Caledonia.

• President Mengistu Haile Mariam of Ethiopia withstood a military coup attempt on May 16, 1989. **Gen. Mered Negussie**, the armed forces chief of staff, and **Ameha Desta**, commander of the air force, were the organizers of the coup. Defense Minister **Hayle Gyorgis Habete Maryam** was informed of the plans and sought to halt the attempt. He was shot to death by the conspirators. Loyalist forces moved in to support Mengistu. **General Demissie Bulto**, of the Asmara Second Army, attempted to join the coup, but he and other high ranking officers were killed when his forces refused to back him. Gen. Mered and Commander Ameha were also arrested and summarily executed in Addis Ababa. Many other senior officers, including eight generals, were subsequently tortured and executed for their perceived role in the rebellion.

• **Grand Mufti Sheikh Hassan Khalid** was killed by a car bomb in Beirut, Lebanon, on May 16, 1989. Over twenty bystanders were also killed in the assassination.

Khalid was born in Beirut to a Sunni family in 1921. He attended the school of Islamic law in Beirut, graduating in 1940. He continued his studies at Al-Azhar University in Cairo, Egypt, and subsequently joined the Shari'ah court in Beirut in an administrative position. Khalid also taught at the Azhar Lubnan school in Beirut. He was named mufti in 1967. He was a critic of the Maronite Christian militias during the civil war of 1975 and a founder of the Islamic coalition At Tajammu al Islami. He remained a leading religious figure in Lebanon until his assassination in 1989 by members of a Syrian-backed militia.

• **Jose Antonio Rodriguez Porth** (1916–89), minister of the president and close advisor to President Alfredo Cristiani of El Salvador, was shot and killed while leaving his home in San Salvador on June 9, 1989. Two bodyguards were also killed during the assassination.

• **Gen. Arnaldo Ochoa Sanchez**, a leading figure in the Cuban revolution of the late 1950s and a highly decorated military figure, was arrested and found guilty on June 14, 1989, by a Cuban military tribunal on charges of conspiring to smuggle drugs into the United States. Ochoa and three other officers, **Amado Padron Trujillo**, **Antonio de la Guardia** and **Jorge Martinez**, were executed by firing squad on July 13, 1989. It was believed that Ochoa was actually purged and executed because his criticism of the Castro regime. A 1997 film, *8-A*, dramatized Ochoa's arrest, trial and execution.

• **Abdolrahman Qassemlu**, a leader of the Iranian opposition group, the Kurdish Democratic Party, was assassinated with his deputy in Vienna, Austria, on July 13, 1989. Qassemlu was reported to have been involved in secret negotiations with the Iranian government and it was believed that the murders were orchestrated by the Iranians.

• **Appapillai Amirthalingam**, the general secretary of the moderate Tamil United Liberation Front, was assassinated by Tamil Tiger terrorists on July 13, 1989, in Sri Lanka. **Vettivelu Yogeshwaran**, a Tamil member

of parliament from Jaffna was also killed in the attack. Three gunmen were slain by security guards following the assault. The director of the Sri Lanka Broadcasting Co., **Themis Guruge** (1929–89), was shot to death the following week on July 23, 1989, in Polhengoda, Sri Lanka.

• **Lt. Col. William Higgins**, a U.S. marine attached to the United Nations monitoring force in Lebanon, was kidnapped in February of 1988 by members of the Shi'ite extremist group Organization for the Oppressed of the Earth. Higgins was reportedly hanged by his captors on July 31, 1989, though there was speculation that he was possibly killed at an earlier date.

• **Romulo Liclican**, the mayor of Diffun, the Philippines, was shot to death by unknown gunmen on August 3, 1989.

• **Luis Carlos Galan Sarmiento** (1945–89), a Colombian senator and the Liberal Party candidate for president of Colombia, was assassinated on August 18, 1989, while speaking at a political rally in the small town of Soacha, near Bogota. A leading critic of Colombia's drug cartels, Galan had escaped an earlier assassination attempt in Medellin two weeks earlier on August 5. The gunmen were believed to be involved with the Medellin drug cartel. Galan had been an unsuccessful presidential candidate in 1982.

Two other leading Colombian officials had been murdered earlier in the week by members of the drug cartel. **Carlos Ernesto Valencia Garcia** (1946–89), an Appeals Court Judge, was murdered in Bogota on August 16, 1989, and **Col. Valdemar Franklin Quinero**, the chief of police in Antioquia province, was shot to death near his home in Medellin on August 18, 1989. Colombia's drug wars continued throughout the year, with **Pablo Palaez Gonzalez**, a former Medellin mayor, shot to death on September 12, 1989, and **Guillermo Gomez Murillo**, a newspaper reporter and outspoken critic of the drug cartels, murdered in Buenaventura on September 16, 1989. Colombia's president, Virgilio Barco, led the country's efforts against the drug lords, and, on December 15, 1989, a military raid on a ranch near Tolu brought an end to leading drug cartel boss **Jose Gonzalo Rodriguez Gacha** (1947–89), who was killed along with his son and over a dozen bodyguards by the Colombian military.

• **Huey P. Newton**, the co-founder of the Black Panther Party in the 1960s, was found shot to death in Oakland, California, on August 22, 1989. Tyrone Robinson (b. 1964), a member of the West Coast Black Guerrilla Family gang, was charged with the murder. Robinson claimed that Newton was killed in self-defense during a confrontation over the theft of drugs. Huey Percy Newton was born in New Orleans, Louisiana, on February 17, 1942. With Bobby Seale, he founded the Black Panther Party in Oakland in 1966 in order to combat racism and police brutality. Newton served as the Black Panthers' "minister of defense," urging blacks to arm themselves against oppression. He was convicted for voluntary manslaughter in regard to the death of a police officer in 1967. His imprisonment led to a large "Free Huey" campaign on college campuses throughout the United States. His conviction was overturned and he was released from prison in 1969. Newton fled the country in 1974, after again being accused of murder. He settled in Cuba for three years before returning to the United States. Two trials resulted in deadlocked juries and Newton went free. He received a doctorate in social philosophy from the University of California at Santa Cruz in 1980. The Panthers were disbanded two years later. Newton was again in trouble with the law in March 1989 when he was charged with misappropriating funds designated for a school founded by the Panthers in Oakland. He pled no contest to the charges. Newton was shot to death five months later.

• **Anton Lubowski** (1952–89), a leading white anti-apartheid activist and member of the South West Africa People's Organization, was shot to death in Windhoek, Namibia, on September 12, 1989. A former South African police officer was arrested for the murder.

• **Commandant Jean-Baptiste Lingani** and **Capt. Henri Zongo** of Burkina Faso, were executed by firing squad on September 19, 1989. The two were accused of plotting against the government of Pres. Blaise Compaore. They had assisted Compaore and former president Thomas Sankara (q.v.) in seizing power in Burkina Faso in 1983. Two other officers were also executed.

• **Nazem al-Kaderi** (1916–89), a leading Sunni Muslim politician and a member of the Lebanese Parliament, was shot to death in Beirut, Lebanon, by three gunmen on September 21, 1989. Kaderi's bodyguard was also killed in the assault.

• **Jesus Jaramillo Monsalve** (1917–89), a Roman Catholic bishop, and the **Rev. Jose Munoz Pareja** were abducted and murdered in Arauca, Colombia, on October 3, 1989. The leftist National Liberation Army were reportedly responsible for the killings.

• **Maj. Moise Giroldi Vega** led an unsuccessful coup attempt against Gen. Manuel Noriega, the leader of Panama, on October 3, 1989. Noriega himself reportedly shot and killed Giroldi after the coup's failure.

• **Francis Minah**, the former vice president of Sierra Leone, was executed with five others on October 10, 1989. The execution came after a lengthy trial and conviction on charges of conspiring to overthrow the government in March of 1987. Minah was born in Sawula, near Pujehun, on August 19, 1929, the son of Paramount Chief M.J. Minah. He was educated locally and in England, and earned a degree in law in the mid–1960s. He established a law practice in Sierra Leone in 1965. He joined President Siaka Steven's All Peoples Congress party in 1973 and served in Steven's cabinet as minister of trade and industry, minister of foreign affairs, attorney general, minister of finance and minister of health over the next fourteen years. He was accused of plotting against Steven's successor, President Joseph Momoh, and was executed by hanging.

- **Gabriel Jaime Santamaria**, a leader of the leftist Patriotic Union in Colombia, was shot to death in Medillin, Colombia, on October 27, 1989. His assailant was killed by security after the assassination.

- **Muhammad Ali Marzouki** (1919–89), a Saudi Arabian diplomat, was assassinated by gunmen in Beirut, Lebanon, on November 1, 1989. Marzouki was the last Saudi Embassy official remaining in Lebanon. The terrorist group, Islamic Jihad, was believed responsible for the murder.

- **Rohana Wijeweera**, the chairman of the Sinhalese People's Liberation Front, was arrested by the Sri Lankan government for inciting rebellion and presumably executed on November 13, 1989. Wijeweera was the founder of the Janatha Vimukthi Peramuna (JVP) party in 1965. He had been a leader of a Communist rebellion in 1971 and had served over a decade in prison.

- Six Jesuit priests—**Ignacio Ellacuria, Segundo Montes, Ignacio Martin-Baro, Joaquin Lopez y Lopez, Juan Ramon Moreno,** and **Amado Lopez**— were murdered at the University of Central America in San Salvador on November 16, 1989. The priests and their housekeeper were slain by members of the Salvadoran military, presumably because of their outspoken criticism of injustices in the country and their support of assistance for the poor.

- **Josu Muguruta**, a member of the Basque separatist organization ETA, was assassinated in Madrid, Spain, on November 20, 1989, shortly before he was to be sworn in to the Spanish Parliament. The right-wing Anti-Terrorist Liberation Group claimed responsibility for the assassination.

- **Rene Moawad** (Rene Mu'awwad), the president of Lebanon, was killed in an explosion on November 22, 1989, while riding in a motorcade returning from Muslim West Beirut. Over twenty others were reportedly killed in the attack. Rene Anis Moawad was born in Zgharta in 1925. He attended the Jesuit University of St. Joseph in Beirut and received a law degree in 1947. He became active in politics and was elected to the Parliament in 1957. Moawad served as chairman of the Administration of Justice Parliamentary Commission from 1959 until 1961 and subsequently served as minister of post, telephone, and telegraph until 1964. He was named minister of public works in 1969. He remained neutral during the 1975 civil war. Moawad returned to the cabinet in 1980 to serve as minister of education until 1981. Moawad was elected president in a special session of Parliament and took office on November 5, 1989. He was a moderate Maronite Christian who had the support of the Syrian government. His term of office was cut short when he was assassinated after less than three weeks as president.

- **Ahmed Abdallah**, the president of the Comoros, was shot to death in the presidential palace during a coup attempt on November 26, 1989. Ahmed Abdallah Abderrahman was born in 1919. He was a leading Comoro businessman and served as a representative of the Comoros in the French Senate from 1959 until 1972. He led the pro-independence Democratic Union of the Comoros party and became president of the Comoro Government Council in December of 1972. Abdallah unilaterally declared the Comoro Islands independent on July 7, 1975. He became president and prime minister in the independent government. On August 3, 1975, he was ousted in a coup led by Ali Soilih (q.v.). Abdallah remained on his home island of Anjouan until September 22, 1975, when Ali Soilih led an invasion force to capture the deposed president, who was arrested and sent into exile in France. Abdallah was returned to power on May 21, 1978, following a coup led by French mercenary Col. Bob Denard. Abdallah established the Islamic Republic of the Comoros and served as co-president of the ruling Political-Military Directorate with Mohammed Ahmed until Ahmed's resignation in October of 1978. Abdallah was elected president in a referendum later in the month. He was reelected unopposed in September of 1984. Abdallah survived a coup attempt in March of

1985 and instituted a crackdown on dissidents. He survived another coup attempt in November of 1987. Abdallah was granted permission to run for another term by a national referendum to amend the constitution in November of 1989. His plans were interrupted when he was killed by rebels attacking the presidential palace on November 26, 1989. It was believed that Col. Denard was behind Abadallah's killing, as the president was under international pressure to drive Denard from the country. Abdallah was succeeded as president by Supreme Court president Mohammad Djohar.

• **Francisco Jose Guerrero** (1925–89), a leading right-wing political figure in El Salvador, was shot to death en route to his office in San Salvador on November 28, 1989. Guerrero was a former foreign minister and president of El Salvador's Supreme Court. He was an unsuccessful candidate for the presidency on the National Conciliation Party ticket in 1984.

• **Alfred Herrhausen**, the chief executive of the Deutsche Bank and a leading German financial expert, was killed in a bomb blast in Bad Homburg on November 30, 1989. His assassination was believed to have been orchestrated by the remnants of the Red Army Faction. Herrhausen was born on January 30, 1930. He joined the Deutsche Bank in 1969 and had served as a member of the bank's board of directors since 1971.

• **Robert S. Vance**, a federal judge with the U.S. Court of Appeals for the 11th District, was killed while opening a mail bomb at his home in Mountain Brook, Alabama, on December 16, 1989. His wife was seriously injured in the blast. Savannah Alderman and civil rights leader **Robert Robinson** was also killed by a mail bomb that exploded in his Atlanta, Georgia, office on December 18, 1989. Walter Leroy Moody, Jr. was convicted of both murders and given the death sentence.

• **Nicolae Ceaucescu**, the leader of Romania, and his wife, **Elena**, were ousted from power and forced to flee the capital on December 22, 1989, after a violent revolt. They

were captured the following day and tried and convicted of genocide and gross abuse of power. Both were summarily executed in Bucharest on December 25, 1989. Nicolae Ceaucescu was born in Scornicesti on January 26, 1918. He worked in a factory in Bucharest and joined the workers movement in his early teens. He became active in the Union of Communist Youth in 1933 and became a leading organizer of the outlawed Romanian Communist party. Ceaucescu was arrested in 1936 and served several years in prison. He served on the party's central committee on youth after his release and was again imprisoned in 1940. He escaped from prison following the Soviet army's invasion of Romania in August of 1944. Ceaucescu again served as a leading figure in the Union of Communist Youth and was elected a candidate member of the Communist Party's Central Committee in October of 1945. He was subsequently appointed to the political directorate of the Romanian army, with the rank of brigadier general. He was also elected to the Grand National Assembly in November of 1946. Ceaucescu was named to the Central Committee of the Romanian Workers' Party in 1952 following the consolidation of power in the party by party leader Gheorghe Gheorghiu-Dej. He was named a full member of the Politburo in December of 1955. He became deputy to the party first secretary, Gheorghiu-Dej, in 1957 and was chosen as Gheorghiu-Dej's successor to lead the party. Ceaucescu was selected as first secretary on March 22, 1965, following Gheorghiu-Dej's death. He also assumed the post of president of the State Council in December of 1967. He continued his predecessor's policy of independence from the Soviet Union and was a critic of Soviet intervention in Czechoslovakia in 1968. While his independent policies earned him respect among the Western powers, Romania's declining economic conditions in the 1980s led to increased dissent against his rule. His attempts to pay off Romania's foreign debts by exporting food and fuel led to widespread shortages throughout the country. His opposition to liberal reforms during the late 1980s led to increasingly repressive measures. Democratic reforms were sweeping Communist nations in Eastern Europe, and demonstrations against the Ceaucescu regime took place throughout Romania. The government ordered troops to open fire on protesters in Timisoara on December 17, 1989. This action led to a violent revolt against the government, resulting in Ceaucescu's ouster and execution.

# 1990

• **Gen. Enrique Lopez Albujar**, the former Peruvian minister of defense, was shot to death by leftist Shining Path guerrillas on January 9, 1990, while driving his car in downtown Lima. Lopez had left the government in May of 1989.

• **William Joyce**, the American finance director of the Panama Canal Commission, was shot by assailants at his home in Panama City, Panama, on January 24, 1990. He died of his wounds the following day.

• **T. Ganeshalingam**, a moderate Sri Lankan Tamil politician who served as provincial minister for the north and east, was assassinated by Tamil Tiger rebels on January 28, 1990.

• **Robert Ouko**, the foreign minister of Kenya, was murdered on February 13, 1990. Robert John Ouko was born at Kisumu on March 31, 1932. He attended Makerere University College and, in 1963, began working with the foreign service office. He was named East African minister for finance and administration in 1969 and, the following year, served as minister for Common Market and economic affairs until 1977. Ouko subsequently served in the Kenyan parliament, becoming minister of community affairs. He was named minister for foreign affairs in 1979. He later became a critic of the government of Daniel Arap Moi. Ouko was reported missing in February of 1990. His burned body was later discovered, and the government an-

nounced that he had committed suicide. It soon became apparent that Ouko had been murdered.

• **Diana Cardona Saldarriaga**, the mayor of Apartado, Colombia, was murdered in Medellin on February 26, 1990, after being kidnapped by gunmen disguised as security police.

• **Bernardo Jaramillo Ossa** (1951–90), a candidate for Colombia's president for the left-wing Patriotic Union (UP) party, was shot to death at a Bogota airport on March 22, 1990. His machine-gun wielding assailant was captured and identified as 15-year-old Andres Gutierrez, an agent of Medellin drug lord Pablo Escobar (q.v.). Gutierrez was too young to be tried for the crime and was placed in a state children's home. Jaramillo was president of the UP and had been elected to the Colombian senate eleven days before his death.

• **Gerald Bull** (1928–90), a Canadian ballistics scientist, was shot to death outside his apartment in Brussels, Belgium, on March 22, 1990. Bull was the head of Space Research Corp., which had been linked to Iraq's missile program development. The Israeli secret service and agents of the Iranian government were among the suspects in the killing.

• **Jose Humberto Hernandez Rodriguez**, a Liberal Party deputy in the Colombian congress, was shot to death by gunmen on April 8, 1990. His assassins were believed to be linked to the Colombian drug trade.

• **Maj. Gen. Abdul-Kader al-Kadro**, the former chief of artillery corps, and **Brig. Muhammad Osman Hamed Karar**, the former governor of the Eastern Region, were executed by a firing squad along with twenty-six junior army officers on April 24, 1990. Kadro and Karar and led an unsuccessful coup attempt against the Sudanese government the previous day and were tried and summarily executed for their rebellion.

• **Kazem Rajavi** (1934–90), a leading opponent of the Iranian government in exile, was shot to death near his home outside

Geneva, Switzerland, on April 24, 1990. Rajavi, a university professor who was an outspoken critic of human rights abuses, was a former ambassador to Switzerland. His brother, Massoud Rajavi, was a leader of the People's Mujaheddin guerrilla movement, who claimed Iranian diplomats participated in the killing.

• **Carlos Pizzaro Leongomez** (1952–90), the leader of the rebel April 19 Movement (M-19) and a candidate for president of Colombia, was shot to death by assassins aboard an airliner en route from Bogota on April 26, 1900. The assassin, Gerardo Gutierrez (1969–90), was killed by Pizzaro's bodyguards. The killer was linked to the Medellin drug cartel. Pizarro, the son of a Colombian vice-admiral, joined M-19 in 1971 and eventually became leader of the rebel organization. He was arrested in 1980 and spent three years in prison before his release in an amnesty. He was an unsuccessful candidate for mayor of Bogota in March of 1990. He represented a coalition of twelve leftist parties in elections scheduled for the following month. He was the third presidential candidate to be slain in Colombian within a year.

• **Sam Tambimuttu**, a Tamil politician and member of the Sri Lankan parliament from Batticoloa, was assassinated with his wife by Tamil extremists on May 7, 1990. Another Sri Lanka parliament member from Batticoloa, **V. Yogasangari**, was assassinated by the Tamil Tigers on June 10, 1990.

• **Luis Fontaine Manriquez**, a retired colonel with the Chilean nation police, was shot to death by two unidentified gunmen in Santiago, Chile, on May 10, 1990.

• **Maulvi Mohammed Farooq**, the leading Muslim cleric in Kashmir, was shot to death at his home in Srinagar, India, by three unidentified gunmen on May 21, 1990.

• **Ahmed Darraz**, a senior deputy for Yasir Arafat's Palestine Liberation Organization in the Lebanese refugee camp Ain Hilwe, was killed on June 15, 1990. His assassins were believed to be agents of Palestinian terrorist Abu Nidal (Sabry al-Banna). The murder

sparked violent fighting between Arafat loyalists and members of Nidal's Fatah Revolutionary Council. Nearly eighty perished before Nidal's forces were defeated.

• **Serge Villard**, a member of the Haitian Council of State, was shot by assassins on June 21, 1990, while attending a meeting with labor leaders. He died of his wounds three days later on June 24. **Jean-Marie Montes**, a leading trade unionist, was also killed in the attack.

• **Abdul Aziz Khan**, the highest-ranking judge in the Kashmiri capital, Srinagar, was shot to death by assassins on June 29, 1990. A Kashmir separatist group claimed responsibility for the killing.

• On July 27, 1990, **Major Gideon Orkar** of Nigeria was shot by a firing squad along with 42 other soldiers for their part in a coup attempt on April 22, 1990.

• **Ian Gow** (1937–90), a Conservative member of the British Parliament, died in an explosion of a car bomb as he was leaving his home in Hankham, East Sussex, England, on July 30, 1990. The Provisional Irish Republican Army claimed responsibility for the slaying. Gow, a member of Parliament since 1974, was a close associate of Prime Minister Margaret Thatcher. He had served as her parliamentary private secretary, and had served in positions in the department of environment and the treasury. Gow, an outspoken critic of the IRA, had resigned from the government in 1985 in opposition to the Anglo-Irish accords, granting the Republic of Ireland a voice in Northern Ireland's government.

• **Alexander Muge**, the Anglican Bishop of Eldoret and a critic of President Daniel Arap Moi's government in Kenya, was killed in a mysterious car crash in August of 1990.

• **Vander Beatty**, a former New York state senator, was shot to death at his Brooklyn, New York, campaign headquarters on August 30, 1990. A leading Democratic politician in Brooklyn, Beatty served as deputy party leader in the state senate. He was an unsuccessful candidate for U.S. Congress in

1982. Beatty was running for election to the Democratic State Committee at the time of his death.

• **Samuel K. Doe**, the president of Liberia, was executed by rebels on September 10, 1990. Samuel Kanyon Doe was born in Tuzon on May 6, 1951. He was educated locally and entered the Liberian military in 1969. He was promoted to corporal in 1975 and subsequently received further military training from United States Special Forces troops. Doe became involved with the People's Progressive party, the leading group opposing the regime of President William Tolbert (q.v.). Doe led a military coup against Tolbert in April of 1980. Tolbert was killed during the coup, and Doe served as chairman of the People's Redemption Council from April of 1980. The government promoted a new constitution in April of 1981 and elections were held in October of 1985. Doe was elected president and survived a coup attempt the following month. The coup was led by Brig. Gen. Thomas Quiwonkpa (q.v.), who was later captured and executed. Doe's regime was threatened by several other coup attempts in the late 1980s. Charles Taylor led a revolt in north-eastern Liberia in 1989 that developed into a major tribal conflict. The Liberian army was unable to prevent the rebels' advance through the country. A second rebel group under Prince Johnson broke with Taylor's National Patriotic Forces of Liberia, and fighting continued among rival groups. The Economic Community of West African States sent a peacekeeping force into Liberia in August of 1990. Johnson's rebels took control of much of the capital. Doe was wounded in a gunfight with the rebels when he emerged from the executive mansion on September 9, 1990. He was taken prisoner by the rebels and killed the following day.

• **Max Veillard**, a French mercenary and associate of Bob Denard, was implicated in a coup attempt in the Comoros in August of 1990. Veillard, also known as Servadac, was shot to death by Comoro security forces in October of 1990.

• **Refaat Mahgoub** (1926–90), the speaker of the Egyptian Parliament and a leading political figure in Egypt, was shot to death in Cairo by four assassins with machine guns on October 12, 1990. Three of Mahgoub's bodyguards and his driver were also killed in the attack. The gunmen escaped, but four suspects were captured shortly afterwards and reportedly confessed to the crime. They admitted membership in the extremist Islamic Jihad terrorist group.

• **Dany Chamoun** (1934–90), a Lebanese Maronite Christian leader, was shot to death at his home in Baabda, a suburb of East Beirut, on October 21, 1990. A band of gunmen disguised as Lebanese army soldiers entered his home and shot to death Chamoun, his wife, Ingrid, and two young sons, ages eight and six. Chamoun was the son of former Lebanese President Camille Chamoun and the leader of the rightist National Liberal Party. He was a supporter of Lebanese militia leader Gen. Michel Aoun. Maronite Christian leader Dr. Samir Geagea was tried and convicted of Chamoun's murder. He was sentenced to life imprisonment in June of 1995.

• **Rabbi Meir Kahane**, the founder of the Jewish Defense League and the extremist anti–Arab Kach party in Israel, was assassinated in a New York City hotel on November 5, 1990. Kahane was fatally shot in the neck after completing a speech at the hotel conference room. The assassin was identified as El Sayyid A. Nosair (b. 1956), an Egyptian-born U.S. citizen. He was captured after having been wounded in a shootout with a U.S. Postal service policeman. Kahane was born Martin David Kahane in Brooklyn, New York, on August 1, 1932. During the 1950s he changed his name to Meir and became an Orthodox rabbi for a Queens congregation. During the 1960s Kahane reportedly acted as an FBI informer for leftist anti-war groups. He formed the Jewish Defense League in 1968, advocating aggressive tactics to protect Jewish interests. He was often involved in campaigns against the Soviet Union's refusal to allow Jews to emigrate. Kahane was convicted of making bombs in New York in 1971, and relocated to Israel. He formed the Kach party and was elected to the Knesset in 1984. He advocated the removal of Arabs from Israel and occupied territories. The Kach was banned in the 1988 elections because of its extremist views. He remained an outspoken proponent of militant Zionism until his death. His assassin, Nosair, was acquitted of Kahane's murder in December of 1991. He was later involved in the conspiracy to bomb the World Trade Center in New York on February 26, 1993. Also convicted on federal charges of Kahane's murder, he and nine other defendants were sentenced to life imprisonment for their role in the World Trade center bombing.

# 1991

• **Abu Iyad** (Salah Khalaf) (1934–91), a leader of the Palestine Liberation Organization (PLO) who was considered a likely successor to Yassir Arafat, was shot to death by gunmen in Tunis, Tunisia, on January 14, 1991. PLO security chief **Abu Hul** and another associate were also killed in the attack. The assassinations were believed to have been orchestrated by terrorists linked to Abu Nidal. Abu Iyad was born in Jaffa in 1934.

• **Col. Enrique Bermudez** (1933–91), the leader of the Nicaraguan contra rebels, was shot to death in front of the Intercontinental Hotel in Managua, Nicaragua, on February 16, 1991. Bermudez was a former colonel in the Nicaraguan National Guard during the rule of Anastasio Somoza Debayle (q.v.). After Somoza's ouster in the late 1970s Bermudez was a leader of the revolt against the Sandinista government that followed. The contras fought a long civil war against the government before returning the Nicaragua in 1990.

• **Ranjan Wijeratne**, the Sri Lankan minister of defense, was killed in a massive car bomb explosion blew apart his armor plated Mercedes on March 2, 1991. The assassination was believed to have been orchestrated by Tamil extremists. Wijeratne had previously served as Sri Lanka's foreign minister from 1989 until 1990.

• **Detlev Rohwedder**, the administrator of Treuhand who was in charge of privatizing former East German companies, was shot to death by members of the radical Red Army Faction on April 1, 1991. The killing was believed to have been an attempt to undermine the unification of West and East Germany.

• **Rajiv Gandhi**, the former prime minister of India, was assassinated by a terrorist bomb hidden in a flower basket held by a female suicide bomber in a reception line while campaigning for the Congress party in Sriperumbudur on May 21, 1991. His assassination was believed to have been orchestrated by members of a radical Tamil separatist organization. Rajiv Gandhi was born in Bombay on August 20, 1944. He was the son of Indira Gandhi (q.v.) and the grandson of Jawaharlal Nehru. His grandfather became prime minister in 1947, and Rajiv was raised in the prime minister's residence. He was educated in India and at Cambridge University in Great Britain, where he studied engineering. He trained as an airline pilot while in Great Britain and became a pilot with Indian Airlines. Rajiv remained aloof from politics until his younger brother, Sanjay, was killed in an airplane crash on June 23, 1980. Sanjay had been widely viewed as a likely successor to his mother, Prime Minister Indira Gandhi. Gandhi and the Congress-I party convinced Rajiv to enter politics, and he was elected to Parliament to fill Sanjay's seat in June of 1981. He became a leading advisor to his mother and was appointed general secretary of the Congress-I party in February of 1983. Rajiv was selected to succeed his mother as party leader and prime minister when Indira Gandhi was assassinated on October 31, 1984. He was confirmed in office by a general election two months later. He was considered to have great integrity and was initially a popular leader. Rajiv Gandhi strengthened India's relationship with the United States and the West and attempted to liberalize his nation's economic system. He lost much public support, however, for his decision to send Indian troops to maintain order in Sri Lanka in 1987. His government also faced continuing violence from militant Sikh nationalists, who were responsible for numerous terrorist acts. Gandhi continued to lose support in the Parliament, and the Congress party was defeated by a coalition of anti-government parties in elections in November of 1989. He stepped down as prime minister on December 1, 1989, and became leader of the Opposition. Gandhi forced the collapse of the government of his successor, Vishwarnath Pratap Singh, in November of 1990. New elections were scheduled for May of 1991, and Gandhi was killed while campaigning to regain his office. On August 20, 1991, police tracked down a leader of the Liberation Tigers of Tamil Eelam, Sivarasan (aka Raja Arumainayagam), who was reportedly the architect of Gandhi's assassination. Sivarasan and six of his associates committed suicide after being cornered by Indian police in a house in Konanakunte, near Bangalore.

• **Andre Cools**, a former deputy prime minister of Belgium, was shot to death on July 18, 1991, as he left his apartment in Liege. Cools was a senior member of the Belgian Socialist Party. Two assassins were apprehended and tried in Tunis, Tunisia, in 1998. They were sentenced to twenty years in prison.

• **Shahpur Bakhtiar**, the last prime minister of Iran under the Shah, was stabbed to death outside of his Paris home on August 6, 1991. Bakhtiar was born in Teheran in 1916. He was educated in Lebanon and France, where he studied political science and law at the Sorbonne. He served in the French army during World War II. Bakhtiar returned to Iran in 1946 and entered the Ministry of Labor. He served as deputy labor minister in the government of Mohammed Mossadegh in 1953. Bakhtiar remained active in the National Front, an anti-shah political organization. His opposition to the shah resulted in his arrest on several occasions. On January 4,

1979, the shah selected Bakhtiar to form a government as prime minister in the hopes of preserving the monarchy. As a condition to accepting the appointment, Bakhtiar insisted that the shah leave the country, which he did on January 16, 1979. Bakhtiar, in hopes of stabilizing the government, tried to delay the return of the Ayatollah Khomeini to Iran. He was forced, however, to allow Khomeini to enter Teheran on February 1, 1979. Bakhtiar was unable to gain the support of the leading anti-shah organization, the National Front. The Islamic fundamentalists forced him to leave office on February 5, 1979. He went into hiding before going into exile in Paris. There he formed the National Movement of the Iranian Resistance in opposition to the rule of the Ayatollah Khomeini. He was the target of several assassination attempts before his murder in August of 1991.

• On September 10, 1991, terrorists ambushed a motorcade carrying the leader of the pro–Kuwait Yemenii Unionist Alliance, Omar al-Jawi. Jawi survived the attack, which killed a Yemeni civil servant, **Hassan Huraibi**.

• **Roger Lafontant**, who had served as head of the Duvalier family's secret police, the Tonton Macoutes, was murdered in prison in late September of 1991. Lafontant had led a coup attempt in Haiti on January 6, 1991, to preempt the inauguration of elected president Jean-Bertrand Aristide the following month. Lafontant had served as minister of defense and the interior in the Duvalier regime. He had fled Haiti during a Duvalierist purge in 1985, and returned to the country in July of 1990. He was denied eligibility to run in the subsequent presidential elections and plotted a coup after Aristide's election. The army crushed the coup and Lafontant was arrested and tried in July of 1991. He was murdered in prison in late September during another coup led by Gen. Raul Cedras that ousted President Aristide. Another leading Haitian politician, the **Rev. Sylvio Claude**, the leader of the Christian Democratic party, was also killed in a separate incident when he was burned to death by a pro–Aristide mob with a tire "necklace." Claude, an Evangelist preacher and two-time presidential candidate, had been a leading advocate of human rights since the Duvalier regimes. He was also a critic of the Aristide government, which led to his brutal murder in Les Cayes on September 29, 1991.

• On November 4, 1991, Mohammed Zahir Shah (b.1914), the exiled former king of Afghanistan, was slightly wounded by a knife-wielding assailant at his Rome villa. The attacker was a Portuguese man posing as a journalist. No motive was given in the attack on the former king, who had been involved in peace talks with the ongoing civil violence in Afghanistan.

• **Clement Oumarou Ouedraogo**, the leader of the opposition to President Blaise Compaore of Burkina Faso, was murdered on December 11, 1991, after leading a boycott of the elections.

# 1992

• **Mohamed Boudiaf**, the president of Algeria, was shot to death by an assassin on January 11, 1992, while addressing a rally in Annaba designed to gain popular support for his government. The machine-gun wielding assassin was a member of Boudiaf's security force. Mohamed Boudiaf was born in M'Sila on June 23, 1919. He fought in the French army during World War II, but joined the Algerian Nationalist Movement seeking independence from France in the early 1950s. He served on the National Liberation Front (FLN) leadership council from 1954. Boudiaf was captured by the French in 1956 along with Ahmed Ben Bella and other Algerian leaders. They remained imprisoned until 1962. Boudiaf and Ben Bella disagreed over the political future of Algeria after the formation of the National Front government in 1962. Boudiaf was imprisoned during Ben Bella's leadership and went into exile in Morocco in

1964. He remained a critic of the National Liberation Front leadership. Boudiaf returned from exile and was chosen by the High State Committee to succeed Chadli Benjedid as president on January 16, 1992. He was selected to lead a government of reconciliation following the suppression of Islamic fundamentalists who had been successful in winning an election victory. Boudiaf led a campaign against government corruption and maintained a hard line against the radical Islamics until his death in January of 1992.

• **Abbas al-Musawi** (1952–92), a Palestinian Hezbollah (Party of God) leader, was killed on February 16, 1992, when his car was attacked by an Israeli helicopter near Jipchit in Lebanon. Musawi, his wife Siham, and their child died in the attack. The killing was in retaliation for the murder of three Israeli soldiers in an army camp.

• **Argelino Duran Quintero**, a former government minister of Colombia, was kidnapped by guerrillas in January of 1992. He died in captivity the following March.

• **Salvatore Lima**, the former mayor of Palermo, Sicily, and a member of the Italian parliament, was shot and killed by Mafia gunmen near his home in Palermo on March 12, 1992. Lima was a member of the Italian Parliament and a leading advisor to Italian Premier Giulio Andreotti. Lima's murder came shortly after another Italian political figure, **Sebastiano Corrado**, had been slain by the Mafia in Naples. Corrado, the local councilor of the Party of the Democratic Left, was shot to death on March 11, 1992.

• On March 21, 1992, Gen. Gustavo Leigh Guzman (1920–99), Chile's former commander-in-chief of the air force who served as a member of Chile's ruling junta under Gen. Augusto Pinochet, was shot and critically wounded at his real estate office in Santiago. Gen. Enrique Ruiz, the former chief of air force intelligence and Leigh's business associate, was also injured in the shooting. Leigh was shot five times and Ruiz three, leaving both men seriously injured. A radical leftist group, the Manuel Rodriguez Patriotic Front, claimed responsibility for the shootings. Leigh was a leader of the military coup that ousted President Salvador Allende (q.v.) in September of 1973 and served in the ruling junta until June of 1974. Leigh recovered from his injuries and died seven years later on September 29, 1999.

• **Giovanni Falcone**, a leading Italian prosecutor of Mafia cases, was killed on May 23, 1992, near Palermo, Sicily, when a bomb exploded under his car. His wife, **Judge Francesca Morvillo**, and three bodyguards were also killed in the explosion. Falcone was born on May 18, 1939. A former bankruptcy judge, he was assigned to Palermo in 1978 to prosecute Mafia cases. He convicted over three hundred Mafioso and was named director general of the criminal affairs division of the Italian Justice Department. Salvatore Riina and 23 others leaders of the Sicilian Mafia were convicted of involvement in the murder and were sentenced to life imprisonment in 1997.

• **Farag Foda** (1945–92), a leading Egyptian writer and human rights activist, was shot to death by two masked men on motorcycles believed to be Islamic extremists, while leaving his office in Nasr City on June 8, 1992.

• Palestine Liberation Organization official **Atef Bseiso** was shot to death outside a Paris hotel on June 8, 1992. Bseiso served as the PLO's director of security affairs and was a leading aide to PLO chairman Yasir Arafat. A group headed by rival Palestinian leader Abu Nidal claimed responsibility for the murder, though the Israeli secret service, the Mosad, was also implicated as possible retaliation for Bseiso's involvement in the murder of Israeli athletes at the 1972 Munich Olympics (q.v.).

• **Paolo Borsellino** (1937–1992), the chief prosecutor in Palermo, Sicily, was killed in a bomb blast near his mother's home on July 19, 1992. Five of his bodyguards were also killed in the explosion. Borsellino was a leading prosecutor of the Mafia and was expected to succeed Giovanni Falcone (q.v.) as head of an anti–Mafia organized crime task force.

• **Tavio Ayao Amorin** (Nov. 20, 1958–1992), a Togo opposition leader with the Parti Socialiste Pan-Africain (PSP), was ambushed and shot while walking in downtown Lome on July 23, 1992. He died of his wounds on July 30, 1992.

• **Jean-Claude Congugu**, leader of the opposition party Alliance for Democracy and Progress in the Central African Republic, was killed in Bangui on August 1, 1992, when government security forces attacked a pro-democracy rally.

• **Lt. Gen. Denzil Kobbekaduwa**, the commander of the Sri Lankan task force battling the Tamil Tigers, was killed on Kayts Island when his vehicle hit a land mine in August of 1992. Nine other leading military officers also perished in the explosion.

• **Dr. Mohammad Sadegh Sharafkandi**, who was also known as Dr. Said, an exiled leader of the Iranian Democratic Party of Kurdistan, was shot to death at the Kykonous Restaurant in Berlin, Germany, on September 17, 1992. Three other Kurdish nationalists were also killed in the attack. Sharafkandi was born in Iranian Kurdistan's Bokan region on January 1, 1938. A chemistry teacher from the early 1960s, he received a doctorate in analytical chemistry in France in 1976. He joined the Kurdish nationalist movement after the fall of the Shah in February of 1979. He became leader of the Iranian Democratic Party of Kurdistan following the assassination of Abdolrahman Qassemlu (q.v.) in July of 1989. It was believed agents of the Iranian government were involved in the assassination.

• **Col. Manuel Tumba**, the third ranking officer in Peru's anti-terrorism unit, was assassinated by Shining Path rebels on November 5, 1992. Tumba's murder came shortly after his participation in the capture of Shining Path leader Abimael Guzman the previous month.

• **Adm. Clancey Fernando**, the chief of the Sri Lanka navy, was killed by a radical Tamil terrorist suicide bomber on November 16, 1992.

• **Amman Moayyed al-Janabi**, an Iraqi nuclear engineer who was seeking to defect to Great Britain, was shot to death on December 7, 1992. It was believed that Janabi's assassination was carried out by agents of the Iraqi government seeking to prevent him from revealing information about the country's nuclear program.

• Peruvian labor leader **Pedro Hullica** (1943–92) was shot to death by a band of machine-gun wielding terrorists on December 18, 1992. Hullica was the leader of the General Federation of Peruvian Workers.

# 1993

• **Hakija Turajlic**, one of three deputy prime ministers of the Bosnia and Herzegovina Government, was shot and killed by Serbian nationalist troops while in a French United Nations vehicle on January 8, 1993. Turajlic was on route from an airport meeting in Sara with a delegation from the Turkish government at the time of the attack.

• **Ugur Mumcu**, a leftist Turkish newspaper columnist and investigative journalist, was assassinated in a car bombing by radical Islamic terrorists outside his home in Ankara on January 24, 1993. Mumcu was an opponent of Kurdish separatism and Islamic fundamentalists.

• **Djilali Liabes**, who had served as minister of education in the Algerian cabinet until July of 1992, was shot to death near his Algiers home on March 16, 1993. The assassination was believed to have been carried out by militant Islamic fundamentalists. Liabes had served as head of the National Institute of Strategic Global Studies after leaving the government. Another Algerian cabinet member, Labor Minister Tahar Hamdi, survived an assassination attempt with only minor injuries shortly after Liabes' murder.

• **Hussein Nagdi** (1950–93), an exiled Iranian opposition leader, was shot to death in the streets of Rome en route to his office on March 16, 1993. Nagdi had served as charge d'affaires of the Iranian embassy in Rome until breaking with the government of the Ayatollah Khomeini in 1982. He later served as head of the opposition group the National Council of Resistance of Iran. His killing was alleged to have been carried out by agents of the Iranian government.

• On March 25, 1993, **Col. Koffi Tepe** (1947–93), the former minister of the interior and deputy commander of the Togolese Armed Forces, led a violent coup attempt against the government of Gnassingbe Eyadema at the Tokoin military barracks near Lome. **Gen. Mawulikplim Amegie** (1948–93), who served as minister of interior from 1988 to 1990 and subsequently minister of defense until his death, and **Lt. Col. Gnandi Akpo** (1947–93), the former commander of the presidential guard, were killed while defending the president. The coup failed resulting in the execution of Col. Tepe, who was beaten to death by loyalist troops.

• **Col. Ihsan Mohammed Salem**, known as **Yunis Awad**, the leader of the Palestine Liberation Organization's Al Fatah group in Beirut, was shot to death in Lebanon on April 1, 2001. Abu Nidal's radical Palestinian group was believed to have been behind Salem's assassination, as well as the murder of other PLO officials during the year.

• **Chris Hani**, the secretary of the South African Communist Party, was assassinated outside of his home near Johannesburg on April 10, 1993. Hani was born in Cofimvaba, Transkei, on June 28, 1942. He joined the ANC Youth League in 1957. A graduate of Rhodes University, Hani went into exile in 1962 following his arrest and sentencing under South Africa's Suppression of Communism Act. Hani was active in the fight against the white government of Rhodesia and, after serving two years in a Botswanan prison for possession of illegal weapons, he moved to Lesotho. He ran a guerrilla network against South Africa and, in 1987, he became chief of staff of the ANC's armed forces. He became secretary general of the South African Communist Party in 1991. He was assassinated by Janus Walus and Clive Derby Lewis, radical members of the anti–Communist Afrikaner Resistance Movement. They were convicted of his murder and sentenced to life imprisonment.

- **Lalith Athulathmudali** (1936–93), the leader of the Sri Lankan Tamil opposition party, was shot to death at a political rally in the town of Kirullapone on April 23, 1993. Athulathmudali was a former minister of national security in Sri Lanka, but had broken with President Ranasingle Premadasa (q.v.) and the United National Party in 1991 and subsequently led the Democratic United National Front. The government alleged that the Tamil Tiger extremists were responsible for the killing, producing the body of the alleged killer, Kandiah Ragunathan, the day after Athulathmudali's murder. Opposition leaders continued to accuse the government of orchestrating the murder.

- **Ranasinghe Premadasa**, the president of Sri Lanka, was killed in an explosion when a bomb-laden bicyclist attacked the president during a May Day parade in Colombo on May 1, 1993. Many of his bodyguards and several aides were also killed in the attack. Premadasa was born to a poor family in Colombo on June 23, 1924. He was educated at St. Joseph College and became active in the trade union movement. He was elected to the Colombo Municipal Council in 1950 and became deputy mayor in 1955. Premadasa joined the United National party in 1956 and was elected to the Parliament in 1960. He held positions in several ministries before being named minister of local government in 1968. He served as chief whip of the Opposition in Parliament from 1970, and was elected deputy leader of the United National party in 1976. Premadasa returned to the cabinet as minister of local government in 1977. He was selected as prime minister to succeed Junius R. Jayewardene in February of 1978, after Jayewardene became president. His government was faced with a faltering economy and continuing unrest from Tamil separatists from northern Sri Lanka. Premadasa defeated Sirimavo Bandaranaike in December of 1988 to become president of Sri Lanka and was sworn into office the following January. Premadasa also held other major positions in the government, including the Ministries of Defense and Planning. Violence between Tamil and Sinhalese extremists continued to plague the country, claiming Premadasa as one of its victims in May of 1993.

- **Babacar Seye**, the vice president of the Senegal Constitutional Council, was shot to death by six gunmen on May 15, 1993. The opposition party leader, Abdoulaye Wade, was charged in connection with the murder.

- **Samuel Gapyisi**, leader of the opposition party Mouvement Democratique Republicain (MDR) in Rwanda, was assassinated on May 18, 1993, allegedly by members of the government sponsored Rwandan Patriotic Front.

- **Juan Jesus Cardinal Posadas Ocampo** was shot to death in the parking lot of the airport of Guadalajara on May 24, 1993, when caught in the crossfire between members of drug cartels. The cardinal and his driver were shot at point-blank range. They had been waiting to greet a fellow bishop at the airport when the slayings occurred. Juan Jesus Posadas Ocampo was born in Salvatierra, Mexico, on November 10, 1926. He attended the Seminary of Morelia and was ordained a priest in September of 1950. He remained in Morelia, where he taught at the seminary and rose to become vice-rector. He was selected as Bishop of Tijuana in March of 1970. He became Bishop of Cuernavaca in December of 1982, and was elevated to Archbishop of Guadalajara in May of 1987. Posadas Ocampo was created a cardinal priest by Pope John Paul II on June 28, 1991.

- **Ramesh More**, a member of the Indian radical party Shiv Sena, was shot to death by assassins in Bombay on May 29, 1993. Two days later, **Premkumar Sharma**, a member of the Bharatiya Janata Party, was also shot and killed by assassins in Bomba. Sharma was a state assemblyman from Maharashtra and a leading Hindu politician from the area.

• **Jorge Carpio Nicolle**, a two-time former presidential candidate in Guatemala, was ambushed and shot to death by nearly thirty gunmen in Guatemala on July 3, 1993. Three of his associates were also killed in the attack. Carpio Nicolle was the editor of the *El Grafico* newspaper and the founder of the Guatemalan National Center Union party. He was the cousin of President Ramiro de Leon Carpio of Guatemala.

• **Viktor Polyanichko**, the military governor of the North Ossetia and Ingushetia region in Russia's Caucasus Mountains, and **Gen. Anatoly Koretsky**, the military commander of the region, were shot and killed by gunmen on horseback while traveling in a motorcade in the region on August 1, 1993.

• United States diplomat **Fred Woodruff** (1948–93) was shot and killed near Tbilisi, Georgia, on August 8, 1993. He was killed while riding in a car with the chief bodyguard of Georgian President Eduard Shevardnadze. Woodruff was a C.I.A. operative working with the Georgian government. He was believed to have been the victim of a robbery attempt.

• **Kasdi Merbah**, a former Algerian premier, was ambushed and assassinated by Muslim militants in Bordj el-Bahri, near Algiers, while returning from a coastal resort on August 21, 1993. Merbah was born in 1939. He fought with the revolution during the 1950s and was a member of the Algerian provisional government's delegation which negotiated independence from France. In 1962 Merbah was appointed director of military security, in charge of army intelligence, and he served in that position until 1978. He was then named to the political bureau of the National Liberation front. From 1982 to 1984 he served in the cabinet as minister of heavy industry. Merbah was moved to the ministry of agriculture in the Brahimi government in 1984. In February of 1988 he was named minister of health, and on November 5, 1988, he replaced Brahimi as premier. Merbah initiated policies that would open the way for a multi-party political system in Algeria. When he was dismissed from office by President Chadli Benjedid after less than a year, the reform-minded Merbah threatened a constitutional crisis when he initially refused to leave office. He was ultimately replaced by Mouloud Hamroch on September 9, 1989. He served as leader of the Algerian Movement for Justice and Development from 1990 until his murder in August of 1993.

• **Fidele Rwambuka**, another Rwanda opposition leader with the National Committee of the Republican National Movement of Democracy and Development (MRND), was also assassinated on August 25, 1993. He was the mayor of the commune of Kanzenze.

• **Mehmet Sincar**, a member of the New Democracy Party (DEP) who served in the Turkish parliament from Mardin, was assassinated by unknown gunmen on a Batman street on September 4, 1993. **Metin Ozdemir**, a DEP official, was also killed in the attack.

• **Antoine Izmery**, a leading Haitian political figure and financial backer of Jean-Bertrand Aristide, was shot to death after being dragged from a Port-au-Prince church by nearly a dozen attackers on September 11, 1993.

• **Abu Shaaban**, a leader of the Palestine Liberation Organization's Al Fatah movement, was shot to death in the Gaza Strip by a rival Palestinian assassin on September 21, 1993

• **Ghulam Haider Wyne**, a Pakistani politician and former Chief Minister of Punjab in 1990, was shot to death in Multan, Pakistan, after attending a political meeting on September 29, 1993. A candidate for the National Assembly, Wyne was a close associate of Nawaz Sharif, the former Prime Minister of Pakistan, and was the provincial leader of the Pakistan Muslim League Party. His murder was allegedly due to a tribal vendetta.

• **Sammy Motha**, the leader of the Inkatha Freedom Party in Kwathelma township, South Africa, was shot to death while leaving his home in the early morning of September 29, 1993.

- Col. Taha Sayyid, the chief military prosecutor of Muslim militants charged with attempting to resurrect the underground organization that assassinated Egyptian President Anwar Sadat in 1981, was shot and wounded by four gunmen in Heliopolis, Egypt, on October 9, 1993.

- **Guy Malary**, Haiti's former minister of justice, was shot to death by machine-gun fire in his car near his office in downtown Port-au-Prince on October 14, 1993. Malary was a supporter of exiled president Jean-Bertrand Aristide. Two of Malary's aides were also killed in the attack.

- **Melchior Ndadaye**, the president of Burundi, was killed during a coup on October 21, 1993, three months after taking office. Ndadaye was born in Nyabinhanga, Burundi, on March 28, 1953. A Hutu, he had spent many years in exile in neighboring Rwanda after the ethnic violence in Burundi in the early 1970s. Trained as a teacher, Ndadaye became a lecturer and part-time instructor. He returned to Burundi in the 1980s to work in the banking industry. He also became an advisor to the rural development ministry in 1989. Ndadaye entered politics as head of the Front for Democracy in Burundi (Frodebu), and became Burundi's first freely elected president, and first Hutu leader, in elections in June of 1993. Ndadaye died in a violent coup allegedly supported by former president Jean-Baptiste Bagaza and Army Commander-in-Chief Jean Bikomagu, in October of 1993, sparking renewed ethnic violence in Burundi and Rwanda.

- **Assad Saftawi** (1935–93) was shot to death in Gaza on October 21, 1993, by two masked Palestinian gunmen. Saftawi was a leading Palestinian moderate and a close associate of Yasir Arafat. He was a founding member of the PLO's Fatah movement in the late 1950s.

- **Col. Abbas Koty**, the leader of an unsuccessful coup attempt against the government of President Idriss Deby of Chad in June of 1992, was shot to death by security police on October 22, 1993, after returning to Chad under an agreement guaranteeing his safety. Koty headed the opposition Chad National Rectification Committee (CNRT).

- **Brig. Gen. Bahtiyar Aydin**, the regional police commander for southern Turkey, was assassinated by snipers with the Kurdish Workers' Party (PKK) in Lice on October 22, 1993.

- **Francisco Velis**, a former leader of the Farabundo Marti National Liberation Movement (FLMN) rebel group running for political office in El Salvador was shot to death on October 25, 1993. Another former rebel leader, **Heleno Castro Guevara**, was killed on October 29, 1993, during a traffic dispute in El Salvador.

- A prominent French jurist, **Fernand Bouland** (1948–93), and two American businessmen, **Coby Hoffman** (1949–93) and **Robert Guidi** (1948–93), were shot and killed in a luxury hotel in Cairo, Egypt, on October 26, 1993. Their assailant was a man with a history of mental illness and the incident was not believed to have been related to Muslim fundamentalists. Hoffman and Guidi were from New Jersey and were employees of an oil service company. Bouland was the former dean of law at Aix-en-Provence University and was the mayor of the French town of Chateauneuf-le-Rouge. He was attending at conference in Cairo sponsored by the Egyptian Association of Criminal Law.

- **Dario Londono Cardona**, the vice president of the Colombian senate, was shot by an assassin in Medellin on November 5, 1993. He died of his wounds two days later.

- **Lt. Col. Mouin Shabaytah**, the deputy commander of the Fatah militia in Lebanon, was shot to death by two gunmen in Sidon, Lebanon, on November 15, 1993. Shabaytah was a leading aide to PLO chairman Yasir Arafat.

- On November 25, 1993, Egyptian Prime Minister Atef Sedki survived a car bomb attack. He was the third high-ranking Egyptian official to survive assassination attempts in 1993. Muhammad Safawat ash-Sharif, the minister of information, was slightly injured in an ambush in April. Hassan Muhammad al-Alfi, the minister of the interior, was uninjured when a terrorist bomb exploded by his motorcade as it approached the interior ministry in August of 1993.

• **Pablo Escobar Gaviria**, the leader of the international Medellin drug cartel, was killed in a shoot out with Colombian soldiers in Medellin on December 2, 1993. Escobar and his bodyguard died while trying to escape from the roof of the house they were hiding in. Escobar's drug network reportedly took in an estimated $20 billion annually and had supplied 80% of the cocaine distributed in the United States. He had been on the run from Colombian authorities since July of 1992, after escaping from prison.

• **Jose Maria Lopez**, a former commander of the rebel Farabundo Marti National Liberation Movement (FMLN) in El Salvador, was shot to death near San Salvador on December 9, 1993. Lopez was a candidate for public office at the time of his murder.

• **Mihajlo Ljesar** (1950–93), the vice premier of Montenegro, was shot to death in his office in Podgorica, the capital, on December 20, 1993. The assassin committed suicide after shooting Ljesar.

• **Zviad Gamsakhurdia**, the first elected president of the Republic of Georgia until his ouster in 1992, died of a gunshot wound on December 31, 1993. His wife, Manan, claimed that Gamsakhurdia had committed suicide while under siege by soldiers from the pro-government paramilitary group. The Georgian government alleged that Gamsakhurdia may have been killed during a quarrel with supporters. Zviad Konstantinovich Gamsakhurdia was born in Tbilisi on March 31, 1939. He was a leading supporter of democratic reform and human rights during the 1970s. He was arrested in 1977 and detained until 1979. Gamsakhurdia became the leader of the Popular Georgian Front in 1989 and

was elected to the Georgia Supreme Soviet the following year. He also served as Chairman of the Supreme Soviet from 1990. Georgia was declared an independent republic following a referendum in April of 1991. Gamsakhurdia was elected president of Georgia in May of 1991. After a period of civil unrest, he was deposed by a military council led by Tengis Sigua on January 6, 1992. Followers of Gamsakhurdia attempted a coup on June 24, 1992, but they were crushed by the Georgian security forces. Gamsakhurdia led rebel forces in an offensive on Tbilisi in September of 1993, but after several weeks of fighting he was forced to retreat. Soon after Gamsakhurdia died, surrounded by troops loyal to President Eduard Shevardnadze.

# 1994

• **Mohammed Bellal**, the governor of Algeria's Tissemsilt province, was ambushed and killed by Islamic extremists in a motorcade outside the town of Tissemsilt on January 11, 1994. Eighteen others were killed by the band of armed men who opened fire on the convoy.

• **Naeb Imran Maaytah**, the first secretary of the Jordanian embassy in Beirut, Lebanon, was shot and fatally injured while driving to work in Beirut on January 29, 1994. Four Palestinians reportedly associated with the Fatah Revolutionary Council were arrested for participating in the assassination.

• **Col. Nikolas Kekelidze**, the deputy defense minister of Georgia, was assassinated on February 3, 1994, when a remote-controlled bomb exploded at his home in Tbilisi. Georgy Karkarashvili, the minister of defense, was injured in a separate booby trapped grenade explosion at the scene of Kekelidze's murder.

• **Dominic McGlinchey** (1954–94), the leader of the extremist Irish National Liberation Army (INLA), was shot to death by three gunmen on February 12, 1994. McGlinchey, known as "Mad Dog," was a leading hitman who was involved in hundreds of shootings, bombings and assassinations.

• **Gaston Aziaduvo Edeh**, a newly elected deputy in the Togolese parliament, was abducted and murdered along with two other members of the opposition, **Prosper Ayite Hillah** and **Martin Agbenou** on February 13, 1994.

• **Felicien Gatabazi**, the leader of the opposition Parti Social Democrate (PSD) and a member of the Rwandan coalition government, was shot to death at the entrance of his house on February 21, 1994. Gatabazi was a Tutsi moderate who appealed to Hutus. **Martin Bucyana**, the leader of the Coalition for the Defense of the Republic (CDR), was assassinated the following day in Butare. Both killing were allegedly orchestrated by the government sponsored Rwandan Patriotic Army.

• **Yann Piat** (1950–94), a member of the French National Assembly, was shot and killed while riding in her car in her hometown of Hyeres on the Riviera. Piat was a member of the Union for French Democracy (UDF). Two assailants were apprehended, Epiphanio Pericolo and Denis Labadie. They were associates of a criminal boss and Piat was believed to have been targeted because of her anti-corruption campaign.

• **Luis Colosio**, Mexico's ruling Institutional Revolutionary Party (PRI) candidate for president was shot to death leaving a campaign rally in Tijuana on March 23, 1994. Colosio was considered the front runner in upcoming elections. His assassin was identified as a young pacifist, Mario Aburto Martinez (b.1971). Colosio was born in Magdalena del Kino, Sonora, Mexico, on February 10, 1950. He joined the Institutional Revolutionary Party (PRI) after receiving a degree in economics in Monterrey. He continued his education at the University of Pennsylvania, earning a master's degree in regional development and urban economics, in 1977. He began working for the government department of budget and planning in 1979 and was elected to the Mexican congress from Sonora in 1985. Colosio won a seat in the Senate in 1988. He also served as campaign manager for the successful presidential race of Carlos Salinas de Gortari in 1988. He subsequently served as leader of the PRI until 1992, when he was named secretary of social development in Salinas' government. He became the ruling PRI's candidate for president in November of 1993 and was expected to become Mexico's next president at the time of his assassination.

• **Epaminondias Gonzalez Dubon**, the president of Guatemala's Constitutional Court, was shot and killed by unknown gunmen in Guatemala City on April 1, 1994.

• **Juvenal Habyarimana**, the president of Rwanda, and **Cyprien Ntaryamira**, the president of Burundi, were killed along with several of their aides when their plane crashed while approaching Kigali airport on April 6, 1994. Habyarimana and Ntaryamira were returning from Tanzania after attending a conference in hopes of ending the bloodshed between the Hutu and Tutsi tribes. The plane was shot down by missiles fired from a farm near Masaka on its approach. It was believed that the Hutu-let Rwandan military, upset at Habyarimana's moderate approach towards Tutsis, were responsible. The Rwanda delegation also included **Maj. Gen. Deogratias Nsabimana**, the chief of staff of the Rwandan Army, Ambassador **Juvenal Renzaho**, an adviser in the president's office; **Col. Elie Sagatwa**, the president's private secretary; **Dr. Emmanuel Akingeneye**, the president's doctor; and **Maj. Thaddee Bagaragaza**. Secretary **Bernard Ciza** and Secretary **Cyriaque Simbizi** were accompanying the Burundi delegation. The French crew of the plane, **Major Jack Heraud**, **Col. Jean-Pierre Minaberry** and **Master Sgt. Jean Marie Perrine**, were also killed in the crash. Thousands of people had been killed in both countries over the previous decade in tribal clashes. The day after the crash Rwandan Prime Minister **Agathe Uwilingiyimana**, a Tutsi, under guard by 10 Belgian soldiers with the UN peace-keeping mission, was seized and shot by members of the presidential guard. The Belgians were also tortured and murdered. Several other government officials including **Fuastin Rucogoza**, the minister of information, and **Marc Rugenera**, the finance minister, **Joseph Kavaruganda**, the Hutu president of the supreme court, **Aloys Habimana**, the former director of the agriculture ministry, **Emmanuel Bahigiki**, the former secretary general of the planning ministry, **Theoneste Mujyanama**, the former attorney general, **Felicien Ngango**, the leader of the Hutu opposition Social Democratic Party, **Vincent Nsengiyumva**, the Archbishop of Kigali, **Thaddee Nsengiyumva**, the Bishop of Kabgayi, **Joseph Ruzindama**, the Bishop of Byumba, and nine priests — **Mgr. Innocent Gasabwoya, Mgr. Jean-Marie Vianney Rwabilinda, Father Emmanuel Uwimaria, Father Sylvestre Ndaberetse, Father Bernard Ntarnugabumwe, Father Francois Xavier Muligo, Father Alfred Kayibanda, Fidele Gahonzire Human** and **Brother Jean Baptiste Nsinga**, the president of the St. Joseph Brothers — were also shot during the ensuing violence on June 5, 1994.

Juvenal Habyarimana was born in Gasiza, Gisenyi, on August 3, 1937. He was educated at Lovanium University in Kinshasa and entered the Officers' Training College at Kigali in 1960. He received further military training in Belgium and served as an officer in the Rwandan armed forces. Habyarimana was promoted to commander of the army in June of 1965 and was named to the cabinet as minister of defense the following November. Continued fighting between the rival Hutu and Tutsi tribes led Habyarimana to lead a military coup that ousted the government of Gregoire Kayibanda on July 5, 1973. He formed a civilian-military government and organized the National Revolutionary Movement for Development as the only legal party in 1976. Habyarimana promoted a new constitution in December of 1978 and was confirmed for an additional term of office as

president. He survived a coup attempt in 1980 and was again unopposed for reelection to the presidency in December of 1988. Habyarimana allowed the formation of rival political parties in 1991 and made plans for multiparty elections. He remained president of Rwanda until his death in an air crash on April 6, 1994.

Cyprien Ntaryamira was born in Burundi in 1956. He had fled Burundi in 1972 to escape from the violence that plagued the country when over 100,000 Hutus were murdered by Tutsis. Ntaryamira returned to Burundi in 1983, joining the foreign ministry. He was a founder of the Front for Democracy party under Melchior Ndadaye (q.v.). When Ndadaye became Burundi's first Hutu president in June of 1993, Ntaryamira served in his cabinet as minister of agriculture. Ndadaye was assassinated in October of 1993 and Ntaryamira was eventually chosen to succeed him as president in January of 1994. Ethnic violence continued during his term of office that ended when he perished in an airplane crash on April 6, 1994.

• **Maj. Gen. Raouf Khayrat** (1941–94), Egypt's top anti-terrorist officer, was assassinated by gunmen while in his car in the Cairo area on April 9, 1994. Khayrat led the government's State Security Investigation Section. The Islamic militant organization, Gamaa al-Aslamiya, claimed responsibility for the killing.

• **Taleb al-Suheil** (1930–94), a leading member of the Iraqi exile group Free Iraqi Council, was shot to death at his home in Beirut on April 12, 1994. Two Iraqi diplomats were arrested in connection with the murder.

• **Selomotsi Baholo**, the Deputy Prime Minister of Lesotho, was killed by rebel soldiers on April 14, 1994, who were apparently angry over a pay dispute. Baholo had also served as Lesotho's finance and economic planning minister.

• **Andrei Aizderdzis**, a Russian businessman and deputy in the Duma, was shot to death in front of his apartment building in a Moscow suburb on April 26, 1994. Aizderdzis' murder was believed to have been related to his business dealings, rather than politically motivated.

- **Yousef Fathallah**, the president of the Algerian Human Rights League since 1991, was shot to death by gunmen in Algiers on June 18, 1994. He was a leading critic of human rights abuses in Algeria.

- **Maj. Gen. Carlos Julio Gil Colorado**, the commander of Colombia's Fourth Army Division, was assassinated on July 19, 1994, in Villavicencio, by the leftist Simon Bolivar Guerrilla Coordinator.

- **Manuel Cepeda Vargas** (1930–94), a member of the leftist Patriotic Union party who served in the Colombian senate, was assassinated while driving to work in Bogota on August 9, 1994.

- **Abdallah Kaci**, a member of Algeria's ruling National Transition Council, was assassinated by Islamic militants on August 24, 1994.

- **Ramdas Nayak**, the president of the Hindu Bharatiya Janata party (BJP) in India was shot to death in Bombay on August 25, 1994. His driver was also killed in the attack when two assassins riding motorcycles fired automatic weapons at his car.

- **John Newman** (1947–94), a member of the state legislature in New South Wales, Australia, was shot to death in front of his home in Cabramatta, a Sydney suburb, on September 5, 1994. Newman had been leading an anti-crime campaign in Australia, targeting Asian gangs.

- **Jose Francisco Ruiz Massieu** (1946–94), the secretary-general of Mexico's ruling Institutional Revolutionary Party (PRI), was assassinated on September 28, 1994, in Mexico City while leaving a party breakfast meeting. Ruiz, who had served as governor of Guerrero from 1987 to 1993, was a member of the federal Congress. He was selected as secretary general of the PRI a month before his murder. His alleged assassin was captured and

identified as Daniel Aguilar Trevino (b. 1966). Several leading political figures were implicated in the assassination plot. Raul Salinas, the brother of Mexican President Carlos Salinas, was tried and convicted in January of 1999 of orchestrating the murder of Ruiz and sentenced to fifty years in prison.

- **Mehmet Topac**, a former Turkish Minister of Justice, was assassinated by the leftist guerrilla group the Revolutionary People's Forces (DHG) on September 29, 1994.

- Naguib Mahfouz, the Nobel Prize winning Egyptian author, was stabbed by an Islamic militant in Cairo on October 14, 1994. Mahfouz survived his injuries.

- **Gamini Dissanayake**, the leader of Sri Lanka's United National Party (UNP) and a candidate for president of Sri Lanka, was assassinated by a Tamil terrorist suicide bomber on October 23, 1994. **Gamini Wijesekera**, the general secretary of the United National Party, and two former cabinet members were also among the dozens killed in the assassination. His widow, Srima, replaced him on the ballot but was unsuccessful in the subsequent election.

- An unsuccessful attempt was made on the life of President Bill Clinton on October 29, 1994, when Francisco Duran (b.1968), of Colorado Springs, Colorado, fired several rounds from an assault rifle at the White House. Clinton was in the White House, but was uninjured in the shooting. Duran was overpowered by bystanders and taken into custody. He was convicted of attempted to assassinate the president in April of 1995, and was sentenced to 40 years in prison on June 2, 1995.

- **Valentin Matemyanov**, a deputy in the Russian Duma, was beaten to death by two unknown attackers in Moscow on November 1, 1994. He was reportedly the victim of a street crime by muggers.

- **Hani Abed**, a Palestinian leader, was killed in Khan Yunis, in the Gaza Strip, on November 2, 1994, when a bomb was planted in his car. Abed was a leading official with the radical Islamic Jihad and a newspaper publisher. The assassination was believed to have been carried out by the Israeli Secret Service.

• **Georgi Chanturia**, a leading opposition leader in Georgia, was shot to death in Tbilisi, the capital, on December 3, 1994. Chanturia headed the opposition National Democratic Party. His wife, Irina Sarishvili-Chanturia, a member of the Georgian parliament, was seriously injured in the attack.

# 1995

• **Salah Nour**, a member of Algeria's temporary parliament, the National Transitional Council, was shot to death by Muslim extremists outside his home in Ben Omar, southern Algeria, on January 15, 1995.

• **Gen. Paata Datuashvili**, the former deputy defense minister of Georgia, was shot to death by two unidentified gunmen in Moscow on January 25, 1995. The former Georgian defense minister, Gen. Georgi Karkarashvili, was also injured in the attack which occurred while they were leaving an apartment building.

• **Sergei Skorchkin**, a deputy in the Russian Duma and a member of Vladimir Zhirinovsky's Liberal Democratic Party, was found dead on February 2, 1995, handcuffed to a railway track in a Moscow suburb. His murder was believed to have been carried out by organized crime elements.

• **Eric Lamothe** (1944–95), a member of the Haitian Chamber of Deputies, was found shot to death in his car in Port-au-Prince on March 2, 1995. Lamothe was a supporter of Haitian President Jean Bertrand Aristide.

• **Pierre-Claver Rwangabo**, the governor of Butare in southern Rwanda, was shot to death on March 4, 1995. Rwangabo, a moderate Hutu, was believed to have been the victim of continued violence in the area

caused by forces loyal to the deposed Hutu government.

• Ethnic violence continued in Burundi where **Ernest Kabusheye**, the minister of energy and a moderate Hutu leader, was assassinated by Tutsi extremists on March 11, 1995. **Lucien Sakubu**, the former Tutsi mayor of Bujumbura and an advisor to the minister of the interior, was kidnapped and brutally murdered, presumably by Hutu extremists, on March 13, 1995.

• On March 13, 1995, **Abdul Ali Mazari**, the leader of the pro–Iranian Afghan Wahdat (Unity) party, became another victim in the ongoing civil war. Mazari's organization controlled areas south of capital after Kabul had fallen to the Taliban in April of 1992. Following a break with other anti–Taliban leaders, Mazari surrendered to the Taliban in 1995. He was murdered soon after while in captivity.

• **Djavadov Rovshan Bahtiarovich**, the vice-minister of the interior of Azerbaijan, died in a hospital on March 17, 1995, reportedly as a result of injuries suffered during an assault at his residence by members of the presidential troops.

• **Maurizio Gucci** (1948–95), the former chairman of the Gucci fashion company, was shot to death in front of his office in Milan, Italy, on March 27, 1995. He had stepped down as head of Guccio Gucci SpA in 1993, turning over leadership of the family business to Investcorp investment bank. Gucci's assailant was believed to have been a professional hitman hired by Gucci's ex-wife, Patrizia Reggiani Martinelli, who was charged with involvement in the slaying in 1997.

• **Mireille Durocher de Bertin** (1956–95), the lawyer and former spokeswoman for Gen. Raoul Cedras' military government of Haiti, was shot to death by three gunmen while riding in her car in Port-au-Prince on March 28, 1995. She was a leading critic of the government of President Bertrand Aristide and had planned to contest the presidential elections as head of the Movement for

National Integration party later in the year. Members of the Aristide government were reportedly implicated in the assassination.

- **Gen. Manken Chigawa**, the commander of the Malawi army, was shot to death on April 20, 1995, allegedly during an attempted theft of his car.

- Mexican prosecutor **Leonardo Lario Guzman** was shot to death by four gunmen in front of his home in Guadalajara, Mexico, on May 10, 1995. Guzman was the chief prosecutor in the investigation of the murder of Roman Catholic Cardinal Juan Jesus Posadas Ocampo (q.v.) in 1993.

- **Soliko Khabeishvili**, a close political ally of Georgian President Edward Shevardnadze and director of the Revival and Democracy Fund, was shot to death in front of his home in Tblisi on June 20, 1995.

- **Mahmud el-Khawaja** (1960–95), a Palestinian leader who worked in the United Nations refugee program, UNWRA, was shot to death while walking to work in the Gaza Strip on June 22, 1995.

- Egyptian President Hosni Mubarak survived an assassination attempt while on a state visit to Addis Ababa, Ethiopia, on June 26. Assassins fired on Mubarak's limousine but the president was uninjured in the assault. Two Ethiopian security officers and two of the assailants were killed during the attack.

- **Shamaradan Jafarov**, an opposition member of the Azerbaijan parliament, was shot and killed by police in Baku on June 29, 1995. Jafarov was a member of the opposition Popular Front of Azerbaijan.

- **Beant Singh** (1922–95), the chief minister of Punjab in India, was killed in an explosion caused by a car bomb in Singh's motorcade outside the government building in Chandigargh, Punjab's capital, on August 31, 1995. At least a dozen other people were also killed in the blast. A militant Sikh terrorist organization, the Babbar Khalsa International, claimed responsibility for the assassination. Singh, a member of the ruling Congress (I) party, had served as Punjab's chief minister

since 1992. He had been involved in repressing Sikh uprisings in the Punjab region in the 1980s.

- **Abdelmagid Benhadid**, an independent candidate for Algeria's president, was shot to death by three men in the town of Boudouaou, 18 miles east of Algiers, on September 17, 1995.

- **Aboubakr Belkaid**, a former Algerian interior minister and outspoken critic of Islamic extremists, was shot to death in Algiers on September 28, 1995.

- **General Henri Max Maynard** (1949–95) of Haiti was ambushed by gunmen as he drove through a busy Port-au-Prince street on October 3, 1995. He was shot to death as he attempted to flee from his automobile. Mayard was a former general in the disbanded Haitian army.

- **Omar Qartilan**, the editor of *El Khabar*, the leading Arabic daily newspaper in Algeria, was shot to death on October 3, 1995. He was the fifth journalist to be assassinated in Algeria in a month.

- Macedonian President Kiro Gligorov (b.1917) was critically injured in a car-bomb attack near the Parliament building in Skopje, Macedonia, on October 3, 1995. His driver and three bystanders were killed in the assault. Gligorov was a leader of Macedonian independence from Yugoslavia in 1991. He recovered from his injuries and remained president of Macedonia until 1999.

- **Dr. Fathi al-Shiqaqi** (1951–95), a Palestinian leader who had been expelled from Gaza in 1988, was shot to death by two men on motorcycle in front of his hotel in Sliema, Malta, on October 26, 1995. Shiqaqi was the leader of the extremist Islamic Jihad movement. The Israeli secret service were blamed by his supporters for the attack.

- **Alvaro Gomez Hurtado** (1919–95), a leader of Colombia's opposition Conservative Party, was shot to death in a Bogota street outside Sergio Arboleda University by unidentified gunmen on November 2, 1995. Gomez was a former Colombian ambassador to the United States who had run for president of Colombia on three occasions. He had served as vice president of Colombia from 1982 until 1984 and was publisher of the Bogota daily newspaper *El Nuevo Siglo*. Gomez's aide, **Jose del Cristo Huertas**, was also killed in the attack. Gomez was a leading critic of drug traffickers and corruption in the Colombian government. Retired Col. Bernardo Ruiz was arrested in April of 1999 on charges of orchestrating the killing.

• **Yitzhak Rabin**, the Prime Minister of Israel, was shot to death while attending a peace rally in Tel Aviv by a right-wing Israeli law student, Yigal Amir (b.1968), who opposed Rabin's policies on November 4, 1995. Yitzhak Rabin was born in Jerusalem on March 1, 1922. He was educated in Palestine and joined the Palmach, the commando unit of the Zionist army, the Haganah, in 1941. He fought with the British army during World War II and rose to the rank of deputy commander. Rabin went underground after the war and fought against the British authorities who were preventing Jewish immigration to Palestine. Rabin was arrested in 1946 for blowing up a British police station in Jenin and was imprisoned for six months. Israel was granted independence in 1948, and Rabin served as commander of the Palmach Har-El brigade in the subsequent war against the Arabs. He was promoted to colonel and served as Israel's military representative to armistice negotiations with the Egyptians in 1949. He remained in the army and served as chief of operations in the early 1950s. Rabin was promoted to brigadier general in 1954 and was named commander of the northern sector two years later. He served as deputy chief of staff from 1960 and became chief of staff of the Israel Defense Forces in January of 1964. He led the Israeli army to victory during the Six-Day War against the Arabs in June of 1967. Rabin retired from the army in January of 1968 and was appointed Israel's ambassador to the United States. He successfully presented his nation's policies to the United States government. Rabin returned to Israel in March of

1973 to enter politics. He was elected to the Knesset as a member of the Labor party in December of 1973 and was named to Golda Meir's cabinet as minister of labor. When Meir resigned in April of 1974, Rabin was elected to replace her as prime minister. He took office on June 3, 1974. He announced his resignation in December of 1976 following his government's defeat in a vote of confidence in Parliament. Rabin remained head of a caretaker government until April 8, 1977, when he resigned from leadership of the Labor party for having violated an Israeli law concerning deposits in foreign banks. The Labor party was subsequently defeated by Menachem Begin's Likud coalition in elections the following month. Rabin remained a member of the Knesset and returned to government as minister of defense in 1984. He remained in the National Unity government until 1990. Rabin defeated Shimon Peres for leadership of the Labor party in February of 1992. The Labor party returned to power the following July and Rabin again became prime minister of July 12, 1992. Rabin pursued a policy of peace with the Palestinians and Israel's Arab neighbors. He signed the Israeli-Palestinian Declaration of Principles in Washington with PLO Chairman Yasser Arafat in September of 1994, and signed the Treaty of Peace between Israel and Jordan in October of 1994. Rabin shared the 1994 Nobel Prize for Peace with Arafat and Israeli Foreign Minister Shimon Peres. He remained head of the Israeli government until his assassination in November of 1995. His assassin, Yigal Amir, was convicted of the murder and sentenced to life imprisonment in March of 1996.

• **Jean-Hubert Feuille**, a Haitian legislator, was shot to death while riding in a car in Port-au-Prince, on November 7, 1995. Feuille was a cousin of Haitian President Jean-Bertrand Aristide. Gabriel Fortune, a fellow legislator riding with Feuille, was seriously injured in the attack.

• **Kenule Saro-Wiwa**, a leading Nigerian human rights campaigner, was executed along with eight other Ogoni activists on the orders of Nigeria's military government on November 10, 1995. Saro-Wiwa was born in Bori, Rivers State, in 1941. He served as the Rivers State commissioner for works, land and transport from 1968. He was internationally known for his many books, including *Tambari* (1973), *Sozaboy* (1985) and *A Forest of Flowers* (1986). As president of the Movement for the Survival of the Ogoni People, Saro-Wiwa had opposed the exploitation of the natural resources in the region. His arrest in May of 1994 let to an international response, and his subsequent execution led to Nigeria's expulsion from the British Commonwealth.

• **Ahmed Ala Nazmi** (1953–95), an Egyptian diplomat, was shot to death in Geneva, Switzerland, on November 13, 1995. Extremist Islamic militants claimed responsibility for the assassination.

• **Sergei Markidonov** (1961–95), a member of the Russian Duma, was shot and killed by his bodyguard while campaigning at a hotel in Petrovsk-Zabaikalsky, Siberia, on November 26, 1995. Markidonov was a member of the small Stability party. **Mikhail Lezhnev** (1947–95), a Duma candidate of the Our Home Is Russia party, was shot to death in front of his home near Chelyabinsk, Ural region, on December 8, 1995.

• **Gen. Mohammed Boutaghene**, the commander of the Algerian coast guard, was shot to death in Algiers by Islamic terrorists on November 27, 1995.

# 1996

• **Yahya Ayyash**, a leader of the Palestinian Hamas militia, was killed by an explosion from his booby-trapped cellular phone in Beit Lahia in the Gaza Strip on January 5, 1996. Ayyash, known as "the Engineer," was the alleged organizer of numerous terrorist acts and his death was believed to have been orchestrated by the Israeli secret service.

• **Ozdemir Sabanci** (1941–96), a leading Turkish businessman, was shot to death at his corporate headquarters, Sabanci Center, in Istanbul on January 9, 1996. Sabanci was the chairman of the Toyotasa car joint venture with Japan. **Haluk Gorgun**, the general manager of Toyotasa, and a secretary were also killed in the attack. A leftist guerrilla group, the Revolutionary People's Liberation Party/ Front (DHKP/C), claimed responsibility for the killings.

• **Mufti Fatkhulla Sharipov**, the highest-ranking Islamic cleric in Tajikistan, was shot to death at his home near Dushanbe, Tajikistan, on January 21, 1996. Four others were also killed in the attack, including his wife and son. Sharipov was a supporter of President Imamali Rakhmanov in the Tajik civil war of 1992.

• **Fernando Mugica Herzog** (1933– 96), a leader of the Socialist Party in San Sebastian, Spain, was shot to death by two gunmen on February 6, 1996. The following week, **Francisco Tomas y Valiente**, the former president of Spain's Constitutional Court, was shot to death at his office in the University of Madrid. Both killings were believed to have been the work of the Basque terrorist group ETA.

• **Hussein Kamel** and **Col. Saddam Kamel al-Majid**, two of Saddam Hussein's sons-in-law who had defected to Jordan in August of 1995, returned to Iraq on promises of amnesty on February 20, 1996. They were seized after entering the country and it was later reported they had been killed in a gunfight with relatives. It was believed that the government had executed the two men and numerous members of their family. Saddam Kamel had led the presidential security forces and Hussein Kamel, as minister of industry and minerals, had headed Iraq's military buildup before the Gulf War.

• **Dzhokar M. Dudayev**, the president of the secessionist Russian republic of Chechnya, was killed in a rocket attack by Russian forces in the village of Gekhi-Chu on April 21, 1996. Dzhokar Musaevich Dudayev was born in February of 1944. He spent much of his early life in Kazahkistan. He returned with his family to his native village of Yalkhori in 1957 and attended pilot school. Dudayev joined the Soviet Communist party in 1968. He served in the Soviet Air Force, rising to the rank of major general in 1987. He retired from the Air Force in 1990. Dudayev was elected head of the Chechan executive committee of the opposition All-National Congress of Chechan People in Grozny in November of 1990. He was an advocate of independence for Chechnya and became president of Chechnya in October of 1991. He declared Chechan succession from the Russian Federation and dissolved the parliament in 1993. Russian troops moved in to oust Dudayev in December of 1994. He continued to lead the rebel troops fighting for independence against the Russians until his death.

• **Mohammed Hardi**, the former Algerian minister of the interior, was shot to death in an Algiers parking lot by three Islamic militants on May 4, 1996. Hardi had served as interior minister in 1992 and 1993.

• **Reza Mazlouman**, who served as deputy minister of education under the Shah in Iran, was shot to death at his apartment near Paris on May 28, 1996. Mazlouman had been in exile in France since the Islamic revolution that had toppled the Shah. He was an active opponent of the Iranian government.

• **Kudirat Abiola** (1952–96), the wife of Nigerian opposition leader Chief Moshood Abiola, was shot to death while riding in the streets of Lagos on June 4, 1996. Her driver was also killed as six armed men fired at her car. Kudirat Abiola had been campaigning for the release of her husband from prison. Chief Abiola had been imprisoned since June of 1994 after the military government had annulled the presidential election that he claimed to have won. He died of a heart attack in prison on July 7, 1998.

• **Djamel Zitouni** (aka **Abu Abderrahman Amin**), the former leader of the extremist Armed Islamic Group (GIA) in Algeria, was killed in an ambush on July 16, 1996.

Zitouni, who had orchestrated numerous brutal acts in the past several years including the massacre of seven French monks in March of 1996, had recently been ousted as the GIA's leader.

• **Bishop Pierre Claverie**, the French Roman Catholic bishop of Oran, was killed by a bomb blast at his home on August 1, 1996. His chauffeur was also killed in the explosion. Bishop Claverie had just returned from a meeting with the French Foreign Minister. Forty French citizens had been murdered in Algeria in the previous three years after the extremist rebel group the Armed Islamic Group (GIA) had warned foreigners to leave the country.

• **Gen. Mohamed Farah Aidid**, a leading Somali warlord, was shot in the liver during a skirmish in Medina, Somalia, in July of 1996. He died a little over a week later on August 1, 1996. Farah Aidid was instrumental in the ouster of Somali dictator Mohamed Siad Barre in 1991. Twelve United States soldiers were killed in a battle with his troops in October of 1993. This marked the beginning of the U.S. withdrawal of troops from Somalia.

• **Jaffar Hasso Guly**, the chief representative of the Kurdistan Democratic Party and the exiled Iraqi Kurdish Autonomous Government in Paris, was murdered by unknown assassins at his home in Paris on August 5, 1996.

• **Antoine Leroy**, a leader of the rightist Haitian opposition party, Mobilization for National Development (MDN), and party member **Jacques Florival** were assassinated in Port-au-Prince on August 20, 1996. Government security forces were alleged to be responsible for the slayings.

• **Hamid Hamidov**, the finance minister of the Caucasian republic of Dagestan in Russia, was killed in a car bomb outside the finance ministry in the capital, Makhachkala. on August 20, 1996. Three others were killed in the explosion and numerous bystanders were injured. It was alleged the Hamidov was murdered by criminal elements seeking to prevent his investigation of corruption in the government.

• Burundian Roman Catholic **Archbishop Joachim Ruhuna** of Gitega and several others were burned to death when they ambushed in a car and firebombed by Hutu extremists on September 9, 1996. Ruhuna, an ethnic Tutsi, was a critic of the ethnic violence plaguing Burundi.

• **Najibullah**, the ousted president of Afghanistan, was captured by rebels at a United Nations enclave in Kabul. He was summarily executed when the rebels shot and stabbed him, then hung him by the neck with a wire from a concrete traffic tower. Sayid Mohammed Najib(ullah), a member of the Pashtun tribe, was born in 1947 in Afghanistan's Paktia Province near Pakistan. His father was a banker, and Najib, then called Najibullah, was raised in Kabul. Nicknamed the "Ox," he joined the Communist party while studying medicine at the University of Kabul in 1956. He joined the Parcham wing of the Communist party and was arrested on several occasions for his political activities. Najib became a member of the ruling Revolutionary Council after the ouster of Mohammed Daud (q.v.) in 1978. Shortly afterwards the Mohammad Taraki (q.v.) government began a purge of Parcham members and named Najib as ambassador to Iran. He then went into exile in Eastern Europe. Following the overthrow of the Khalq regime of Hafizullah Amin (q.v.) in December of 1979, Najib returned to Afghanistan to become leader of the Afghan secret police, or KHAD. Najib's successes in this position impressed the Soviets to the extent that he was named to replace Babrak Karmal as general secretary of the People's Democratic party on May 4, 1986. Najib assumed the post of president of the Revolutionary Council on September 30, 1987, and on November 30 he was elected president of Afghanistan under a new constitution. Najib proved a more popular figure with Afghan religious leaders than his predecessors, and the intelligence network he supervised while head of the KHAD helped to secure more support of tribal leaders in the ongoing civil war. Nevertheless, the violence continued as Najib

sought a political solution to the Islamic guerrilla war. Pressure for a settlement increased following the withdrawal of Soviet troops in February of 1989. Najib survived several coup attempts in early 1990. In June, Najib founded a new political party in Afghanistan, the Homeland party, in an effort to win mass support for his government. The new party was primarily composed of his Communist allies and did little to improve his situation. Najib was forced to resign in April of 1992 as the rebels advanced on the capital. He took refuge in the United Nations compound in Kabul on April 16, 1992. The Islamic government that succeeded him attempted to have him turned over to the government to stand trial for war crimes.

• **Choi Duck Keun**, a South Korean diplomat, was assassinated in Vladivostok, Russia, on October 1, 1996. Agents of the North Korean government were allegedly involved in the slaying.

• **Andrei Lukanov**, the former Premier of Bulgaria, was shot to death outside his home in Sofia on October 2, 1996. Andrei Kalov Lukanov was born in Moscow on September 26, 1938. He was educated in Moscow and joined the Dimitrov Young Communist League in 1957. He worked in the Bulgarian Ministry of Foreign Affairs from 1963 and was a member of the Bulgarian Communist party from 1966. From 1976 until 1986 he served as deputy chairman of the Council of Ministers and was first deputy chairman until 1987. Lukanov served as minister for foreign economic relations from 1987 until 1990. He was named premier of Bulgaria on February 3, 1990, serving until December 7, 1990, when he stepped down after a series of strikes. Lukanov was arrested in July of 1992 and charged with misappropriating state funds, but remained a leading political figure in Bulgaria. A critic of Premier Zhan Videnov, he had been removed as chairman of Topenergy, an oil and gas transport company, in July of 1996.

• **Ali Boucetta**, the mayor of Algiers, was shot to death in his car by Islamic militants on October 21, 1996

• Zairian Jesuit Roman Catholic Archbishop **Christophe Muzihirwa Mwene Ngabo** (1923–96) was killed in a guerilla attack in Bukavu on October 29, 1996.

• **Yevhen Shcherban**, a member of the Ukrainian parliament and a leading businessman, was shot to death at the Donetsk airport on November 3, 1996. His wife was also killed in the assault. Shcherban was head of the Aton Transnational trading company.

• **Liu Pang-yu**, the Nationalist Party Taoyuan County magistrate in Taiwan, was shot to death at his home in a Taipei suburb on November 21, 1996. Seven others were also killed in a massacre believed to have been orchestrated by local crimelords. Liu had been indicted for corruption earlier in the year.

# 1997

• **'Abd al-Haq Benhamouda**, a leading Algerian labor union leader, was shot to death in Algiers on January 28, 1997. Islamic extremists in the Algerian Jihad Islamic Front claimed responsibility for the killing. Benhamouda headed the Union Generale des Travailleurs Algeriens and was a leading supporter of the government of President Liamine Zeroual. He was expected to become the leader of the National Democratic Rally (RND) party. Two days later **Gen. Habib Khelili**, a retired army officer, was assassinated in Oran, western Algeria, by Islamic extremists.

• **Rafael Martinez Emperador**, a Spanish Supreme Court judge, was shot to death by an unidentified gunman near his apartment in Madrid on February 10, 1997. The assassination was believed to have been the work of radical Basque separatists in the ETA.

• **Vincent Nkezabaganwa**, a Rwandan Supreme Court justice, was shot to death in his car in the driveway of his home in Kigali by three unidentified gunmen on February 15,

1997. Two others, including his driver, were also killed in the assault.

• **Gerardo Bedoya Borrero** (1942–97), the chief editorial writer for the Colombian paper, *El Pais*, was shot to death in Cali on March 20, 1997. The gunmen were believed to be agents of drug traffickers who objected to Bedoya's recent series of articles advocating extradition for drug crimes.

• **Radovan Stojicic**, the Serbian deputy minister of the interior, was shot to death by a masked gunman at a Sofia restaurant on April 11, 1997.

• On December 17, 1996, leftist Tupac Amaru rebels seized over a hundred hostages in an assault on the Japanese Ambassador's home in Lima. Following months of unsuccessful negotiations where rebel leader **Nestor Cerpa** tried to arrange freedom for captured associates, the Peruvian military stormed the residence to free the hostages. Cerpa and all of his fellow rebels were slain in the assault.

• **Son Sen**, a leading official in the Khmer Rouge rebel group in Cambodia, was shot to death on June 10, 1997, after Pol Pot purged the top leadership of the Khmer Rouge. Fourteen members of Son Sen's family, including his wife, **Yun Yat**, and his grandchildren, were also slain under orders of Pol Pot. Son Sen served as defense minister in the Khmer Rouge government. General Tak Mok, who was also on Pol Pot's death list, ousted Pol Pot from the Khmer Rouge leadership a week later and captured him on June 19, 1997. He was sentenced to life imprisonment by a people's tribunal for Son Sen's murder.

• **A. Thangathurai**, a Tamil member of the Sri Lankan parliament from Trincomalee, was assassinated by radical Tamil terrorists on July 2, 1997.

• **Jorge Cristo**, a Colombian senator and ally of President Ernest Samper, was shot to death in Cucuta, Colombia, on August 8, 1997. Cristo was an advisor to the Liberal Party candidate in upcoming presidential elections. A radical guerrilla group, the National Liberation Army (ELN), claimed responsibility for the assassination.

• **Borys Derevyanko**, the editor of the leading independent newspaper in Odessa, Ukraine, was assassinated on August 11, 1997.

• **Mikhail Manevich**, a leading reformer and the deputy governor of St. Petersburg, was shot to death by a sniper while in his car on August 18, 1997. His wife was also injured in the shooting.

• On August 23, 1995, Kenneth Kaunda, who served as president of Zambia from 1964 to 1991, suffered minor injuries when he was shot by Zambian police while trying to address an opposition meeting in Kabwe, central Zambia. Kaunda, a leading opponent of Zambian President Frederick Chiluba's government, had his car fired upon while trying to escape when police broke up the rally. Another opposition leader, Roger Chongwe, was seriously injured in the assault.

• **Alfred Enrique Vargas**, the Venezuelan ambassador to Jamaica, was shot to death in his Kingston, Jamaica, apartment by an unknown gunman on November 6, 1997.

• **Maj. Gen. Shehu Musa Yar'Adua** (1943–97), a leading Nigerian military and political figure, died in prison on December 8, 1997. The government reported the death was from natural causes, but there was widespread speculation that Yar'Adua had been killed for his opposition to the regime of Gen. Sani Abacha. Yar'Adua had served as Supreme Military Council vice chairman after the assassination of Gen. Murtala Ramat Muhammed (q.v.) in 1976. He retired from the military in 1979 following the election of a new president. In 1989 Yar'Adua was a founder of the People's Front of Nigeria party and a supporter of Chief M.K.O. Abiola's presidential bid in 1993. Gen. Abacha nullified the results of the election, which Abiola seemingly had won. Yar'Adua subsequently began making plans for his own presidential bid, serving on the Constitution Conference in 1994. He was arrested in March of 1995 on charges of conspiring against the government and sentenced

to life imprisonment. He died in captivity two years later.

• **Billy Wright**, a Protestant guerrilla leader from Northern Ireland, was shot to death in a maximum security prison in Belfast by radical members of the Irish National Liberation Army (INLA) on December 27, 1997. He was shot five times by INLA gunmen who had smuggled weapons into the prison. Wright, known as "King Rat," was the leader of the Loyalist Volunteer Force (LVA) and was serving an eight year term in Belfast's Maze prison.

# 1998

• **Rubicel Ruiz Gamboa**, a Mexican peasant leader, was shot and killed near his home in Tuxtla Gutierrez, Chiapas, Mexico, on January 28, 1998. Ruiz was a member of the leftist opposition party in the region, the Democratic Revolutionary Party (PRD).

• **Alberto Jimenez Becerril**, a member of the city council in Seville, Spain, and his wife, **Ascension Garcia Ortiz**, a lawyer, were shot to death in the streets of Seville on January 30, 1998. Members of the Basque separatist group ETA claimed responsibility.

• **Desmir Vasic**, a local Serbian officer in Kosovo, was assassinated by guerrillas with the Kosovo Liberation Army (UCK) on January 23, 1998.

• On February 9, 1998, Eduard Shevardnadze (b.1928), the president of Georgia and former foreign minister of the Soviet Union, survived an assassination attempt when his motorcade was attacked by gunmen with automatic weapons and grenade launchers in Tbilisi. Two of Shevardnadze's bodyguards were killed in the assault, though Shevardnadze escaped without injury. The assailants were believed to have been followers of the late President Zviad Gamsakhurdia (q.v.). Shevardnadze had survived a previous assassination attempt in August of 1995 when a bomb exploded near his car. He had suffered minor injuries in that attack.

• **Claude Erignac** (1937–98), the prefect in the French territory of Corsica, was shot to death by two gunmen outside a theatre in Ajaccio on February 16, 1998. Erignac had been promoting tourism in Corsica and his assassins were believed to be members of a radical separatist group.

• **Eduardo Umana Mendoza**, a leading Colombian lawyer and human rights activist, was shot to death at his Bogota office on April 18, 1998. Known for his work defending workers and accused leftists, he was believed murdered by right-wing extremists.

• **Vadym Hetman**, the chairman of Ukraine's Interbank Currency Exchange and a leader of the Group of Independent Deputies in parliament, was shot to death upon entering his apartment in the Ukraine on April 22, 1998.

• Two leading Islamic clerics in Iraq were killed in 1998. **Ayatollah Sheikh Murtada Al-Burujerdi** (1929–98) was assassinated with two of his followers in Najaf in April of 1998. **Grand Ayatollah Sheikh Mirza Ali Al-Gharawi** (1930–98) was shot to death with his son and son-in-law en route to Najaf in June of 1998. The government of Saddam Hussein was believed responsible for the killings.

• **Pol Pot**, the leader of Cambodia's Khmer Rouge regime from 1976 until his ouster in 1979, reportedly died of a heart attack while under house arrest near the town of Anlong Veng on the Cambodia-Thailand border, on April 15, 1998. Pol Pot's Khmer Rouge forces had continued to wage a civil war against the Cambodian government since his ouster nearly twenty years earlier. A power struggle had culminated in 1997 with the execution of Pol Pot's longtime associate, Son Sen (q.v.). Forces loyal to his slain rival captured the ailing Pol Pot on June 21, 1997. The Cambodian government wanted Pol Pot to be tried on charges of genocide by an international tribunal, but his death ended hopes of bringing him to justice.

• **Bishop Juan Jose Gerardi Conedera**, a leading Guatemalan Roman Catholic prelate and human rights activist, was beaten to death with a concrete block in the garage of his home in Guatemala City on April 26, 1998. Gerardi was born in Guatemala City on December 27, 1922. He headed the Recovery of Historical Memory project, detailing human rights abuses orchestrated by the military that took place during Guatemala's 36-year-long civil war. His murder took place two days after the final report had been made public.

• **Commandant Alois Estermann** (1955–98), the newly appointed leader of the Vatican's Swiss Guard, was shot to death with his wife, Gladys, at his residence in the Vatican on May 4, 1998. The killer was identified as Corporal Cedric Tornay (1977–98), who was reportedly displeased over not receiving a promotion he felt he deserved. Tornay committed suicide after killing Estermann and his wife.

• **Luis Yat Zapeta**, the Mayor of Santa Cruz del Ruiche, Guatemala, was shot to death at his home by five masked men on May 6, 1998. Zapeta became mayor in February of 1998 following the resignation of Silverio Perez.

• **Tomas Caballero Pastor**, a member of the town council in Pamplona, Spain, was shot to death on May 6, 1998, while driving in his car near his home. Caballero was a member of the ruling Popular Party. The Basque separatist group ETA claimed responsibility for the assassination.

• **Gen. Fernando Landazabal Reyes** (1922–98), the former Colombian minister of defense, was assassinated near his apartment in Bogota on May 12, 1998. Landazabal had been a leading critic of the government's negotiations with leftist rebels during the 1980s. He was an advisor to Gen. Harold Bedoya Pizarro, a rightist presidential candidate, at the time of his death. His assassination was alleged to have been orchestrated by the Colombian drug cartel.

• **Seth Sendashonga**, a former Rwandese government minister, was shot to death in his car in Nairobi, Kenya, on May 16, 1998. His driver was also killed. Sendashonga had survived a previous assassination attempt in February of 1996 when he and his nephew where injured in a shooting in Nairobi. Sendashonga was a member of the Rwandese Patriotic Front, which overthrew the Rwandese government in July of 1994. He served as minister of interior in the new government until he was dismissed in August of 1995. He subsequently went to Kenya, where he formed an opposition group to the Rwandese government. He was a leading proponent of human rights in Rwanda.

• **Mrs. Sarojini Yogeshwaran**, the Mayor of Jaffna, Sri Lanka, and a moderate Tamil politician, was shot to death at her home by Tamil Tiger extremists on May 19, 1998. Her husband, V. Yogasangari (q.v.), had been murdered by terrorists eight years earlier.

• **Lt. Gen. Lev Rokhlin**, the chairman of the Russian Duma Committee on National Security and commander of Russian troops during the Chechnyan war, was shot to death in bed at his home in a Moscow suburb on July 3, 1998. Rokhlin's wife, Tamara Rokhlin, confessed to the murder, though some opposition leaders believed she was coerced and that his killing was politically motivated.

• **Khalifi Athmane**, a leader of the Algerian rebel force Armed Islamic Group (GIA), was killed in a gun battle outside of Algiers by Algerian security forces on July 8, 1998.

• The ouster of Prince Norodom Ranariddhi from leadership in the Cambodian government by forces loyal to Hun Sen, resulted in numerous acts of political violence and murder. **Hor Sok** the Secretary of State at the Ministry of the Interior, was arrested on July 7, 1998, while attempting to flee the country. He was executed soon after. Two leading officials with FUNCINPEC, Prince Norodom Ranaraddhi's political party, were captured trying to flee Phnom Penh with a group of soldiers. **Gen. Krauch Yeuam**, the Ministry of Defense's under-secretary, and **Gen. Chao Sambath**, were summarily executed.

• **S. Shanmuganathan**, a moderate Tamil politician and district member of parliament from Vavunia, was assassinated by Tamil Tiger terrorists on July 15, 1998.

• On July 24, 1998, Russell Weston, Jr., began firing in the United States Capitol. Officer **Jacob J. Chestnut** and Detective **John M. Gibson** were shot to death by Weston, before Capitol guards shot and killed him.

• **Otakhon Latifi**, a leader of the United Tajik Opposition (UTO), was assassinated in Tajikistan in September of 1998.

• **P. Sivapalan**, a moderate Tamil political leader in Sri Lanka and the mayor of Jaffna, was killed in a bomb explosion in the municipal offices of Jaffna on September 11, 1998. The town military commander, **Brigadier Susanthan Mendis**, and city architect **Mallika Rajaratnam** were also killed in the blast. Sivapalan became the second mayor of Jaffna to die at the hands of Tamil Tiger terrorists in four months.

• **Azem Hajdari**, an Albanian Democratic Party leader, was shot to death with his bodyguard by unidentified gunmen on September 12, 1998. The killing spurred riots and demonstrations against the government of Premier Fatos Nano, who was forced to temporarily flee his offices in the capital of Tirana during the unrest.

• **Jorge Humberto Gonzalez**, a Liberal Colombian congressional deputy, was shot to death by an unidentified gunman in Medellin on September 15, 1998.

• **Ahmet Krashnigi**, a member of the ethnic Albanian government in Kosovo, was shot and killed by unidentified gunmen on September 21, 1998.

• **Sanjaasurengiyn Zorig** (1962–98), the Mongolian minister of infrastructure development and telecommunications and a leader of the democratic revolution in 1989, was axed and stabbed to death at his home in Ulan Bator on October 2, 1998. Zorig was a leading candidate for prime minister at the time of his murder. Zorig's wife, Banzaragchiin Bulgan, was arrested as a suspect in her husband's death the following year.

• **Canagasabai Rajathurai**, a moderate Tamil political leader in Sri Lanka, was assassinated by Tamil extremists on October 6, 1998.

• **Tommy Burks**, a member of the Tennessee state senate, was shot to death while in his pickup truck on a road near Monterey, Tennessee, on October 19, 1998. Burks was born in Cookeville, Tennessee, on May 22, 1940. A Democrat, he served in the Tennessee state house of representatives from 1970 until his election to the state senate in 1978. His opponent in the general election several weeks away, Byron 'Low Tax' Looper, was arrested and convicted of the assassination. Burks' widow, Charlotte Gentry Burks, contested the election as a write-in candidate and won an overwhelming victory to succeed her husband in office.

• **Jorge Ortega**, a Colombian labor leader who served as vice president of the Unitary Workers' Federation, was shot to death in front of his home on October 20, 1998. His assailant was not identified, but union leaders believed the rightist paramilitary organization was involved.

• **Barnett Slepian**, a doctor who performed abortions, was shot to death by a sniper in the kitchen of his home in Amherst, New York, on October 23, 1998.

• **Shadid Bargishev**, who had recently been named to head the office in charge of fighting kidnapping in Chechnya was killed when a bomb exploded outside of his office on October 26, 1998. Bargishe had been planning to initiate a major effort against kidnappers who had abducted hundreds of people following the conclusion of the war between Chechnya and Russia in 1996.

• **Galina Starovoytova** (1936–88), a member of the Russian State Duma, was shot to death in the entryway of her St. Petersburg apartment building on November 20, 1998. Her aide, Ruslan Linkov, was also seriously wounded in the assault. Starovoytova was a leading liberal member of the Russian legislature. She was first elected to the Supreme Soviet of the Soviet Union as Yerevan's representative in 1988. She was an aide to President Boris Yeltsin on ethnic issues in the early 1990s. Starovoitova was elected to the lower house of the Russian parliament in 1995 and was co-chair of the Democratic Russia movement.

• **Darius Foruhar**, a leading nationalist and critic of the Islamic government of Iran, and his wife, Parvaneh, were stabbed to death at their home in Teheran on November 22, 1998. Foruhar had briefly served as minister of labor in the cabinet of the 1979 provisional government after the ouster of the shah. He was the leader of the small Iranian Nation's Party.

• **Mohammad Mokhtari**, a leading Iranian poet, was found dead near the outskirts of Tehran on December 4, 1998. Mokhtari was a prominent spokesman against censorship laws in Iran. His death was believed to have been politically motivated.

• **Ceci Cunha**, a member of the Brazilian congress, her husband and two in-laws were murdered in the northeastern state of Alagoas in December of 1998. Cunha had defeated Talvane Albuquerque in elections two months earlier. Albuquerque was selected as Cunha's replacement in the Chamber of Deputies, but was expelled in March under suspicion that he had ordered Cunha's killing.

• **Zvonko Bojanic**, the mayor of Kosovo Polje in Serbia, was kidnapped and shot to death by five masked assailants on December 17, 1998. His body was found dumped along a roadside the following day. The killing was believed to have been carried out by the Kosovo Liberation Army (KLA) in retaliation for the killings of 36 KLA members three days earlier.

# 1999

• **Ener Maloku**, a close aide to Dr. Ibrahim Rugova, the Kosovo ethnic Albanian leader, was shot outside his home in Pristina on January 12, 1999. He died soon after at a hospital. He had been the target of an unsuccessful assassination attempt the previous November.

• **Robinson Manolo Morales Canales**, a Guatemalan trade union leader and member of the Executive Council of the Workers Union, was shot to death by unidentified assassins in Zacapa, Guatemala, on January 12, 1999. Morales was an outspoken critic of local corruption in Zacapa and a leading spokesman for trade union freedoms.

• **Sifiso Nkabinde**, the secretary general of the South African opposition United Democratic Movement (UDM), was killed in Kwa-Zulu-Natal province while leaving a grocery store in Richmond, South Africa, on January 23, 1999. His assassination began a series of retaliatory killings. A second UDM official, deputy chairman **Valindlela Matiyase**, was shot to death near his Capetown home by two unidentified gunmen on January 24, 1999. The ruling African National Congress (ANC) councilor **Zwelinzima Hlazo** was shot and killed en route to his home in Nyanga on March 7, 1999. Later that day UDM politician **Mncedisi Mpongwana** was shot to death in Guguletu. The following day **Bhabha Dyonise**, the Nyanga chairman of the UDM, and UDM member **Zolile Tyandela**, were murdered in Nyanga. **Patata Nqwaru**, the vice chairman of the local chapter of the UDM, was assassinated on March 9, 1999, near Cape Town.

• **Jaime Hurtado**, a leader of the opposition Popular Democratic Movement in Ecuador, was shot to death as he was leaving the congress building in Quito on February 17, 1999. Hurtado's aide and driver were also killed in the assault. Members of a right-wing terrorist group were believed responsible for the murder.

• **Ayatollah Mohammed Sadiq al-Sader**, the leading Shiite cleric in Iraq, was shot to death with his two sons, **Hojjatue Al-Islam Al-Sayyid Mostafa Al-Sadr** and **Al-Sayyid Mu'ammai Al-Sadr**, in the holy city of Najaf by unidentified gunmen on February 19, 1999. The Ayatollah was a critic of the government's restrictions on religious freedom. He was the third leading Shiite cleric killed within a year.

• **Jean-Yvon Toussaint** (1951–99), a leading leftist member of the Haitian senate, was shot to death by an unidentified assassin outside his home near Port-au-Prince, Haiti, on March 1, 1999. Toussaint was a leader of the Struggling People's Organization party and the Senate's treasurer. He had served in the senate since 1995.

• **Rosemary Nelson** (1959–99), a leading Roman Catholic attorney and human rights activist in Northern Ireland, was killed on March 15, 1999, when a bomb exploded beneath her car in Lurgan, Northern, Ireland. The Red Hand Defenders, a radical Protestant guerrilla group, claimed responsibility for the murder.

• **Jozo Leutar** (1953–99), a leading Bosnian Croat politician and deputy minister of the interior of Bosnia's Moslem-Corat federation, was badly injured en route to work in a car bomb in Sarajevo on March 16, 1999. Leutar remained in a coma until he died from his injuries two weeks later on March 28, 1999.

• Paraguayan Vice President **Luis Maria Argana** (1933–99) was shot to death on March 23, 1999, by four gunmen on an Asuncion, Paraguay, street, when the assassins blocked his jeep with a car, threw a grenade and riddled it with bullets. His driver was also killed in the ambush. Argana was a leading rival to Paraguayan President Raul Cubas, and Argana's faction of the ruling Colorado Party had been threatening the president with impeachment. Argana had been a leading official in the Colorado Party during the dictatorship of Gen. Alfredo Stroessner until Stroessner's ouster in a coup in 1989. He subsequently served as a minister in the military government that followed during the transitional period before Paraguay was transformed into a democracy. Argana was defeated for the Colorado Party's presidential nomination by Gen. Lino Oviedo, a former army chief of staff who had led a coup attempt against President Juan Carlos Wasmosy in 1996. Oviedo was disqualified because of a jail sentence resulting from his unsuccessful coup attempt. Oviedo's supporter, Cubas, was selected to replace him and Argana automatically became his deputy. Cubas was elected to the presidency and soon pardoned Oviedo from jail. Argana and his supporters engaged in a fierce rivalry with the president, threatening him with impeachment for what they considered an unconstitutional pardon.

• **Ibrahim Bare Mainassara**, the president of Niger, was ambushed and assassinated on April 9, 1999, by members of the Presidential Guard at the military airport in Niamey, in what was believed to be a coup attempt. The military seized control of the country under Maj. Daouda Malam Wanke, commander of the Presidential Guard. Ibrahim Bare Mainassara was born in Maradi, Niger, on May 9, 1949. He entered the Niger army in 1970 and became a senior aide to President Seyni Kountche in 1973. Kountche named him leader of the Presidential Guard in 1976. Mainassara commanded Niger's airborne regiment from 1978 to the mid–1980s. He was named to the government as minister of health in 1987 and was sent to France as ambassador the following year. He served as Niger's ambassador to Algeria from 1990 to 1992. He returned to Niger to serve as a defense adviser to the prime minister in 1992 and became chief of staff for Pres. Mahamane Ousmane, Niger's first democratically elected president, in 1993. He was named army chief of staff in March of 1995. Mainassara staged a bloodless coup in January of 1996, proclaiming himself the leader of the National

Salvation Council. He was elected president the following July in an election of dubious fairness. He survived several coup attempts until April 9, 1999, when he and his personal bodyguards were shot to death by machine-gun wielding members of the Presidential Guard.

• **Brig. Gen. Ali Sayyad Shirazi**, the deputy chief of staff of the Iranian armed forces, was shot to death near his home as he left for work on April 10, 1999. The People's Mujahedden, an Iraqi-based opposition group, claimed responsibility for the assassination, giving Shirazi's activities during the 1980s war between Iran and Iraq as the cause.

• **Robert Belarino Gonzalez**, a member of the leftist Democratic Front for the New Guatemala, was shot to death by unidentified gunmen in front of his home in Guatemala City on May 13, 1999.

• **Amin Kayed**, an official in the Palestinian Liberation Organization, was shot to death with his wife in a suburb of Sidon, Lebanon, on May 19, 1999. Two days later, Jamal ad-Dayekh, another PLO official, was seriously injured when a bomb exploded in his car in Sido. Dayekh lost his legs in the explosion. Both men were members of the Al Fatah organization headed by Yasser Arafat.

• **Euclides Francisco de Paula** (1962–99), the leader of the Farm Workers Union in Parauapebas, in northern Brazil, was shot to death by two gunmen on motorcycles on May 20, 1999. De Paula was shot twice in the head, and died en route to a hospital.

• **Massimo D'Antona** (1948–99), an adviser to Italian Labor Minister Antonio Bassolino, was shot to death in an ambush near his home in Rome as he walked to work on May 20, 1999. The Red Brigade terrorist group claimed credit for the assassination. D'Antona was instrumental in drafting the Italian government's labor-management policies and served as a representative on the steering committee for the "Pact for Jobs and Development." He was also a law teacher at La Sapienza University in Rome.

- **Francisco Stanley Albaiter** (1943–99), a Mexican television host known as Paco Stanley, was shot to death by three unidentified gunmen who attacked his car in Mexico City on June 7, 1999. A bystander was killed in the attack and several others were wounded. Stanley had worked with TV Azteca and Televvisa since the mid–1970s, hosting numerous variety series. It was believed that Stanley's killing was drug related.

- **Luagalau Levaula Kamu** (1955–99), Samoa's minister for public works, was shot to death at a political rally at a high school in the capital city, Apia, on July 16, 1999. Levaula had introduced Prime Minister Tuila'epa Sailele Malielegaoi and stepped off stage when a sniper shot him once in the back. Levaula was pronounced dead at a nearby hospital shortly afterwards. This was the first political assassination since Samoa gained independence in 1962. Leafa Vitale (b. 1942), the former minister of women's affairs, and Toi Aukuso (b. 1931), the former minister of communications, were charged and convicted of planning Kamu's murder and sentenced to death in April of 2000. Vitale's son, Alatise Vitale (b. 1965) had previously been convicted of carrying out the murder and received a sentence of life imprisonment.

- **Neelan Tiruchelvam**, a Sri Lankan moderate political leader and member of parliament, was killed in the capital of Colombo on July 29, 1999, when an assassin with a bomb hurled himself at Tiruchelvam's car, killing himself and the politician. Tiruchelvam, a member of the Tamil United Liberation Front party and an adviser to President Chandrika Kumeratunga, was involved in a peace proposal between the dominant Sinhalese and the Tamil minority, which had been fighting a civil war in the north and east of Sri Lanka for the previous 16 years. A constitutional lawyer and human rights activist, Tiruchelvam had entered parliament in August of 1994. The rebel group The Liberation Tigers of Tamil Eelam were suspected of being responsible for the assassination. The Tamil Tigers had previously orchestrated the murders of three other Tamil United Liberation Front political leaders in the 1980s, including the party's founder, Appapillai Amritalingam (q.v.).

- **Jaime Garzon** (1960–99), a leading political satirist in Colombia, was shot to death by two gunmen aboard a motorcycle on a Bogota street on August 13, 1999. Garzon was the host of a talk show on a local radio station and wrote a weekly magazine column. He was also a familiar face on Colombian television, known for his political humor. Right-wing terrorists were believed responsible for the killing.

- **Rafa Daham Mujawwal al-Takriti**, the head of Iraq's intelligence bureau and Saddam Hussein's second cousin, died on October 11, 1999, three days after having been removed from his position. He was the former Iraqi ambassador to Turkey. His death was announced as having been the result of a heart attack and also from injuries received in an auto accident, but it was considered likely he had been executed by the government because of his rivalry with Hussein's son, Uday.

- **Vazgen Sarkisyan** (1959–99), the premier of Armenia, was killed when five gunmen attacked the capitol while parliament was in session on October 27, 1999. Other leading Armenian politicians were also killed in the assault including Parliament Speaker **Karen Demirchyan**, Deputy Speakers **Yuri Bakhshyan** and **Ruben Miroyan**, Energy Minister **Leonard Petrosyan**, economic advisor **Mikhail Kotanyan** and legislators **Genrikh Arbamyan** and **Armenak Armenakyan**. Sarkisyan, who had become prime minister the previous June, had been addressing the parliament when a gunman stepped forward and shot him several times. The other assailants then began firing on the parliament. The leader of the terrorists that killed Sarkisyan was identified as Nairi Unanyan, a former Armenian Revolutionary Federation party members, who claimed to be staging a coup against the government. Several other legislators were wounded in the assault and approximately 40 people were held hostage until the following day, when President Robert Kocharyan negotiated their freedom for a promise of a fair trial for the assassins.

- **Atputharaja Nadarajah**, a moderate Tamil politician in Sri Lanka, was assassinated by Tamil Tiger terrorists on November 2, 1999.

- **Wezi Kaunda** (1952–99), the son of former Zambian President Kenneth Kaunda and a leader of the opposition United National Independence Party, was shot to death near his home in Lusaka, Zambia, on November 3, 1999. The gunman took Kaunda's car and the government indicated that the killing had occurred during the course of a car-jacking. Opposition leaders believed the murder to have been politically motivated.

- **Abdelkader Hachani** (1949–99), a leader of the outlawed Islamic Salvation Front (FIS) in Algeria, was assassinated at a dental clinic in Algiers on November 22, 1999. Hachani had been a supporter of the government's attempts to settle the civil war against the Islamic fundamentalist rebels that had been going on since 1992.

- Three senior officers were executed by the Iraqi government on charges of treason and conspiracy on November 22, 1999. **Maj. Gen. Abd Al-Karim Al-Hamadani**, a retired officer, was executed for his criticism of the Iraqi government's war with Iran and Kuwaiti invasion. **Lt. Col. Falah Hamdan al-Dulaymi** and **Lt. Col. Ahmad Battah al-Dulaymi** were also put to death.

- Chandrika Kumaratunga (b.1945), the president of Sri Lanka, was wounded in an assassination attempt by a suicide bomber on December 18, 1999. Over thirty people were killed in the blast. Thirteen people were killed several weeks later on January 5, 2000, when a suicide bomber detonated explosives in front of Prime Minister Sirimavo Bandaranaike's office. The premier, the mother of President Kumaratunga, was not in her office at the time.

# 2000

- **Kumar Ponnambalam**, a leading Tamil politician and president of the All Ceylon Tamil Congress, was shot to death by unidentified gunmen while leaving his residence in Wellawatte, Sri Lanka, on January 5, 2000. Ponnambalam was born on August 12, 1938. He became involved in politics in Sri Lanka in the early 1960s, serving as president of the Tamil Congress' Young Wing from 1966. A practicing lawyer since 1974, Ponnambalam was an unsuccessful candidate for president of Sri Lanka in 1982.

- **Zeljko Raznjatovic**, a leading Serbian warlord known as **Arkan**, was shot to death in a Belgrade hotel lobby on January 15, 2000. **Milovan "Manda" Mandic**, Raznjatovic's business associate, and **Dragan Garic**, an interior ministry executive, were also killed in the shooting. Dobrosav Gavric (b.1976), a former police officer, was arrested for the murder on January 22, 2000. Arkan's followers suspected the government of Slobodan Milosevic of involvement in the slaying. Raznjatovic was born in Brezice, Slovenia, on April 17, 1952. He led the Serbian National Guard paramilitary unit, known as the Tigers, during Serbia's battles with Bosnia and Croatia in the 1990s. He was elected a deputy in the Yugoslav parliament from Kosovo in December of 1992 and allied himself with Milosevic the following year. He had been indicted by the International Tribunal for war crimes in 1997.

- **Col. Akl Hashem** (1952–2000), a leader of the South Lebanon Army (SLA), was killed by a remote detonated bomb near his home in Dibel, southern Lebanon, on January 30, 2000. The Hezballah claimed responsibility for the bomb attack that killed Hashem, whose forces were allied with the Israelis. A Maronite from the village of Debel, he served as a surgeon in the Lebanese army before defecting to the SLA. He was considered a likely successor the his commander, Antoine Lahd.

- **Pavle Bulatovic**, the defense minister of Yugoslavia and a close associate of President Slobodan Milosevic, was shot to death by an unidentified gunman while dining in a Serbian restaurant on February 7, 2000. Bulatovic was born in northern Montenegro on December 13, 1948. He studied economics and taught at the Montenegrin Podgorica University. A member of the opposition Montenegrin Socialist People's Party, Bulatovic had served as minister of the interior in Montenegro from 1993 to 1996. He became minister of defense in 1998, serving in that position during the NATO air strikes against Serbia.

- **Erwin Aroldo Ochoa Lopez** and **Julio Armando Vasquez Ramirez**, two leading conservationists in Guatemala, were shot to death while leaving a restaurant in Puerto Barrios, Guatemala, on February 29, 2000. Ochoa and Vasquez worked with the National Protected Areas Council (CONAP). Ochoa served as CONAP's legal advisor and Vasquez was the region's administrative assistant.

- **Iqbal Raad**, the top defense attorney for former Pakistani prime minister Nawaz Sharif, was shot to death in his Karachi office by three gunmen on March 10, 2000. Raad was leading the defense of Sharif on charges of attempting to prevent an airplane carrying Gen. Pervez Musharraf from landing at Karachi in October of 1999. Musharraf subsequently deposed Sharif's government.

- **Jean Leoppold Dominique** (1930–2000), the owner of Radio Haiti Inter, a pro-government radio station in Haiti, and a leading advisor to President Rene Preval, was shot to death en route to work on April 3, 2000. Dominique, one of Haiti's best known political commentators, founded Radio Haiti Inter in the 1960s. He was an outspoken advocate of human rights and had been exiled on several occasions over the years for his criticism of repressive governments in Haiti.

- **Arif Khan** (1954–2000), the governor of the northern Afghanistan province of Kunduz, was shot to death in his vehicle near Peshawar, Pakistan, near the Afghan border, on April 5, 2000, while on vacation. Khan was also a senior member of the Taliban army and his assassins were believed to be members of rival Afghan factions.

- **Manva Ngele**, Gabon's charge d'affaires in Togo, was shot to death in front of Gabon's embassy in Lome, Togo, by two unidentified gunmen on April 15, 2000. Ngele had served as his country's senior diplomat in Togo for the previous four years.

- **Zivorad "Zika" Petrovic** (1938–2000), the chief executive of Yugoslavia's national airline, JAT, was shot to death in front of his Belgrade home on April 26, 2000. Petrovic was a close associate of Yugoslav president Slobodan Milosevic and a member of the political party run by Milosevic's wife, Mira Markovic.

- **Luis Terrero Gil**, an official with the ruling Dominican Liberation Party (PLD) in Moca, Dominican Republic, was shot to death in front of his home on April 29, 2000. Bodyguards of opposition party candidate Hipolito Mejia Dominguez fired the shots that killed Terrero and another PLD supporter, claiming the car carrying Mejia had been fired upon from Terrero's house.

- **Jose Luis Lopez de la Calle** (1930–2000), a political reporter for the Spanish daily newspaper *El Mundo*, was shot to death at his home in the Basque region of Spain on May 5, 2000. Lopez was an outspoken critic of the militant Basque separatist organization, the ETA, and it was believed they were responsible for his murder.

- **Bosko Perosevic**, another close associate of Yugoslav President Slobodan Milosevic, was shot to death in Novi Sad, Yugoslavia, on May 13, 2000. Perosevic was the leader of the Novi Sad's Socialist Party and headed the regional government in the province of Vojvodina.

- **Ghulam Hassan Bhatt**, the junior power minister in the Indian state of Jammu and Kashmir, died in a bomb explosion planted in his car on May 15, 2000. Four others also died in the attack, which was believed to have been planted by guerrillas.

- **Saifullo Rakhimov**, the chairman of Tajikistan's government-run radio and television, was shot to death by unidentified gunmen as he was driving near his home in Dushanbe, Tajikistan, on May 20, 2000.

- **Goran Zugic**, the security advisor to Montenegro President Milo Djukanovic, was shot to death outside his home in Podgorica on May 31, 2000.

- **Jesus Maria Pedrosa** (1943–2000), a member of Spain's ruling Popular Party, was shot to death in his hometown of Durango, Spain, on June 4, 2000. Pedrosa was an opponent of Basque separatists in the province of Vizcaya and his assassination was believed to have been carried out by the extremist ETA.

- **C.V. Gooneratne** (1935–2000), the Sri Lankan minister of industry, was assassinated by a Tamil Tiger suicide bomber on June 7, 2000, in Colombo while he was collecting money for soldiers killed by Tamil extremists. Gooneratne's wife, Shyama, several bodyguards and nearly twenty others were also killed in the attack. **Kanapathipillai Navaratnarajah**, a moderate Tamil political leader, **Anura Silva**, the deputy mayor of Mount Lavinia Municipal Council, were among those killed in the terrorist attack.

- **Brig. Stephen Saunders**, the senior British military representative in Greece, was shot to death while driving in Athens on June 8, 2000. A leftist terrorist organization known as "November 17" claimed responsibility for the killing.

- **Jose Maria Martin Carpena**, an official with Spain's ruling Popular Party in Malaga, Spain, was shot to death in front of his home in Malaga on July 15, 2000. The ETA, a militant Basque separatist organization, were believed responsible for the murder.

- **Jean-Michel Rossi** (1957–2000), a leading Corsican nationalist, was shot to death in a bar in the Ile Rousse on August 7, 2000. His bodyguard, Jean-Claude Fratacci, was also slain in the machine-gun attack.

Rossi was a founding member of the National Liberation Front. It was believed that Rossi's murder had been carried out by Corsica's organized crime syndicate.

- **Virgil Sahleanu**, a Romanian engineer and trade union leader, was stabbed to death by two strangers near the door to the building where he lived on September 27, 2000. Sahleanu had been involved in fighting against the privatization of Tepro Iasi, a leading metallurgical company.

- **Mylvaganam Nimalrajan** (1961–2000), a leading Sri Lankan journalist, was shot to death by unknown assassins on October 20, 2000. A Tamil fluent in Sinhalese, he covered the ongoing civil war in Sri Lanka for over a decade. Nimalrajan reported for numerous overseas news organizations during the fighting, sometimes incurring the anger of both the government and the rebels.

- Spanish Supreme Court justice **Gen. Jose Francisco Querol** (1931–2000), was killed when a bomb exploded underneath his car in Madrid on October 30, 2000. Querol's driver and bodyguard were also killed in the attack. He was president of the Supreme Court's military section. The militant Basque separatist group, the ETA, were believed to be responsible for the assassination.

- **Hussein Obaiyat**, the leader of the Tanzim militia, a Palestinian radical organization loyal to Yasir Arafat's Al Fatah, was killed when his truck was fired upon by Israeli helicopter gunships near Bethlehem in the West Bank on November 9, 2000. The Israeli military alleged the Obaiyat was the mastermind behind several assaults on Israeli soldiers and civilians.

- **Ernest Lluch i Martin**, the former Spanish minister of Health during the 1980s, was shot to death by an unknown gunman in Barcelona on November 21, 2000. Lluch was a member of the Socialist Party and a leading economics. His killers were believed to be members of the Basque separatist group ETA. Lluch was born in Vilassar de Mar, Spain, on January 21, 1937. He became a professor of economics at the University of Barcelona during the Franco dictatorship, but was expelled after supporting a students' union. He was elected to the Spanish chamber of deputies for Barcelona in the first post–Franco parliament in 1977. A Socialist, he became minister of health in Felipe Gonzalez's government in 1982. He stepped down from the cabinet in 1986 and subsequently served as Chancellor of the Universidad Internacional de Menendez Pelayo from 1989 to 1995.

• **Carlos Cardoso** (1951–2000), a leading Mozambican journalist and publisher of the independent newspaper *Metical*, was shot to death by unknown gunmen while leaving his office by car in the capital of Mozambique, Maputo, on November 22, 2000. Cardoso began writing free-lance for various newspapers in the mid–1970s. He became head of Mozambique's first independent new organization, MediaCo-op, in 1992.

• **Xhemajl Mustafa**, an adviser to moderate Kosovo Albanian leader Ibrahim Rugova, was shot four times by unknown gunmen in front of his home in Pristina, Yugoslavia, on November 23, 2000. He died of his injuries en route to a hospital.

• **Gen. Ansumane Mane**, the former army chief of staff who ousted President Bernardo Vieira of Guinea-Bissau in May of 1999, was killed in a gun battle with soldiers in Blom on November 30, 2000. Mane had led the ruling military junta that succeeded Vieira until civilian government had been restored. He had led a coup attempt against the subsequent government and was killed by loyalist troops after the coup failed.

# BIBLIOGRAPHY

## Books

*Afghanistan: A Country Study*. Washington, DC: U.S. Government Printing Office, 1986.

Alexander, Robert J., ed. *Biographical Dictionary of Latin American and Caribbean Political Leaders*. New York: Greenwood Press, 1988.

*Algeria: A Country Study*. Washington, DC: U.S. Government Printing Office, 1986.

Alisky, Marvin. *Historical Dictionary of Peru*. Metuchen, NJ: Scarecrow, 1979.

Ameringer, Charles D. *Don Pepe: A Political Biography of Jose Figueres of Costa Rica*. Albuquerque, NM: University of New Mexico Press, 1978.

Amirsadeghi, Hossein. *Twentieth Century Iran*. New York: Holmes and Meier, 1977.

Andersson, Ingvar. *A History of Sweden*. London: Weidenfeld and Nicolson, 1956.

Archer, Jules. *The Dictators*. New York: Bantam, 1968.

Arvil, Pierre. *Politics in France*. Baltimore: Penguin, 1969.

*The Australian Encyclopedia*. Sydney, Australia: Grolier Society of Australia, 1983.

Ayany, Samuel G. *A History of Zanzibar*. Nairobi: East Africa Literature Bureau, 1970.

Ayling, S.E. *Portraits of Power*. New York: Barns and Noble, 1961.

Azimi, Fakhreddin. *Iran: The Crisis of Democracy, 1941–1953*. New York: St. Martin's, 1989.

Banani, Amin. *The Modernization of Iran, 1921–1941*. Stanford, CA: Stanford University Press, 1961.

Barteau, Harry C. *Historical Dictionary of Luxembourg*. Lanham, MD: Scarecrow, 1996.

Bizzaro, Salvatore. *Historical Dictionary of Chile*. Metuchen, NJ: Scarecrow, 1972.

Bolloten, Burnett. *The Spanish Civil War*. Chapel Hill, NC: University of North Carolina Press, 1995.

Boorman, Howard L., ed. *Biographical Dictionary of the Republic of China*. New York: Columbia University Press, 1967.

Brace, Richard M. *Morocco Algeria Tunisia*. Englewood Cliffs, NJ: Prentice–Hall, 1964.

Brown, Archie, ed. *The Soviet Union: A Biographical Dictionary*. New York: Macmillan, 1991.

Bruegel, J.W. *Czechoslovakia Before Munich*. London: Cambridge University Press, 1973.

Bullock, Alan, and R.B. Woodlings, eds. *Twentieth Century Culture*. New York: Harper & Row, 1983.

Burns, E. Bradford. *A History of Brazil*. New York: Columbia University Press, 1980.

Calder, Bruce J. *The Impact of Intervention*. Austin: University of Texas Press, 1984.

*Cambridge History of Japan*. 6 vols. New York: Cambridge University Press, 1988.

Cammaerts, Emile. *Albert of Belgium*. London: Ivor Nicholson & Watson Ltd., 1935.

Carr, Raymond. *Spain, 1808–1975*. Oxford: Claredon Press, 1983.

Chapman, Charles E. *A History of the Cuban Republic*. New York: Octagon Books, 1969.

Collier, Simon, Harold Blakemore, and Thomas E. Skidmore, eds. *The Cambridge Encyclopedia of Latin American and the Caribbean*. Cambridge: Cambridge University Press, 1985.

*Columbia Encyclopedia*. Morningside Heights, NJ: Columbia University Press, 1950.

Coutouvidis, John, and Jaime Reynolds. *Poland 1939–1947*. New York: Holmes & Meir, 1986.

Creedman, Theodore S. *Historical Dictionary of Costa Rica*. Metuchen, NJ: Scarecrow, 1977.

Davis, Robert H. *Historical Dictionary of Colombia*. Metuchen, NJ: Scarecrow, 1977.

Delpar, Helen, ed. *Encyclopedia of Latin America.* New York: McGraw-Hill, 1974.

Derry, T.K. *A History of Modern Norway 1814–1972.* Clarendon Press: Oxford, 1973.

Dunn, E. Elmwood, and Svend E. Holcoe. *Historical Dictionary of Liberia.* Metuchen, NJ: Scarecrow, 1985.

Dupree, Louis. *Afghanistan.* Princeton, NJ: Princeton University Press, 1973.

Edelman, Marc, and Joanne Kennen, eds. *The Costa Rica Reader.* New York: Grove Weidenfeld, 1989.

*Egypt: A Country Study.* Washington, DC: U.S. Government Printing Office, 1991.

Embree, Ainslie T., ed. *Encyclopedia of Asian History.* New York: Scribner's.

*Encyclopaedia Britannica.* Chicago: Encyclopaedia Britannica, various editions.

*Encyclopedia of Asian History.* New York: Scribner's, 1988.

*Encyclopedia of the Modern Middle East.* 4 vols. New York: Macmillan, 1996.

Eyck, Erich. *History of the Weimar Republic.* Cambridge, MA: Harvard University Press, 1963.

Ezergails, Andrew. *The 1917 Revolution in Latvia.* London: Columbia University Press, 1974.

Flemion, Philip F. *Historical Dictionary of El Salvador.* Metuchen, NJ: Scarecrow, 1972.

Fryxell, Anders. *History of Sweden.* London: Richard Bently, 1944.

Galdames, Louis. *A History of Chile.* New York: Russell & Russell, 1964.

Galindez, Jesus de. *The Era of Trujillo.* Tucson, AZ: University of Arizona Press, 1973.

Gjerset, Knut. *The History of Norwegian People.* New York: Arno Press, 1969.

Goldstein, Melvyn C. *A History of Modern Tibet, 1913–1951.* Berkeley: University of California Press, 1989.

Goldwert, Marvin. *Democracy, Militarism, and Nationalism in Argentina, 1930–1966.* Austin: University of Texas Press, 1972.

Gregorian, Vartan. *The Emergence of Modern Afghanistan.* Stanford: Stanford University Press, 1972.

Griffiths, John C. *Modern Iceland.* New York: Frederick A. Praeger, 1969.

Hayes, Paul M. *Quisling.* New York: Newton Abbot, 1971.

Heath, Dwight B. *Historical Dictionary of Bolivia.* Metuchen, NJ: Scarecrow, 1972.

Hedrick, Basil C., and Anne Hedrick. *Historical Dictionary of Panama.* Metuchen, NJ: Scarecrow, 1970.

Heinl, Robert Debs, Jr., and Nancy Gordon Heinl. *Written in Blood: The Story of the Haitian People 1492–1971.* Boston: Houghton-Mifflin, 1978.

Held, Joseph. *The Columbia History of Eastern Europe in the Twentieth Century.* New York: Columbia University Press, 1991.

Hilton, Ronald, ed. *Who's Who in Latin America.* 2 vols. Stanford: Stanford University Press, 1971.

Holborn, Hajo. *History of Modern Germany, 1840–1945.* New York: Alfred A. Knopf, 1969.

Holden, David, and Richard Johns. *The House of Saud.* New York: Holt, Rinehart and Winston, 1981.

Hoptner, J.B. *Yugoslavia in Crisis, 1934–1941.* New York: Columbia University Press, 1962.

Howarth, David. *The Desert King—A Life of Ibn Saud.* London: Collins, 1964.

Hutton, Patrick H., ed. *Historical Dictionary of the Third French Republic.* 2 vols. New York: Greenwood Press, 1994.

*The International Who's Who.* London: Europa, various editions.

*Iran: A Country Study.* Washington, DC: U.S. Government Printing Office, 1989.

*Iraq: A Country Study.* Washington, DC: U.S. Government Printing Office, 1990.

Jackson, Gabriel. *The Spanish Republic and the Civil War, 1931–1939.* Princeton, NJ: Princeton University Press, 1972.

Jackson, George, ed. *Dictionary of the Russian Revolution.* New York: Greenwood Press, 1989.

Jelavich, Barbara. *History of the Balkans,* 2 vols. Cambridge, MA: Cambridge University Press, 1983.

*Jordan: A Country Study.* Washington, DC: U.S. Government Printing Office, 1991.

Karnow, Stanley. *Vietnam: A History.* New York: Viking, 1983.

Keller, Edmond J. *Revolutionary Ethiopia.* Bloomington & Indianapolis: Indiana University Press, 1988.

Khoury, Philip S. *Syria and the French Mandate.* Princeton, NJ: Princeton University Press, 1987.

Kinross, Lord. *Ataturk.* New York: William Morrow, 1965.

Knight, Alan. *The Mexican Revolution.* 2 vols. Cambridge: Cambridge University Press, 1986.

*Kodansha Encyclopedia of Japan.* New York: Harper & Roe, 1983.

Kolinski, Charles J. *Historical Dictionary of Paraguay.* Metuchen, NJ: Scarecrow, 1973.

Komarnicki, Titus. *Rebirth of the Polish Republic.* London: William Heinemann Ltd., 1957.

Korbani, Agnes. *The Political Dictionary of the Modern Middle East.* Lanham, New York, London: Univesity Press of America, 1995.

Korbel, Josef. *Poland Between East and West.* Princeton, NJ: Princeton University Press, 1963.

Kousoulas, D. George. *Modern Greece: Profile of a Nation.* New York: Scribner's, 1974.

Langley, Lester D. *Central America: The Real Story.* New York: Crown, 1985.

Langville, Alan R. *Modern World Rulers: A Chronology*. Metuchen, NJ: Scarecrow, 1979.

Lauring, Palle. *A History of the Kingdom of Denmark*. Copenhagen: Host & Son, 1963.

Levine, Robert M. *Historical Dictionary of Brazil*. Metuchen, NJ: Scarecrow, 1979.

Levy, Felice, comp. *Obituaries on File*. 2 vols. New York: Facts on File, 1979.

Lewis, Bernard. *The Emergence of Modern Turkey*. London: Oxford University Press, 1958.

Liebenow, J. Gus. *Liberia: The Quest for Democracy*. Bloomington, IN: Indiana University Press, 1925.

Lipschutz, Mark R., and R. Kent Rasmussen. *Dictionary of African Historical Biography*. Chicago: Aldine, 1978.

Livermore, H.L. *A New History of Portugal*. Cambridge, MA: Cambridge University Press, 1966.

Loppa, Frank J. *Dictionary of Modern Italian History*. Westport, CT: Greenwood Press, 1985.

Loveman, Brian. *Chile — The Legacy of Hispanic Capitalism*. New York: Oxford University Press, 1979.

Luck, James Murray. *A History of Switzerland*. Palo Alto, CA: Sposs Inc. 1985.

MacDonald, John. *The Eastern Europe Collection*, 2 vols. New York: Arno Press, 1971.

MacDonnell, John De Courcy. *King Leopold II*. New York: University Press, 1905.

McLauchlan, Gordon, ed. *New Zealand Encyclopedia*. Auckland, NZ: David Bateman Ltd., 1984.

McLintock, A.H., ed. *An Encyclopedia of New Zealand*. Wellington, New Zealand: Owen, 1966.

Mamatey, Victor S., and Radomir Luza. *A History of the Czechoslovak Republic, 1918–1948*. Princeton, NJ: Princeton University Press, 1973.

Mansor, Menahem, ed. *Political and Diplomatic History of the Arab World, 1900–1967*. 7 vols. Washington, DC: NCR/Microcard Editions, 1972.

Maude, George. *Historical Dictionary of Finland*. Lanham, MD: Scarecrow, 1995.

May, Author J. *The Passing of the Hapsburg Monarchy 1914–1918*. 2 vols. University of Pennsylvania Press: Philadelphia, 1968.

Meyer, Harvey K. *Historical Dictionary of Honduras*. Metuchen, NJ: Scarecrow, 1977.

_____. *Historical Dictionary of Nicaragua*. Metuchen, NJ: Scarecrow, 1972.

Moore, Richard E. *Historical Dictionary of Guatemala*. Metuchen, NJ: Scarecrow, 1973.

Newton, Gerald. *The Netherlands, 1795–1977*. London: Westview Press, 1978.

Nousiainen, Jaakko. *The Finnish Political System*. Cambridge, MA: Harvard University Press, 1971.

Oakley, Stewart. *The Story of Denmark*. London: Faber & Faber, 1972.

Olson, James S., ed. *Historical Dictionary of the Spanish Empire, 1402–1975*. New York: Greenwood, 1992.

Opello, Walter C., Jr. *Portugal: From Monarchy to Pluralist Democracy*. Boulder, CO: Westview Press, 1991.

Otetea, Andrei. *A Concise History of Poland*. Robert Hale: London, 1985.

Palmer, Alan. *The Facts on File Dictionary of 20th Century History*. New York: Facts on File, 1979.

Palomlenyi, Erving. *A History of Hungary*. Zrinyi Printing House: Budapest, 1975.

Perusse, Roland I. *Historical Dictionary of Haiti*. Metuchen, NJ: Scarecrow, 1977.

Petran, Tabitha. *Syria*. New York: Praeger, 1972.

Petrovich, Michael Boro. *A History of Modern Serbia*. 2 vols. New York: Harcourt Brace Jovanovich, 1976.

Plummer, Brenda Gayle. *Haiti and the Great Powers, 1902–1915*. Baton Rouge: Louisiana State University Press, 1988.

Pollo, Stefanaq, and Arben Puto. *The History of Albania*. London: Routledge & Kegan Paul, 1981.

Polonsky, Antony. *Politics in Independent Poland 1921–39*. Oxford: Clarendon Press, 1972.

Poullada, Leon B. *Reform and Rebellion in Afghanistan, 1919–1929*. London: Cornell University Press, 1973.

Prouty, Chris, and Eugene Rosenfeld. *Historical Dictionary of Ethiopia and Eritrea*. Metuchen, NJ: Scarecrow, 1981.

Raun, Toivo U. *Estonia and the Estonians*. Stanford, CA: Hoover Institute, 1991.

Renwick, George. *Luxembourg*. New York: Charles Scribner's Sons, 1970.

Richmond, J.C.B. *Egypt 1798–1952*. London: Methuen, 1977.

Robertson, William Spence. *History of Latin American Nations*. New York: D. Appleton-Century, 1943.

Roos, Hans. *A History of Modern Poland*. New York: Alfred A. Knopf, 1966.

Rose, Leo E., and John T. Scholz. *Nepal Profile of a Himalayan Kingdom*. Boulder, CO: Westview, 1980.

Rudolph, Donna K., and G.A. Rudolph. *Historical Dictionary of Venezuela*. Metuchen, NJ: Scarecrow, 1971.

Ryder, A.J. *Twentieth Century Germany: From Bismarck to Brandt*. New York: Columbia University Press, 1973.

Sabaliunas, Leonas. *Lithuania in Crisis, 1939–1940*. Bloomington: Indiana University Press, 1972.

Sanders, Alan J.K. *Historical Dictionary of Mongolia*. Lanham, MD: Scarecrow, 1996.

Sedwick, Frank. *The Tragedy of Manuel Azana*. Ohio: Ohio State University Press, 1963.

Senn, Alfred Erich. *The Emergence of Modern Lithuania*. Westport, CT: Greenwood Press, 1975.

Seton-Watson, R.W. *A History of the Czechs and Slovaks*. Hamden, CT: Arcon Books, 1965.

_____. *A History of the Roumanians*. Hamden, CT: Arcon Books, 1963.

Shimoni, Yaacov, and Evyatar Levine, eds. *Political Dictionary of the Middle East in the 20th Century*. New York: Quadrangle, 1974.

Shreshtha, Kusum. *Monarchy in Nepal*. Bombay: Popular Prakashan, 1984.

Simon, Reeva. *Iraq Between the Two World Wars*. New York: Columbia University Press, 1986.

Singleton, Fred. *Twentieth Century Yugoslavia*. New York: Columbia Universty Press, 1976.

Smith, Harold. *Historical Dictionary of Thailand*. Metuchen, NJ: Scarecrow, 1976.

Spuler, Bertold, C.G. Allen, and Neil Saunders. *Rulers and Governments of the World*. 3 vols. London and New York: Bowker, 1977.

Stewart, Donald E.J. *Historical Dictionary of Cuba*. Metuchen, NJ: Scarecrow, 1981.

Stewart, John. *African States and Rulers*. Jefferson, NC: McFarland, 1989.

Stomberg, Andrew A. *A History of Sweden*. New York: Macmillan, 1969.

Storry, Richard. *A History of Modern Japan*. Baltimore: Penguin, 1968.

Sudoplatov, Pavel, and Anatoli Sudoplatov. *Special Tasks: The Memoirs of an Unwanted Witness—A Soviet Spymaster*. New York: Little, Brown, 1994.

Sykes, Sir Percy. *A History of Persia*. 2 vols. London: Macmillan, 1963.

Tenenbaum, Barbara A., ed. *Encyclopedia of Latin American History and Culture*. (5 vols.). New York: Charles Scribner's Sons, 1996.

*Thailand: A Country Study*. Washington, DC: U.S. Government Printing Office, 1989.

Thomas, Hugh. *The Spanish Civil War*. New York: Harper and Row, 1961.

Tunny, Christopher. *A Biographical Dictionary of World War II*. New York: St. Martin's, 1972.

*Turkey: A Country Study*. Washington, DC: U.S. Government Printing Office, 1988.

Volgyes, Ivan. *Hungary in Revolution 1918–1919*. Lincoln: University of Nebraska Press, 1971.

von Ranke, Leopold. *The History of Servia and the Servian Revolution*. New York: De Capo Press, 1973.

Walker, Thomas W. *Nicaragua: The Land of Sandino*. Boulder, CO: Westview Press, 1991.

Wallace, William V. *Czechoslovakia*. Boulder, CO: Westview Press, 1976.

Warren, Harris Gaylord. *Rebirth of the Paraguayan Republic*. Pittsburgh, PA: University of Pittsburgh Press, 1985.

*Webster's Biographical Dictionary*. Springfield, MA: Merriam, various editions.

Weinstein, Martin. *Uruguay: The Politics of Failure*. Westport, CT: Greenwood, 1975.

Werlich, David P. *Peru: A Short History*. Carbondale and Edwardsville, IL: Southern Illinois University Press, 1978.

Whatt, David K. *Thailand: A Short History*. New Haven, CT: Yale University Press, 1984.

Whitfield, Danny J. *Historical Dictionary of Vietnam*. Metuchen, NJ: Scarecrow, 1976.

*Who's Who in the World*. Chicago: Marquis Who's Who, various editions.

Wilbur, Donald Newton, ed. *The Nations of Asia*. New York: Hart, 1966.

Willis, Jean L. *Historical Dictionary of Uruguay*. Metuchen, NJ: Scarecrow, 1974.

Win, May Kyi, and Harold E. Smith. *Historical Dictionary of Thailand*. Lanham, MD: Scarecrow, 1995.

Wise, L.F., and E.W. Egan. *Kings, Rulers and Statesmen*. New York: Sterling, 1967.

Wright, Ione, and Lisa M. Nekhom. *Historical Dictionary of Argentina*. Metuchen, NJ: Scarecrow, 1978.

Wuorinen, John H. *A History of Finland*. New York: Columbia University Press, 1965.

Wyatt, David K. *Thailand: A Short History*. New Haven: Yale University Press, 1984.

Wynot, Edward D., Jr. *Polish Politics in Transition*. Athens, GA: University of Georgia, 1974.

Young, A. Morgan. *Imperial Japan, 1926–1938*. Westport, CT: Greenwood Press, 1938.

# Periodicals

*Annual Register of World Events* (London), 1900–1950.

*Current Biography* (New York), 1940–1950.

*Encyclopaedia Britannica Book of the Year* (Chicago), 1940–1970.

*Facts on File* (New York), 1940–1965.

*Memphis Commercial Appeal* (Memphis), 1900–1965.

*Memphis Press Scimitar* (Memphis), 1920–1965.

*Times of London* (London), 1900–1965.

# Index

# Index